© Copyright 2022 - All rights reserved.

The content contained within this book may not be reproduced, duplicated or transmitted without direct written permission from the author or the publisher.

Under no circumstances will any blame or legal responsibility be held against the publisher, or author, for any damages, reparation, or monetary loss due to the information contained within this book. Either directly or indirectly.

Legal Notice:

This book is copyright protected. This book is only for personal use. You cannot amend, distribute, sell, use, quote or paraphrase any part, or the content within this book, without the consent of the author or publisher.

Disclaimer Notice:

Please note the information contained within this document is for educational and entertainment purposes only. All effort has been executed to present accurate, up to date, and reliable, complete information. No warranties of any kind are declared or implied. Readers acknowledge that the author is not engaging in the rendering of legal, financial, medical or professional advice. The content within this book has been derived from various sources. Please consult a licensed professional before attempting any techniques outlined in this book.

By reading this document, the reader agrees that under no circumstances is the author responsible for any losses, direct or indirect, which are incurred as a result of the use of information contained within this document, including, but not limited to, errors, omissions, or inaccuracies.

Table Of Contents

CHAPTER 1: WHAT IS AN AIR FRYER? HOW TO USE IT? 14

- What Is an Air Fryer? 14
- How to Use an Air Fryer 14
- Purchasing Your Fryer 15
- Benefits of Using an Air fryer 16
- Best Practices When Air Frying 17
- Basic Parts, Accessories, and Their Importance 18
- Air Fryer Cooking Chart 19
- Air Fryer Tips 21
- Air Fryer Safety 22
- Control Dials 22
- Mistakes to Avoid With Your Air Fryer 23
- Tips for Cleaning 24
- FAQ 24

CHAPTER 2: BREAKFAST 26

1. Banana Bread Pudding 27
2. Air Fried German Pancakes 27
3. Air-Fried Flax Seed French Toast Sticks With Berries 28
4. Breakfast Frittatas 28
5. Air-Fried Breakfast Bombs 29
6. Banana Bread 29
7. Scrambled Eggs 30
8. Bacon And Eggs 30
9. Sausage Breakfast Casserole 30
10. Breakfast Burritos 31
11. Baked Bacon Egg Cups 31
12. Breakfast Chicken Strips 32
13. No-Bun Breakfast Bacon Burger 32
14. Breakfast Coconut Porridge 32
15. Morning Time Sausages 33
16. Scrambled Pancake Hash 33
17. Breakfast Meatloaf Slices 34
18. Seed Porridge 34
19. Kale Breakfast Fritters 34
20. Keto Air Bread 35
21. Herbed Breakfast Eggs 35
22. Eggs In Zucchini Nests 36
23. Breakfast Liver Pate 36
24. Bread-Free Breakfast Sandwich 36
25. Egg Butter 37
26. Awesome Lemon Bell Peppers 37
27. Avocado Rolls 38
28. Portobello Hearty Mushroom Burgers .. 38
29. Crazy Mac And Cheese 38
30. Zucchini Noodles With Avocado Sauce 39
31. Candied Walnut And Strawberry 39
32. Blueberry Spelt Pancakes 40
33. Good Morning Energy Crackers 40
34. Masala Quinoa Meal 40
35. Toasted Quinoa Chunks 41
36. Lime And Cumin Quinoa 41
37. Fancy Breakfast Quinoa 41
38. Dr. Sebi Kamut Puff Cereal 42
39. Fresh Sautéed Apple 42
40. Perfect Vegetable Roast 42
41. Herb Frittata 43
42. Zucchini Bread 43
43. Blueberry Muffins 44
44. Baked Eggs 44
45. Bagels 45
46. Cauliflower Hash Browns 45
47. Cheese And Red Pepper Egg Cups 46
48. Coconut Porridge With Flax Seed 46
49. Easy Chocolate Doughnut 46
50. Cheesy Spinach Omelet 47
51. Roasted Garlic And Thyme Dipping Sauce 47
52. Cheesy Sausage And Egg Rolls 47
53. Baked Berry Oatmeal 47
54. Broccoli And Cheddar Cheese Quiche 48
55. Egg And Cheese Puff Pastry Tarts 48
56. French Toast 49
57. Grilled Gruyere Cheese Sandwich 49
58. Pancakes 50
59. Breakfast Sandwich 50
60. Egg Muffins 50
61. Cream Cheese Pancakes 50
62. Eggs On The Go 51
63. Breakfast Muffins 51
64. Egg Porridge 51
65. Delicious Breakfast Soufflé 52
66. Yummy Breakfast Italian Frittata 52
67. Savory Cheese and Bacon Muffins 52
68. Best Air-Fried English Breakfast 53
69. Sausage and Egg Breakfast Burrito ... 53
70. French Toast Sticks 54
71. Home-Fried Potatoes 54
72. Homemade Cherry Breakfast Tarts ... 55
73. Sausage and Cream Cheese Biscuits . 55
74. Fried Chicken and Waffles 56
75. Cheesy Tater Tot Breakfast Bake 56
76. Breakfast Scramble Casserole 57
77. Breakfast Grilled Ham and Cheese 57

#	Title	Page
78.	Classic Hash Browns	58
79.	Canadian Bacon and Cheese English Muffins	58
80.	Radish Hash Browns	59
81.	Vegetable Egg Cups	59
82.	Spinach Frittata	59
83.	Omelet Frittata	60
84.	Cheese Soufflés	60
85.	Simple Egg Soufflé	60
86.	Vegetable Egg Soufflé	61
87.	Asparagus Frittata	61
88.	Spicy Cauliflower Rice	61
89.	Broccoli Stuffed Peppers	62
90.	Zucchini Muffins	62
91.	Jalapeño Breakfast Muffins	62
92.	Zucchini Noodles	63
93.	Mushroom Frittata	63
94.	Egg Muffins	64
95.	Blueberry Breakfast Cobbler	64
96.	Granola	65
97.	Mixed Berry Muffins	65
98.	Homemade Strawberry Breakfast Tarts	66
99.	Everything Bagels	67
100.	Easy Maple-Glazed Doughnuts	67
101.	Chocolate-Filled Doughnut Holes	68
102.	Delicious Original Hash Browns	68
103.	Waffles and Chicken	69
104.	Puffed Egg Tarts	70
105.	Early Morning Steak and Eggs	70
106.	Breakfast Potatoes	71
107.	Baked Potato Breakfast Boats	71
108.	Greek Frittata	72
109.	Mini Shrimp Frittata	72
110.	Spinach and Mushroom Mini Quiche	73
111.	Italian Egg Cups	73
112.	Mexican Breakfast Pepper Rings	74
113.	Cajun Breakfast Muffins	74
114.	Hearty Blueberry Oatmeal	75

CHAPTER 3: SNACKS 76

#	Title	Page
115.	Air Fried Chicken Tenders	77
116.	Parmesan Zucchini Chips	77
117.	Cattle Ranch Garlic Pretzels	77
118.	Herby Sweet Potato Chips	78
119.	Cumin Tortilla Chips With Guacamole	78
120.	Oven-Dried Strawberries	78
121.	Chili Cheese Toasts	79
122.	Cheese Sticks	79
123.	Blended Veggie Chips	79
124.	Sweet Apple And Pear Chips	80
125.	Cocoa Banana Chips	80
126.	Coriander Roasted Chickpeas	81
127.	Corn Nuts	81
128.	Baked Potatoes	81
129.	Coconut Chicken Bites	81
130.	Buffalo Cauliflower Snack	82
131.	Banana Snack	82
132.	Potato Spread	82
133.	Mexican Apple Snack	83
134.	Shrimp Muffins	83
135.	Zucchini Cakes	84
136.	Cauliflower Bars	84
137.	Pesto Crackers	84
138.	Pumpkin Muffins	85
139.	Zucchini Chips	85
140.	Beef Jerky Snack	85
141.	Honey Party Wings	85
142.	Salmon Party Patties	86
143.	Banana Chips	86
144.	Sesame Tofu Cubes	86
145.	Thyme Salty Tomatoes	87
146.	Creamy Chicken Liver	87
147.	Catfish Sticks	88
148.	Honey Banana Chips	88
149.	Ginger Apple Chips	88
150.	Maple Carrot Fries	89
151.	Sweet Potato Fries	89
152.	Squid Rings	89
153.	Carrot Chips	90
154.	Corn Okra Bites	90
155.	Salty Potato Chips	90
156.	Corn & Beans Fries	91
157.	Sugary Apple Fritters	91
158.	Oregano Onion Rings	91
159.	Cinnamon Mixed Nuts	92
160.	Apple & Cinnamon Chips	92
161.	Sesame Cabbage & Prawns Egg Roll Wraps	92
162.	Rosemary Potatoes	93
163.	Crunchy Mozzarella Sticks With Sweet Thai Sauce	93
164.	Chili Cheese Crisps	94
165.	Parmesan Baked Tomatoes	94
166.	Gingered Scallops	94
167.	Baked Bacon Potatoes	95
168.	Coconut Shrimps	95
169.	Guacamole Tortilla Chips	96
170.	Roasted Chickpeas	96
171.	Supreme French Fries	97
172.	Butter Cashews	97
173.	Cinnamon Banana Chips	98
174.	Easy Baked Chocolate Mug Cake	98
175.	Fried Peaches	98

CHAPTER 4: DEHYDRATE 100

#	Title	Page
176.	Pineapple Slices	100
177.	Apple Slices	100
178.	Pear Slices	100

#		Page	#		Page
179.	Mango Slices	101	230.	Parsley Kohlrabi Fritters	121
180.	Zucchini Slices	101	231.	Chives Bamboo Shoots	122
181.	Dragon Fruit Slices	101	232.	Summer Eggplant & Zucchini	122
182.	Broccoli Florets	101	233.	Zucchini Hassel Back	122
183.	Avocado Slices	102	234.	Butternut Squash Hash	123
184.	Sweet Potato Chips	102	235.	Butter Mushrooms With Chives	123
185.	Kiwi Chips	102	236.	Fennel & Spinach Quiche	123

CHAPTER 5: LUNCH 104

#		Page	#		Page
			237.	Lemony Baby Potatoes	124
186.	Marinated Duck Breasts	105	238.	White Mushrooms With Snow Peas	124
187.	Chicken And Radish Mix	105	239.	Gold Potatoes And Bell Pepper Mix	125
188.	Chicken Breasts And BBQ Chili Sauce	105	240.	Potato With Bell Peppers	125
189.	Duck Breasts And Mango Mix	106	241.	Chinese Long Beans Mix	125
190.	Quick Creamy Chicken Casserole	106	242.	Portobello Mushrooms With Spinach	125
191.	Chicken And Peaches	107	243.	Summer Squash Mix	126
192.	Tea Glazed Chicken	107	244.	Corn With Tomatoes Salad	126
193.	Ratatouille	107	245.	Colored Veggie Mix	126
194.	Vegetable Egg Rolls	108	246.	Minty Leeks Medley	127
195.	Grilled Cheese And Greens Sandwiches	108	247.	Juicy Pork Chops	127
196.	Veggie Tuna Melts	109	248.	Crispy Meatballs	128
197.	California Melts	109	249.	Flavorful Steak	128
198.	Vegetable Pita Sandwiches	109	250.	Lemon Garlic Lamb	128
199.	Falafel	110	251.	Honey Mustard Pork Tenderloin	128
200.	Stuffed Tomatoes	110	252.	Easy Rosemary Lamb Chops	129
201.	Loaded Mini Potatoes	111	253.	BBQ Pork Ribs	129
202.	Crustless Veggie Quiche	111	254.	Juicy Steak Bites	129
203.	Scrambled Eggs With Broccoli And Spinach	112	255.	Greek Lamb Chops	130
204.	Beans And Greens Pizza	112	256.	Easy Beef Roast	130
205.	Grilled Chicken Mini Pizzas	112	257.	Herb Butter Rib Eye Steak	130
206.	Chicken Croquettes	113	258.	Classic Beef Jerky	131
207.	Pork Chops And Yogurt Sauce	113	259.	BBQ Pork Chops	131
208.	Lamb And Macadamia Nuts Mix	114	260.	Simple Beef Patties	131
209.	Beef, Cucumber And Eggplants	114	261.	Simple Beef Sirloin Roast	132
210.	Rosemary Pork And Artichokes	114	262.	Seasoned Beef Roast	132
211.	Mustard Lamb Loin Chops	114	263.	Bacon Wrapped Filet Mignon	132
212.	Herbed Lamb Chops	115	264.	Beef Burger	133
213.	Za'atar Lamb Loin Chops	115	265.	Season and Salt-Cured Beef	133
214.	Pesto Coated Rack Of Lamb	116	266.	Sweet & Spicy Meatballs	134
215.	Spiced Lamb Steaks	116	267.	Spiced Pork Shoulder	135
216.	Leg Of Lamb With Brussels Sprout	116	268.	Seasoned Pork Tenderloin	135
217.	Honey Mustard Cheesy Meatballs	117	269.	Garlicky Pork Tenderloin	136
218.	Spicy Lamb Kebabs	117	270.	Glazed Pork Tenderloin	136
219.	Simple Beef Burgers	117	271.	Country Style Pork Tenderloin	136
220.	Lamb With Potatoes	118	272.	Seasoned Pork Chops	137
221.	Nutmeg Beef Mix	118	273.	Breaded Pork Chops	137
222.	Oregano Daikon	118	274.	Crusted Rack of Lamb	138
223.	Creamy Spinach	119	275.	Lamb Burgers	139
224.	Eggplant With Grated Cheddar	119	276.	Salmon	139
225.	Coriander Garlic Bulbs	120	277.	Parmesan Shrimp	139
226.	Parmesan Sticks	120	278.	Shrimp with Lemon and Chile	140
227.	Creamy Snow Peas	120	279.	Tilapia	140
228.	Sesame Okra	121	280.	Tomato Basil Scallops	140
229.	Fennel Oregano Wedges	121	281.	Shrimp Scampi	141
			282.	Salmon Cakes	141

#	Title	Page
283.	Cilantro Lime Shrimps	142
284.	Cajun Style Shrimp	142

CHAPTER 6: DINNER 144

#	Title	Page
285.	Crispy Indian Wrap	145
286.	Easy Peasy Pizza	145
287.	Eggplant Parmigiana	146
288.	Luscious Lazy Lasagna	147
289.	Pasta With Creamy Cauliflower Sauce	147
290.	Lemony Lentils With "Fried" Onions	148
291.	Our Daily Bean	149
292.	Taco Salad With Creamy Lime Sauce	149
293.	Bbq Jackfruit Nachos	150
294.	10-Minute Chimichanga	150
295.	Mexican Stuffed Potatoes	151
296.	Kids' Taquitos	151
297.	Immune-Boosting Grilled Cheese Sandwich	152
298.	Tamale Pie With Cilantro Lime Cornmeal Crust	152
299.	Herbed Eggplant	153
300.	Spices Stuffed Eggplants	154
301.	Salsa Stuffed Eggplants	154
302.	Sesame Seeds Bok Choy	154
303.	Basil Tomatoe	155
304.	Overloaded Tomatoes	155
305.	Sweet & Spicy Cauliflower	155
306.	Herbed Potatoes	156
307.	Spicy Potatoes	156
308.	Crispy Kale Chips	157
309.	Grilled Buffalo Cauliflower	157
310.	Faux Fried Pickles	157
311.	Greatest Green Beans	158
312.	Summer Grilled Corn	158
313.	Cheesy Bean Bake	158
314.	Barbacoa Beef	158
315.	Maple Smoked Brisket	159
316.	Philly Cheesesteak Sandwiches	159
317.	Pot Roast And Potatoes	160
318.	Butter Chicken	160
319.	Curried Chicken Meatball Wraps	160
320.	Fall-Off-The-Bone Chicken	161
321.	White Chicken Chili	161
322.	Coconut Curry Vegetable Rice Bowls	162
323.	Egg Roll In A Bowl	162
324.	Frittata Provencal	162
325.	Ramekin Eggs	163
326.	Easter Ham	163
327.	Korean Lamb Chops	163
328.	Air Fryer Chicken Kabobs	164
329.	Chicken Fried Rice In Air Fryer	164
330.	Air Fried Chicken Tikkas	165
331.	Nashville Hot Chicken In Air Fryer	165
332.	Air Fryer Panko Breaded Chicken Parmesan	166
333.	Air Fryer Rosemary Turkey	167
334.	Air Fryer Lamb Chops	167
335.	Air Fried Shrimp And Sauce	168
336.	Air Fryer Italian Meatball	168
337.	Air Fryer Coconut Milk Chicken	169
338.	Air Fryer Cauliflower Rice	169
339.	Buttery Cod	170
340.	Creamy Chicken	170
341.	Mushroom And Turkey Stew	170
342.	Basil Chicken	171
343.	Eggplant Bake	171
344.	Meatball Casserole	171
345.	Herbed Lamb Rack	172
346.	Baked Beef	172
347.	Old-Fashioned Pork Chops	172
348.	Turkey Pillows	173
349.	Chicken Wings	173
350.	Sesame Chicken	174
351.	Chicken And Potatoes	174
352.	Polish Sausage And Sourdough Kabobs	174
353.	Ranch Meatloaf With Peppers	175
354.	Indian Beef Samosas	175
355.	Grilled Vienna Sausage With Broccoli	176
356.	Aromatic T-Bone Steak With Garlic	176
357.	Sausage Scallion Balls	176
358.	Cube Steak With Cowboy Sauce	177
359.	Steak Fingers With Lime Sauce	177
360.	Beef Kofta Sandwich	178
361.	Classic Beef Ribs	178
362.	Spicy Short Ribs With Red Wine Sauce	179
363.	Crispy Salt and Pepper Tofu	179
364.	Air Fryer Chicken Wings	180
365.	Spicy Parmesan Chicken Wings	180
366.	Buffalo Cauliflower Bites	181
367.	Spicy Dry-Rubbed Chicken Wings	181
368.	Air Fryer Steak Bites and Mushrooms	181
369.	Pecan Crusted Chicken	182
370.	Chicken Tikka Kebab	182
371.	Air Fryer Brussels sprouts	183
372.	Crispy Air Fried Tofu	183
373.	Buttermilk Fried Mushrooms	183
374.	Crispy Baked Avocado Tacos	184
375.	Chicken Cordon Bleu	184
376.	Fried Chicken	185
377.	Seasoned Tomatoes	185
378.	Filled Tomatoes	186
379.	Parmesan Asparagus	186
380.	Almond Asparagus	186
381.	Spicy Butternut Squash	187
382.	Sweet & Spicy Parsnips	187
383.	Pesto Tomatoes	188
384.	Roasted Cauliflower with Nuts & Raisins	188
385.	Spicy Herb Chicken Wings	188

386.	LAMB MEATBALLS	189
387.	SWEET & SOUR CHICKEN SKEWER	189
388.	GREEN STUFFED PEPPERS	189
389.	BEEF MEATBALLS IN TOMATO SAUCE	190
390.	MUSTARD PORK BALLS	190
391.	GARLIC PORK CHOPS	190
392.	HONEY GINGER SALMON FILLETS	191
393.	ROSEMARY & LEMON SALMON	191
394.	FISH WITH CAPERS & HERB SAUCE	191
395.	LEMON HALIBUT	192
396.	FRIED COD & SPRING ONION	192

CHAPTER 7: MAINS 194

397.	GARLIC PUTTER PORK CHOPS	195
398.	CAJUN PORK STEAKS	195
399.	CAJUN SWEET-SOUR GRILLED PORK	195
400.	PORK LOIN WITH POTATOES	196
401.	ROASTED CHAR SIEW (PORK BUTT)	196
402.	ASIAN PORK CHOPS	196
403.	MARINATED PORK CHOPS	197
404.	STEAK WITH CHEESE BUTTER	197
405.	MUSSELS BOWLS	197
406.	CHICKEN AND PEPPERCORNS MIX	197
407.	SALMON PATTIES	198
408.	SHRIMP WITH VEGGIE	198
409.	CHILI GARLIC CHICKEN WINGS	198
410.	FUNKY-GARLIC AND TURKEY BREASTS	199
411.	CHILI CHICKEN WINGS	199
412.	LEMON DRUMSTICKS	199
413.	SALSA VERDE CHICKEN	200
414.	MADEIRA BEEF	200
415.	CREAMY PORK AND ZUCCHINIS	200
416.	AIR-FRYER TOFU SATAY	201
417.	STICKY-SWEET BBQ TOFU	201
418.	VEGGIE BOWL	201
419.	AIR FRIED FISH SKIN	202
420.	BAKED THAI FISH	202
421.	OVEN BRAISED CORNED BEEF	202
422.	CRISPY KETO PORK BITES	202
423.	SOY AND GARLIC MUSHROOMS	203
424.	CRACK CHICKEN	203
425.	BULLET-PROOF BEEF ROAST	203
426.	AIR FRIED CATFISH	204
427.	LEMON FISH FILLET	204
428.	COCONUT SHRIMP	204
429.	RIB EYE STEAK	205
430.	DELICIOUS HOT STEAKS	205
431.	CREAMY BEEF LIVER CAKES	205
432.	PORK CHOPS IN CREAM	206
433.	FIVE SPICE PORK BELLY	206
434.	FAST RIB EYE STEAK	206
435.	PORK TENDERLOINS WITH APPLE	207
436.	AWESOME BEEF BULGOGI WITH MUSHROOMS	207
437.	HOMEMADE BEEF LIVER SOUFFLÉ	207
438.	AUTHENTIC WIENER BEEF SCHNITZEL	207
439.	HERBED BEEF ROAST	208
440.	EFFORTLESS BEEF SCHNITZEL	208
441.	SWEET MARINATED PORK CHOPS	208
442.	SAGE SAUSAGES BALLS	209
443.	PORK BELLY WITH HONEY	209
444.	COCKTAIL FRANKS IN BLANKET	209
445.	SEASONED PORK SHOULDER	210
446.	GLAZED PORK SHOULDER	210
447.	SIMPLE PORK LOIN	211
448.	BACON WRAPPED PORK TENDERLOIN	211

CHAPTER 8: POULTRY 214

449.	QUICK & EASY LEMON PEPPER CHICKEN	215
450.	SPICY JALAPENO HASSEL BACK CHICKEN	215
451.	TASTY HASSEL BACK CHICKEN	215
452.	WESTERN TURKEY BREAST	216
453.	LEMON PEPPER TURKEY BREAST	216
454.	TENDER TURKEY LEGS	216
455.	PERFECT CHICKEN BREASTS	217
456.	RANCH GARLIC CHICKEN WINGS	217
457.	RANCH CHICKEN THIGHS	217
458.	TACO RANCH CHICKEN WINGS	217
459.	SIMPLE CAJUN CHICKEN WINGS	218
460.	SIMPLE AIR FRIED CHICKEN	218
461.	BUFFALO WINGS	218
462.	HONEY LIME CHICKEN WINGS	219
463.	SIMPLE CHICKEN DRUMSTICKS	219
464.	HEALTHY CHICKEN WINGS	219
465.	THAI CHICKEN THIGHS	220
466.	CHICKEN PATTIES	220
467.	CAJUN SEASONED CHICKEN DRUMSTICKS	220
468.	HONEY GARLIC CHICKEN	221
469.	SRIRACHA CHICKEN WINGS	221
470.	SWEET & SPICY CHICKEN WINGS	221
471.	GINGER GARLIC CHICKEN	221
472.	HERB ROASTED CHICKEN	222
473.	HONEY & MUSTARD CHICKEN THIGHS	222
474.	FRIED CHICKEN TENDERLOINS	222
475.	THYME TURKEY NUGGETS	223
476.	FRUITY CHICKEN BREASTS WITH BBQ SAUCE	223
477.	SAVORY HONEY & GARLIC CHICKEN	223
478.	HOT CHICKEN WINGS	224
479.	SWEET CHICKEN DRUMSTICKS	224
480.	SAVORY BUFFALO CHICKEN	224
481.	ROSEMARY CHICKEN BREASTS	224
482.	CHICKEN WITH AVOCADO & RADISH BOWL	225
483.	SAVORY CHICKEN WITH ONION	225
484.	BUTTERED CRISPY TURKEY	225
485.	CHINESE CHICKEN WINGS RECIPE	226
486.	CHICKEN AND ASPARAGUS RECIPE	226
487.	HONEY DUCK BREASTS RECIPE	226

#	Recipe	Page
488.	Coconut Creamy Chicken	227
489.	Lemony Chicken	227
490.	Buttermilk Marinated Chicken	227
491.	Roasted Duck	227
492.	Roasted Turkey Breast	228
493.	Lemon Pepper Turkey	228
494.	Maple Chicken Thighs	229
495.	Italian Chicken Bake	229
496.	Pesto Chicken Bake	230
497.	Lemon Garlic Chicken	230
498.	Grilled Ranch Chicken	230
499.	Chicken Breast Pita Sandwiches	231
500.	Asian Style Turkey Meatballs	231
501.	Sweet And Spicy Chicken Stir-Fry	232
502.	Crispy Chicken Parmigiana	232
503.	Chicken Fajitas With Avocados	233
504.	Fried Chicken With Buttermilk	233
505.	Panko-Crusted Chicken Nuggets	233
506.	Crusted Chicken Tenders	234
507.	Chicken With Greek Yogurt Buffalo Sauce	234
508.	Baked Chicken Fajita Roll-Ups	235
509.	Garlicky Chicken And Potatoes	235
510.	Chicken Thighs With Lemon Garlic	236
511.	Lemony Chicken With Barbecue Sauce	236
512.	Chicken Popcorn	237
513.	Quick & Easy Meatballs	237
514.	Lemon Pepper Chicken Wings	238
515.	BBQ Chicken Wings	238
516.	Yummy Chicken Nuggets	238
517.	Italian Seasoned Chicken Tenders	239
518.	Classic Chicken Wings	239
519.	Simple Spice Chicken Wings	240
520.	Herb Seasoned Turkey Breast	240
521.	Tasty Rotisserie Chicken	240
522.	Spicy Asian Chicken Thighs	241
523.	Tomato, Eggplant 'N Chicken Skewers	241
524.	Teriyaki Glazed Chicken Bake	242
525.	Sriracha-Ginger Chicken	242
526.	Naked Cheese, Chicken Stuffing 'N Green Beans	242
527.	Grilled Chicken Pesto	243
528.	Healthy Turkey Shepherd's Pie	243
529.	Chicken Fillet Strips	243
530.	Chicken Chili Verde	244
531.	Lemon Curry Chicken	244
532.	Turkey Joint	245
533.	Cilantro Drumsticks	245
534.	Mozzarella Turkey Rolls	245
535.	Sage & Onion Turkey Balls	245
536.	Turkey Loaf	246
537.	Moroccan Chicken	246
538.	Herbed Cornish Game Hen	247
539.	Cajun Spiced Whole Chicken	247
540.	Lemony Whole Chicken	248
541.	Crispy Chicken Legs	249
542.	Marinated Spicy Chicken Legs	249
543.	Gingered Chicken Drumsticks	250
544.	Crispy Chicken Drumsticks	251
545.	Lemony Chicken Thighs	252
546.	Chinese Chicken Drumsticks	252
547.	Crispy Chicken Thighs	253
548.	Oat Crusted Chicken Breasts	254
549.	Crispy Chicken Cutlets	254
550.	Brie Stuffed Chicken Breasts	255
551.	Chicken Kabobs	256
552.	Simple Turkey Breast	256
553.	Herbed Duck Breast	257

CHAPTER 9: SEAFOOD 258

#	Recipe	Page
554.	Citrusy Branzini On The Grill	259
555.	Cajun-Seasoned Lemon Salmon	259
556.	Grilled Salmon Fillets	259
557.	Cheesy Breaded Salmon	259
558.	Coconut Crusted Shrimp	260
559.	Rice Flour Coated Shrimp	260
560.	Buttered Scallops	260
561.	Fish Sticks	261
562.	Butter Trout	261
563.	Pesto Almond Salmon	261
564.	Garlic Lemon Shrimp	261
565.	Air-Fried Crab Sticks	262
566.	Cajun Salmon	262
567.	E-Z Catfish	262
568.	Fish Nuggets	263
569.	Grilled Shrimp	263
570.	Honey & Sriracha Tossed Calamari	263
571.	Salmon Croquettes	264
572.	Spicy Cod	264
573.	Air Fried Lobster Tails	264
574.	Air Fryer Salmon	265
575.	Simple Scallops	265
576.	3-Ingredient Air Fryer Catfish	266
577.	Pecan-Crusted Catfish	266
578.	Flying Fish	266
579.	Air Fryer Fish Tacos	267
580.	Bacon Wrapped Scallops	267
581.	Quick Fried Catfish	267
582.	Air-Fried Herbed Shrimp	268
583.	Creamy Air Fryer Salmon	268
584.	Barbecued Lime Shrimp	268
585.	Spicy Air-Fried Cheese Tilapia	268
586.	Cheese Salmon	269
587.	Air-Fryer Baked Salmon & Asparagus	269
588.	Parmesan Baked Salmon	269
589.	Grilled Prawns	270
590.	Pesto Scallops	270

#	Title	Page
591.	Creamy Parmesan Shrimp	270
592.	Delicious Garlic Butter Salmon	271
593.	Horseradish Salmon	271
594.	Pesto Shrimp	271
595.	Garlic Butter Shrimp	272
596.	Honey Mustard Salmon	272
597.	Classic Tilapia	272
598.	Coconut Crusted Fish Fillets	273
599.	Tuna Patties	273
600.	Fish With Vegetables	273
601.	Balsamic Salmon	274
602.	Dijon Fish Fillets	274
603.	Perfect Salmon Dinner	274
604.	Steam Clams	275
605.	Breaded Coconut Shrimp	275
606.	Breaded Cod Sticks	275
607.	Cajun Shrimp	276
608.	Cod Fish Nuggets	276
609.	Creamy Salmon	276
610.	Crumbled Fish	277
611.	Easy Crab Sticks	277
612.	Fried Catfish	277
613.	Grilled Sardines	277
614.	Zucchini with Tuna	278
615.	Caramelized Salmon Fillet	278
616.	Deep Fried Prawns	278
617.	Mussels with Pepper	279
618.	Monkfish with Olives and Capers	279
619.	Shrimp, Zucchini and Cherry Tomato Sauce	279
620.	Salmon with Pistachio Bark	280
621.	Salted Marinated Salmon	280
622.	Sautéed Trout with Almonds	280
623.	Calamari Slices	280
624.	Honey Glazed Salmon	281
625.	Sweet & Sour Glazed Salmon	281
626.	Ranch Tilapia	282
627.	Breaded Flounder	282
628.	Simple Haddock	282
629.	Breaded Hake	283
630.	Sesame Seeds Coated Tuna	283
631.	Cheese and Ham Patties	284
632.	Air-Fried Seafood	284
633.	Fish with Chips	284
634.	Crumbly Fishcakes	285
635.	Bacon Wrapped Shrimp	285
636.	Crab Legs	285
637.	Fish Sticks	285
638.	Crusty Pesto Salmon	286
639.	Salmon Patties	286
640.	Cajun Salmon	286
641.	Buttery Cod	287
642.	Sesame Tuna Steak	287
643.	Lemon Garlic Shrimp	287
644.	Foil Packet Salmon	288
645.	Foil Packet Lobster Tail	288
646.	Avocado Shrimp	288
647.	Lemon Butter Scallops	289
648.	Cheesy Lemon Halibut	289
649.	Spicy Mackerel	290

CHAPTER 10: VEGETABES 292

#	Title	Page
650.	Zucchini Curry	293
651.	Healthy Carrot Fries	293
652.	Simple Stuffed Potatoes	293
653.	Simple Roasted Carrots	293
654.	Broccoli & Cheese	294
655.	Fried Plantains	294
656.	Bacon-Wrapped Asparagus	294
657.	Air Fried Roasted Corn On The Cob	295
658.	Green Beans & Bacon	295
659.	Air Fried Honey Roasted Carrots	295
660.	Air Fried Roasted Cabbage	296
661.	Burrata-Stuffed Tomatoes	296
662.	Broccoli With Parmesan Cheese	296
663.	Caramelized Broccoli	297
664.	Brussels Sprouts With Balsamic Oil	297
665.	Spiced Butternut Squash	297
666.	Garlic Thyme Mushrooms	297
667.	Zucchini Parmesan Chips	298
668.	Jicama Fries	298
669.	Cauliflower Pizza Crust	298
670.	Savoy Cabbage And Tomatoes	299
671.	Cauliflower Steak	299
672.	Tomato, Avocado And Green Beans	299
673.	Dill And Garlic Green Beans	300
674.	Eggplant Stacks	300
675.	Air Fried Spaghetti Squash	300
676.	Beets And Blue Cheese Salad	301
677.	Broccoli Salad	301
678.	Roasted Brussels Sprouts With Tomatoes	301
679.	Cheesy Brussels Sprouts	302
680.	Sweet Baby Carrots Dish	302
681.	Seasoned Leeks	302
682.	Crispy Potatoes And Parsley	302
683.	Garlic Tomatoes	303
684.	Easy Green Beans And Potatoes	303
685.	Green Beans And Tomatoes	303
686.	Flavored Asparagus	303
687.	Avocado Fries	304
688.	Spaghetti Squash Tots	304
689.	Cinnamon Butternut Squash Fries	304
690.	Lemon Bell Peppers	304
691.	Pesto Tomatoes	305
692.	Seasoned Potatoes	305
693.	Spicy Zucchini	305
694.	Seasoned Yellow Squash	306

#	Title	Page
695.	BUTTERED ASPARAGUS	306
696.	BUTTERED BROCCOLI	306
697.	SEASONED CARROTS WITH GREEN BEANS	307
698.	SWEET POTATO WITH BROCCOLI	307
699.	SEASONED VEGGIES	308
700.	POTATO GRATIN	308
701.	GARLIC EDAMAME	308
702.	SPICY CHICKPEAS	309
703.	EGG ROLL PIZZA STICKS	309
704.	CAJUN ZUCCHINI CHIPS	310
705.	CRISPY OLD BAY CHICKEN WINGS	310
706.	CINNAMON AND SUGAR PEACHES	311
707.	CHICKEN WINGS WITH PROVENCAL HERBS IN AIR FRYER	311
708.	SPICED CHICKEN WINGS IN AIRFRYER	312
709.	ROSTI (SWISS POTATOES)	312
710.	CRISPY BRUSSELS SPROUTS	312
711.	FLATBREAD	313
712.	CREAMY CABBAGE	313
713.	CREAMY POTATOES	313
714.	GREEN BEANS AND CHERRY TOMATOES	314
715.	CRISPY BRUSSELS SPROUTS AND POTATOES	314
716.	HERBED TOMATOES	314
717.	AIR FRIED LEEKS	314
718.	CRISPY BROCCOLI	315
719.	GARLIC-ROASTED BELL PEPPERS	315
720.	ASPARAGUS WITH GARLIC	315
721.	CHEESY ROASTED SWEET POTATOES	316
722.	SALTY LEMON ARTICHOKES	316
723.	ASPARAGUS & PARMESAN	316
724.	CORN ON COBS	317
725.	ONION GREEN BEANS	317
726.	DILL MASHED POTATO	318
727.	CREAM POTATO	318
728.	CHILI SQUASH WEDGES	318
729.	HONEY CARROTS WITH GREENS	319
730.	SOUTH ASIAN CAULIFLOWER FRITTERS	319
731.	SUPREME AIR-FRIED TOFU	319
732.	NOT YOUR AVERAGE ZUCCHINI PARMESAN CHIPS	320
733.	SKY-HIGH ROASTED CORN	320
734.	RAVISHING AIR-FRIED CARROTS WITH HONEY GLAZE	320
735.	FLAMING BUFFALO CAULIFLOWER BITES	321
736.	PLEASANT AIR-FRIED EGGPLANT	321
737.	CAULIFLOWER HASH	322
738.	ASPARAGUS WITH ALMONDS	322
739.	ZUCCHINI CUBES	322
740.	SWEET POTATO & ONION MIX	323
741.	SPICY EGGPLANT CUBES	323
742.	ROASTED GARLIC HEAD	324
743.	WRAPPED ASPARAGUS	324
744.	BAKED YAMS WITH DILL	324
745.	HONEY ONIONS	324
746.	DELIGHTFUL ROASTED GARLIC SLICES	325
747.	COCONUT OIL ARTICHOKES	325
748.	ROASTED MUSHROOMS	325
749.	MASHED YAMS	326
750.	CAULIFLOWER RICE	326
751.	SHREDDED CABBAGE	326
752.	FRIED LEEKS RECIPE	327
753.	BRUSSELS SPROUTS AND TOMATOES MIX RECIPE	327
754.	RADISH HASH RECIPE	327
755.	BROCCOLI SALAD RECIPE	327
756.	CHILI BROCCOLI	328
757.	PARMESAN BROCCOLI AND ASPARAGUS	328
758.	BUTTER BROCCOLI MIX	328
759.	BALSAMIC KALE	329
760.	KALE AND OLIVES	329
761.	KALE AND MUSHROOMS MIX	329
762.	OREGANO KALE	329
763.	KALE AND BRUSSELS SPROUTS	330

CHAPTER 11: SOUPS AND STEWS 332

#	Title	Page
764.	POTATO AND CHEESE SOUP	333
765.	SPLIT PEA SOUP	333
766.	CORN SOUP	333
767.	BEEF AND RICE SOUP	334
768.	CHICKEN NOODLE SOUP	334
769.	ZUPPA TOSCANA	335
770.	MINESTRONE SOUP	335
771.	CHICKEN AND WILD RICE SOUP	336
772.	CREAMY TOMATO SOUP	336
773.	TOMATO SOUP	337
774.	CARROT SOUP	337
775.	CABBAGE SOUP	338
776.	CREAM OF ASPARAGUS	338
777.	VEGGIE NOODLE SOUP	339
778.	CARROT GINGER SOUP	339
779.	CREAMY TOMATO BASIL SOUP	339
780.	CREAM OF MUSHROOM SOUP	340
781.	CHIPOTLE SWEET POTATO CHOWDER	340
782.	COCONUT SWEET POTATO STEW	341
783.	ITALIAN VEGETABLE STEW	341
784.	SPINACH MINT STEW	342
785.	CREAMY CAULIFLOWER AND SAGE SOUP	342
786.	CURRIED PUMPKIN SOUP	343
787.	MY SIGNATURE LEMON CHICKEN SOUP	343
788.	FUSS-FREE FRENCH ONION SOUP	344
789.	CREAMY BROCCOLI AND APPLE SOUP	344
790.	IMMUNE-BOOST CHARD AND SWEET POTATO STEW	345
791.	MOROCCAN LENTIL SOUP	346
792.	SALMON MEATBALLS SOUP	346
793.	TURMERIC CHICKEN SOUP	347
794.	EGG DROP SOUP WITH SHREDDED CHICKEN	347
795.	ASIAN EGG DROP SOUP	347

796.	LEEK AND SALMON SOUP	348
797.	THAI COCONUT SOUP	348
798.	GINGER HALIBUT SOUP	348
799.	SALMON HEAD SOUP	348
800.	CHICKEN CURRY SOUP	349
801.	SALMON STEW	349
802.	COCONUT SEAFOOD SOUP	350
803.	CHICKEN SOUP	350
804.	POACHED EGG SOUP	350
805.	SIMPLE CHICKEN AND KALE SOUP	351
806.	ASPARAGUS SOUP	351
807.	LEFTOVER SHREDDED CHICKEN SOUP	352
808.	CREAM OF BROCCOLI SOUP	352
809.	TURKEY WITH GINGER AND TURMERIC SOUP	353
810.	BUTTERNUT SQUASH SOUP	353

CHAPTER 12: DESSERTS 354

811.	APPLE CHIPS	355
812.	SWEETENED PLANTAINS	355
813.	ROASTED BANANAS	355
814.	PEAR CRISP	355
815.	EASY PEARS DESSERT	355
816.	VANILLA STRAWBERRY MIX	356
817.	SWEET BANANAS AND SAUCE	356
818.	CINNAMON APPLES AND MANDARIN SAUCE	356
819.	CHOCOLATE VANILLA BARS	357
820.	RASPBERRY BARS	357
821.	COCOA BERRIES CREAM	357
822.	COCOA PUDDING	357
823.	BLUEBERRY COCONUT CRACKERS	358
824.	CAULIFLOWER PUDDING	358
825.	SWEET VANILLA RHUBARB	358
826.	PINEAPPLE PUDDING	358
827.	BLUEBERRY JAM	359
828.	PLUM JAM	359
829.	COCONUT PANCAKE	359
830.	APPLES AND RED GRAPE JUICE	359
831.	COCONUT AND AVOCADO PUDDING	360
832.	CINNAMON ROLLS	360
833.	CHERRIES AND RHUBARB BOWLS	360
834.	PUMPKIN BOWLS	361
835.	APPLE JAM	361
836.	YOGURT AND PUMPKIN CREAM	361
837.	RAISINS RICE MIX	361
838.	ORANGE BOWLS	362
839.	STRAWBERRY JAM	362
840.	CARAMEL CREAM	362
841.	WRAPPED PEARS	362
842.	LEMON BARS	363
843.	COCONUT DONUTS	363
844.	BLUEBERRY CREAM	363
845.	BLACKBERRY CHIA JAM	364
846.	MIXED BERRIES CREAM	364
847.	AIR FRIED CRUMBED FISH	364
848.	AIR FRYER MEATLOAF	364
849.	AIR FRYER SHRIMP A LA BANG	365
850.	BALSAMIC-GLAZED CARROTS	365
851.	BAKED POTATOES WITH YOGURT AND CHIVES	366
852.	BUTTERED BROCCOLI WITH PARMESAN	366
853.	CREAMY CORN CASSEROLE	367
854.	CHARRED GREEN BEANS WITH SESAME SEEDS	367
855.	CINNAMON-SPICED ACORN SQUASH	368
856.	PARMESAN ASPARAGUS FRIES	368
857.	CHILI CORN ON THE COB	369
858.	SPICY CABBAGE	369
859.	SPICY BROCCOLI WITH HOT SAUCE	370
860.	CHEESY BROCCOLI GRATIN	370
861.	PERFECT CINNAMON TOAST	371
862.	ANGEL FOOD CAKE	371
863.	APPLE DUMPLINGS	371
864.	CHOCOLATE DONUTS	372
865.	APPLE HAND PIES	372
866.	SWEET CREAM CHEESE WONTONS	372
867.	FRENCH TOAST BITES	373
868.	CINNAMON SUGAR ROASTED CHICKPEAS	373
869.	BROWNIE MUFFINS	373
870.	CHOCOLATE MUG CAKE	374
871.	GRILLED PEACHES	374
872.	SIMPLE & DELICIOUS SPICED APPLES	374
873.	TANGY MANGO SLICES	375
874.	DRIED RASPBERRIES	375
875.	SWEET PEACH WEDGES	375
876.	AIR FRYER OREO COOKIES	375
877.	AIR FRIED BUTTER CAKE	376
878.	AIR FRYER S'MORES	376
879.	PEANUT BUTTER COOKIES	377
880.	SWEET PEAR STEW	377
881.	VANILLA APPLE COMPOTE	377
882.	APPLE DATES MIX	378
883.	CHOCOLATE RICE	378
884.	RAISINS CINNAMON PEACHES	378
885.	LEMON PEAR COMPOTE	378
886.	STRAWBERRY STEW	379
887.	WALNUT APPLE PEAR MIX	379
888.	CINNAMON PEAR JAM	379
889.	PEAR SAUCE	380
890.	SWEET PEACH JAM	380
891.	WARM PEACH COMPOTE	380
892.	SPICED PEAR SAUCE	381
893.	HONEY FRUIT COMPOTE	381

CHAPTER 1:

What Is an Air Fryer? How to Use It?

What Is an Air Fryer?

The air fryer is an equipment with the distinction that it uses hot water to cook the food. The fryer utilizes warm water, up to about 200ºC, to cook the food instead of traditionally cooking meals using oil. The latest version of the fryer allows temperature adjustment for accurate, uniform cooking.

It does this by circulating hot air quickly with a built-in fan, a process that builds temperatures high enough to mimic conventional frying. Because of this, air fryers can fry food without the hazards of traditional oil frying—such as oil burns or fire damage—and can do it in a more systematic, controlled manner.

An air fryer uses hot air, so some may argue it works the same as a conventional oven. However, you must remember that the two appliances produce different results, often due to their differences in technology. While ovens apply dry air and heat directly to the dish and take longer cooking times, air fryers contain technology that rapidly spirals air around the dish, resulting in faster cooking times and a more fried appearance.

An air fryer is one of the magical cooking appliances that help to cook various delicious and tasty dishes at home. You can fry French fries with very little oil. Saves more than 80% of oil when frying or cooking food. Most people are disappointed due to the lack of crispiness in their food. The air fryer makes your food crispy and tasty.

How to Use an Air Fryer

Since 2010, there have been countless versions of the air fryer, often with different styles and mechanisms. That said, it's usually best to consult your service provider when it comes to how to use it, and if you're looking to replace your current brand with another, how it differs from your newer appliance. However, there are some similarities:

- **Use the right attachment:** Before anything else, clarify what attachment you'll need for the dish with the recipe. Do you need a mixer? A grill? And the extra pan? Ensure that you have everything ready.
- **Ungrease your pan:** While air fryers don't need oil to work, not using oil often means a larger chance of certain dishes sticking to the pan or basket. You can spray the pan lightly with oil to keep your food from sticking or add parchment paper to it for a true oil-free alternative. Nonetheless, unsticking your pan is crucial.

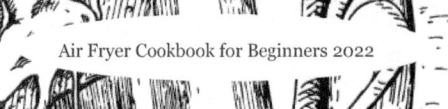

- **Set the temperature:** Whether you're using Fahrenheit, Celsius, or amount of wattage, be sure you set your fryer at the right temperature or power level, so it doesn't over or undercook your dish. Some air fryers also provide "modes" or cooking options for certain types of food like fries and pastries.
- **Set the timer:** Once you're done with your temperature, just set the timer as indicated in the recipe and let it fly. You can experiment a little with this. You can also take out the pan now and then to add more *ingredients* or check your cooking time. All you need is to pause the machine.

Purchasing Your Fryer

If you're considering buying an air fryer, make sure you look at the features of the fryer you're buying. Price often depends on the equipment's characteristics. Some designs might be a little cheaper than others. You should look for features, such as an automatic timer, a simple navigation touch screen surface or an embedded dial, simple cleaning, and space effectiveness. Some machines are completely capable of cooking a large quantity of food, while others are not. If you have a big group at all times, then choose a larger machine. Three types of Air Fryers are available on the market today and include:

- **Halogen:** It uses a halogen light bulb to cook. These often have a transparent glass cover so you can watch the whole cooking process without opening the air fryer.
- **Dynamic:** It has a paddle that rotates the food while cooking, so there is no need to turn it. This is nice when you are making fries, but not so good for other foods. If I put my empanadas or dumplings in one of these and the paddle spins it around, it would have stuffed all over the place.
- **Static air:** It is where everything stays still except the air inside heated by coil elements and circulated by a fan. This is what most people have when getting an air fryer.

Air fryers come in many different sizes. My air fryer cooks 1.8 pounds of food at a time and has a basket about 6-inches in diameter. Other types cook 1.5 and up to 2.5 pounds of food at a time.

Things to Know Before You Buy an Air Fryer

The convection mechanism utilizes super-heated air to cook food in a special chamber. Technically speaking, a mechanical fan blows heat around the space so the hot air circulates around your food at high speed, cooking evenly from all sides, producing crispy browning results. This is called the Maillard effect.

This intelligent but straightforward machine radiates heat from heating elements and uses rapid air technology to fry, roast, and bake your food with less oil. The air fryer can also warm your food. You don't have to slave over a hot stove as the air fryer features automatic temperature control. Thanks to its convection settings, it produces crispier and tastier food than using conventional cooking methods.

If you think of cutting down on fat consumption, here is a great solution. Studies have shown that air-fried veggies contain up to 80% less fat than deep-fried veggies. To give you an idea of the calorie content—deep-fried onion rings contain about 411 calories versus air-fried ones, which have about 176 calories. Deep-fried chicken nuggets contain 305 calories versus air-fried chicken nuggets containing 180 calories.

Air fryers come with accessories, such as baking dishes, pans, trays, grill pans, skewer racks, and so forth, which will vary from model to model. However, make sure to use pans and racks that are designed to fit into the air fryer.

Benefits of Using an Air fryer

Air fryers' major advantage is that it keeps the cooked meals healthier. It reduces the fat part of the meal by not using oil to heat and boil the meat. This is not the case with conventional fryers, where oil use increases saturated fat content. Another benefit of using air fryers is that modern ones are equipped with an exhaust system that filters out surplus air. It's pleasant to the surroundings because it's eco-friendly.

While the equipment is perfect for a healthy lifestyle, one drawback of using an air fryer is that it uses air to cook the food, so it is essential not to overload the cooking zone, resulting in irregular cooking. Thicker meat cuts may also require extra cooking time to cook completely. Price can also be a problem, as some designs are costly in the market today.

Health

Is air frying a healthy cooking method? Deep-fried foods absorb fat, which significantly increases their calorie content. Furthermore, these foods are typically coated in breadcrumbs, flour, or eggs before frying. For instance, a medium-sized baked potato (approximately 100 grams) contains about 93 calories, 0 grams of fat, and 0 milligrams of cholesterol. On the other hand, 100 grams of French fries have 319 calories and 17 grams of fat; they also contain high amounts of trans-fats and sodium (approximately 234 milligrams).

In fact, there is no need to be afraid of fat. The harmful fat in the fryer oil, which contains free radicals, should be avoided. Vegetable oils to avoid include soybean oil, corn oil, cottonseed oil, sunflower oil, peanut oil, and rice bran oil. Oils with health benefits include olive oil, coconut oil, grapeseed oil, flaxseed oil, avocado oil, walnut oil, and sesame oil. Butter, tallow, and lard are excellent for frying because they have a high smoke point. Unfortunately, healthy and unrefined oils have a low smoke point, and they become unhealthy under the heat in deep fryers. It is better to save them for salad dressings and cook your food with minimum oil.

Fast Cooking

The Air Fryer's cooking times are shorter compared to a standard convection oven or convection toaster oven. Your Air Fryer heats up in a few minutes, then hot air circulates quickly, cooking your food evenly on all sides. It can take about 50 minutes to roast chicken in a conventional oven; in an Air Fryer, it gets perfectly cooked, beautifully browned with crispy edges in 30–35 minutes. Many Air Fryer models come with dividers to cook different dishes at the same time. The Air Fryer is a real winner for one-pot meals too. This is a space, cost, and frustration-saving solution!

More Flavor

These fried foods do not taste like fat. These fried foods are delicious! Extraordinary chips are only the beginning. Old-fashioned casseroles, spicy chilies, perfect mac and cheese, sophisticated appetizers, ooey-gooey bread puddings, and delicious snacks turn out great in the Air Fryer.

Requires Less Oil and Fats

Compared to other traditional fryers, the air requires very little oil for frying. It saves more than 80% of the oil during cooking. Just a tablespoon of oil fries your French fries make it tender from inside and crispy from outside.

Saves Nutritional Values

The traditional method of frying destroys essential vitamins and minerals in your food. Air fryer fries your food by blowing the very hot air into a food basket. Air frying your food helps maintain essential vitamins and nutrients in your food.

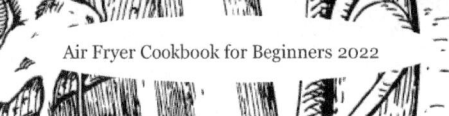

Reduces the Risk of Heart-Related Diseases
Eating fried deep food is not a healthy choice for your body. The air fryer keeps the essential vitamins and nutrients in your food. This will help to reduce heart-related diseases.

Automatic Cooking Programs
Most of the air fryer comes with pre-programmed auto cook buttons. These auto-cooking functions are nothing but commonly used programs like French fries, chicken fries, chips, etc. Just press the auto cook function button, and your air fryer will automatically adjust the time and temperature of your air fryer.

Versatile
An air fryer is not only a fryer to cook different foods. You can use it for baking bread, making popcorn, or even making roasted vegetables.

Cost-Effective
Since no oil is used for cooking, you can save a lot of money on purchasing cooking oil.

Easy to Cook
Never mind if you are a kitchen novice. Since air fryers are digital, it requires less skill to cook delicious dishes even if you are not good at cooking.

Fewer Calories
Since you do not add any oil to cook your food compared to traditional frying methods, you don't add a few calories to cook your food. Remember that a cup of oil is already equivalent to 800 calories alone, so deep-frying increases the caloric value of your food to a dangerously high level.

The fact is that there are many benefits to using an air fryer, and you can enjoy a healthier and more comfortable life.

Best Practices When Air Frying
While it is easy to use an air fryer, using it for the first time can present some challenges. But this should not scare you from air frying your foods. After all, you get more health benefits than frying foods in oil. Below are the best practices and tips that you can do to successfully air fry your favorite foods.

- **Shake the basket**: To distribute the ingredients within the basket, you can shake the basket a few times while cooking.
- **Spray a little amount of oil**: If you are not satisfied with how brown your food is, you can spray oil halfway through the cooking process. Be sure to spray foods lightly and not lather them with oil.
- **Preheat the air fryer before you place your food inside**: Just like cooking in an oven, you need to preheat your air fryer so that your food will cook properly.
- **Never put too many foods inside the basket**: While it is very tempting to cook more food at a time, overcrowding your air fryer prevents the hot air from circulating properly within the fryer thus, you end up with food that is not evenly brown or crispy.
- **Add water to the air fryer drawer**: If you are cooking greasy foods, add water to the air fryer drawer located under the basket. This prevents the grease from getting too hot and causing it to smoke.
- **Hold your food properly**: Since air fryers have strong fans that can blow off light food particles, secure them in place using toothpicks. If food gets stuck in the fan or heating element of the air fryer, it might get burned and cause smoke to form during the cooking process.
- **Flip your food:** Halfway through the cooking time, flip your food over just as you would when cooking on a grill. This will ensure that the food will brown evenly on all sides.

- ***Press the breading on your food firmly***: An air fryer has a strong fan that can blow off parts of your food; thus, if you are putting breading on your food, make sure that you press it firmly to help it stay in place while you are cooking.
- ***Use oven-safe accessories***: When cooking with an air fryer, use oven-safe accessories like small baking pans or tins where you can place your food. Oven-safe accessories can withstand extremely high temperatures, so they aren't damaged once you are cooking your food.

Basic Parts, Accessories, and Their Importance

Air fryer accessories come in different shapes and functions. Air fryer accessories can take it to the next level by preparing all types of foods and frying them. You can get many types of air fryer accessories, and they will help you create meals that you would never think possible that you can make in an air fryer. These include baked goodies, grilled, and even barbecued meats.

So, here is a quick list and description of each air fryer accessory available in the market. It also includes how to use it and when best to use it.

Skewers on Double-Layer Rack

The double-layer rack accessory allows you to maximize the cooking space within the fryer. You can bake, fry, or grill fish, chicken, pork, or beef on the bottom rack while cooking other types of food on the upper rack, such as burgers and sausages. This accessory also comes with four skewers so that you can make kabobs, meat on skewers, and grill.

The rack is dishwasher safe; thus, clean-up is a breeze, as it is dishwasher-friendly. It is also compatible with most air fryer models, but make sure that you ask the store where you are buying it if it is compatible with the brand and model of air fryer.

Grill Pan

The grill pan comes with a rapid air technology design thanks to the perforated surface, making it ideal for the air to flow throughout the food while grilling.

Since the grill pan is placed at the bottom of the air fryer, it comes with an Easy Click removable handle so that you can place the grill pan in the air fryer or take them out to clean. The perforations on the surface of the grill pan also allow the extra fat to drip away so that you can make the perfect grilled surface on the meat. Moreover, the surface of the grill pan is non-stick, so that you can easily remove the food from the pan. It also has a very large enough surface to grill a big steak fish, a whole fillet of fish, and a generous amount of vegetables.

Baking Dish

The air fryer baking dish or pan does not only help you cook baked goodies such as cakes and bread, but you can also cook quiche, lasagna, shepherd's pie, and other deep-dish recipes that you usually cook in an oven. It comes with a non-stick surface; thus, clean-up is effortless and dishwasher safe. The non-stick surface also ensures that you can easily take out your food, so you get perfect results all the time.

The air fryer-baking dish allows you to use your air fryer as an oven to bake cakes, muffins, and bread. Using a suitable baking dish for your air fryer ensures that you can cook your recipes properly, as they are designed to ensure that the proper airflow is distributed within the air fryer to cook food evenly.

Prepare and place your ingredients in the basket and set the timer. The warm air goes to work, and the timer goes off with a ding noise when its job is finished, showing that your food is prepared. You can even inspect your food to see its progress without interfering with the fixed moment. The fryer will stop once you take out the pan; heating will resume when you put the pan back. The Air fryer is a straightforward appliance, with no assembling required and no complications. It consists of three main items: the cooking basket, the pan, and the main fryer unit.

You're putting your meals in the cooking basket. It has a basket handle where you place your hand to avoid burns or accidents while handling the appliance and cooked meals when the air fryer is switched on. The basket fits into the pan perfectly. The pan gathers food, and surplus oil remains and fits completely into the air fryer. The main fryer unit is made up of many components. Other useful components include a rack, double grill layer, basketball, and food separators that allow various dishes to be prepared at once.

Air Fryer Cooking Chart

Over time, many manufacturers have tweaked the cooking settings of the air fryer to suit their different inventions. However, you will have many recipes falling along the time and temperature patterns as in the chart below.

It is essential to read your manufacturer's time and temperature instructions, and then you can adjust both to fit the recipe in question to ensure that you have well-cooked meals. Also, work with a food thermometer to aid you in reaching the accurate internal temperature of meats and seafood for safe consumption.

Vegetables

	Temp (°F)	Time (mins)		Temp (°F)	Time (mins)
Asparagus (1-inch slices)	400ºF	5	Onions (quartered)	400ºF	11
Beets (whole)	400ºF	40	Parsnips (½-inch chunks)	380ºF	15
Bell peppers (1-inch chunks)	400ºF	15	Pearl onions	400ºF	10
Broccoli (florets)	400ºF	6	Potatoes (whole baby pieces)	400ºF	15
Broccoli rabe (chopped)	400ºF	6	Potatoes (1-inch chunks)	400ºF	12
Brussel sprouts (halved)	380ºF	15	Potatoes (baked whole)	400ºF	40
Cabbage (diced)	380ºF	15	Pumpkin (½-inch chunks)	380ºF	13
Carrots (halved)	380ºF	15	Radishes	380ºF	15
Cauliflower (florets)	400ºF	12	Squash (½-inch chunks)	400ºF	12
Collard greens	250ºF	12	Sweet potato (baked)	380ºF	30–35
Corn on the cob	390ºF	6	Tomatoes (halves)	350ºF	10
Cucumber (½-inch slices)	370ºF	4	Tomatoes (cherry)	400ºF	4
Eggplant (2-inch cubes)	400ºF	15	Turnips (½-inch chunks)	380ºF	15
Fennel (quartered)	370ºF	15	Zucchini (½-inch sticks)	400ºF	12
Green beans	400ºF	5	Mushrooms (¼-inch slices)	400ºF	5
Kale (halved)	250ºF	12			

Chicken

	Temp (°F)	Time (mins)		Temp (°F)	Time (mins)
Breasts, bone-in (1 ¼ pound)	370ºF	25	Legs, bone-in (1 ¾ pound)	380ºF	30
Breasts, boneless (4 ounces)	380ºF	12	Thighs, boneless (1 ½ pound)	380ºF	18–20
Drumsticks (2 ½ pounds)	370ºF	20	Wings (2 pounds)	400ºF	12
Game hen (halved 2 pounds)	390ºF	20	Whole chicken	360ºF	75
Thighs, bone-in (2 pounds)	380ºF	22	Tenders	360ºF	8–10

Beef

	Temp (°F)	Time (mins)		Temp (°F)	Time (mins)
Beef eye round roast (4 pounds)	400ºF	45–55	Meatballs (1-inch)	370ºF	7
Burger patty (4 ounces)	370ºF	16–20	Meatballs (3-inch)	380ºF	10
Filet mignon (8 ounces)	400ºF	18	Ribeye, bone-in (1-inch, 8 ounces)	400ºF	10–15
Flank steak (1.5 pounds)	400ºF	12	Sirloin steaks (1-inch, 12 ounces)	400ºF	9–14
Flank steak (2 pounds)	400ºF	20–28			

Pork & Lamb

	Temp (°f)	Time (mins)		Temp (°f)	Time (mins)
Bacon (regular)	400ºF	5–7	Pork tenderloin	370ºF	15
Bacon (thick cut)	400ºF	6–10	Sausages	380ºF	15
Pork loin (2 pounds)	360ºF	55	Lamb loin chops (1-inch thick)	400ºF	8–12
Pork chops, bone in (1-inch, 6.5 ounces)	400ºF	12	Rack of lamb (1.5–2 pounds)	380ºF	22

Fish & Seafood

	Temp (°f)	Time (mins)		Temp (°f)	Time (mins)
Calamari (8 ounces)	400ºF	4	Tuna steak	400ºF	7–10
Fish fillet (1-inch, 8 ounces)	400ºF	10	Scallops	400ºF	5–7
Salmon, fillet (6 ounces)	380ºF	12	Shrimp	400ºF	5
Swordfish steak	400ºF	10			

Frozen Foods

	Temp (°F)	Time (mins)		Temp (°F)	Time (mins)
Breaded shrimp	400ºF	9	French fries (thick - 17 ounces)	400ºF	18
Chicken nuggets (12 ounces)	400ºF	10	Mozzarella sticks (11 ounces)	400ºF	8
Fish sticks (10 ounces)	400ºF	10	Onion rings (12 ounces)	400ºF	8
Fish fillets (½-inch, 10 ounces)	400ºF	14	Pot stickers (10 ounces)	400ºF	8
French fries (thin - 20 ounces)	400ºF	14			

Air Fryer Tips

Air fryers can provide you with crispier foods that satisfy your cravings, and in closing, here are some tips to ensure success while using your air fryer.

- ***Do not overcrowd food while cooking:*** Make sure you give foods lots of space for the hot air to circulate effectively around what you are cooking. This will give you the crispy results you crave! Also, it is best to work in small batches.
- ***Spray foods:*** On occasion, your air fryer will pick up foods that are light and blow them around the fryer. Secure foods you cook with toothpicks!
- ***Check your food's doneness frequently:*** One of the best benefits of cooking with an air fryer is that you do not have to worry about how often you open it up to check for doneness. If you are an anxious chef, this can give you peace of mind to create yummy meals and snacks every single time!
- ***Take out the basket before removing the food:*** If you go to invert the air fryer basket when it is still locked tightly in the drawer, you will pour out all the grease that has been released from your food.
- ***Clean the drawer after each use:*** The air fryer drawer is extremely easy to clean and quite hassle-free. But if you leave it unwashed, you can risk contaminating future food you cook, and an unpleasant odor may take over your kitchen. To avoid this, simply clean it after each use.
- ***Use the air dryer to dry the appliance out:*** After washing the basket and air fryer drawer, you can pop them back into the fryer and turn on the appliance for 2–3 minutes. This is a great way to dry it for your next use thoroughly!

If you miss the traditional fried food, try melting butter and sprinkling in your favorite herbs and spices to shake things up. Then, you can whip up a healthy avocado mayo and a few drizzles of hot sauce for a custom dip.

How to achieve that delicious, crispy surface? Pat your food dry before adding spices and oil. 1 tablespoon or 2 of oil should be brushed onto foods; experts recommend using oil sprays or misters with your favorite oil (olive, vegetable, or coconut oil). Avoid aerosol spray cans because they have harsh agents that can damage the coating on Air Fryer baskets.

Although most foods need some oil to help them crisp, certain foods naturally have some fat, such as fatty cuts of meat; therefore, you do not have to add extra fat to these foods, but anyway, do not forget to grease the cooking basket.

Allow your food to rest for 5–10 seconds before removing them from the cooking basket unless the recipe indicates otherwise. If you want to shake or add ingredients during the cooking cycle, simply remove the cooking basket; the machine will automatically shut down. Place the cooking basket back into the air fryer drawer, and the cooking cycle will automatically resume.

Use your air fryer to reheat leftovers by setting the temperature to 300ºF for up to 10 minutes. As for French fries, baking this food is much healthier than frying them. Here's the secret to perfect fries. Cut your potatoes into 1/4-inch pieces lengthwise; make sure the pieces are uniform in size. Soak them in cold water for 30 minutes (45 minutes for sweet potato fries). You can add vinegar to the water as well. Your fries will turn out slightly crispier, and vinegar can improve their flavor, too.

Air Fryer Safety

- Your air fryer gets hot. Do not touch any of its surfaces when cooking. When cooking is done, use oven mitts or potholders to touch it and wait for it to cool down.
- Avoid immersing the cord, plug, or the air fryer unit in water or other liquid due to electric shocks.
- Persons with reduced physical, sensory or mental capabilities, or lack of experience and knowledge, should not use your air fryer without supervision.
- Always keep children away from your air fryer.
- Avoid using your air fryer if it has a damaged plug or power cord.
- Avoid using your air fryer outdoors due to adverse weather conditions.
- Avoid letting the cord hang over the edge of the table or countertop, especially if you have pets around the house.
- Avoid placing your air fryer close to a hot gas or electric burner.
- Ensure that both the timer dial and temperature dial are off when disconnecting your air fryer from the power outlet.
- Ensure that the frying basket is locked into position when turning on your air fryer.
- Ensure that the frying basket drawer is fully closed and the handle locked securely in the drawer when using your air fryer.
- Carefully handle your air fryer after frying because the frying basket and the food inside of it are extremely hot.

Control Dials

- The temperature control dial allows you to select frying temperatures from 175–400°F. Temperatures can be adjusted at any time before or during the cooking period.
- The control panel shows the HEAT ON light when the cooking temperature is reached. It also shows the red POWER light, which will turn on when you use your fryer. The shortcut functions are specifically designed for certain kinds of food, like poultry and fish, and you can select these if you think they are a better option than manually setting the frying temperature.

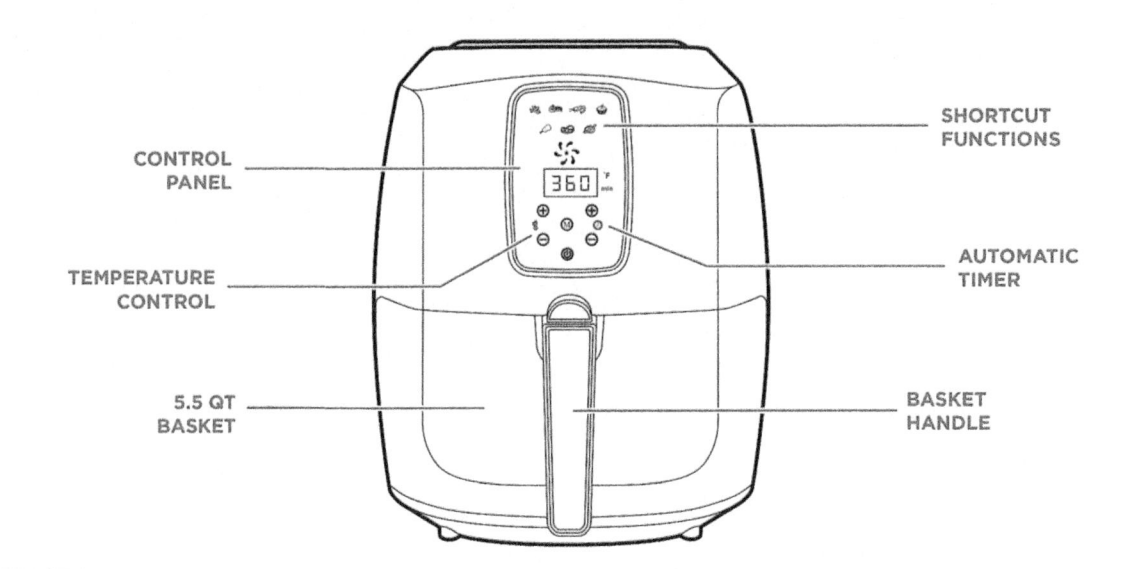

Diagram labels: CONTROL PANEL, SHORTCUT FUNCTIONS, TEMPERATURE CONTROL, AUTOMATIC TIMER, 5.5 QT BASKET, BASKET HANDLE. Display shows 360.

The automatic timer button allows you to select how long your food will cook and automatically count down during the cooking period. Typically, one beep sounds when frying time has reached 0 minutes. Most Air fryers turn OFF automatically, but you should always check and turn both the temperature control dial and the timer dial to 0 (OFF).

Mistakes to Avoid With Your Air Fryer

You don't read instructions before beginning: When using an electrical appliance, basic manufacturer's instructions should always be followed; this is extremely important for safety reasons. That way, you'll avoid common mistakes.

You cook too small and lightweight items: An Air Fryer has a powerful fan on top of the unit, as we said before. It is not suitable for foods such as egg roll wrappers and lightweight freeze-dried foods, so be careful.

Your food comes out dry and tasteless: Foods can dry out quickly at high temperatures; they can also stick together. If your veggies turn out limp and mushy, this is a timing issue. Therefore, you should modify the temperature and time. If you are unsure, simply go 30ºF below and cut the time by 20–30%. Then, check your food and increase the cooking time if necessary.

You do not want to invest in some accessories: Accessories such as baking pans and oven-safe dishes have to be able to fit inside the cooking basket. Another important rule—they shouldn't be exposed to the heating element.

You're using wet coatings: Do not worry; wet battered foods such as tempura can be adapted to the Air Fryer. Coat your food generously with a crisp coating like breadcrumbs, crushed crackers, crushed tortilla chips, or pork rinds. Try to apply a classic three-step breading procedure (flour, eggs, and breadcrumbs) to reduce splattering.

You are afraid of mistakes: Mistakes are natural; they are also a big part of learning. Give yourself enough time to learn and enjoy a new cooking method. Remember, there is a time to plant and a time to harvest. Recipes can't be rushed if you want delicious, perfectly cooked food.

Tips for Cleaning

Cleaning the air fryer is easy, and it does not require you to do many complicated tasks. The first thing that you need to do is to unplug the air fryer before cleaning to prevent electrocution. The basket is dishwasher-friendly, so you can take it out from the fryer's chamber and clean them in the sink or the dishwasher.

Once you remove the fryer basket, give extra attention to the base of the fryer, where most of the drippings from the food have collected and dried. Make sure that you remove the browning that has accumulated at the base, as this can lead to burning in future cooking. You can remove the browning by spraying it with warm soapy water and allowing it to soak for at least an hour. This will soften the browning, so you can easily wipe it clean. Aside from taking care of the inside of the air fryer, it is also important to clean the exterior using a warm moist cloth.

- The frying basket may be coasted in grease from repeated and frequent use. Smoking can occur when bits of burnt food get recooked many times. So, you should get into the habit of cleaning your frying basket after every use.
- The pan, basket, and the inside of the appliance have a non-stick coating, so you should avoid using abrasive materials to clean them.
- Wipe the outside of the appliance with a damp kitchen towel.
- Clean the frying basket with hot water, some washing-up liquid, and a non-abrasive sponge. You can use a degreasing agent to remove grease and grime. Hint: The frying basket is dishwasher-proof.
- Clean the inside of your air fryer (after you have taken out the frying basket) with warm water and a non-abrasive sponge.

FAQ

Does It Cook Healthier Foods and Eco-Friendly?

Air fryers are designed to work without fattening oils and produce healthier foods with up to 80% less fat. This makes it easier to lose weight because you can still eat your fried dishes while preserving calories and saturated fat. Using this device makes the switch to a healthier life more achievable. Your home also gets rid of the aroma that comes with deep-fried foods that often stay around the atmosphere after deep-frying for several hours.

Can It Be Used for Multipurpose Cooking Tasks?

The air fryer allows you to multi-task as various dishes can be prepared at once. Your all-in-one appliance can grill the meals you enjoy, bake, fry, and roast! For different cooking practices, you no longer need multiple types of equipment. It can cook meat, boil veggies, and bake pastries. It serves to replace your oven, profound fryer, and stovetop effectively.

Unquestionably, the air fryer's most important advantage is its use of hot air circulation to cook food products from all perspectives, eliminating the need for oil use. This allows individuals on a low-fat diet to prepare deliciously healthy meals comfortably.

Is It Safe to Use?

Remember how careful it is to throw chicken or other ingredients into the deep fryer. You want to make sure you don't spill the warm oil and burn your skin because it's always very hot. You wouldn't have to worry about burnt skin from the spillage of warm oil with your air fryer. It does all the frying, and it's totally safe. However, while repositioning your fryer, use cooking gloves to prevent heat risks. Also, keep your air fryer out of the reach of children.

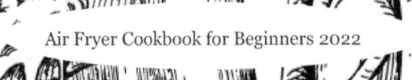

Is It Easy to Clean Up?

There is no grease left by the Air Fryer and, therefore, no mess. Clean-up time is pleasant, as there is no scraping or scrubbing of pans to clean on walls and floors. There's no need to spend time making sure it's all squeaky clean. The sections of the Air Fryer are made of a non-stick material that keeps food from sticking to surfaces, making it easier to clean. These sections can be easily cleaned and well maintained. They are also removable and safe for the dishwasher.

Does It Consume Much Time?

People on tight schedules can use the air fryer's speed to create delicious dishes. For example, in less than 15 minutes you can prepare French fries, and in 25 minutes you can bake a cake. You can also enjoy crispy chicken tenders or golden fries within minutes. The air fryer is just appropriate for you if you're always on the go because you're going to spend less time in the kitchen. It allows you to manage your daily life, which is hectic and busy, making your day more manageable.

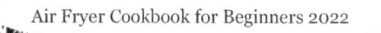

CHAPTER 2:

Breakfast

1. Banana Bread Pudding

Intermediate Recipe
Preparation Time: 10 minutes
Cooking Time: 20 minutes
Servings: 4
Ingredients:

- Olive oil
- 2 medium ripe bananas, mashed
- ½ cup low-fat milk
- 2 tablespoons peanut butter
- 2 tablespoons maple syrup
- 1 teaspoon ground cinnamon
- 1 teaspoon vanilla extract
- 2 slices whole-grain bread, torn into bite-sized pieces
- ¼ cup quick oats

Directions:

- Lightly spray four individual ramekins or one air fryer–safe baking dish with olive oil.
- In a large mixing bowl, combine the bananas, milk, peanut butter, maple syrup, cinnamon, and vanilla. Using an electric mixer or whisk, mix until fully combined.
- Add the bread pieces and stir to coat in the liquid mixture.
- Add the oats and stir until everything is combined.
- Transfer the mixture to the baking dish or divide between the ramekins. Cover with aluminum foil.
- Place 2 ramekins in the fryer basket and air fry until heated through, 10 to 12 minutes
- Remove the foil and cook for 6 to 8 more minutes
- Repeat with the remaining 2 ramekins. Make It Even Lower Calorie: Reduce the calories by using sugar-free maple syrup or by replacing the peanut butter with PB2 (powdered peanut butter). Combine 4 tablespoons of powdered peanut butter with 2 tablespoons of water to equal 2 tablespoons of peanut butter.

Nutrition:
Calories 212
Fat 6g
Saturated Fat 2g
Carbs 38g
Protein 6g
Sodium: 112mg

2. Air Fried German Pancakes

Basic Recipe
Preparation Time: 5 minutes
Cooking Time: 8 Minutes
Servings: 5
Ingredients:

- Serving size: 1/2 cup batter
- 3 Full eggs
- Whole wheat flour: 1 cup
- Almond milk: 1 cup
- A pinch of salt
- Apple sauce: 2 heaping tablespoons (optional but recommended to replace the need for added oil or butter)
- For Garnishing:
- Berries
- Greek yogurt
- Confectioner sugar
- Maple syrup (optional)

Directions:

- Set the air fryer temperature to 390°F/199°C. Inside the air fryer, set the cast iron tray or ramekin as it heats. Take the blender and add all the batter ingredients to it, and combine until smooth. If the batter is too thick, simply add milk or applesauce tablespoons to smooth out. Use nonstick baking spray and spray the cast iron tray or ramekin, and then dump in a batter serving.
- Air fry the batter for 6-8 minutes
- Do not worry if top gets hard to touch. This is the advantage of using the air fryer –

it provides the pancake with a good firm outer coating/edges that softens as it cools. Place the remaining batter in the refrigerator in an airtight container to freshen it up every morning.

Garnish, and serve.

Nutrition:
Calories 139
Protein 8 g
Fat 4 g
Carbs 18 g
Fiber 3 g
Sugar 1 g

3. Air-Fried Flax Seed French Toast Sticks With Berries

Intermediate Recipe
Preparation Time: 25 minutes
Cooking Time: 35 minutes
Servings: 4
Ingredients:
- Whole-grain bread: 4 slices (1 1/2-oz.)
- 2 Big Eggs
- 1/4 cup 2% reduced-fat milk
- Vanilla extract: 1 teaspoon
- Ground cinnamon: ½ teaspoon
- 1/4 cup of light brown sugar, split,
- 2/3 cup flax seed cooking spray
- 2 Cups of fresh-cut strawberries
- Maple syrup: 8 teaspoons
- Powdered sugar: 1 teaspoon

Directions:
- Cut each of the bread slices into four long sticks. In a shallow dish, whisk together eggs, milk, cinnamon, vanilla extract, and 1 tablespoon brown sugar. In a second, shallow dish, combine flaxseed meal and remaining 3 tablespoons of brown sugar.
- Dip the pieces of bread in a mixture of eggs, soak them slightly, and allow any excess to drip away. Dredge each piece in a mixture of flax seeds and coat on all sides. Cover the bits of bread with cooking oil.
- Place pieces of bread in a single layer in the air fryer basket, leave room between each piece and cook at 375 ° F in batches until golden brown and crunchy, 10 minutes, turn slices over halfway through cooking. Place 4 sticks of French toast on each plate to serve. Finish with 1/2 cup of strawberries, 2 teaspoons of maple syrup, and a powdered sugar layer. Serve right now.

Nutrition:
Calories 361 Fat 10g
Saturated Fat 1g
Unsaturated Fat 7g
Protein 14g
Carbs 56g
Fiber 10g
Sugars: 30g
Sodium: 218mg

4. Breakfast Frittatas

Preparation Time: 15 minutes
Cooking Time: 20 minutes
Servings: 2
Ingredients:
- Breakfast sausage: ¼ pound, completely cooked and crumbled
- Eggs: 4, lightly beaten
- Shredded cheddar cheese: ½ cup
- Red pepper: 2 tablespoons, chopped
- Green onion: 1 chopped
- Cayenne pepper: 1 pinch
- Cooking spray

Directions:
- Combine the sausage, eggs, cheddar cheese, onion, bell pepper, and cayenne in a bowl and blend. Set the temperature of the air-fryer to 360°F (180°C). Sprinkle a 6x2-inch non-stick cake pan with a cooking spray.

Put the mixture of the eggs in the prepared cake pan. Cook in the air fryer for 18 to 20 minutes until the frittata is set.

Nutrition:
Calories 379.8 Protein 31.2g
Carbs 2.9g Cholesterol 443mg
Sodium: 693.5mg

5. Air-Fried Breakfast Bombs
Basic Recipe
Preparation Time: 20 minutes
Cooking Time: 5 minutes
Servings: 2
Ingredients:
- Bacon: 3 slices, center-cut
- 3 Big, lightly beaten eggs
- 1 1/3-ounce fat cream cheese, softened
- Fresh chives: 1 tablespoon, chopped
- 4 Ounces of new whole wheat flour pizza dough
- Cooking spray

Directions:
- Cook the bacon over medium to very crisp in a medium skillet, around 10 minutes Take bacon off the pan. In a pan, add eggs to the bacon drippings; cook for about 1 minute, frequently stirring, until almost set, but still loose. Transfer eggs to a bowl; add cream cheese, chives, and crumbled bacon to taste.
- Divide the dough into four pieces equal to each. Roll each piece into a 5-inch circle onto a lightly floured surface—place one-fourth of each dough circle in the middle of the egg mixture. Brush the outside edge of the dough with water; wrap the dough around the mixture of the eggs to form a bag, pinch the dough at the seams together.
- In air fryer tray, put dough bags in a single layer; coat thoroughly with cooking spray. Cook for 5 to 6 minutes at 350 ° F until golden brown, then test for 4 minutes

Nutrition:
Calories 305 Fat 15g
Saturated fat 5g Unsaturated fat 8g
Protein 19g Sodium 548mg
Calcium 5% DV Potassium 2% DV
Carbs 26g Fiber 2g Sugars 1g Added sugars 0g

6. Banana Bread
Basic Recipe
Preparation Time: 5 minutes
Cooking Time: 30 minutes
Servings: 4
Ingredients:
- Banana: 1, ripe and mashed - 1 egg
- Brown sugar: 2-3 tablespoons
- Canola oil: 2 tablespoons
- Milk: 1/4 cup
- Plain flour: ¾ cup mixed with 1/2 tablespoon baking soda

Directions:
- Whisk the egg into the mashed banana in a small bowl. Add the sugar, butter, and milk and whisk again.
- Add the flour and baking soda in the mixture and blend until mixed.
- If using an air fryer, preheat for 3 minutes to 320°F/160°C.
- Pour the batter into the dish of air fryer (apply a little butter on the basket) and cook for 32 to 35 minutes, or until a toothpick inserted into the cake's bottom comes out clean. A touch of stickiness is all right.
- Let the tin/dish cool for 10 minutes, then transfer to a wire rack to cool down.

Nutrition:
Calories 233 kcal Carbs 34g
Sugar: 13g Vitamin A: 105IU
Cholesterol 42mg Sodium: 25mg
Protein 5g Fat 9g Saturated Fat 1g
Potassium: 178mg Fiber 1g
Vitamin C: 2.6mg Calcium: 34mg
Iron: 1.4m

7. Scrambled Eggs
Basic Recipe
Preparation Time: 4 Minutes
Cooking Time: 10 minutes
Servings: 2
Ingredients:
- Unsalted butter: 1/3 tablespoon
- 2 Eggs
- Milk: 2 tablespoons
- Salt and black pepper to try
- Cheddar cheese: 1/8 cup

Directions:
- Place fresh butter in a fryer-safe oven/air saucepan and place it inside the fryer. Cook, about 2 minutes, at 300 degrees until fresh butter get melted.
- Whisk the milk and eggs all together then add some pepper and salt for taste. Cook for 3-4 minutes at 300 degrees, then put eggs to the inside of the fry pan and stir.
- Cook for another 2-3 minutes, then add (cheddar) cheese and stir the eggs once more. Cook another 2 minutes. Remove that pan from air fryer and instantly serve.

Nutrition:
Calories 126 kcal
Fat 9g
Cholesterol 200mg
Carbs 1g
Protein 9g
Sugar: 0g

8. Bacon And Eggs
Basic Recipe
Preparation Time: 4 minutes
Cooking Time: 10 minutes
Servings: 3
Ingredients:
- 6 nitrate-free bacon strips
- Eggs: 6
- Spinach: 6 cups
- Olive oil: ½ tablespoon

Directions:
- Place the eggs on top of the second air fryer rack. Set the temperature at 270 degrees F. Air fry in hard-boiled for 15 minutes, for medium-boiled for 12 minutes and for soft boiled for 10 minutes Lift for 2 minutes and put in the ice water bath and peel shell.
- Place bacon in the lower rack. Set temperature for 12-14 minutes at 375°F and cook. 14 minutes are preferable to get extra crispy bacon. Serve with sautéed cooked spinach in olive oil.

Nutrition:
Calories 427
Fat 29g
Saturated Fat 9.3g
Trans Fat 0g

9. Sausage Breakfast Casserole
Intermediate Recipe
Preparation Time: 10 minutes
Cooking Time: 20 minutes
Servings: 6
Ingredients:
- Hash browns: 1 Lb.
- Breakfast Sausage: 1 lb.
- Eggs: 4
- Green Bell Pepper: 1, diced
- Red Bell Pepper: 1, diced
- Yellow Bell Pepper: 1, diced
- Sweet onion: ¼ cup, diced

Directions:
- Cover the air fryer basket lined with foil. Put the hash browns on the bottom basket of the air fryer.
- Place the uncooked sausage over it.
- Place the peppers and the onions evenly on top.
- Cook it 10 minutes on 355°F.
- When needed, open the air fryer and mix the casserole up a bit.

Whisk each egg in a bowl, and then pour right over the saucepan.

Cook another 10 minutes on 355°F.

Serve with a sprinkle of salt and pepper.

Nutrition:
Calories 517
Fat 37g
Saturated Fat 10g
Trans Fat 0g
Unsaturated Fat 25g
Cholesterol 189mg
Sodium: 1092mg
Carbs 27g
Fiber 3g
Sugar: 4g
Protein 21g

10. Breakfast Burritos
Basic Recipe
Preparation Time: 20 minutes
Cooking Time: 3Minutes
Servings: 8
Ingredients:
- Breakfast sausage: 1 pound
- 1 Chopped bell pepper
- Eggs: 12, lightly beaten
- Black pepper: ½ teaspoon
- Sea salt: 1 teaspoon
- Flour tortillas: 8 (burrito style)
- Shredded cheddar cheese: 2 cups

Directions:
- Crumble and cook the sausage until brown in a large skillet. Add chopped peppers. Dry out grease put the sausage on a towel-lined sheet of paper, cover, and set aside.
- Melt 1 spoonful of butter in a large saucepan, add eggs, salt, and pepper and cook over medium heat, stirring continuously until almost set and no longer runny.
- Remove from heat and whisk in cooked sausage.
- In the center of a tortilla, add some of the egg and sausage mixtures, top with some of the bacon, fold sides, and roll-up. Preheat the fryer until 390 degrees.
- Spray burritos gently with a drop of olive oil. Place as many burritos as fit into the air fryer and cook for 3 minutes at 390 degrees, rotating trays halfway through. Cook extra for 3 minutes for crispier burritos Immediately remove and serve, or allow cooling slightly, then wrapping well and freezing for meal preparation.

Nutrition:
Calories 283kcal
Carbs 16g
Protein 16g
Fat 17g

11. Baked Bacon Egg Cups
Intermediate Recipe
Preparation Time: 10 minutes
Cooking Time: 12 Minutes
Servings: 2
Ingredients:
- 2 eggs
- 1 tablespoon chives, fresh, chopped
- ½ teaspoon paprika
- ½ teaspoon cayenne pepper
- 3-ounces cheddar cheese, shredded
- ½ teaspoon butter
- ¼ teaspoon salt
- 4-ounces bacon, cut into tiny pieces

Directions:
- Slice bacon into tiny pieces and sprinkle it with cayenne pepper, salt, and paprika. Mix the chopped bacon. Spread butter in bottom of ramekin dishes and beat the eggs there. Add the chives and shredded cheese. Add the chopped bacon over egg mixture in ramekin dishes.
- Place the ramekins in your air fryer basket. Preheat your air fryer to

360Fahrenheit. Place the air fryer basket in your air fryer and cook for 12-minutes. When the cook time is completed, remove the ramekins from air fryer and serve warm.

Nutrition:
Calories 553 Fat 43.3g
Carbs 2.3g Protein 37.3g

12. Breakfast Chicken Strips
Intermediate Recipe
Preparation Time: 10 minutes
Cooking Time: 12 minutes
Servings: 4
Ingredients:
- 1 teaspoon paprika - 1 tablespoon cream
- 1 lb. chicken fillet - ½ teaspoon salt
- ½ teaspoon black pepper

Directions:
- Cut the chicken fillet into strips. Sprinkle the chicken fillets with salt and pepper.
- Preheat the air fryer to 365Fahrenheit.
- Place the butter in the air basket tray and add the chicken strips. Cook the chicken strips for 6-minutes
- Turn the chicken strips to the other side and cook them for an additional 5-minute after strips are cooked, sprinkle them with cream and paprika, then transfer them to serving plates.
- Serve warm.

Nutrition:
Calories 245 Fat 11.5g
Carbs 0.6g Protein 33g

13. No-Bun Breakfast Bacon Burger
Intermediate Recipe
Preparation Time: 10 minutes
Cooking Time: 8 minutes
Servings: 2
Ingredients:
- 8-ounces ground beef
- 2-ounces lettuce leaves
- ½ teaspoon minced garlic
- 1 teaspoon olive oil
- ½ teaspoon sea salt
- 1 teaspoon ground black pepper
- 1 teaspoon butter
- 4-ounces bacon, cooked
- 1 egg
- ½ yellow onion, diced
- ½ cucumber, slice finely
- ½ tomato, slice finely

Directions:
- Begin by whisking the egg in a bowl, then add the ground beef and combine well.
- Add cooked, chopped bacon to the ground beef mixture.
- Add butter, ground black pepper, minced garlic, and salt.
- Mix and make burgers.
- Preheat your air fryer to 370Fahrenheit.
- Spray the air fryer basket with olive oil and place the burgers inside of it.
- Cook the burgers for 8-minutes on each side. Meanwhile, slice the cucumber, onion, and tomato finely.
- Place the tomato, onion, and cucumber onto the lettuce leaves.
- When the burgers are cooked, allow them to chill at room temperature, and place them over the vegetables and serve.

Nutrition:
Calories 618 Fat 37.8g
Carbs 8.6g Protein 59.4g

14. Breakfast Coconut Porridge
Intermediate Recipe
Preparation Time: 5 minutes
Cooking Time: 7 minutes
Servings: 4
Ingredients:
- 1 cup coconut milk
- 3 tablespoons blackberries

2 tablespoons walnuts
1 teaspoon butter
1 teaspoon ground cinnamon
5 tablespoons chia seeds
3 tablespoons coconut flakes
¼ teaspoon salt

Directions:
Pour the coconut milk into the air fryer basket tray. Add the coconut, salt, chia seeds, ground cinnamon, and butter.

Ground up the walnuts and add them to the air fryer basket tray. Sprinkle the mixture with salt.

Mash the blackberries with a fork and add them also to the air fryer basket tray.

Cook the porridge at 375Fahrenheit for 7-minutes when the cook time is over, remove the air fryer basket from air fryer and allow sitting and resting for 5-minutes Stir porridge with a wooden spoon and serve warm.

Nutrition:
Calories 169 Fat 18.2g
Carbs 9.3g Protein 4.2g

15. Morning Time Sausages
Intermediate Recipe
Preparation Time: 10 minutes
Cooking Time: 12 minutes
Servings: 6
Ingredients:
7-ounces ground chicken
7-ounces ground pork
1 teaspoon ground coriander
1 teaspoon basil, dried
½ teaspoon nutmeg
1 teaspoon olive oil
1 teaspoon minced garlic
1 tablespoon coconut flour
1 egg
1 teaspoon soy sauce
1 teaspoon sea salt
½ teaspoon ground black pepper

Directions:
Combine the ground pork, chicken, soy sauce, ground black pepper, garlic, basil, coriander, nutmeg, sea salt, and egg. Add the coconut flour and mix the mixture well to combine. Preheat your air fryer to 360Fahrenheit. Make medium-sized sausages with the ground meat mixture. Spray the inside of the air fryer basket tray with the olive oil. Place prepared sausages into the air fryer basket and place inside of air fryer. Cook the sausages for 6-minutes. Turn the sausages over and cook for 6-minutes more. When the cook time is completed, let the sausages chill for a little bit. Serve warm.

Nutrition:
Calories 156 Fat 7.5g
Carbs 1.3g Protein 20.2g

16. Scrambled Pancake Hash
Intermediate Recipe
Preparation Time: 10 minutes
Cooking Time: 9Minutes
Servings: 6
Ingredients:
1 egg
¼ cup heavy cream
5 tablespoons butter
1 cup coconut flour
1 teaspoon ground ginger
1 teaspoon salt
1 tablespoon apple cider vinegar
1 teaspoon baking soda

Directions:
Combine the salt, baking soda, ground ginger and flour in a mixing bowl. In a separate bowl, crack the egg into it. Add butter and heavy cream. Mix well using a hand mixer. Combine the liquid and dry mixtures and stir until smooth. Preheat your air fryer to

400Fahrenheit. Pour the pancake mixture into the air fryer basket tray. Cook the pancake hash for 4-minutes. After this, scramble the pancake hash well and continue to cook for another 5-minute more. When dish is cooked, transfer it to serving plates, and serve hot!

Nutrition:
Calories 178 Fat 13.3g
Carbs 10.7g Protein 4.4g

17. Breakfast Meatloaf Slices
Intermediate Recipe
Preparation Time: 10 minutes
Cooking Time: 20 minutes
Servings: 6
Ingredients:
- 8-ounces ground pork
- 7-ounces ground beef
- 1 teaspoon olive oil
- 1 teaspoon butter
- 1 tablespoon oregano, dried
- 1 teaspoon cayenne pepper
- 1 teaspoon salt
- 1 tablespoon chives
- 1 tablespoon almond flour
- 1 egg
- 1 onion, diced

Directions:
Beat egg in a bowl. Add the ground beef and ground pork. Add the chives, almond flour, cayenne pepper, salt, dried oregano, and butter. Add diced onion to ground beef mixture. Use hands to shape a meatloaf mixture. Preheat the air fryer to 350Fahrenheit. Spray the inside of the air fryer basket with olive oil and place the meatloaf inside it. Cook the meatloaf for 20-minutes. When the meatloaf has cooked, allow it to chill for a bit. Slice and serve it.

Nutrition:
Calories 176 Fat 6.2g
Carbs 3.4g Protein 22.2g

18. Seed Porridge
Basic Recipe
Preparation Time: 10 minutes
Cooking Time: 12 minutes
Servings: 3
Ingredients:
- 1 tablespoon butter
- ¼ teaspoon nutmeg
- 1/3 cup heavy cream
- 1 egg
- ¼ teaspoon salt
- 3 tablespoons sesame seeds
- 3 tablespoons chia seeds

Directions:
Place the butter in your air fryer basket tray. Add the chia seeds, sesame seeds, heavy cream, nutmeg, and salt. Stir gently. Beat the egg in a cup and whisk it with a fork. Add the whisked egg to air fryer basket tray. Stir the mixture with a wooden spatula. Preheat your air fryer to 375Fahrenheit. Place the air fryer basket tray into air fryer and cook the porridge for 12-minutes stir it about 3 times during the cooking process. Remove the porridge from air fryer basket tray immediately and serve hot!

Nutrition:
Calories 275 Fat 22.5g
Carbs 13.2g Protein 7.9g

19. Kale Breakfast Fritters
Intermediate Recipe
Preparation Time: 8 minutes
Cooking Time: 8 minutes
Servings: 8
Ingredients:
- 12-ounces kale, chopped

1 teaspoon oil
1 tablespoon cream
1 teaspoon paprika
½ teaspoon sea salt
2 tablespoons almond flour
1 egg
1 tablespoon butter
½ yellow onion, diced

Directions:

Wash and chop the kale. Add the chopped kale to blender and blend it until smooth. Dice up the yellow onion. Beat the egg and whisk it in a mixing bowl. Add the almond flour, paprika, cream and salt into bowl with whisked egg and stir. Add the diced onion and blended kale to mixing bowl and mix until you get fritter dough. Preheat your air fryer to 360Fahrenheit. Spray the inside of the air fryer basket with olive oil. Make medium-sized fritters with prepared mixture and place them into air fryer basket. Cook the kale fritters 4-minutes on each side. Once they are cooked, allow them to chill then serve.

Nutrition:
Calories 86
Fat 5.6g
Carbs 6.8g
Protein 3.6g

20. Keto Air Bread
Intermediate Recipe
Preparation Time: 10 minutes
Cooking Time: 25 minutes
Servings: 19
Ingredients:

1 cup almond flour
¼ sea salt
1 teaspoon baking powder
¼ cup butter
3 eggs

Directions:

Crack the eggs into a bowl then using a hand blender mix them up. Melt the butter at room temperature. Take the melted butter and add it to the egg mixture. Add the salt, baking powder and almond flour to egg mixture and knead the dough. Cover the prepared dough with a towel for 10-minutes to rest. Meanwhile, preheat your air fryer to 360Fahrenheit. Place the prepared dough in the air fryer tin and cook the bread for 10-minutes. Then reduce the heat to 350Fahrenheit and cook the bread for additional 15-minutes you can use a toothpick to check to make sure the bread is cooked. Transfer the bread to a wooden board to allow it to chill. Once the bread has chilled, then slice and serve it.

Nutrition:
Calories 40
Fat 3.9g
Carbs 0.5g
Protein 1.2g

21. Herbed Breakfast Eggs
Intermediate Recipe
Preparation Time: 10 minutes
Cooking Time: 17 minutes
Servings: 2
Ingredients:

4 eggs
1 teaspoon oregano
1 teaspoon parsley, dried
½ teaspoon sea salt
1 tablespoon chives, chopped
1 tablespoon cream
1 teaspoon paprika

Directions:

Place the eggs in the air fryer basket and cook them for 17-minutes at 320Fahrenheit. Meanwhile, combine the parsley, oregano, cream, and salt in shallow bowl. Chop the chives and add them to cream mixture. When the eggs are cooked, place them in cold water and allow them to chill. After this, peel the eggs and cut them into halves. Remove the egg yolks and add yolks to cream mixture and mash to blend well with a fork. Then fill the egg whites with the cream-egg yolk mixture. Serve immediately.

Nutrition:
Calories 136 Fat 9.3g
Carbs 2.1g Protein 11.4g

22. Eggs In Zucchini Nests
Basic Recipe
Preparation Time: 10 minutes
Cooking Time: 7 minutes
Servings: 2
Ingredients:
- 4 teaspoons butter
- ½ teaspoon paprika
- ½ teaspoon black pepper
- ¼ teaspoon sea salt
- 4-ounces cheddar cheese, shredded
- 4 eggs
- 8-ounces zucchini, grated

Directions:
Grate the zucchini and place the butter in ramekins. Add the grated zucchini in ramekins in the shape of nests. Sprinkle the zucchini nests with salt, pepper, and paprika. Beat the eggs and pour over zucchini nests.

Top egg mixture with shredded cheddar cheese. Preheat the air fryer basket and cook the dish for 7-minutes. When the zucchini nests are cooked, chill them for 3-minutes and serve them in the ramekins.

Nutrition:
Calories 221 Fat 17.7g
Carbs 2.9g Protein 13.4g

23. Breakfast Liver Pate
Intermediate Recipe
Preparation Time: 5 minutes
Cooking Time: 10 minutes
Servings: 7
Ingredients:
- 1 lb. chicken liver
- 1 teaspoon salt
- ½ teaspoon cilantro, dried
- 1 yellow onion, diced
- 1 teaspoon ground black pepper
- 1 cup water
- 4 tablespoons butter

Directions:
Chop the chicken liver roughly and place it in the air fryer basket tray. Add water to air fryer basket tray and add diced onion. Preheat your air fryer to 360Fahrenheit and cook chicken liver for 10-minutes. Dry out the chicken liver when it is finished cooking.

Transfer the chicken liver to blender, add butter, ground black pepper and dried cilantro and blend. Once you get a pate texture, transfer to liver pate bowl and serve immediately or keep in the fridge for later.

Nutrition:
Calories 173
Fat 10.8g
Carbs 2.2g
Protein 16.1g

24. Bread-Free Breakfast Sandwich
Intermediate Recipe
Preparation Time: 10 minutes
Cooking Time: 10 minutes
Servings: 2
Ingredients:
- 6-ounces ground chicken
- 2 slices of cheddar cheese
- 2 lettuce leaves

1 tablespoon dill, dried
½ teaspoon sea salt
1 egg
1 teaspoon cayenne pepper
1 teaspoon tomato puree

Directions:

Combine the ground chicken with the pepper and sea salt. Add the dried dill and stir. Beat the egg into the ground chicken mixture. Make 2 medium-sized burgers from the ground chicken mixture. Preheat your air fryer to 380Fahrenheit. Spray the air fryer basket tray with olive oil and place the ground chicken burgers inside of it. Cook the chicken burgers for 10-minutes Flip over burgers and cook for an additional 6-minutes. When the burgers are cooked, transfer them to the lettuce leaves. Sprinkle the top of them with tomato puree and with a slice of cheddar cheese. Serve immediately!

Nutrition:
Calories 324
Fat 19.2g
Carbs 2.3g
Protein 34.8g

25. Egg Butter
Basic Recipe
Preparation Time: 5 minutes
Cooking Time: 17 minutes
Servings: 2
Ingredients:
    4 eggs
    4 tablespoons butter
    1 teaspoon salt

Directions:

Cover the air fryer basket with foil and place the eggs there. Transfer the air fryer basket into the air fryer and cook the eggs for 17 minutes at 320Fahrenheit. When the time is over, remove the eggs from the air fryer basket and put them in cold water to chill them. After this, peel the eggs and chop them up finely. Combine the chopped eggs with butter and add salt. Mix it until you get the spread texture. Serve the egg butter with the keto almond bread.

Nutrition:
Calories 164
Fat 8.5g
Carbs 2.67g
Protein 3g

26. Awesome Lemon Bell Peppers
Intermediate Recipe
Preparation Time: 10 minutes
Cooking Time: 5 minutes
Servings: 4
Ingredients:
    4 bell peppers
    1 teaspoon olive oil
    1 tablespoon lemon juice
    1/4 teaspoon garlic, minced
    1 teaspoon parsley, chopped
    1 pinch sea salt
    Pinch of pepper

Directions:

Preheat your Air Fryer to 390 degrees F in "AIR FRY" mode
Add bell pepper in the Air fryer
Drizzle with it with the olive oil and air fry for 5 minutes
Take a serving plate and transfer it
Take a small bowl and add garlic, parsley, lemon juice, salt, and pepper
Mix them well and Drizzle with the mixture over the peppers
Serve and enjoy!

Nutrition:
Calories 59 kcal Carbs 6g
Fat 4g Protein 2g

27. Avocado Rolls
Intermediate Recipe
Preparation Time: 10 minutes
Cooking Time: 25 minutes
Servings: 4
Ingredients:
- 10 friendly wrappers
- 3 avocados, sliced
- 1 tomato, diced
- Salt and pepper to taste
- 1 tablespoon olive oil
- 4 tablespoon peppers
- 2 tablespoons date sugar
- 1 tablespoon hemp seed oil
- 1 tablespoon alkaline vinegar

Directions:
- Take a bowl and mash avocados
- Stir in tomatoes, salt, and pepper, mix well
- Arrange wrappers and scoop mix on top
- Roll and seal edges
- Cook in your Air fryer for 5 minutes at 350 degrees F
- Take a bowl and mix remaining ingredients, serve with sauce
- Enjoy!

Nutrition:
Calories 422 kcal
Carbs 38 g
Fat 15 g

28. Portobello Hearty Mushroom Burgers
Intermediate Recipe
Preparation Time: 10 minutes
Cooking Time: 20 minutes
Servings: 4
Ingredients:
- 2 cups Portobello mushroom caps
- 1 avocado, sliced
- 1 plum tomato, sliced
- 1 cup torn lettuce
- 1 cup purslane
- 1/2 teaspoon cayenne
- 1 teaspoon oregano
- 2 teaspoons basil
- 3 tablespoons olive oil

Directions:
- Remove mushroom stems and cut off ½ inch slices from top slice
- Take a bowl and mix in onion powder, cayenne, oregano, olive oil, and basil
- Cover Air Fryer basket with a baking sheet, brush grape seed oil
- Put caps on baking sheet
- Pour mixture on top and let them sit for 10 minutes
- Preheat your Air Fryer 400 degrees F and transfer to Fryer, bake it for 8 minutes, flip and Bake it for 8 minutes more
- Lay caps on serving dish, layer sliced avocado, tomato, lettuce, purslane
- Cover with another mushroom cap
- Serve and enjoy!

Nutrition:
Calories 358 kcal Carbs 49 g
Fat 13 g Protein 15g

29. Crazy Mac And Cheese
Intermediate Recipe
Preparation Time: 10 minutes
Cooking Time: 20 minutes
Servings: 4
Ingredients:
- 12 ounces alkaline pasta
- 1/4 cup chickpea flour
- 1 cup raw Brazilnut
- 1/2 teaspoon onion powder
- 1 teaspoon salt
- 2 teaspoons grape seed oil
- 1 cup hemp seed milk
- 1 cup of water
- 1/2 key lime, juiced

Directions:
- Take a bowl and add nuts, soak overnight. Cook pasta according to package Preheat your Air Fryer to 325 degrees F.

- Transfer cooked pasta to a baking dish and Drizzle with oil, add remaining ingredients to a blender and blend until smooth
- Pour mix over mac and mix
- Transfer to Air Fryer and Bake it for 25 minutes
- Serve and enjoy!

Nutrition:
Calories 255 kcal Carbs 1 g
Fat 23 g Protein 12 g

30. Zucchini Noodles With Avocado Sauce

Basic Recipe
Preparation Time: 10 minutes
Cooking Time: 15 minutes
Servings: 4
Ingredients:
- 3 medium zucchinis
- 1 and 1/2 cup cherry tomatoes
- 1 avocado
- 2 green onions, sliced
- 1 garlic clove
- 3 tablespoons olive oil
- Juice of 1 key lemon
- 1 tablespoon spring water
- Salt and cayenne to taste

Directions:
- Preheat your Air Fryer to 385 degrees F
- Take your Air Fryer cooking basket and cover with parchment paper
- Put tomatoes and Drizzle with olive oil, season with salt and cayenne
- Transfer to your Fryer and cook for 10-15 minutes until starting to split
- Add quartered avocado, parsley, sliced green onion, garlic, spring water, lemon juice, 1/2 teaspoon salt to a food processor
- Blend until creamy
- Cut zucchini ends using use spiralizer to turn into zoodles
- Mix zoodles with sauce
- Divide into 3 bowls and serve with tomatoes
- Enjoy!

Nutrition:
Calories 180 kcal
Carbs 14 g
Fat 14 g
Protein 2g

31. Candied Walnut And Strawberry

Intermediate Recipe
Preparation Time: 10 minutes
Cooking Time: 10 minutes
Servings: 4
Ingredients:
- 1/2 cup walnuts, chopped
- 1 tablespoon raw agave nectar
- 1/4 teaspoon salt
- Dressing
- 1/2 cup strawberries, sliced
- 2 tablespoons shallots
- 1/2 cup grape seed oil
- 2 teaspoons raw agave nectar
- 1 and 1/2 teaspoon lime juice
- 1 teaspoon onion powder
- 1/2 teaspoon ginger
- 1/4 teaspoon dill
- 1/4 teaspoon salt

Directions:
- Coat walnuts with agave and salt
- Transfer to a cooking basket lined with parchment
- Preheat your Air Fryer to 300 degrees F roast for 6-8 minuteslet them cool. Add dressing ingredients to a bowl, blend for half a minute
- Add walnuts. Mix and enjoy!

Nutrition:
Calories 260 kcal
Carbs 28 g
Fat 16 g
Protein 4g

32. Blueberry Spelt Pancakes
Intermediate Recipe
Preparation Time: 10 minutes
Cooking Time: 10 minutes
Servings: 4
Ingredients:
- 2 cups spelt flour
- 1 cup hemp milk
- 1/2 cup spring water
- 2 tablespoons grape seed
- 1/2 cup Agave
- 1/2 cup blueberries
- 1/4 teaspoon Sea Moss
- 2 tablespoons Hemp Seeds
- Grape seed oil

Directions:
- Place Moss, agave, hemp seeds, grape seed oil, spelt in a large bowl
- Mix well
- Add milk and water, mix until you have your desired consistency
- Toss in blueberries and toss well
- Preheat your Air Fryer to 325 degrees F
- Transfer batter to Air Fryer basket lined with parchment paper
- Cook for 3-4 minutes, flip and cook for 3 minutes more until golden on both side
- Serve and enjoy!

Nutrition:
Calories 276 kcal
Carbs 36 g
Fat 11 g
Protein 9g

33. Good Morning Energy Crackers
Intermediate Recipe
Preparation Time: 10 minutes
Cooking Time: 25 minutes
Servings: 4
Ingredients:
- 1/2 cup hemp seeds
- 1/2 cup quinoa
- 1/2 cup sunflower seeds
- 1/2 cup sesame seeds
- 1 garlic clove, crushed
- 1/2 teaspoon cayenne pepper
- Salt and pepper to taste
- 1 and 1/4 cup spring water

Directions:
- Preheat your oven to 280 degrees F
- Take a bowl and mix everything, spread the mix in your cooking basket lined with baking sheet
- Bake it for 20-25 minutes
- Break into pieces and serve
- Enjoy!

Nutrition:
Calories 148 kcal
Carbs 1.4 g
Fat 1.6 g
Protein 4.8g

34. Masala Quinoa Meal
Intermediate Recipe
Preparation Time: 10 minutes
Cooking Time: 45 minutes
Servings: 4
Ingredients:
- 1/2 white onion, chopped
- Pinch of salt
- 1 red bell pepper, chopped
- 1/2 jalapeno pepper, seeded and chopped
- 2 tablespoons ginger, peeled and grated
- 1 tablespoon masala powder
- 1 cup quinoa
- 2 cups Sebi friendly vegetable stock
- 1/2 lemon, juiced

Directions:
- Preheat your Air Fryer to 350 degrees F
- Take a large skillet and place it over medium heat, add onion and salt, Sauté for 3 minutes
- Add pepper, jalapeno, ginger, garam masala and Sauté for 1 minute
- Add quinoa to the stock, stir

Transfer mix to Air Fryer cooking basket
Cook for about 3-40 minutes until fluffy
Add lemon juice and fluff more
Adjust the seasoning accordingly and serve
Enjoy!

Nutrition:
Calories 503 kcal
Carbs 103 g
Fat 3 g
Protein 32g

35. Toasted Quinoa Chunks
Basic Recipe
Preparation Time: 10 minutes
Cooking Time: 15 minutes
Servings: 4
Ingredients:
- 8 ounces walnuts
- 1/2 cup uncooked quinoa
- 1 teaspoon salt
- 1 tablespoon olive oil
- 1 teaspoon ground onion powder
- 1 teaspoon paprika powder

Directions:
Preheat your Air Fryer to 400 degrees F
Take a bowl and mix everything
Transfer mixture to Air Fryer cooking basket lined with parchment paper
Bake it for 10 minutes
Break into pieces and serve
Enjoy!

Nutrition:
Calories 187 kcal
Carbs 6 g Fat 3 g
Protein 5 g

36. Lime And Cumin Quinoa
Intermediate Recipe
Preparation Time: 10 minutes
Cooking Time: 30 minutes
Servings: 4
Ingredients:
- 2 tablespoons avocado oil
- 1/4 white onion, chopped
- Pinch of salt
- 2 garlic cloves, minced
- 1 cup quinoa
- 1/2 lime, juiced
- 1 tablespoon onion powder
- 1 teaspoon chili powder
- 1/4 teaspoon paprika
- 2 cups Sebi friendly vegetable stock

Directions:
Preheat your Air Fryer to 300 degrees F
Take a pan and place it over medium heat
Add onion and salt, Sauté for 3 minutes
Add garlic, quinoa, lime, cumin, chili, paprika and Sauté for 2 minutes
Transfer mix to Air Fryer cooking basket
Add stock and cook for 20-25 minutes
Serve and enjoy

Nutrition:
Calories 266 kcal
Carbs 40g
Fat 8g
Protein 9g

37. Fancy Breakfast Quinoa
Basic Recipe
Preparation Time: 10 minutes
Cooking Time: 3Minutes
Servings: 4
Ingredients:
- 1/2 cup walnuts, soaked and chopped
- 4 ounces sesame seeds, soaked
- 2 ounces hemp seeds, soaked overnight
- 1 teaspoon date sugar
- 1/2 teaspoon ground cinnamon
- 5 ounces quinoa puff
- 1 teaspoon hemp seed oil
- 1 cup of coconut milk

Directions:
Take a bowl and mix in all the seeds and spices
Add hemp seed oil
Stir well until the mixture is thick

Flatten mixture on your cooking basket

Preheat your Air Fryer to 330 degrees F

Transfer to your Air fryer and cook for 2-3 minutes until light brown

Transfer mix to a serving bowl

Add quinoa puff, stir well and add coconut milk stir again

Serve and enjoy

Nutrition:
Calories 510 kcal
Carbs 50 g
Fat 8 g
Protein 21g

38. Dr. Sebi Kamut Puff Cereal
Basic Recipe
Preparation Time: 10 minutes
Cooking Time: 12 minutes
Servings: 4
Ingredients:

Agave nectar

6 ounces bag of Kamut puff

Directions:

Begin by spreading Kamut Puffs over your Air Fryer cooking basket, Drizzle with agave nectar on top

Stir well

Transfer to Air Fryer and cook for 8-12 minutes

Let the puffs cool for 10-15 minutes

Enjoy with coconut milk and use it as needed!

Nutrition:
Calories 196 kcal
Carbs 29 g Fat 8 g Protein 2g

39. Fresh Sautéed Apple
Basic Recipe
Preparation Time: 10 minutes
Cooking Time: 10 minutes
Servings: 4
Ingredients:

2 tablespoons olive oil

3 apples, peeled, cored and sliced

1 tablespoon garlic clove, grated

1 tablespoon date sugar

Pinch of salt

Directions:

Preheat your Air Fryer 300 degrees F. Add coconut oil to the cooking basket, add remaining ingredients and stir well.

Transfer to Air Fryer, cook for 5-10 minutes, making sure to shake the basket occasionally until golden. Serve and enjoy!

Nutrition:
Calories 32 kcal
Carbs 32g
Fat 9g
Protein 3g

40. Perfect Vegetable Roast
Basic Recipe
Preparation Time: 10 minutes
Cooking Time: 10 minutes
Servings: 4
Ingredients:

2 cups Roma tomatoes

1/2 cup mushrooms halved

1 red bell pepper, seeded and cut into bite-sized portions

1 tablespoon coconut oil

1 tablespoon garlic powder

1 teaspoon salt

Directions:

Preheat your Air Fryer 400 degrees F

Take a bowl and add mushrooms, Roma tomatoes, bell pepper, oil, salt, garlic powder and mix well

Transfer to Air Fryer cooking basket

Cook for 12-15 minutes, making sure to shake occasionally

Serve and enjoy once crispy!

Nutrition:
Calories 19 kcal Carbs 19 g
Fat 16 g Protein 7g

41. Herb Frittata

Preparation Time: 10 minutes
Cooking Time: 25 minutes
Servings: 4
Ingredients:
- 2 tablespoons chopped green scallions
- 1/2 teaspoon ground black pepper
- 2 tablespoons chopped cilantro
- 1/2 teaspoon salt
- 2 tablespoons chopped parsley
- 1/2 cup half and half, reduced-fat
- 4 eggs, pastured
- 1/3 cup shredded cheddar cheese, reduced-fat

Direction:
- Switch on the air fryer, insert fryer basket, grease it with olive oil, then shut with its lid, set the fryer at 330 degrees F and preheat for 10 minutes.
- Meanwhile, take a round heatproof pan that fits into the fryer basket, grease it well with oil and set aside until required.
- Crack the eggs in a bowl, beat in half-and-half, then add remaining ingredients, beat until well mixed and pour the mixture into prepared pan.
- Open the fryer, place the pan in it, close with its lid and cook for 15 minutes at the 330 degrees F until its top is nicely golden, frittata has set and inserted toothpick into the frittata slides out clean.
- When air fryer beeps, open its lid, take out the pan, then transfer frittata onto a serving plate, cut it into pieces and serve.

Nutrition:
Calories 141 Cal
Carbs 2 g
Fat 10 g
Protein 8 g
Fiber 0 g

42. Zucchini Bread

Preparation Time: 25 minutes
Cooking Time: 40 minutes
Servings: 8
Ingredients:
- ¾ cup shredded zucchini
- 1/2 cup almond flour
- 1/4 teaspoon salt
- 1/4 cup cocoa powder, unsweetened
- 1/2 cup chocolate chips, unsweetened, divided
- 6 tablespoons erythritol sweetener
- 1/2 teaspoon baking soda
- 2 tablespoons olive oil
- 1/2 teaspoon vanilla extract, unsweetened
- 2 tablespoons butter, unsalted, melted
- 1 egg, pastured

Direction:
- Switch on the air fryer, insert fryer basket, grease it with olive oil, then shut with its lid, set the fryer at 310 degrees F and preheat for 10 minutes.
- Meanwhile, place flour in a bowl, add salt, cocoa powder, and baking soda and stir until mixed.
- Crack the eggs in another bowl, whisk in sweetener, egg, oil, butter, and vanilla until smooth and then slowly whisk in flour mixture until incorporated.
- Add zucchini along with 1/3 cup chocolate chips and then fold until just mixed.
- Take a mini loaf pan that fits into the air fryer, grease it with olive oil, then pour in the prepared batter and sprinkle remaining chocolate chips on top.
- Open the fryer, place the loaf pan in it, close with its lid and cook for 30 minutes at the 310 degrees F until inserted toothpick into the bread slides out clean.
- When air fryer beeps, open its lid, remove the loaf pan, then place it on a wire rack

and let the bread cool in it for 20 minutes.

Take out the bread, let it cool completely, then cut it into slices and serve.

Nutrition:
Calories 356 Cal Carbs 49 g
Fat 17 g Protein 5.1 g
Fiber 2.5 g

43. Blueberry Muffins

Preparation Time: 10 minutes
Cooking Time: 30 minutes
Servings: 14
Ingredients:
- 1 cup almond flour
- 1 cup frozen blueberries
- 2 teaspoons baking powder
- 1/3 cup erythritol sweetener
- 1 teaspoon vanilla extract, unsweetened
- ½ teaspoon salt
- ¼ cups melted coconut oil
- 1 egg, pastured
- ¼ cup applesauce, unsweetened
- ¼ cup almond milk, unsweetened

Direction:
- Switch on the air fryer, insert fryer basket, grease it with olive oil, then shut with its lid, set the fryer at 360 degrees F and preheat for 10 minutes.
- Meanwhile, place flour in a large bowl, add berries, salt, sweetener, and baking powder and stir until well combined.
- Crack the eggs in another bowl, whisk in vanilla, milk, and applesauce until combined and then slowly whisk in flour mixture until incorporated.
- Take fourteen silicone muffin cups, grease them with oil, and then evenly fill them with the prepared batter.
- Open the fryer; stack muffin cups in it, close with its lid and cook for 10 minutes until muffins are nicely golden brown and set.
- When air fryer beeps, open its lid, transfer muffins onto a serving plate and then remaining muffins in the same manner. Serve straight away.

Nutrition:
Calories 201 Cal Carbs 27.3g
Fat 8.8 g Protein 3g Fiber 1.2g

44. Baked Eggs

Preparation Time: 5 minutes
Cooking Time: 17 minutes
Servings: 2
Ingredients:
- 2 tablespoons frozen spinach, thawed
- ½ teaspoon salt
- ¼ teaspoon ground black pepper
- 2 eggs, pastured
- 3 teaspoons grated parmesan cheese, reduced-fat
- 2 tablespoons milk, unsweetened, reduced-fat

Direction:
- Switch on the air fryer, insert fryer basket, grease it with olive oil, then shut with its lid, set the fryer at 330 degrees F and preheat for 5 minutes.
- Meanwhile, take two silicon muffin cups, grease them with oil, then crack an egg into each cup and evenly add cheese, spinach, and milk.
- Season the egg with salt and black pepper and gently stir the ingredients, without breaking the egg yolk.
- Open the fryer, add muffin cups in it, close with its lid and cook for 8 to 12 minutes until eggs have cooked to desired doneness.
- When air fryer beeps, open its lid, take out the muffin cups and serve.

Nutrition:
Calories 161 Cal Carbs 3 g
Fat 11.4 g Protein 1.1 g
Fiber 1.1 g

45. Bagels

Preparation Time: 10 minutes
Cooking Time: 20 minutes
Servings: 6
Ingredients:
- 2 cups almond flour
- 2 cups shredded mozzarella cheese, low-fat
- 2 tablespoons butter, unsalted
- 1 1/2 teaspoon baking powder
- 1 teaspoon apple cider vinegar
- 1 egg, pastured

For Egg Wash:
- 1 egg, pastured
- 1 teaspoon butter, unsalted, melted

Direction:
- Place flour in a heatproof bowl, add cheese and butter, then stir well and microwave for 90 seconds until butter and cheese has melted.
- Then stir the mixture until well combined, let it cool for 5 minutes and whisk in the egg, baking powder, and vinegar until incorporated and dough comes together.
- Let the dough cool for 10 minutes, then divide the dough into six pieces, shape each piece into a bagel and let the bagels rest for 5 minutes.
- Prepare the egg wash and for this, place the melted butter in a bowl, whisk in the egg until blended and then brush the mixture generously on top of each bagel.
- Take a fryer basket, line it with parchment paper and then place prepared bagels in it in a single layer.
- Switch on the air fryer, insert fryer, then shut with its lid, set the fryer at 350 degrees F and cook for 10 minutes at the 350 degrees F until bagels are nicely golden and thoroughly cooked, turning the bagels halfway through the frying.
- When air fryer beeps, open its lid, transfer bagels to a serving plate and cook the remaining bagels in the same manner. Serve straight away.

Nutrition:
Calories 408.7 Cal   Carbs 8.3 g
Fat 33.5 g   Protein 20.3g   Fiber 4g

46. Cauliflower Hash Browns

Preparation Time: 10 minutes
Cooking Time: 25 minutes
Servings: 6
Ingredients:
- 1/4 cup chickpea flour
- 4 cups cauliflower rice
- 1/2 medium white onion, peeled and chopped
- 1/2 teaspoon garlic powder
- 1 tablespoon xanthan gum
- 1/2 teaspoon salt
- 1 tablespoon nutritional yeast flakes
- 1 teaspoon ground paprika

Direction:
- Switch on the air fryer, insert fryer basket, grease it with olive oil, then shut with its lid, set the fryer at 375 degrees F and preheat for 10 minutes.
- Meanwhile, place all the ingredients in a bowl, stir until well mixed and then shape the mixture into six rectangular disks, each about ½-inch thick.
- Open the fryer, add hash browns in it in a single layer, close with its lid and cook for 25 minutes at the 375 degrees F until nicely golden and crispy, turning halfway through the frying.
- When air fryer beeps, open its lid, transfer hash browns to a serving plate and serve.

Nutrition:
Calories 115.2 Cal   Carbs 6.2 g
Fat 7.3 g   Protein 7.4 g
Fiber 2.2 g

47. Cheese And Red Pepper Egg Cups

Preparation Time: 10 minutes
Cooking Time: 15 minutes
Servings: 4
Ingredients:
- Large free-range eggs, 4.
- Shredded cheese, 1 cup
- Diced red pepper, 1 cup
- Half and half, 4 tbsps.
- Salt and Pepper.

Directions:
- Preheat your air fryer to 300°F and grease four ramekins.
- Grab a medium bowl and add the eggs. Whisk well.
- Add the red pepper, half the cheese, half and half, and salt and pepper. Stir well to combine.
- Pour the mixture between the ramekins and pop into the air fryer.
- Cook for 15 minutes then serve and enjoy.

Nutrition:
Calories: 195
Carbs: 7g
Protein: 13g
Fat: 12g

48. Coconut Porridge With Flax Seed

Preparation Time: 5 minutes
Cooking Time: 30 minutes
Servings: 3
Ingredients:
Unsweetened almond milk, 1 ½ cup
Coconut flour, 2 tbsp.
Vegan vanilla protein powder, 2 tbsp.
Powdered erythritol, ¼ tsp.
Golden flaxseed meal, 3 tbsp.

Directions:
- Preheat your Air Fryer at a temperature of about 375° F
- Combine coconut flour with the golden flaxseed meal and the protein powder in a bowl
- Spray your Air Fryer with cooking spray, then pour the mixture in the air fryer pan
- Pour the milk and top with chopped blueberries and chopped raspberries
- Move the pan in the air fryer and seal the lid
- Set the temperature at about 375° F and the timer to about 30 minutes
- When the timer beeps, turn off your Air Fryer and remove the baking pan
- Serve and enjoy your delicious porridge!

Nutrition:
Calories: 249
Fats: 13.7 g
Carbs: 6 g
Protein: 17 g

49. Easy Chocolate Doughnut

Preparation Time: 10 minutes
Cooking Time: 12 minutes
Servings: 6
Ingredients:
- Melted unsalted butter, 3 tbsps.
- Powdered sugar, ¼ cup
- Refrigerated biscuits, 8.
- Semisweet chocolate chips, 48

Directions:
- Cut the biscuits into thirds then flatten them and place 2 chocolate chips at the center.
- Wrap the chocolate with dough to seal the edges.
- Rub each dough hole with some butter.
- Set the dough into the air fryer to cook for 12 minutes at 3400F.
- Set aside to add powdered sugar.
- Serve and enjoy.

Nutrition:
Calories: 393 Fat: 17g
Carbs: 55g Protein: 5g

50. Cheesy Spinach Omelet

Preparation Time: 5 minutes
Cooking Time: 10 minutes
Servings: 2
Ingredients:
Eggs, 3
Chopped fresh spinach, 2 tbsps.
Shredded cheese, ½ cup
Pepper.
Salt.

Directions:
- Mix the eggs with pepper and salt then whisk and put in an oven-safe tray.
- Add spinach and cheese but do not stir.
- Allow to cook in the air fryer for 8 minutes at 390°F.
- Cook for 2 more minutes to brown the omelet.
- Serve on plates to enjoy.

Nutrition:
Calories: 209 Fat: 15.9g
Carbs: 1g
Protein: 15.4g

51. Roasted Garlic And Thyme Dipping Sauce

Preparation Time: 5 minutes
Cooking Time: 30 minutes
Servings: 1
Ingredients:
Minced fresh thyme leaves, ½ tsp.
Salt, 1/8 tsp.
Light mayonnaise, ½ cup
Crushed roasted garlic, 2 tbsps.
Pepper, 1/8 tsp.

Directions:
- Wrap garlic in foil. Put it in the cooking basket of the Air Fryer and roast for 30 minutes at 390 degrees.
- Combine all the ingredients to serve.

Nutrition:
Calories: 485 Fat: 39.4g
Carbs: 34.1g Protein: 2.2g

52. Cheesy Sausage And Egg Rolls

Preparation Time: 15 minutes
Cooking Time: 15 minutes
Servings: 8
Ingredients:
Cooked breakfast sausage links, 8 pieces.
Eggs, 3.
Salt and Pepper,
Cheddar cheese slices, 4.
Refrigerated crescent rolls, 8 oz.

Directions:
- Set the air fryer at 325 degrees Fahrenheit to preheat.
- Beat the eggs; reserve one tablespoon as egg wash and scramble the rest.
- Halve the cheese slices.
- Separate the dough into 8 triangles.
- Fill each triangle with a half-slice of cheese, a tablespoon of scrambled eggs, and a sausage link.
- Loosely roll up all filled triangles before placing in the air fryer basket. Brush with the egg wash that was set aside and sprinkle all over with pepper and salt.
- Cook for 15 minutes.
- Serve right away.

Nutrition:
Calories: 270
Fat: 20.0g
Protein: 10.0 g
Carbs: 13.0 g

53. Baked Berry Oatmeal

Preparation Time: 5 minutes
Cooking Time: 25 minutes
Servings: 2-4
Ingredients:
1 medium-size egg
1 cup of whole milk
1 cup of rolled oats
2½ tablespoons of brown sugar

½ teaspoon of baking powder
½ teaspoon of ground cinnamon
Oil
2 cups of divided, mixed berries
2 tablespoons of slivered almonds
Sprinkling of nutmeg

Directions:
- In a bowl, combine the egg with the milk, mixing well to combine.
- In a second bowl, combine the oats with the brown sugar, baking powder, and cinnamon. Mix thoroughly.
- Spritz your air fryer safe pan with oil spray.
- Add ¼ cup of the mixed berries to the air fryer.
- Pour the oatmeal mixture over the fruit, followed by the egg and milk mixture.
- Allow to rest for approximately 10 minutes before adding the remaining fruit on top.
- Scatter the slivered almonds over the berries and season with a sprinkling of nutmeg.
- Place the pan in your air fryer and bake at 320 degrees F, for 10 minutes. Check the progress and either continue to bake or remove from the appliance.
- Set aside to rest for 4-5 minutes and serve.

Nutrition:
Calories: 151 kcal
Fat: 7.1g
Carbs: 17.9g
Protein: 3.6g

54. Broccoli And Cheddar Cheese Quiche

Preparation Time: 5 Minutes
Cooking Time: 10 Minutes
Servings: 1
Ingredients:
- 1 medium-size egg
- 3-4 tablespoons of heavy cream
- 4-5 very small-size broccoli florets
- 1 tablespoon of finely grated Cheddar cheese

Directions:
- In a bowl, whisk the egg along with the heavy cream.
- Lightly grease a 5" circular, ceramic quiche-style dish.
- Arrange the broccoli florets evenly on the bottom of the dish.
- Pour in the egg-cream mixture.
- Scatter the grated Cheddar cheese over the top and air fry at 325 degrees F for 10 minutes.
- Serve and enjoy.

Nutrition:
Calories: 162 kcal
Fat: 5.23g
Carbs: 14.3
Protein: 9.4

55. Egg And Cheese Puff Pastry Tarts

Preparation Time: 10 minutes
Cooking Time: 20 Minutes
Servings: 4
Ingredients:
- All-purpose flour
- 1 (9") square sheet of frozen, thawed puff pastry
- ¾ cup of shredded Cheddar cheese
- 4 large-size eggs
- 1 tablespoon of minced fresh chives

Directions:
- Preheat the air fryer to 390 ° F.
- On a lightly floured clean work surface, unfold the sheet of pastry and cut it into 4 even squares.
- Put 2 of the pastry squares in the air fryer basket, spacing them apart from one another.
- Air fry until the pastry is a light golden brown, for approximately 10 minutes.

Open the basket, and with a metal spoon, press down the middles of each pastry square to create an indentation. Scatter 3 tablespoons of shredded cheese into each indent. Crack an egg carefully into the middle of each pastry.

Air fry for 8-10 minutes, until the eggs are cooked to your preferred level of doneness.

Transfer the tarts to a wire baking rack set over wax paper and allow it to cool for 4-5 minutes.

Repeat Steps 2-4 with the remaining ingredients.

Garnish with half of the chives and serve warm.

Nutrition:
Calories: 231 kcal
Fat: 6.5g
Carbs: 10.3g
Protein: 6.4g

56. French Toast

Preparation Time: 5 Minutes
Cooking Time: 3 Minutes
Servings: 4
Ingredients:

2 medium-size eggs
⅔ cup of whole milk
1 tablespoon of cinnamon
1 teaspoon of vanilla extract
4 slices of whole wheat bread

Directions:

In a small-size bowl, combine the eggs with the milk, cinnamon, and vanilla extract. Beat to break up the eggs and incorporate them.

Dip each side of bread in the egg mixture, shaking off any excess.

Add the dipped bread slices into the pan and air fryer for a few minutes at 320 degrees F. Flip the bread over and air fry for an additional 3 minutes.

Serve.

Nutrition:
Calories: 231 kcal
Fat: 6.3g
Carbs: 13.6g
Protein: 4.6g

57. Grilled Gruyere Cheese Sandwich

Preparation Time: 5 Minutes
Cooking Time: 10 Minutes
Servings: 1
Ingredients:

2 ounces of thinly sliced Gruyere cheese
2 slices of whole-grain bread
1 tablespoon of butter

Directions:

Lay the Gruyere cheese between the 2 slices of bread.

Butter up the outside of the bread slices.

Place the cheese sandwich in the air fryer basket. You may need to use toothpicks to secure.

Air fry the sandwich for approximately 3-5 minutes at 360 degrees F until the cheese melts.

Flip the sandwich over and turn the heat up to 380 degrees F until crisp.

Continue to air fryer for approximately 5 minutes, until the sandwich is to your desired texture. You will need to check continually that the sandwich doesn't burn.

Set to one side to cool slightly before enjoying.

Nutrition:
Calories: 151 kcal
Fat: 7.1g
Carbs: 17.9g
Protein: 3.6g

58. Pancakes

Preparation Time: 5 minutes
Cooking Time: 10 minutes
Servings: 2
Ingredients:
- 2 tbsps. coconut oil
- 1 tsp. maple extract
- 2 tbsps. cashew milk
- 2 eggs
- 2/3 oz. /20g pork rinds

Directions:
- Grind up the pork rinds until fine and mix with the rest of the ingredients, except the oil.
- Add the oil to a skillet. Add a quarter-cup of the batter and fry until golden on each side. Continue adding the remaining batter.

Nutrition:
Calories: 280 Carbs: 31 g
Fat: 2 g
Protein: 5 g

59. Breakfast Sandwich

Preparation Time: 5 minutes
Cooking Time: 5 minutes
Servings: 1
Ingredients:
- 2 oz. /60g cheddar cheese
- 1/6 oz. /30g smoked ham
- 2 tbsps. butter
- 4 eggs

Directions:
- Fry all the eggs and sprinkle the pepper and salt on them.
- Place an egg down as the sandwich base. Top with the ham and cheese and a drop or two of Tabasco.
- Place the other egg on top and enjoy.

Nutrition:
Calories: 180 Carbs: 19 g
Fat: 7 g
Protein: 10 g

60. Egg Muffins

Preparation Time: 10 minutes
Cooking Time: 15-20 minutes
Servings: 1
Ingredients:
- 1 tbsp. green pesto
- Oz/75g shredded cheese
- Oz/150g cooked bacon
- 1 scallion, chopped
- Eggs

Directions:
- You should set your fryer to 350°F/175°C.
- Place liners in a regular cupcake tin. This will help with easy removal and storage.
- Beat the eggs with pepper, salt, and the pesto. Mix in the cheese.
- Pour the eggs into the cupcake tin and top with the bacon and scallion.
- Cook for 15-20 minutes, or until the egg is set.

Nutrition:
Calories: 160
Carbs: 11 g
Fat: 6 g
Protein: 8 g

61. Cream Cheese Pancakes

Preparation Time: 10 minutes
Cooking Time: 10 minutes
Servings: 1
Ingredients:
- 2 oz. cream cheese
- 2 eggs
- ½ tsp. cinnamon
- 1 tbsp coconut flour
- ½ to 1 packet of Sugar

Directions:
- Mix together all the ingredients until smooth.
- Heat up a non-stick skillet with butter or coconut oil on medium-high.
- Make them as you would normal pancakes.

Cook it on one side and then flip to cook the other side!

Top with some butter and/or sugar.

Nutrition:
Calories: 190 Carbs: 15 g
Fat: 8 g Protein: 9 g

---

62. Eggs On The Go

Preparation Time: 5 minutes
Cooking Time: 15 minutes
Servings: 1

Ingredients:
- 110g bacon, cooked
- Pepper - Salt
- Eggs

Directions:
- You should set your fryer to 400°F/200°C.
- Place liners in a regular cupcake tin. This will help with easy removal and storage.
- Crack an egg into each of the cups and sprinkle some bacon onto each of them. Season with some pepper and salt.
- Bake for 15 minutes, or once the eggs are set.

Nutrition:
Calories: 140 Carbs: 10 g
Fat: 5 g Protein: 7 g

---

63. Breakfast Muffins

Preparation Time: 10 minutes
Cooking Time: 15-20 minutes
Servings: 1

Ingredients:
- 1 medium egg
- ¼ cup heavy cream
- 1 slice cooked bacon (cured, pan-fried, cooked)
- 1 oz. cheddar cheese
- Salt and black pepper (to taste)

Directions:
- Preheat your fryer to 350°F/175°C.
- In a bowl, combine the eggs with the cream, salt and pepper.
- Spread into muffin tins and fill the cups half full.
- Place 1 slice of bacon into each muffin hole and half ounce of cheese on top of each muffin.
- Bake for around 15-20 minutes or until slightly browned.
- Add another ½ oz. of cheese onto each muffin and broil until the cheese is slightly browned. Serve!

Nutrition:
Calories: 250 Carbs: 15 g
Fat: 10 g Protein: 12 g

---

64. Egg Porridge

Preparation Time: 5 minutes
Cooking Time: 10 minutes
Servings: 1

Ingredients:
- 2 organic free-range eggs
- 1/3 cup organic heavy cream without food additives
- 2 packages of your preferred sweetener
- 2 tbsp grass-fed butter ground organic cinnamon to taste

Directions:
- In a bowl add the eggs, cream and sweetener, and mix together.
- Melt the butter in a saucepan over a medium heat. Lower the heat once the butter is melted.
- Combine together with the egg and cream mixture.
- While cooking, mix until it thickens and curdles. When you see the first signs of curdling, remove the saucepan immediately from the heat.
- Pour the porridge into a bowl. Sprinkle cinnamon on top and serve immediately.

Nutrition:
Calories: 120 Carbs: 7 g
Fat: 5 g Protein: 6 g

65. Delicious Breakfast Soufflé

Preparation Time: 5 minutes
Cooking Time: 15 minutes
Servings: 4
Ingredients:
- 6 eggs
- ⅓ cup milk
- ½ cup shredded mozzarella cheese
- 1 tbsp. freshly chopped parsley
- ½ cup chopped ham
- 1 tsp. salt
- 1 tsp. black pepper
- ½ tsp. garlic powder
- Cooking spray

Directions:
- Grease 4 ramekins with a non-stick cooking spray. Preheat your Air Fryer Oven to 350ºF.
- Using a large bowl, add and stir all the ingredients until they are mixed properly.
- Pour the egg mixture into the greased ramekins and place it inside your Air Fryer Oven.
- Cook it inside your air fryer for 8 minutes. Then carefully remove the soufflé from your air fryer and allow it to cool off.
- Serve and enjoy!

Nutrition:
- Calories: 195
- Fats: 15 g
- Carbs: 6 g
- Protein: 9 g

66. Yummy Breakfast Italian Frittata

Preparation Time: 5 minutes
Cooking Time: 10 minutes
Servings: 6
Ingredients:
- 6 eggs
- ⅓ cup milk
- 4-oz. chopped Italian sausage
- 3 cups stemmed and roughly chopped kale
- 1 red seeded and chopped bell pepper
- ½ cup a grated feta cheese
- 1 chopped zucchini
- 1 tbsp. freshly chopped basil
- 1 tsp. garlic powder
- 1 tsp. onion powder
- 1 tsp. salt
- 1 tsp. black pepper

Directions:
- Preheat your Air Fryer Oven to 360°F.
- Grease the air fryer pan with a non-stick cooking spray.
- Add the Italian sausage to the pan and cook it inside your Air Fryer Oven for 5 minutes.
- While doing that, add and stir in the remaining ingredients until they mix properly.
- Add the egg mixture to the pan and allow it to cook inside your Air Fryer Oven for 5 minutes.
- Then carefully remove the pan and allow it to cool off until it gets chill enough to serve.
- Serve and enjoy!

Nutrition:
- Calories: 225
- Fats: 14 g
- Carbs: 4.5 g
- Protein: 20 g

67. Savory Cheese and Bacon Muffins

Preparation Time: 5 minutes
Cooking Time: 17 minutes
Servings: 4
Ingredients:
- 1 ½ cup all-purpose flour
- 2 tsp. baking powder
- ½ cup milk
- 2 eggs

1 tbsp. freshly chopped parsley
4 cooked and chopped bacon slices
1 thinly chopped onion
½ cup shredded cheddar cheese
½ tsp. onion powder
1 tsp. salt
1 tsp. black pepper

Directions:

Turn on your Air Fryer Oven and let it heat up to 360ºF.

In a large bowl, add and stir all the ingredients until they mix properly.

Then grease the muffin cups with a non-stick cooking spray or line it with parchment paper. The pour the batter proportionally into each muffin cup.

Place it inside your Air Fryer Oven and bake it for 15 minutes.

Then carefully remove it from your Air Fryer Oven and allow it to chill.

Serve and enjoy!

Nutrition:

Calories: 180 Fats: 18 g
Carbs: 16 g Protein: 15 g

68. Best Air-Fried English Breakfast

Preparation Time: 5 minutes
Cooking Time: 20 minutes
Servings: 4
Ingredients:

8 sausages
8 bacon slices
4 eggs
1 (16-oz.) can baked beans
8 slices of toast

Directions:

Add the sausages and bacon slices to your air fryer and cook them for 10 minutes at a 320°F.

In a ramekin or heat-resistant bowl, add the baked beans, place another ramekin, and add the eggs and whisk.

Increase the temperature to 290°F.

Place it inside your air fryer and cook it for an additional 10 minutes, or until everything is done.

Serve and enjoy!

Nutrition:

Calories: 850 Fats: 40 g
Carbs: 20 g Protein: 48 g

69. Sausage and Egg Breakfast Burrito

Preparation Time: 5 minutes
Cooking Time: 30 minutes
Servings: 6
Ingredients:

6 eggs
Salt
Pepper
Cooking oil
½ cup chopped red bell pepper
½ cup chopped green bell pepper
8 oz. ground chicken sausage
½ cup salsa
6 medium (8-inch) flour tortillas
½ cup shredded Cheddar cheese

Directions:

In a medium bowl, whisk the eggs, and add salt and pepper to taste.

Place a skillet in the air fryer on medium-high heat. Spray with cooking oil. Add the egg and scramble them for 2–3 minutes, until the eggs are fluffy. Remove the eggs from the skillet and set aside.

If needed, spray the skillet with more oil. Add the chopped red and green bell peppers. Cook for 2–3 minutes, or until the peppers are soft.

Add the ground sausage to the skillet. Break the sausage into smaller pieces using a

- spatula or spoon. Then cook for 3–4 minutes, or until the sausage is brown.
- Add the salsa and scrambled eggs. Stir to combine. Remove the skillet from heat.
- Spoon the mixture evenly onto the tortillas.
- To form the burritos, fold the sides of each tortilla toward the middle and then roll up from the bottom. You can secure each burrito with a toothpick. Alternatively, you can moisten the outside edge of the tortilla with a small amount of water. I prefer to use a cooking brush, but you can also dab with your fingers.
- Spray the burritos with cooking oil and place them in the Air Fryer Oven. Do not stack. Cook the burritos in batches if they do not all fit in the basket. Cook for 8 minutes
- Open the Air Fryer Oven and flip the burritos. Heat it for an additional 2 minutes or until crisp.
- If necessary, repeat steps 8 and 9 for the remaining burritos.
- Sprinkle the Cheddar cheese over the burritos. Cool before serving.

Nutrition:
- Calories: 236 Fats: 13 g
- Carbs: 16 g Protein: 15 g

70. French Toast Sticks

Preparation Time: 5 minutes
Cooking Time: 15 minutes
Servings: 12
Ingredients:
- 4 slices Texas toast (or any thick bread, such as challah)
- 1 tbsp. butter
- 1 egg
- 1 tsp. stevia
- 1 tsp. ground cinnamon
- ¼ cup milk
- 1 tsp. vanilla extract
- Cooking oil

Directions:
- Cut each bread slice into 3 pieces (for 12 sticks total).
- Place the butter in a small, microwave-safe bowl. Heat for 15 seconds or until the butter has melted.
- Remove the bowl from the microwave. Add the egg, stevia, cinnamon, milk, and vanilla extract. Whisk until fully combined.
- Spray the air fry basket with cooking oil.
- Dredge each of the bread sticks in the egg mixture.
- Place the French toast sticks in the Air Fryer Oven —it is okay to stack them. Spray the French toast sticks with cooking oil. Cook for 8 minutes
- Open the Air Fryer Oven and flip each of the French toast sticks. Cook for an additional 4 minutes or until the French toast sticks are crisp.
- Cool before serving.

Nutrition:
- Calories: 52
- Fats: 2 g
- Carbs: 7 g
- Protein: 2 g

71. Home-Fried Potatoes

Preparation Time: 5 minutes
Cooking Time: 25 minutes
Servings: 4
Ingredients:
- 3 large russet potatoes
- 1 tbsp. canola oil
- 1 tbsp. extra-virgin olive oil
- 1 tsp. paprika
- Salt
- Pepper
- 1 cup chopped onion
- 1 cup chopped red bell pepper
- 1 cup chopped green bell pepper

Directions:

- Cut the potatoes into ½-inch cubes. Place the potatoes in a large bowl of cold water and allow them to soak for at least 30 minutes, preferably an hour.
- Dry out the potatoes and wipe thoroughly with paper towels. Then return them to the empty bowl.
- Add the canola and olive oils, paprika, and salt and pepper to flavor. Toss to fully coat the potatoes.
- Transfer the potatoes to the Air Fryer Oven. Cook for 20 minutes, shaking the air fryer basket every 5 minutes (a total of 4 times). Place the onion and red and green bell peppers in the air fry basket. Fry for an additional 3–4 minutes, or until the potatoes are cooked through and the peppers are soft.
- Cool before serving.

Nutrition:

Calories: 279 Fats: 8 g
Carbs: 50 g Protein: 6 g

72. Homemade Cherry Breakfast Tarts

Preparation Time: 15 minutes
Cooking Time: 20 minutes
Servings: 6
Ingredients:
For the Tarts:

- 2 refrigerated piecrusts
- ⅓ cup cherry preserves
- 1 tsp. cornstarch
- Cooking oil

For the Frosting:

- ½ cup vanilla yogurt
- 1 oz. cream cheese
- 1 tsp. stevia
- 1 tsp. Rainbow sprinkles

Directions:

- To make the tarts, Place the piecrusts on a flat surface. Then cut each piecrust with a pizza cutter, for 6 in total. (I discard the unused dough left from slicing the edges).
- In a small bowl, combine the preserves and cornstarch. Mix well.
- Scoop 1 tbsp. of the preserve mixture onto the top half of each piece of piecrust.
- Fold the bottom of each piece up to close the tart. Press along the edges of each tart to seal them using the back of a fork.
- Sprinkle the breakfast tarts with cooking oil and place them in the Air Fryer Oven. I do not recommend piling the breakfast tarts because they will stick together if piled, so you may need to prepare them in two batches. Cook for 10 minutes.
- Allow the breakfast tarts to cool fully before removing them from the Air Fryer Oven.
- If needed, repeat steps 5 and 6 for the remaining breakfast tarts.
- To make the frosting, mix well the yogurt, cream cheese, and stevia in a small bowl.
- Spread the breakfast tarts with frosting, top with sprinkles, and serve.

Nutrition:

Calories: 119
Fats: 4 g
Carbs: 19 g
Protein: 2 g

73. Sausage and Cream Cheese Biscuits

Preparation Time: 5 minutes
Cooking Time: 15 minutes
Serving: 5
Ingredients:

- 12 oz. chicken breakfast sausage
- 1 (6-oz.) can biscuits
- ⅛ cup cream cheese

Direction:

- Form 5 sausage patties out of the sausages.
- Place the sausage patties in the Air Fryer Oven and cook for 5 minutes
- Open the air fryer, flip the patties, and cook for an additional 5 minutes.
- Remove the cooked sausages from the air fryer.
- Form 5 biscuits out of the biscuit dough.
- Place the biscuits in the air fryer and cook for 3 minutes.
- Open the Air Fryer Oven, flip the biscuits, and cook for an additional 2 minutes.
- Remove the cooked biscuits from the air fryer.
- Split each biscuit in half. Spread 1 tsp. of cream cheese onto the bottom of each biscuit. Top with a sausage patty and the other half of the biscuit. Serve.

Nutrition:

Calories: 24 g Fats: 13 g
Carbs: 20 g Protein: 9 g

74. Fried Chicken and Waffles

Preparation Time: 10 minutes
Cooking Time: 30 minutes
Servings: 4
Ingredients:

- 8 whole chicken wings
- 1 tsp. garlic powder
- Chicken seasoning or rub
- Pepper
- ½ cup all-purpose flour
- Cooking oil
- 8 frozen waffles
- Maple syrup (optional)

Directions:

- In a medium bowl, spice the chicken with garlic powder, chicken seasoning, and pepper to flavor.
- Put the chicken in a sealable plastic bag and add the flour. Shake to thoroughly coat the chicken.
- Spray the air fry basket with cooking oil.
- With the use of tongs, transfer the chicken from the bag to the air fryer. Pile the chickens on top of each other. Sprinkle them with cooking oil. Heat for five minutes
- Unlock the air fryer and shake the basket. Proceed to cook the chicken. Keep shaking every 5 minutes until 20 minutes has passed, or until the chicken is completely cooked.
- Take out the cooked chicken from the air fryer and set it aside.
- Wash the basket with warm water. Then transfer them back to the air fryer.
- Lower the temperature of the Air Fryer Oven to 370ºF.
- Put the frozen waffles in the Air Fryer Oven, without piling them. Depending on how big your air fryer is, you may need to cook the waffles in batches. Sprinkle the waffles with cooking oil. Cook for 6 minutes.
- If necessary, take out the cooked waffles from the Air Fryer Oven, then repeat step 9 for the leftover waffles.
- Serve the waffles with the chicken and a bit of maple syrup if desired.

Nutrition:

Calories: 461 Fats: 22 g
Carbs: 45 g Protein: 28 g

75. Cheesy Tater Tot Breakfast Bake

Preparation Time: 5 minutes
Cooking Time: 20 minutes
Servings: 4
Ingredients:

- 4 eggs
- 1 cup milk
- 1 tsp. onion powder
- Salt
- Pepper
- Cooking oil

12 oz. ground chicken sausage
1-lb. frozen tater tots
¾ cup shredded Cheddar cheese

Directions:

Whisk the eggs in medium bowls. Add the milk, onion powder, and salt and pepper to taste. Stir to combine.

Spray a skillet with cooking oil and place it over medium-high heat. Add the ground sausage. Using a spatula or spoon, cut the sausage into smaller pieces. Cook for 3–4 minutes, or until the sausage is brown. Remove from heat and set aside.

Spray a barrel pan with cooking oil. Make sure to oil the bottom and sides of the pan.

Place the tater tots in the barrel pan. Cook for 6 minutes in the Air Fryer Oven.

Open the Air Fryer Oven and shake the pan, then add the egg mixture and cooked sausage. Cook for an additional 6 minutes. Open the Air Fryer Oven and sprinkle the cheese over the tater tot bake. Cook for an additional 2–3 minutes

Cool before serving.

Nutrition:

Calories: 518
Fats: 30 g
Carbs: 31 g
Protein: 30 g

76. Breakfast Scramble Casserole

Preparation Time: 20 minutes
Cooking Time: 10 minutes
Servings: 4
Ingredients:

6 slices bacon
6 eggs
Salt
Pepper
Cooking oil
½ cup chopped red bell pepper
½ cup chopped green bell pepper
½ cup chopped onion
¾ cup shredded Cheddar cheese

Directions:

In a pan over medium-high heat, cook the bacon for 5–7 minutes, flipping until evenly crisp. Dry out on paper towels, crumble the bacon, and set aside. In a medium bowl, whisk the eggs. Add salt and pepper to taste.

Spray a barrel pan with cooking oil, especially the bottom and sides of the pan. Add the beaten eggs, crumbled bacon, red bell pepper, green bell pepper, and onion to the pan. Place the pan in the Air Fryer Oven. Cook for 6 minutes Open the air fryer and sprinkle the cheese over the casserole. Cook for an additional 2 minutes. Cool before serving.

Nutrition:

Calories: 348
Fats: 26 g
Carbs: 4 g
Protein: 25 g

77. Breakfast Grilled Ham and Cheese

Preparation Time: 5 minutes
Cooking Time: 10 minutes
Servings: 2
Ingredients:

1 tsp. butter
4 slices bread
4 slices smoked country ham
4 slices Cheddar cheese
4 thick slices tomato

Directions:

Spread ½ tsp. of butter onto one side of 2 bread slices. Each sandwich will have 1 bread slice with butter and 1 slice without.

- Assemble each sandwich by layering 2 ham slices, 2 cheese slices, and 2 tomato slices on the unbuttered bread pieces. Top with the other bread slices buttered-side up.
- Place the sandwiches in the air fryer buttered-side down. Cook for 4 minutes
- Open the air fryer, flip the grilled cheese sandwiches, and cook for an additional 4 minutes
- Cool before serving. Cut each sandwich in half and enjoy.

Nutrition:
Calories: 525
Fats: 25 g
Carbs: 34 g
Protein: 41 g

78. Classic Hash Browns

Preparation Time: 15 minutes
Cooking Time: 20 minutes
Servings: 4
Ingredients:
- 4 russet potatoes
- 1 tsp. paprika
- Salt
- Pepper
- Cooking oil

Directions:
- Peel the potatoes using a vegetable peeler. Shred the potatoes with a cheese grater. If your grater has differently sized holes, use the area of the tool with the largest holes.
- Put the shredded potatoes in a large bowl of cold water. Let sit for 5 minutes Cold water helps remove excess starch from the potatoes. Stir to help dissolve the starch.
- Dry out the potatoes with paper towels or napkins. Make sure the potatoes are completely dry.
- Season the potatoes with paprika and salt and pepper to taste.
- Spray the potatoes with cooking oil and transfer them to the Air Fryer Oven. Cook for 20 minutes and shake the basket every 5 minutes (a total of 4 times).
- Cool before serving.

Nutrition:
Calories: 150
Sodium: 52 mg
Carbs: 34 g
Fiber: 5 g
Protein: 4 g

79. Canadian Bacon and Cheese English Muffins

Preparation Time: 5 minutes
Cooking Time: 10 minutes
Servings: 4
Ingredients:
- 4 English muffins
- 8 slices Canadian bacon
- 4 slices cheese
- Cooking oil

Directions:
- Split each English muffin. Assemble the breakfast sandwiches by layering 2 Canadian bacon slices and 1 cheese slice into each English muffin bottom. Put the other half on top of the English muffin. Place the sandwiches in the Air Fryer Oven. Spray the top of each with cooking oil. Cook for 4 minutes.
- Open the Air Fryer Oven and flip the sandwiches. Cook for an additional 4 minutes.
- Cool before serving.

Nutrition:
Calories: 333
Fats: 14 g
Carbs: 27 g
Protein: 24 g

80. Radish Hash Browns

Preparation Time: 10 minutes
Cooking Time: 13 minutes
Servings: 4
Ingredients:
- 1 lb. radishes, washed and cut off roots
- 1 tbsp. olive oil
- ½ tsp. paprika
- ½ tsp. onion powder
- ½ tsp. garlic powder
- 1 medium onion
- ¼ tsp. pepper
- ¾ tsp. sea salt

Directions:
- Slice the onion and radishes using a mandolin slicer.
- Add the sliced onion and radishes to a large mixing bowl and toss with olive oil.
- Transfer the onion and radish slices in an air fryer basket and cook at 360ºF for 8 minutes. Shake the basket twice.
- Return the onion and radish slices to the mixing bowl and toss with seasonings.
- Again, cook onion and radish slices in the air fry basket for 5 minutes at 400ºF. Shake the basket halfway through.
- Serve and enjoy.

Nutrition:
Calories: 62 Fats: 3.7 g
Carbs: 7.1 g Protein: 1.2 g

81. Vegetable Egg Cups

Preparation Time: 10 minutes
Cooking Time: 20 minutes
Servings: 4
Ingredients:
- 4 eggs
- 1 tbsp. cilantro, chopped
- 4 tbsp. half and half
- 1 cup cheddar cheese, shredded
- 1 cup vegetables, diced
- Pepper
- Salt

Directions:
- Sprinkle 4 ramekins with cooking spray and set aside.
- In a mixing bowl, whisk the eggs with cilantro, half and half, vegetables, ½ cup cheese, pepper, and salt.
- Pour the egg mixture into the 4 ramekins.
- Place ramekins in air fry basket and cook at 300ºF for 12 minutes.
- Top with the remaining ½ cup of cheese and cook for 2 minutes more at 400ºF.
- Serve and enjoy.

Nutrition:
Calories: 194 Fats: 11.5 g
Carbs: 6 g Protein: 13 g

82. Spinach Frittata

Preparation Time: 5 minutes
Cooking Time: 8 minutes
Servings: 1
Ingredients:
- 3 eggs
- 1 cup spinach, chopped
- 1 small onion, minced
- 2 tbsp. mozzarella cheese, grated
- Pepper
- Salt

Directions:
- Preheat the Air Fryer Oven to 350ºF, and spray the sheet pan with cooking spray.
- In a bowl, whisk the eggs with the remaining ingredients until well combined.
- Pour the egg mixture into the prepared pan and place the pan in the air fry basket.
- Cook the frittata for 8 minutes or until set. Serve and enjoy.

Nutrition:
Calories: 384 Fats: 23.3 g
Carbs: 10.7 g Protein: 34.3 g

83. Omelet Frittata

Preparation Time: 10 minutes
Cooking Time: 6 minutes
Servings: 2
Ingredients:
- 3 eggs, lightly beaten
- 2 tbsp. cheddar cheese, shredded
- 2 tbsp. heavy cream
- 2 mushrooms, sliced
- ¼ small onion, chopped
- ¼ bell pepper, diced
- Pepper
- Salt

Directions:
- In a bowl, whisk the eggs with the cream, vegetables, pepper, and salt.
- Preheat the Air Fryer Oven to 400ºF.
- Pour the egg mixture into the sheet pan. Place the pan in the Air Fryer Oven and cook for 5 minutes.
- Add the shredded cheese on top of the frittata and cook for 1 minute more.
- Serve and enjoy.

Nutrition:
- Calories: 160 Fats: 10 g
- Carbs: 4 g
- Protein: 12 g

84. Cheese Soufflés

Preparation Time: 10 minutes
Cooking Time: 6 minutes
Servings: 8
Ingredients:
- 6 large eggs, separated
- ¾ cup heavy cream
- ¼ tsp. cayenne pepper
- ½ tsp. xanthan gum
- ½ tsp. pepper
- ¼ tsp. cream of tartar
- 2 tbsp. chives, chopped
- 2 cups cheddar cheese, shredded
- 1 tsp. salt
- 3 cups Almond flour

Directions:
- Preheat the Air Fryer Oven to 325ºF.
- Spray 8 ramekins with cooking spray and set them aside.
- In a bowl, whisk together the almond flour, cayenne pepper, pepper, salt, and xanthan gum.
- Slowly add the heavy cream and mix to combine.
- Whisk in the egg yolks, chives, and cheese until well combined.
- In a large bowl, add the egg whites and tartar cream and beat until stiff peaks form.
- Fold the egg white mixture into the almond flour mixture until combined.
- Pour the mixture into the prepared ramekins. Divide the ramekins into batches.
- Place the first batch of ramekins into the air fry basket.
- Cook the soufflé for 20 minutes.
- Serve and enjoy.

Nutrition:
- Calories: 210 Fats: 16 g
- Carbs: 1 g Protein: 12 g

85. Simple Egg Soufflé

Preparation Time: 5 minutes
Cooking Time: 8 minutes
Servings: 2
Ingredients:
- 2 eggs
- ¼ tsp. chili pepper
- 2 tbsp. heavy cream
- ¼ tsp. pepper
- 1 tbsp. parsley, chopped
- Salt

Directions:
- In a bowl, whisk the eggs with the remaining gradients.
- Spray two ramekins with cooking spray.

Pour egg mixture into the prepared ramekins and place into the air fryer basket.

Cook the soufflé at 390ºF for 8 minutes. Serve and enjoy.

Nutrition:
Calories: 116 Fats: 10 g
Carbs: 1.1 g Protein: 6 g

86. Vegetable Egg Soufflé
Preparation Time: 10 minutes
Cooking Time: 20 minutes
Servings: 4
Ingredients:
- 4 large eggs
- 1 tsp. onion powder
- 1 tsp. garlic powder
- 1 tsp. red pepper, crushed
- ½ cup broccoli florets, chopped
- ½ cup mushrooms, chopped

Directions:
Sprinkle four ramekins with cooking spray and set them aside.

In a bowl, whisk the eggs with onion powder, garlic powder, and red pepper.

Add the mushrooms and broccoli and stir well. Pour the egg mixture into the prepared ramekins and place the ramekins into the air fry basket.

Cook at 350ºF for 15 minutes. Make sure the soufflé is cooked; if the soufflé is not cooked, then cook for 5 minutes more.

Serve and enjoy.

Nutrition:
Calories: 91 Fats: 5.1 g
Carbs: 4.7 g Protein 7.4 g

87. Asparagus Frittata
Preparation Time: 10 minutes
Cooking Time: 10 minutes
Servings: 4
Ingredients:
- 6 eggs
- 3 mushrooms, sliced
- 10 asparagus, chopped
- ¼ cup half and half
- 2 tsp. butter, melted
- 1 tsp. pepper
- 1 tsp. salt

Directions:
Toss the mushrooms and asparagus with the melted butter and add them into the air fry basket. Cook mushrooms and asparagus at 350ºF for 5 minutes Shake basket twice.

Meanwhile, in a bowl, whisk together eggs, half and half, pepper, and salt. Transfer the cooked mushrooms and asparagus into the sheet pan. Pour the egg mixture over mushrooms and asparagus.

Place the sheet pan in the Air Fryer Oven and cook at 350ºF for 5 minutes, or until eggs are set. Slice and serve.

Nutrition:
Calories: 211
Fats: 13 g
Carbs: 4 g
Protein: 16 g

88. Spicy Cauliflower Rice
Preparation Time: 10 minutes
Cooking Time: 22 minutes
Servings: 2
Ingredients:
- 1 cauliflower head, cut into florets
- ½ tsp. cumin
- ½ tsp. chili powder
- 6 onion spring, chopped
- 2 jalapeños, chopped
- 4 tbsp. olive oil
- 1 zucchini, trimmed and cut into cubes
- ½ tsp. paprika
- ½ tsp. garlic powder
- ½ tsp. cayenne pepper
- ½ tsp. pepper
- ½ tsp. salt

Directions:

Preheat the air fryer to 370ºF.

Add the cauliflower florets into the food processor and process until it looks like rice.

Transfer the cauliflower rice onto the sheet pan and drizzle with half of the oil.

Place the sheet pan in the Air Fryer Oven and cook for 12 minutes, stir halfway through.

Heat the remaining oil in a small pan over medium heat.

Add the zucchini and cook for 5–8 minutes

Add the onion and jalapeños and cook for 5 minutes.

Add the spices and stir well. Set aside.

Add the cauliflower rice to the zucchini mixture and stir well.

Serve and enjoy.

Nutrition:

Calories: 254 Fats: 28 g

Carbs: 12.3 g Protein: 4.3 g

---

89. Broccoli Stuffed Peppers

Preparation Time: 10 minutes
Cooking Time: 40 minutes
Servings: 2
Ingredients:
- 4 eggs
- ½ cup cheddar cheese, grated
- 2 bell peppers cut in half and remove seeds
- ½ tsp. garlic powder
- 1 tsp. dried thyme
- ¼ cup feta cheese, crumbled
- ½ cup broccoli, cooked
- ¼ tsp. pepper
- ½ tsp. salt

Directions:

Preheat the Air Fryer Oven to 325ºF.

In a bowl, beat the eggs and mix them with the seasonings, then pour the egg mixture into the pepper halves over feta and broccoli. Place the bell pepper halves into the air fry basket and cook for 35–40 minutes.

Top with the grated cheddar cheese and cook until the cheese is melted.

Serve and enjoy.

Nutrition:

Calories: 340 Fats: 22 g

Carbs: 12 g Protein: 22 g

---

90. Zucchini Muffins

Preparation Time: 10 minutes
Cooking Time: 20 minutes
Servings: 8
Ingredients:
- 6 eggs
- 4 drops stevia
- ¼ cup Swerve®
- ⅓ cup coconut oil, melted
- 1 cup zucchini, grated
- ¾ cup coconut flour
- ¼ tsp. ground nutmeg
- 1 tsp. ground cinnamon
- ½ tsp. baking soda

Directions:

Preheat the air fryer to 325ºF.

Add all the ingredients except the zucchini in a bowl and mix well.

Add the zucchini and stir well.

Pour the batter into the silicone muffin molds and place into the air fry basket.

Cook the muffins for 20 minutes.

Serve and enjoy.

Nutrition:

Calories: 136 Fats: 12 g

Carbs: 1 g Protein: 4 g

---

91. Jalapeño Breakfast Muffins

Preparation Time: 10 minutes
Cooking Time: 15 minutes
Servings: 8
Ingredients:
- 5 eggs

⅓ cup coconut oil, melted
2 tsp. baking powder
3 tbsp. erythritol
3 tbsp. jalapeños, sliced
¼ cup unsweetened coconut milk
2/3 cup coconut flour
¾ tsp. sea salt

Directions:

Preheat the air fryer to 325ºF.

In a large bowl, mix together the coconut flour, baking powder, erythritol, and sea salt.

Stir in the eggs, jalapeños, coconut milk, and coconut oil until well combined.

Pour the batter into the silicone muffin molds and place into the air fry basket.

Cook muffins for 15 minutes.

Serve and enjoy.

Nutrition:

Calories: 125
Fats: 12 g
Carbs: 7 g
Protein: 3 g

92. Zucchini Noodles

Preparation Time: 10 minutes
Cooking Time: 44 minutes
Servings: 3
Ingredients:

1 egg
½ cup parmesan cheese, grated
½ cup feta cheese, crumbled
1 tbsp. thyme
1 garlic clove, chopped
1 onion, chopped
2 medium zucchinis, trimmed and spiralized
2 tbsp. olive oil
1 cup mozzarella cheese, grated
½ tsp. pepper
½ tsp. salt

Directions:

Preheat the air fryer to 350ºF.

Add the spiralized zucchini and salt to a colander and set aside for 10 minutes. Wash the zucchini noodles and pat dry with a paper towel.

Heat the oil in a pan over medium heat. Add the garlic and onion and sauté for 3–4 minutes.

Add the zucchini noodles and cook for 4–5 minutes or until softened.

Add the zucchini mixture into the air fryer baking pan. Add the egg, thyme, cheeses. Mix well and season.

Place the pan in the air fryer and cook for 30–35 minutes.

Serve and enjoy.

Nutrition:

Calories: 435 Fats: 29 g
Carbs: 10.4 g
Protein: 25 g

93. Mushroom Frittata

Preparation Time: 10 minutes
Cooking Time: 13 minutes
Servings: 1
Ingredients:

1 cup egg whites
1 cup spinach, chopped
2 mushrooms, sliced
2 tbsp. parmesan cheese, grated
Salt

Directions:

Sprinkle the sheet pan with cooking spray and place it in the Air Fryer Oven on medium heat. Add the mushrooms and sauté for 2–3 minutes. Add the spinach and cook for 1–2 minutes, or until wilted.

Transfer the mushroom spinach mixture to the sheet pan. Beat the egg whites in a mixing bowl until frothy. Season it with a pinch of salt.

Pour the egg white mixture into the spinach and mushroom mixture and sprinkle with parmesan cheese. Place the pan in Air Fryer Oven and cook the frittata at 350ºF for 8 minutes.

Slice and serve.

Nutrition:
Calories: 176
Fats: 3 g
Carbs: 4 g
Protein: 31 g

94. Egg Muffins

Preparation Time: 10 minutes
Cooking Time: 15 minutes
Servings: 12
Ingredients:
- 9 eggs
- ½ cup onion, sliced
- 1 tbsp. olive oil
- 8 oz. ground sausage
- ¼ cup coconut milk
- ½ tsp. oregano
- 1 ½ cups spinach
- ¾ cup bell peppers, chopped
- Pepper
- Salt

Directions:
Preheat the Air Fryer Oven to 325ºF.

Add the ground sausage in a pan and sauté over medium heat for 5 minutes.

Add the olive oil, oregano, bell pepper, and onion and sauté until the onion is translucent.

Put the spinach in the pan and cook for 30 seconds.

Remove pan from heat and set aside.

In a mixing bowl, whisk together the eggs, coconut milk, pepper, and salt until well beaten.

Add the sausage and vegetable mixture into the egg mixture and mix well.

Pour the egg mixture into the silicone muffin molds and place it into the air fry basket. (Cook in batches.)

Cook muffins for 15 minutes.

Serve and enjoy.

Nutrition:
Calories: 135 Fats: 11 g
Carbs: 1.5 g Protein: 8 g

95. Blueberry Breakfast Cobbler

Preparation Time: 5 minutes
Cooking Time: 15 minutes
Servings: 4
Ingredients:
- ⅓ cup whole wheat pastry flour
- ¾ tsp. baking powder
- Dash sea salt
- ½ cup 2% milk
- 2 tbsp. pure maple syrup
- ½ tsp. vanilla extract
- Cooking oil spray
- ½ cup fresh blueberries
- ¼ cup granola, or plain store-bought granola

Directions:
In a medium bowl, whisk the flour, baking powder, and salt. Add the milk, maple syrup, and vanilla extract and gently whisk, just until thoroughly combined.

Preheat the Air Fryer Oven by selecting "Bake" setting, the temperature to 350°F, and "Time" setting to 3 minutes. Select "Start/Pause" to start.

Spray a 6x6-inch round baking pan with cooking oil and pour the batter into the pan. Top evenly with the blueberries and granola.

Once the unit is preheated, place the pan into the air fry basket.

Select "Bake," set the temperature to 350°F, and set the time to 15 minutes. Select "Start/Pause" to begin.

When the cooking is complete, the cobbler should be nicely browned, and a knife inserted into the middle should come out clean. Enjoy plain or topped with a little vanilla yogurt.

Nutrition:
Calories: 112
Fats: 1 g
Carbs: 23 g
Protein: 3 g

96. Granola

Preparation Time: 5 minutes
Cooking Time: 40 minutes
Servings: 2
Ingredients:
- 1 cup rolled oats
- 3 tbsp. pure maple syrup
- 1 tbsp. sugar
- 1 tbsp. neutral-flavored oil, such as refined coconut, sunflower, or safflower
- ¼ tsp. sea salt
- ¼ tsp. ground cinnamon
- ¼ tsp. vanilla extract

Directions:
- Insert the crisper plate into the air fry basket and the basket into the Air Fryer Oven. Preheat it by selecting "Bake," setting the temperature to 250°F, and setting the time to 3 minutes. Select "Start/Pause" to start.
- In a medium bowl, stir together the oats, maple syrup, sugar, oil, salt, cinnamon, and vanilla until thoroughly combined. Transfer the granola to a 6x6-inch round baking pan.
- Once the unit is preheated, place the pan into the basket.
- Select "Bake," set the temperature to 250°F and set the time to 40 minutes. Select "Start/Pause" to begin. After 10 minutes, stir the granola well. Resume cooking, stirring the granola every 10 minutes, for a total of 40 minutes, or until the granola is lightly browned and mostly dry.
- Place the granola on a plate to cool. When the cooking is complete, it will become crisp as it cools. Store the completely cooled granola in an air-tight container in a cool, dry place for 1 to 2 weeks.

Tip: You can change this recipe to include some of your favorite granola ingredients, such as dried fruits, different types of nuts, and even goodies such as chocolate chips.
Stir them in after the granola is done, but before it's completely cool.

Nutrition:
Calories: 165
Fats: 5 g
Carbs: 27 g
Protein: 3 g

97. Mixed Berry Muffins

Preparation Time: 15 minutes
Cooking Time: 15 minutes
Servings: 8
Ingredients:
- 1 ⅓ cups plus 1 tbsp. all-purpose flour, divided
- ¼ cup granulated sugar
- 2 tbsp. light brown sugar
- 2 tsp. baking powder
- 2 eggs
- ⅔ cup whole milk
- ⅓ cup safflower oil
- 1 cup mixed fresh berries

Directions:
- In a medium bowl, stir together 1 ⅓ cups of flour, the granulated sugar, brown sugar, and baking powder until mixed well.
- In a small bowl, whisk the eggs, milk, and oil until combined. Mix the egg mixture into the dry ingredients just until combined.
- In another small bowl, toss the mixed berries with the leftover flour until

coated. Gently stir the berries into the batter.
- Insert the crisper plate into the air fry basket and the basket into the Air Fryer Oven . Preheat it by selecting "Bake," setting the temperature to 315°F, and setting the time to 3 minutes. Select "Start/Pause" to start.
- Once the unit is preheated, place 4 cups into the basket and fill each ¾ full with the batter.
- Select "Bake," set the temperature to 315°F, and set the time for 17 minutes. Select "Start/Pause" to begin.
- After about 12 minutes, check the muffins. If they spring back when lightly touched with your finger, they are done. If not, resume cooking. When the cooking is done, transfer the muffins to a wire rack to cool. Repeat steps 6, 7, and 8 with the remaining muffin cups and batter. Let the muffins cool for 10 minutes before serving.

Nutrition:
Calories: 230
Fats: 11 g
Carbs: 30 g
Protein: 4 g

98. Homemade Strawberry Breakfast Tarts

Preparation Time: 15 minutes
Cooking Time: 20 minutes
Servings: 6
Ingredients:
2 refrigerated piecrusts
½ cup strawberry preserves
1 tsp. cornstarch
Cooking oil spray
½ cup low-Fat vanilla yogurt
1 oz. cream cheese, at room temperature
3 tbsp. confectioners' sugar
Rainbow sprinkles for decorating

Directions:
- Place the piecrusts on a flat surface. Cut each piecrust into 3 rectangles using a knife or pizza cutter, for 6 in total. Discard any unused dough from the piecrust edges.
- In a small bowl, stir together the preserves and cornstarch. Mix well and ensure there are no lumps of cornstarch remaining.
- Scoop 1 tbsp. of the strawberry mixture onto the top half of each piece of piecrust.
- Fold the bottom of each piece up to enclose the filling. Press along the edges of each tart to seal using the back of a fork.
- Insert the crisper plate into the basket and the air fry basket into the Air Fryer Oven . Preheat it by selecting "Bake," setting the temperature to 375°F, and setting the time to 3 minutes Select "Start/Pause" to start.
- Once the unit is preheated, spray the crisper plate with cooking oil. Work in batches, spray the breakfast tarts with cooking oil, and place them into the basket in a single layer. Do not stack the tarts.
- Select "Bake," set the temperature to 375°F, and set the time to 10 minutes. Select "Start/Pause" to begin.
- When the cooking is complete, the tarts should be light golden brown. Let the breakfast tarts cool fully before removing them from the air fry basket.
- Repeat steps 5, 6, 7, and 8 for the remaining breakfast tarts.
- In a small bowl, stir together the yogurt, cream cheese, and confectioners' sugar. Spread the breakfast tarts with the frosting and top with sprinkles.

Nutrition:
Calories: 408 Fats: 20.5 g
Carbs: 56 g Protein: 1 g

99. Everything Bagels

Preparation Time: 10 minutes
Cooking Time: 10 minutes
Servings: 2
Ingredients:
- ½ cup self-rising flour, plus more for dusting
- ½ cup plain Greek yogurt
- 1 egg
- 1 tbsp. water
- 4 tsp. everything bagel spice mix
- Cooking oil spray
- 1 tbsp. butter, melted

Directions:
- In a large bowl, and using a wooden spoon, stir together the flour and yogurt until a tacky dough forms. Transfer the dough to a lightly floured work surface and roll the dough into a ball.
- Cut the dough into 2 pieces and roll each piece into a log. Form each log into a bagel shape, pinching the ends together.
- In a small bowl, whisk the egg and water. Brush the egg wash on the bagels.
- Sprinkle 2 tsp. of the spice mix on each bagel and gently press it into the dough.
- Insert the crisper plate into the basket and the basket into the Air Fryer Oven . Preheat it by selecting "Bake," setting the temperature to 330°F, and setting the time to 3 minutes. Select "Start/Pause" to begin.
- Once the Air Fryer Oven is hot enough, spray the crisper plate with cooking spray. Drizzle the bagels with the butter and place them into the basket.
- Select "Bake," set the temperature to 330°F, and set the time to 10 minutes. Select "Start/Pause" to begin.
- When the cooking is complete, the bagels should be lightly golden on the outside. Serve warm.

Nutrition:
Calories: 271 Fats: 13 g
Carbs: 28 g Protein: 10 g

100. Easy Maple-Glazed Doughnuts

Preparation Time: 10 minutes
Cooking Time: 14 minutes
Servings: 8
Ingredients:
- 1 (8-count) can Jumbo® Flaky Biscuits
- Cooking oil spray
- ½ cup light brown sugar
- ¼ cup butter
- 3 tbsp. milk
- 2 cups confectioners' sugar, plus more for dusting (optional)
- 2 tsp. pure maple syrup

Directions:
- Insert the crisper plate into the air fry basket and the basket into the Air Fryer Oven . Preheat it by selecting "Air Fry," setting the temperature to 350°F, and setting the time to 3 minutes. Select "Start/Pause" to begin.
- Remove the biscuits from the tube and cut out the center of each biscuit with a small, round cookie cutter.
- Once the Ai Fry Oven is hot enough, spray the crisper plate with cooking oil. Work in batches, place 4 doughnuts into the basket.
- Select "Air Fry," set the temperature to 350°F, and set the time to 5 minutes. Select "Start/Pause" to begin.
- When the cooking is complete, place the doughnuts on a plate. Repeat steps 3 and 4 with the remaining doughnuts.
- In a small saucepan over medium heat, combine the brown sugar, butter, and milk. Heat until the butter is melted, and the sugar is dissolved, about 4 minutes.
- Remove the pan from the heat and whisk in the confectioners' sugar and maple syrup until smooth.
- Dip the slightly cooled doughnuts into the maple sauce. Place them on a wire rack

and dust with confectioners' sugar (if using). Let rest just until the sauce is set. Enjoy the doughnuts warm.

Nutrition:
Calories: 219 Fats: 10 g
Carbs: 30 g
Protein: 2 g

101. Chocolate-Filled Doughnut Holes

Preparation Time: 10 minutes
Cooking Time: 30 minutes
Servings: 12
Ingredients:
- 1 (8-count) can refrigerated biscuits
- Cooking oil spray
- 48 semisweet chocolate chips
- 3 tbsp. melted unsalted butter
- ¼ cup confectioners' sugar

Directions:
- Separate the biscuits and cut each biscuit into thirds for 24 pieces.
- Flatten each biscuit piece slightly and put 2 chocolate chips in the center of each. Wrap the dough around the chocolate and seal the edges well.
- Insert the crisper plate into the air fry basket and the basket into the Air Fryer Oven. Preheat the unit by selecting air fry, setting the temperature to 330°F, and setting the time to 3 minutes Select "Start/Pause" to begin.
- Once the Air Fryer Oven is hot enough, spray the crisper plate with cooking oil. Brush each doughnut hole with a bit of the butter and place it into the basket. Select "Air Fry," set the temperature to 330°F, and set the time between 8–12 minutes. Select "Start/Pause" to begin.
- The doughnuts are done when they are golden brown. When the cooking is complete, place the doughnut holes on a plate and dust with the confectioners' sugar. Serve warm.

Nutrition:
Calories: 393 Fats: 17 g
Carbs: 55 g Protein: 5 g

102. Delicious Original Hash Browns

Preparation Time: 15 minutes
Cooking Time: 20 minutes
Servings: 4
Ingredients:
- 4 russet potatoes, peeled
- 1 tsp. paprika
- Salt
- Black pepper, freshly ground
- Cooking oil spray

Directions:
- Shred the potatoes with a box grater. If your grater has different hole sizes, use the largest ones.
- Place the shredded potatoes in a large bowl of cold water. Let it sit for 5 minutes (cold water helps remove excess starch from the potatoes.) Stir them to help dissolve the starch.
- Insert the crisper plate into the air fry basket and the basket into the Air Fryer Oven. Preheat it by selecting "Air Fry," setting the temperature to 360°F, and setting the time to 3 minutes. Select "Start/Pause" to begin.
- Dry out the potatoes and pat them with paper towels until the potatoes are completely dry. Season the potatoes with paprika, salt, and pepper.
- Once the Air Fryer Oven is hot enough, spray the crisper plate with cooking oil. Spray also the potatoes with the cooking oil and place them into the basket.

- Select "Air Fry," set the temperature to 360°F, and set the time to 20 minutes Select "Start/Pause" to begin.
- After 5 minutes, remove the basket and shake the potatoes. Reinsert the basket to resume cooking. Continue shaking the basket every 5 minutes (a total of 4 times), or until the potatoes are done.
- When the cooking is complete, remove the hash browns from the basket and serve warm.

Nutrition:
Calories: 150 Carbs: 34 g
Protein: 4 g

103. Waffles and Chicken

Preparation Time: 15 minutes
Cooking Time: 30 minutes
Servings: 4

Ingredients:
- 8 whole chicken wings
- 1 tsp. garlic powder
- Chicken seasoning, for preparing the chicken
- Freshly ground black pepper
- ½ cup all-purpose flour
- Cooking oil spray
- 8 frozen waffles
- Pure maple syrup, for serving (optional)

Directions:
- In a medium bowl, combine the chicken and garlic powder and season with chicken seasoning and pepper. Toss to coat.
- Transfer the chicken to a resealable plastic bag and add the flour. Seal the bag and shake it to coat the chicken thoroughly.
- Insert the crisper plate into the air fry basket and the basket into the unit. Preheat the unit by selecting "Air Fry," setting the temperature to 400°F, and setting the time to 3 minutes Select "Start/Pause" to begin.
- Once the Air Fryer Oven is hot enough, spray the crisper plate with cooking oil. Using tongs, transfer the chicken from the bag to the basket. (It is okay to stack the chicken wings on top of each other). Spray them with cooking oil.
- Select "Air Fry," set the temperature to 400°F, and set the time to 20 minutes. Select "Start/Pause" to begin.
- After 5 minutes, remove the basket and shake the wings. Reinsert the basket to resume cooking. Remove and shake the basket every 5 minutes until the chicken is fully cooked.
- When the cooking is complete, remove the cooked chicken from the basket, and cover it to keep it warm.
- Rinse the basket and crisper plate with warm water and insert it back into the Air Fryer Oven.
- Select "Air Fry," set the temperature to 360°F, and set the time to 3 minutes. Select "Start/Pause" to begin.
- Once the Air Fryer Oven is hot enough, spray the crisper plate with cooking spray. Work in batches, place the frozen waffles into the basket. Do not stack them. Spray the waffles with cooking oil.
- Select "Air Fry," set the temperature to 360°F, and set the time to 6 minutes. Select "Start/Pause" to begin.
- Repeat steps 10 and 11 with the remaining waffles when the cooking is complete.
- Serve the waffles with the chicken, and a touch of maple syrup if desired.

Nutrition:
Calories: 461
Fats: 22 g
Carbs: 45 g
Protein: 28 g

104. Puffed Egg Tarts

Preparation Time: 10 minutes
Cooking Time: 20 minutes
Servings: 4
Ingredients:
- ⅓ sheet frozen puff pastry, thawed
- Cooking oil spray
- ½ cup shredded Cheddar cheese
- 2 eggs
- ¼ tsp. salt, divided
- 1 tsp. minced fresh parsley (optional)

Directions:
- Insert the crisper plate into the air fry basket and the basket into the Air Fryer Oven. Preheat it by selecting "Bake," setting the temperature to 390°F, and setting the time to 3 minutes. Select "Start/Pause" to begin.
- Lay the puff pastry sheet on a piece of parchment paper and cut it in half.
- Once the Air Fryer Oven is hot enough, spray the crisper plate with cooking oil. Transfer the 2 squares of pastry to the basket, keeping them on the parchment paper.
- Select "Bake," set the temperature to 390°F, and set the time to 20 minutes. Select "Start/Pause" to begin.
- After 10 minutes, use a metal spoon to press down the center of each pastry square to make a sort of well. Divide the cheese equally between the baked pastries. Carefully, crack an egg on top of the cheese, and sprinkle each with the salt. Resume cooking for 7–10 minutes.
- When the cooking is complete, the eggs will be cooked through. Sprinkle each with parsley (if using) and serve.

Nutrition:
- Calories: 322
- Fats: 24 g
- Carbs: 12 g
- Protein: 15 g

105. Early Morning Steak and Eggs

Preparation Time: 10 minutes
Cooking Time: 30 minutes
Servings: 4
Ingredients:
- Cooking oil spray
- 4 (4 oz.) New York strip steaks
- 1 tsp. granulated garlic, divided
- 1 tsp. salt, divided
- 1 tsp. freshly ground black pepper, divided
- 4 eggs
- ½ tsp. paprika

Directions:
- Insert the crisper plate into the air fry basket and the basket into the Air Fryer Oven. Preheat it by selecting "Air Fry," setting the temperature to 360°F, and setting the time to 3 minutes. Select "Start/Pause" to begin.
- Once the unit is hot enough, spray the crisper plate with cooking oil. Place 2 steaks into the basket; do not oil or season them at this time.
- Select "Air Fry," set the temperature to 360°F, and set the time to 9 minutes. Select "Start/Pause" to begin.
- After 5 minutes, open the Air Fryer Oven and flip the steaks. Sprinkle each with ¼ tsp. of granulated garlic, ¼ tsp. of salt, and ¼ tsp. of pepper. Resume cooking until the steaks register at least 145°F on a food thermometer.
- When the cooking is complete, transfer the steaks to a plate and tent with aluminum foil to keep warm. Repeat steps 2, 3, and 4 with the remaining steaks.
- Spray 4 ramekins with olive oil. Crack 1 egg into each ramekin. Sprinkle the eggs with the paprika and the remaining ½ tsp. each of salt and pepper. Work in

batches, place 2 ramekins into the basket.
- Select "Bake," set the temperature to 330°F, and set the time to 5 minutes. Select "Start/Pause" to begin. When the cooking is complete and the eggs are cooked to 160°F, remove the ramekins and repeat step 7 with the remaining 2 ramekins.
- Serve the eggs with the steaks.

Nutrition:
Calories: 304
Fats: 19 g
Carbs: 2 g
Protein: 31 g

106. Breakfast Potatoes

Preparation Time: 10 minutes
Cooking Time: 20 minutes
Serving: 6
Ingredients:
- 1 ½ tsp. olive oil, divided, plus more for misting
- 4 large potatoes, skin-on, cut into cubes
- 2 tsp. seasoned salt, divided
- 1 tsp. minced garlic, divided
- 2 large green or red bell peppers, cut into 1-inch pieces
- ½ onion, diced

Directions:
- Lightly, spray the air fryer basket with cooking oil.
- In a medium bowl, toss the potatoes with ½ tsp. of olive oil. Sprinkle with 1 tsp. of seasoned salt and ½ tsp. of minced garlic. Stir to coat.
- Place the seasoned potatoes in the fryer basket in a single layer.
- Cook for 5 minutes Shake the basket and cook for another 5 minutes
- Meanwhile, in a medium bowl, toss the bell peppers and onion with the remaining ½ tsp. of olive oil.
- Sprinkle the peppers and onions with the remaining 1 tsp. of seasoned salt and ½ tsp. of minced garlic. Stir to coat.
- Add the seasoned peppers and onions to the fryer basket with the potatoes.
- Cook for 5 minutes Shake the basket and cook for an additional 5 minutes

Nutrition:
Calories: 199
Fats: 1 g
Carbs: 43 g
Protein: 5 g

107. Baked Potato Breakfast Boats

Preparation Time: 10 minutes
Cooking Time: 20 minutes
Serving: 4
Ingredients:
- 2 large russet potatoes, scrubbed
- Olive oil
- Salt
- Black pepper, freshly ground
- 4 eggs
- 2 tbsp. chopped, cooked bacon
- 1 cup shredded cheddar cheese

Directions:
- Poke holes in the potatoes with a fork and microwave on full power for 5 minutes. Turn potatoes over and cook for an additional 3–5 minutes, or until the potatoes are fork-tender.
- Cut the potatoes in half lengthwise and use a spoon to scoop out the inside of the potato. Be careful to leave a layer of potato so that it makes a sturdy 'boat.' Lightly, spray the fry basket with olive oil. Spray the skin side of the potatoes with oil and sprinkle with salt and pepper to taste.
- Place the potato skins in the fryer basket skin-side down. Crack one egg into each potato skin.

Sprinkle ½ tbsp. of bacon pieces and ¼ cup of shredded cheese on top of each egg. Sprinkle with salt and pepper to taste.

Air fry until the yolk is slightly runny, 5–6 minutes, or until the yolk is fully cooked, 7–10 minutes.

Nutrition:
Calories: 338
Fats: 15 g
Saturated Fat: 8 g
Cholesterol: 214 mg
Carbs: 35 g
Protein: 17 g
Fiber: 3 g
Sodium: 301 mg

108. Greek Frittata

Preparation Time: 10 minutes
Cooking Time: 20 minutes
Serving: 4
Ingredients:
- Olive oil
- 5 eggs
- ¼ tsp. salt
- ⅛ tsp. freshly ground black pepper
- 1 cup baby spinach leaves, shredded
- ½ cup halved grape tomatoes
- ½ cup crumbled feta cheese

Directions:

Spray a small round air fryer-friendly pan with olive oil.

In a medium bowl, whisk together the eggs, salt, and pepper and whisk to combine.

Add the spinach and stir to combine.

Pour ½ cup of the egg mixture into the pan.

Sprinkle ¼ cup of the tomatoes and ¼ cup of the feta on top of the egg mixture.

Cover the pan with aluminum foil and secure it around the edges.

Place the pan carefully into the fryer basket.

Air-fry for 12 minutes.

Remove the foil from the pan and cook until the eggs are set, 5–7 minutes.

Remove the frittata from the pan and place on a serving platter. Repeat with the remaining ingredients.

Nutrition:
Calories: 146
Fats: 10 g
Saturated Fats: 5 g
Cholesterol: 249 mg
Carbs: 3 g
Protein: 11 g
Fiber: 1 g
Sodium: 454 mg

109. Mini Shrimp Frittata

Preparation Time: 15 minutes
Cooking Time: 20 minutes
Serving: 4
Ingredients:
- 1 tsp. olive oil, plus more for spraying
- ½ small red bell pepper, finely diced
- 1 tsp. minced garlic
- 1 (4-oz.) can of tiny shrimp, dried out
- Salt
- Black pepper, freshly ground
- 4 eggs, beaten
- 4 tsp. ricotta cheese

Directions:

Spray four ramekins with olive oil. Heat 1 tsp. of oil in a medium skillet over medium-high heat. Add the bell pepper and garlic and sauté until the pepper is soft, about 5 minutes.

Add the shrimp, season with salt and pepper for 5–7 minutes, or until soft. Remove from the heat.

Add the eggs and stir to combine. Pour one-quarter of the mixture into each ramekin.

Place 2 ramekins in the fry basket and cook for 6 minutes. Remove the fryer basket from the Air Fryer Oven and stir the mixture in each ramekin. Top each frittata with 1 tsp. of ricotta cheese.

Return the basket to the Air Fryer Oven and cook until eggs are set, and the top is lightly browned, about 4–5 minutes. Repeat with the remaining two ramekins.

Nutrition:
Calories: 114
Fats: 7 g
Carbs: 1 g
Protein: 12 g

Nutrition:
Calories: 183
Fats: 13 g
Saturated Fats: 7 g
Cholesterol: 206 mg
Carbs: 3 g
Protein: 14 g
Fiber: 1 g
Sodium: 411 mg

110. Spinach and Mushroom Mini Quiche

Preparation Time: 10 minutes
Cooking Time: 15 minutes
Serving: 4
Ingredients:
- 1 tsp. olive oil, plus more for spraying
- 1 cup coarsely chopped mushrooms
- 1 cup fresh baby spinach, shredded
- 4 eggs, beaten
- ½ cup shredded Cheddar cheese
- ½ cup shredded mozzarella cheese
- ¼ tsp. salt
- ¼ tsp. black pepper

Directions:
Spray 4 silicone baking cups with olive oil and set aside. In a medium sauté pan over medium heat, warm 1 tsp. of olive oil. Add the mushrooms and sauté until soft, 3 to 4 minutes.

Add the spinach and cook until wilted, 1–2 minutes Set aside.

In a medium bowl, whisk together the eggs, Cheddar cheese, mozzarella cheese, salt, and pepper. Gently fold the mushrooms and spinach into the egg mixture.

Pour ¼ of the mixture into each silicone baking cup. Place the baking cups into the fryer basket and air fry for 5 minutes Stir the mixture in each ramekin slightly and air fry until the egg has set, an additional 3–5 minutes.

111. Italian Egg Cups

Preparation Time: 5 minutes
Cooking Time: 10 minutes
Serving: 4
Ingredients:
- Olive oil
- 1 cup marinara sauce
- 4 eggs
- 4 tbsp. shredded mozzarella cheese
- 4 tsp. grated Parmesan cheese
- Salt
- Freshly ground black pepper
- Chopped fresh basil, for garnish

Directions:
Lightly, spray 4 individual ramekins with olive oil.

Pour ¼ cup of marinara sauce into each ramekin.

Crack 1 egg into each ramekin on top of the marinara sauce.

Sprinkle 1 tbsp. of mozzarella and 1 tbsp. of Parmesan on top of each egg. Season it with salt and pepper.

Cover each ramekin with aluminum foil. Place 2 of the ramekins in the air fry basket.

Air-fry for 5 minutes and remove the aluminum foil. Air-fry until the top is lightly browned and the egg white is cooked, another 2–4 minutes. If you prefer the yolk to be firmer, cook for 3 to 5 more minutes.

Repeat with the remaining 2 ramekins. Garnish with the basil and serve.

Nutrition:
Calories: 135
Fats: 8 g
Saturated Fats: 3 g
Cholesterol: 191 mg
Carbs: 6 g
Protein: 10 g
Fiber: 1 g
Sodium: 407 mg

112. Mexican Breakfast Pepper Rings

Preparation Time: 5 minutes
Cooking Time: 10 minutes
Serving: 4
Ingredients:

Olive oil
1 large red, yellow, or orange bell pepper, cut into four ¾-inch rings
4 eggs
Salt
Black pepper, freshly ground
2 tsp. salsa

Directions:

Lightly, spray a small round air fryer–friendly pan with olive oil.

Place 2 bell pepper rings on the pan. Crack 1 egg into each bell pepper ring. Season with salt and black pepper.

Spoon ½ tsp. of salsa on top of each egg. Place the pan in the fryer basket. Air-fry until the yolks are slightly runny, about 5–6 minutes, or until the yolks are fully cooked, 8–10 minutes.

Repeat with the remaining 2 pepper rings. Serve hot.

Pair it with turkey sausage or turkey bacon to make this a healthier morning meal.

Tip: To air-fry like a pro, use a silicone spatula to easily move the rings from the pan to your plate.

Nutrition:
Calories: 84 Fats: 5 g
Saturated Fats: 2 g
Cholesterol: 186 mg Carbs: 3 g
Protein: 7 g Fiber: 1 g Sodium: 83 mg

113. Cajun Breakfast Muffins

Preparation Time: 10 minutes
Cooking Time: 10 minutes
Serving: 6
Ingredients:

Olive oil
4 eggs, beaten
2 ¼ cups frozen hash browns, thawed
1 cup diced ham
½ cup shredded Cheddar cheese
½ tsp. Cajun seasoning

Directions:

Lightly spray 12 silicone muffin cups with olive oil.

In a medium bowl, mix together the eggs, hash browns, ham, Cheddar cheese, and Cajun seasoning.

Spoon 1 ½ tbsp. of the hash brown mixture into each muffin cup.

Place the muffin cups in the air fry basket.

Air-fry until the muffins are golden brown on top and the center has set up, about 8–10 minutes.

Tip: To make it even lower in calories, reduce or eliminate the cheese.

Nutrition:
Calories: 178
Fats: 9 g
Saturated Fats: 4 g
Cholesterol: 145 mg
Carbs: 13 g
Protein: 11 g
Fiber: 2 g
Sodium: 467 mg

114. Hearty Blueberry Oatmeal

Preparation Time: 10 minutes
Cooking Time: 25 minutes
Serving: 6

Ingredients:
- 1 ½ cups quick oats
- 1 ¼ tsp. ground cinnamon, divided
- ½ tsp. baking powder
- A Pinch salt
- 1 cup unsweetened vanilla almond milk
- ¼ cup honey
- 1 tsp. vanilla extract
- 1 egg, beaten
- 2 cups blueberries
- Olive oil
- 1 ½ tsp. sugar, divided
- 6 tbsp. low-Fat whipped topping (optional)

Directions:
- In a large bowl, mix together the oats, 1 tsp. of cinnamon, baking powder, and salt.
- In a medium bowl, whisk together the almond milk, honey, vanilla and egg.
- Pour the liquid ingredients into the oats mixture and stir to combine. Fold in the blueberries.
- Lightly, spray a round air fryer–friendly pan with oil.
- Add half the blueberry mixture to the pan.
- Sprinkle ⅛ tsp. of cinnamon and ½ tsp. of sugar over the top.
- Cover the pan with aluminum foil and place gently in the air fry basket. Air-fry for 20 minutes remove the foil and air fry for an additional 5 minutes Transfer the mixture to a shallow bowl.
- Repeat with the remaining blueberry mixture, ½ tsp. of sugar, and ⅛ tsp. of cinnamon.
- To serve, spoon into bowls and top with the whipped topping.

Nutrition:
Calories: 170
Fats: 3 g
Saturated Fats: 1 g
Cholesterol: 97 mg
Carbs: 34 g
Protein: 4 g
Fiber: 4 g
Sodium: 97 mg

CHAPTER 3:

Snacks

115. Air Fried Chicken Tenders
Basic Recipe
Preparation Time: 10 minutes
Cooking Time: 10 minutes
Servings: 4
Ingredients:
- 1/8 cup flour
- Pepper and salt to taste
- Olive spray
- 1 egg white
- 12 oz, chicken breasts
- 1-¼ oz. panko bread crumbs

Directions:
Trim off excess fat from your chicken breast. Cut into tenders. Season it with pepper and salt. Dip the tenders into flour and after that Into egg whites and bread crumbs. Keep in the fryer basket. Apply olive spray and cook for 10 minutes at 350 degrees F. Serve.

Nutrition:
Calories 399
Carbs 18g
Fat 11g
Protein 57g

116. Parmesan Zucchini Chips
Basic Recipe
Preparation Time: 15 minutes
Cooking Time: 10 minutes
Servings: 4
Ingredients:
- Salt to taste
- 3 medium zucchinis
- 1 cup grated Parmesan cheese

Directions:
Preheat the oven in Air Fryer mode at 110 F for 2 to 3 minutes Use a mandolin slicer to very finely slice the zucchinis, season with salt, and coat well with the Parmesan cheese. In batches, arrange as lots of zucchini pieces as possible in a single layer on the cooking tray. When the device is ready, move the cooking tray onto the leading rack of the oven and close the oven. Set the timer to 7 minutes and press Start. Cook till the cheese melts while turning the midway. Transfer the chips to serving bowls to cool and make the remaining. Serve warm.

Nutrition:
Calories 107
Fat 6.99 g
Carbs 3.73 g
Protein 7.33 g

117. Cattle Ranch Garlic Pretzels
Basic Recipe
Preparation Time: 10 minutes
Cooking Time: 15 minutes
Servings: 4
Ingredients:
- ½ tsp garlic powder
- 2 cups pretzels
- 1 ½ tsp ranch dressing mix
- 1 tbsp melted butter

Directions:
Preheat the oven in Air Fryer mode at 270 F for 2 to 3 minutes. In a medium bowl, blend all the ingredients up until well-integrated, pour into the rotisserie basket and near to seal. Repair the basket onto the lever in the oven and close the oven. Set the timer to 15 minutes, press Start and cook until the pretzels are gently browner. After, open the oven, secure the basket utilizing the rotisserie lift and transfer the snack into serving bowls. Permit cooling and delight in.

Nutrition:
Calories 35 Fat 3.72 g
Carbs 0.4 g Protein 0.12 g

118. Herby Sweet Potato Chips
Basic Recipe
Preparation Time: 10 minutes
Cooking Time: 10 minutes
Servings: 4
Ingredients:
- 1 tsp dried mixed herbs
- 2 medium sweet potatoes, peeled
- 1 tbsp olive oil

Directions:
- Pre-heat the oven in Air Fry mode at 375 F for 2 to 3 minutes. On the other hand, utilize a mandolin slicer to thinly slice the sweet potatoes, transfer to a medium bowl and blend well with the herbs and olive oil till well coated. In batches, organize as numerous sweet potato pieces as possible in a single layer on the cooking tray. When the device is ready, slide the cooking tray onto the top rack of the oven and close the oven. Set the timer to 7 minutes and press Start. Cook till the sweet potatoes are crispy while turning midway. Transfer the chips to serving bowls when prepared and make the remaining in the same manner. Delight in.

Nutrition:
Calories 87
Fat 3.48 g
Carbs 13.38 g
Protein 1.03 g

119. Cumin Tortilla Chips With Guacamole
Basic Recipe
Preparation Time: 5 minutes
Cooking Time: 15 minutes
Servings: 4
Ingredients:
- For the tortilla chips:
- 2 tablespoon olive oil
- 12 corn tortillas
- 1 tbsp paprika powder
- 1 tbsp cumin powder
- Salt and black pepper to taste
- For the guacamole:
- 1 little company tomato, sliced
- A pinch dried parsley
- 1 big avocado, pitted and peeled

Directions:
- Preheat the oven in Air Fry mode at 375 F for 2 to 3 minutes in a medium bowl, mix all the ingredients for the tortilla chips well and put the mix into the rotisserie basket. Close to seal. Fix the basket onto the lever in the oven and close the oven. Set the timer to 15 minutes, press Start and cook until the tortillas are golden brown.
- After, open the oven, take out the basket using the rotisserie lift and transfer the chips to serving bowls. Meanwhile, as the chips cooked, in a little bowl, mash the avocados and blend with the tomato and parsley up until well combined.
- Serve the tortilla chips with the guacamole.

Nutrition:
Calories 159
Fat 14.74 g
Carbs 7.82 g
Protein 1.94 g

120. Oven-Dried Strawberries
Basic Recipe
Preparation Time: 10 minutes
Cooking Time: 10 minutes
Servings: 4
Ingredients:
- 1-pound large strawberries

Directions:
- Pre-heat the air fryer in Dehydrate mode at 110 F for 2 to 3 minutes Use a mandolin slicer to thinly slice the strawberries. In batches, arrange a few of the

strawberry pieces in a single layer on the cooking tray.

When the device is ready, move the cooking tray onto the top rack of the oven and close the oven

Set the timer to 7 minutes and press Start. Cook until the fruits are crispy.

Transfer the fruit chips to serving bowls when all set and make the remaining in the same manner. Delight in.

Nutrition:
Calories 36
Fat 0.34 g
Carbs 8.71 g
Protein 0.76 g

121. Chili Cheese Toasts
Basic Recipe
Preparation Time: 5 minutes
Cooking Time: 10 minutes
Servings: 4
Ingredients:
- 1 tsp garlic powder
- 1 tsp red chili flakes
- 6 pieces sandwich bread
- 4 tablespoon butter
- 1 cup grated cheddar cheese
- 2 little fresh red chilies, deseeded and minced
- ½ tsp salt
- 1 tablespoon sliced fresh parsley

Directions:
Pre-heat the oven in Broil mode at 375 F for 2 to 3 minutes Spread the butter on one side of each bread pieces and lay on a tidy, flat surface. Divide the cheddar cheese on top and followed with the remaining ingredients. Lay 3 pieces of the bread on the cooking tray, slide the tray onto the middle rack of the oven, and close the oven. Set the timer for 3 to 4 minutes and press Start. Cook till the cheese melts and is golden brown on top. Remove the first batch when ready and prepare the other three bread pieces. Slice them into triangle halves and serve immediately.

Nutrition:
Calories 105
Fat 11.53 g
Carbs 0.68 g
Protein 0.29 g

122. Cheese Sticks
Basic Recipe
Preparation Time: 10 minutes
Cooking Time: 10 minutes
Servings: 6
Ingredients:
- 1 teaspoon garlic powder
- 1 teaspoon of Italian spices
- ¼ teaspoon rosemary, ground
- 2 eggs
- 1 cheese sticks
- ¼ cup parmesan cheese, grated
- ¼ cup whole-wheat flour

Directions:
Unwraps the cheese sticks. Keep aside. Beat the eggs into a bowl. Mix the cheese, flavorings, and flour in another bowl. Now roll the sticks in the egg and then into the batter. Coat well. Keep them in your air fryer basket. Cook for 7 minutes at 370 degrees F. Serve hot.

Nutrition:
Calories 76 Carbs 5g
Fat 4g Protein 5g

123. Blended Veggie Chips
Basic Recipe
Preparation Time: 20 minutes
Cooking Time: 10 minutes
Servings: 4
Ingredients:
- 1 big carrot
- 1 tsp salt

1 tsp Italian spices
1 zucchini
1 sweet potato peeled
½ tsp pepper
1 red beet, peeled
A pinch cumin powders

Directions:

Preheat the air fryer in Dehydrate mode at 110 F for 2 to 3 minutes

Utilize a mandolin slicer to thinly slice all the vegetables and transfer to a medium bowl. Season it with salt, Italian spices, and cumin powder. In batches, organize some of the veggies in a single layer on the cooking tray.

When the device is ready, move the cooking tray onto the top rack of the oven and close the oven then set the timer to 7 or 9 minutes and press Start. Cook up until the veggies are crispy. Transfer the vegetables to serving bowls when all set and make the staying in the same manner. Delight in.

Nutrition:
Calories 84
Fat 0.15 g
Carbs 18.88 g
Protein 2.25 g

124. Sweet Apple And Pear Chips

Basic Recipe
Preparation Time: 15 minutes
Cooking Time: 10 minutes
Servings: 4
Ingredients:

6 pears, peeled
6 Honey crisp apples

Directions:

Pre-heat the air fryer in Dehydrate mode at 110 F for 2 to 3 minutes. On the other hand, utilize a mandolin slicer to very finely slice the apples and pears. In batches, set up a few of the fruit slices in a single layer on the cooking tray.

When the device is ready, move the cooking tray onto the top rack of the oven and close the oven

Set the timer to 7 minutes and press Start. Cook till the fruits are crispy. Transfer the fruit chips to serving bowls when all set and make the staying in the same manner. Take pleasure in.

Nutrition:
Calories 142 Fat 0.46 g
Carbs 37.7g Protein 0.71g

125. Cocoa Banana Chips

Basic Recipe
Preparation Time: 5 minutes
Cooking Time: 7 minutes
Servings: 4
Ingredients:

¼ tsp cocoa powder
5 large firm bananas, peeled
A pinch of cinnamon powder

Directions:

Preheat the air fryer in Dehydrate mode at 110 F for 2 to 3 minutes. On the other hand, utilize a mandolin slicer to very finely slice the bananas, and coat well with the cocoa powder and the cinnamon powder. In batches, organize as many banana pieces as possible in a single layer on the cooking tray.

When the device is ready, slide the cooking tray onto the top rack of the oven and close the oven set the timer to 7 minutes and press Start. Cook until the banana pieces are crispy. Transfer the chips to serving bowls when all set and make the remaining in the same manner. Take pleasure in.

Nutrition:
Calories 152 Fat 0.57 g
Carbs 38.89 g Protein 1.87 g

126. Coriander Roasted Chickpeas

Basic Recipe
Preparation Time: 10 minutes
Cooking Time: 45minutes
Servings: 2
Ingredients:

¼ tsp garlic powder
1 (15 oz) can chickpeas, Dry-out pipes
¼ tsp ground coriander - 1/8 tsp salt
¼ tsp chili pepper powder
¼ tsp curry powder
¼ tsp ground cumin
¼ tsp paprika
Olive oil for spraying

Directions:

Pre-heat the oven in Air Fryer mode at 375 F for 2 to 3 minutes in a medium bowl, mix the chickpeas with all the spices until well-integrated and pour into the rotisserie basket. Grease lightly with olive oil, shake the basket, and close the seal. Fix the basket onto the lever in the oven and close the oven. Set the timer to 35 or 45 minutes, press Start and cook up until the chickpeas are golden brown. After, open the oven, take out the basket utilizing the rotisserie lift and transfer the treat into serving bowls. Allow cooling and delight in.

Nutrition:
Calories 91 Fat 1.82 g
Carbs 14.87 g Protein 4.61 g

127. Corn Nuts

Basic Recipe
Preparation Time: 10 minutes
Cooking Time: 20 minutes
Servings: 8
Ingredients:

3 tablespoons of vegetable oil
1 oz. white corn
1-½ teaspoons salt

Directions:

Cover the corn with water in a bowl. Keep aside. Dry out the corn. Spread it on a flat pan and use paper towels to pat dry.
Pre-heat your air fryer to 400 degrees F. Transfer the corn to a bowl then include salt and oil. Stir to coat uniformly.
Keep the corn in your air fryer basket. Cook for 8 minutes Shake the basket and cook for 10 minutes more. Transfer to a plate lined with a paper towel. Set aside to cool.

Nutrition:
Calories 240 Fat 8g
Carbs 36g
Protein 6g

128. Baked Potatoes

Intermediate Recipe
Preparation Time: 10 minutes
Cooking Time: 1hour
Servings: 2
Ingredients:

½ teaspoon of coarse sea salt
1 tablespoon peanut oil
2 large potatoes, scrubbed

Directions:

Pre-heat your air fryer to 400 degrees F. Brush peanut oil on your potatoes and sprinkle some salt. Then keep them in the basket of your air fryer.
Cook the potatoes for an hour. Serve hot.

Nutrition:
Calories 360 Carbs 64g
Fat 8g Protein 8g

129. Coconut Chicken Bites

Basic Recipe
Preparation Time: 10 minutes
Cooking Time: 15 minutes
Servings: 4
Ingredients:

2 teaspoons garlic powder

2 eggs
Salt and black pepper to the taste
¾ cup panko bread crumbs
¾ cup coconut, shredded
Cooking spray
8 chicken tenders

Directions:

- Using a bucket, mix pepper, salt and eggs with garlic powder and whisk well.
- In another bowl, mix coconut with panko and stir well.
- Dip the chicken tenders in eggs mix and then coat in coconut one well.
- Spray chicken bites with cooking spray, place them in your air fryer's basket and cook them at 350 degrees F for 10 minutes
- Serve.
- Enjoy!

Nutrition:
Calories 252
Fat 4
Carbs 14
Protein 24

130. Buffalo Cauliflower Snack

Basic Recipe
Preparation Time: 10 minutes
Cooking Time: 15 minutes
Servings: 4
Ingredients:

4 cups cauliflower florets
1 cup panko bread crumbs
¼ cup butter, melted
¼ cup buffalo sauce
Mayonnaise for serving

Directions:

- In a bowl, mix the buffalo sauce and butter and beat well. Soak cauliflower florets in this mix and coat with breadcrumbs. Put them in the air fryer basket and cook at 350 degrees Fahrenheit for 15 minutes.
- Arrange them on a platter and serve with mayo on the side. Enjoy!

Nutrition:
Calories 241 Fat 4
Carbs 8 Protein 4

131. Banana Snack

Basic Recipe
Preparation Time: 10 minutes
Cooking Time: 5 minutes
Servings: 8
Ingredients:

16 baking cups crust
¼ cup peanut butter
¾ cup chocolate chips
1 banana, peeled and sliced into 16 pieces
1 tablespoon vegetable oil

Directions:

- Put chocolate chips in a small pot, heat up over low heat, stir until it melts and take off heat.
- In a bowl, mix peanut butter with coconut oil and whisk well.
- Spoon 1 teaspoon chocolates mix in a cup, add 1 banana slice and top with 1 teaspoon butter mix
- Repeat with the rest of the cups, place them all into a dish that fits your air fryer, cook at 320 degrees F for 5 minutes, transfer to a freezer and keep there until you serve them as a snack.

Enjoy!
Nutrition:
Calories 70 Fat 4 Carbs 10 Protein 1

132. Potato Spread

Basic Recipe
Preparation Time: 10 minutes
Cooking Time: 10 minutes
Servings: 10
Ingredients:

19 ounces canned garbanzo beans, Dried
1 cup sweet potatoes, peeled and chopped

¼ cup tahini
2 tablespoons lemon juice
1 tablespoon olive oil
5 garlic cloves, minced
½ teaspoon cumin, ground
2 tablespoons water
A pinch of salt and white pepper

Directions:

Put potatoes in your air fryer's basket, cook them at 360 degrees F for 15 minutes, cool them down, peel, put them in your food processor and pulse well. Basket, add sesame paste, garlic, beans, lemon juice, cumin, water and oil and pulse really well. Add salt and pepper, pulse again, divide into bowls and serve.

Enjoy!

Nutrition:
Calories 200
Fat 3
Carbs 20
Protein 11

133. Mexican Apple Snack

Basic Recipe
Preparation Time: 10 minutes
Cooking Time: 5 minutes
Servings: 4
Ingredients:

3 big apples, cored, peeled and cubed
2 teaspoons lemon juice
¼ cup pecans, chopped
½ cup dark chocolate chips
½ cup clean caramel sauce

Directions:

In a bowl, mix apples with lemon juice, stir and transfer to a pan that fits your air fryer.

Add chocolate chips, pecans, Drizzle with the caramel sauce, toss, introduce in your air fryer and cook at 320 degrees F for 5 minutes

Toss gently, divide into small bowls and serve right away as a snack.

Enjoy!

Nutrition:
Calories 200 Fat 4
Carbs 20
Protein 3

134. Shrimp Muffins

Basic Recipe
Preparation Time: 10 minutes
Cooking Time: 26 minutes
Servings: 6
Ingredients:

1 spaghetti squash, peeled and halved
2 tablespoons mayonnaise
1 cup mozzarella, shredded
8 ounces shrimp, peeled, cooked and chopped
1 and ½ cups panko
1 teaspoon parsley flakes
1 garlic clove, minced
Salt and black pepper to the taste
Cooking spray

Directions:

Put squash halves in your air fryer, cook at 350 degrees F for 16 minutes, leave aside to cool down and scrape flesh into a bowl. Add salt, pepper, parsley flakes, panko, shrimp, mayo and mozzarella and stir well.

Spray a muffin tray that fits your air fryer with cooking spray and divide squash and shrimp mix in each cup. Introduce in the fryer and cook at 360 degrees F for 10 minutes

Arrange muffins on a platter and serve as a snack.

Enjoy!

Nutrition:
Calories 60 Fat 2g
Carbs 4g
Protein 4g

135. Zucchini Cakes

Basic Recipe
Preparation Time: 10 minutes
Cooking Time: 12 minutes
Servings: 8

Ingredients:
- Cooking spray
- ½ cup dill, chopped
- 1 egg
- ½ cup whole wheat flour
- Salt and black pepper to the taste
- 1 yellow onion, chopped
- 2 garlic cloves, minced
- 3 zucchinis, grated

Directions:
- In a bowl, mix zucchinis with garlic, onion, flour, salt, pepper, egg and dill, stir well, shape small patties out of this mix, spray them with cooking spray, place them in the air fryer's basket and boil at 370 degrees F for 6 minutes on each side.
- Serve them as a snack right away.
- Enjoy!

Nutrition:
Calories 60
Fat 1g
Carbs 6g
Protein 2g

136. Cauliflower Bars

Basic Recipe
Preparation Time: 10 minutes
Cooking Time: 25 minutes
Servings: 12

Ingredients:
- 1 big cauliflower head, florets separated
- ½ cup mozzarella, shredded
- ¼ cup egg whites
- 1 teaspoon Italian seasoning
- Salt and black pepper to the taste

Directions:
- Put cauliflower florets in your food processor, pulse well, spread on a lined baking sheet that fits your air fryer, introduce in the fryer and cook at 360 degrees F for 10 minutes
- Transfer cauliflower to a bowl, add salt, pepper, cheese, egg whites and Italian seasoning, stir really well, spread this into a rectangle pan that fits your air fryer, press well, introduce in the fryer and cook at 360 degrees F for 15 minutes more. Cut into 12 bars, arrange them on a platter and serve as a snack
- Enjoy!

Nutrition:
Calories 50 Fat 1g
Carbs 3g Protein 3 g

137. Pesto Crackers

Basic Recipe
Preparation Time: 10 minutes
Cooking Time: 17 minutes
Servings: 6

Ingredients:
- ½ teaspoon baking powder
- Salt and black pepper to the taste
- 1 and ¼ cups flour
- ¼ teaspoon basil, dried
- 1 garlic clove, minced
- 2 tablespoons basil pesto
- 3 tablespoons butter

Directions:
- In a bowl, mix salt, pepper, baking powder, flour, garlic, cayenne, basil, pesto and butter and stir until you obtain a dough.
- Spread this dough on a lined baking sheet that fits your air fryer, introduce in the fryer at 325 degrees F and Bake it for 17 minutes
- Leave aside to cool down, cut crackers and serve them as a snack.
- Enjoy!

Nutrition:
Calories 200 Fat 20
Carbs 4 Protein 7

138. Pumpkin Muffins
Basic Recipe
Preparation Time: 10 minutes
Cooking Time: 15 minutes
Servings: 8
Ingredients:
- ¼ cup butter
- ¾ cup pumpkin puree
- 2 tablespoons flaxseed meal
- ¼ cup flour
- ½ cup sugar
- ½ teaspoon nutmeg, ground
- 1 teaspoon cinnamon powder
- ½ teaspoon baking soda
- 1 egg
- ½ teaspoon baking powder

Directions:
- In a bowl, mix butter with pumpkin puree and egg and blend well.
- Add flaxseed meal, flour, sugar, baking soda, baking powder, nutmeg and cinnamon and stir well. Spoon this into a muffin pan that fits your fryer introduces in the fryer at 350 degrees F and Bake it for 15 minutes I Serve muffins cold as a snack.
- Enjoy!

Nutrition:
Calories 50 Fat 3
Carbs 2 Protein 2

139. Zucchini Chips
Basic Recipe
Preparation Time: 10 minutes
Cooking Time: 1hour
Servings: 6
Ingredients:
- 3 zucchinis, thinly sliced
- Salt and black pepper to the taste
- 2 tablespoons olive oil
- 2 tablespoons balsamic vinegar

Directions:
- Using a bucket, mix vinegar with oil adding pepper with salt and stir well.
- Add zucchini slices, toss to coat well, introduce in your air fryer and cook at 200 degrees F for 1 hour.
- Serve zucchini chips cold as a snack.
- Enjoy!

Nutrition:
Calories 40
Fat 3 Carbs 3
Protein 7

140. Beef Jerky Snack
Intermediate Recipe
Preparation Time: 2 hours
Cooking Time: 1hour and 30 minutes
Servings: 6
Ingredients:
- 2 cups soy sauce
- ½ cup Worcestershire sauce
- 2 tablespoons black peppercorns
- 2 tablespoons black pepper
- 2 pounds beef round, sliced

Directions:
- In a bowl, mix soy sauce with black peppercorns, black pepper and Worcestershire sauce and whisk well.
- Add beef slices, toss to coat and leave aside in the fridge for 6 hours.
- Introduce beef rounds in your air fryer and cook them at 370 degrees F for 1 hour and 30 minutes
- Transfer to a bowl and serve cold.
- Enjoy!

Nutrition:
Calories 300 Fat 12
Carbs 3 Protein 8 g

141. Honey Party Wings
Intermediate Recipe
Preparation Time: 1hour and 12 minutes
Cooking Time: 10 minutes
Servings: 8
Ingredients:
- 16 chicken wings

2 tablespoons soy sauce
2 tablespoons of honey
Salt and black pepper taste to taste
2 tablespoons lime juice

Directions:

In a bowl, mix the wings with soy sauce, honey, salt, pepper and lime juice, mix well and put in the refrigerator for 1 hour. Transfer the wings to an air fryer, cook at 360 degrees F for 12 minutes, and turn it over halfway.

Serve on a plate and serve as an appetizer. Enjoy!

Nutrition:
Calories 211
Fat 4
Carbs 14
Protein 3

142. Salmon Party Patties
Basic Recipe
Preparation Time: 10 minutes
Cooking Time: 22 minutes
Servings: 4
Ingredients:

3 big potatoes, boiled, Dried and mashed
1 big salmon fillet, skinless, boneless
2 tablespoons parsley, chopped
2 tablespoon dill, chopped
Salt and black pepper to the taste
1 egg
2 tablespoons bread crumbs
Cooking spray

Directions:

Place salmon in your air fryer's basket and cook for 10 minutes at 360 degrees F. Transfer salmon to a cutting board, cool it down, flake it and put it in a bowl. Add mashed potatoes, salt, pepper, dill, parsley, egg and bread crumbs, stir well and shape 8 patties out of this mix. Place salmon patties in your air fryer's basket, spry them with cooking oil, and for 12 minutes cook at 360 degrees F, flipping them halfway, transfer them to a platter and serve as an appetizer. Enjoy!

Nutrition:
Calories 231
Fat 3
Carbs 14
Protein 4

143. Banana Chips
Basic Recipe
Preparation Time: 10 minutes
Cooking Time: 15 minutes
Servings: 4
Ingredients:

4 bananas, peeled and sliced
A pinch of salt
½ teaspoon turmeric powder
½ teaspoon chaat masala
1 teaspoon olive oil

Directions:

In a bowl, mix banana slices with salt, turmeric, chaat masala and oil, toss and leave aside for 10 minutes Transfer banana slices to your preheated air fryer at 360 degrees F and cook them for 15 minutes flipping them once.

Serve as a snack.
Enjoy!

Nutrition:
Calories 121
Fat 1
Carbs 3
Protein 3

144. Sesame Tofu Cubes
Basic Recipe
Preparation Time: 20 minutes
Cooking Time: 20 minutes
Servings: 2
Ingredients:

8 oz tofu

1 teaspoon cornstarch
1 teaspoon scallions, chopped
1 teaspoon rice vinegar
1 teaspoon sesame oil
1 teaspoon soy sauce

Directions:
Cut the tofu into the cubes.
Put the tofu cubes in the bowl and sprinkle with the rice vinegar, sesame oil, and soy sauce.
Shake the mixture.
Leave the tofu for 10 minutes to marinate.
Preheat the air fryer to 370 F.
Sprinkle the marinated tofu with the cornstarch and put in the air fryer basket.
Cook tofu for 20 minutes
Shake the tofu after 11 minutes of cooking.
Then chill the tofu gently and sprinkle with the chopped scallions.
Enjoy!

Nutrition:
Calories 108
Fat 7
Carbs 3.4
Protein 9.5

145. Thyme Salty Tomatoes
Basic Recipe
Preparation Time: 10 minutes
Cooking Time: 10 minutes
Servings: 2
Ingredients:
2 tomatoes
1 tablespoon thyme
1 pinch salt
1 teaspoon olive oil

Directions:
Preheat the air fryer to 375 F.
Slice the tomatoes.
Then combine together thyme and salt. Shake the mixture.
Sprinkle the sliced tomatoes with the thyme mixture. Place the sliced tomatoes in the air fryer and spray with the olive oil.
Cook the tomatoes for 10 minutes
When the tomatoes are cooked – they should have tender and little bit dry texture.
Enjoy!

Nutrition:
Calories 46 Fat 2.7
Carbs 5.6 Protein 1.2

146. Creamy Chicken Liver
Basic Recipe
Preparation Time: 10 minutes
Cooking Time: 10 minutes
Servings: 2
Ingredients:
7 oz chicken liver
¼ cup water
1 tablespoon butter
2 teaspoon cream
1 tablespoon fresh dill, chopped
1 pinch salt

Directions:
Preheat the air fryer to 390 F.
Combine together water, chicken liver, and salt.
Mix the mixture and place it in the air fryer basket.
Cook the chicken liver for 10 minutes
Stir it after 5 minutes of cooking.
Then transfer the cooked chicken liver to the bowl.
Add cream and butter.
Blend the mixture until smooth.
After this, add chopped fresh dill and stir gently.
Serve the meal and enjoy!

Nutrition:
Calories 223 Fat 12.5
Carbs 1.9 Protein 24

147. Catfish Sticks
Basic Recipe
Preparation Time: 10 minutes
Cooking Time: 10 minutes
Servings: 2
Ingredients:
- 8 oz catfish fillet
- ½ teaspoon salt
- ½ teaspoon ground black pepper
- ¼ cup panko breadcrumbs
- 1 egg
- ½ teaspoon olive oil

Directions:
- Cut the catfish fillet into 2 medium pieces (sticks).
- Then sprinkle the catfish with the salt and ground black pepper.
- Beat the egg in the bowl and whisk it.
- Dip the catfish fillets in the whisked egg.
- After this, coat the fish in the panko breadcrumbs.
- Preheat the air fryer to 380 F.
- Put the fish sticks in the air fryer basket and spray with the olive oil.
- Cook the fish sticks for 10 minutes
- Flip the sticks into another side after 10 minutes of cooking.
- When the fish sticks are cooked – let them chill gently.
- Serve the meal!

Nutrition:
Calories 231 Fat 12.2
Carbs 8 Protein 21.5

148. Honey Banana Chips
Basic Recipe
Preparation Time: 10 minutes
Cooking Time: 6 minutes
Servings: 2
Ingredients:
- 2 bananas
- 1 teaspoon honey
- 1 pinch white pepper
- ½ teaspoon olive oil

Directions:
- Peel the bananas and slice them into the chip's pieces. Then sprinkle the bananas with the honey and white pepper.
- Spray the olive oil over the bananas and mix them gently with the help of the hands.
- Preheat the air fryer to 320 F. Put the banana chips in the air fryer basket and cook for 6 minutes
- Serve the cooked banana chips immediately.
- Enjoy!

Nutrition:
Calories 126 Fat 1.6
Carbs 29.9 Protein 1.3

149. Ginger Apple Chips
Basic Recipe
Preparation Time: 10 minutes
Cooking Time: 10 minutes
Servings: 2
Ingredients:
- ½ teaspoon olive oil
- 3 apples
- 1 pinch ground ginger

Directions:
- Peel the apples and remove the seeds. Slice the apples and sprinkle them with the ground ginger and olive oil.
- Preheat the air fryer to 400 F.
- Place the apple slices on the air fryer rack.
- Cook the apple chips for 10 minutes
- Shake the apple chips carefully after 4 minutes of cooking.
- Then chill the apple chips carefully.
- Serve the meal immediately or keep it in the paper bag in the dry place.
- Enjoy!

Nutrition:
Calories 184 Fat 1.8
Fiber 8.1 Carbs 46.3
Protein 0.9

150. Maple Carrot Fries
Basic Recipe
Preparation Time: 5 minutes
Cooking Time: 10 minutes
Servings: 2
Ingredients:
- 1 cup baby carrot
- ¼ cup maple syrup
- 1 pinch salt
- ½ teaspoon thyme
- ½ teaspoon ground black pepper
- 1 teaspoon dried oregano
- 1 tablespoon olive oil

Directions:
- Preheat the air fryer to 410 F.
- Place the baby carrot in the air fryer basket.
- Sprinkle the baby carrot with the thyme, salt, ground black pepper, and dried oregano.
- Then spray the olive oil over the baby carrot and shake it well.
- Cook the baby carrot fries for 10 minutes
- Shake the carrot fries after 6 minutes of cooking.
- Chill the cooked meal for 5 minutes
- Enjoy!

Nutrition:
Calories 197
Fat 7.3
Carbs 34.4
Protein 0.7

151. Sweet Potato Fries
Basic Recipe
Preparation Time: 10 minutes
Cooking Time: 15 minutes
Servings: 2
Ingredients:
- 2 sweet potatoes
- 1 tablespoon coconut oil
- 1/3 teaspoon salt
- ½ teaspoon ground black pepper
- ½ teaspoon onion powder

Directions:
- Preheat the air fryer to 370 F.
- Peel the sweet potatoes and cut them into the fries.
- Sprinkle the vegetables with the salt, ground black pepper, and onion powder.
- Shake the sweet potatoes and sprinkle with the coconut oil.
- Put the uncooked sweet potato fries in the air fryer basket and cook for 15 minutes
- Shake the sweet potato fries every 5 minutes
- When the sweet potato fries are cooked – let them chill gently
- Serve the meal!

Nutrition:
Calories 225 Fat 6.8
Carbs 42.1 Protein 2.6

152. Squid Rings
Basic Recipe
Preparation Time: 10 minutes
Cooking Time: 4 minutes
Servings: 2
Ingredients:
- 2 squid tubes
- 2 eggs
- 1/3 cup flour
- ¼ teaspoon salt
- ½ teaspoon onion powder
- ½ teaspoon garlic powder

Directions:
- Wash and peel the squid cubes carefully. Then slice the squid cubes into the rings.
- Beat the eggs in the bowl and whisk them.
- Then dip the squid rings in the whisked eggs.
- Combine together flour, salt, onion powder, and garlic powder. Stir the mixture with the help of the fork.
- Then coat the squid rings with the flour mixture.
- Preheat the air fryer to 400 F.
- Put the squid rings onto the air fryer rack.

Cook the squid rings for 4 minutes

Shake the squid rings after 3 minutes of cooking.

When the squid rings are cooked – let them chill till the room temperature

Enjoy!

Nutrition:
Calories 383 Fat 10.5
Carbs 17.2 Protein 55.8

153. Carrot Chips
Basic Recipe
Preparation Time: 10 minutes
Cooking Time: 20 minutes
Servings: 2
Ingredients:
- 3 carrots
- ½ teaspoon salt
- ½ teaspoon ground black pepper
- 1 tablespoon canola oil

Directions:

Peel the carrot and slice into the chips.

Then sprinkle the uncooked carrot chips with the salt, ground black pepper, and canola oil.

Shake the carrot chips carefully.

Preheat the air fryer to 360 F.

Put the carrot chips in the air fryer basket.

Shake the carrot chips in halfway.

Check the doneness of the carrot chips while cooking.

Chill the carrot chips and serve.

Enjoy!

Nutrition:
Calories 101 Fat 7 Carbs 9.3 Protein 0.8

154. Corn Okra Bites
Basic Recipe
Preparation Time: 10 minutes
Cooking Time: 4 minutes
Servings: 2
Ingredients:
- 4 tablespoon corn flakes, crushed
- 9 oz okra
- 1 egg
- ½ teaspoon salt
- 1 teaspoon olive oil

Directions:

Preheat the air fryer to 400 F.

Chop the okra roughly.

Combine together the corn flakes and salt.

Crack the egg into the bowl and whisk it.

Toss the chopped okra in the whisked egg.

Then coat the chopped okra with the corn flakes.

Put the chopped okra in the air fryer basket and sprinkle with the olive oil.

Cook the okra for 4 minutes

Shake the okra after 2 minutes of cooking.

When the okra is cooked – let it chill gently.

Enjoy!

Nutrition:
Calories 115
Fat 4.8
Carbs 12.7
Protein 5.2

155. Salty Potato Chips
Basic Recipe
Preparation Time: 10 minutes
Cooking Time: 19 minutes
Servings: 2
Ingredients:
- 3 potatoes
- 1 tablespoon canola oil
- ½ teaspoon salt

Directions:

Wash the potatoes carefully and do not peel them. Slice the potatoes into the chips.

Sprinkle the potato chips with the olive oil and salt. Mix the potatoes carefully.

Preheat the air fryer to 400 F. Put the potato chips in the air fryer basket and cook for 19 minutes

Shake the potato chips every 3 minutes

When the potato chips are cooked – chill them well.

Enjoy!

Nutrition:
Calories 282 Fat 7.3 Carbs 50.2 Protein 5.4

156. Corn & Beans Fries
Basic Recipe
Preparation Time: 10 minutes
Cooking Time: 10 minutes
Servings: 2
Ingredients:
¼ cup corn flakes crumbs
1 egg - 10 oz green beans
1 tablespoon canola oil
½ teaspoon salt
1 teaspoon garlic powder

Directions:
Preheat the air fryer to 400 F.
Put the green beans in the bowl.
Beat the egg in the green beans and stir carefully until homogenous.
Then sprinkle the green beans with the salt and garlic powder.
Shake gently. Then coat the green beans in the corn flakes crumbs well.
Put the green beans in the air fryer basket in one layer. Cook the green beans for 7 minutes
Shake the green beans twice during the cooking. When the green beans are cooked – let them chill and serve.
Enjoy!

Nutrition:
Calories 182 Fat 9.4 Carbs 21 Protein 6.3

157. Sugary Apple Fritters
Basic Recipe
Preparation Time: 10 minutes
Cooking Time: 10 minutes
Servings: 2
Ingredients:
2 red apples
1 teaspoon sugar
1 tablespoon flour
1 tablespoon semolina
1 teaspoon lemon juice
½ teaspoon ground cinnamon
1 teaspoon butter
1 egg

Directions:
Peel the apples and grate them.
Sprinkle the grated apples with the lemon juice.
Then add sugar, flour, semolina, and ground cinnamon.
Mix the mixture and crack the egg.
Mix the apple mixture carefully.
Preheat the air fryer to 370 F.
Toss the butter in the air fryer basket and melt it.
When the butter is melted – make the medium fritters from the apple mixture. Use 2 spoons for this step.
Place the fritters in the air fryer basket and cook for 6 minutes
After this, flip the fritters to another side and cook for 2 minutes more.
Dry the cooked fritters with the help of the paper towel and serve.
Enjoy!

Nutrition:
Calories 207
Fat 4.6
Carbs 40.3
Protein 4.5

158. Oregano Onion Rings
Basic Recipe
Preparation Time: 14 minutes
Cooking Time: 10 minutes
Servings: 2
Ingredients:
1 tablespoon oregano
1 tablespoon flour
½ teaspoon cornstarch

1 egg
½ teaspoon salt
2 white onions, peeled
1 tablespoon olive oil

Directions:
- Crack the egg into the bowl and whisk it. Combine together the flour and cornstarch in the separate bowl.
- Add oregano and salt. Shake the mixture gently. Peel the onions and slice them to get the "rings".
- Then dip the onion rings in the whisked egg. After this, coat the onion rings in the flour mixture.
- Preheat the air fryer to 365 F.
- Spray the air fryer basket with the olive oil inside. Then place the onion rings in the air fryer and cook for 8 minutes
- Shake the onion rings after 4 minutes of cooking. Let the cooked meal chill gently.
- Serve it!

Nutrition:
Calories 159 Fat 9.6
Carbs 15.5 Protein 4.6

159. Cinnamon Mixed Nuts
Basic Recipe
Preparation Time: 5 minutes
Cooking Time: 20 minutes
Servings: 5
Ingredients:
- ½ cup pecans
- ½ cup walnuts
- ½ cup almonds
- A pinch of cayenne pepper
- 2 tbsp sugar
- 2 tbsp egg whites
- 2 tsp cinnamon

Directions:
- Add the pepper, sugar, and cinnamon to a bowl and mix them well; set aside. In another bowl, mix in the pecans, walnuts, almonds, and egg whites. Add the spice mixture to the nuts and give it a good mix. Lightly grease the frying basket with cooking spray. Pour in the nuts, and cook them for 10 minutes on Air Fry function at 350 F. Stir the nuts using a wooden vessel, and cook for further for 10 minutes Pour the nuts in the bowl. Let cool.

Nutrition:
Calories 180 Fat 12g
Carbs 13g Protein 6g

160. Apple & Cinnamon Chips
Basic Recipe
Preparation Time: 15 minutes
Cooking Time: 10 minutes
Servings: 2
Ingredients:
- 1 tsp sugar
- 1 tsp salt
- 1 whole apple, sliced
- ½ tsp cinnamon
- Confectioners' sugar for serving

Directions:
- Preheat your Air Fryer to 400 F. In a bowl, mix cinnamon, salt and sugar; add the apple slices. Place the prepared apple spices in the cooking basket and cook for 10 minutes on Bake function. Dust with sugar and serve.

Nutrition:
Calories 110 Fat 0g
Carbs 27g Protein 1g

161. Sesame Cabbage & Prawns Egg Roll Wraps
Basic Recipe
Preparation Time: 32 minutes
Cooking Time: 18 minutes
Servings: 4
Ingredients:
- 2 tbsp vegetable oil

1-inch piece fresh ginger, grated
1 tbsp minced garlic - 1 carrot, cut into strips
¼ cup chicken broth
2 tbsp reduced-sodium soy sauce
1 tbsp sugar - 1 cup shredded Napa cabbage
1 tbsp sesame oil - 8 cooked prawns, minced
1 egg
8 egg roll wrappers

Directions:

In a skillet over high heat, heat vegetable oil, and cook ginger and garlic for 40 seconds, until fragrant. Stir in carrot and cook for another 2 minutes Pour in chicken broth, soy sauce, and sugar and bring to a boil.

Add cabbage and let simmer until softened, for 4 minutes Remove skillet from the heat and stir in sesame oil. Let cool for 15 minutes Strain cabbage mixture, and fold in minced prawns. Whisk an egg in a small bowl. Fill each egg roll wrapper with prawn mixture, arranging the mixture just below the center of the wrapper.

Fold the bottom part over the filling and tuck under. Fold in both sides and tightly roll up. Use the whisked egg to seal the wrapper. Place the rolls into a greased frying basket, spray with oil and cook for 12 minutes at 370 F on Air Fry function, turning once halfway through.

Nutrition:
Calories 149.3 Fat 3.5g
Carbs 20g Protein 8.8 g

162. Rosemary Potatoes
Basic Recipe
Preparation Time: 10 minutes
Cooking Time: 25 minutes
Servings: 2
Ingredients:

pounds potatoes, halved
2 tbsp olive oil
3 garlic cloves, grated
1 tbsp minced fresh rosemary
1 tsp salt
¼ tsp freshly ground black pepper

Directions:

In a bowl, mix potatoes, olive oil, garlic, rosemary, salt, and pepper, until they are well-coated. Arrange the potatoes in the basket and cook t 360 F on Air Fry function for 25 minutes, shaking twice during the cooking. Cook until crispy on the outside and tender on the inside.

Nutrition:
Calories 132
Fats: 2.5g
Carbs 18.3g
Protein 9.5g

163. Crunchy Mozzarella Sticks With Sweet Thai Sauce
Intermediate Recipe
Preparation Time: 2 hours
Cooking Time: 20 minutes
Servings: 2
Ingredients:

12 mozzarella string cheese
2 cups breadcrumbs
3 eggs
1 cup sweet Thai sauce
4 tbsp skimmed milk

Directions:

Pour the crumbs in a bowl. Crack the eggs into another bowl and beat with the milk. One after the other, dip each cheese sticks in the egg mixture, in the crumbs, then egg mixture again and then in the crumbs again.

Place the coated cheese sticks on a cookie sheet and freeze for 1 to 2 hours. Preheat Air Fry function to 380 F. Arrange the sticks in the frying basket without overcrowding. Cook for 8 minutes, flipping them halfway through cooking to brown evenly. Cook in batches. Serve with a sweet Thai sauce.

Nutrition:
Calories 173 Fat 5.6g Carbs 27g Protein 3.3g

164. Chili Cheese Crisps
Basic Recipe
Preparation Time: 17 minutes
Cooking Time: 10 minutes
Servings: 3
Ingredients:
- 4 tbsp grated cheese + extra for rolling
- 1 cup flour + extra for kneading
- ¼ tsp chili powder
- ½ tsp baking powder - 3 tsp butter
- A pinch of salt

Directions:
- In a bowl, mix in the cheese, flour, baking powder, chili powder, butter, and salt. The mixture should be crusty. Add some drops of water and mix well to get dough. Remove the dough on a flat surface.
- Rub some extra flour in your palms and on the surface, and knead the dough for a while. Using a rolling pin, roll the dough out into a thin sheet.
- With a pastry cutter, cut the dough into your desired lings' shape. Add the cheese lings to the basket, and cook for 8 minutes at 350 F on Air Fry function, flipping once halfway through.

Nutrition:
Calories 1085 Fat 71g Carbs 64g Protein 55g

165. Parmesan Baked Tomatoes
Basic Recipe
Preparation Time: 10 minutes
Cooking Time: 10 minutes
Servings: 4
Ingredients:
- 1 cup grated mozzarella cheese
- 1 cup grated Parmesan cheese
- ½ cup chopped basil
- Olive oil
- 4 tomatoes, halved

Directions:
- Grease a baking pan with some cooking spray. Place tomato halves over the pan; stuff with cheese and basil.
- Preheat the Air Fryer Grill to 400°F.
- When it is pre-heated, open the door, and take out the middle roasting tray.
- Place the pan over the tray and push it back; close door and cooking will start. Midway, it will display "Turn Food" on its screen; ignore it, and it will continue to cook after 10 seconds. Cook until cheese is bubbly.
- Open the door after the cooking cycle is over; serve warm.

Nutrition:
Calories 486
Fat 7.5g
Carbs 11g
Protein 17.5g

166. Gingered Scallops
Basic Recipe
Preparation Time: 10 minutes
Cooking Time: 15 minutes
Servings: 4-6
Ingredients:
- 6 very large sea scallops
- ¼ cup tamarind sauce
- 1 tablespoon dark brown sugar
- 6 slices bacon, cut in half crosswise
- 1 ½ teaspoon minced ginger

Directions:
- In a mixing bowl, add tamarind sauce, brown sugar, ginger, and scallops. Combine the ingredients to mix well with each other. Set aside for 15-20 minutes

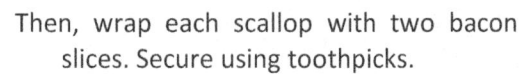

Then, wrap each scallop with two bacon slices. Secure using toothpicks.

Grease a baking pan with some cooking spray. Place scallops over the pan.

Place the air fryer over the kitchen platform. Arrange to drip pan in the lower position. Press "Air Fry," set the timer to 15 minutes, and set the temperature to 350°F.

When the air fryer is pre-heated, it will display "Add Food" on its screen. Open the door, and take out the middle roasting tray.

Place the pan over the tray and push it back; close door and cooking will start. Midway, it will display "Turn Food" on its screen; flip scallops and close door. Cook until bacon is crispy and brown.

Open the door after the cooking cycle is over; serve warm.

Nutrition:
Calories 173
Fat 14g
Carbs 3g
Protein 5.5g

---

167. Baked Bacon Potatoes
Basic Recipe
Preparation Time: 5 minutes
Cooking Time: 10 minutes
Servings: 4
Ingredients:
- ¼ cup chopped scallions
- 1 cup grated cheddar cheese
- 3 russet potatoes, cleaned and cut into 1-inch rounds
- ¼ cup butter
- 3 tablespoon bacon bits, cooked and crumbled

Directions:
Grease a baking pan with some cooking spray. Place potato over the pan; brush with butter and top with scallions and cheese.

Preheat the Air Fryer Grill to 400°F, then open the door, and take out the middle roasting tray.

Place the pan over the tray and push it back; close door and cooking will start. Midway, it will display "Turn Food" on its screen; ignore it, and it will continue to cook after 10 seconds. Cook until cheese is bubbly.

Open the door after the cooking cycle is over; serve warm with bacon on top.

Nutrition:
Calories 330
Fat 12g
Carbs 48g
Protein 7.5g

---

168. Coconut Shrimps
Basic Recipe
Preparation Time: 10 minutes
Cooking Time: 12 minutes
Servings: 4
Ingredients:
- 8 ounces coconut milk
- ½ cup panko breadcrumbs
- 8 large shrimp, peeled and deveined
- Salt and ground black pepper, to taste
- ½ teaspoon cayenne pepper

Directions:
In a mixing bowl, add salt, black pepper, and coconut milk. Combine the ingredients to mix well with each other.

In another bowl, add breadcrumbs, cayenne pepper, Ground black pepper, and salt. Combine the ingredients to mix well with each other. Coat the shrimps evenly with first coconut mixture and then with crumbs. Grease a baking pan with some cooking spray. Place shrimps over the pan.

Preheat the Air Fryer Grill to 350°F.

When it is pre-heated, it will display "Add Food" on its screen. Open the door, and take out the middle roasting tray. Place the pan over the tray and push it back; close door and cooking will start. Midway, it will display "Turn Food" on its screen; flip shrimps and close door.

Open the door after the cooking cycle is over; serve warm.

Nutrition:
Calories 209
Fat 15g
Carbs 6g
Protein 4.5g

169. Guacamole Tortilla Chips
Basic Recipe
Preparation Time: 10 minutes
Cooking Time: 15 minutes
Servings: 4
Ingredients:
Chips:
- 1 tablespoon cumin powder
- 1 tablespoon paprika powder
- 12 corn tortillas
- 2 tablespoon olive oil
- Ground black pepper and salt to taste

Guacamole:
- 1 small firm tomato, chopped
- 1 large avocado, pitted, peeled and mashed
- A pinch dried parsley

Directions:
In a mixing bowl, add all chips ingredients. Combine the ingredients to mix well with each other. In another bowl, add guacamole ingredients. Combine the ingredients to mix well with each other.

Preheat the Air Fryer Grill to 375°F and set the timer to 15 minutes.

In the basket, add chips mixture.

When the air fryer is pre-heated, it will display "Add Food" on its screen. Open the door and lock the basket. Press the red lever and arrange the basket on the left side; now, just simply rest the basket rod over the right side.

Close door and press "Rotate"; cooking will start. Cook until chips are evenly golden.

Open the door after the cooking cycle is over; serve chips with guacamole.

Nutrition:
Calories 140
Fat 13g
Carbs 11g
Protein 2.5g

170. Roasted Chickpeas
Intermediate Recipe
Preparation Time: 10 minutes
Cooking Time: 45 minutes
Servings: 2
Ingredients:
- 1 (15 ounces) can chickpeas, Dry outed
- 1/4 teaspoon garlic powder
- 1/4 teaspoon ground cumin
- 1/4 teaspoon ground coriander
- 1/4 teaspoon curry powder
- 1/8 teaspoon salt
- 1/4 teaspoon chili pepper powder
- 1/4 teaspoon paprika
- Olive oil

Directions:
In a mixing bowl, add chickpeas and spices. Combine the ingredients to mix well with each other.

Preheat the Air Fryer Grill to 375°F and set the timer to 35 minutes.

In the basket, add chickpea mixture.

When the air fryer is pre-heated, it will display "Add Food" on its screen. Open the door and lock the basket. Press the red lever and arrange the basket on the left side; now, just simply rest the basket rod over the right side.

Close door and press "Rotate"; cooking will start. Cook until evenly toasted and golden brown. Cook for 5-10 minutes more if needed.

Open the door after the cooking cycle is over; serve warm

Nutrition:
Calories 132
Fat 13g
Carbs 11g
Protein 2.4g

171. Supreme French Fries
Basic Recipe
Preparation Time: 10 minutes
Cooking Time: 10 minutes
Servings: 2
Ingredients:
- ½ teaspoon onion powder
- ½ teaspoon garlic powder
- 1-pound potatoes, peeled and cut into strips
- 3 tablespoons olive oil
- 1 teaspoon paprika
- Salt to taste (optional)

Directions:
In a mixing bowl, add potato strips and water. Soak for an hour; Dry out and dry pieces completely over paper towels.

In a mixing bowl, add a strip and other ingredients. Combine the ingredients to mix well with each other.

Preheat the Air Fryer Grill to 375°F and set the timer to 30 minutes.

In the basket, add potato mix.

When it is pre-heated, it will display "Add Food" on its screen. Open the door and lock the basket. Press the red lever and arrange the basket on the left side; now, just simply rest the basket rod over the right side.

Close door and press "Rotate"; cooking will start.

Open the door after the cooking cycle is over; serve warm.

Nutrition:
Calories 176 Fat 11g
Carbs 17g
Protein 3g

172. Butter Cashews
Basic Recipe
Preparation Time: 5 minutes
Cooking Time: 5 minutes
Servings: 5-6
Ingredients:
- 1 teaspoon butter, melted
- 1 ½ cups raw cashew nut
- Salt and black pepper to taste

Directions:
In a mixing bowl, add cashews and other ingredients. Combine the ingredients to mix well with each other.

Grease a baking tray with some cooking spray. Place cashews over the tray.

Preheat the Air Fryer Grill to 355°F and set timer to 5 minutes.

When the air fryer is pre-heated, it will display "Add Food" on its screen. Open the door, and take out the middle roasting tray.

Place the baking tray over the roasting tray and push it back; close door and cooking will start. Midway it will display "Turn Food" on its screen; shake baking tray and close door.

Open the door after the cooking cycle is over; serve warm.

Nutrition:
Calories 233
Fat 15g
Carbs 12g
Protein 6g

173. Cinnamon Banana Chips
Basic Recipe
Preparation Time: 10 minutes
Cooking Time: 6 minutes
Servings: 4
Ingredients:
- ¼ teaspoon cocoa powder
- A pinch of cinnamon powder
- 5 large firm bananas, peeled

Directions:
- Slice bananas thinly in a horizontal manner and combine with cocoa and cinnamon in a bowl.
- Preheat the Air Fryer Grill to 380°F set timer to 7 minutes.
- When the air fryer is pre-heated, it will display "Add Food" on its screen. Open the door, and take out the middle roasting tray.
- Place slices (cook in batches if needed) over the tray and push it back; close door and cooking will start. Midway, it will display "Turn Food" on its screen; ignore it, and it will continue to cook after 10 seconds. Cook until the slices crisps.
- Open the door after the cooking cycle is over; serve warm.

Nutrition:
Calories 173
Fat 0.5g
Carbs 34g
Protein 2.5g

174. Easy Baked Chocolate Mug Cake
Basic Recipe
Preparation Time: 5 minutes
Cooking Time: 10 minutes
Servings: 3
Ingredients:
- ½ cup cocoa powder
- ½ cup stevia powder
- 1 cup coconut cream
- 1 package cream cheese, room temperature
- 1 tablespoon vanilla extract
- tablespoons butter

Directions:
- Preheat the air fryer oven for 5 minutes
- In a mixing bowl, combine all ingredients.
- Use a hand mixer to mix everything until fluffy.
- Pour into greased mugs.
- Place the mugs in the fryer basket.
- Bake it for 15 minutes at 350°F.
- Place in the fridge to chill before serving.

Nutrition:
Calories 744 Fat 69.7g
Protein 13.9g
Carbs: 4g

175. Fried Peaches
Intermediate Recipe
Preparation Time: 2 hours 10 minutes
Cooking Time: 15 minutes
Servings: 4
Ingredients:
- 4 ripe peaches (1/2 a peach = 1 serving)
- 1 1/2 cups flour
- Salt
- 2 egg yolks
- 3/4 cups cold water
- 1 1/2 tablespoons olive oil
- 2 tablespoons brandy
- 4 egg whites
- Cinnamon/sugar mix

Directions:
- Mix flour, egg yolks, and salt in a mixing bowl. Slowly mix in water, then add brandy. Set the mixture aside for 2 hours and go do something for 1 hour 45 minutes
- Boil a large pot of water and cut and X at the bottom of each peach. While the water boils fill another large bowl with water and ice. Boil each peach for about a minute, then plunge it in the ice bath. Now the peels should basically fall off the peach. Beat the egg whites and mix

into the batter mix. Dip each peach in the mix to coat.

Pour the coated peach into the Oven rack/basket. Place the Rack on the middle-shelf of the Air fryer oven. Set temperature to 360°F, and set time to 10 minutes

Prepare a plate with cinnamon/sugar mix, roll peaches in mix and serve.

Nutrition:
Calories 306 Fat 3g
Protein 10g Carbs: 2.7g

CHAPTER 4:

Dehydrate

176. Pineapple Slices
Preparation Time: 10 minutes
Cooking Time: 14 hours
Servings: 12
Ingredients:
- 12 pineapple slices

Directions:
- Select "Dehydrate" mode.
- Select "LEVEL 2," then set time for 14 hours and set the temperature to 125ºF.
- Place the pineapple slices in the air fry basket and place the basket in the Air Fryer Oven. Press "Start."

Nutrition:
- Calories: 374
- Fats: 0.9 g
- Carbs: 99 g
- Sugar: 74.5 g
- Protein: 4.1 g

177. Apple Slices
Preparation Time: 10 minutes
Cooking Time: 8 hours
Servings: 4
Ingredients:
- 2 apple, cored and cut into ⅛-inch thick slices
- 1 tsp. ground cinnamon

Directions:
- Select "Dehydrate" mode.
- Select "LEVEL 2," then set time for 8 hours and set the temperature to 145ºF.
- Place the apple slices in the air fry basket and place the basket in the Air Fryer Oven.
- Sprinkle cinnamon on top of the apple slices. Press "Start."

Nutrition:
- Calories: 60
- Fats: 0.2 g
- Carbs: 16 g
- Sugar: 11.6 g
- Protein: 0.3 g

178. Pear Slices
Preparation Time: 10 minutes
Cooking Time: 5 hours
Servings: 4
Ingredients:
- 2 pears, cut into ¼-inch thick slices

Directions:
- Select "Dehydrate" mode.
- Select "LEVEL 2," then set time for 5 hours and set the temperature to 160ºF.
- Place the pear slices in the air fry basket and place the basket in the Air Fryer Oven. Press "Start."

Nutrition:
- Calories: 61 Fats: 0.2 g
- Carbs: 16 g
- Sugar: 10.2 g
- Protein: 0.4 g

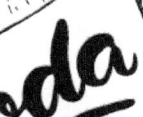

179. Mango Slices

Preparation Time: 10 minutes
Cooking Time: 12 hours
Servings: 4
Ingredients:
- 2 large mangoes, peeled and cut into ¼ -inch thick slices

Directions:
- Select "Dehydrate" mode.
- Select "LEVEL 2," then set time for 12 hours and set the temperature to 135ºF.
- Place the mango slices in the air fry basket and place the basket in the Air Fryer Oven. Press "Start."

Nutrition:
- Calories: 102
- Fats: 0.6 g
- Carbs: 25 g
- Sugar: 23 g
- Protein: 1.4 g

180. Zucchini Slices

Preparation Time: 10 minutes
Cooking Time: 12 hours
Servings: 4
Ingredients:
- 1 zucchini, sliced thinly

Directions:
- Select "Dehydrate" mode.
- Select "LEVEL 2," then set time for 12 hours and set the temperature to 135ºF.
- Place the zucchini slices in the air fry basket and place the basket in the Air Fryer Oven. Press "Start."

Nutrition:
- Calories: 10
- Fats: 0.1 g
- Carbs: 2.1 g
- Sugar: 0.9 g
- Protein: 0.6 g

181. Dragon Fruit Slices

Preparation Time: 10 minutes
Cooking Time: 12 hours
Servings: 4
Ingredients:
- 2 dragon fruit, peeled and cut into ¼ -inch thick slices

Directions:
- Select "Dehydrate" mode.
- Select "LEVEL 2," then set time for 12 hours and set the temperature to 115ºF.
- Place the dragon fruit slices in the air fry basket and place the basket in the Air Fryer Oven. Press "Start."

Nutrition:
- Calories: 25
- Carbs: 6 g
- Sugar: 6 g

182. Broccoli Florets

Preparation Time: 10 minutes
Cooking Time: 12 hours
Servings: 6
Ingredients:
- 1 lb. broccoli florets
- Pepper
- Salt

Directions:
- Select "Dehydrate" mode.
- Select "LEVEL 2," then set time for 12 hours and set the temperature to 115ºF.
- Place the broccoli florets in the air fry basket and place the basket in the Air Fryer Oven. Press "Start."

Nutrition:
- Calories: 25
- Fats: 0.3 g
- Carbs: 5 g
- Sugar: 1.3 g
- Protein: 2.1 g

183. Avocado Slices

Preparation Time: 10 minutes
Cooking Time: 10 hours
Servings: 4
Ingredients:
- 4 avocados, halved and pitted

Directions:
- Select "Dehydrate" mode.
- Select "LEVEL 2," then set time for 10 hours and set the temperature to 160ºF.
- Place the avocado slices in the air fry basket and place the basket in the Air Fryer Oven. Press "Start."

Nutrition:
- Calories: 415
- Fats: 39 g
- Carbs: 17.5 g
- Sugar: 1.1 g
- Protein: 3.9 g

184. Sweet Potato Chips

Preparation Time: 10 minutes
Cooking Time: 12 hours
Servings: 2
Ingredients:
- 2 sweet potatoes, peel and sliced thinly
- 1 tsp. olive oil
- ⅛ tsp. cinnamon
- Salt

Directions:
- Add the sweet potato slices in a bowl. Add the cinnamon, oil, and salt and toss well.
- Select "Dehydrate" mode.
- Select "LEVEL 2," then set time for 12 hours and set the temperature to 125ºF.
- Place the sweet potato slices in the air fry basket and place the basket in the Air Fryer Oven. Press "Start."

Nutrition:
- Calories: 195
- Fats: 2 g
- Carbs: 41 g
- Sugar: 0.8 g
- Protein: 2.3 g

185. Kiwi Chips

Preparation Time: 5 minutes
Cooking Time: 10 hours
Servings: 4
Ingredients:
- 6 kiwis, peeled & cut into ¼-inch thick slices

Directions:
- Select "Dehydrate" mode.
- Select "LEVEL 2," then set time for 10 hours and set the temperature to 135ºF.
- Place kiwi slices in the air fry basket and place the basket in the Air Fryer Oven. Press "Start."

Nutrition:
- Calories: 71
- Fats: 0.6 g
- Carbs: 16 g
- Sugar: 10.3 g
- Protein: 1.3 g

CHAPTER 5:

Lunch

186. Marinated Duck Breasts
Intermediate Recipe
Preparation Time: 1 day
Cooking Time: 20 minutes
Servings: 2
Ingredients:
- duck breasts
- 1 cup white wine
- ¼ cup soy sauce
- garlic cloves, minced
- tarragon springs
- Salt and black pepper to the taste
- 1 tablespoon butter
- ¼ cup sherry wine

Directions:
- In a bowl, mix duck breasts with white wine, soy sauce, garlic, tarragon, salt and pepper, toss well and keep in the fridge for 1 day. Transfer duck breasts to your preheated air fryer at 350 degrees F and cook for 10 minutes, flipping halfway.
- Meanwhile, pour the marinade in a pan, heat up over medium heat, add butter and sherry, stir, bring to a simmer, cook for 5 minutes and take off heat. Divide duck breasts on plates, Drizzle with sauce all over and serve. Enjoy!

Nutrition:
Calories 475
Fat 12
Carbs 10
Protein 48

187. Chicken And Radish Mix
Basic Recipe
Preparation Time: 10 minutes
Cooking Time: 30 minutes
Servings: 4
Ingredients:
- chicken things, bone-in
- Salt and black pepper to the taste
- 1 tablespoon olive oil
- 1 cup chicken stock
- radishes, halved
- 1 teaspoon sugar
- carrots cut into thin sticks
- tablespoon chives, chopped

Directions:
- Heat up a pan that fits your air fryer over medium heat, add stock, carrots, sugar and radishes, stir gently, reduce heat to medium, cover pot partly and simmer for 20 minutes Rub chicken with olive oil, season with salt and pepper, put in your air fryer and cook at 350 degrees F for 4 minutes.
- Add chicken to radish mix, toss, introduce everything in your air fryer, cook for 4 minutes more, divide among plates and serve. Enjoy!

Nutrition:
Calories 237
Fat 10
Carbs 19
Protein 29

188. Chicken Breasts And BBQ Chili Sauce
Basic Recipe
Preparation Time: 10 minutes
Cooking Time: 20 minutes
Servings: 6
Ingredients:
- cups chili sauce
- cups ketchup
- 1 cup pear jelly
- ¼ cup honey
- ½ teaspoon liquid smoke
- 1 teaspoon chili powder
- 1 teaspoon mustard powder
- 1 teaspoon sweet paprika
- Salt and black pepper to the taste
- 1 teaspoon garlic powder
- chicken breasts, skinless and boneless

Directions:

Season chicken breasts with salt and pepper, put in preheated air fryer and cook at 350 degrees F for 10 minutes Meanwhile, heat up a pan with the chili sauce over medium heat, add ketchup, pear jelly, honey, liquid smoke, chili powder, mustard powder, sweet paprika, salt, pepper and the garlic powder, stir, bring to a simmer and cook for 10 minutes Add air fried chicken breasts, toss well, divide among plates and serve. Enjoy!

Nutrition:
Calories 473
Fat 13
Carbs 39
Protein 33

189. Duck Breasts And Mango Mix

Intermediate Recipe
Preparation Time: 1 hour
Cooking Time: 20 minutes
Servings: 4
Ingredients:

duck breasts
1 and ½ tablespoons lemongrass, chopped
tablespoons lemon juice
tablespoons olive oil
Salt and black pepper to the taste
garlic cloves, minced
For the mango mix:
1 mango, peeled and chopped
1 tablespoon coriander, chopped
1 red onion, chopped
1 tablespoon sweet chili sauce
1 and ½ tablespoon lemon juice
1 teaspoon ginger, grated
¾ teaspoon sugar

Directions:

In a bowl, mix duck breasts with salt, pepper, lemongrass, 3 tablespoons lemon juice, olive oil and garlic, toss well, keep in the fridge for 1 hour, transfer to your air fryer and cook at 360 degrees F for 10 minutes, flipping once. Meanwhile, in a bowl, mix mango with coriander, onion, chili sauce, lemon juice, ginger and sugar and toss well. Divide duck on plates, add mango mix on the side and serve. Enjoy!

Nutrition:
Calories 465
Fat 11
Carbs 29
Protein 38

190. Quick Creamy Chicken Casserole

Basic Recipe
Preparation Time: 10 minutes
Cooking Time: 15 minutes
Servings: 4
Ingredients:

ounces spinach, chopped
tablespoons butter
tablespoons flour
1 and ½ cups milk
½ cup parmesan, grated
½ cup heavy cream
Salt and black pepper to the taste
cup chicken breasts, skinless, boneless and cubed
1 cup bread crumbs

Directions:

Heat up a pan with the butter over medium heat, add flour and stir well. Add milk, heavy cream and parmesan, stir well, cook for 1-2 minutes more and take off heat. In a pan that fits your air fryer, spread chicken and spinach. Add salt and pepper and toss. Add cream mix and spread, sprinkle bread crumbs on top, introduce in your air fryer and cook at 350 for 12 minutes Divide chicken and spinach mix on plates and serve. Enjoy!

Nutrition:
Calories 321
Fat 9
Carbs 22
Protein 17

191. Chicken And Peaches
Basic Recipe
Preparation Time: 10 minutes
Cooking Time: 30 minutes
Servings: 6
Ingredients:
- 1 whole chicken, cut into medium pieces
- ¾ cup water
- 1/3 cup honey
- Salt and black pepper to the taste
- ¼ cup olive oil
- peaches, halved

Directions:
- Put the water in a pot, bring to a simmer over medium heat, add honey, whisk really well and leave aside. Rub chicken pieces with the oil, season with salt and pepper, place in your air fryer's basket and cook at 350 degrees F for 10 minutes Brush chicken with some of the honey mix, cook for 6 minutes more, flip again, brush one more time with the honey mix and cook for 7 minutes more. Divide chicken pieces on plates and keep warm. Brush peaches with what's left of the honey marinade, place them in your air fryer and cook them for 3 minutes Divide among plates next to chicken pieces and serve. Enjoy!

Nutrition:
Calories 430
Fat 14
Carbs 15
Protein 20

192. Tea Glazed Chicken
Basic Recipe
Preparation Time: 10 minutes
Cooking Time: 30 minutes
Servings: 6
Ingredients:
- ½ cup apricot preserves
- ½ cup pineapple preserves
- chicken legs - 1 cup hot water
- black tea bags
- 1 tablespoon soy sauce
- 1 onion, chopped
- ¼ teaspoon red pepper flakes
- 1 tablespoon olive oil
- Salt and black pepper to the taste
- chicken legs

Directions:
- Put the hot water in a bowl, add tea bags, leave aside covered for 10 minutes, discard bags at the end and transfer tea to another bowl. Add soy sauce, pepper flakes, apricot and pineapple preserves, whisk really well and take off heat.
- Season chicken with salt and pepper, rub with oil, put in your air fryer and cook at 350 degrees F for 5 minutes Spread onion on the bottom of a baking dish that fits your air fryer, add chicken pieces, Drizzle with the tea glaze on top, introduce in your air fryer and cook at 320 degrees F for 25 minutes Divide everything on plates and serve. Enjoy!

Nutrition:
Calories 298 Fat 14
Carbs 14 Protein 30

193. Ratatouille
Basic Recipe
Preparation Time: 10 minutes
Cooking Time: 20 minutes
Servings: 4
Ingredients:
- Roma tomatoes, seeded and chopped

garlic cloves, sliced
1 baby eggplant, peeled and chopped
1 red bell pepper, chopped
1 yellow bell pepper, chopped
1 small onion, chopped
1 teaspoon Italian seasoning
1 teaspoon olive oil

Directions:

In a medium metal bowl, gently combine the tomatoes, garlic, eggplant, red and yellow bell peppers, onion, Italian seasoning, and olive oil. Place the bowl in the air fryer. Roast for 12 to 16 minutes, stirring once, until the vegetables are tender. Serve warm or cold.

Nutrition:
Calories 69
Fat 2g
Protein 2g
Carbs 11g

194. Vegetable Egg Rolls
Basic Recipe
Preparation Time: 15 minutes
Cooking Time: 10 minutes
Servings: 4
Ingredients:

½ cup chopped yellow summer squash
⅓ cup grated carrot
½ cup chopped red bell pepper
scallions, white and green parts, chopped
1 teaspoon low-sodium soy sauce
egg roll wrappers (see Tip)
1 tablespoon cornstarch
1 egg, beaten

Directions:

In a medium bowl, mix the yellow squash, carrot, red bell pepper, scallions, and soy sauce.

Place the egg roll wrappers on a work surface. Top each with about 3 tablespoons of the vegetable mixture.

In a small bowl, thoroughly mix the cornstarch and egg. Brush some egg mixture on the edges of each wrapper. Roll up the wrappers, folding over the sides so the filling is contained. Brush the egg mixture on the outside of each egg roll.

Air-fry it for 7 to 10 minutes or until brown and crunchy then serve immediately.

Nutrition:
Calories 130
Fat 2g
Protein 6g
Carbs 23g

195. Grilled Cheese And Greens Sandwiches
Basic Recipe
Preparation Time: 15 minutes
Cooking Time: 10 minutes
Servings: 4
Ingredients:

1½ cups chopped mixed greens (kale, chard, collards; see Tip)
garlic cloves, thinly sliced
teaspoons olive oil
slices low-sodium low-fat Swiss cheese
slices low-sodium whole-wheat bread
Olive oil spray, for coating the sandwiches

Directions:

In a 6-by-2-inch pan, mix the greens, garlic, and olive oil. Cook in the air fryer for 4 to 5 minutes, stirring once, until the vegetables are tender. Dry out, if necessary.

Make 2 sandwiches, dividing half of the greens and 1 slice of Swiss cheese between 2 slices of bread. Lightly spray the outsides of the sandwiches with olive oil spray.

Grill the sandwiches in the air fryer for 6 to 8 minutes, turning with tongs halfway through, until the bread is toasted and the cheese melts.

Cut each sandwich in half to serve.

Nutrition:
Calories 176 Fat 6g
Protein 10g Carbs 24g

196. Veggie Tuna Melts
Basic Recipe
Preparation Time: 15 minutes
Cooking Time: 10 minutes
Servings: 4
Ingredients:
- low-sodium whole-wheat English muffins split
- 1 (6-ounce) can chunk light low-sodium tuna, Dry outed
- 1 cup shredded carrot
- ⅓ cup chopped mushrooms
- scallions, white and green parts, sliced
- ⅓ cup nonfat Greek yogurt
- tablespoons low-sodium stone-ground mustard
- slices low-sodium low-fat Swiss cheese, halved

Directions:
- Place the English muffin halves in the air fryer basket. Grill for 3 to 4 minutes, or until crisp. Remove from the basket and set aside.
- In a medium bowl, thoroughly mix the tuna, carrot, mushrooms, scallions, yogurt, and mustard. Top each half of the muffins with one-fourth of the tuna mixture and a half slice of Swiss cheese.
- Grill in the air fryer for 4 to 7 minutes, or until the tuna mixture is hot and the cheese melts and starts to brown. Serve immediately.

Nutrition:
Calories 191 Fat 4g
Protein 23g Carbs 16g

197. California Melts
Basic Recipe
Preparation Time: 10 minutes
Cooking Time: 5 minutes
Servings: 4
Ingredients:
- low-sodium whole-wheat English muffins split
- tablespoons nonfat Greek yogurt
- fresh baby spinach leaves
- 1 ripe tomato, cut into 4 slices
- ½ ripe avocados, peeled, pitted, and sliced lengthwise (see Tip)
- fresh basil leaves
- tablespoons crumbled fat-free low-sodium feta cheese, divided

Directions:
- Put the English muffin halves into the air fryer. Toast for 2 minutes, or until light golden brown. Transfer to a work surface.
- Spread each muffin half with 1½ teaspoons of yogurt.
- Top each muffin half with 2 spinach leaves, 1 tomato slice, one-fourth of the avocado, and 2 basil leaves. Sprinkle each with 1 tablespoon of feta cheese. Toast the sandwiches in the air fryer for 3 to 4 minutes, or until the cheese softens and the sandwich is hot. Serve immediately.

Nutrition:
Calories 110 Fat 3g
Protein 8g Carbs 13g

198. Vegetable Pita Sandwiches
Basic Recipe
Preparation Time: 10 minutes
Cooking Time: 20 minutes
Servings: 4
Ingredients:
- 1 baby eggplant peeled and chopped (see Tip)

1 red bell pepper, sliced
½ cup diced red onion
½ cup shredded carrot
1 teaspoon olive oil
⅓ cup low-fat Greek yogurt
½ teaspoon dried tarragon
low-sodium whole-wheat pita breads, halved crosswise

Directions:

In a 6-by-2-inch pan, stir together the eggplant, red bell pepper, red onion, carrot, and olive oil. Put the vegetable mixture into the air fryer basket and roast for 7 to 9 minutes, stirring once, until the vegetables are tender. Dry out if necessary.

In a small bowl, thoroughly mix the yogurt and tarragon until well combined.

Stir the yogurt mixture into the vegetables. Stuff one-fourth of this mixture into each pita pocket.

Place the sandwiches in the air fryer and cook for 2 to 3 minutes, or until the bread is toasted. Serve immediately.

Nutrition:
Calories 176
Fat 4g
Protein 7g
Carbs 27g

199. Falafel
Basic Recipe
Preparation Time: 10 minutes
Cooking Time: 20 minutes
Servings: 4
Ingredients:

1 (16-ounce) can no-salt-added chickpeas rinsed and Dry outed
⅓ cup whole-wheat pastry flour
⅓ cup minced red onion
garlic cloves, minced
tablespoons minced fresh cilantro
1 tablespoon olive oil
½ teaspoon ground cumin
¼ teaspoon cayenne pepper

Directions:

In a medium bowl, mash the chickpeas with a potato masher until mostly smooth.

Stir in the pastry flour, red onion, garlic, cilantro, olive oil, cumin, and cayenne until well mixed. Firm the chickpea mixture into 12 balls. Air-fry the falafel balls, in batches, for 11 to 13 minutes, or until the falafel are firm and light golden brown. Serve.

Nutrition:
Calories 172
Fat 5g
Protein 7g
Carbs 25g

200. Stuffed Tomatoes
Basic Recipe
Preparation Time: 5 minutes
Cooking Time: 20 minutes
Servings: 4
Ingredients:

medium beefsteak tomatoes, rinsed and patted dry
1 medium onion, chopped
½ cup grated carrot
1 garlic clove, minced
teaspoons olive oil
cups fresh baby spinach
¼ cup crumbled low-sodium feta cheese
½ teaspoon dried basil

Directions:

Cut about ½ inch off the top of each tomato. Gently hollow them out (see Tip), leaving a wall about ½ inch thick. Dry out the tomatoes, upside down, on paper towels while you prepare the filling.

In a 6-by-2-inch pan, mix the onion, carrot, garlic, and olive oil. Bake it for 4 to 6 minutes, or until the vegetables are crisp-tender.

Stir in the spinach, feta cheese, and basil.

Fill each tomato with one-fourth of the vegetable mixture. Bake the tomatoes in the air fryer basket for 12 to 14 minutes, or until hot and tender.

Serve immediately.

Nutrition:
Calories 79 Fat 3g
Protein 3g
Carbs 9g

201. Loaded Mini Potatoes
Basic Recipe
Preparation Time: 5 minutes
Cooking Time: 25 minutes
Servings: 2
Ingredients:
- 24 small new potatoes, or creamer potatoes, rinsed, scrubbed, and patted dry
- 1 teaspoon olive oil
- ½ cup low-fat Greek yogurt
- 1 tablespoon low-sodium stone-ground mustard (see Tip)
- ½ teaspoon dried basil
- Roma tomatoes, seeded and chopped
- scallions, white and green parts, chopped
- tablespoons chopped fresh chives

Directions:
- In a large bowl, toss the potatoes with the olive oil. Transfer to the air fryer basket. Roast for 20 to 25 minutes, shaking the basket once, until the potatoes are crisp on the outside and tender within. Meanwhile, in a small bowl, stir together the yogurt, mustard, and basil.
- Place the potatoes on a serving platter and carefully smash each one slightly with the bottom of a drinking glass. Top the potatoes with the yogurt mixture. Sprinkle with the tomatoes, scallions, and chives. Serve immediately.

Nutrition:
Calories 100
Fat 2g
Protein 5g
Carbs 19g

202. Crustless Veggie Quiche
Basic Recipe
Preparation Time: 5 minutes
Cooking Time: 20 minutes
Servings: 3
Ingredients:
- egg whites
- 1 egg
- 1 cup frozen chopped spinach, thawed and Dry outed
- 1 red bell pepper, chopped
- ½ cup chopped mushrooms
- ⅓ cup minced red onion
- 1 tablespoon low-sodium mustard
- 1 slice low-sodium low-fat Swiss cheese, torn into small pieces
- Nonstick cooking spray with flour, for greasing the pan

Directions:
- In a medium bowl, beat the egg whites and egg until blended.
- Stir in the spinach, red bell pepper, mushrooms, onion, and mustard.
- Mix in the Swiss cheese.
- Spray a 6-by-2-inch pan with nonstick cooking spray.
- Pour the egg mixture into the prepared pan.
- Bake it for 18 to 22 minutes, or until the egg mixture is puffed, light golden brown, and set. Cool for 5 minutes before serving.

Nutrition:
Calories 76
Fat 3g
Protein 8g
Carbs 4g

203. Scrambled Eggs With Broccoli And Spinach

Basic Recipe
Preparation Time: 15 minutes
Cooking Time: 20 minutes
Servings: 4
Ingredients:

- teaspoons unsalted butter
- 1 medium onion, chopped
- 1 red bell pepper, chopped
- 1 cup small broccoli florets
- ½ teaspoon dried marjoram
- egg whites
- eggs
- 1 cup fresh baby spinach

Directions:

- In a 6-by-2-inch pan in the air fryer, heat the butter for 1 minute, or until it melts.
- Add the onion, red bell pepper, broccoli, marjoram, and 1 tablespoon of water. Air-fry for 3 to 5 minutes, or until the vegetables are crisp-tender. Dry out, if necessary.
- Meanwhile, in a medium bowl, beat the egg whites and eggs until frothy.
- Add the spinach and eggs to the vegetables in the pan. Air-fry for 8 to 12 minutes, stirring three times during cooking, until the eggs are set and fluffy and reach 160°F on a meat thermometer. Serve immediately.

Nutrition:
Calories 86 Fat 3g
Protein 8g
Carbs 5g

204. Beans And Greens Pizza

Basic Recipe
Preparation Time: 10 minutes
Cooking Time: 20 minutes
Servings: 4
Ingredients:

- ¾ cup whole-wheat pastry flour
- ½ teaspoon low-sodium baking powder
- 1 tablespoon olive oil, divided
- 1 cup chopped kale
- cups chopped fresh baby spinach
- 1 cup canned no-salt-added cannellini beans, rinsed and Dry outed (see Tip)
- ½ teaspoon dried thyme
- 1 piece low-sodium string cheese, torn into pieces

Directions:

- In a small bowl, mix the pastry flour and baking powder until well combined.
- Add ¼ cup of water and 2 teaspoons of olive oil. Mix until a dough form.
- On a floured surface, press or roll the dough into a 7-inch round. Set aside while you cook the greens.In a 6-by-2-inch pan, mix the kale, spinach, and remaining teaspoon of the olive oil. Air-fry it for 3 to 5 minutes until the greens are wilted. Dry out well.
- Put the pizza dough into the air fryer basket. Top with the greens, cannellini beans, thyme, and string cheese. Air-fry for 11 to 14 minutes or until the crust is golden brown and the cheese is melted. Cut into quarters to serve.

Nutrition:
Calories 175
Fat 5g
Protein 9g
Carbs 24g

205. Grilled Chicken Mini Pizzas

Basic Recipe
Preparation Time: 15 minutes
Cooking Time: 10 minutes
Servings: 4
Ingredients:

- low-sodium whole-wheat pita breads, split (see Tip)
- ½ cup no-salt-added tomato sauce

1 garlic clove, minced
½ teaspoon dried oregano
1 cooked shredded chicken breast
1 cup chopped button mushrooms
½ cup chopped red bell pepper
½ cup shredded part skim low-sodium mozzarella cheese

Directions:
Place the pita breads, insides up, on a work surface.
In a small bowl, stir together the tomato sauce, garlic, and oregano. Spread about 2 tablespoons of the sauce over each pita half.
Top each with ¼ cup of shredded chicken, ¼ cup of mushrooms, and 2 tablespoons of red bell pepper. Sprinkle with the mozzarella cheese.
Bake the pizzas for 3 to 6 minutes, or until the cheese melts and starts to brown and the pita bread is crisp. Serve immediately.

Nutrition:
Calories 249 Fat 7g
Protein 23g
Carbs 25g

206. Chicken Croquettes
Basic Recipe
Preparation Time: 15 minutes
Cooking Time: 10 minutes
Servings: 4
Ingredients:
(5-ounce) cooked chicken breasts, finely chopped (see Tip)
⅓ cup low-fat Greek yogurt
tablespoons minced red onion
celery stalks, minced
1 garlic clove, minced
½ teaspoon dried basil
egg whites, divided
slices low-sodium whole-wheat bread, crumbled

Directions:
In a medium bowl, thoroughly mix the chicken, yogurt, red onion, celery, garlic, basil, and 1 egg white. Form the mixture into 8 ovals and gently press into shape.
In a shallow bowl, beat the remaining egg white until foamy.
Put the bread crumbs on a plate.
Dip the chicken croquettes into the egg white and then into the bread crumbs to coat.
Air-fry the croquettes, in batches, for 7 to 10 minutes, or until the croquettes reach an internal temperature of 160°F on a meat thermometer and their color is golden brown. Serve immediately.

Nutrition:
Calories 207
Fat 4g
Protein 32g
Carbs 8g,

207. Pork Chops And Yogurt Sauce
Basic Recipe
Preparation Time: 10 minutes
Cooking Time: 30 minutes
Servings: 4
Ingredients:
tablespoons avocado oil
pounds pork chops
1 cup yogurt
garlic cloves, minced
1 teaspoon turmeric powder
Salt and black pepper to the taste
tablespoon oregano, chopped

Directions:
In the air fryer's pan, mix the pork chops with the yogurt and the other ingredients, toss and cook at 400 degrees F for 30 minutes

Divide the mix between plates and serve.
Nutrition:
Calories 301 Fat 7
Carbs 19
Protein 22

208. Lamb And Macadamia Nuts Mix
Basic Recipe
Preparation Time: 10 minutes
Cooking Time: 20 minutes
Servings: 4
Ingredients:
- pounds lamb stew meat, cubed
- tablespoons macadamia nuts, peeled
- 1 cup baby spinach
- ½ cup beef stock
- garlic cloves, minced
- Salt and black pepper to the taste
- 1 tablespoon oregano, chopped

Directions:
In the air fryer's pan, mix the lamb with the nuts and the other ingredients,
Cook at 380 degrees F for 20 minutes,
Divide between plates and serve.
Nutrition:
Calories 280 Fat 12
Carbs 20 Protein 19

209. Beef, Cucumber And Eggplants
Basic Recipe
Preparation Time: 10 minutes
Cooking Time: 20 minutes
Servings: 4
Ingredients:
- 1 pound beef stew meat, cut into strips
- 2 eggplants, cubed
- 2 cucumbers, sliced
- 2 garlic cloves, minced
- 1 cup heavy cream
- 2 tablespoons olive oil
- Salt and black pepper to the taste

Directions:
In a baking dish that fits your air fryer, mix the beef with the eggplants and the other ingredients, toss, introduce the pan in the fryer and cook at 400 degrees F for 20 minutes
Divide everything into bowls and serve.
Nutrition:
Calories 283 Fat 11
Carbs 22 Protein 14

210. Rosemary Pork And Artichokes
Basic Recipe
Preparation Time: 10 minutes
Cooking Time: 25 minutes
Servings: 4
Ingredients:
- 1 pound pork stew meat, cubed
- 1 cup canned artichoke hearts, Dry outed and halved - 2 tablespoons olive oil
- 2 tablespoons rosemary, chopped
- ½ teaspoon cumin, ground
- ½ teaspoon nutmeg, ground
- ½ cup sour cream
- Salt and black pepper to the taste

Directions:
In a pan that fits your air fryer, mix the pork with the artichokes and the other ingredients, introduce in the fryer and cook at 400 degrees F for 25 minutes
Divide everything into bowls and serve.
Nutrition:
Calories 280 Fat 13
Carbs 22 Protein 18

211. Mustard Lamb Loin Chops
Basic Recipe
Preparation Time: 15 minutes
Cooking Time: 30 minutes
Servings: 4
Ingredients:
- 4-ounces lamb loin chops

tablespoons Dijon mustard
1 tablespoon fresh lemon juice
½ teaspoon olive oil
1 teaspoon dried tarragon
Salt and black pepper, to taste

Directions:
- Preheat the Air fryer to 390-degree F and grease an Air fryer basket.
- Mix the mustard, lemon juice, oil, tarragon, salt, and black pepper in a large bowl.
- Coat the chops generously with the mustard mixture and arrange in the Air fryer basket.
- Cook for about 15 minutes, flipping once in between and dish out to serve hot.

Nutrition:
Calories 433, Fat 17.6g,
Carbs 0.6g, Protein 64.1g,

212. Herbed Lamb Chops
Basic Recipe
Preparation Time: 10 minutes
Cooking Time: 10 minutes
Servings: 2
Ingredients:
- 4: 4-ounceslamb chops
- 1 tablespoon fresh lemon juice
- 1 tablespoon olive oil
- 1 teaspoon dried rosemary
- 1 teaspoon dried thyme
- 1 teaspoon dried oregano
- ½ teaspoon ground cumin
- ½ teaspoon ground coriander
- Salt and black pepper, to taste

Directions:
- Preheat the Air fryer to 390-degree F and grease an Air fryer basket.
- Mix the lemon juice, oil, herbs, and spices in a large bowl.
- Coat the chops generously with the herb mixture and refrigerate to marinate for about 1 hour.
- Arrange the chops in the Air fryer basket and cook for about 7 minutes, flipping once in between.
- Dish out the lamb chops in a platter and serve hot.

Nutrition:
Calories 491
Fat 24g
Carbs 1.6g
Protein 64g

213. Za'atar Lamb Loin Chops
Basic Recipe
Preparation Time: 10 minutes
Cooking Time: 30 minutes
Servings: 4
Ingredients:
- 8: 3½-ouncesbone-in lamb loin chops, trimmed
- garlic cloves, crushed
- 1 tablespoon fresh lemon juice
- 1 teaspoon olive oil
- 1 tablespoon Za'ataro
- Salt and black pepper, to taste

Directions:
- Preheat the Air fryer to 400-degree F and grease an Air fryer basket.
- Mix the garlic, lemon juice, oil, Za'atar, salt, and black pepper in a large bowl
- Coat the chops generously with the herb mixture and arrange the chops in the Air fryer basket.
- Cook for about 15 minutes, flipping twice in between and dish out the lamb chops to serve hot.

Nutrition:
Calories 433
Fat 17.6g
Carbs 0.6g
Protein 64.1g

214. Pesto Coated Rack Of Lamb

Basic Recipe
Preparation Time: 15 minutes
Cooking Time: 15 minutes
Servings: 4
Ingredients:
- ½ bunch fresh mint
- 1: 1½-pounds rack of lamb
- 1 garlic clove
- ¼ cup extra-virgin olive oil
- ½ tablespoon honey
- Salt and black pepper, to taste

Directions:
- Preheat the Air fryer to 200-degree F and grease an Air fryer basket.
- Put the mint, garlic, oil, honey, salt, and black pepper in a blender and pulse until smooth to make pesto.
- Coat the rack of lamb with this pesto on both sides and arrange in the Air fryer basket.
- Cook for about 15 minutes and cut the rack into individual chops to serve.

Nutrition:
Calories 406
Fat 27.7g
Carbs 2.9g
Protein 34.9g

215. Spiced Lamb Steaks

Basic Recipe
Preparation Time: 15 minutes
Cooking Time: 14 minutes
Servings: 3
Ingredients:
- ½ onion, roughly chopped
- 1½ pounds boneless lamb sirloin steaks
- garlic cloves, peeled
- 1 tablespoon fresh ginger, peeled
- 1 teaspoon garam masala
- 1 teaspoon ground fennel
- ½ teaspoon ground cumin
- ½ teaspoon ground cinnamon
- ½ teaspoon cayenne pepper
- Salt and black pepper, to taste

Directions:
- Preheat the Air fryer to 330-degree F and grease an Air fryer basket.
- Put the onion, garlic, ginger, and spices in a blender and pulse until smooth.
- Coat the lamb steaks with this mixture on both sides and refrigerate to marinate for about 24 hours.
- Arrange the lamb steaks in the Air fryer basket and cook for about 15 minutes, flipping once in between.
- Dish out the steaks in a platter and serve warm.

Nutrition:
Calories 252 Fat 16.7g
Carbs 4.2g Protein 21.7g

216. Leg Of Lamb With Brussels Sprout

Intermediate Recipe
Preparation Time: 20 minutes
Cooking Time: 1 hour 30 minutes
Servings: 4
Ingredients:
- 2¼ pounds leg of lamb
- 1 tablespoon fresh rosemary, minced
- 1 tablespoon fresh lemon thyme
- 1½ pounds Brussels sprouts, trimmed
- tablespoons olive oil, divided
- 1 garlic clove, minced
- Salt and ground black pepper, as required
- tablespoons honey

Directions:
Preheat the Air fryer to 300-degree F and grease an Air fryer basket.
- Make slits in the leg of lamb with a sharp knife.
- Mix 2 tablespoons of oil, herbs, garlic, salt, and black pepper in a bowl.

- Coat the leg of lamb with oil mixture generously and arrange in the Air fryer basket.
- Cook for about 75 minutes and set the Air fryer to 390-degree F.
- Coat the Brussels sprout evenly with the remaining oil and honey and arrange them in the Air fryer basket with leg of lamb. Cook for about 15 minutes and dish out to serve warm.

Nutrition:
Calories 449 Fats 19.9g
Carbs 16.6g Protein 51.7g

217. Honey Mustard Cheesy Meatballs

Basic Recipe
Preparation Time: 15 minutes
Cooking Time: 15 minutes
Servings: 8
Ingredients:
- onions, chopped
- 1-pound ground beef
- tablespoons fresh basil, chopped
- tablespoons cheddar cheese, grated
- teaspoons garlic paste
- teaspoons honey
- Salt and black pepper, to taste
- teaspoons mustard

Directions:
- Preheat the Air fryer to 385₀F and grease an Air fryer basket.
- Mix all the ingredients in a bowl until well combined.
- Shape the mixture into equal-sized balls gently and arrange the meatballs in the Air fryer basket.
- Cook for about 15 minutes and dish out to serve warm.

Nutrition:
Calories 134 Fat 4.4g
Carbs 4.6g Protein 18.2g

218. Spicy Lamb Kebabs

Basic Recipe
Preparation Time: 20 minutes
Cooking Time: 10 minutes
Servings: 6
Ingredients:
- eggs, beaten
- 1 cup pistachios, chopped
- 1-pound ground lamb
- tablespoons plain flour
- tablespoons flat-leaf parsley, chopped
- teaspoons chili flakes - garlic cloves, minced
- tablespoons fresh lemon juice
- teaspoons cumin seeds
- 1 teaspoon fennel seeds
- teaspoons dried mint
- teaspoons salt - Olive oil
- 1 teaspoon coriander seeds
- 1 teaspoon freshly ground black pepper

Directions:
- Preheat the Air fryer to 355-degree F and grease an Air fryer basket.
- Mix lamb, pistachios, eggs, lemon juice, chili flakes, flour, cumin seeds, fennel seeds, coriander seeds, mint, parsley, salt and black pepper in a large bowl.
- Thread the lamb mixture onto metal skewers to form sausages and coat with olive oil.
- Place the skewers in the Air fryer basket and cook for about 8 minutes
- Dish out in a platter and serve hot.

Nutrition:
Calories 284 Fat 15.8g
Carbs 8.4g Protein 27.9g

219. Simple Beef Burgers

Basic Recipe
Preparation Time: 20 minutes
Cooking Time: 10 minutes
Servings: 6
Ingredients:
- pounds ground beef

cheddar cheese slices
dinner rolls
tablespoons tomato ketchup
Salt and black pepper, to taste

Directions:
- Preheat the Air fryer to 390-degree F and grease an Air fryer basket.
- Mix the beef, salt and black pepper in a bowl.
- Make small equal-sized patties from the beef mixture and arrange half of patties in the Air fryer basket.
- Cook for about 12 minutes and top each patty with 1 cheese slice.
- Arrange the patties between rolls and Drizzle with ketchup.
- Repeat with the remaining batch and dish out to serve hot.

Nutrition:
Calories 537 Fat 28.3g
Carbs 7.6g Protein 60.6g

220. Lamb With Potatoes
Basic Recipe
Preparation Time: 20 minutes
Cooking Time: 20 minutes
Servings: 2
Ingredients:
- ½ pound lamb meat
- small potatoes, peeled and halved
- ½ small onion, peeled and halved
- ¼ cup frozen sweet potato fries
- 1 garlic clove, crushed
- ½ tablespoon dried rosemary, crushed
- 1 teaspoon olive oil

Directions:
- Preheat the Air fryer to 355-degree F and arrange a divider in the Air fryer. Rub the lamb evenly with garlic and rosemary and place on one side of Air fryer divider.
- Cook for about 20 minutes and meanwhile, microwave the potatoes for about 4 minutes. Dish out the potatoes in a large bowl and stir in the olive oil and onions.
- Transfer into the Air fryer divider and change the side of lamb ramp.
- Cook for about 15 minutes, flipping once in between and dish out in a bowl.

Nutrition:
Calories 399 Fat 18.5g
Carbs 32.3g Protein 24.5g

221. Nutmeg Beef Mix
Basic Recipe
Preparation Time: 10 minutes
Cooking Time: 30 minutes
Servings: 4
Ingredients:
- pounds beef stew meat, cubed
- 1 teaspoon nutmeg, ground
- tablespoons avocado oil
- ½ teaspoon chili powder
- ¼ cup beef stock
- 2 tablespoons chives, chopped
- Salt and black pepper to the taste

Directions:
- In a pan that fits your air fryer, mix the beef with the nutmeg and the other ingredients, toss, introduce the pan in the fryer and cook at 400 degrees F for 30 minutes
- Divide the mix into bowls and serve.

Nutrition:
Calories 280 Fat 12
Carbs 17 Protein 14

222. Oregano Daikon
Basic Recipe
Preparation Time: 10 minutes
Cooking Time: 10 minutes
Servings: 5
Ingredients:
- 1-pound daikon
- ½ teaspoon sage

1 teaspoon salt
1 tablespoon olive oil
1 teaspoon dried oregano

Directions:
Peel the daikon and cut it into cubes.
Sprinkle the daikon cubes with sage, salt, and dried oregano.
Mix well
Preheat the air fryer to 360 F.
Place the daikon cubes in the air fryer rack and Drizzle with olive oil.
Cook the daikon for 6 minutes
Turn the daikon and cook for 4 minutes more or until soft and golden brown.

Nutrition:
Calories 43
Fat 2.8
Carbs 3.9
Protein 1.9

223. Creamy Spinach
Basic Recipe
Preparation Time: 10 minutes
Cooking Time: 12 minutes
Servings: 4
Ingredients:
oz chive stems
cup spinach
1 cup chicken stock
1 cup heavy cream
1 teaspoon salt
1 teaspoon paprika
½ teaspoon chili flakes
1 teaspoon ground black pepper
½ teaspoon minced garlic
oz. Parmesan, shredded

Directions:
Preheat the air fryer to 390 F.
Chop the spinach roughly.
Place the spinach in the air fryer basket bowl.
Add the chicken stock and heavy cream.
Add salt, paprika, chili flakes, and ground black pepper.
Add the chives and minced garlic.
Mix gently and cook it for 10 minutes
Blend using a hand blender. You should get the creamy texture of a soup.
Sprinkle with the shredded cheese and cook it for 2 minutes at 400 F.
Serve hot.

Nutrition:
Calories 187
Fat 16
Carbs 4.4
Protein 8.4

224. Eggplant With Grated Cheddar
Basic Recipe
Preparation Time: 15 minutes
Cooking Time: 10 minutes
Servings: 10
Ingredients:
eggplants
1 teaspoon minced garlic
1 teaspoon olive oil
oz. Cheddar cheese, grated
½ teaspoon ground black pepper

Directions:
Wash the eggplants carefully and slice them.
Rub the slices with minced garlic, salt, and ground black pepper.
Leave the slices for 5 minutes to marinade.
Preheat the air fryer to 400 F.
Place the eggplant circles in the air fryer rack and cook them for 6 minutes
Then turn them over cook for 5 minutes more.
Sprinkle the eggplants with the grated cheese and cook for 30 seconds.
Serve hot.

Nutrition:
Calories 97 Fat 6.2
Carbs 7.7 Protein 5.2

225. Coriander Garlic Bulbs

Basic Recipe
Preparation Time: 10 minutes
Cooking Time: 10 minutes
Servings: 18
Ingredients:
- 1-pound garlic heads
- tablespoons olive oil
- 1 teaspoon dried oregano
- 1 teaspoon dried basil
- 1 teaspoon ground coriander
- ¼ teaspoon ground ginger

Directions:
- Cut the ends of the garlic bulbs.
- Place each bulb on foil.
- Coat them with olive oil, dried oregano, dried basil, ground coriander, and ground ginger.
- Preheat the air fryer to 400 F.
- Wrap the garlic in foil and place in the air fryer.
- Cook for 10 minutes until soft.
- Let them cool for at least 10 minutes before serving.

Nutrition:
Calories 57
Fat 1.4
Carbs 8.2
Protein 1.3

226. Parmesan Sticks

Basic Recipe
Preparation Time: 10 minutes
Cooking Time: 10 minutes
Servings: 3
Ingredients:
- oz. Parmesan
- 1 egg
- ½ cup heavy cream
- tablespoons almond flour
- ¼ teaspoon ground black pepper

Directions:
- Crack the egg in a bowl and whisk.
- Add the heavy cream and almond flour.
- Sprinkle the mixture with ground black pepper.
- Whisk carefully or use a hand mixer.
- Cut the cheese into thick short sticks
- Dip the sticks in the heavy cream mixture.
- Place the cheese sticks in freezer bags and freeze them.
- Preheat the air fryer to 400 F.
- Place the cheese sticks in the air fryer rack.
- Cook for 8 minutes

Nutrition:
Calories 389 Fat 29.5
Carbs 5.5 Protein 28.6

227. Creamy Snow Peas

Basic Recipe
Preparation Time: 10 minutes
Cooking Time: 5 minutes
Servings: 5
Ingredients:
- ½ cup heavy cream
- 1 teaspoon butter
- 1 teaspoon salt
- 1 teaspoon paprika
- 1-pound snow peas
- ¼ teaspoon nutmeg

Directions:
- Preheat the air fryer to 400 F.
- Wash the snow peas carefully and place them in the air fryer basket tray.
- Then sprinkle the snow peas with the butter, salt, paprika, nutmeg, and heavy cream.
- Cook the snow peas for 5 minutes
- When the time is over – shake the snow peas gently and transfer them to the serving plates.
- Enjoy!

Nutrition:
Calories 98 Fat 5.9
Carbs 6.9 Protein 3.5

228. Sesame Okra
Basic Recipe
Preparation Time: 10 minutes
Cooking Time: 4 minutes
Servings: 4
Ingredients:
- 1 tablespoon sesame oil
- 1 teaspoon sesame seed
- oz. okra
- ½ teaspoon salt
- 1 egg

Directions:
- Wash the okra and chop it roughly.
- Crack the egg into a bowl and whisk it.
- Add the chopped okra to the whisked egg.
- Sprinkle with the sesame seeds and salt.
- Preheat the air fryer to 400 F.
- Mix the okra mixture carefully.
- Place the mixture in the air fryer basket.
- Drizzle with olive oil.
- Cook the okra for 4 minutes
- Stir and serve.

Nutrition:
Calories 81 Fat 5
Carbs 6.1 Protein 3

229. Fennel Oregano Wedges
Basic Recipe
Preparation Time: 15 minutes
Cooking Time: 6 minutes
Servings: 4
Ingredients:
- 1 teaspoon stevia extract
- ½ teaspoon fresh thyme
- ½ teaspoon salt - 1 teaspoon olive oil
- 14 oz. fennel
- 1 teaspoon butter
- 1 teaspoon dried oregano
- ½ teaspoon chili flakes

Directions:
- Slice the fennel into wedges. Melt the butter. Combine the butter, olive oil, dried oregano, and chili flakes in a bowl. Combine well.
- Add salt, fresh thyme, and stevia extract. Whisk gently.
- Brush the fennel wedges with the mixture. Preheat the air fryer to 370 F.
- Place the fennel wedges in the air fryer rack.
- Cook the fennel wedges for 3 minutes on each side.

Nutrition:
Calories 41 Fat 1.9
Carbs 6.1 Protein 1

230. Parsley Kohlrabi Fritters
Basic Recipe
Preparation Time: 10 minutes
Cooking Time: 7 minutes
Servings: 4
Ingredients:
- oz. kohlrabi
- 1 egg
- 1 tablespoon almond flour
- ½ teaspoon salt
- 1 teaspoon olive oil
- 1 teaspoon ground black pepper
- 1 tablespoon dried parsley
- ¼ teaspoon chili pepper

Directions:
- Peel the kohlrabi and grate it. Combine the grated kohlrabi with salt, ground black pepper, dried parsley, and chili pepper.
- Crack the egg into the mixture and whisk it. Make medium fritters from the mixture.
- Preheat the air fryer to 380 F. Grease the air fryer basket tray with olive oil and place the fritters inside. Cook the fritters for 4 minutes Turn the fritters and cook for 3 minutes more. Allow to cool slightly before serving.

Nutrition:
Calories 66
Fat 4.7
Carbs 4.4
Protein 3.2

231. Chives Bamboo Shoots
Basic Recipe
Preparation Time: 10 minutes
Cooking Time: 4 minutes
Servings: 2
Ingredients:
- oz. bamboo shoots
- garlic cloves, sliced
- 1 tablespoon olive oil
- ½ teaspoon chili flakes
- tablespoon chives
- ½ teaspoon salt
- tablespoons fish stock

Directions:
- Preheat the air fryer to 400 F. Cut the bamboo shoots into strips.
- Combine the sliced garlic cloves, olive oil, chili flakes, salt, and fish stock in the air fryer basket tray. Cook for 1 minute.
- Stir the mixture gently. Add the bamboo strips and chives.
- Stir the dish carefully and cook for 3 minutes more.
- Stir again before serving.

Nutrition:
Calories 100
Fat 7.6
Carbs 7
Protein 3.7

232. Summer Eggplant & Zucchini
Basic Recipe
Preparation Time: 15 minutes
Cooking Time: 15 minutes
Servings: 8
Ingredients:
- 1 eggplant
- 1 tomato
- 1 zucchini
- oz chive stems
- green peppers
- 1 teaspoon paprika
- 1 tablespoon olive oil
- ½ teaspoon ground nutmeg
- ½ teaspoon ground thyme
- 1 teaspoon salt

Directions:
- Preheat the air fryer to 390 F.
- Wash the eggplant, tomato, and zucchini carefully.
- Chop all the vegetables roughly.
- Place the chopped vegetables in the air fryer basket tray.
- Coat the vegetables with the paprika, olive oil, ground nutmeg, ground thyme, and salt.
- Stir the vegetables using two spatulas.
- Cut the green peppers into squares.
- Add the squares into the vegetable mixture. Stir gently.
- Cook for 15 minutes, stirring after 10 minutes then serve.

Nutrition:
Calories 48 Fat 2.1
Fiber 3.3 Carbs 7.4
Protein 1.4

233. Zucchini Hassel Back
Basic Recipe
Preparation Time: 15 minutes
Cooking Time: 12 minutes
Servings: 2
Ingredients:
- 1 zucchini
- oz. Cheddar, sliced
- ½ teaspoon salt
- ½ teaspoon dried oregano
- ½ teaspoon ground coriander
- ½ teaspoon paprika
- tablespoons heavy cream
- 1 teaspoon olive oil
- ¼ teaspoon minced garlic

Directions:
- Cut the zucchini into a Hassel back shape.
- Then fill the zucchini with the sliced cheese.

Coat the zucchini Hassel back with salt, dried oregano, ground coriander, paprika, minced garlic, olive oil, and heavy cream.

Preheat the air fryer to 400 F.

Wrap the zucchini Hassel back in foil and place in the preheated air fryer.

Cook for 12 minutes

When the zucchini is cooked, remove it from the foil and cut into 2 pieces.

Nutrition:
Calories 215 Fat 14.9
Carbs 5.7 Protein 15.6

234. Butternut Squash Hash
Basic Recipe
Preparation Time: 10 minutes
Cooking Time: 14 minutes
Servings: 4
Ingredients:
- 1 cup chicken stock
- oz. butternut squash
- 1 teaspoon salt
- 1 tablespoon butter
- 1 teaspoon dried dill
- ¼ teaspoon paprika

Directions:
Peel the butternut squash and chop it.
Preheat the air fryer to 370 F.
Pour the chicken stock into the air fryer basket tray.
Add salt, chopped butternut squash, butter, dried dill, and paprika.
Stir gently.
Cook for 14 minutes
Transfer to a bowl.
Use a fork to mash.
Serve immediately.

Nutrition:
Calories 61
Fat 3.3
Carbs 6.2
Protein 0.9

235. Butter Mushrooms With Chives
Basic Recipe
Preparation Time: 10 minutes
Cooking Time: 10 minutes
Servings: 2
Ingredients:
- 1 cup white mushrooms
- oz chive stems
- 1 tablespoon butter
- 1 teaspoon olive oil
- 1 teaspoon dried rosemary
- 1/3 teaspoon salt
- ¼ teaspoon ground nutmeg

Directions:
Preheat the air fryer to 400 F.
Pour the olive oil and butter in the air fryer basket tray.
Add dried rosemary, salt, and ground nutmeg.
Stir gently.
Dice the chives.
Add the diced chives in the air fryer basket tray.
Cook for 5 minutes
Meanwhile, chop the white mushrooms.
Add the mushrooms.
Stir the mixture and cook it for a further 5 minutes at the same temperature.
Stir then serve.

Nutrition:
Calories 104
Fat 8.4
Carbs 6.8
Protein 1.8

236. Fennel & Spinach Quiche
Basic Recipe
Preparation Time: 15 minutes
Cooking Time: 10 minutes
Servings: 5
Ingredients:
- oz. fennel, chopped

1 cup spinach
eggs
½ cup almond flour
1 teaspoon olive oil
1 tablespoon butter
1 teaspoon salt
¼ cup heavy cream
1 teaspoon ground black pepper

Directions:
- Chop the spinach and combine it with the chopped fennel in a large bowl.
- Crack the egg in a separate bowl and whisk.
- Combine the whisked eggs with the almond flour, butter, salt, heavy cream, and ground black pepper.
- Whisk together to mix
- Preheat the air fryer to 360 F.
- Grease the air fryer basket tray with the olive oil.
- Add both mixtures.
- Cook the quiche for 18 minutes
- Let the quiche cool.
- Remove it from the air fryer and slice into servings.

Nutrition:
Calories 209 Fat 16.1
Carbs 7.4 Protein 8.3

237. Lemony Baby Potatoes
Basic Recipe
Preparation Time: 10 minutes
Cooking Time: 25 minutes
Servings: 6
Ingredients:
- tablespoons olive oil
- springs rosemary, chopped
- tablespoons parsley, chopped
- tablespoons oregano, chopped
- Salt and black pepper to the taste
- 1 tablespoon lemon rind, grated
- garlic cloves, minced
- tablespoons lemon juice
- pounds baby potatoes

Directions:
- In a bowl, mix baby potatoes with oil, rosemary, parsley, oregano, salt, pepper, lemon rind, garlic and lemon juice, toss, transfer potatoes to your air fryer's basket and cook at 356 degrees F for 25 minutes
- Divide potatoes between plates and serve as a side dish.
- Enjoy!

Nutrition:
Calories 204 Fat 4
Carbs 17 Protein 6

238. White Mushrooms With Snow Peas
Basic Recipe
Preparation Time: 10 minutes
Cooking Time: 15 minutes
Servings: 2
Ingredients:
- Salt and black pepper to the taste
- ounces snow peas
- ounces white mushrooms, halved
- 1 yellow onion, cut into rings
- tablespoons coconut aminos
- 1 teaspoon olive oil

Directions:
- In a bowl, snow peas with mushrooms, onion, aminos, oil, salt and pepper, toss well, transfer to a pan that fits your air fryer, introduce in the fryer and cook at 350 degrees F for 15 minutes. Divide between plates and serve as a side dish. Enjoy!

Nutrition:
Calories 175
Fat 4
Carbs 12
Protein 7

239. Gold Potatoes And Bell Pepper Mix

Basic Recipe
Preparation Time: 10 minutes
Cooking Time: 25 minutes
Servings: 4
Ingredients:
- gold potatoes, cubed
- 1 yellow onion, chopped
- teaspoons olive oil
- 1 green bell pepper, chopped
- Salt and black pepper to the taste
- ½ teaspoon thyme, dried

Directions:
- Heat up your air fryer at 350 degrees F, add oil, heat it up, add onion, bell pepper, salt and pepper, stir and cook for 5 minutes
- Add potatoes and thyme, stir, cover and cook at 360 degrees F for 20 minutes
- Divide between plates and serve as a side dish.
- Enjoy!

Nutrition:
Calories 201 Fat 4
Carbs 12 Protein 7

240. Potato With Bell Peppers

Basic Recipe
Preparation Time: 10 minutes
Cooking Time: 25 minutes
Servings: 6
Ingredients:
- ounces jarred roasted red bell peppers, chopped
- garlic cloves, minced
- tablespoons parsley, chopped
- Salt and black pepper to the taste
- tablespoons chives, chopped
- potatoes, peeled and cut into wedges
- Cooking spray

Directions:
- In a pan that fits your air fryer, combine roasted bell peppers with garlic, parsley, salt, pepper, chives, potato wedges and the oil, toss, transfer to your air fryer and cook at 350 degrees F for 25 minutes
- Divide between plates and serve as a side dish.
- Enjoy!

Nutrition:
Calories 212 Fat 6
Carbs 11 Protein 5

241. Chinese Long Beans Mix

Basic Recipe
Preparation Time: 10 minutes
Cooking Time: 10 minutes
Servings: 4
Ingredients:
- ½ teaspoon coconut aminos
- 1 tablespoon olive oil
- A pinch of salt and black pepper
- garlic cloves, minced
- long beans, trimmed and sliced

Directions:
- In a pan that fits your air fryer, combine long beans with oil, aminos, salt, pepper and garlic, toss, introduce in your air fryer and cook at 350 degrees F for 10 minutes
- Divide between plates and serve as a side dish.
- Enjoy!

Nutrition:
Calories 170 Fat 3
Carbs 7 Protein 3

242. Portobello Mushrooms With Spinach

Basic Recipe
Preparation Time: 10 minutes
Cooking Time: 12 minutes
Servings: 4
Ingredients:
- big Portobello mushroom caps

1 tablespoon olive oil
1 cup spinach, torn
1/3 cup vegan breadcrumbs
¼ teaspoon rosemary, chopped

Directions:
- Rub mushrooms caps with the oil, place them in your air fryer's basket and cook them at 350 degrees F for 2 minutes
- Meanwhile, in a bowl, mix spinach, rosemary and breadcrumbs and stir well.
- Stuff mushrooms with this mix, place them in your air fryer's basket again and cook at 350 degrees F for 10 minutes
- Divide them between plates and serve as a side dish.
- Enjoy!

Nutrition:
Calories 152 Fat 4 Carbs 9 Protein 5

243. Summer Squash Mix
Basic Recipe
Preparation Time: 10 minutes
Cooking Time: 10 minutes
Servings: 4
Ingredients:
- ounces coconut cream
- ½ teaspoon oregano, dried
- Salt and black pepper
- 1 big yellow summer squash, peeled and cubed
- 1/3 cup carrot, cubed
- tablespoons olive oil

Directions:
- In a pan that fits your air fryer, combine squash with carrot, oil, oregano, salt, pepper and coconut cream, toss, transfer to your air fryer and cook at 400 degrees F for 10 minutes
- Divide between plates and serve as a side dish. Enjoy!

Nutrition:
Calories 170 Fat 4
Carbs 8 Protein 6

244. Corn With Tomatoes Salad
Basic Recipe
Preparation Time: 10 minutes
Cooking Time: 10 minutes
Servings: 4
Ingredients:
- cups corn
- A Drizzle with of olive oil
- Salt and black pepper to the taste
- 1 teaspoon sweet paprika
- 1 tablespoon stevia
- ½ teaspoon garlic powder
- ½ iceberg lettuce head, cut into medium strips
- ½ romaine lettuce head, cut into medium strips
- 1 cup canned black beans, Dry outed
- tablespoons cilantro, chopped
- green onions, chopped
- cherry tomatoes, sliced

Directions:
- Put the corn in a pan that fits your air fryer, Drizzle with the oil, add salt, pepper, paprika, stevia and garlic powder, introduce in your air fryer and cook at 350 degrees F for 10 minutes
- Transfer corn to a salad bowl, add lettuce, black beans, tomatoes, green onions and cilantro, toss, divide between plates and serve as a side salad.
- Enjoy!

Nutrition:
Calories 162 Fat 6
Carbs 7 Protein 6

245. Colored Veggie Mix
Basic Recipe
Preparation Time: 10 minutes
Cooking Time: 12 minutes
Servings: 6
Ingredients:
- 1 zucchini, sliced in half and roughly chopped

1 orange bell pepper, roughly chopped
1 green bell pepper, roughly chopped
1 red onion, roughly chopped
ounces brown mushrooms, halved
Salt and black pepper to the taste
1 teaspoon Italian seasoning
1 cup cherry tomatoes, halved
½ cup kalamata olives, pitted and halved
¼ cup olive oil
tablespoons balsamic vinegar
tablespoons basil, chopped

Directions:
In a bowl, mix zucchini with mushrooms, orange bell pepper, green bell pepper, red onion, salt, pepper, Italian seasoning and oil, toss well, transfer to preheated air fryer at 380 degrees F and cook them for 12 minutes

In a large bowl, combine mixed veggies with tomatoes, olives, vinegar and basil, toss, divide between plates and serve cold as a side dish.

Enjoy!

Nutrition:
Calories 180
Fat 5
Carbs 10
Protein 6

246. Minty Leeks Medley

Basic Recipe
Preparation Time: 10 minutes
Cooking Time: 12 minutes
Servings: 4
Ingredients:
leeks, roughly chopped
1 tablespoon cumin, ground
1 tablespoon mint, chopped
1 tablespoon parsley, chopped
1 teaspoon garlic, minced
A Drizzle with of olive oil
Salt and black pepper to the taste

Directions:
In a pan that fits your air fryer, combine leeks with cumin, mint, parsley, garlic, salt, pepper and the oil, toss, introduce in your air fryer and cook at 350 degrees F for 12 minutes

Divide Minty Leeks Medley between plates and serve as a side dish.

Enjoy!

Nutrition:
Calories 131 Fat 7
Carbs 10 Protein 6

247. Juicy Pork Chops

Preparation Time: 10 minutes
Cooking Time: 16 minutes
Servings: 4
Ingredients:
4 pork chops, boneless
2 tsp. olive oil
½ tsp. celery seed
½ tsp. parsley
½ tsp. granulated onion
½ tsp. granulated garlic
¼ tsp. sugar
½ tsp. salt

Directions:
In a small bowl, mix together the olive oil, celery seed, parsley, granulated onion, granulated garlic, sugar, and salt.

Rub the seasoning mixture all over the pork chops.

Place the pork chops on the sheet pan and cook at 350°F for 8 minutes.

Turn the pork chops to the other side and cook for 8 minutes more.

Serve and enjoy.

Nutrition:
Calories: 279
Fats: 22.3 g
Carbs: 0.6 g
Protein: 18.1 g

248. Crispy Meatballs

Preparation Time: 10 minutes
Cooking Time: 12 minutes
Servings: 8
Ingredients:
- 1 lb. ground pork
- 1 lb. ground beef
- 1 tbsp. Worcestershire sauce
- ½ cup feta cheese, crumbled
- ½ cup breadcrumbs
- 2 eggs, lightly beaten
- ¼ cup fresh parsley, chopped
- 1 tbsp. garlic, minced
- 1 onion, chopped
- ¼ tsp. pepper
- 1 tsp. salt

Directions:
- Add all the ingredients into the mixing bowl and mix until well combined.
- Spray the sheet pan with cooking spray.
- Make small balls from the meat mixture and arrange them on a pan and air-fry at 400°F for 10–12 minutes.
- Serve and enjoy.

Nutrition:
- Calories: 263
- Fats: 9 g
- Carbs: 7.5 g
- Protein: 35.9 g

249. Flavorful Steak

Preparation Time: 10 minutes
Cooking Time: 18 minutes
Servings: 2
Ingredients:
- 2 steaks, rinsed and pat dry
- ½ tsp. garlic powder
- 1 tsp. olive oil
- Pepper
- Salt

Directions:
- Rub the steaks with olive oil and season with garlic powder, pepper, and salt.
- Preheat the Air Fryer Oven to 400°F.
- Place the steaks on the air fryer oven pan and air-fry for 10–18 minutes, turning halfway through.
- Serve and enjoy.

Nutrition:
- Calories: 361 Fats: 10.9 g
- Carbs: 0.5 g Protein: 61.6 g

250. Lemon Garlic Lamb

Preparation Time: 10 minutes
Cooking Time: 6 minutes
Servings: 6
Ingredients:
- 6 lamb loin chops
- 2 tbsp. fresh lemon juice
- 1 ½ tbsp. lemon zest
- 1 tbsp. dried rosemary
- 1 tbsp. olive oil
- 1 tbsp. garlic, minced
- Pepper
- Salt

Directions:
- Add the lamb chops to a mixing bowl. Add the remaining ingredients on top of the lamb chops and coat well.
- Arrange the lamb chops on Air Fryer Oven tray and air fry at 400°F for 3 minutes. Turn lamb chops to another side and air-fry for 3 minutes more.
- Serve and enjoy.

Nutrition:
- Calories: 69 Fats: 6 g
- Carbs: 1.2 g Protein: 3 g

251. Honey Mustard Pork Tenderloin

Preparation Time: 10 minutes
Cooking Time: 26 minutes
Servings: 4
Ingredients:
- 1 lb. pork tenderloin
- 1 tsp. sriracha sauce

1 tbsp. garlic, minced
2 tbsp. soy sauce
1 ½ tbsp. honey
¾ tbsp. Dijon mustard
1 tbsp. mustard

Directions:

Add the sriracha sauce, garlic, soy sauce, honey, Dijon mustard, and mustard into a large Ziploc® bag and mix well.

Add the pork tenderloin into the bag. Seal bag and place it in the refrigerator overnight. Preheat the Air Fryer Oven to 380°F. Spray the Air Fryer Oven tray with cooking spray, then place the marinated pork tenderloin on a tray and air-fry for 26 minutes. Turn the pork tenderloin after every 5 minutes. Slice and serve.

Nutrition:

Calories: 195 Fats: 4.1 g
Carbs: 8 g
Protein: 30.5 g

252. Easy Rosemary Lamb Chops

Preparation Time: 10 minutes
Cooking Time: 6 minutes
Servings: 4
Ingredients:

4 lamb chops
2 tbsp. dried rosemary
¼ cup fresh lemon juice
Pepper
Salt

Directions:

In a small bowl, mix together the lemon juice, rosemary, pepper, and salt. Brush the lemon juice rosemary mixture over the lamb chops.

Place the lamb chops in the air fry basket and air-fry at 400°F for 3 minutes. Turn the lamb chops to the other side and cook for 3 minutes more. Serve and enjoy.

Nutrition:

Calories: 267
Fats: 21.7 g
Carbs: 1.4 g
Protein: 16.9 g

253. BBQ Pork Ribs

Preparation Time: 10 minutes
Cooking Time: 12 minutes
Servings: 6
Ingredients:

1 slab baby back pork ribs, cut into pieces
½ cup BBQ sauce
½ tsp. paprika
Salt

Directions:

Add the pork ribs in a mixing bowl. Add the BBQ sauce, paprika, and salt over the pork ribs, coat them well and set aside for 30 minutes.

Preheat the Air Fryer Oven to 350°F. Arrange the marinated pork ribs in the Air Fryer Ovenpan and cook for 10–12 minutes, turning halfway through.

Serve and enjoy.

Nutrition:

Calories: 145 Fats: 7 g
Carbs: 10 g Protein: 9 g

254. Juicy Steak Bites

Preparation Time: 10 minutes
Cooking Time: 9 minutes
Servings: 4
Ingredients:

1 lb. sirloin steak, cut into bite-size pieces
1 tbsp. steak seasoning
1 tbsp. olive oil
Pepper
Salt

Directions:

Preheat the Air Fryer Oven to 390°F.

Add the steak pieces into a large mixing bowl. Add the steak seasoning, oil, pepper, and salt over steak pieces and toss until well coated.

Transfer the steak pieces in the Air Fryer Oven pan and air-fry for 5 minutes.

Turn the steak pieces to the other side and cook for 4 minutes more.

Serve and enjoy.

Nutrition:
Calories: 241 Fats: 10.6 g Protein: 34.4 g

255. Greek Lamb Chops

Preparation Time: 10 minutes
Cooking Time: 10 minutes
Servings: 4
Ingredients:
- 2 lbs. lamb chops
- 2 tsp. garlic, minced
- 1 ½ tsp. dried oregano
- ¼ cup fresh lemon juice
- ¼ cup olive oil
- ½ tsp. pepper
- 1 tsp. salt

Directions:

Add the lamb chops in a mixing bowl. Add the remaining ingredients over the lamb chops and coat well.

Arrange the lamb chops on the air fry basket and cook at 400°F for 5 minutes.

Turn the lamb chops and cook for 5 minutes more.

Serve and enjoy.

Nutrition:
Calories: 538 Fats: 29.4 g
Carbs: 1.3 g Protein: 64 g

256. Easy Beef Roast

Preparation Time: 10 minutes
Cooking Time: 45 minutes
Servings: 6
Ingredients:
- 2 ½ lb. beef roast
- 2 tbsp. Italian seasoning

Directions:

Arrange the roast on the rotisserie spite.

Rub the roast with the Italian seasoning then insert into the the Air Fryer Oven oven.

Air-fry at 350°F for 45 minutes or until the internal temperature of the roast reaches 145°F.

Slice and serve.

Nutrition:
Calories: 365 Fats: 13.2 g
Carbs: 0.5 g
Protein: 57.4 g

257. Herb Butter Rib Eye Steak

Preparation Time: 10 minutes
Cooking Time: 14 minutes
Servings: 4
Ingredients:
- 2 lb. rib eye steak, bone-in
- 1 tsp. fresh rosemary, chopped
- 1 tsp. fresh thyme, chopped
- 1 tsp. fresh chives, chopped
- 2 tsp. fresh parsley, chopped
- 1 tsp. garlic, minced
- ¼ cup butter softened
- Pepper
- Salt

Directions:

In a small bowl, combine together the butter and the herbs.

Rub the herb-butter mixture on the rib eye steak and place it in the refrigerator for 30 minutes.

Place the marinated steak in the Air Fryer Ovenpan and cook at 400°F for 12–14 minutes.

Serve and enjoy.

Nutrition:
Calories: 416
Fats: 36.7 g
Carbs: 0.7 g
Protein: 20.3 g

258. Classic Beef Jerky

Preparation Time: 10 minutes
Cooking Time: 4 hours
Servings: 4
Ingredients:
- 2 lbs. London broil, sliced thinly
- 1 tsp. onion powder
- 3 tbsp. brown sugar
- 3 tbsp. soy sauce
- 1 tsp. olive oil
- ¾ tsp. garlic powder

Directions:
- Add all the ingredients except the meat in a large Ziploc® bag.
- Mix until well combined. Add the meat in the bag.
- Seal the bag and massage gently to cover the meat with marinade.
- Let the meat marinate for 1 hour.
- Arrange the marinated meat slices in the Air Fryer Oven tray and dehydrate at 160°F for 4 hours.

Nutrition:
- Calories: 133
- Fats: 4.7 g
- Carbs: 9.4 g
- Protein: 13.4 g

259. BBQ Pork Chops

Preparation Time: 10 minutes
Cooking Time: 7 minutes
Servings: 4
Ingredients:
- 4 pork chops

For the Rub:
- ½ tsp. allspice
- ½ tsp. dry mustard
- 1 tsp. ground cumin
- 1 tsp. garlic powder
- ½ tsp. chili powder
- ½ tsp. paprika
- 1 tbsp. brown sugar
- 1 tsp salt

Directions:
- In a small bowl, mix together all the rub ingredients and rub all over the pork chops.
- Arrange the pork chops in the air fry basket and air-fry at 400°F for 5 minutes.
- Turn the pork chops to other side and air-fry for 2 minutes more.
- Serve and enjoy.

Nutrition:
- Calories: 273
- Fats: 20.2 g
- Carbs: 3.4 g
- Protein: 18.4 g

260. Simple Beef Patties

Preparation Time: 10 minutes
Cooking Time: 13 minutes
Servings: 4
Ingredients:
- 1 lb. ground beef
- ½ tsp. garlic powder
- ¼ tsp. onion powder
- Pepper
- Salt

Directions:
- Preheat the Air Fryer Oven to 400°F.
- Add the ground meat, garlic powder, onion powder, pepper, and salt into the mixing bowl and mix until well combined.
- Make even-shaped patties from the meat mixture and arrange them in the air fryer pan.
- Place the pan in the Air Fryer Oven oven.
- Cook the patties for 10 minutes Turn patties after 5 minutes.
- Serve and enjoy.

Nutrition:
- Calories: 212
- Fats: 7.1 g
- Carbs: 0.4 g
- Protein: 34.5 g

261. Simple Beef Sirloin Roast

Preparation Time: 10 minutes
Cooking Time: 50 minutes
Servings: 8
Ingredients:
- 2 ½ lb. sirloin roast
- Salt and ground black pepper, as required

Directions:
- Rub the roast with salt and black pepper generously.
- Insert the rotisserie rod through the roast.
- Insert the rotisserie forks, one on each side of the rod to secure the rod to the chicken.
- Arrange the drip pan in the bottom of the Air Fryer Oven cooking chamber.
- Select "Roast" and then adjust the temperature to 350°F.
- Set the timer for 50 minutes and press "Start."
- When the display shows "Add Food," press the red lever down and load the left side of the rod into the Air Fryer Oven.
- Now, slide the rod's left side into the groove along the metal bar so it doesn't move. Then, close the door and touch "Rotate." Press the red lever to release the rod when cooking time is complete.
- Remove from the Air Fryer Oven and place the roast onto a platter for about 10 minutes before slicing. With a sharp knife, cut the roast into the desired slice sizes and serve.

Nutrition:
Calories: 201 Fats: 8.8 g
Protein: 28.9 g

262. Seasoned Beef Roast

Preparation Time: 10 minutes
Cooking Time: 45 minutes
Servings: 10
Ingredients:
- 3 lb. beef top roast
- 1 tbsp. olive oil
- 2 tbsp. Montreal steak seasoning

Directions:
- Coat the roast with oil and then rub with the seasoning generously.
- With the help of kitchen twines, tie the roast to keep it compact. Arrange the roast onto the cooking tray.
- Arrange the drip pan in the bottom of the Air Fryer Oven cooking chamber.
- Select "Air Fry" and then adjust the temperature to 360°F. Set the timer for 45 minutes and press "Start."
- When the display shows "Add Food," insert the cooking tray in the center position.
- When the display shows "Turn Food," do nothing.
- When cooking time is complete, remove the tray from Air Fryer Oven and place the roast onto a platter for about 10 minutes before slicing. With a sharp knife, cut the roast into desired slice sizes and serve.

Nutrition:
Calories: 269
Fats: 9.9 g

263. Bacon Wrapped Filet Mignon

Preparation Time: 10 minutes
Cooking Time: 15 minutes
Servings: 2
Ingredients:
- 2 bacon slices
- 2 (4-oz.) filet mignon
- Salt and ground black pepper, as required
- Olive oil cooking spray

Directions:
- Wrap 1 bacon slice around each filet mignon and secure with toothpicks.
- Season the filets lightly with the salt and black pepper.

- Arrange the filet mignon onto a coking rack and spray with cooking spray.
- Place the drip pan in the bottom of the Air Fryer Oven cooking chamber.
- Select "Air Fry" and then adjust the temperature to 375°F.
- Set the timer for 15 minutes and press "Start."
- When the display shows "Add Food," insert the cooking rack in the center position.
- Turn the filets when the display shows "Turn Food."
- When cooking time is complete, remove the rack from the Air Fryer Oven and serve hot.

Nutrition:
Calories: 360
Fats: 19.6 g
Carbs: 0.4 g
Protein: 42.6 g

264. Beef Burger

Preparation Time: 15 minutes
Cooking Time: 18 minutes
Servings: 4
Ingredients:
For the Burgers:
- 1 lb. ground beef
- ½ cup panko breadcrumbs
- ¼ cup onion, chopped finely
- 3 tbsp. Dijon mustard
- 3 tsp. low-sodium soy sauce
- 2 tsp. fresh rosemary, chopped finely
- Salt, to taste

For the Sauce:
- 2 tbsp. Dijon mustard
- 1 tbsp. brown sugar
- 1 tsp. soy sauce
- 4 slices Gruyére cheese

Directions:
- In a large bowl, add all the ingredients and mix until well combined.
- Make 4 equal-sized patties from the mixture.
- Arrange the patties onto a cooking tray.
- Arrange the drip pan in the bottom of the Air Fryer Oven cooking chamber.
- Select "Air Fry" and then adjust the temperature to 370°F.
- Set the timer for 15 minutes and press "Start."
- When the display shows "Add Food" insert the cooking rack in the center position.
- Turn the burgers when the display shows "Turn Food."
- To make the sauce, add the mustard, brown sugar and soy sauce and mix well.
- When cooking time is complete, remove the tray from the Air Fryer Oven and coat the burgers with the sauce.
- Top each burger with 1 cheese slice.
- Return the tray to the cooking chamber and select "Broil."
- Set the timer for 3 minutes and press "Start."
- When cooking time is complete, remove the tray from the Air Fryer Oven and serve hot.

Nutrition:
Calories: 402 Fats: 18 g
Carbs: 6.3 g
Protein: 44.4 g

265. Season and Salt-Cured Beef

Preparation Time: 15 minutes
Cooking Time: 3 hours
Servings: 4
Ingredients:
- 1 ½ lb. beef round, trimmed
- ½ cup Worcestershire sauce
- ½ cup low-sodium soy sauce
- 2 tsp. honey
- 1 tsp. liquid smoke
- 2 tsp. onion powder

½ tsp. red pepper flakes
Ground black pepper, as required

Directions:
- In a ziploc® bag, place the beef and freeze for 1–2 hours.
- Place the meat onto a cutting board and cut against the grain into ⅛–¼-inch strips.
- In a large bowl, add the remaining ingredients and mix until well combined.
- Add the steak slices and coat with the mixture generously.
- Refrigerate to marinate for about 4-6 hours.
- Remove the beef slices from the bowl and with paper towels, pat dry them.
- Divide the steak strips onto the cooking trays and arrange in an even layer.
- Select "Dehydrate" and then adjust the temperature to 160°F.
- Set the timer for 3 hours and press "Start."
- When the display shows "Add Food," insert 1 tray in the top position and another in the center position.
- After 1 ½ hours, switch the position of cooking trays.
- Meanwhile, in a small pan, add the remaining ingredients over medium heat and cook for about 10 minutes, stirring occasionally.
- When cooking the time is complete, remove the trays from the Air Fryer Oven.

Nutrition:
Calories: 372 Fats: 10.7 g
Carbs: 12 g Protein: 53.8 g

266. Sweet & Spicy Meatballs

Preparation Time: 20 minutes
Cooking Time: 30 minutes
Servings: 8
Ingredients:

For the Meatballs:
- 2 lb. lean ground beef
- 2/3 cup quick-cooking oats
- ½ cup Ritz® crackers, crushed
- 1 (5-oz.) can evaporated milk
- 2 large eggs, lightly beaten
- 1 tsp. honey
- 1 tbsp. dried onion, minced
- 1 tsp. garlic powder
- 1 tsp. ground cumin
- Salt and ground black pepper, as required

For the Sauce:
- ⅓ cup orange marmalade
- ⅓ cup honey
- ⅓ cup brown sugar
- 2 tbsp. cornstarch
- 2 tbsp. soy sauce
- 1-2 tbsp. hot sauce
- 1 tbsp. Worcestershire sauce

Directions:
- To make the meat balls, add all the ingredients and mix until well combined.
- Make 1 ½-inch balls from the mixture.
- Arrange half of the meatballs onto a cooking tray in a single layer.
- Arrange the drip pan in the bottom of the Air Fryer Oven cooking chamber.
- Select "Air Fry" and then adjust the temperature to 380°F.
- Set the timer for 15 minutes and press "Start."
- When the display shows "Add Food," insert the cooking tray in the center position.
- Turn the meat balls when the display shows "Turn Food."
- When cooking time is complete, remove the tray from the Air Fryer Oven.
- Repeat with the remaining meatballs.
- To make the sauce, add all the ingredients in a small pan over medium heat and stir continuously.
- Serve the meatballs with the sauce.

Nutrition:
Calories: 411 Fats: 11.1 g
Carbs: 38.8 g Protein: 38.9 g

267. Spiced Pork Shoulder

Preparation Time: 15 minutes
Cooking Time: 55 minutes
Servings: 6
Ingredients:
- 1 tsp. ground cumin
- 1 tsp. cayenne pepper
- 1 tsp. garlic powder
- Salt and ground black pepper, as required
- 2 lb. pork shoulder, skin-on

Directions:
- In a small bowl, mix together the spices, salt and black pepper.
- Arrange the pork shoulder skin-side down on a cutting board.
- Season the inner side of the pork shoulder with salt and black pepper.
- With kitchen twines, tie the pork shoulder into a long round cylinder shape.
- Season the outer side of the pork shoulder with the spice mixture.
- Insert the rotisserie rod through the pork shoulder.
- Insert 1 rotisserie fork on each side of the rod to secure the pork shoulder.
- Arrange the drip pan in the bottom of the Air Fryer Oven cooking chamber.
- Select "Roast" and then adjust the temperature to 350°F.
- Set the timer for 55 minutes and press the "Start."
- When the display shows "Add Food," press the red lever down and load the left side of the rod into the Air Fryer Oven.
- Now slide the rod's left side into the groove along the metal bar so it doesn't move.
- Then close the door and touch "Rotate."
- Press the red lever to release the rod when cooking time is complete.
- Remove the pork from the Air Fryer Oven and place onto a platter for about 10 minutes before slicing.
- With a sharp knife, cut the pork shoulder into the desired slice sizes and serve.

Nutrition:
- Calories: 445
- Fats: 32.5 g
- Carbs: 0.7 g
- Protein: 35.4 g

268. Seasoned Pork Tenderloin

Preparation Time: 10 minutes
Cooking Time: 45 minutes
Servings: 5
Ingredients:
- 1 ½ lb. pork tenderloin
- 2–3 tbsp. BBQ pork seasoning

Directions:
- Rub the pork with seasoning generously. Insert the rotisserie rod through the pork tenderloin.
- Insert the rotisserie forks, one on each side of the rod to secure the pork tenderloin.
- Arrange the drip pan in the bottom of the Air Fryer Oven cooking chamber.
- Select "Roast" and then adjust the temperature to 360 degrees F.
- Set the timer for 45 minutes and press "Start."
- When the display shows "Add Food," press the red lever down and load the left side of the rod into the Air Fryer Oven.
- Now, slide the rod's left side into the groove along the metal bar so it doesn't move.
- Then, close the door and touch "Rotate."
- Press the red lever to release the rod when cooking time is complete.
- Remove the pork from the Air Fryer Oven and place onto a platter for about 10 minutes before slicing.
- With a sharp knife, cut the roast into desired slice sizes and serve.

Nutrition:
- Calories: 195 Fats: 4.8 g
- Protein: 35.6 g

269. Garlicky Pork Tenderloin

Preparation Time: 15 minutes
Cooking Time: 20 minutes
Servings: 5
Ingredients:
- 1 ½ lb. pork tenderloin
- Non-stick cooking spray
- 2 small heads roasted garlic
- Salt and ground black pepper, as required

Directions:
- Lightly, spray all the sides of pork with cooking spray and season with salt and black pepper.
- Now, rub the pork with roasted garlic. Arrange the roast onto the lightly greased cooking tray.
- Arrange the drip pan in the bottom of the Air Fryer Oven cooking chamber.
- Select "Air Fry" and then adjust the temperature to 400°F. Set the timer for 20 minutes and press the "Start."
- When the display shows "Add Food" insert the cooking tray in the center position.
- Turn the pork when the display shows "Turn Food."
- When cooking time is complete, remove the tray from the Air Fryer Oven and place the pork onto a platter for about 10 minutes before slicing. With a sharp knife, cut the pork into desired slice sizes and serve.

Nutrition:
- Calories: 202
- Fats: 4.8 g
- Carbs: 1.7 g
- Protein: 35.9 g

270. Glazed Pork Tenderloin

Preparation Time: 15 minutes
Cooking Time: 20 minutes
Servings: 3
Ingredients:
- 1-lb. pork tenderloin
- 2 tbsp. Sriracha
- 2 tbsp. honey
- Salt, as required

Directions:
- Insert the rotisserie rod through the pork tenderloin.
- Insert 1 rotisserie fork on each side of the rod to secure the pork tenderloin.
- In a small bowl, add the Sriracha, honey and salt and mix well.
- Brush the pork tenderloin evenly with honey mixture.
- Arrange the drip pan in the bottom of the Air Fryer Oven cooking chamber.
- Select "Air Fry" and then adjust the temperature to 350°F.
- Set the timer for 20 minutes and press the "Start."
- When the display shows "Add Food," press the red lever down and load the left side of the rod into the Air Fryer Oven.
- Now, slide the rod's left side into the groove along the metal bar so it doesn't move.
- Then, close the door and touch "Rotate."
- Press the red lever to release the rod when cooking time is complete.
- Remove the pork from the Air Fryer Oven and place onto a platter for about 10 minutes before slicing.
- With a sharp knife, cut the pork into desired slice sizes and serve.

Nutrition:
- Calories: 269 Fats: 5.3 g
- Carbs: 13.5 g
- Protein: 39.7 g

271. Country Style Pork Tenderloin

Preparation Time: 15 minutes
Cooking Time: 25 minutes
Servings: 3
Ingredients:
- 1 lb. pork tenderloin

1 tbsp. garlic, minced
2 tbsp. soy sauce
2 tbsp. honey
1 tbsp. Dijon mustard
1 tbsp. grain mustard
1 tsp. Sriracha sauce

Directions:

In a large bowl, add all the ingredients except the pork and mix well.

Add the pork tenderloin and coat with the mixture generously.

Refrigerate to marinate for 2–3 hours.

Remove the pork tenderloin from the bowl, reserving the marinade.

Place the pork tenderloin on a lightly greased cooking tray.

Arrange the drip pan in the bottom of the Air Fryer Oven cooking chamber.

Select "Air Fry" and then adjust the temperature to 380°F.

Set the timer for 25 minutes and press the "Start."

When the display shows "Add Food," insert the cooking tray in the center position.

Turn the pork when the display shows "Turn Food" and coat it with the reserved marinade.

When cooking time is complete, remove the tray from the Air Fryer Oven and place the pork tenderloin onto a platter for about 10 minutes before slicing.

With a sharp knife, cut the pork tenderloin into the desired slice sizes and serve.

Nutrition:

Calories: 277 Fats: 5.7 g
Carbs: 14.2 g Protein: 40.7 g

272. Seasoned Pork Chops

Preparation Time: 10 minutes
Cooking Time: 12 minutes
Servings: 4
Ingredients:

4 (6-oz.) pork chops, boneless
2 tbsp. pork rub
1 tbsp. olive oil

Directions:

Coat both sides of the pork chops with the oil and the pork rub.

Place the pork chops onto the lightly greased cooking tray.

Arrange the drip pan in the bottom of the Air Fryer Oven cooking chamber.

Select "Air Fry" and then adjust the temperature to 400°F.

Set the timer for 12 minutes and press "Start."

When the display shows "Add Food," insert the cooking tray in the center position.

Turn the pork chops when the display shows "Turn Food."

When cooking time is complete, remove the tray from the Air Fryer Oven and serve hot.

Nutrition:

Calories: 285
Fats: 9.5 g
Carbs: 1.5 g
Protein: 44.5 g

273. Breaded Pork Chops

Preparation Time: 15 minutes
Cooking Time: 28 minutes
Servings: 2
Ingredients:

2 (5-oz.) boneless pork chops
1 cup buttermilk
½ cup flour
1 tsp. garlic powder
Salt and ground black pepper, as required
Olive oil cooking spray

Directions:

In a bowl, place the chops and buttermilk and refrigerate, covered for about 12 hours.

Remove the chops from the bowl and discard the buttermilk.

In a shallow dish, mix together the flour, garlic powder, salt, and black pepper.

Coat the chops generously with flour mixture.

Place the pork chops onto the cooking tray and spray with the cooking spray.

Arrange the drip pan in the bottom of the Air Fryer Oven cooking chamber.

Select "Air Fry" and then adjust the temperature to 380°F.

Set the timer for 28 minutes and press the "Start."

When the display shows "Add Food," insert the cooking tray in the center position.

Turn the pork chops when the display shows "Turn Food."

When cooking time is complete, remove the tray from the Air Fryer Oven and serve hot.

Nutrition:
Calories: 370
Fats: 6.4 g
Carbs: 30.7 g
Protein: 44.6 g

274. Crusted Rack of Lamb

Preparation Time: 15 minutes
Cooking Time: 19 minutes **Servings:** 4
Ingredients:
- 1 rack of lamb, fat removed
- Salt and ground black pepper, as required
- ⅓ cup pistachios, chopped finely
- 2 tbsp. panko breadcrumbs
- 2 tsp. fresh thyme, chopped finely
- 1 tsp. fresh rosemary, chopped finely
- 1 tbsp. butter, melted
- 1 tbsp. Dijon mustard

Directions:

Insert the rotisserie rod through the rack on the meaty side of the ribs, right next to the bone.

Insert 1 rotisserie fork on each side of the rod to secure the rack.

Season the rack with salt and black pepper evenly.

Arrange the drip pan in the bottom of the Air Fryer Oven cooking chamber.

Select "Air Fry" and then adjust the temperature to 380°F.

Set the timer for 12 minutes and press the "Start."

When the display shows "Add Food," press the red lever down and load the left side of the rod into the Air Fryer Oven.

Now slide the rod's left side into the groove along the metal bar so it doesn't move.

Then, close the door and touch "Rotate."

Mix together the remaining ingredients in a small bowl, except the mustard.

Press the red lever to release the rod when cooking time is complete.

Remove the rack from the Air Fryer Oven and brush the meaty side with the mustard.

Then coat the pistachio mixture on all sides of the rack and press firmly.

Now place the rack of lamb onto the cooking tray, meat side up.

Select "Air Fry" and adjust the temperature to 380°F.

Set the timer for 7 minutes and press the "Start."

When the display shows "Add Food," insert the cooking tray in the center position.

When the display shows "Turn Food" do nothing.

When cooking time is complete, remove the tray from the Air Fryer Oven and place the rack onto a cutting board for at least 10 minutes

Cut the rack into individual chops and serve.

Nutrition:
Calories: 824 Fats: 39.3 g
Carbs: 10.3 g Protein: 72 g

275. Lamb Burgers

Preparation Time: 15 minutes
Cooking Time: 8 minutes
Servings: 6
Ingredients:
- 2 lb. ground lamb
- 1 tbsp. onion powder
- Salt and ground black pepper, as required

Directions:
- In a bowl, add all the ingredients and mix well.
- Make 6 equal-sized patties from the mixture.
- Arrange the patties on a cooking tray.
- Arrange the drip pan in the bottom of Air Fryer Oven cooking chamber.
- Select "Air Fry" and then adjust the temperature to 360 degrees F.
- Set the timer for 8 minutes and press "Start."
- When the display shows "Add Food," insert the cooking rack in the center position.
- Turn the burgers when the display shows "Turn Food."
- When cooking time is complete, remove the tray from Air Fryer Oven and serve hot.

Nutrition:
- Calories: 285
- Fats: 11.1 g
- Carbs: 0.9 g
- Protein: 42.6 g

276. Salmon

Preparation Time: 5 minutes
Cooking Time: 12 minutes
Servings: 2
Ingredients
- 2 salmon fillets, wild-caught, each about 1 ½-inch thick
- 1 tsp. ground black pepper
- 2 tsp. paprika
- 1 tsp. salt
- 2 tsp. olive oil

Directions:
- Switch the Air Fryer Oven on, insert the basket, grease it with olive oil, close it and set it at 390ºF. Meanwhile, rub each salmon fillet with oil and then season with black pepper, paprika, and salt.
- Open the , add seasoned salmon in it, close the Air Fryer Oven and cook for 7 minutes, or until nicely golden and cooked, flipping the fillets halfway through the frying. When the Air Fryer Oven beeps, open its lid and transfer the salmon onto a serving plate and serve.

Nutrition:
- Calories: 288
- Carbs: 1.4 g
- Fats: 18.9 g
- Protein: 28.3 g

277. Parmesan Shrimp

Preparation Time: 10 minutes
Cooking Time: 10 minutes
Servings: 6
Ingredients
- 2 lb. jumbo shrimp, wild-caught, peeled, deveined
- 2 tbsp. minced garlic
- 1 tsp. onion powder
- 1 tsp. basil
- 1 tsp. ground black pepper
- ½ tsp. dried oregano
- 2 tbsp. olive oil
- 2/3 cup grated parmesan cheese, reduced fat
- 2 tbsp. lemon juice

Directions:
- Switch the Air Fryer Oven on, insert the basket, grease it with olive oil, close it and set it at 350ºF.
- Meanwhile, place the cheese in a bowl, add the remaining ingredients except the

shrimps and the lemon juice, and stir until combined.

Add the shrimps and then toss until well coated.

Open the Air Fryer Oven, add the shrimps, spray oil over them, close the Air Fryer Oven and cook for 10 minutes, or until nicely golden and crispy, shaking halfway through the frying. When air fryer beeps, open its lid, transfer chicken onto a serving plate, and drizzle with lemon juice and serve.

Nutrition:
Calories: 307 Carbs: 12 g
Fats: 16.4 g Protein: 27.6 g

278. Shrimp with Lemon and Chile

Preparation Time: 5 minutes
Cooking Time: 12 minutes
Servings: 2
Ingredients:

1 lb. shrimp, wild-caught, peeled, deveined
1 lemon, sliced
1 small red chili pepper, sliced
½ tsp. ground black pepper
½ tsp. garlic powder
1 tsp. salt
1 tbsp. olive oil

Directions:

Switch the Air Fryer Oven on, insert the basket, grease it with olive oil, close it and set it at 400ºF.

Meanwhile, place the shrimps in a bowl, add the garlic, salt, black pepper, oil, and lemon slices and toss until combined. Open the Air Fryer Oven, add shrimps and lemon in it, close it, and cook for 5 minutes, shaking halfway through the frying. Then add the chili slices, shake the basket until mixed and continue cooking for 2 minutes or until shrimps are opaque and crispy. When the Air Fryer Oven beeps, open its lid, transfer shrimps and lemon slices onto a serving plate and serve.

Nutrition:
Calories: 112.5
Carbs: 1 g
Fats: 1 g
Protein: 2 g

279. Tilapia

Preparation Time: 5 minutes
Cooking Time: 12 minutes
Servings: 2
Ingredients:

2 tilapia fillets, wild-caught, 1 ½ inch thick
1 tsp. OLD BAY® seasoning
¾ tsp. lemon pepper seasoning
½ tsp. salt

Directions:

Switch the Air Fryer Oven on, insert the basket, grease it with olive oil, close it and set it at 400ºF.

Meanwhile, spray the tilapia fillets with the oil and then season with the salt, lemon pepper, and OLD BAY® seasoning until evenly coated. Open the fryer, add the tilapia in it, close it and cook for 7 minutes, or until nicely golden and cooked, turning the fillets halfway through the frying. When Air Fryer Oven beeps, open its lid, transfer tilapia fillets onto a serving plate and serve.

Nutrition:
Calories: 36
Fats: 0.75 g
Protein: 7.4 g

280. Tomato Basil Scallops

Preparation Time: 5 minutes
Cooking Time: 15 minutes
Servings: 2
Ingredients:

8 jumbo sea scallops, wild-caught

- 1 tbsp. tomato paste
- 12 lb. frozen spinach, thawed and dried out
- 1 tbsp. fresh basil, chopped
- 1 tsp. ground black pepper
- 1 tsp. minced garlic
- 1 tsp. salt
- ¾ cup heavy whipping cream, reduced fat

Directions:
- Switch the Air Fryer Oven on, insert the basket, grease it with olive oil, close it and set it at 350ºF.
- Meanwhile, take a 7-inch baking pan, grease it with oil and place the spinach in it in an even layer.
- Spray the scallops with oil, sprinkle with ½ tsp. each of salt and black pepper and then place the scallops over the spinach.
- Place the tomato paste in a bowl, whisk in the cream, basil, garlic, and remaining salt and black pepper until smooth, and then pour over the scallops.
- Open the fryer, place the pan in it, close it and cook for 10 minutes, or until thoroughly cooked and hot.
- Serve straight away.

Nutrition:
- Calories: 359
- Carbs: 6 g
- Fats: 33 g
- Protein: 9 g

281. Shrimp Scampi

Preparation Time: 5 minutes
Cooking Time: 12 minutes
Servings: 4
Ingredients:
- 1 lb. shrimp, peeled, deveined
- 1 tbsp. minced garlic
- 1 tbsp. minced basil
- 1 tbsp. lemon juice
- 1 tsp. dried chives
- 1 tsp. dried basil
- 2 tsp. red pepper flakes
- 4 tbsp. butter, unsalted
- 2 tbsp. chicken stock

Directions:
- Switch the Air Fryer Oven on, insert the basket, grease it with olive oil, close it and set it at 350ºF.
- Add the butter in it along with the red pepper and garlic and cook for 2 minutes or until the butter has melted.
- Then add the remaining ingredients in the pan, stir until mixed and continue cooking for 5 minutes, or until shrimps have cooked, stirring halfway through.
- When done, remove the pan from the Air Fryer Oven, stir the shrimp scampi, let it rest for 1 minute and then stir again.
- Garnish the shrimps with the basil leaves and serve.

Nutrition:
- Calories: 221
- Carbs: 1 g
- Fats: 13 g
- Protein: 23 g

282. Salmon Cakes

Preparation Time: 5 minutes
Cooking Time: 12 minutes
Servings: 2
Ingredients:
- ½ cup almond flour
- 15 oz. cooked pink salmon
- ¼ tsp. ground black pepper
- 2 tsp. Dijon mustard
- 2 tbsp. chopped fresh dill
- 2 tbsp. mayonnaise, reduced fat
- 1 egg, pastured
- 2 lemon wedges

Directions:
- Switch the Air Fryer Oven on, insert the basket, grease it with olive oil, close it and set it at 350ºF.
- Meanwhile, place all the ingredients in a bowl, except for the lemon wedges, stir

until combined and then shape into four patties, each about 4 inches. Open the fryer, add the salmon patties in it, spray oil over them, close it and cook for 12 minutes or until nicely golden and crispy, flipping the patties halfway through the frying.

When Air Fryer Oven beeps, open its lid, transfer salmon patties onto a serving plate and serve.

Nutrition:
Calories: 517
Carbs: 15 g
Fats: 27 g
Protein: 52 g

283. Cilantro Lime Shrimps
Preparation Time: 25 minutes
Cooking Time: 21 minutes
Servings: 4
Ingredients:
- ½-lb. shrimp, peeled, deveined
- ½ tsp. minced garlic
- 1 tbsp. cilantro, chopped
- ½ tsp. paprika
- ¾ tsp. salt
- ½ tsp. ground cumin
- 2 tbsp. lemon juice

Directions:
- Take 6 wooden skewers and let them soak in warm water for 20 minutes
- Meanwhile, switch the Air Fryer Oven on, insert the basket, grease it with olive oil, close it and set it at 350ºF.
- Whisk together the lemon juice, paprika, salt, cumin, and garlic in a large bowl, then add the shrimps and toss until well coated.
- Dry out the skewers and then thread the shrimps in them.
- Open the fryer, add the shrimps in it in a single layer, spray oil over them, close it and cook for 8 minutes or until nicely golden and cooked, turning the skewers halfway through the frying.
- When Air Fryer Oven beeps, open it, transfer shrimps onto a serving plate and keep them warm.
- Cook the remaining shrimp skewers in the same manner and serve.

Nutrition:
Calories: 59
Carbs: 0.3 g
Fats: 1.5 g
Protein: 11 g

284. Cajun Style Shrimp
Preparation Time: 3 minutes
Cooking Time: 10 minutes
Servings: 2
Ingredients:
- ⅛ oz. salt
- 1/16 oz. smoked paprika
- 1/16 oz. garlic powder
- 1/16 oz. Italian seasoning
- 1/16 oz. chili powder
- ⅟32 oz. onion powder
- ⅟32 oz. cayenne pepper
- ⅟32 oz. black pepper
- ⅟32 oz. dried thyme
- 1 lb. large shrimp, peeled and unveiled
- 2 tbsp. olive oil
- Lime wedges, for serving

Directions:
- Select "Preheat" in the Air Fryer Oven , set the temperature to 190°C and press "Start/Pause." Combine all the seasonings in a large bowl. Set aside
- Mix the shrimp with the olive oil until they are evenly coated. Sprinkle the dressing mixture over the shrimp and stir until well coated. Place the shrimp in the preheated Air Fryer Oven .

Select the Shrimp set the time to 5 minutes and press "Start/Pause." Shake the baskets in the middle of cooking. Serve with lime wedges.

Nutrition:
Calories: 126
Fats: 6 g
Carbs: 2 g
Protein: 33 g

CHAPTER 6:

Dinner

285. Crispy Indian Wrap
Basic Recipe
Preparation Time: 20 minutes
Cooking Time: 8 minutes
Servings: 4
Ingredients:
- Cilantro Chutney
- 2¾ cups diced potato, cooked until tender
- teaspoons oil (coconut, sunflower, or safflower)
- large garlic cloves, minced or pressed
- 1½ tablespoons fresh lime juice
- 1½ teaspoons cumin powder
- 1 teaspoon onion granules
- 1 teaspoon coriander powder
- ½ teaspoon sea salt
- ½ teaspoon turmeric
- ¼ teaspoon cayenne powder
- large flour tortillas, preferably whole grain or sprouted
- 1 cup cooked garbanzo beans (canned are fine), rinsed and Dry out
- ½ cup finely chopped cabbage
- ¼ cup minced red onion or scallion
- Cooking oil spray (sunflower, safflower, or refined coconut)

Directions:
- Make the Cilantro Chutney and set aside.
- In a large bowl, mash the potatoes well, using a potato masher or large fork. Add the oil, garlic, lime, cumin, onion, coriander, salt, turmeric, and cayenne. Stir very well, until thoroughly combined. Set aside.
- Lay the tortillas out flat on the counter. In the middle of each, evenly distribute the potato filling. Add some of the garbanzo beans, cabbage, and red onion to each, on top of the potatoes.
- Spray the air fryer basket with oil and set aside. Enclose the Indian wraps by folding the bottom of the tortillas up and over the filling, then folding the sides in—and finally rolling the bottom up to form, essentially, an enclosed burrito.
- Place the wraps in the air fryer basket, seam side down. They can touch each other a little bit, but if they're too crowded, you'll need to cook them in batches. Fry for 5 minutes Spray with oil again, flip over, and cook an additional 2 or 3 minutes, until nicely browned and crisp. Serve topped with the Cilantro Chutney.

Nutrition:
Calories 288 Fat 7g
Carbs 50g Protein 9g

286. Easy Peasy Pizza
Basic Recipe
Preparation Time: 5 minutes
Cooking Time: 10 minutes
Servings: 4
Ingredients:
- Cooking oil spray (coconut, sunflower, or safflower)
- 1 flour tortilla, preferably sprouted or whole grain
- ¼ cup vegan pizza or marinara sauce
- ⅓ Cup grated vegan mozzarella cheese or Cheesy Sauce
- Toppings of your choice

Directions:
- Spray the air fryer basket with oil. Place the tortilla in the air fryer basket. If the tortilla is a little bigger than the base, no problem! Simply fold the edges up a bit to form a semblance of a "crust."
- Pour the sauce in the center, and evenly distribute it around the tortilla "crust" (I like to use the back of a spoon for this purpose).
- Sprinkle evenly with vegan cheese, and add your toppings. Bake it for 9 minutes, or until nicely browned.

Remove carefully, cut into four pieces, and enjoy.

Nutrition:
Calories 210
Fat 6g
Carbs 33g
Protein 5g

287. Eggplant Parmigiana
Basic Recipe
Preparation Time: 15 minutes
Cooking Time: 40 minutes
Servings: 4
Ingredients:
- 1 medium eggplant (about 1 pound), sliced into ½-inch-thick rounds
- tablespoons tamari or shoyu
- tablespoons nondairy milk, plain and unsweetened
- 1 cup chickpea flour (see Substitution Tip)
- 1 tablespoon dried basil
- 1 tablespoon dried oregano
- teaspoons garlic granules
- teaspoons onion granules
- ½ teaspoon sea salt
- ½ teaspoons freshly ground black pepper
- Cooking oil spray (sunflower, safflower, or refined coconut)
- Vegan marinara sauce (your choice)
- Shredded vegan cheese (preferably mozzarella; see Ingredient Tip)

Directions:
- Place the eggplant slices in a large bowl, and pour the tamari and milk over the top. Turn the pieces over to coat them as evenly as possible with the liquids. Set aside.
- Make the coating: In a medium bowl, combine the flour, basil, oregano, garlic, onion, salt, and pepper and stir well. Set aside.
- Spray the air fryer basket with oil and set aside.
- Stir the eggplant slices again and transfer them to a plate (stacking is fine). Do not discard the liquid in the bowl.
- Bread the eggplant by tossing an eggplant round in the flour mixture. Then, dip in the liquid again. Double up on the coating by placing the eggplant again in the flour mixture, making sure that all sides are nicely breaded. Place in the air fryer basket.
- Repeat with enough eggplant rounds to make a (mostly) single layer in the air fryer basket. (You'll need to cook it in batches, so that you don't have too much overlap and it cooks perfectly.)
- Spray the tops of the eggplant with enough oil so that you no longer see dry patches in the coating. Fry for 8 minutes. Remove the air fryer basket and spray the tops again. Turn each piece over, again taking care not to overlap the rounds too much. Spray the tops with oil, again making sure that no dry patches remain. Fry for another 8 minutes, or until nicely browned and crisp.
- Repeat steps 5 to 7 one more time, or until all of the eggplant is crisp and browned.
- Finally, place half of the eggplant in a 6-inch round, 2-inch deep baking pan and top with marinara sauce and a sprinkle of vegan cheese. Fry for 3 minutes, or until the sauce is hot and cheese is melted (be careful not to overcook, or the eggplant edges will burn). Serve immediately, plain or over pasta. Otherwise, you can store the eggplant in the fridge for several days and then make a fresh batch whenever the mood strikes by repeating this step!

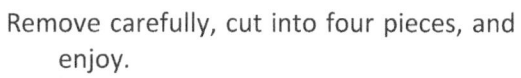

Nutrition:
Calories 217 Fat 9g
Carbs 38g Protein 9g

288. Luscious Lazy Lasagna

Basic Recipe
Preparation Time: 15 minutes
Cooking Time: 15 minutes
Servings: 4
Ingredients:

- ounces lasagna noodles, preferably bean-based, but any kind will do
- 1 tablespoon extra-virgin olive oil
- cups crumbled extra-firm tofu, Dry out and water squeezed out
- cups loosely packed fresh spinach
- tablespoons nutritional yeast
- tablespoons fresh lemon juice
- 1 teaspoon onion granules
- 1 teaspoon sea salt
- ⅛ Teaspoon freshly ground black pepper
- large garlic cloves, minced or pressed
- cups vegan pasta sauce, your choice
- ½ cup shredded vegan cheese (preferably mozzarella)

Directions:

- Cook the noodles until a little firmer than al dente (they'll get a little softer after you air-fry them in the lasagna). Dry out and set aside.
- While the noodles are cooking, make the filling. In a large pan over medium-high heat, add the olive oil, tofu, and spinach. Stir-fry for a minute, then add the nutritional yeast, lemon juice, onion, salt, pepper, and garlic. Stir well and cook just until the spinach is nicely wilted. Remove from heat.
- To make half a batch (one 6-inch round, 2-inch deep baking pan) of lasagna: Spread a thin layer of pasta sauce in the baking pan. Layer 2 or 3 lasagna noodles on top of the sauce. Top with a little more sauce and some of the tofu mixture. Place another 2 or 3 noodles on top, and add another layer of sauce and then another layer of tofu. Finish with a layer of noodles, and then a final layer of sauce. Sprinkle about half of the vegan cheese on top (omit if you prefer; see the Ingredient Tip from the Eggplant Parmigiana). Place the pan in the air fryer and Bake it for 15 minutes, or until the noodles are browning around the edges and the cheese is melted. Cut and serve.

Nutrition:
Calories 317
Fat 8g
Carbs 46g
Protein 20g

289. Pasta With Creamy Cauliflower Sauce

Basic Recipe
Preparation Time: 10 minutes
Cooking Time: 20 minutes
Servings: 4
Ingredients:

- cups cauliflower florets
- Cooking oil spray (sunflower, Safflower, or refined coconut)
- 1 medium onion, chopped
- ounces pasta, your choice (about 4 cups cooked; use gluten-free pasta if desired)
- Fresh chives or scallion tops, for garnish
- ½ cup raw cashew pieces (see Ingredient Tip)
- 1½ cups water
- 1 tablespoon nutritional yeast
- large garlic cloves, peeled
- tablespoons fresh lemon juice
- 1½ teaspoons sea salt
- ¼ teaspoons freshly ground black pepper

Directions:

- Place the cauliflower in the air fryer basket, sprits the tops with oil spray, and roast for 8 minutes Remove the air fryer basket, stir, and add the onion. Sprits with oil again and roast for another 10

minutes, or until the cauliflower is browned and the onions are tender.
- While the vegetables are roasting in the air fryer, cook the pasta according to the package directions and mince the chives or scallions. Set aside.
- In a blender jar, place the roasted cauliflower and onions along with the cashews, water, nutritional yeast, garlic, lemon, salt, and pepper. Blend well, until very smooth and creamy. Serve a generous portion of the sauce on top of the warm pasta, and top with the minced chives or scallions. The sauce will store, refrigerated in an airtight container, for about a week.

Nutrition:
Calories 341
Fat 9g
Carbs 51g
Protein 14g

290. Lemony Lentils With "Fried" Onions

Basic Recipe
Preparation Time: 10 minutes
Cooking Time: 30 minutes
Servings: 4
Ingredients:
- 1 cup red lentils
- cups water
- Cooking oil spray (coconut, sunflower, or safflower)
- 1 medium-size onion, peeled and cut into ¼-inch-thick rings
- Sea salt
- ½ cup kale, stems removed, thinly sliced
- large garlic cloves, pressed or minced
- tablespoons fresh lemon juice
- teaspoons nutritional yeast
- 1 teaspoon sea salt
- 1 teaspoon lemon zest (see Ingredient Tip)
- ¾ teaspoons freshly ground black pepper

Directions:
- In a medium-large pot, bring the lentils and water to a boil over medium-high heat.
- Reduce the heat to low and simmer, uncovered, for about 30 minutes (or until the lentils have dissolved completely), making sure to stir every 5 minutes or so as they cook (so that the lentils don't stick to the bottom of the pot).
- While the lentils are cooking, get the rest of your dish together.
- Spray the air fryer basket with oil and place the onion rings inside, separating them as much as possible. Spray them with the oil and sprinkle with a little salt. Fry for 5 minutes.
- Remove the air fryer basket, shake or stir, spray again with oil, and fry for another 5 minutes.
- (Note: You're aiming for all of the onion slices to be crisp and well browned, so if some of the pieces begin to do that, transfer them from the air fryer basket to a plate.)
- Remove the air fryer basket, spray the onions again with oil, and fry for a final 5 minutes or until all the pieces are crisp and browned.
- To finish the lentils: Add the kale to the hot lentils, and stir very well, as the heat from the lentils will steam the thinly sliced greens.
- Stir in the garlic, lemon juice, nutritional yeast, salt, zest, and pepper.
- Stir very well and then distribute evenly in bowls. Top with the crisp onion rings and serve.

Nutrition:
Calories 220
Fat 1g
Carbs 39g
Protein 15g

291. Our Daily Bean

Basic Recipe
Preparation Time: 5 minutes
Cooking Time: 10 minutes
Servings: 4

Ingredients:
- 1 (15-ounce) can pinto beans, Dry out
- ¼ cup tomato sauce
- tablespoons nutritional yeast
- large garlic cloves, pressed or minced
- ½ teaspoon dried oregano
- ½ teaspoon cumin
- ¼ teaspoon sea salt
- ⅛ Teaspoon freshly ground black pepper
- Cooking oil spray (sunflower, safflower, or refined coconut)

Directions:
- In a medium bowl, stir together the beans, tomato sauce, nutritional yeast, garlic, oregano, cumin, salt, and pepper until well combined.
- Spray the 6-inch round, 2-inch deep baking pan with oil and pour the bean mixture into it. Bake it for 4 minutes Remove, stir well, and Bake it for another 4 minutes, or until the mixture has thickened and is heated through. It will most likely form a little crust on top and be lightly browned in spots. Serve hot. This will keep, refrigerated in an airtight container, for up to a week.

Nutrition:
Calories 284
Fat 4g
Carbs 47g
Protein 20g

292. Taco Salad With Creamy Lime Sauce

Basic Recipe
Preparation Time: 10 minutes
Cooking Time: 10 minutes
Servings: 4

Ingredients:
For The Sauce
- 1 (12.3-ounce) package of silken-firm tofu
- ¼ cup plus 1 tablespoon fresh lime juice
- Zest of 1 large lime (1 teaspoon)
- 1½ tablespoons coconut sugar
- large garlic cloves, peeled
- 1 teaspoon sea salt
- ½ teaspoon ground chipotle powder

For The Salad
- cups romaine lettuce, chopped (1 large head)
- 1 (15-ounce) can vegan refried beans (or whole pinto or black beans if you prefer)
- 1 cup chopped red cabbage
- medium tomatoes, chopped
- ½ cup chopped cilantro
- ¼ cup minced scallions
- Double batch of garlic lime tortilla chips

Directions:
To Make the Sauce
- Dry out the tofu (pour off any liquid) and place in a blender.
- Add the lime juice and zest, coconut sugar, garlic, salt, and chipotle powder. Blend until very smooth. Set aside.

To Make the Salad
- Distribute the lettuce equally into three big bowls.
- In a small pan over medium heat, warm the beans, stirring often, until hot (this should take less than a minute). Place on top of the lettuce.
- Top the beans with the cabbage, tomatoes, cilantro, and scallions.
- Drizzle with generously with the Creamy Lime Sauce and serve with the double batch of air-fried chips. Enjoy immediately.

Nutrition:
Calories 422
Fat 7g
Carbs 71g
Protein 22g

293. Bbq Jackfruit Nachos
Basic Recipe
Preparation Time: 30 minutes
Cooking Time: 20 minutes
Servings: 4
Ingredients:
1 (20-ounce) can jackfruit, dry out
- ⅓ cup prepared vegan bbq sauce
- ¼ cup water - tablespoons tamari or shoyu
- 1 tablespoon fresh lemon juice
- large garlic cloves, pressed or minced
- 1 teaspoon onion granules
- ⅛ Teaspoon cayenne powder
- ⅛ Teaspoon liquid smoke
- Double batch garlic lime tortilla chips
- 2½ cups prepared cheesy sauce
- medium-size tomatoes, chopped
- ¾ cup guacamole of your choice
- ¾ cup chopped cilantro
- ½ cup minced red onion
- 1 jalapeño, seeds removed and thinly sliced (optional)

Directions:
- In a large skillet over high heat, place the jackfruit, BBQ sauce, water, tamari, lemon juice, garlic, onion granules, cayenne, and liquid smoke. Stir well and break up the jackfruit a bit with a spatula.
- Once the mixture boils, reduce the heat to low. Continue to cook, stirring often (and breaking up the jackfruit as you stir), for about 20 minutes, or until all of the liquid has been absorbed. Remove from the heat and set aside.
- Assemble the nachos: Distribute the chips onto three plates, and then top evenly with the jackfruit mixture, warmed Cheesy Sauce, tomatoes, guacamole, cilantro, onion, and jalapeño (if using). Enjoy immediately, because soggy chips are tragic.

Nutrition:
Calories 661
Fat 15g
Carbs 124g
Protein 22g

294. 10-Minute Chimichanga
Basic Recipe
Preparation Time: 5 minutes
Cooking Time: 10 minutes
Servings: 4
Ingredients:
- 1 whole-grain tortilla
- ½ cup vegan refried beans
- ¼ cup grated vegan cheese (optional)
- Cooking oil spray (sunflower, safflower, or refined coconut)
- ½ cup fresh salsa (or Green Chili Sauce)
- cups chopped romaine lettuce (about ½ head)
- Guacamole (optional)
- Chopped cilantro (optional)
- Cheesy Sauce (optional)

Directions:
- Lay the tortilla on a flat surface and place the beans in the center. Top with the cheese, if using. Wrap the bottom up over the filling, and then fold in the sides. Then roll it all up so as to enclose the beans inside the tortilla (you're making an enclosed burrito here).
- Spray the air fryer basket with oil, place the tortilla wrap inside the basket, seam-side down, and spray the top of the chimichanga with oil. Fry for 5 minutes Spray the top (and sides) again with oil, flip over, and spray the other side with oil. Fry for an additional 2 or 3 minutes, until nicely browned and crisp.
- Transfer to a plate. Top with the salsa, lettuce, guacamole, cilantro, and/or Cheesy Sauce, if using.

Serve immediately.

Nutrition:
Calories 317
Fat 6g
Carbs 55g
Protein 13g

295. Mexican Stuffed Potatoes
Intermediate Recipe
Preparation Time: 15 minutes
Cooking Time: 40 minutes
Servings: 4
Ingredients:
- large potatoes, any variety (I like Yukon Gold or russets for this dish; see Cooking Tip)
- Cooking oil spray (sunflower, safflower, or refined coconut)
- 1½ cups Cheesy Sauce
- 1 cup black or pinto beans (canned beans are fine; be sure to Dry out and rinse)
- medium tomatoes, chopped
- 1 scallion, finely chopped
- ⅓ Cup finely chopped cilantro
- 1 jalapeño, finely sliced or minced (optional)
- 1 avocado, diced (optional)

Directions:
- Scrub the potatoes, prick with a fork, and spray the outsides with oil. Place in the air fryer (leaving room in between so the air can circulate) and Bake it for 30 minutes
- While the potatoes are cooking, prepare the Cheesy Sauce and additional items. Set aside.
- Check the potatoes at the 30-minute mark by poking a fork into them. If they're very tender, they're done. If not, continue to cook until a fork inserted proves them to be well-done. (As potato sizes vary, so will your cook time—the average cook time is usually about 40 minutes)
- When the potatoes are getting very close to being tender, warm the Cheesy Sauce and the beans in separate pans.
- To assemble: Plate the potatoes and cut them across the top. Then, pry them open with a fork—just enough to get all the goodies in there. Top each potato with the Cheesy Sauce, beans, tomatoes, scallions, cilantro, and jalapeño and avocado, if using. Enjoy immediately.

Nutrition:
Calories 420
Fat 5g
Carbs 80g
Fiber 17g
Protein 15g

296. Kids' Taquitos
Basic Recipe
Preparation Time: 5 minutes
Cooking Time: 10 minutes
Servings: 4
Ingredients:
- corn tortillas
- Cooking oil spray (coconut, sunflower, or safflower)
- 1 (15-ounce) can vegan refried beans
- 1 cup shredded vegan cheese
- Guacamole (optional)
- Cheesy Sauce (optional)
- Vegan sour cream (optional)
- Fresh salsa (optional)

Directions:
- Warm the tortillas (so they don't break): Run them under water for a second, and then place in an oil-sprayed air fryer basket (stacking them is fine). Fry for 1 minute.
- Remove to a flat surface, laying them out individually. Place an equal amount of the beans in a line down the center of

each tortilla. Top with the vegan cheese.
- Roll the tortilla sides up over the filling and place seam-side down in the air fryer basket (this will help them seal so the tortillas don't fly open). Add just enough to fill the basket without them touching too much (you may need to do another batch, depending on the size of your air fryer basket).
- Spray the tops with oil. Fry for 7 minutes, or until the tortillas are golden-brown and lightly crisp.
- Serve immediately with your preferred toppings.

Nutrition:
Calories 286 Fat 9g
Carbs 44g
Protein 9g

297. Immune-Boosting Grilled Cheese Sandwich

Basic Recipe
Preparation Time: 5 minutes
Cooking Time: 15 minutes
Servings: 4
Ingredients:
- slices sprouted whole-grain bread (or substitute a gluten-free bread)
- 1 teaspoon vegan margarine or neutral-flavored oil (sunflower, safflower, or refined coconut)
- slices vegan cheese (Violife cheddar or Chao creamy original) or Cheesy Sauce
- 1 teaspoon mellow white miso
- 1 medium-large garlic clove, pressed or finely minced
- tablespoons fermented vegetables, kimchi, or sauerkraut
- Romaine or green leaf lettuce

Directions:
- Spread the outsides of the bread with the vegan margarine. Place the sliced cheese inside and close the sandwich back up again (buttered sides facing out). Place the sandwich in the air fryer basket and fry for 6 minutes Flip over and fry for another 6 minutes, or until nicely browned and crisp on the outside.
- Transfer to a plate. Open the sandwich and evenly spread the miso and garlic clove over the inside of one of the bread slices. Top with the fermented vegetables and lettuce, close the sandwich back up, cut in half, and serve immediately.

Nutrition:
Calories 288
Fat 13g
Carbs 34g
Protein 8g

298. Tamale Pie With Cilantro Lime Cornmeal Crust

Basic Recipe
Preparation Time: 25 minutes
Cooking Time: 20 minutes
Servings: 4
Ingredients:
For the filling
- 1 medium zucchini, diced (1¼ cups)
- teaspoons neutral-flavored oil (sunflower, safflower, or refined coconut)
- 1 cup cooked pinto beans, Dry out
- 1 cup canned diced tomatoes (unsalted) with juice
- large garlic cloves, minced or pressed
- 1 tablespoon chickpea flour
- 1 teaspoon dried oregano
- 1 teaspoon onion granules
- ½ teaspoon salt
- ½ teaspoon crushed red chili flakes
- Cooking oil spray (sunflower, safflower, or refined coconut)

For the crust
- ½ cup yellow cornmeal, finely ground
- 1½ cups water
- ½ teaspoon salt
- 1 teaspoon nutritional yeast
- 1 teaspoon neutral-flavored oil (sunflower, safflower, or refined coconut)
- tablespoons finely chopped cilantro
- ½ teaspoon lime zest

Directions:

To make the filling

- In a large skillet set to medium-high heat, sauté the zucchini and oil for 3 minutes or until the zucchini begins to brown.
- Add the beans, tomatoes, garlic, flour, oregano, onion, salt, and chili flakes to the mixture. Cook it over medium heat, stirring often, for 5 minutes, or until the mixture is thickened and no liquid remains. Remove from the heat.
- Spray a 6-inch round, 2-inch deep baking pan with oil and place the mixture in the bottom. Smooth out the top and set aside.

To make the crust

- In a medium pot over high heat, place the cornmeal, water, and salt. Whisk constantly as you bring the mixture to a boil. Once it boils, reduce the heat to very low. Add the nutritional yeast and oil and continue to cook, stirring very often, for 10 minutes or until the mixture is very thick and hard to whisk. Remove from the heat.
- Stir the cilantro and lime zest into the cornmeal mixture until thoroughly combined. Using a rubber spatula, gently spread it evenly onto the filling in the baking pan to form a smooth crust topping. Place in the air fryer basket and Bake it for 20 minutes, or until the top is golden-brown. Let it cool for 5 to 10 minutes, then cut and serve.

Nutrition:
Calories 165 Fat 5g
Carbs 26g
Protein 6g

299. Herbed Eggplant
Basic Recipe
Preparation Time: 15 minutes
Cooking Time: 15 minutes
Servings: 2

Ingredients
- ½ teaspoon dried marjoram, crushed
- ½ teaspoon dried oregano, crushed
- ½ teaspoon dried thyme, crushed
- ½ teaspoon garlic powder
- Salt and ground black pepper, as required
- 1 large eggplant, cubed
- Olive oil cooking spray

Directions:
- Set the temperature of air fryer to 390 degrees F. Grease an air fryer basket.
- In a small bowl, mix well herbs, garlic powder, salt, and black pepper.
- Spray the eggplant cubes evenly with cooking spray and then, rub with the herbs mixture.
- Arrange eggplant cubes into the prepared air fryer basket in a single layer.
- Air fry for about 6 minutes
- Flip and spray the eggplant cubes with cooking spray.
- Air fry for another 6 minutes
- Flip and again, spray the eggplant cubes with cooking spray.
- Air fry for 2-3 more minutes
- Remove from air fryer and transfer the eggplant cubes onto serving plates.
- Serve hot.

Nutrition:
Calories 62
Carbs 14.5g
Protein 2.4g
Fat 0.5g

300. Spices Stuffed Eggplants
Basic Recipe
Preparation Time: 15 minutes
Cooking Time: 12 minutes
Servings: 4

Ingredients
- teaspoons olive oil, divided
- ¾ tablespoon dry mango powder
- ¾ tablespoon ground coriander
- ½ teaspoon ground cumin
- ½ teaspoon ground turmeric
- ½ teaspoon garlic powder
- Salt, to taste
- baby eggplants

Directions:
- In a small bowl, mix together one teaspoon of oil, and spices.
- From the bottom of each eggplant, make 2 slits, leaving the stems intact.
- With a small spoon, fill each slit of eggplants with spice mixture.
- Now, brush the outer side of each eggplant with remaining oil.
- Set the temperature of air fryer to 369 degrees F. Grease an air fryer basket.
- Arrange eggplants into the prepared air fryer basket in a single layer.
- Air fry for about 8-12 minutes
- Remove from air fryer and transfer the eggplants onto serving plates.
- Serve hot.

Nutrition:
Calories 317 Carbs 65g
Protein 10.9g Fat 6.7g

301. Salsa Stuffed Eggplants
Basic Recipe
Preparation Time: 15 minutes
Cooking Time: 25 minutes
Servings: 2

Ingredients
- 1 large eggplant
- teaspoons olive oil, divided
- teaspoons fresh lemon juice, divided
- cherry tomatoes, quartered
- tablespoons tomato salsa
- ½ tablespoon fresh parsley
- Salt and ground black pepper, as required

Directions:
- Set the temperature of air fryer to 390 degrees F. Grease an air fryer basket.
- Place eggplant into the prepared air fryer basket. Air fry for about 15 minutes
- Remove from air fryer and cut the eggplant in half lengthwise.
- Drizzle with the eggplant halves evenly with one teaspoon of oil.
- Now, set the temperature of air fryer to 355 degrees F. Grease the air fryer basket.
- Arrange eggplant into the prepared air fryer basket, cut-side up.
- Air fry for another 10 minutes
- Remove eggplant from the air fryer and set aside for about 5 minutes
- Carefully, scoop out the flesh, leaving about ¼-inch away from edges.
- Drizzle with the eggplant halves with one teaspoon of lemon juice.
- Transfer the eggplant flesh into a bowl.
- Add the tomatoes, salsa, parsley, salt, black pepper, remaining oil, and lemon juice and mix well.
- Stuff the eggplant haves with salsa mixture and serve.

Nutrition:
Calories 192 Carbs 33.8g
Protein 6.9g Fat 6.1g

302. Sesame Seeds Bok Choy
Basic Recipe
Preparation Time: 10 minutes
Cooking Time: 6 minutes
Servings: 4

Ingredients
- bunches baby bok choy, bottoms removed and leaves separated

Olive oil cooking spray
1 teaspoon garlic powder
1 teaspoon sesame seeds

Directions:

Set the temperature of air fryer to 325 degrees F.

Arrange bok choy leaves into the air fryer basket in a single layer.

Spray with the cooking spray and sprinkle with garlic powder.

Air fry for about 5-6 minutes, shaking after every 2 minutes

Remove from air fryer and transfer the bok choy onto serving plates.

Garnish with sesame seeds and serve hot.

Nutrition:
Calories 26 Carbs 4g
Protein 2.5g Fat 0.7g

303. Basil Tomatoe
Basic Recipe
Preparation Time: 10 minutes
Cooking Time: 10 minutes
Servings: 2

Ingredients:

tomatoes, halved - Olive oil cooking spray
Salt and ground black pepper, as required
1 tablespoon fresh basil, chopped

Directions:

Set the temperature of air fryer to 320 degrees F. Grease an air fryer basket.

Spray the tomato halves evenly with cooking spray and sprinkle with salt, black pepper and basil.

Arrange tomato halves into the prepared air fryer basket, cut sides up.

Air-fry it for about 10 minutes or until desired doneness.

Remove from air fryer and transfer the tomatoes onto serving plates.

Serve warm.

Nutrition:
Calories 22 Carbs 4.8g
Protein 1.1g Fat 4.8g

304. Overloaded Tomatoes
Basic Recipe
Preparation Time: 15 minutes
Cooking Time: 22 minutes
Servings: 4

Ingredients:

tomatoes
1 teaspoon olive oil
1 carrot, peeled and finely chopped
1 onion, chopped
1 cup frozen peas, thawed
1 garlic clove, minced
cups cold cooked rice
1 tablespoon soy sauce

Directions:

Cut the top of each tomato and scoop out pulp and seeds. In a skillet, heat oil over low heat and sauté the carrot, onion, garlic, and peas for about 2 minutes

Stir in the soy sauce and rice and remove from heat. Set the temperature of air fryer to 355 degrees F. Grease an air fryer basket.

Stuff each tomato with the rice mixture.

Arrange tomatoes into the prepared air fryer basket.

Air fry for about 20 minutes

Remove from air fryer and transfer the tomatoes onto a serving platter.

Set aside to cool slightly.

Serve warm.

Nutrition:
Calories 421 Carbs 89.1g
Protein 10.5g
Fat 2.2g

305. Sweet & Spicy Cauliflower
Basic Recipe
Preparation Time: 15 minutes
Cooking Time: 30 minutes
Servings: 4

Ingredients

1 head cauliflower, cut into florets

¾ cup onion, thinly sliced
garlic cloves, finely sliced
1½ tablespoons soy sauce
1 tablespoon hot sauce
1 tablespoon rice vinegar
1 teaspoon coconut sugar
Pinch of red pepper flakes
Ground black pepper, as required
scallions, chopped

Directions:
Set the temperature of air fryer to 350 degrees F. Grease an air fryer pan. Arrange cauliflower florets into the prepared air fryer pan in a single layer.
Air fry for about 10 minutes
Remove from air fryer and stir in the onions.
Air fry for another 10 minutes
Remove from air fryer and stir in the garlic.
Air fry for 5 more minutes
Meanwhile, in a bowl, mix well soy sauce, hot sauce, vinegar, coconut sugar, red pepper flakes, and black pepper.
Remove from the air fryer and stir in the sauce mixture.
Air fry for about 5 minutes
Remove from air fryer and transfer the cauliflower mixture onto serving plates. Garnish with scallions and serve.

Nutrition:
Calories 72 Carbs 13.8g
Protein 3.6g Fat 0.2g

306. Herbed Potatoes
Basic Recipe
Preparation Time: 10 minutes
Cooking Time: 16 minutes
Servings: 4

Ingredients
small potatoes, chopped
tablespoons olive oil
teaspoons mixed dried herbs
Salt and ground black pepper, as required
tablespoons fresh parsley, chopped

Directions:
Set the temperature of air fryer to 356 degrees F. Grease an air fryer basket.
In a large bowl, add the potatoes, oil, herbs, salt and black pepper and toss to coat well. Arrange the chopped potatoes into the prepared air fryer basket in a single layer.
Air fry it for about 16 minutes, tossing once halfway through.
Remove from air fryer and transfer the potatoes onto serving plates. Garnish with parsley and serve.

Nutrition:
Calories 268
Carbs 40.4g
Protein 4.4g
Fat 10.8g

307. Spicy Potatoes
Basic Recipe
Preparation Time: 10 minutes
Cooking Time: 20 minutes
Servings: 6

Ingredients
1¾ pounds waxy potatoes, peeled and cubed
1 tablespoon olive oil
½ teaspoon ground cumin
½ teaspoon ground coriander
½ teaspoon paprika
Salt and freshly ground black pepper, as required

Directions:
In a large bowl of water, add the potatoes and set aside for about 30 minutes
Dry out the potatoes completely and dry with paper towels.

In a bowl, add the potatoes, oil, and spices and toss to coat well.

Set the temperature of air fryer to 355 degrees F. Grease an air fryer basket.

Arrange potato pieces into the prepared air fryer basket in a single layer.

Air fry for about 20 minutes

Remove from air fryer and transfer the potato pieces onto serving plates.

Serve hot.

Nutrition:
Calories 113 Fat 2.5g
Carbs 21g Protein 2.3g

308. Crispy Kale Chips
Basic Recipe
Preparation Time: 5 minutes
Cooking Time: 7 minutes
Servings: 3
Ingredients:
3 cups kale leaves, stems removed
1 tablespoon olive oil
Salt and pepper, to taste
Directions:

In a bowl, combine all of the ingredients. Toss to coat the kale leaves with oil, salt, and pepper.

Arrange the kale leaves on the double layer rack and insert inside the air fryer.

Close the air fryer and cook for 7 minutes at 3700F. Allow to cool before serving.

Nutrition:
Calories 48 Carbs 1.4g
Protein 0.7g Fat 4.8g

309. Grilled Buffalo Cauliflower
Basic Recipe
Preparation Time: 5 minutes
Cooking Time: 5 minutes
Servings: 1
Ingredients:
1 cup cauliflower florets
Cooking oil spray
Salt and pepper, to taste
½ cup buffalo sauce
Directions:

Place the cauliflower florets in a bowl and spray with cooking oil. Season it with salt and pepper.

Toss to coat.

Place the grill pan in the air fryer and add the cauliflower florets.

Close the lid and cook for 5 minutes at 3900F.

Once cooked, place in a bowl and pour the buffalo sauce over the top. Toss to coat.

Nutrition:
Calories 25 Fat 0.1g
Carbs 5.3g
Protein 2g

310. Faux Fried Pickles
Basic Recipe
Preparation Time: 5 minutes
Cooking Time: 5 minutes
Servings: 2
Ingredients:
1 cup pickle slices
1 egg, beaten
½ cup grated Parmesan cheese
½ cup almond flour
¼ cup pork rinds, crushed
Salt and pepper, to taste
Directions:

Place the pickles in a bowl and pour the beaten egg over the top. Allow to soak.

In another dish or bowl, combine the Parmesan cheese, almond flour, pork rinds, salt, and pepper.

Dredge the pickles in the Parmesan cheese mixture and place on the double layer rack.

Place the rack with the pickles inside of the air fryer.

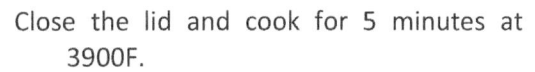

Close the lid and cook for 5 minutes at 3900F.

Nutrition:
Calories 664 Carbs 17.9g Protein 42g Fat 49.9g

311. Greatest Green Beans
Basic Recipe
Preparation Time: 5 minutes
Cooking Time: 5 minutes
Servings: 2
Ingredients:
- 1 cup green beans, trimmed
- ½ teaspoon oil
- Salt and pepper, to taste

Directions:
- Place the green beans in a bowl and add in oil, salt, and pepper.
- Toss to coat the beans.
- Place the grill pan in the air fryer and add the green beans in a single layer.
- Close the lid and cook for 5 minutes at 3900F.

Nutrition:
Calories 54 Fat 2.5g
Carbs 7.7g Protein 2g

312. Summer Grilled Corn
Basic Recipe
Preparation Time: 5 minutes
Cooking Time: 10 minutes
Servings: 2
Ingredients:
- corns on the cob cut into halves widthwise
- ½ teaspoon oil
- Salt and pepper, to taste

Directions:
- Brush the corn cobs with oil and season with salt and pepper.
- Place the grill pan accessory into the air fryer.
- Place the corn cobs on the grill pan.
- Close the lid and cook for 3 minutes at 3900F. Open the air fryer and turn the corn cobs. Cook for another 3 minutes at the same temperature.

Nutrition:
Calories 173 Carbs 29g
Protein 4.5 g Fat 4.5g

313. Cheesy Bean Bake
Basic Recipe
Preparation Time: 5 minutes
Cooking Time: 55 minutes
Servings: 6
Ingredients:
- tbsp. extra-virgin olive oil
- ½ tsp. black pepper
- 1 1/3 cups mozzarella coarsely grated
- 1 1/2 tsp. garlic, sliced
- tbsp. tomato paste
- 1 1/3 cups dried beans
- ½ tsp. kosher salt

Directions:
- Pressure Cook beans with 4 cups water on High for 25 minutes. Sauté beans with oil.
- Add garlic and cook for 1 minute. Add beans, tomato paste, water, a pinch of salt and pepper.
- Top with cheese.
- Press Broil for 7 minutes with Air Fryer Lid. Serve with toasted bread or nacho chips

Nutrition:
Calories 761 kcal Fat 28 g
Carbs 54 g Protein 45 g

314. Barbacoa Beef
Basic Recipe
Preparation Time: 15 minutes
Cooking Time: 1hour and 20 minutes
Servings: 10
Ingredients:
- 2/3 cup beer

cloves garlic
chipotles in adobo sauce
1 tsp. black pepper
1/4 tsp. ground cloves
1 tbsp. olive oil
3-pound beef chuck roast, 2-inch chunks
bay leaves
1 onion, chopped
oz. chopped green chilies
1/4 cup lime juice
tbsp. apple cider vinegar
1 tbsp. ground cumin
1 tbsp. dried Mexican oregano
tsp. salt

Directions:

Puree beer, garlic, chipotles, onion, green chilies, lime juice, vinegar, and seasonings.
Sauté roast in oil.
Add the bay leaves and pureed sauce.
Cook on High Pressure for 60 minutes
Discard the leaves.
Shred beef and serve with sauce.

Nutrition:
Calories 520 kcal
Fat 23g
Carbs 56 g
Protein 31g

315. Maple Smoked Brisket
Basic Recipe
Preparation Time: 15 minutes
Cooking Time: 1hour and 20 minutes
Servings: 4
Ingredients:

lb. beef brisket
tbsp. maple sugar
c. bone broth or stock of choice
1 tbsp. liquid smoke
fresh thyme sprigs
tsp. smoked sea salt
1 tsp. black pepper
1 tsp. mustard powder
1 tsp. onion powder
½ tsp. smoked paprika

Directions:

Coat the brisket with all spices and sugar.
Sauté brisket in oil for 3 minutes
Add broth, liquid smoke, and thyme to the Air fryer and cover.
Cook at High Pressure for 50 minutes
Remove brisket.
Sauté sauce for 10 minutes
Serve sliced brisket with any whipped vegetable and sauce.

Nutrition:
Calories 1671 kcal
Fat 43g
Carbs 98 g
Protein 56g

316. Philly Cheesesteak Sandwiches
Basic Recipe
Preparation Time: 5 minutes
Cooking Time: 30 minutes
Servings: 8
Ingredients:

3-pound beef top sirloin steak, sliced
onions, julienned
1 can condensed French onion soup, undiluted
garlic cloves, minced
1 package Italian salad dressing mix
tsp. beef base
1/2 tsp. pepper
large red peppers, julienned
1/2 cup pickled pepper rings
hoagie buns, split
slices provolone cheese

Directions:

Combine the first 7 ingredients in the pressure cooker. Adjust to pressure-cook on High for 10 minutes. Add peppers and pepper rings. Pressure-cook on High for 5 minutes

Put beef, cheese, and vegetables on bun bottoms. Broil 1-2 minutes and serve.

Nutrition:
Calories 4852 kcal Fat 67g
Carbs 360 g Protein 86g

317. Pot Roast And Potatoes
Basic Recipe
Preparation Time: 15 minutes
Cooking Time: 1 hour and 15 minutes
Servings: 8
Ingredients:
- tbsp. all-purpose flour
- 1 tbsp. kosher salt
- lb. chuck roast
- 1 tbsp. black pepper
- c. low-sodium beef broth
- 1/2 c. red wine
- 1 lb. baby potatoes, halved
- 1 tbsp. Worcestershire sauce
- carrots, sliced
- 1 onion, chopped
- 1 tbsp. extra-virgin olive oil
- cloves garlic, minced
- 1 tsp. thyme, chopped
- tsp. rosemary, chopped
- tbsp. tomato paste

Directions:
Coat chuck roast with pepper and salt.
Sauté the beef for 5 minutes on each side then set aside.
Cook onion for 5 minutes
Add herbs, garlic, and tomato paste and cook for 1 minute.
Add four and wine and cook for 2 minutes
Add Worcestershire sauce, broth, carrots, potatoes, salt and pepper.
Put beef on top of the mixture
High-Pressure Cook for an hour and serve.

Nutrition:
Calories 3274 kcal
Fat 42 g
Carbs 286 g
Protein 78 g

318. Butter Chicken
Intermediate Recipe
Preparation Time: 10 minutes
Cooking Time: 1hour and 10 minutes
Servings: 6
Ingredients:
- 1 tbsp. vegetable oil
- 1 tbsp. butter
- 1 onion, diced
- tsp. grated ginger
- 1 tsp. ground cumin
- 1/2 tsp. turmeric
- 1/ 2 tsp. kosher salt
- ½ tsp. black pepper
- 3/4 c. heavy cream
- cloves garlic, chopped
- oz. tomato paste
- lb. boneless chicken thighs, 1" pieces
- 1 tbsp. garam masala
- 1 tsp. paprika
- 1 tbsp. sugar

Directions:
Sauté the onion, ginger, and garlic in oil and butter
Add tomato paste and cook for 3 minutes
Add ½ cup water, chicken, and spices to the Pot.
Pressure Cook on High for 5 minutes
Add heavy cream.
Serve with rice, naan, yogurt, and cilantro.

Nutrition:
Calories 3841 Fat 100g
Carbs 244g Protein 150g

319. Curried Chicken Meatball Wraps
Basic Recipe
Preparation Time: 5 minutes
Cooking Time: 15 minutes
Servings: 12
Ingredients:
- 1 egg, beaten
- 1 onion, chopped

1/2 cup Rice Krispies
1/4 cup golden raisins
1/4 cup minced cilantro
tsp. curry powder
1/2 tsp. salt
Boston lettuce leaves
1 carrot, shredded
1/2 cup chopped salted peanuts
1-pound lean ground chicken
tbsp. olive oil
1 cup plain yogurt

Directions:
Mix the first 7 ingredients.
Shape mixture into 24 balls.
Sauté meatballs on medium with oil
Add water to pot.
Put meatballs on the trivet in the pressure cooker.
Pressure-cook on High for 7 minutes
Mix yogurt and cilantro.
Place 2 teaspoons sauce and 1 meatball in each lettuce leaf; top with remaining ingredients and serve.

Nutrition:
Calories 2525
Fat 80g
Carbs 225g
Protein 120g

---

320. Fall-Off-The-Bone Chicken
Intermediate Recipe
Preparation Time: 10 minutes
Cooking Time: 1hour and 10 minutes
Servings: 4
Ingredients:
1 tbsp. packed brown sugar
1 tbsp. chili powder
1 tbsp. smoked paprika
1 tsp. chopped thyme leaves
¼ tbsp. kosher salt
¼ tbsp. black pepper
1 whole small chicken
1 tbsp. extra-virgin olive oil
2/3 c. low-sodium chicken broth
tbsp. chopped parsley

Directions:
Coat chicken with brown sugar, chili powder, sugar, pepper, paprika, and thyme.
Sauté chicken in oil for 3-4 minutes
Pour broth in the Pot.
Pressure Cook on High for 25 minutes
Garnish sliced chicken with parsley and serve.

Nutrition:
Calories 1212
Fat 10g
Carbs 31g
Protein 15g

---

321. White Chicken Chili
Basic Recipe
Preparation Time: 5 minutes
Cooking Time: 30 minutes
Servings: 6
Ingredients:
1 tbsp. vegetable oil
1 red bell pepper, diced
oz. condensed cream of chicken soup
tbsp. shredded Cheddar cheese
green onions, sliced
1 cup Kernel corn
1 tbsp. chili powder
oz. (2) boneless, skinless chicken breast
oz. white cannellini beans
1 cup Chunky Salsa

Directions:
Sauté pepper, corn, and chili powder in oil for 2 minutes
Season chicken with salt and pepper.
Layer the beans, salsa, water, chicken, and soup over the corn mixture.
Pressure Cook on High for 4 minutes
Shred chicken and return to pot.

Serve topped with cheese and green onions.
Nutrition:
Calories 1848
Fat 70g
Carbs 204g
Protein 90g

322. Coconut Curry Vegetable Rice Bowls
Basic Recipe
Preparation Time: 5 minutes
Cooking Time: 40minutes
Servings: 6
Ingredients:
- 2/3 cup uncooked brown rice
- 1 tsp. curry powder
- 3/4 tsp. salt divided
- 1 cup chopped green onion
- 1 cup sliced red bell pepper
- 1 tbsp. grated ginger
- 1 1/2 tbsp. sugar
- 1 cup matchstick carrots
- 1 cup chopped red cabbage
- oz. sliced water chestnuts
- oz. no salt added chickpeas
- oz. coconut milk

Directions:
Add rice, water, curry powder, and 1/4 tsp. of the salt in the Air fryer. Pressure Cook for 15 minutes. Sauté for 2 minutes and serve.

Nutrition:
Calories 1530 Fat 110g
Carbs 250g
Protein 80g

323. Egg Roll In A Bowl
Basic Recipe
Preparation Time: 5 minutes
Cooking Time: 20 minutes
Servings: 4
Ingredients:
- 1/3 cup low-sodium soy sauce
- tbsp. sesame oil
- 1 cup matchstick cut carrots
- 1 bunch green onions, sliced
- bags coleslaw mix
- 1 lb. ground chicken
- tbsp. sesame seeds
- cloves garlic, minced
- oz. shiitake mushrooms, sliced
- 1 1/2 cups chicken broth

Directions:
Add sesame oil, ground chicken, soy sauce, garlic, chicken broth and mushrooms to Air fryer.
Cook for 2 minutes on High Pressure.
Add in coleslaw mix and carrots.
Let sit for 5 minutes
Serve with sesame seeds and green onions.

Nutrition:
Calories 3451 Fat 130g
Carbs 301g Protein 150g

324. Frittata Provencal
Basic Recipe
Preparation Time: 5 minutes
Cooking Time: 45 minutes
Servings: 6
Ingredients:
- eggs
- 1 tsp. minced thyme
- 1 tsp. hot pepper sauce
- 1/2 tsp. salt
- 1/4 tsp. pepper
- oz. goat cheese, divided
- 1/2 cup chopped sun-dried tomatoes
- 1 tbsp. olive oil
- 1 potato, peeled and sliced
- 1 onion, sliced
- 1/2 tsp. smoked paprika

Directions:
Sauté potato, paprika, and onion in oil for 5-7 minutes
Transfer potato mixture to a greased baking dish.

Pour the first 6 ingredients over potato mixture.
Cover baking dish with foil.
Add water and trivet to pot.
Use a foil sling to lower the dish onto the trivet.
Adjust to pressure-cook on high for 35 minutes and serve.

Nutrition:
Calories 2554 Fat 70g
Carbs 190g Protein 80g

325. Ramekin Eggs
Basic Recipe
Preparation Time: 2 minutes
Cooking Time: 3minutes
Servings: 2
Ingredients:
1 tbsp. ghee, plus more for greasing
cups mushrooms, chopped
¼ tsp. salt
1 tbsp. chives, chopped
eggs
tbsp. heavy cream

Directions:
Sauté mushrooms with ghee and salt until tender.
Put mushrooms into greased ramekins.
Add chives, egg, and cream.
Add water, trivet, and ramekins to pot.
Pressure Cook on Low for 1-2 minutes
Serve with freshly toasted bread.

Nutrition:
Calories 703 Fat 5g
Carbs 20g Protein 7g

326. Easter Ham
Basic Recipe
Preparation Time: 5 minutes
Cooking Time: 15 minutes
Servings: 8
Ingredients:
1/2 c. orange marmalade
¼ tsp. black pepper
1 (4-6 lb.) fully cooked, spiral, bone-in ham
1/4 c. brown sugar
1/4 c. orange juice
tbsp. Dijon mustard

Directions:
Mix marmalade, brown sugar, orange juice, Dijon, and black pepper.
Coat ham with glaze.
Cook on Meat for 15 minutes
Serve ham with more glaze from the Pot.

Nutrition:
Calories 3877 Fat 80g
Carbs 207g Protein 100g

327. Korean Lamb Chops
Intermediate Recipe
Preparation Time: 10 minutes
Cooking Time: 50minutes
Servings: 6
Ingredients:
lbs. Lamb chops
1/2 tsp. Red pepper powder
tbsp. granulated sugar
1 tbsp. curry powder
1/2 tbsp. soy sauce
tbsp. rice wine
tbsp. garlic, minced
1 tsp. ginger, minced
bay leaves
1 cup carrots, diced
cups onions, diced
1 cup celery, diced
tbsp. Korean red pepper paste
tbsp. ketchup
tbsp. Corn syrup
1/2 tbsp. sesame oil
1/2 tsp. cinnamon powder
1 tsp. sesame seeds
1 tsp. black pepper
1/3 cup Asian pear ground
1/3 cup onion powder
1/2 tbsp. Green plum extract

1 cup red wine

Directions:

Put all ingredients except cilantro and green onions into the Air fryer.

Pressure Cook for 20 minutes

Sauté until sauce is thickened.

Add water and lamb on trivet to pot.

Broil at 400°F for 5 minutes

Serve with chopped cilantro and green onions.

Nutrition:

Calories 2728

Fat 220g

Carbs 551g

Protein 250g

328. Air Fryer Chicken Kabobs

Basic Recipe

Preparation Time: 15 minutes

Cooking Time: 15 minutes

Servings: 2

Ingredients:

Chicken breasts, chopped

Mushrooms cut into halves

⅓ Cup honey

⅓ Cup Soy sauce -

1 teaspoon Pepper, crushed

1 teaspoon Sesame seeds

Bell peppers, in different colors

Cooking oil spray as required

Directions:

Cut the chicken breasts into small cubes, wash and pat dry. Rub little pepper and salt over the chicken. Sprits some oil on it. In a small bowl, combine honey and soy sauce thoroughly.

Add the sesame seeds into the mix. Drive in chicken, bell peppers and mushrooms onto the skewers.

Set the air fryer at 170 degrees Celsius and preheat.

Drizzle with the kabobs with the honey and soy sauce mixture.

Put all the skewed chicken kabobs into the air fryer basket and cook for 20 minutes

Rotate the skewer intermittently in between.

Serve hot.

Nutrition:

Calories 392 Fat 5g

Carbs 65.4g Protein 6.7g

329. Chicken Fried Rice In Air Fryer

Basic Recipe

Preparation Time: 20 minutes

Cooking Time: 20 minutes

Servings: 4

Ingredients:

cups cooked cold white rice

1 cup chicken cooked & diced

1 cup carrots and peas, frozen

1 tablespoon vegetable oil

1 tablespoon soy sauce

½ cup onion

¼ teaspoon salt

Directions:

In a large bowl, put the cooked cold rice.

Stir in soy sauce and vegetable oil.

Now add the frozen carrots and peas, diced chicken, diced onion, salt and combine.

Transfer the rice mixture into the mix.

Take a non-stick pan which you can comfortably place in the air fryer and transfer the complete rice mixture into the pan.

Place the pan in the air fryer.

Set the temperature at 180 degree Celsius and timer for 20 minutes

Remove the pan after the set time elapse.

Serve hot.

Nutrition:

Calories 618

Fat 5.5g

Carbs 116.5g

Protein 21.5g

330. Air Fried Chicken Tikkas
Basic Recipe
Preparation Time: 10 minutes
Cooking Time: 15 minutes
Servings: 4
Ingredients:
For marinade:
- 1¼ pounds chicken, bones cut into small bite size
- ¼ pound cherry tomatoes
- 1 cup yogurt
- 1 tablespoon ginger garlic paste (fresh)
- bell peppers, 1" cut size
- tablespoons chili powder
- tablespoons cumin powder
- 1 tablespoon turmeric powder
- tablespoons coriander powder
- 1 teaspoon garam masala powder
- teaspoons olive oil
- Salt – to taste

For garnishing:
- 1 lemon, cut into half
- ⅓ cup Coriander, fresh, chopped
- 1 medium Onion, nicely sliced
- Mint leaves, fresh – few

Directions:
- In a large bowl mix all the marinade ingredients and coat it thoroughly on the chicken pieces.
- Cover the bowl and set aside for 2 hours minimum. If you can refrigerate overnight, it can give better marinade effect.
- Thread the chicken in the skewers along with bell peppers and tomatoes alternately.
- Preheat your air fryer at 200 degrees Celsius.
- Spread an aluminum liner on the air fryer basket and arrange the skewers on it.
- Set the timer for 15 minutes and grill it.
- Turn the skewer intermittently for an even grilling.
- Once done, put into a plate and garnish with the given ingredients before serving.

Nutrition:
Calories 400 Fat 20g
Carbs 17.4g Protein 46.9g

331. Nashville Hot Chicken In Air Fryer
Basic Recipe
Preparation Time: 10 minutes
Cooking Time: 27 minutes
Servings: 4
Ingredients:
- pounds chicken with bones, 8 pieces
- tablespoons vegetable oil
- cups all-purpose flour
- 1 cup buttermilk
- tablespoons paprika
- 1 teaspoon onion powder
- 1 teaspoon garlic powder
- 1 teaspoon ground black pepper
- teaspoons salt

For Hot sauce:
- 1 tablespoon cayenne pepper
- ¼ cup vegetable oil
- 1 teaspoon salt
- slices white bread
- Dill pickle, as required

Directions:
- Clean and wash chicken thoroughly, pat dry and keep ready aside.
- In a bowl, whisk buttermilk and eggs.
- Combine garlic powder, black pepper, paprika, onion powder, All-purpose flour and salt in a bowl.
- Now dip the chicken in the egg and buttermilk and put in the second bowl marinade bowl and toss to get an even coating. Maybe you need to repeat the process twice for a better coat.
- After that spray some vegetable oil and keep aside.

- Before cooking the chicken, pre-heat the fryer at 190 degrees Celsius.
- Brush vegetable oil on the fry basket before start cooking.
- Now place the coated chicken in the air fryer at 190 degrees Celsius and set the timer for 20 minutes. Do not crowd the air fryer. It would be better if you can do the frying in 2 batches.
- Keep the flipping the chicken intermittently for even frying.
- Once the set timer elapsed, remove the chicken to a plate and keep it there without covering.
- Now start the second batch. Do the same process.
- After 20 minutes, reduce the temperature to 170 degrees Celsius and place the first batch of chicken over the second batch, which is already in the air fry basket.
- Fry it again for another 7 minutes
- While the chicken is air frying, make the hot sauce.
- In a bowl mix salt and cayenne pepper thoroughly.
- In a small saucepan, heat some vegetable oil.
- When the oil becomes hot add the spice mix and continue stirring to become smooth.
- While serving, place the chicken over the white bread and spread the hot sauce over the chicken.
- Use dill pickle to top it.
- Serve hot.

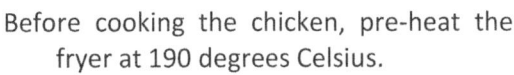

Nutrition:
Calories 1013
Fat 22.2g
Carbs 53.9g
Protein 140.7g

332. Air Fryer Panko Breaded Chicken Parmesan

Basic Recipe
Preparation Time: 10 minutes
Cooking Time: 20 minutes
Servings: 4
Ingredients:
- ounces chicken breasts, skinless
- 1 cup panko bread crumbs
- ⅛ cup egg whites
- ½ cup parmesan cheese, shredded
- ½ cup mozzarella cheese, grated
- ¾ cup marinara sauce
- ½ teaspoon salt
- 1 teaspoon ground pepper
- teaspoons italian seasoning
- Cooking spray, as required

Directions:
- Cut each chicken breast into halves to make 4 breast pieces. Wash and pat dry.
- Place the chicken in a chopping board and pound to flatten.
- Sprits the air fryer basket with cooking oil.
- Set the temperature of air fryer to 200 degrees Celsius and preheat.
- In a large bowl, mix cheese, panko breadcrumbs, and seasoning ingredients.
- Put the egg white in a large bowl.
- Dip the pounded chicken into the egg whites and dredge into breadcrumb mixture.
- Now place the coated chicken into the air fryer basket and spray some cooking oil.
- Start cooking the chicken breasts for 7 minutes
- Dress on top of the chicken breasts with shredded mozzarella and marinara sauce.

Continue cooking for another 3 minutes and remove for serving when the cheese starts to melt.

Nutrition:
Calories 347
Fat 15g
Carbs 7.4g
Protein 37g

333. Air Fryer Rosemary Turkey
Basic Recipe
Preparation Time: 5 minutes
Cooking Time: 30 minutes
Servings: 6
Ingredients:
- 2½ pounds turkey breast
- teaspoons fresh rosemary, chopped
- ¼ cup olive oil
- cloves garlic, minced
- 1 teaspoon crushed pepper
- ¼ cup maple syrup
- 1 tablespoon ground mustard
- 1 tablespoon butter
- 1½ teaspoon salt

Directions:
- Combine thoroughly, minced garlic, olive oil, shredded rosemary, pepper and salt in medium bowl.
- Rub the herb seasoning and oil all over the turkey breast loins.
- Cover and refrigerate for at least 2 hours for better marinade effect.
- Before cooking, allow it to thaw for half an hour.
- Spray some cooking oil on the air fryer basket and place the turkey breast on it.
- Set the temperature at 200 degrees Celsius for 20 minutes
- Flip the turkey breast intermittently.
- While cooking in progress, melt a tablespoon of butter in a microwave oven.
- Stir in mustard powder and maple syrup in the melted butter.
- Pour the sauce mix over the turkey breast and continue cooking for another 10 minutes
- After the cooking is over, slice it for serving.

Nutrition:
Calories 292
Fat 13.5g
Carbs 9.5g
Protein 15g

334. Air Fryer Lamb Chops
Basic Recipe
Preparation Time: 5 minutes
Cooking Time: 30 minutes
Servings: 2
Ingredients:
- lamb chops
- ½ tablespoon oregano, fresh, coarsely chopped
- 1½ tablespoons olive oil
- 1 teaspoon black pepper, ground
- 1 clove garlic
- ½ teaspoon salt

Directions:
- Set the air fryer temperature to 200 degrees Celsius.
- Spray olive on garlic clove and place it in the air fryer basket.
- Bake it for 12 minutes
- Combine herbs with pepper, olive oil, and salt.
- Rub half of the mix over the lamb chops and set aside for 3 minutes
- Remove the roasted garlic clove from the air fryer.
- Set the temperature at 200 degrees Celsius and preheat the air fryer.

- Layer the lamb chops into the air fryer basket and cook for 5 minutes or until it becomes brown.
- Do not roast the lambs altogether by overlapping one over the other. You can do the roasting in batches.
- After finish roasting, squeeze the garlic into the herb sauce.
- Add some more salt and pepper if required.
- Serve the dish along with garlic sauce.

Nutrition:
Calories 97
Fat 10.7g
Carbs 1.3g
Protein 0.3g

335. Air Fried Shrimp And Sauce
Basic Recipe
Preparation Time: 10 minutes
Cooking Time: 20 minutes
Servings: 4
Ingredients:
    1 pound shrimps
    ½ cup all-purpose flour
    1 egg white
    ¾ cup panko breadcrumbs
    tablespoons chicken seasoning
    1 teaspoon paprika
    1 teaspoon pepper
    ½ teaspoon salt
    Cooking spray, as required
    To make the sauce:
    ⅓ cup of greek yogurt, non-fat
    ¼ cup sweet chili sauce
    tablespoons sriracha

Directions:
- Peel, devein, clean, wash and pat dry the shrimps.
- Marinate the shrimps by using the seasoning.
- Put egg white, all-purpose flour and breadcrumbs in three separate bowls.
- Set the temperature to 200 degree Celsius and preheat the air fryer.
- Dip the seasoned shrimp in flour, then in the egg white and finally dredge in the breadcrumbs.
- Sprits cooking oil on the coated shrimp.
- Put the shrimps in the air fryer basket and cook for 4 minutes
- Flip the shrimps and cook further 4 minutes
- For making the sauce, blend all the sauce ingredients in a medium bowl thoroughly.
- Serve the shrimps along with the sauce.

Nutrition:
Calories 318
Fat 6.7g
Carbs 30.7g
Protein 31.3g

336. Air Fryer Italian Meatball
Basic Recipe
Preparation Time: 6minutes
Cooking Time: 15 minutes
Servings: 6
Ingredients:
    pounds ground beef
    eggs
    1¼ cup bread crumbs
    ¼ cup fresh parsley, chopped
    1 teaspoon dried oregano
    ¼ cup parmigiano reggiano, grated
    1 teaspoon light cooking oil
    Salt to taste
    Pepper, as required
    Tomato sauce, for serving

Directions:
- In a mixing bowl put the meat and all ingredients except the cooking oil.
- Hand mix all the ingredients. Once the mix blended thoroughly, make a small ball with your hand. The given quantity is enough to make 24 balls.

- Spread a liner paper in the air fryer basket and lightly coat it with cooking oil.
- Place the bowls in the air fryer basket without overlapping one another.
- Set the temperature to 200 degrees Celsius and cook for 12-14 minutes until its side becomes brown.
- Once the sides become brown, turn the balls and cook for another 5 minutes
- Serve hot along with tomato sauce.

Nutrition:
Calories 405
Fat 13.1g
Carbs 16.5g
Protein 52.1g

337. Air Fryer Coconut Milk Chicken
Basic Recipe
Preparation Time: 10 minutes
Cooking Time: 18 minutes
Servings: 6
Ingredients:
- 1¾ pounds Chicken thighs with skin and bone -

Marinade:
- cups coconut milk
- teaspoons ground black pepper
- 1 teaspoon cayenne pepper, ground
- 1 teaspoon salt

Seasoned flour:
- 1 tablespoon baking powder
- 1 tablespoon paprika powder
- cups all-purpose flour
- 1 tablespoon garlic powder
- 1 teaspoon salt

Directions:
- Clean, wash the chicken thighs and pat dry.
- Combine paprika, cayenne pepper, black pepper, salt in a large bowl.
- Put chicken into it and toss to coat the ingredients.
- Pour buttermilk until chicken covered.
- Refrigerate the coated chicken for a minimum of 6 hours.
- Set the air fryer temperature to 180 degrees Celsius.
- In another bowl combine the seasoning flour such as baking powder, paprika, all-purpose flour, garlic powder, and salt.
- Now take out the chicken from the refrigerator and thaw it for some time.
- Dredge the chicken into the flour and remove excess flour by shaking off it.
- Place the coated chicken into the air fryer basket.
- Cook it for 8 minutes
- After 8 minutes flip the chicken pieces and cook for another 10 minutes
- Transfer the cooked chicken onto a paper towel, so that the excess juice can dry out quickly.
- Serve hot.

Nutrition:
Calories 384
Fat 21.7g
Carbs 39.2g
Protein 12.1g

338. Air Fryer Cauliflower Rice
Basic Recipe
Preparation Time: 10 minutes
Cooking Time: 20 minutes
Servings: 3
Ingredients:
Segment - 1
- ½ firm tofu
- ½ cup onion, chopped
- tablespoons low sodium soy sauce
- 1 cup carrot diced
- ½ teaspoon turmeric powder

Segment – 2
- cups cauliflower rice
- ½ cup frozen peas
- tablespoons low sodium soy sauce

1½ teaspoons sesame oil, toasted
1 tablespoon rice vinegar
1 tablespoon ginger, grated
½ cup broccoli, finely chopped
cloves garlic, minced

Directions:

Crumble tofu in a large bowl. Toss the crumbled tofu with sector 1 ingredients.

Set the air fryer temperature to 190 degree Celsius and cook for 10 minutes. Shake the air fryer basket 2-3 times during the cooking in progress.

In another large bowl, combine all the ingredients mentioned in the segment 2.

After 10 minutes of cooking, transfer the second segment ingredients over the cooked food. Shake the air basket tray and cook for 10 minutes at 190 degrees Celsius. Make sure to shake the air fryer basket intermittently for a better baking result. When the cauliflower rice becomes tender, it is ready to serve.

Serve hot along with your favorite sauce.

Nutrition:
Calories 126 Fat 5g
Carbs 14g
Protein 7.8g

339. Buttery Cod
Basic Recipe
Preparation Time: 5 minutes
Cooking Time: 15 minutes
Servings: 4
Ingredients:
tbsp parsley, chopped
tbsp butter, melted
cherry tomatoes, halved
0.25 cup tomato sauce
cod fillets, cubed

Directions:
Turn on the air fryer to 390 degrees. Combine all of the ingredients and put them into a pan that works with the air fryer. After 12 minutes of baking, you can divide this between the four bowls and enjoy.

Nutrition:
Calories 232
Fat 8g
Carbs 5g
Protein 11g

340. Creamy Chicken
Basic Recipe
Preparation Time: 5 minutes
Cooking Time: 15 minutes
Servings: 4
Ingredients:
Pepper and salt
1 tsp olive oil
1 0.5 tsp sweet paprika
0.25 cup coconut cream
chicken breasts, cubed

Directions:
Turn on the air fryer to 370 degrees. Prepare a frying pan that fits into the machine with some oil before adding the ingredients inside. Add this to the air fryer and let it bake. After 17 minutes, you can divide between the few plates and serve!

Nutrition:
Calories 250
Fat 12g
Carbs 5g
Protein 11g

341. Mushroom And Turkey Stew
Basic Recipe
Preparation Time: 5 minutes
Cooking Time: 25 minutes
Servings: 4
Ingredients:
Pepper and salt

1 tbsp parsley, chopped
0.25 cup tomato sauce
1 turkey breast cubed
0.5 lb. Brown mushrooms, sliced

Directions:

Turn on the air fryer to 350 degrees. Pick out a pan and mix the tomato sauce, pepper, salt, mushrooms, and turkey together. Add to the air fryer.

After 25 minutes, the stew is done—divides between four bowls and top with the parsley.

Nutrition:
Calories 220
Fat 12g
Carbs 5g
Protein 12g

342. Basil Chicken
Basic Recipe
Preparation Time: 5 minutes
Cooking Time: 15 minutes
Servings: 4
Ingredients:

Pepper and salt
tsp smoked paprika
0.5 tsp dried basil
0.5 cup chicken stock
1 0.5 lb chicken breasts, cubed

Directions:

Turn on the air fryer to 390 degrees.

Bring out a pan and toss the ingredients inside before putting it into the air fryer.

After 25 minutes of baking, divide this between a few plates and serve with a side salad.

Nutrition:
Calories 223
Fat 12g
Carbs 5g
Protein 13g

343. Eggplant Bake
Basic Recipe
Preparation Time: 5 minutes
Cooking Time: 15 minutes
Servings: 4
Ingredients:

tsp olive oil
Pepper and salt
spring onions, chopped
1 hot chili pepper, chopped
eggplants, cubed
garlic cloves, minced
0.5 cup cilantro, chopped
0.5 lb cherry tomatoes, cubed

Directions:

Turn on the air fryer and let it heat up to 380 degrees.

Prepare a baking pan that will go into the air fryer and mix all of the ingredients onto it.

Place into the air fryer to cook. After 15 minutes, divide between four bowls and serve.

Nutrition:
Calories 232
Fat 12g
Carbs 5g
Protein 10g

344. Meatball Casserole
Basic Recipe
Preparation Time: 5 minutes
Cooking Time: 15 minutes
Servings: 6
Ingredients:

1 tbsp thyme, chopped
0.25 cup parsley, chopped
0.33 lb turkey sausage
1 egg, beaten
0.66 lb ground beef
tbsp olive oil
1 shallot, minced
1 tbsp Dijon mustard

garlic cloves, minced
tbsp whole milk
1 tbsp rosemary, chopped

Directions:
- Turn on the air fryer to a High setting and then give it time to heat up with some oil inside.
- Add the garlic and onions and cook for a few minutes to make soft.
- Add the milk and bread crumbs to a bowl and then mix. Then add in the rest of the ingredients and set aside to soak.
- Use this mixture, after five minutes, to prepare some small meatballs. Add these to the air fryer.
- Turn the heat up to 400 degrees to cook. After 10 minutes, take the lid off and shake the basket. Cook another five minutes before serving.

Nutrition:
Calories 168
Fat 11g
Carbs 4g
Protein 12g

345. Herbed Lamb Rack
Basic Recipe
Preparation Time: 5 minutes
Cooking Time: 10 minutes
Servings: 2
Ingredients:
- tbsp olive oil
- 0.5 tsp pepper
- 1 tbsp dried thyme
- tbsp dried rosemary
- 0.5 tsp salt
- tsp garlic, minced
- 1 lb rack of lamb

Directions:
- Turn on the air fryer to 400 degrees. In a bowl, combine the herbs and olive oil well.
- Use this to coat the lamb before adding to the basket of the air fryer.
- Close the lid, and then let this cook. Halfway through, you can shake the basket to make sure nothing sticks.
- After ten minutes, take the lamb out and enjoy.

Nutrition:
Calories 542 Fat 37g
Carbs 3g Protein 45g

346. Baked Beef
Intermediate Recipe
Preparation Time: 10 minutes
Cooking Time: 60minutes
Servings: 5
Ingredients:
- 1 bunch garlic cloves
- 1 bunch fresh herbs, mixed
- sliced onions
- Olive oil
- lbs beef
- celery sticks, chopped
- carrots, chopped

Directions:
- Great up a pan and then add the herbs, olive oil, beef roast, and vegetables inside.
- Turn the air fryer on to 400 degrees and place the pan inside. Let this heat up and close the lid.
- After an hour of cooking, open the lid and then serve this right away.

Nutrition:
Calories 306 Fat 21g
Carbs 10g Protein 32g

347. Old-Fashioned Pork Chops
Basic Recipe
Preparation Time: 5 minutes
Cooking Time: 15 minutes
Servings: 6
Ingredients:
- Salt

0.5 tsp onion powder
0.25 tsp chili powder
0.25 tsp. Pepper
1 tsp smoked paprika
1 cup pork rind
tbsp parmesan, grated
boneless pork chops
beaten eggs

Directions:
Use the pepper and salt to season the pork chops. Blend the rind to make some crumbs.

In another bowl, beat the eggs and then coat this onto the pork chops with the crumbs.

Take out the air fryer and set it to 400 degrees to heat up.

When this is done, add the pork chops into the air fryer and let it heat up. When this is halfway done, flip the pork chops over and cook a little more.

After 15 minutes of cooking, turn off the air fryer and serve.

Nutrition:
Calories 391 Fat 18g
Carbs 17g Protein 38g

348. Turkey Pillows
Basic Recipe
Preparation Time: 5 minutes
Cooking Time: 10 minutes
Servings: 4
Ingredients:
  slices turkey breast
  jars Cream cheese
  1 Egg yolk
  cups Flour
  20.5 tbsp Dried granular yeast
  tbsp Sugar
  tsp Salt
  0.25 cup Olive oil
  0.33 cup Water
  1 cup Milk with an egg inside

Directions:
Mix the ingredients for the dough with your hands until smooth. Make it into small balls and put on a floured surface. Open the dough balls with a roller to make it square. Cut into small pieces. Fill with the turkey breast and a bit of cream cheese. Close the points together.

Turn on the air fryer to 400 degrees. Place a few of the balls inside and let them cook. After five minutes, take these out and repeat with the rest of the pillows until done.

Nutrition:
Calories 528
Fat 30g
Carbs 23g
Protein 44g

349. Chicken Wings
Basic Recipe
Preparation Time: 5 minutes
Cooking Time: 25 minutes
Servings: 2
Ingredients:
  tbsp. chives
  0.5 tbsp. salt
  1 tbsp lime
  0.5 tbsp ginger, chopped
  1 tbsp garlic, minced
  1 tbsp chili paste
  tbsp honey
  0.5 tbsp cornstarch
  1 tbsp soy sauce
  Oil
  chicken wings

Directions:
Dry the chicken and then cover it with spray. Add into the air fryer that is preheated to 400 degrees.

Let this cook for a bit. During that time, add the rest of the ingredients to a bowl and set aside.

After 25 minutes, the chicken is done. Add the chicken into a bowl and top with the sauce. Sprinkle the chives on top and serve.

Nutrition:
Calories 81 Fat 5g
Carbs 0g Protein 8g

350. Sesame Chicken
Basic Recipe
Preparation Time: 5 minutes
Cooking Time: 50minutes
Servings: 4
Ingredients:
- Soy sauce
- Pepper
- Salt
- Olive oil
- Breadcrumbs
- Egg
- 1 lb. Chicken breast

Directions:
Slice the chicken into fillets and add to the bowl with the sesame and soy sauce. Let this marinate for half an hour. Beat the eggs and then pass the chicken through it.

Add to the grill of the air fryer at 350 degrees. Let it grill for a bit.

After 20 minutes, take the chicken off and let it cool down before serving.

Nutrition:
Calories 375 Fat 18g
Carbs 6g Protein 35g

351. Chicken And Potatoes
Basic Recipe
Preparation Time: 5 minutes
Cooking Time: 55minutes
Servings: 2
Ingredients:
- Pepper and salt
- Provencal herbs
- Chicken pieces
- Potatoes
- Olive oil

Directions:
Peel the skin from the potatoes and cut into slices. Add some pepper and place into the air fryer.

Preheat to 340 degrees. Cover the chicken with the herbs, pepper, salt, and oil and add it in with the potatoes.

Cook this until well done. After forty minutes, turn the chicken around and let it cook another 15 minutes before serving.

Nutrition:
Calories 200 Fat 4g
Carbs 18g Protein 22g

352. Polish Sausage And Sourdough Kabobs
Basic Recipe
Preparation Time: 5 minutes
Cooking Time: 15 minutes
Servings: 4
Ingredients:
- 1 pound smoked Polish beef sausage, sliced
- 1 tablespoon mustard - 1 tablespoon olive oil
- tablespoons Worcestershire sauce
- bell peppers, sliced
- cups sourdough bread, cubed
- Salt and ground black pepper, to taste

Directions:
Toss the sausage with the mustard, olive, and Worcestershire sauce. Thread sausage, peppers, and bread onto skewers.

Sprinkle with salt and black pepper.

Cook in the preheated Air Fryer at 360 degrees F for 11 minutes

Brush the skewers with the reserved marinade. Bon appétit!

Nutrition:
Calories 284 Fat 13.8g
Carbs 16.5g Protein 23.1g

353. Ranch Meatloaf With Peppers

Basic Recipe
Preparation Time: 5 minutes
Cooking Time: 30 minutes
Servings: 5
Ingredients:
- 1 pound beef, ground
- 1/2 pound veal, ground
- 1 egg
- tablespoons vegetable juice
- 1 cup crackers, crushed
- bell peppers, chopped
- 1 onion, chopped
- garlic cloves, minced
- tablespoons tomato paste
- tablespoons soy sauce
- 1 (1-ounce) package ranch dressing mix
- Sea salt, to taste
- 1/2 teaspoon ground black pepper, to taste
- ounces tomato paste
- 1 tablespoon Dijon mustard

Directions:
- Start by preheating your Air Fryer to 330 degrees F.
- In a mixing bowl, thoroughly combine the ground beef, veal, egg, vegetable juice, crackers, bell peppers, onion, garlic, tomato paste, and soy sauce, ranch dressing mix, salt, and ground black pepper. Mix until everything is well incorporated and press into a lightly greased meatloaf pan.
- Cook approximately 25 minutes in the preheated Air Fryer. Whisk the tomato paste with the mustard and spread the topping over the top of your meatloaf.

Continue to cook 2 minutes more. Let it stand on a cooling rack for 6 minutes before slicing and serving. Enjoy!

Nutrition:
Calories 411 Fat 31.4g
Carbs 10g Protein 28.2g

354. Indian Beef Samosas

Basic Recipe
Preparation Time: 5 minutes
Cooking Time: 30 minutes
Servings: 8
Ingredients:
- 1 tablespoon sesame oil
- tablespoons shallots, minced
- cloves garlic, minced
- tablespoons green chili peppers, chopped
- 1/2 pound ground chuck
- ounces bacon, chopped
- Salt and ground black pepper, to taste
- 1 teaspoon cumin powder
- 1 teaspoon turmeric
- 1 teaspoon coriander
- 1 cup frozen peas, thawed
- 1 (16-ounce) of phyllo dough
- 1 egg, beaten with 2 tablespoons of water (egg wash)

Directions:
- Heat the oil in a saucepan over medium-high heat. Once hot, sauté the shallots, garlic, and chili peppers until tender, about 3 minutes
- Then, add the beef and bacon; continue to sauté an additional 4 minutes, crumbling with a fork. Season it with salt, pepper, cumin powder, turmeric, and coriander. Stir in peas.
- Then, preheat your Air Fryer to 330 degrees F. Brush the Air Fryer basket with cooking oil.
- Place 1 to 2 tablespoons of the mixture onto each phyllo sheet. Fold the sheets into

triangles, pressing the edges. Brush the tops with egg wash.

Bake it for 7 to 8 minutes, working with batches. Serve with Indian tomato sauce if desired. Enjoy!

Nutrition:
Calories 266 Fat 13g
Carbs 24.5g Protein 12.2g

355. Grilled Vienna Sausage With Broccoli
Basic Recipe
Preparation Time: 5 minutes
Cooking Time: 20 minutes
Servings: 4
Ingredients:
- 1 pound beef Vienna sausage
- 1/2 cup mayonnaise
- 1 teaspoon yellow mustard
- 1 tablespoon fresh lemon juice
- 1 teaspoon garlic powder
- 1/4 teaspoon black pepper
- 1 pound broccoli

Directions:
Start by preheating your Air Fryer to 380 degrees F. Spritz the grill pan with cooking oil.

Cut the sausages into serving sized pieces. Cook the sausages for 15 minutes, shaking the basket occasionally to get all sides browned. Set aside.

In the meantime, whisk the mayonnaise with mustard, lemon juice, garlic powder, and black pepper. Toss the broccoli with the mayo mixture.

Turn up temperature to 400 degrees F. Cook broccoli for 6 minutes, turning halfway through the cooking time. Serve the sausage with the grilled broccoli on the side. Bon appétit!

Nutrition:
Calories 477 Fat 43.2g
Carbs 7.3g Protein 15.9g

356. Aromatic T-Bone Steak With Garlic
Basic Recipe
Preparation Time: 5 minutes
Cooking Time: 15 minutes
Servings: 3
Ingredients:
- 1-pound T-bone steak
- garlic cloves, halved
- 1/4 cup all-purpose flour
- tablespoons olive oil
- 1/4 cup tamari sauce
- teaspoons brown sugar
- tablespoons tomato paste
- 1 teaspoon Sriracha sauce
- tablespoons white vinegar
- 1 teaspoon dried rosemary
- 1/2 teaspoon dried basil
- heaping tablespoons cilantro, chopped

Directions:
Rub the garlic halves all over the T-bone steak. Toss the steak with the flour.

Drizzle with the oil all over the steak and transfer it to the grill pan; grill the steak in the preheated Air Fryer at 400 degrees F for 10 minutes

Meanwhile, whisk the tamari sauce, sugar, tomato paste, Sriracha, vinegar, rosemary, and basil. Cook an additional 5 minutes

Serve garnished with fresh cilantro. Bon appétit!

Nutrition:
Calories 463 Fat 24.6g
Carbs 16.7g Protein 44.7g

357. Sausage Scallion Balls
Basic Recipe
Preparation Time: 5 minutes
Cooking Time: 15 minutes
Servings: 4
Ingredients:
- 1 ½ pounds beef sausage meat

1 cup rolled oats
tablespoons scallions, chopped
1 teaspoon worcestershire sauce
Flaky sea salt and freshly ground black pepper, to taste
1 teaspoon paprika
1/2 teaspoon granulated garlic
1 teaspoon dried basil
1/2 teaspoon dried oregano
teaspoons mustard
pickled cucumbers

Directions:

Start by preheating your Air Fryer to 380 degrees F. Spritz the Air Fryer basket with cooking oil.

In a mixing bowl, thoroughly combine the sausage meat, oats, scallions, Worcestershire sauce, salt, black pepper, paprika, garlic, basil, and oregano.

Then, form the mixture into equal sized meatballs using a tablespoon.

Place the meatballs in the Air Fryer basket and cook for 15 minutes, turning halfway through the cooking time. Serve with mustard and cucumbers. Bon appétit!

Nutrition:
Calories 560
Fat 42.2g
Carbs 21.5g
Protein 31.1g

358. Cube Steak With Cowboy Sauce

Basic Recipe
Preparation Time: 5 minutes
Cooking Time: 15 minutes
Servings: 4
Ingredients:

1 ½ pounds cube steak
Salt, to taste
1/4 teaspoon ground black pepper, or more to taste
ounces butter
garlic cloves, finely chopped
scallions, finely chopped
tablespoon fresh parsley, finely chopped
1 tablespoon fresh horseradish, grated
1 teaspoon cayenne pepper

Directions:

Pat dry the cube steak and season it with salt and black pepper. Spritz the Air Fryer basket with cooking oil. Add the meat to the basket.

Cook in the preheated Air Fryer at 400 degrees F for 14 minutes

Meanwhile, melt the butter in a skillet over a moderate heat. Add the remaining ingredients and simmer until the sauce has thickened and reduced slightly. Top the warm cube steaks with Cowboy sauce and serve immediately.

Nutrition:
Calories 469
Fat 30.4g
Carbs 0.6g
Protein 46g

359. Steak Fingers With Lime Sauce

Basic Recipe
Preparation Time: 5 minutes
Cooking Time: 15 minutes
Servings: 4
Ingredients:

1 ½ pounds sirloin steak
1/4 cup soy sauce
1/4 cup fresh lime juice
1 teaspoon garlic powder
1 teaspoon shallot powder
1 teaspoon celery seeds
1 teaspoon mustard seeds
Coarse sea salt and ground black pepper, to taste

1 teaspoon red pepper flakes
eggs, lightly whisked
1 cup breadcrumbs
1/4 cup parmesan cheese
1 teaspoon paprika

Directions:
- Place the steak, soy sauce, lime juice, garlic powder, shallot powder, celery seeds, mustard seeds, salt, black pepper, and red pepper in a large ceramic bowl; let it marinate for 3 hours.
- Tenderize the cube steak by pounding with a mallet; cut into 1-inch strips.
- In a shallow bowl, whisk the eggs. In another bowl, mix the breadcrumbs, parmesan cheese, and paprika.
- Dip the beef pieces into the whisked eggs and coat on all sides. Now, dredge the beef pieces in the breadcrumb mixture.
- Cook at 400 degrees F for 14 minutes, flipping halfway through the cooking time.
- Meanwhile, make the sauce by heating the reserved marinade in a saucepan over medium heat; let it simmer until thoroughly warmed. Serve the steak fingers with the sauce on the side. Enjoy!

Nutrition:
Calories 471
Fat 26.3g
Carbs 13.9g
Protein 42.5g

360. Beef Kofta Sandwich
Basic Recipe
Preparation Time: 5 minutes
Cooking Time: 25 minutes
Servings: 4
Ingredients:
1/2 cup leeks, chopped
garlic cloves, smashed
1-pound ground chuck
1 slice of bread, soaked in water until fully tender
Salt, to taste
1/4 teaspoon ground black pepper, or more to taste
1 teaspoon cayenne pepper
1/2 teaspoon ground sumac
saffron threads
tablespoons loosely packed fresh continental parsley leaves
tablespoons tahini sauce
warm flatbreads
ounces baby arugula
tomatoes cut into slices

Directions:
- In a bowl, mix the chopped leeks, garlic, ground meat, soaked bread, and spices; knead with your hands until everything is well incorporated.
- Now, mound the beef mixture around a wooden skewer into a pointed-ended sausage.
- Cook in the preheated Air Fryer at 360 degrees F for 25 minutes
- To make the sandwiches, spread the tahini sauce on the flatbread; top with the kofta kebabs, baby arugula and tomatoes. Enjoy!

Nutrition:
Calories 436 Fat 20.5g
Carbs 32g Protein 33.7g

361. Classic Beef Ribs
Basic Recipe
Preparation Time: 5 minutes
Cooking Time: 30 minutes
Servings: 4
Ingredients:
pounds beef back ribs
1 tablespoon sunflower oil
1/2 teaspoon mixed peppercorns, cracked
1 teaspoon red pepper flakes
1 teaspoon dry mustard

Coarse sea salt, to taste

Directions:
- Trim the excess fat from the beef ribs. Mix the sunflower oil, cracked peppercorns, red pepper, dry mustard, and salt.
- Rub over the ribs.
- Cook in the preheated Air Fryer at 395 degrees F for 11 minutes
- Turn the heat to 330 degrees F and continue to cook for 18 minutes more. Serve warm.

Nutrition:
Calories 532 Fat 39g Carbs 0.4g
Protein 44.7g

362. Spicy Short Ribs With Red Wine Sauce

Basic Recipe
Preparation Time: 5 minutes
Cooking Time: 15 minutes
Servings: 4
Ingredients:
- 1 ½ pounds short rib
- 1 cup red wine
- 1/2 cup tamari sauce
- 1 lemon, juiced
- 1 teaspoon fresh ginger, grated
- 1 teaspoon salt
- 1 teaspoon black pepper
- 1 teaspoon paprika
- 1 teaspoon chipotle chili powder
- 1 cup ketchup
- 1 teaspoon garlic powder
- 1 teaspoon cumin

Directions:
- In a ceramic bowl, place the beef ribs, wine, tamari sauce, lemon juice, ginger, salt, black pepper, paprika, and chipotle chili powder.
- Cover and let it marinate for 3 hours in the refrigerator.
- Discard the marinade and add the short ribs to the Air Fryer basket. Cook in the preheated Air fry at 380 degrees F for 10 minutes, turning them over halfway through the cooking time.
- In the meantime, heat the saucepan over medium heat; add the reserved marinade and stir in the ketchup, garlic powder, and cumin.
- Cook until the sauce has thickened slightly.
- Pour the sauce over the warm ribs and serve immediately. Bon appétit!

Nutrition:
Calories 505
Fat 31g
Carbs 22.1g
Protein 35.2g

363. Crispy Salt and Pepper Tofu

Preparation Time: 5 minutes
Cooking Time: 15 minutes
Servings: 4
Ingredients:
- ¼ cup chickpea flour
- ¼ cup arrowroot (or cornstarch)
- 1 tsp. sea salt
- 1 tsp. granulated garlic
- ½ tsp. freshly grated black pepper
- 1 (15-oz.) package tofu, firm or extra-firm
- Cooking oil spray (sunflower, safflower, or refined coconut)
- Asian Spicy Sweet Sauce, optional

Directions:
- In a medium bowl, combine the flour, arrowroot, salt, garlic, and pepper. Stir well to combine.
- Cut the tofu into cubes (no need to press—if it's a bit watery, that's fine!). Place the cubes into the flour mixture. Toss well to coat. Spray the tofu with oil and toss again. (The spray will help the coating better stick to the tofu.)
- Spray the air fry basket with the oil. Place the tofu in a single layer in the air fry

basket (you may have to do this in 2 batches, depending on the size of your appliance) and spray the tops with oil. Fry for 8 minutes. Remove the air fry basket and spray again with oil. Toss gently or turn the pieces over. Spray with oil again and fry for another 7 minutes, or until golden-browned and very crisp.

Serve immediately, either plain or with the Asian Spicy Sweet Sauce.

Nutrition:
Calories: 148
Total Fats: 5 g
Sodium: 473 mg
Carbs: 14 g Fiber: 1 g
Protein: 11 g

364. Air Fryer Chicken Wings

Preparation Time: 5 minutes
Cooking Time: 20 minutes
Servings: 4
Ingredients:
- 4 Chicken wings
- ½ tsp. Sea salt
- ½ tsp. Black pepper
- 1 oz. Smoked paprika
- ½ tsp. Garlic powder
- ½ tsp. Onion powder
- ½ tsp. Baking powder
- 2 tbsp. Olive oil

Directions:
Take the chicken wing out of the refrigerator and pat them dry (if you remove as much moisture as possible, you will get a crispy wing skin).

Mix the sea salt, black pepper, smoked paprika, garlic powder, onion powder and baking powder in a small bowl or baking dish.

Sprinkle the spice mixture on the wings and throw it to cover.

Place the wings on the respective basket. In Air Fryer Oven this is known as the "Cook&Crisp" basket.

Drizzle the chicken wings with olive oil.

Use the "Air Crisp" setting at 400°F on the Air Fryer Oven to cook the wings for 14 minutes on each side.

Enjoy hot wings!

Nutrition:
Calories: 32
Protein: 2 g
Fats: 1.73 g
Carbs: 2.56 g

365. Spicy Parmesan Chicken Wings

Preparation Time: 5 minutes
Cooking Time: 35 minutes
Servings: 5
Ingredients:
- 2 Chicken wings
- ½ tsp. Sea salt
- ½ tsp. Black pepper
- 2 Bell pepper
- ½ tsp. Garlic powder
- ½ tsp. Onion powder
- ½ tsp. Baking powder
- 1 lb. Parmesan cheese

Directions:
Take the chicken wing out of the refrigerator and pat them dry.

Mix sea salt, black pepper, bell pepper, garlic powder, onion powder and baking powder in a small bowl.

Sprinkle some of the spice mixture on the wings and throw it to cover.

Place the wings on a flat layer in the Air Fryer Oven .

Place the chicken in the Air Fryer Oven at 400°F and cook for 30 minutes. To make the wings crispy quickly, you have to turn them about halfway.

Serve the chicken wings with the rest of the spicy parmesan sauce.

Nutrition:
Calories: 176
Protein: 2.02 g
Fats: 15.19 g
Carbs: 9.79 g

366. Buffalo Cauliflower Bites

Preparation Time: 5 minutes
Cooking Time: 25 minutes
Servings: 4
Ingredients:
- 2 lb. Cauliflower
- 2 Garlic cloves
- 3 tbsp Oil
- ½ tsp. Salt
- 1 lb. Blue cheese

For the Buffalo Sauce:
- 1 lb. Hot Sauce
- 1 tbsp Butter
- 1 lb. Worcestershire sauce

Directions:
- Cut the cauliflower into florets of equal size and place in a large bowl.
- Cut each clove of garlic into 3 pieces and smash them with the side of your knife. Don't be afraid to smash the garlic. You want to expose as much of the garlic surface as possible so that it cooks well. Add this to the cauliflower.
- Pour over the oil and add salt. Mix well until the cauliflower is well covered with oil and salt.
- Turn on the Air Fryer Oven at 400°F for 20 minutes and add the cauliflower. Turn it in half once.
- To make the Sauce, whisk the hot sauce, butter and Worcestershire sauce in a small bowl.
- Once the cauliflower is cooked, place it in a large bowl. Pour the hot sauce over the cauliflower and mix well.
- Put the cauliflower back in the Air Fryer Oven. Set it to 400F for 3-4 minutes so the sauce becomes a little firm.
- Serve with the blue cheese.

Nutrition:
Calories: 69 Protein: 1.87 g
Fats: 6.06 g Carbs: 1.99 g

367. Spicy Dry-Rubbed Chicken Wings

Preparation Time: 5 minutes
Cooking Time: 45 minutes
Servings: 6
Ingredients:
- 2 Chicken wings
- ¼ cup Spicy dry massage

Directions:
- Take the chicken out of the fridge and let it approach room temperature (30 minutes). Preheat the oven to 400°F.
- Place the chicken in a Ziploc® bag with the spicy dry massage.
- Shake the bag so that the mixture covers the chicken evenly.
- Store in the refrigerator for at least 4 hours, ideally overnight.

Nutrition:
Calories: 230 Protein: 31.02 g
Fats: 11.54 g Carbs: 1.11 g

368. Air Fryer Steak Bites and Mushrooms

Preparation Time: 5 minutes
Cooking Time: 25 minutes
Servings: 4
Ingredients:
- 1 lb. Beef cut into cubes
- 3 tbsp Olive oil
- ½ tbsp Montreal steak seasoning
- 2 Mushrooms

Directions:
- Preheat the empty air fryer to 390 °F with a crisp plate or basket for 4 minutes.

Pat the meat dry. As the Air Fryer Oven heats up, throw beef cubes with olive oil and Montreal spices.

Halve the mushrooms. Put the beef cubes and halved mushrooms into the preheated Air Fryer Oven and gently shake to combine.

Set the Air Fryer Oven temperature to 390°F and the timer to 8 minutes.

Stop after 3 minutes and shake the basket. Repeat this process every 2 minutes, or until the beef cubes have reached the desired degree of cooking. Lift a large piece out and test it with a meat thermometer or cut and look in the middle to see the progress. Note that the meat will continue to cook as soon as it is removed from the Air Fryer Oven and resting.

Let the meat rest for a few minutes before serving and then enjoy.

Nutrition:
Calories: 583 Protein: 32.38 g
Fats: 27.25 g Carbs: 61.98 g

369. Pecan Crusted Chicken

Preparation Time: 10 minutes
Cooking Time: 25 minutes
Servings: 6
Ingredients:
- 2 lb. Chicken tenders
- ½ tsp. Salt
- ½ tsp. Pepper
- 1 Smoked paprika
- 1 tbsp Honey
- 1 lb. Mustard
- 1 lb. Pecans, finely chopped

Directions:

Place the chicken tenders in a large bowl.

Add the salt, pepper and smoked paprika and mix well until the chicken is covered with the spices.

Pour in the honey and mustard and mix well.

Place the finely chopped pecans on a plate.

Roll the tenders into the shredded pecans, one chicken tender at a time, until both sides are covered. Brush off excess material.

Place the chicken tenders in the air fry basket and continue until all the tenders have been coated and are in the air fry basket.

Set the Air Fryer Oven to 350°F for 12 minutes until the chicken is cooked through and the pecans are golden brown before serving.

Nutrition:
Calories: 95 Protein: 3.08 g
Fats: 8.18 g
Carbs: 3.16 g

370. Chicken Tikka Kebab

Preparation Time: 10 minutes
Cooking Time: 30 minutes
Servings: 6
Ingredients:
- 2 lb. Chicken
- 1 lb. Marinade
- 2 tbsp Oil
- 2 Onions
- 2 Green Pepper
- 2 Red Pepper

Directions:

Add the chicken and spread the marinade on each side. Let it rest in the fridge for between 30 minutes and 8 hours.

Add the oil, onions, green and red peppers to the marinade for cooking. Mix well.

Thread the marinated chicken, peppers and onions into the skewers in between.

Lightly, grease the air fry basket.

Arrange the chicken sticks in the Air Fryer Oven. Cook them at 356°F for 10 minutes.

Turn the chicken sticks and cook for another 7 minutes, then serve.

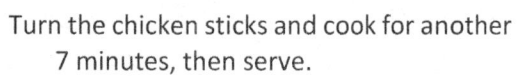

Nutrition:
Calories: 147 Protein: 10.25 g
Fats: 10.68 g Carbs: 1.85 g

371. Air Fryer Brussels sprouts
Preparation Time: 10 minutes
Cooking Time: 15 minutes
Servings: 2
Ingredients:
- ¼ c. balsamic vinegar
- 3 tbsp. extra-virgin olive oil
- ½ tsp. Kosher salt
- ½ tsp. Freshly ground black pepper

Directions:
- Remove the hard ends of the Brussels sprouts and remove any damaged outer leaves. Rinse them under cold water and pat dry. If the sprouts are large, cut them in half. Add the oil, salt and pepper.
- Arrange the Brussels sprouts in a single layer in your Air Fryer Oven and work in batches if not all fit. Cook for 8–12 minutes at 374°F and shake the pan halfway through the cooking process to brown it evenly. They are done when they are lightly browned and crispy at the edges.
- Serve the sprouts warm, optionally with balsamic reduction and parmesan.

Nutrition:
Calories: 1197 Protein: 125.58 g
Fats: 65.97 g
Carbs: 16.97 g

372. Crispy Air Fried Tofu
Preparation Time: 10 minutes
Cooking Time: 50 minutes
Servings: 8
Ingredients:
- 2 c. almond flour
- ½ tsp. baking soda
- ¼ tsp. kosher salt
- ¼ c. butter, room temperature
- ¼ c. almond butter
- 3 tbsp. honey
- 1 large egg
- 1 tsp. pure vanilla extract
- 1 c. semisweet chocolate chips
- ½ tsp. Flaky sea salt
- 1 lb. Tofu

Directions:
- Squeeze the tofu for at least 15 minutes by placing either a heavy pan or a pan on top and letting the moisture drain. When you're done, cut the tofu into bite-sized blocks and put it in a bowl.
- Mix all the remaining ingredients in a small bowl. Drizzle over the tofu and toss to cover. Let the tofu marinate for another 15 minutes.
- Preheat your air fryer to 374°F. Add the tofu blocks to your air fry basket in a single layer. Let cook for 10–15 minutes and shake the pan occasionally for an even cooking.

Nutrition:
Calories: 247
Protein: 3.83 g
Fats: 18.05 g
Carbs: 21.99 g

373. Buttermilk Fried Mushrooms
Preparation Time: 5 minutes
Cooking Time: 30 minutes
Servings: 2
Ingredients:
- 2 tbsp. olive oil
- 1 tsp. kosher salt
- 1 tsp. cayenne
- 1 tsp. paprika
- 1 tsp. garlic powder
- 1 tsp. onion powder

1 tsp. oregano
2 lemons, sliced thinly crosswise
2 lb. Mushrooms
1 lb. Buttermilk
2 cups Flour

Directions:

Preheat the Air Fryer Oven to 374°C. Clean the mushrooms and place them in a large bowl with buttermilk. Let marinate for 15 minutes.

Mix the flour and spices in a large bowl. Put the mushrooms out of the buttermilk (keep the buttermilk). Dip each mushroom in the flour mixture, shake off any excess flour, dip again in the buttermilk and then again in the flour.

Grease the bottom of your air pan well and place the mushrooms in a layer, leaving space between the mushrooms. Let it cook for 5 minutes, then roughly coat all sides with a little oil to promote browning. Cook for another 5–10 minutes until golden brown and crispy.

Nutrition:
Calories: 380
Protein: 49.65 g
Fats: 18.15 g
Carbs: 6.86 g

374. Crispy Baked Avocado Tacos

Preparation Time: 10 minutes
Cooking Time: 20 minutes
Servings: 5
Ingredients:
2 Avocado
1 cup Flour
1 Panko

For the Sauce:
6 slices of ham (we used Applegate brand)
4 eggs
¼ cup full-fat coconut milk
¼ cup orange bell peppers, chopped
¼ cup red bell peppers, chopped
¼ cup yellow onions, chopped
½ tsp. Salt & pepper, to taste
1 tbsp Olive oil or coconut oil to sauté veggies

Directions:

Combine all the salsa ingredients and put them in the fridge.

Halve the avocado lengthwise and remove the pit. Lay the avocado skin-face down and cut each half into 4 equal pieces. Then gently peel off the skin.

Preheat the oven to 446°C or the Air Fryer Oven to 374°F. Arrange your work area so that you have a bowl of flour, a bowl of sauce, a bowl of panko with salt and pepper, and a baking sheet lined with parchment at the end.

Dip each avocado slice first in the flour, then in the sauce and then in the panko. Place on the prepared baking sheet and bake for 10 minutes or fry in the air. Lightly brown after half of the cooking process.

While cooking avocados, combine all the ingredients in the bowls.

Pour some mixture on each tortilla, top with 2 pieces of avocado and drizzle with sauce. Serve immediately and enjoy!

Nutrition:
Calories: 193
Protein: 13.7 g
Fats: 13.25 g
Carbs: 4.69 g

375. Chicken Cordon Bleu

Preparation Time: 60 minutes
Cooking Time: 40 minutes
Servings: 6
Ingredients:
1 garlic clove
2 eggs
2 tsp. butter, melted

1 cup bread, ground
¼ cup flour
2 tsp. fresh thyme
16 slices Swiss cheese
8 slices ham
4 chicken breasts

Directions:

Preheat the Air Fryer Oven to 350ºF.

Flatten out the chicken breasts and then fill them with 2 cheese slices, 2 ham slices, and then cheese again.

Roll the chicken breasts, using a toothpick to keep them together.

Mix the garlic, thyme, and bread together with the butter. Beat the eggs and season the flour with pepper and salt.

Pass the chicken rolls through the flour, then the eggs, and then the breadcrumbs. Add to the Air Fryer Oven to cook.

After 20 minutes, take the chicken rolls out and them cool down before serving.

Nutrition:

Calories: 387
Carbs: 18 g
Fats: 20 g
Protein: 33 g

376. Fried Chicken

Preparation Time: 20 minutes
Cooking Time: 25 minutes
Servings: 4
Ingredients:

1 lemon
1 ginger, grated
½ tsp. Ground pepper, salt, and garlic powder
1 lb. chopped chicken
1 tbsp Oil

Directions:

Add the chicken to a bowl with the rest of the ingredients. Let it set for a bit to marinate.

After 15 minutes, add some oil to the Air Fryer Oven and let it heat up to 320°F.

Place the chicken in the Air Fryer Oven to cook for 25 minutes, shaking it a few times to cook through. Serve warm.

Nutrition:

Calories: 345
Carbs: 23 g
Fats: 3 g
Protein: 3 g

377. Seasoned Tomatoes

Preparation Time: 10 minutes
Cooking Time: 10 minutes
Servings: 2
Ingredients:

3 tomatoes, halved
Olive oil cooking spray
Salt and ground black pepper
1 tbsp. fresh basil, chopped

Directions:

Drizzle the tomatoes halves with the olive oil.

Sprinkle with salt, black pepper and basil.

Press the "Power" button of the Air Fryer Oven and turn the dial to select the "Air Fry" mode.

Press the "Time" button and again turn the dial to set the cooking time to 10 minutes.

Now push the "Temp" button and rotate the dial to set the temperature at 320°F.

Press the "Start/Pause" button to start.

Open the unit when it has reached the temperature, when it beeps.

Arrange the tomatoes in the air fry basket and insert them in the oven.

Serve warm.

Nutrition:

Calories: 34
Fats: 0.4 g
Carbs: 7.2 g
Protein: 1.7 g

378. Filled Tomatoes

Preparation Time: 15 minutes
Cooking Time: 15 minutes
Servings: 4
Ingredients:
- 2 large tomatoes
- ½ cup broccoli, chopped finely
- ½ cup Cheddar cheese, shredded
- Salt and ground black pepper
- ½ tsp. dried thyme, crushed

Directions:
- Carefully, cut the top of each tomato d scoop out the pulp and seeds.
- In a bowl, mix together the chopped broccoli, cheese, salt and black pepper.
- Stuff each tomato with the broccoli mixture evenly.
- Press the "Power" button of the Air Fryer Oven and turn the dial to select the "Air Fry" mode.
- Press the "Time" button and again turn the dial to set the cooking time to 15 minutes.
- Now push the "Temp" button and rotate the dial to set the temperature at 355°F.
- Press the "Start/Pause" button to start.
- Open the unit when it has reached the temperature, when it beeps.
- Arrange the tomatoes in a basket and insert them in the Air Fryer Oven.
- Serve warm with the garnishing of thyme.

Nutrition:
- Calories: 206
- Fats: 15.6 g
- Carbs: 9 g
- Protein: 9.4 g

379. Parmesan Asparagus

Preparation Time: 10 minutes
Cooking Time: 10 minutes
Servings: 3
Ingredients:
- 1 lb. fresh asparagus, trimmed
- 1 tbsp. Parmesan cheese, grated
- 1 tbsp. butter, melted
- 1 tsp. garlic powder
- Salt and ground black pepper

Directions:
- In a bowl, mix together the asparagus, cheese, butter, garlic powder, salt, and black pepper.
- Press the "Power" button of the Air Fryer Oven and turn the dial to select the "Air Fry" mode.
- Press the "Time" button and again turn the dial to set the cooking time to 10 minutes.
- Now push the "Temp" button and rotate the dial to set the temperature at 400°F.
- Press the "Start/Pause" button to start.
- Open the unit when it has reached the temperature, when it beeps.
- Arrange the veggie mixture in a basket and insert them in the Air Fryer Oven.
- Serve hot.

Nutrition:
- Calories: 73
- Fats: 4.4 g
- Carbs: 6.6 g
- Protein: 4.2 g

380. Almond Asparagus

Preparation Time: 15 minutes
Cooking Time: 16 minutes
Servings: 3
Ingredients:
- 1 lb. asparagus
- 2 tbsp. olive oil
- 2 tbsp. balsamic vinegar
- Salt and ground black pepper

Directions:
- In a bowl, mix together the asparagus, oil, vinegar, salt, and black pepper.
- Press the "Power" button of the Air Fryer Oven and turn the dial to select the "Air Fry" mode.

Press the "Time" button and again turn the dial to set the cooking time to 6 minutes.

Now push the "Temp" button and rotate the dial to set the temperature at 400°F.

Press the "Start/Pause" button to start.

Open the unit when it has reached the temperature, when it beeps.

Arrange the veggie mixture in a basket and insert them in the Air Fryer Oven.

Serve hot.

Nutrition:

Calories: 173
Fats: 14.8 g
Carbs: 8.2 g
Protein: 5.6 g

381. Spicy Butternut Squash

Preparation Time: 15 minutes
Cooking Time: 20 minutes
Servings: 4
Ingredients:

- 1 medium butternut squash, peeled, seeded and cut into chunks
- 2 tsp. cumin seeds
- ⅛ tsp. garlic powder
- ⅛ tsp. chili flakes, crushed
- Salt and ground black pepper
- 1 tbsp. olive oil
- 2 tbsp. pine nuts
- 2 tbsp. fresh cilantro, chopped

Directions:

In a bowl, mix together the squash, spices, and oil.

Press the "Power" button of the Air Fryer Oven and turn the dial to select the "Air Fry" mode.

Press the "Time" button and again turn the dial to set the cooking time to 20 minutes.

Now push the "Temp" button and rotate the dial to set the temperature at 375°F.

Press the "Start/Pause" button to start.

Open the unit when it has reached the temperature, when it beeps.

Arrange the squash chunks in a basket and insert them in the Air Fryer Oven.

Serve hot with the garnishing of pine nuts and cilantro.

Nutrition:

Calories: 191
Fats: 7 g
Carbs: 34.3 g
Protein: 3.7 g

382. Sweet & Spicy Parsnips

Preparation Time: 15 minutes
Cooking Time: 44 minutes
Servings: 5
Ingredients:

- 1 ½ lb. parsnip, peeled and cut into 1-inch chunks
- 1 tbsp. butter, melted
- 2 tbsp. honey
- 1 tbsp. dried parsley flakes, crushed
- ¼ tsp. red pepper flakes, crushed
- Salt and ground black pepper

Directions:

In a large bowl, mix together the parsnips and butter.

Press the "Power" button of the Air Fryer Oven and turn the dial to select the "Air Fry" mode.

Press the "Time" button and again turn the dial to set the cooking time to 44 minutes.

Now push the "Temp" button and rotate the dial to set the temperature at 355°F.

Press the "Start/Pause" button to start.

Open the unit when it has reached the temperature, when it beeps.

Arrange the squash chunks in a basket and insert them in the Air Fryer Oven.

Meanwhile, in another large bowl, mix together the remaining ingredients.

After 40 minutes of cooking, press the "Start/Pause" button to pause the unit. Transfer the parsnips chunks into the bowl of honey mixture and toss to coat well.

Again, arrange the parsnip chunks in the air fry basket and insert in the Air Fryer Oven.

Serve hot.

Nutrition:
Calories: 149 Fats: 2.7 g
Carbs: 31.5 g Protein: 1.7 g

383. Pesto Tomatoes

Preparation Time: 15 minutes
Cooking Time: 20 minutes
Servings: 4
Ingredients:
- 3 large heirloom tomatoes cut into ½ inch thick slices.
- 8 oz. feta cheese, cut into ½ inch thick slices.
- ½ cup red onions, thinly sliced
- 1 tbsp. olive oil

Directions:
Spread some pesto on each tomato slice. Top each tomato slice with a feta slice, onion and drizzle with oil.

Press the "Power" button of the Air Fryer Oven and turn the dial to select the "Air Fry" mode. Press the "Time" button and again turn the dial to set the cooking time to 14 minutes.

Now push the "Temp" button and rotate the dial to set the temperature at 390°F. Press the "Start/Pause" button to start.

Open the unit when it has reached the temperature, when it beeps. Arrange the tomatoes in a basket and insert them in the Air Fryer Oven.

Serve warm.

Nutrition:
Calories: 480 Fats: 41.9 g
Carbs: 13 g Protein: 15.4 g

384. Roasted Cauliflower with Nuts & Raisins

Preparation Time: 5 minutes
Cooking Time: 20 minutes
Servings: 4
Ingredients:
- 1 small cauliflower head, cut into florets
- 2 tbsp. pine nuts, toasted
- 2 tbsp. raisins soak in boiling water and dried
- 1 tsp. curry powder
- ½ tsp. sea salt
- 3 tbsp. olive oil

Directions:
Preheat your Air Fryer Oven to 320°F for 2 minutes. Add all the ingredients to a bowl and toss to combine.

Add the cauliflower mixture to the air fry basket and cook for 15 minutes.

Nutrition:
Calories: 264
Fats: 26 g
Carbs: 8 g
Protein: 2 g

385. Spicy Herb Chicken Wings

Preparation Time: 15 minutes
Cooking Time: 15 minutes
Servings: 6
Ingredients:
- 4 lbs. chicken wings
- ½ tbsp. ginger
- 2 tbsp. vinegar
- 1 fresh lime juice
- 1 tbsp. olive oil
- 2 tbsp. soy sauce
- 6 garlic cloves, minced
- 1 habanero, chopped
- ¼ tsp. cinnamon
- ½ tsp. sea salt

Directions:
Preheat your Air Fryer Oven to 390°F.

Add all the ingredients except the chicken to a large bowl and combine well.

Place the chicken wings into the marinade mix and store in the fridge for 2 hours.

Add the chicken wings to the Air Fryer Oven and cook for 15 minutes. Serve hot!

Nutrition:
Calories: 673
Fats: 29 g
Carbs: 9 g
Protein: 39 g

386. Lamb Meatballs
Preparation Time: 5 minutes
Cooking Time: 15 minutes
Servings: 4
Ingredients:
- 1 lb. ground lamb
- 1 egg white
- ½ tsp. sea salt
- 2 tbsp. parsley, fresh, chopped
- 1 tbsp. coriander, chopped
- 2 garlic cloves, minced
- 1 tbsp. olive oil
- 1 tbsp. mint, chopped

Directions:
Preheat your Air Fryer Oven to 320°F.

Add all the ingredients in a mixing bowl and combine well.

Form small meatballs from the mixture and place them in air fry basket and cook for 15 minutes. Serve hot!

Nutrition:
Calories: 312 Fats: 9.8 g
Carbs: 12.3 g Protein: 23 g

387. Sweet & Sour Chicken Skewer
Preparation Time: 5 minutes
Cooking Time: 18 minutes
Servings: 4
Ingredients:
- 1 lb. chicken tenders
- ¼ tsp. pepper
- 4 garlic cloves, minced
- 1 ½ tbsp. soy sauce
- 2 tbsp. pineapple juice
- 1 tbsp. sesame oil
- ½ tsp. ginger, minced

Directions:
Preheat your Air Fryer Oven to 390°F.

Combine all the ingredients in a bowl, except for the chicken.

Skewer the chicken tenders, them then soak them in the marinade for 2 hours.

Add tenders to the Air Fryer Oven and cook for 18 minutes. Serve hot!

Nutrition:
Calories: 217
Fats: 3 g
Carbs: 15.3 g
Protein: 21.3 g

388. Green Stuffed Peppers
Preparation Time: 5 minutes
Cooking Time: 25 minutes
Servings: 3
Ingredients:
- 3 green bell peppers, tops and seeds removed
- 1 onion, medium-sized, diced
- 1 carrot, thinly diced
- 1 small cauliflower, shredded
- 1 tsp. garlic powder
- 1 tsp. coriander
- 1 tsp. mixed spices
- 1 tsp. Chinese five spice
- 1 tbsp. olive oil
- 3 tbsp. any soft cheese
- 1 zucchini, thinly diced
- ¼ yellow pepper, thinly diced

Directions:
Sauté the onion with the olive oil in a wok over medium heat.

Add the cauliflower and seasonings. Cook for 5 minutes, stirring to combine.

Add the vegetables (carrot, zucchini, yellow pepper) and cook for an additional 5 minutes more.

Fill each of the green peppers with 1 tbsp. of soft cheese.

Then stuff them with cauliflower mixture.

Cap the stuffed peppers with the pepper tops and cook in the Air Fryer Oven for 15 minutes at 390°F.

Nutrition:
Calories: 272
Fats: 12.7 g
Carbs: 26 g
Protein: 17 g

389. Beef Meatballs in Tomato Sauce

Preparation Time: 5 minutes
Cooking Time: 12 minutes
Servings: 3
Ingredients:
- 11 oz. minced beef
- 1 onion, chopped finely
- 1 tbsp. fresh parsley, chopped
- 1 cup tomato sauce
- 1 egg
- Salt and pepper to taste
- 1 tbsp. fresh thyme, chopped

Directions:

Mix all the ingredients in a mixing bowl, except the tomato sauce. Form 11 meatballs with the mixture. Preheat your Air Fryer Oven to 390°F.

Add the meatballs to the air fry basket and cook for 7 minutes. Transfer the meatballs to an oven-safe dish and pour the tomato sauce over them.

Put the dish in the air fry basket and cook for an additional 5 minute at 320°F.

Nutrition:
Calories: 275 Fats: 16 g
Carbs: 2 g
Protein: 20 g

390. Mustard Pork Balls

Preparation Time: 5 minutes
Cooking Time: 15 minutes
Servings: 4
Ingredients:
- 7 oz. minced pork
- 1 tsp. organic honey
- 1 tsp. Dijon mustard
- 1 tbsp. cheddar cheese, grated
- ⅓ cup onion, diced
- Salt and pepper to taste
- A handful of fresh basil, chopped
- 1 tsp. garlic purée

Directions:

In a bowl, mix the meat with all of the seasonings and form balls.

Place the pork balls into the Air Fryer Oven and cook for 15 minutes at 392°F.

Nutrition:
Calories: 121
Fats: 6.8 g
Carbs: 2.7 g
Protein: 11.3 g

391. Garlic Pork Chops

Preparation Time: 5 minutes
Cooking Time: 16 minutes
Servings: 4
Ingredients:
- 4 pork chops
- 1 tbsp. coconut butter
- 2 tsp. minced garlic cloves
- 1 tbsp. coconut butter
- 2 tsp. parsley, chopped
- Salt and pepper to taste

Directions:

Preheat your air fryer to 350°F.

In a bowl, mix the coconut oil, seasonings, and butter. Coat the pork chops with this mixture.

Place the chops on the grill pan of your Air Fryer Oven cook them for 8 minutes per side.

Nutrition:
Calories: 356
Fats: 30 g
Carbs: 2.3 g
Protein: 19 g

392. Honey Ginger Salmon Fillets

Preparation Time: 5 minutes
Cooking Time: 10 minutes
Servings: 2
Ingredients:
2 salmon fillets
2 tbsp. fresh ginger, minced
2 garlic cloves, minced
¼ cup honey
⅓ cup orange juice
⅓ cup soy sauce
1 lemon, sliced

Directions:
Mix all the ingredients in a bowl.
Marinate the salmon fillets in the sauce for 2 hours in the fridge.
Add the marinated salmon to the air fry basket and cook at 395°F for 10 minutes. Garnish with fresh ginger and lemon slices.

Nutrition:
Calories: 514
Fats: 22 g
Carbs: 39.5 g
Protein: 41 g

393. Rosemary & Lemon Salmon

Preparation Time: 5 minutes
Cooking Time: 10 minutes
Servings: 2
Ingredients:
2 salmon fillets
1 dash pepper
2 lb. Fresh rosemary, chopped
2 slices of lemon

Directions:
Rub the rosemary over the salmon fillets, then season them with salt and pepper, and place lemon slices on top of salmon fillets.
Place in the fridge for 2 hours.
Preheat your Air Fryer Oven to 320°F. Cook for 10 minutes.

Nutrition:
Calories: 363
Fats: 22 g
Carbs: 8 g
Protein: 40 g

394. Fish with Capers & Herb Sauce

Preparation Time: 5 minutes
Cooking Time: 15 minutes
Servings: 4
Ingredients:
2 cod fillets
¼ cup almond flour
1 tsp. Dijon Mustard
1 egg

For the Sauce:
2 tbsp. light sour cream
2 tsp. capers
1 tbsp. tarragon, chopped
1 tbsp. fresh dill, chopped
2 tbsp. red onion, chopped
2 tbsp. dill pickle, chopped

Directions:
Add all of the sauce ingredients into a small mixing bowl and mix until well blended then place in the fridge.
In a bowl, mix the Dijon mustard and the egg and sprinkle the flour over a plate.
Dip the cod fillets first in the egg mixture to coat, and then dip them into the flour, coating them on both sides.

Preheat your Air Fryer Oven to 300°F, place the fillets into the Air Fryer Oven and cook for 10 minutes.

Place the fillets on the serving dishes, drizzle with the sauce and serve.

Nutrition:
Calories: 198
Fats: 9.4 g
Carbs: 17.6 g
Protein: 11 g

395. Lemon Halibut

Preparation Time: 5 minutes
Cooking Time: 20 minutes
Servings: 4
Ingredients:
4 halibut fillets
1 egg, beaten
1 lemon, sliced
½ tsp. Salt and pepper to taste
1 tbsp. parsley, chopped

Directions:
Sprinkle the lemon juice over the halibut fillets.

In a food processor mix the lemon slices, salt, pepper, and parsley.

Take fillets and coat them with this mixture; then dip the fillets into the beaten egg.

Cook the fillets in your Air Fryer Oven at 350°F for 15 minutes.

Nutrition:
Calories: 48
Fats: 1 g
Carbs: 2.5 g
Protein: 9 g

396. Fried Cod & Spring Onion

Preparation Time: 5 minutes
Cooking Time: 20 minutes
Servings: 4
Ingredients:
7 oz. cod fillet, washed and dried
1 Spring onion, white and green parts, chopped
A dash of sesame oil
5 tbsp. light soy sauce
1 tsp. dark soy sauce
3 tbsp. olive oil
5 slices of ginger
1 cup water
½ tsp. Salt and pepper to taste

Directions:
Season the cod fillet with a dash of sesame oil, salt, and pepper. Preheat your Air Fryer Oven to 356ºF. Cook the cod fillet in air fryer for 12 minutes.

For the seasoning sauce, boil water in a pan along with both light and dark soy sauce on the stovetop and stir.

In a small saucepan, heat the olive oil and add the ginger and white part of the spring onion. Fry until the ginger browns, then remove the ginger and onions.

Top the cod fillet with shredded green onion. Pour the olive oil over the fillet and add the seasoning sauce on top.

Nutrition:
Calories: 233
Fats: 16 g
Carbs: 15.5 g
Protein: 6.7 g

CHAPTER 7:

Mains

397. Garlic Putter Pork Chops
Preparation Time: 10 minutes
Cooking Time: 10 minutes
Servings: 4
Ingredients:
- tsp. parsley
- tsp. grated garlic cloves
- 1 tbsp. coconut oil
- 1 tbsp. coconut butter
- pork chops

Directions:
- Preparing the Ingredients. Ensure your air fryer is preheated to 350 degrees.
- Mix butter, coconut oil, and all seasoning together. Then rub seasoning mixture over all sides of pork chops. Place in foil, seal, and chill for 1 hour.
- Remove pork chops from foil and place into air fryer.
- Air Frying. Set temperature to 350°F, and set time to 7 minutes. Cook 7 minutes on one side and 8 minutes on the other.
- Drizzle with olive oil and serve alongside a green salad.

Nutrition:
Calories: 526; Fat: 23g; Protein:41g; Sugar:4g

---

398. Cajun Pork Steaks
Preparation Time: 5 minutes
Cooking Time: 20 minutes
Servings: 6
Ingredients:
- 4-6 pork steaks
- BBQ sauce:
- Cajun seasoning
- 1 tbsp. vinegar
- 1 tsp. low-sodium soy sauce
- ½ C. brown sugar

Directions:
- Preparing the Ingredients. Ensure your air fryer is preheated to 290 degrees.
- Sprinkle pork steaks with Cajun seasoning.
- Combine remaining ingredients and brush onto steaks. Add coated steaks to air fryer.
- Air Frying. Set temperature to 290°F, and set time to 20 minutes. Cook 15-20 minutes till just browned.

Nutrition:
Calories: 209;
Fat: 11g;
Protein:28g;
Sugar:2g

---

399. Cajun Sweet-Sour Grilled Pork
Preparation Time: 5 minutes
Cooking Time: 12 minutes
Servings: 3
Ingredients:
- ¼ cup brown sugar
- 1/4 cup cider vinegar
- 1-lb pork loin, sliced into 1-inch cubes
- tablespoons Cajun seasoning
- tablespoons brown sugar

Directions:
- Preparing the Ingredients. In a shallow dish, mix well pork loin, 3 tablespoons brown sugar, and Cajun seasoning. Toss well to coat. Marinate in the ref for 3 hours.
- In a medium bowl mix well, brown sugar and vinegar for basting.
- Thread pork pieces in skewers. Baste with sauce and place on skewer rack in air fryer.
- Air Frying. For 12 minutes, cook on 360°F. Halfway through Cooking Time, turnover skewers and baste with sauce. If needed, cook in batches.
- Serve and enjoy.

Nutrition:
Calories: 428;
Fat: 16.7g;
Protein:39g;
Sugar:2g

400. Pork Loin With Potatoes

Preparation Time: 10 minutes
Cooking Time: 25 minutes
Servings: 2
Ingredients:
- pounds pork loin
- large red potatoes, chopped
- ½ teaspoon garlic powder
- ½ teaspoon red pepper flakes, crushed
- Salt and black pepper, to taste

Directions:
- In a large bowl, put all of the ingredients together except glaze and toss to coat well. Preheat the Air fryer to 325 degrees F. Place the loin in the air fryer basket.
- Arrange the potatoes around pork loin.
- Cook for about 25 minutes.

Nutrition:
Calories:260
Fat: 8g
Carbs: 27g
Protein: 21g

401. Roasted Char Siew (Pork Butt)

Preparation Time: 10 minutes
Cooking Time: 25 minutes
Servings: 4
Ingredients:
- 1 strip of pork shoulder butt with a good amount of fat marbling
- Marinade:
- 1 tsp. sesame oil
- tbsp. raw honey
- 1 tsp. light soy sauce
- 1 tbsp. rose wine

Directions:
- Mix all of the marinade ingredients together and put it to a Ziploc bag. Place pork in bag, making sure all sections of pork strip are engulfed in the marinade. Chill 3-24 hours.
- Take out the strip 30 minutes before planning to cook and preheat your air fryer to 350 degrees.
- Place foil on small pan and brush with olive oil. Place marinated pork strip onto prepared pan.
- Set temperature to 350°F, and set time to 20 minutes. Roast 20 minutes.
- Glaze with marinade every 5-10 minutes.
- Remove strip and leave to cool a few minutes before slicing.

Nutrition:
Calories: 289;
Fat: 13g;
Protein:33g;
Sugar:1g

402. Asian Pork Chops

Preparation Time: 2 hours and 10 minutes
Cooking Time: 15 minutes
Servings: 2
Ingredients:
- 1/2 cup hoisin sauce
- tablespoons cider vinegar
- 1 tablespoon Asian sweet chili sauce
- (1/2-inch-thick) boneless pork chops
- salt and pepper

Directions:
- Stir together hoisin, chili sauce, and vinegar in a large mixing bowl. Separate a quarter cup of this mixture, then add pork chops to the bowl and let it sit in the fridge for 2 hours. Take out the pork chops and place them on a plate. Sprinkle each side of the pork chop evenly with salt and pepper.
- Cook at 360 degrees for 14 minutes, flipping half way through. Brush with reserved marinade and serve.

Nutrition:
Calories: 338; Fat: 21g;
Protein:19g;
Fiber:1g

403. Marinated Pork Chops

Preparation Time: 10 minutes
Cooking Time: 30 minutes
Servings: 2
Ingredients:
- pork chops, boneless
- 1 tsp garlic powder
- ½ cup flour
- 1 cup buttermilk
- Salt and pepper

Directions:
- Add pork chops and buttermilk in a zip-lock bag. Seal the bag and set aside in the refrigerator overnight.
- In another zip-lock bag add flour, garlic powder, pepper, and salt.
- Remove marinated pork chops from buttermilk and add in flour mixture and shake until well coated.
- Preheat the Air Fryer Grill to 380 F.
- Spray air fryer tray with cooking spray.
- Arrange pork chops on a tray and air fryer for 28-30 minutes. Turn pork chops after 18 minutes.
- Serve and enjoy.

Nutrition:
Calories 424
Fat 21.3 g
Carbs 30.8 g
Protein 25.5 g

404. Steak With Cheese Butter

Preparation Time: 10 minutes
Cooking Time: 8-10 minutes
Servings: 2
Ingredients:
- rib-eye steaks
- tsp garlic powder
- 1/2 tbsp blue cheese butter
- 1 tsp pepper
- tsp kosher salt

Directions:
- Preheat the air fryer to 400 F.
- Mix together garlic powder, pepper, and salt and rub over the steaks.
- Spray air fryer basket with cooking spray.
- Put the steak in the air fryer basket and cook for 4-5 minutes on each side.
- Top with blue butter cheese.
- Serve and enjoy.

Nutrition:
Calories 830
Fat 60 g
Carbohydrates 3 g
Sugar 0 g
Protein 70g
Cholesterol 123 mg

405. Mussels Bowls

Preparation Time: 5 minutes
Cooking Time: 15 minutes
Servings: 2
Ingredients:
- pounds mussels, scrubbed
- ounces black beer
- 1 yellow onion, chopped
- ounces spicy sausage, chopped
- 1 tablespoon paprika

Directions:
- Combine all the ingredients in a pan that fits your air fryer.
- Put the pan in the air fryer and cook at 400 degrees F for 12 minutes.
- Divide the mussels into bowls, serve, and enjoy!

Nutrition:
Calories 201, Fat 6,
Fiber 7, Carbs 17, Protein 7

406. Chicken And Peppercorns Mix

Preparation Time: 5 minutes
Cooking Time: 20 minutes
Servings: 2
Ingredients:
- chicken thighs, boneless

Salt and black pepper to taste
½ cup balsamic vinegar
garlic cloves, minced
½ cup soy sauce

Directions:

In a container that fits your air fryer, mix the chicken with all the other ingredients and toss.

Put the pan in the fryer and cook at 380 degrees F for 20 minutes.

Divide everything between plates and serve.

Nutrition:
Calories 261, Fat 7,
Fiber 5, Carbs 15, Protein 16

407. Salmon Patties

Preparation Time: 10 minutes
Cooking Time: 7 minutes
Servings: 2
Ingredients:

oz salmon fillet, minced
1 lemon, sliced
1/2 tsp garlic powder
1 egg, lightly beaten
1/8 tsp salt

Directions:

Add all ingredients except lemon slices into the bowl and mix until well combined.

Spray air fryer basket with cooking spray.

Place lemon slice into the air fryer basket.

Make the equal shape of patties from salmon mixture and place on top of lemon slices into the air fryer basket.

Cook at 390 F for 7 minutes.

Serve and enjoy.

Nutrition:
Calories 184
Fat 9.2 g
Carbohydrates 1 g
Sugar 0.4 g
Protein 24.9 g
Cholesterol 132 mg

408. Shrimp With Veggie

Preparation Time: 10 minutes
Cooking Time: 20 minutes
Servings: 2
Ingredients:

50 small shrimp
1 tbsp Cajun seasoning
1 bag of frozen mix vegetables
1 tbsp olive oil

Directions:

Line air fryer basket with aluminum foil.

In a large bowl, set all of the ingredients and toss well.

Transfer shrimp and vegetable mixture into the air fryer basket and cook at 350 F for 10 minutes.

Toss well and cook for 10 minutes more.

Serve and enjoy.

Nutrition:
Calories 101
Fat 4 g
Carbohydrates 14 g
Sugar 1 g
Protein 2 g
Cholesterol 3 mg

409. Chili Garlic Chicken Wings

Preparation Time: 10 minutes
Cooking Time: 35 minutes
Servings: 2
Ingredients:

lbs. chicken wings
tsp seasoned salt
1/2 cup coconut flour
1/4 tsp garlic powder
1/4 tsp chili powder

Directions:

Preheat the air fryer to 370 F.

In a bowl, put all of the ingredients but the chicken wings and mix well.

Add chicken wings into the bowl coat well.

Spray air fryer basket with cooking spray.

Add the chicken wings by batches into the air fryer basket.

Cook for 35-40 minutes. Shake halfway through.

Serve and enjoy.

Nutrition:
Calories 440 Fat 17.1 g
Carbohydrates 1 g
Sugar 0.2 g
Protein 65 g

410. Funky-Garlic And Turkey Breasts

Preparation Time: 10 minutes
Cooking Time: 25 minutes
Servings: 2
Ingredients:
- ½ teaspoon garlic powder
- tablespoons butter
- ¼ teaspoon dried oregano
- 1-pound turkey breasts, boneless
- 1 teaspoon pepper and salt

Directions:
Season turkey on both sides generously with garlic, dried oregano, salt and pepper

Set your air fryer to sauté mode and add butter, let the butter melt

Add turkey breasts and sauté for 2 minutes on each side

Lock the lid and select the "Bake/Roast" setting, bake for 15 minutes at 355 degrees F

Serve and enjoy

Nutrition:
Calories 223, Fat 13g,
Carbohydrates 5g, Protein 19g

411. Chili Chicken Wings

Preparation Time: 10 minutes
Cooking Time: 35 minutes
Servings: 2
Ingredients:
- ½ cup hot sauce
- ½ cup water
- tbsp butter
- 32 ounces frozen chicken wings
- ½ tsp paprika

Directions:
Add all the ingredients into the cook and crisp basket and place the basket inside the air fryer

Place the pressure cooker lid on top of the pot and close the pressure valve to the seal position. Set the pressure cooker function to high heat and set the timer for 5 minutes

The moment once cooking is done, release the pressure quickly by carefully opening the steamer valve

Serve hot

Nutrition:
Calories 311,
Fat 23g,
Carbohydrates 0g,
Protein 24g

412. Lemon Drumsticks

Preparation Time: 10 minutes
Cooking Time: 28 minutes
Servings: 2
Ingredients:
- ½ cup hot sauce
- tbsp butter
- ½ cup water
- 1/3 cup lemon juice
- 1-pound drumstick

Directions:
Add all the ingredients into the cook and crisp basket and place the basket inside the air fryer

Place the pressure cooker lid on top of the pot and close the pressure valve to the seal position. Set the pressure cooker function to high heat and set the timer for 5 minutes

Immediately after the cooking is done, release the pressure quickly by carefully opening the steamer valve.

Serve hot

Nutrition:
Calories 414, Fat 26g,
Carbohydrates 3g,
Protein 42g.

413. Salsa Verde Chicken

Preparation Time: 5 minutes
Cooking Time: 25 minutes
Servings: 2
Ingredients:
- ounces Salsa Verde
- 1 tablespoon paprika
- 1-pound boneless chicken breasts
- 1 teaspoon ground coriander
- 1 teaspoon cilantro

Directions:
- Rub the boneless chicken breasts with the paprika, ground black pepper, and cilantro. Set the pressure cooker to "Pressure" mode.
- Place the boneless chicken into the pressure cooker. Sprinkle the meat with the salsa Verde and stir well.
- Close the pressure cooker lid and cook for 30 minutes.
- When the Cooking Time ends, release the pressure and transfer the chicken to the mixing bowl. Shred the chicken well. Serve it.

Nutrition:
Calories: 160 Fat: 4g
Carbs: 5g Protein: 26g

414. Madeira Beef

Preparation Time: 5 minutes
Cooking Time: 25 minutes
Servings: 6
Ingredients:
- 1 cup Madeira
- 1 and ½ pounds beef meat, cubed
- Salt and black pepper to the taste
- 1 yellow onion, thinly sliced
- 1 chili pepper, sliced

Directions:
- Put the reversible rack in the Air fryer, add the baking pan inside and mix all the ingredients in it.
- Cook on Baking mode at 380 degrees F for 25 minutes, divide the mix into bowls and serve.

Nutrition:
Calories 295,
Fat 16,
Fiber 9,
Carbs 20,
Protein 15.

415. Creamy Pork And Zucchinis

Preparation Time: 5 minutes
Cooking Time: 25 minutes
Servings: 4
Ingredients:
- 1 and ½ pounds pork stew meat, cubed
- 1 cup tomato sauce
- 1 tablespoon olive oil
- zucchinis, sliced
- Salt and black pepper to the taste

Directions:
- Put the reversible rack in the Air fryer, add the baking pan inside and mix all the ingredients in it.
- Cook on Baking mode at 380 degrees F, divide the mix into bowls and serve.

Nutrition:
Calories 284,
Fat 12,
Fiber 9,
Carbs 17,
Protein 12.

416. Air-Fryer Tofu Satay

Preparation Time: 30 minutes
Cooking Time: 25 minutes
Servings: 2
Ingredients:

- 1 block tofu, extra firm
- tbsp. soy sauce
- tsp ginger garlic paste
- 1 tsp sriracha sauce
- 1 tbsp. maple syrup + lime juice

Directions:

- Mix the maple syrup with lime juice, ginger garlic paste, sriracha, and soy sauce in a food processor or blender. Blend it until smooth.
- Cut the tofu into strips. Add the puree over the strips and let it marinate for 15 to 30 minutes.
- Soak 6 bamboo skewers in water while the tofu marinates.
- With a wire cutter, cut each skewer into two, as a full skewer will not fit inside the air-fryer.
- Skewer one strip of tofu to each bamboo stick. Peirce it through the uncut side of the skewer.
- Place the skewers in the air-fryer. Set the temperature to 370 F and let it cook for 15 minutes. You do not have to toss the contents.
- Serve with peanut butter sauce.

Nutrition:
Calories: 236
Fat: 11g
Carbs: 17g
Protein: 17g

417. Sticky-Sweet Bbq Tofu

Preparation Time: 10 minutes
Cooking Time: 50 minutes
Servings: 2
Ingredients:

- 1 ½ cups BBQ sauce
- 1 block tofu, extra firm
- Oil for greasing

Directions:

- Fix the temperature to 400°F and preheat the air-fryer.
- Press down the tofu and slice it into 1" cubes.
- Place them on a greased baking sheet.
- Apply a coat of BBQ sauce and let it cook in the air-fryer for 20 minutes. Keep it aside.
- Add ½ cup of BBQ sauce into a glass saucepan. The sauce should evenly spread in the pan. Place the cooked tofu cubes on top and add another layer of the sauce on it.
- Transfer them to the air-fryer again and let it cook for 30 minutes.
- Enjoy!

Nutrition:
Calories: 173 Fat: 10g
Carbs 9g Protein: 16g

418. Veggie Bowl

Preparation Time: 10 minutes
Cooking Time: 30 minutes
Servings: 2
Ingredients:

- cups Brussel sprouts
- cups sweet potato
- tsp garlic powder
- tbsp. soy sauce, low sodium
- Cooking spray

Directions:

- Place the sweet potatoes in the air-fryer. Add a light layer of oil for tossing.
- Top it with 1 tsp of garlic powder and toss.
- Set the temperature to 400 F and cook for 15 minutes. Toss after 5 minutes.
- Transfer the Brussels sprouts to the cooking basket and spray a layer of oil and the remaining garlic powder. Toss them well and cook at 400 F for 5 minutes.

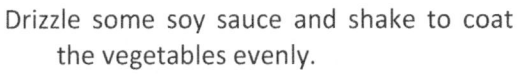

Drizzle some soy sauce and shake to coat the vegetables evenly.

Set to the same temperature and cook for 5 minutes. Check it when it hits 2 minutes and toss the contents.

Cooking Time will depend on the vegetable. Once the vegetables are done, they will be soft and brown.

Nutrition:
Calories: 261 Fat: 8g
Carbs: 28g Protein: 14g

419. Air Fried Fish Skin
Preparation Time: 10 minutes
Cooking Time: 15 minutes
Servings: 2
Ingredients:
- ½ pound salmon skin
- tbsp. heart-healthy oil
- Salt and pepper, as needed

Directions:
Fix the temperature to 400° F and preheat the air-fryer for 5 minutes.

Make sure the salmon skin is patted dry.

In a bowl, add all components and combine well.

Transfer the ingredients to the air-fryer basket and close it

Allow it to cook for 10 minutes at a temperature of 400 F.

Shake the items halfway through the Cooking Time, to make sure that the skin is cooked evenly.

Nutrition:
Calories:150 Fat:13
Carbs:3 Protein: 9

420. Baked Thai Fish
Preparation Time: 10 minutes
Cooking Time: 25 minutes
Servings: 2
Ingredients:
- 1 pound cod fillet
- 1 tbsp. lime juice
- ¼ cup of coconut milk
- Salt and pepper, as needed

Directions:
Cut the cod fillet into small pieces.

Fix the temperature to 325°F and preheat the fryer for 5 minutes.

Add all the ingredients to a baking dish and transfer it to an air-fryer.

Let it cook for 20 minutes at a temperature of 325 F. Enjoy!

Nutrition:
Calories: 333 Fat: 5g
Carbs: 56g Protein: 18g

421. Oven Braised Corned Beef
Preparation Time: 10 minutes
Cooking Time: 55 minutes
Servings: 2
Ingredients:
- 1 medium onion, chopped
- cups of water
- tbsp. Dijon mustard
- pounds corned beef brisket

Directions:
Fix the temperature to 400° F and preheat the air-fryer for 5 minutes.

Slice the brisket to chunks

Add all the ingredients to a baking tray that fits inside the air-fryer.

Let it cook for 50 minutes at a temperature of 400 F.

Enjoy!

Nutrition:
Calories: 320 Fat: 22g
Carbs: 10g Protein: 21g

422. Crispy Keto Pork Bites
Preparation Time: 5 minutes
Cooking Time: 25 minutes
Servings: 2
Ingredients:
- 1 medium onion

½ pound pork belly
tbsp. coconut cream
1 tbsp. butter
Salt & pepper, to taste

Directions:

Slice the pork belly into even and thin strips
The onion has to be diced.
Transfer all the ingredients into a mixing bowl and allow it to marinate in the fridge for the next two hours.
Fix the temperature to 350 F and preheat the air-fryer for 5 minutes.
Keep the pork strips inside the air-fryer and let it cook for 25 minutes at a temperature of 350 F.
Enjoy!

Nutrition:
Calories: 448
Fat: 42g
Carbs: 2g
Protein: 20g

423. Soy And Garlic Mushrooms

Preparation Time: 2 hours and 5 minutes
Cooking Time: 25 minutes
Servings: 2
Ingredients:

pounds mushrooms
garlic cloves
¼ cup coconut amino
tbsp. olive oil

Directions:

Transfer all the ingredients to a dish and combine until well incorporated.
Let it marinate for 2 hours in a fridge
Fix the temperature to 350 F and preheat for 5 minutes.
Transfer the mushrooms to a heatproof dish that can fit in an air-fryer
Let it cook for 20 minutes at a temperature of 350 F.
Enjoy!

Nutrition:
Calories: 216 Fat: 16g
Carbs: 13g Protein: 11g

424. Crack Chicken

Preparation Time: 5 minutes
Cooking Time: 30 minutes
Servings: 2
Ingredients:

1 block cream cheese
chicken breasts
slices of bacon
¼ cup olive oil
Salt and pepper

Direction:

Fix the temperature to 350 °F and let the air-fryer preheat for 5 minutes
In a baking dish that can fit the air-fryer, place the chicken.
Apply the cream cheese and olive oil on it. Fry the bacon and crumble it on top of the chicken.
Season as needed.
Transfer the dish into the air-fryer and cook it for 25 minutes at a temperature of 350 F.
Enjoy!

Nutrition:
Calories: 250
Carbs: 14 g
Fat: 19 g
Protein: 22 g

425. Bullet-Proof Beef Roast

Preparation Time: 2 hours
Cooking Time: 2 hours and 5 minutes
Servings: 2
Ingredients:

1 cup of organic beef
tbsp. olive oil
pounds beef round roast
Salt and pepper, to taste

Directions:
- Place all of the ingredients in a resealable bag and let it marinate in the fridge for about two hours.
- Fix the temperature to 400° F and preheat the air-fryer for 5 minutes.
- Place the ingredients in the Ziploc bag in a baking tray that will fit the air-fryer.
- Let it cook for 2 hours at a temperature of 400 F.
- Serve while it is warm.

Nutrition:
Calories: 280
Carbs: 13 g
Fat: 15 g
Protein: 26 g

426. Air Fried Catfish

Preparation Time: 5 minutes
Cooking Time: 20 minutes
Servings: 2
Ingredients:
- 1 whole egg
- catfish fillets
- ¼ cup almond flour
- Salt and Pepper, to taste
- tbsp. olive oil

Directions:
- Fix the temperature to 350 F and preheat the air-fryer for 5 minutes.
- Sprinkle some salt and pepper on the catfish fillet.
- Beat the eggs, soak the catfish in it and dip it in almond flour.
- Remove any excess and apply a coat of olive oil on its surface.
- Transfer the fish to the air-fryer and let it cook for 15 minutes at a temperature of 350 F.
- Enjoy!

Nutrition:
Calories: 210   Carbs: 9 g
Fat: 11 g   Protein: 17 g

427. Lemon Fish Fillet

Preparation Time: 5 minutes
Cooking Time: 20 minutes
Servings: 2
Ingredients:
- salmon fish fillets
- ½ cup almond flour
- 1 lemon
- tbsp. vegetable oil
- 1 whole egg

Directions:
- Fix the temperature to 400° F and preheat the air-fryer for 5 minutes.
- Season the fish with lemon, salt, pepper and vegetable oil.
- Beat the egg and soak the fillet in it. Cover the fillet with almond flour.
- Transfer the fish into the cooking basket and let it cook for 15 minutes at a temperature of 400 F.
- Enjoy!

Nutrition:
Calories: 230
Carbs: 10 g
Fat: 12 g
Protein: 20 g

428. Coconut Shrimp

Preparation Time: 10 minutes
Cooking Time: 10 minutes
Servings: 2
Ingredients:
- 1 cup coconut, unsweetened and dried
- large shrimps
- 1 cup white flour
- 1 cup egg white
- 1 cup panko breadcrumbs

Directions:
- Keep the shrimp on some paper towels.
- Combine the breadcrumbs and coconut in a pan and keep it aside.
- In another pan, mix the cornstarch and the flour and keep it aside.

Keep the egg whites in a bowl

Put the shrimp, one at a time, first in the flour mixture. Then dip it in the egg whites and finally into the breadcrumbs mixture.

Transfer all the shrimp into the air-fryer basket.

Adjust the temperature to 400 F and time to 10 minutes.

Halfway through the Cooking Time, you can turn over the shrimp if needed.

Enjoy!

Nutrition:
Calories: 220
Carbs: 11 g
Fat: 10 g
Protein: 16 g

429. Rib Eye Steak

Preparation Time: 5 minutes
Cooking Time: 25 minutes
Servings: 2
Ingredients:
    1 tbsp. olive oil
    pounds rib eye steak
    1 tbsp. steak rub

Directions:

Adjust the Cooking Time of the air-fryer to 4 minutes and then set the temperature to 400 F to preheat.

Rub both sides of the steak with the rub and olive oil.

Transfer the steak into the air fry basket.

Set the Cooking Time to 14 minutes and temperature to 400 F.

Once 7 minutes is done, turn the steak to its other side.

When the cooking is done, remove the steak from the fryer and let it cool down for 10 minutes before serving.

Nutrition:
Calories: 310 Carbs: 16 g
Fat: 19 g Protein: 34 g

430. Delicious Hot Steaks

Preparation Time: 5 minutes
Cooking Time: 10 minutes
Servings: 2
Ingredients:
    steaks, 1-inch thick
    ½ tsp black pepper
    1 tbsp olive oil
    ½ tsp ground paprika
    Salt and black pepper to taste

Directions:

Warm up the air fryer to 390° F. Mix olive oil, black pepper, paprika, salt and pepper and rub onto steaks. Spread evenly. Put the steaks in the fryer, and cook for 6 minutes, turning them halfway through.

Nutrition:
Calories: 300
Carbs: 15 g
Fat: 19 g
Protein: 32 g

431. Creamy Beef Liver Cakes

Preparation Time: 5 minutes
Cooking Time: 20 minutes
Servings: 2
Ingredients:
    1 lb beef liver, sliced
    large eggs
    1 tbsp butter
    ½ tbsp black truffle oil
    1 tbsp cream
    Salt and black pepper

Directions:

Preheat the Air Fryer to 320 F. Cut the liver into thin slices and refrigerate for 10 minutes. Separate the whites from the yolks and put each yolk in a cup. In another bowl, add the cream, truffle oil, salt and pepper and mix with a fork. Arrange half of the mixture in a small ramekin.

Pour the white of the egg and divide it equally between ramekins. Top with the egg yolks. Surround each yolk with a liver. Cook for 15 minutes and serve cool.

Nutrition:
Calories: 215
Carbs: 11 g
Fat: 10 g
Protein: 20 g

432. Pork Chops In Cream
Preparation Time: 5 minutes
Cooking Time: 20 minutes
Servings: 4
Ingredients:
- pork chops, center-cut
- tbsp flour
- tbsp sour cream
- Salt and black pepper
- ½ cup breadcrumbs

Directions:
Coat the chops with flour. Drizzle the cream over and rub gently to coat well. Spread the breadcrumbs onto a bowl, and coat each pork chop with crumbs. Spray the chops with oil and arrange them in the basket of your Air Fryer. Cook for 14 minutes at 380 F, turning once halfway through. Serve with salad, slaw or potatoes.

Nutrition:
Calories: 250
Carbs: 13 g
Fat: 13 g
Protein: 24 g

433. Five Spice Pork Belly
Preparation Time: 10 minutes
Cooking Time: 3 hours
Servings: 2
Ingredients:
- 1 ½ lb pork belly, blanched
- 1 tsp five spice seasoning
- ½ tsp white pepper
- ¾ tsp garlic powder
- 1 tsp salt

Directions:
After blanching the pork belly leave it at room temperature for 2 hours to air dry. Pat with paper towels if there is excess water. Preheat the air fryer to 330 F. Take a skewer and pierce the skin as many times as you can, so you can ensure crispiness. Combine the seasonings in a small bowl, and rub it onto the pork.

Place the pork into the air fryer and cook for 30 minutes. Heat up to 350 F and cook for 30 more minutes. Let cool slightly before serving.

Nutrition:
Calories: 280
Carbs: 14 g
Fat: 17 g
Protein: 29 g

434. Fast Rib Eye Steak
Preparation Time: 5 minutes
Cooking Time: 10 minutes
Servings: 2
Ingredients:
- pounds rib eye steak
- 1 tbsp olive oil
- Salt and black pepper to taste

Directions:
Preheat your fryer to 350 F. Rub both sides of the steak with oil; season with salt and pepper. Place the steak in your Air Fryer's cooking basket and cook for 8 minutes. Serve and enjoy!

Nutrition:
Calories: 300 Carbs: 15 g
Fat: 19 g
Protein: 32 g

435. Pork Tenderloins With Apple

Preparation Time: 5 minutes
Cooking Time: 50 minutes
Servings: 4
Ingredients:
- pork tenderloins
- 1 apple, wedged
- 1 cinnamon quill
- 1 tbsp soy sauce
- Salt and black pepper

Directions:
In a bowl, add pork, apple, cinnamon, soy sauce, salt, and black pepper into; stir to coat well. Let sit at room temperature for 25-35 minutes. Put the pork and apples into the air fryer, and a little bit of marinade. Cook at 380 F for 14 minutes, turning once halfway through. Serve hot!

Nutrition:
Calories: 200
Carbs: 10 g
Fat: 10 g
Protein: 18 g

436. Awesome Beef Bulgogi With Mushrooms

Preparation Time: 3 hours
Cooking Time: 20 minutes
Servings: 2
Ingredients:
- oz beef
- ½ cup sliced mushrooms
- tbsp bulgogi marinade
- 1 tbsp diced onion

Directions:
Slice the beef into bite-size pieces and place them in a bowl. Add the bulgogi and mix to coat the beef completely. Cover the bowl and place in the fridge for 3 hours to marinate. Preheat the air fryer to 350 F. Transfer the beef to a baking dish; stir in the mushroom and onion. Cook for 10 minutes, until nice and tender. Serve with some roasted potatoes and a green salad.

Nutrition:
Calories: 220
Carbs: 12 g
Fat: 11 g
Protein: 23 g

437. Homemade Beef Liver Soufflé

Preparation Time: 15 minutes
Cooking Time: 30 minutes
Servings: 2
Ingredients:
- ½ lb of beef liver
- eggs
- oz buns
- 1 cup warm milk
- Salt and black pepper to taste

Directions:
Cut the liver in slices and put it in the fridge for 15 minutes. Divide the buns into pieces and soak them in milk for 10 minutes. Put the liver in a blender, and add the yolks, the bread mixture, and the spices. Grind the components and stuff in the ramekins. Line the ramekins in the Air Fryer's basket; cook for 20 minutes at 350 F.

Nutrition:
Calories: 230 Carbs: 15 g
Fat: 11 g Protein: 26 g

438. Authentic Wiener Beef Schnitzel

Preparation Time: 5 minutes
Cooking Time: 30 minutes
Servings: 4
Ingredients:
- beef schnitzel cutlets

½ cup flour
eggs, beaten
Salt and black pepper
1 cup breadcrumbs

Directions:

Coat the beef cutlets in flour and take away any excess. Dip the coated cutlets into the egg mixture. Season it with salt and black pepper. Then dip it into the crumbs and coat well. Drizzle them generously with oil and cook for 10 minutes at 360 F, turning once halfway through.

Nutrition:
Calories: 195
Carbs: 12 g
Fat: 11 g
Protein: 18 g

439. Herbed Beef Roast

Preparation Time: 5 minutes
Cooking Time: 45 minutes
Servings: 2
Ingredients:

tsp olive oil
1 lb. beef Roast
½ tsp dried rosemary
½ tsp dried oregano
Salt and black pepper to taste

Directions:

Preheat the Air Fryer to 400 F. Drizzle oil over the beef, and sprinkle with salt, pepper, and herbs. Rub onto the meat with hands. Cook for 45 minutes for medium-rare and 50 minutes for well-done.

Check halfway through, and flip to ensure they cook evenly. Wrap the beef in foil for 10 minutes after cooking to allow the juices to reabsorb into the meat. Slice the beef and serve with a side of steamed asparagus.

Nutrition:
Calories: 235
Carbs: 12 g
Fat: 13 g
Protein: 28 g

440. Effortless Beef Schnitzel

Preparation Time: 5 minutes
Cooking Time: 20 minutes
Servings: 2
Ingredients:

tbsp vegetable oil
oz breadcrumbs
1 whole egg, whisked
1 thin beef schnitzel, cut into strips
1 whole lemon

Directions:

Preheat your fryer to 356 F. In a bowl, add breadcrumbs and oil and stir well to get a loose mixture. Dip schnitzel in egg, then dip in breadcrumbs coat well. Place the prepared schnitzel your Air Fryer's cooking basket and cook for 12 minutes. Serve with a drizzle of lemon juice.

Nutrition:
Calories: 205
Carbs: 12 g
Fat: 11 g
Protein: 25 g

441. Sweet Marinated Pork Chops

Preparation Time: 5 minutes
Cooking Time: 20 minutes
Servings: 3
Ingredients:

pork chops, ½-inch thick
Salt and black pepper to taste
1 tbsp maple syrup
1 ½ tbsp minced garlic
tbsp mustard

Directions:
- In a bowl, add all ingredients except the pork, and mix well. Add the pork and toss it in the mustard sauce to coat well. Slide-out the fryer basket and place the chops in the basket; cook at 350 F for 6 minutes.
- Halfway through, flip the pork and cook further for 6 minutes. Once ready, remove them onto a serving platter and serve with a side of steamed asparagus.

Nutrition:
Calories: 260 Carbs: 13 g
Fat: 15 g Protein: 27 g

442. Sage Sausages Balls

Preparation Time: 5 minutes
Cooking Time: 20 minutes
Servings: 4
Ingredients:
- ½ oz sausages, sliced
- Salt and black pepper to taste
- 1 cup onion, chopped
- tbsp breadcrumbs - 1 tsp sage

Directions:
- Heat up your Air Fryer to 340 F. In a bowl, mix onions, sausage meat, sage, salt and pepper. Add breadcrumbs to a plate. Form balls using the mixture and roll them in breadcrumbs. Add onion balls in your Air Fryer's cooking basket and cook for 15 minutes. Serve and enjoy!

Nutrition:
Calories: 185 Carbs: 10 g
Fat: 11 g Protein: 17 g

443. Pork Belly With Honey

Preparation Time: 5 minutes
Cooking Time: 30 minutes
Servings: 8
Ingredients:
- pounds pork belly
- ½ tsp pepper
- 1 tbsp olive oil
- 1 tbsp salt
- tbsp honey

Directions:
- Preheat your Air Fryer to 400 F. Season the pork belly with salt and pepper. Grease the basket with oil. Add seasoned meat and cook for 15 minutes. Add honey and cook for 10 minutes more. Serve with green salad.

Nutrition:
Calories: 250
Carbs: 12 g
Fat: 14 g
Protein: 25 g

444. Cocktail Franks In Blanket

Preparation Time: 5 minutes
Cooking Time: 20 minutes
Servings: 4
Ingredients:
- oz cocktail franks
- oz can crescent rolls

Directions:
- Use a paper towel to pat the cocktail franks to drain completely. Cut the dough in 1 by 1.5-inch rectangles using a knife. Gently roll the franks in the strips, making sure the ends are visible Place in freezer for 5 minutes.
- Preheat the fryer to 330 F. Take the franks out of the freezer and place them in the air fryer's basket and cook for 6-8 minutes. Increase the temperature to 390 F. cook for another 3 minutes until a fine golden texture appears.

Nutrition:
Calories: 170
Carbs: 10 g
Fat: 10 g
Protein: 16 g

445. Seasoned Pork Shoulder

Preparation Time: 15 minutes
Cooking Time: 1 hour
Servings: 10
Ingredients:
- pounds skin-on, bone-in pork shoulder
- 2-3 tablespoons adobo seasoning
- Salt, as required

Directions:
- Arrange the pork shoulder onto a cutting board, skin-side down.
- Season the inner side of pork shoulder with adobo seasoning and salt.
- Season the inner side of pork shoulder with salt and adobo seasoning
- With kitchen twines, tie the pork shoulder into a long round cylinder shape.
- Season the outer side of pork shoulder with salt.
- Insert the rotisserie rod through the pork shoulder.
- Insert the rotisserie forks, one on each side of the rod to secure the pork shoulder.
- Arrange the drip pan in the bottom of Instant Omni Plus Toaster Oven.
- Now, slide the rod's left side into the groove along the metal bar so it doesn't move.
- Then, close the door and touch "Rotate".
- Select "Roast" and then adjust the temperature to 350 degrees F.
- Set the timer for 60 minutes and press the "Start".
- When Cooking Time is complete, press the red lever to release the rod.
- Remove the pork from toaster oven and place onto a platter for about 10 minutes before slicing.
- With a knife, slice the pork shoulder into desired sized slices and serve.

Nutrition:
Calories 397
Total Fat 29.1 g
Saturated Fat 10.7 g
Cholesterol 122 mg
Sodium 176 mg
Total Carbs 0 g
Fiber 0 g
Sugar 0 g
Protein 31.7 g

446. Glazed Pork Shoulder

Preparation Time: 15 minutes
Cooking Time: 20 minutes
Servings: 5
Ingredients:
- 1/3 cup soy sauce
- tablespoons brown sugar
- 1 tablespoon maple syrup
- pounds pork shoulder, cut into 1½-inch thick slices

Directions:
- In a large bowl, mix together the soy sauce, brown sugar, and maple syrup.
- Add the pork shoulder and coat with marinade generously.
- Cover and refrigerate to marinate for about 4-6 hours.
- Place the pork shoulder into a greased air fryer basket.
- Arrange the air fryer basket in the center of Instant Omni Plus Toaster Oven.
- Press "Air Fry" and then set the temperature to 355 degrees F.
- Set the timer for 10 minutes and press "Start".
- When the display shows "Turn Food" "do nothing.
- After 10 minutes adjust the temperature to 390 degrees F for 8 minutes.
- When Cooking Time is complete, remove the air fryer basket from Toaster Oven.
- Place the pork shoulder onto a cutting board for about 10 minutes before slicing.

With a sharp knife, cut the tenderloin into desired sized slices and serve.

Nutrition:
Calories 563
Total Fat 38.8 g
Saturated Fat 14.3 g
Cholesterol 163 mg
Sodium 1000 mg
Total Carbs 7.5 g
Fiber 0.1 g
Sugar 6.2 g
Protein 43.3 g

447. Simple Pork Loin

Preparation Time: 10 minutes
Cooking Time: 30 minutes
Servings: 6
Ingredients:
- pounds pork loin
- tablespoons olive oil, divided
- Salt and ground black pepper, as required

Directions:
- Arrange a wire rack in a greased air fryer basket.
- Coat the pork loin with oil and then, rub with salt and black pepper.
- Arrange the pork loin into the prepared baking pan.
- Arrange the air fryer basket in the bottom of Instant Omni Plus Toaster Oven.
- Place the baking pan over the drip pan.
- Select "Bake" and then adjust the temperature to 350 degrees F.
- Set the timer for 30 minutes and press "Start".
- When Cooking Time is complete, remove the air frying basket from Toaster Oven.
- Place the pork loin onto a cutting board.
- With a piece of foil, cover the pork loin for about 10 minutes before slicing.
- With a knife, slice the pork loin into desired size slices and serve.

Nutrition:
Calories 406
Total Fat 25.7 g
Saturated Fat 8.6 g
Cholesterol 121 mg
Sodium 121 mg
Protein 41.3 g
Total Carbs 12.5 g
Fiber 0.6 g
Sugar 11.6 g
Protein 39.7 g

448. Bacon Wrapped Pork Tenderloin

Preparation Time: 15 minutes
Cooking Time: 30 minutes
Servings: 4
Ingredients:
- 1 (1½ pound) pork tenderloin
- tablespoons Dijon mustard
- 1 tablespoon honey
- bacon strips

Directions:
- Coat the tenderloin with mustard and honey.
- Wrap the pork tenderloin with bacon strips.
- Place the pork loin into a greased air fryer basket.
- Arrange the air fryer basket in the center of Instant Omni Plus Toaster Oven.
- Press "Air Fry" and then set the temperature to 360 degrees F.
- Set the timer for 30 minutes and press "Start".
- When the display shows "Turn Food" "flip the pork tenderloin.
- When Cooking Time is complete, remove the air fryer basket from Toaster Oven.
- Place the pork loin onto a cutting board for about 10 minutes before slicing.

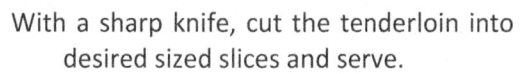

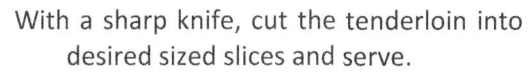

With a sharp knife, cut the tenderloin into desired sized slices and serve.

Nutrition:
Calories 386 Total Fat 16.1 g
Saturated Fat 5.7 g
Cholesterol 164 mg
Sodium 273 mg
Total Carbs 4.8 g
Fiber 0.3 g
Sugar 4.4 g
Protein 52.6 g
Cholesterol 15 mg
Sodium 798 mg
Total Carbs 20.3 g
Fiber 2.6 g
Sugar 1.7 g
Protein 43.9 g

CHAPTER 8:

Poultry

449. Quick & Easy Lemon Pepper Chicken

Preparation Time: 10 minutes
Cooking Time: 30 minutes
Servings: 4
Ingredients:

- chicken breasts, boneless & skinless
- 1 1/2 tsp granulated garlic
- 1 tbsp lemon pepper seasoning
- 1 tsp salt

Directions:

- Preheat the air fryer to 360 F.
- Season chicken breasts with lemon pepper seasoning, granulated garlic, and salt.
- Place chicken into the air fryer basket and cook for 30 minutes. Turn chicken halfway through.
- Serve and enjoy.

Nutrition:
Calories 285
Fat 10.9 g
Carbohydrates 1.8 g
Sugar 0.3 g
Protein 42.6 g
Cholesterol 130 mg

450. Spicy Jalapeno Hassel Back Chicken

Preparation Time: 10 minutes
Cooking Time: 15 minutes
Servings: 2
Ingredients:

- chicken breasts, boneless and skinless
- 1/2 cup cheddar cheese, shredded
- tbsp pickled jalapenos, chopped
- oz cream cheese, softened
- bacon slices, cooked and crumbled

Directions:

- Make five to six slits on top of chicken breasts.
- In a bowl, mix together 1/2 cheddar cheese, pickled jalapenos, cream cheese, and bacon.
- Stuff cheddar cheese mixture into the slits.
- Place chicken into the air fryer basket and cook at 350 F for 14 minutes.
- Sprinkle remaining cheese on top of the chicken and air fry for 1 minute more.
- Serve and enjoy.

Nutrition:
Calories 736
Fat 49 g
Carbohydrates 3.7 g
Sugar 0.2 g
Protein 65.5 g
Cholesterol 233 mg

451. Tasty Hassel Back Chicken

Preparation Time: 10 minutes
Cooking Time: 18 minutes
Servings: 2
Ingredients:

- chicken breasts, boneless and skinless
- 1/2 cup sauerkraut, squeezed and remove excess liquid
- thin Swiss cheese slices, tear into pieces
- thin deli corned beef slices, tear into pieces
- Salt and Pepper

Directions:

- Make five slits on top of chicken breasts. Season chicken with pepper and salt.
- Stuff each slit with beef, sauerkraut, and cheese.
- Spray chicken with cooking spray and place in the air fryer basket.
- Cook chicken at 350 F for 18 minutes.
- Serve and enjoy.

Nutrition:
Calories 724
Fat 39.9 g
Carbohydrates 3.6 g
Sugar 2.6 g
Protein 83.6 g
Cholesterol 260 mg

452. Western Turkey Breast

Preparation Time: 10 minutes
Cooking Time: 60 minutes
Servings: 8
Ingredients:
- lbs. turkey breast, boneless
- 1 tbsp olive oil
- 1 1/2 tsp paprika
- 1 1/2 tsp garlic powder
- Salt and pepper

Directions:
- Preheat the air fryer to 350 F.
- In a bowl, mix paprika, garlic powder, pepper, and salt together.
- Rub oil and spice mixture all over turkey breast.
- Place turkey breast skin side down in the air fryer basket and cook for 25 minutes.
- Turn turkey breast and cover with foil and cook for 35-45 minutes more or until the internal temperature of the turkey reaches 160 F.
- Remove turkey breast from the air fryer and allow it to cool for 10 minutes.
- Slice and serve.

Nutrition:
Calories 254 Fat 5.6 g
Carbohydrates 10.4 g
Sugar 8.1 g
Protein 38.9 g
Cholesterol 98 mg

453. Lemon Pepper Turkey Breast

Preparation Time: 10 minutes
Cooking Time: 60 minutes
Servings: 6
Ingredients:
- lbs turkey breast, de-boned
- 1 tsp lemon pepper seasoning
- 1 tbsp Worcestershire sauce
- tbsp olive oil
- 1/2 tsp salt

Directions:
- Add olive oil, Worcestershire sauce, lemon pepper seasoning, and salt into the zip-lock bag. Add turkey breast to the marinade and coat well and marinate for 1-2 hours.
- Remove turkey breast from marinade and place it into the air fryer basket.
- Cook at 350 F for 25 minutes. Turn turkey breast and cook for 35 minutes more or until the internal temperature of turkey breast reaches 165 F.
- Slice and serve.

Nutrition:
Calories 279 Fat 8.4 g
Carbohydrates 10.3 g
Sugar 8.5 g
Protein 38.8 g
Cholesterol 98 mg

454. Tender Turkey Legs

Preparation Time: 10 minutes
Cooking Time: 27 minutes
Servings: 4
Ingredients:
- turkey legs
- 1/4 tsp oregano
- 1/4 tsp rosemary
- 1 tbsp butter
- Salt and Pepper

Directions:
- Season turkey legs with pepper and salt.
- In a small bowl, mix together butter, oregano, and rosemary.
- Rub the butter mixture all over turkey legs.
- Preheat the air fryer to 350 F.
- Place turkey legs into the air fryer basket and cook for 27 minutes.
- Serve and enjoy.

Nutrition:
Calories 182 Fat 9.9 g
Carbohydrates 1.9 g Sugar 0.1 g
Protein 20.2 g Cholesterol 68 mg

455. Perfect Chicken Breasts

Preparation Time: 10 minutes
Cooking Time: 15 minutes
Servings: 4
Ingredients:
- 1 lb chicken breasts, skinless and boneless
- 1 tsp poultry seasoning
- tsp olive oil
- 1 tsp salt

Directions:
- Drizzle oil on the chicken breasts and season with poultry seasoning and salt.
- Place chicken breasts into the air fryer basket and cook at 360 F for 10 minutes. Flip chicken and cook for 5 minutes more.
- Serve and enjoy.

Nutrition:
Calories 237
Fat 10.8 g
Carbohydrates 0.3 g
Sugar 0 g
Protein 32.9 g
Cholesterol 101 mg

456. Ranch Garlic Chicken Wings

Preparation Time: 10 minutes
Cooking Time: 25 minutes
Servings: 4
Ingredients:
- lbs. chicken wings
- garlic cloves, minced
- 1/4 cup butter, melted
- tbsp ranch seasoning mix

Directions:
- Add chicken wings into the zip-lock bag.
- Mix together butter, garlic, and ranch seasoning and pour over chicken wings. Seal bag shakes well and places in the refrigerator overnight.
- Place marinated chicken wings into the air fryer basket and cook at 360 F for 20 minutes. Shake air fryer basket twice.
- Turn temperature to 390 F and cook chicken wings for 5 minutes more.
- Serve and enjoy.

Nutrition:
Calories 552
Fat 28.3 g
Carbohydrates 1.3 g
Sugar 0.1 g
Protein 66 g
Cholesterol 232 mg

457. Ranch Chicken Thighs

Preparation Time: 10 minutes
Cooking Time: 23 minutes
Servings: 4
Ingredients:
- chicken thighs, bone-in & skin-on
- 1/2 tbsp ranch dressing mix

Directions:
- Add chicken thighs into the mixing bowl and sprinkle with ranch dressing mix. Toss well to coat.
- Spray chicken thighs with cooking spray and place into the air fryer basket.
- Cook at 380 F for 23 minutes. Turn chicken halfway through.
- Serve and enjoy.

Nutrition:
Calories 558 Fat 21.7 g
Carbohydrates 0.5 g Sugar 0.3 g
Protein 84.6 g Cholesterol 260 mg

458. Taco Ranch Chicken Wings

Preparation Time: 10 minutes
Cooking Time: 30 minutes
Servings: 4
Ingredients:
- lbs. chicken wings
- 1 tsp ranch seasoning

1 1/2 tsp taco seasoning
1 tsp olive oil

Directions:
Preheat the air fryer to 400 F.
In a mixing bowl, add chicken wings, ranch seasoning, taco seasoning, and oil and toss well to coat.
Place chicken wings into the air fryer basket and cook for 15 minutes.
Turn chicken wings to another side and cook for 15 minutes more.
Serve and enjoy.

Nutrition:
Calories 444 Fat 18 g
Carbohydrates 0 g Sugar 0 g
Protein 65.6 g Cholesterol 202 mg

459. Simple Cajun Chicken Wings

Preparation Time: 10 minutes
Cooking Time: 25 minutes
Servings: 4
Ingredients:
lbs. chicken wings
1/3 cup ranch dressing
1 tbsp + 1/2 tsp Cajun seasoning

Directions:
Rub 1 tablespoon Cajun seasoning all over chicken wings.
Place chicken wings into the air fryer basket and cook at 400 F for 25 minutes. Turn chicken wings halfway through.
Meanwhile, in a small bowl, mix together ranch dressing and 1 teaspoon Cajun seasoning.
Serve chicken wings with Cajun ranch dressing.

Nutrition:
Calories 437 Fat 16.9 g
Carbohydrates 1.1 g
Sugar 0.5 g Protein 65.9 g
Cholesterol 202 mg

460. Simple Air Fried Chicken

Preparation Time: 10 minutes
Cooking Time: 10 minutes
Servings: 4
Ingredients:
oz chicken, skinless and boneless
1/2 tsp black pepper
1/2 tsp salt
1/2 cup almond meal
1 egg, beaten

Directions:
Preheat the air fryer at 330 F/ 165 C.
Add egg in a bowl and whisk until frothy and season with pepper and salt.
In a shallow dish, mix together almond meal and salt.
Dip chicken into the egg mixture then coats with almond meal.
Place coated chicken into the air fryer basket and cook for 10 minutes.
Serve and enjoy.

Nutrition:
Calories 285;
Fat 12.8 g;
Carbohydrates 3.7 g;
Protein 38.1 g;

461. Buffalo Wings

Preparation Time: 5 minutes
Cooking Time: 15 minutes
Servings: 4
Ingredients:
32 oz chicken wings
1/4 cup hot sauce
tbsp grass-fed butter, melted
Salt

Directions:
Add chicken wings into the bowl. Pour hot sauce and butter over chicken wings and toss well.
Place marinated chicken wings into the refrigerator for 1-2 hours.

Preheat the air fryer at 400 F/ 204 C for 3 minutes

Place marinated chicken wings into the air fryer basket and cook for 12 minutes. shake basket halfway through.

Serve and enjoy.

Nutrition:
Calories 678; Fat 34 g;
Carbohydrates 0.4 g; Sugar 0.3 g;
Protein 87.7 g;
Cholesterol 300 mg

462. Honey Lime Chicken Wings

Preparation Time: 10 minutes
Cooking Time: 50 minutes
Servings: 6
Ingredients:
  lbs chicken wings
  tbsp fresh lime juice
  salt and black pepper
  1/4 tsp white pepper powder
  tbsp honey

Directions:
In a bowl, place all the ingredients and coat well.

Place marinated chicken wings into the refrigerator for 1-2 hours.

Preheat the air fryer to 182 C/ 360 F.

Place marinated chicken wings into the air fryer basket and cook for 12 minutes. Shake air fryer basket halfway through.

Turn temperature to 400 F/ 204 C and cook for 3 minutes more.

Serve and enjoy.

Nutrition:
Calories 311;
Fat 11.2 g;
Carbohydrates 6.1 g;
Sugar 5.8 g;
Protein 43.8 g;
Cholesterol 135 mg

463. Simple Chicken Drumsticks

Preparation Time: 10 minutes
Cooking Time: 16 minutes
Servings: 4
Ingredients:
  1 1/2 lbs chicken drumsticks
  tbsp chicken seasoning
  1 tsp black pepper
  1 tbsp olive oil
  1 tsp salt

Directions:
In a small bowl, mix together chicken seasoning, olive oil, pepper, and salt.

Rub seasoning mixture all over the chicken.

Place seasoned chicken into the air fryer basket and cook for 10 minutes. Flip halfway through.

Turn temperature to 300 F/ 148 C and cook for 6 minutes more.

Serve and enjoy.

Nutrition:
Calories 319;
Fat 13.2 g;
Carbohydrates 0.3 g;
Sugar 0 g;
Protein 46.8 g;
Cholesterol 150 mg

464. Healthy Chicken Wings

Preparation Time: 10 minutes
Cooking Time: 25 minutes
Servings: 4
Ingredients:
  lbs. chicken wings
  1 tbsp pepper
  1 tbsp garlic powder
  tbsp seasoning salt

Directions:
In a bowl, mix all of the ingredients except for the chicken wings.

Add chicken wings in a bowl and toss until well coated.

Preheat the air fryer at 370 F/ 187 C for 5 minutes.

Put the chicken wings into the basket of the air fryer and cook for 20 minutes. Shake basket halfway through.

Serve and enjoy.

Nutrition:
Calories 442; Fat 16.9 g;
Carbohydrates 2.6 g;
Sugar 0.5 g;
Protein 66.1 g;
Cholesterol 202 mg

465. Thai Chicken Thighs
Preparation Time: 10 minutes
Cooking Time: 20 minutes
Servings: 4
Ingredients:
- 1 lb chicken thighs, boneless and skinless
- tsp ginger, minced
- garlic cloves, chopped
- 1/2 cup coconut milk
- tbsp curry paste

Directions:

Add all ingredients into the zip-lock bag and shake well and place bag in the refrigerator for overnight.

Add marinated chicken and the sauce in a pie dish.

Place dish in air fryer and cook for 20 minutes at 165 F/ 73 C.

Serve and enjoy.

Nutrition:
Calories 341; Fat 20 g;
Carbohydrates 5.2 g; Sugar 1.1 g;
Protein 34.1 g; Cholesterol 101 mg

466. Chicken Patties
Preparation Time: 10 minutes
Cooking Time: 13 minutes
Servings: 8
Ingredients:
- lbs ground chicken
- 1 cup homemade salsa
- 1/2 small onion, chopped
- 1 1/2 cups egg whites
- Salt and Pepper

Directions:

Add egg whites, salsa, and onion into the blender and blend until combined.

Add ground chicken and egg mixture into the large mixing bowl. Season with pepper and salt and mix until well combined.

Make small patties from meat mixture.

Spray air fryer basket with cooking spray.

Place chicken patties in air fryer and cook for 12-13 minutes. Cook in batches.

Serve and enjoy.

Nutrition:
Calories 357; Fat 12.7 g;
Carbohydrates 2.8 g; Sugar 1.5 g;
Protein 54.7 g; Cholesterol 151 mg

467. Cajun Seasoned Chicken Drumsticks
Preparation Time: 5 minutes
Cooking Time: 15 minutes
Servings: 2
Ingredients:
- chicken drumsticks, skinless
- 1 tbsp Cajun seasoning
- tsp olive oil

Directions:

Add all ingredients to the zip-lock bag. Shake bag well and place in refrigerator for half hour.

Place marinated chicken drumsticks in air fryer basket and cook for 15 minutes at 400 F/ 204 C.

Serve and enjoy.

Nutrition:
Calories 118; Fat 7.3 g;
Carbohydrates 0 g; Sugar 0 g;
Protein 12.7 g; Cholesterol 40 mg

468. Honey Garlic Chicken

Preparation Time: 10 minutes
Cooking Time: 15 minutes
Servings: 2
Ingredients:
- chicken drumsticks, skinless
- 1/2 tsp garlic, minced
- tsp honey
- tsp olive oil

Directions:
- Put all of the ingredients to a bowl and mix until well coated.
- Place chicken in refrigerator for half hour.
- Place marinated chicken into the air fryer and cook for 15 minutes at 400 F/ 204 C.
- Serve and enjoy.

Nutrition:
Calories 140; Fat 7.3 g; Carbohydrates 6 g; Sugar 5.8 g; Protein 12.7 g;

469. Sriracha Chicken Wings

Preparation Time: 10 minutes
Cooking Time: 35 minutes
Servings: 2
Ingredients:
- 1 lb. chicken wings - 1/2 lime juice
- 1 tbsp grass-fed butter
- tbsp sriracha sauce
- 1/4 cup honey

Directions:
- Preheat the air fryer to 182 C/ 360 F.
- Add chicken wings in air fryer basket and cook for 30 minutes.
- Meanwhile, in a pan, add all remaining ingredients and bring to boil for 3 minutes. Once chicken wings are done then toss with sauce and serve.

Nutrition:
Calories 711; Fat 32.6 g; Carbohydrates 35.9 g; Sugar 35.8 g; Protein 65.8 g; Cholesterol 227 mg

470. Sweet & Spicy Chicken Wings

Preparation Time: 10 minutes
Cooking Time: 20 minutes
Servings: 8
Ingredients:
- lbs. chicken wings
- tbsp honey
- 1/2 cup buffalo sauce
- tbsp grass-fed butter, melted
- Salt and Pepper

Directions:
- Put the chicken wings into the basket of the air fryer and cook for 20 minutes at 400 F/ 204 C. Shake air fryer basket 2 times during the cooking.
- In a large bowl, combine together honey, buffalo sauce, butter, pepper, and salt.
- Add cooked chicken wings into the bowl and toss until well coated with sauce.
- Serve and enjoy.

Nutrition:
Calories 262;
Fat 11.7 g;
Carbohydrates 4.6 g;
Sugar 4.4 g;
Protein 32.9 g;
Cholesterol 109 mg

471. Ginger Garlic Chicken

Preparation Time: 10 minutes
Cooking Time: 30 minutes
Servings: 2
Ingredients:
- chicken thighs, skinless and boneless
- 1/2 tsp ground ginger
- 1 garlic clove, minced
- tbsp ketchup
- 1/2 cup honey

Directions:
- Cut chicken thighs into the small pieces and place them into the air fryer basket and cook for 25 minutes at 390 F/ 198 C.

- Meanwhile, in a pan heat together honey, ketchup, garlic, and ground ginger for 4-5 minutes.
- Once the chicken is cooked then transfer into the mixing bowl.
- Pour honey mixture over the chicken and toss until well coated.
- Serve and enjoy.

Nutrition:
Calories 554;
Fat 16.3 g;
Carbohydrates 37.2 g;
Sugar 36.5 g;
Protein 63.7 g;
Cholesterol 195 mg

472. Herb Roasted Chicken

Preparation Time: 5 minutes
Cooking Time: 20 minutes
Servings: 4
Ingredients:
- chicken drumsticks
- 1 tbsp lemon juice
- 1 tsp garlic salt
- 1 tsp chili powder
- 1 1/2 tsp mixed herbs

Direction
- Preheat the air fryer to 180 C/ 356 F for 5 minutes.
- In a small bowl, mix together garlic salt, chili powder, and mixed herbs.
- Rub lemon juice all over the chicken then rub garlic salt mixture.
- Place chicken into the air fryer basket and cook for 10 minutes at 200 C/ 392 F.
- Turn heat to 180 C/ 356 F and cook for 5 minutes more.
- Serve and enjoy.

Nutrition:
Calories 86; Fat 2.8 g;
Carbohydrates 1.3 g; Sugar 0.3 g;
Protein 13 g;
Cholesterol 40 mg

473. Honey & Mustard Chicken Thighs

Preparation Time: 5 minutes
Cooking Time: 25 minutes
Servings: 4
Ingredients:
- thighs, skin-on
- tbsp honey
- tbsp Dijon mustard
- ½ tbsp garlic powder
- Salt and black pepper to taste

Directions:
- In a bowl, mix honey, mustard, garlic, salt, and black pepper. Coat the thighs in the mixture and arrange them on the greased basket. Fit in the baking tray and cook for 16 minutes at 400 F on Air Fry function, turning once halfway through. Serve warm.

Nutrition:
Calories 285;
Fat 12.8 g;
Carbohydrates 3.7 g;
Protein 38.1 g;

474. Fried Chicken Tenderloins

Preparation Time: 5 minutes
Cooking Time: 10 minutes
Servings: 4
Ingredients:
- chicken tenderloins
- tbsp butter, softened
- oz breadcrumbs
- 1 large egg, whisked

Directions:
- Preheat Cuisinart on Air Fry function to 380 F. Combine butter and breadcrumbs in a bowl. Keep mixing and stirring until the mixture gets crumbly. Dip the chicken in the egg, then in the crumb mix. Place in the greased basket and fit in the baking tray; cook for 10 minutes, flipping once until crispy.

Set on Broil function for crispier taste. Serve.
Nutrition:
Calories 245;
Fat 11 g;
Carbohydrates 4.8 g;
Protein 28.5 g;

475. Thyme Turkey Nuggets
Preparation Time: 5 minutes
Cooking Time: 20 minutes
Servings: 4
Ingredients:
- oz turkey breast
- 1 egg, beaten
- 1 cup breadcrumbs
- ½ tsp dried thyme
- Salt and black pepper to taste

Directions:
Preheat Cuisinart on Air Fry function to 350 F. Pulse the turkey in a food processor and transfer to a bowl. Stir in thyme, salt, and pepper.

Form nugget-sized balls out of turkey mixture and dip in breadcrumbs, then in egg, and finally in the breadcrumbs again. Place the nuggets on a greased Air Fryer basket and fit in the baking tray. Cook for 10 minutes, shaking once until golden brown. Serve warm.

Nutrition:
Calories 285;
Fat 12.8 g;
Carbohydrates 3.7 g;
Protein 38.1 g;

476. Fruity Chicken Breasts With BBQ Sauce
Preparation Time: 5 minutes
Cooking Time: 20 minutes
Servings: 2
Ingredients:
- chicken breasts, cubed
- green bell peppers, sliced
- ½ onion, sliced
- 1 can drain pineapple chunks
- ½ cup barbecue sauce

Directions:
Preheat air fryer on Bake function to 370 F. Thread the green bell peppers, chicken cubes, onions, and pineapple chunks on the skewers. Brush with barbecue sauce and cook in your air fryer for 20 minutes until slightly crispy. Serve.

Nutrition:
Calories 296
Fat 10g;
Carbohydrates 5 g;
Protein 34 g;

477. Savory Honey & Garlic Chicken
Preparation Time: 35 minutes
Cooking Time: 20 minutes
Servings: 4
Ingredients:
- chicken drumsticks, skin removed
- tbsp olive oil
- tbsp honey
- ½ tbsp garlic, minced

Directions:
Add garlic, olive oil, and honey to a sealable zip bag. Add chicken and toss to coat; set aside for 30 minutes. Add the coated chicken to the basket and fit in the baking sheet; cook for 15 minutes at 400 F on Air Fry function, flipping once. Serve and enjoy!

Nutrition:
Calories 364;
Fat 8 g;
Carbohydrates 5g;
Protein 32 g;

478. Hot Chicken Wings

Preparation Time: 5 minutes
Cooking Time: 20 minutes
Servings: 2
Ingredients:
- chicken wings
- 1 tbsp water
- tbsp potato starch
- tbsp hot curry paste
- ½ tbsp baking powder

Directions:
Combine hot curry paste and water in a small bowl. Add in the wings toss to coat. Cover the bowl with plastic wrap and refrigerate for 30 minutes.

Preheat Cuisinart on Air Fry function to 370 degrees. In a bowl, mix the baking powder with potato starch. Remove the wings from the fridge and dip them in the starch mixture.

Place on a lined baking dish and cook in your Cuisinart for 7 minutes. Flip over and cook for 5 minutes.

Nutrition:
Calories 283;
Fat 12g;
Carbohydrates 3.8 g;
Protein 29 g;

479. Sweet Chicken Drumsticks

Preparation Time: 35 minutes
Cooking Time: 20 minutes
Servings: 2
Ingredients:
- chicken drumsticks, skin removed
- tbsp olive oil
- tbsp honey
- ½ tbsp garlic, minced

Directions:
Add all the ingredients to a resealable bag; massage until well-coated. Set aside the chicken for 30 minutes in the fridge to marinate.

Preheat Cuisinart on Air Fry function to 390 F. Remove the chicken drumsticks from the fridge and add them to the greased basket. Fit in the baking tray and cook for 15 minutes, shaking once. Serve hot.

Nutrition:
Calories 245;
Fat 9 g;
Carbohydrates 8 g;
Protein 34 g;

480. Savory Buffalo Chicken

Preparation Time: 5 minutes
Cooking Time: 25 minutes
Servings: 4
Ingredients:
- pounds chicken wings
- ½ cup cayenne pepper sauce
- ½ cup coconut oil
- 1 tbsp Worcestershire sauce
- 1 tbsp kosher salt

Directions:
In a bowl, mix cayenne pepper sauce, coconut oil, Worcestershire sauce, and salt; set aside. Put chicken in the basket of the Air Fryer and fit in the baking tray. Cook for 25 minutes at 380 F on Air Fry function. Transfer to a large-sized plate and drizzle with the prepared sauce to serve.

Nutrition:
Calories 285;
Fat 12.8 g;
Carbohydrates 3.7 g;
Protein 38.1 g;

481. Rosemary Chicken Breasts

Preparation Time: 5 minutes
Cooking Time: 15 minutes
Servings: 4
Ingredients:
- chicken breasts
- Salt and black pepper to taste

½ cup dried rosemary
1 tbsp butter, melted

Directions:
- Preheat Cuisinart on Air Fry function to 390 F. Lay a foil on a flat surface. Place the breasts on the foil, sprinkle with rosemary, tarragon, salt, and pepper and drizzle the butter.
- Wrap the foil around the breasts. Place the wrapped chicken in the Air Fryer basket and fit in the baking tray; cook for 12 minutes. Remove and carefully unwrap. Serve with the sauce extract and steamed veggies.

Nutrition:
Calories 312;
Fat 7.5 g;
Carbohydrates 6 g;
Protein 42 g;

482. Chicken With Avocado & Radish Bowl

Preparation Time: 5 minutes
Cooking Time: 15 minutes
Servings: 2
Ingredients:
- chicken breasts
- 1 avocado, sliced
- radishes, sliced
- 1 tbsp chopped parsley
- Salt and black pepper to taste

Directions:
- Preheat Cuisinart on Air Fry function to 300 F. Cut the chicken into small cubes. Mix all of the ingredients in a bowl and transfer to the Air Fryer pan. Cook for 14 minutes, shaking once. Serve with cooked rice or fried red kidney beans.

Nutrition:
Calories 285;
Fat 12. g;
Carbohydrates 3.6 g;
Protein 35.7 g;

483. Savory Chicken With Onion

Preparation Time: 5 minutes
Cooking Time: 20 minutes
Servings: 4
Ingredients:
- chicken breasts, cubed
- 1 ½ cup onion soup mix
- 1 cup mushroom soup
- ½ cup heavy cream

Directions:
- Preheat your Cuisinart oven to 400 F on Bake function. Add mushrooms, onion mix, and heavy cream in a frying pan. Heat on low heat for 1 minute. Pour the warm mixture over chicken and allow to sit for 25 minutes. Place the marinated chicken in the basket and fit in the baking tray; cook for 15 minutes. Serve and enjoy!

Nutrition:
Calories 246;
Fat 11.3g;
Carbohydrates 4.3 g;
Protein 31g;

484. Buttered Crispy Turkey

Preparation Time: 5 minutes
Cooking Time: 20 minutes
Servings: 4
Ingredients:
- 1-pound turkey breast, halved
- cups panko breadcrumbs
- Salt and black pepper to taste
- ½ tsp cayenne pepper
- 1 stick butter, melted

Directions:
- In a bowl, combine the breadcrumbs, salt, cayenne and black peppers. Brush the butter onto the turkey breast and coat in the crumb mixture. Transfer to a lined baking dish.

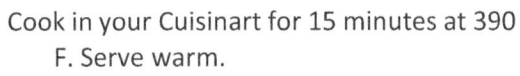

Cook in your Cuisinart for 15 minutes at 390 F. Serve warm.

Nutrition:
Calories 282; Fat 12.4g;
Carbohydrates 3.4 g; Protein 36.2g;

485. Chinese Chicken Wings Recipe

Preparation Time: 2 hours and 5 minutes
Cooking Time: 10 minutes
Servings: 4
Ingredients:
  chicken wings
  3-tbsp. lime juice
  2-tbsp. soy sauce
  2-tbsp. honey
  Salt and black pepper to the taste.

Directions:
  In a bowl, mix honey with soy sauce, salt, black and lime juice, whisk well, add chicken pieces, toss to coat and keep in the fridge for 2 hours.
  Transfer chicken to your air fryer, cook at 370 °F, for 6 minutes on each side, increase heat to 400 °F and cook for 3 minutes more. Serve hot.

Nutrition:
Calories: 372;
Fat: 9g;
Fiber: 10g;
Carbs: 37g;
Protein: 24g

486. Chicken And Asparagus Recipe

Preparation Time: 5 minutes
Cooking Time: 25 minutes
Servings: 4
Ingredients:
  asparagus spears
  chicken wings, halved.
  one-tablespoon rosemary, chopped.
  one-teaspoon cumin, ground.
  Salt and black pepper to the taste.

Directions:
  Pat dry chicken wings, season with salt, pepper, cumin and rosemary, put them in your air fryer's basket and cook at 360 °F, for 20 minutes
  Meanwhile, heat up a pan over medium heat, add asparagus, add water to cover, steam for a few minutes; transfer to a bowl filled with ice water, drain and arrange on plates. Add chicken wings on the side and serve.

Nutrition:
Calories: 270;
Fat: 8g;
Fiber: 12g;
Carbs: 24g;
Protein: 22g

487. Honey Duck Breasts Recipe.

Preparation Time: 5 minutes
Cooking Time: 30 minutes
Servings: 2
Ingredients:
  1 smoked duck breast, halved.
  one-tablespoon mustard
  one-teaspoon tomato paste
  ½-tsp. apple vinegar
  one-teaspoon honey

Directions:
  In a bowl, mix honey with tomato paste, mustard and vinegar, whisk well, add duck breast pieces, toss to coat well, transfer to your air fryer and cook at 370 °F, for 15 minutes
  Take duck breast out of the fryer, add to honey mix, toss again, return to air fryer and cook at 370 °F, for 6 minutes more. Divide among plates and serve with a side salad.

Nutrition:
Calories: 274; Fat: 11g; Fiber: 13g;
Carbs: 22g; Protein: 13g

488. Coconut Creamy Chicken

Preparation Time: 2 hours
Cooking Time: 25 minutes
Servings: 4
Ingredients:
- big chicken legs - 4-tbsp. coconut cream
- 2-tbsp. ginger, grated.
- 5-tsp. turmeric powder
- Salt and black pepper to the taste.

Directions:
- In a bowl, mix cream with turmeric, ginger, salt and pepper, whisk, add chicken pieces, toss them well and leave aside for 2 hours.
- Transfer chicken to your preheated air fryer, cook at 370 °F, for 25 minutes; divide among plates and serve with a side salad

Nutrition:
Calories: 300; Fat: 4g;
Fiber: 12g; Carbs: 22g; Protein: 20g

489. Lemony Chicken

Preparation Time: 5 minutes
Cooking Time: 30 minutes
Servings: 6
Ingredients:
- 1 whole chicken; cut into medium pieces
- Zest from 2 lemons, grated.
- Juice from 2 lemons
- one-tablespoon olive oil
- Salt and black pepper to the taste.

Directions:
- Season chicken with salt, pepper, rub with oil and lemon zest, drizzle lemon juice, put in your air fryer and cook at 350 °F, for 30 minutes; flipping chicken pieces halfway. Divide among plates and serve with a side salad.

Nutrition:
Calories: 334; Fat: 24g;
Fiber: 12g; Carbs: 26g;
Protein: 20g

490. Buttermilk Marinated Chicken

Preparation Time: 10 minutes
Cooking Time: 25 minutes
Servings: 6
Ingredients
- 3-lb. whole chicken
- 1 tablespoon salt
- 1-pint buttermilk

Directions:
- Place the whole chicken in a large bowl and drizzle salt on top.
- Pour the buttermilk over it and leave the chicken soaked overnight.
- Cover the chicken bowl and refrigerate overnight.
- Remove the chicken from the marinade and fix it on the rotisserie rod in the Air fryer oven.
- Turn the dial to select the "Air Roast" mode.
- Hit the Time button and again use the dial to set the Cooking Time to 25 minutes.
- Now push the Temp button and rotate the dial to set the temperature at 370 degrees F.
- Close its lid and allow the chicken to roast.
- Serve warm.

Nutrition:
Calories 284 Total Fat 7.9 g
Saturated Fat 1.4 g Cholesterol 36 mg
Sodium 704 mg Total Carbs 46 g
Fiber 3.6 g
Sugar 5.5 g
Protein 17.9 g

491. Roasted Duck

Preparation Time: 10 minutes
Cooking Time: 3 hours
Servings: 12
Ingredients
- lb. whole Pekin duck
- garlic cloves chopped

lemons; 1chopped; 1 juiced
1/2 cup balsamic vinegar
1/4 cup honey

Directions:
- Place the Pekin duck in a baking tray and add garlic, lemon, and salt on top.
- Whisk honey, vinegar, and honey in a bowl.
- Brush this glaze over the duck liberally. Marinate overnight in the refrigerator.
- Remove the duck from the marinade and fix it on the rotisserie rod in the Air fryer oven.
- Turn the dial to select the "Air Roast" mode.
- Hit the Time button and again use the dial to set the Cooking Time to 3 hours.
- Now push the Temp button and rotate the dial to set the temperature at 350 degrees F.
- Close its lid and allow the duck to roast.
- Serve warm.

Nutrition:
Calories 387
Total Fat 6 g
Saturated Fat 9.9 g
Cholesterol 41 mg
Sodium 154 mg
Total Carbs 37.4 g
Fiber 2.9 g
Sugar 15.3 g
Protein 14.6 g

492. Roasted Turkey Breast

Preparation Time: 10 minutes
Cooking Time: 50 minutes
Servings: 6
Ingredients
- lb. boneless turkey breast
- ¼ cup mayonnaise
- teaspoon poultry seasoning
- salt and black pepper
- ½ teaspoon garlic powder

Directions:
- Whisk all the ingredients, including turkey in a bowl, and coat it well.
- Place the boneless turkey breast in the Air fryer basket.
- Rotate the dial to select the "Air fry" mode.
- Press the Time button and again use the dial to set the Cooking Time to 50 minutes.
- Now press the Temp button and rotate the dial to set the temperature at 350 degrees F.
- Once preheated, place the air fryer basket in the Ninja oven and Close its lid to bake.
- Slice and serve.

Nutrition:
Calories 322
Total Fat 11.8 g
Saturated Fat 2.2 g
Cholesterol 56 mg
Sodium 321 mg
Total Carbs 14.6 g
Dietary Fiber 4.4 g
Sugar 8 g
Protein 17.3 g

493. Lemon Pepper Turkey

Preparation Time: 10 minutes
Cooking Time: 45 minutes
Servings: 6
Ingredients
- lbs. turkey breast
- tablespoons oil
- 1 tablespoon Worcestershire sauce
- 1 teaspoon lemon pepper
- 1/2 teaspoon salt

Directions:
- Whisk everything in a bowl and coat the turkey liberally.
- Place the turkey in the Air fryer basket.
- Press "Power Button" of the Air Fryer Grill and turn the dial to select the "Air Fry" mode.

- Press the Time button and again turn the dial to set the Cooking Time to 45 minutes.
- Now push the Temp button and rotate the dial to set the temperature at 375 degrees F.
- Once preheated, place the air fryer basket inside and close its lid.
- Serve warm.

Nutrition:
Calories 391 Total Fat 2.8 g
Saturated Fat 0.6 g Cholesterol 330 mg
Sodium 62 mg Total Carbs 36.5 g
Fiber 9.2 g Sugar 4.5 g Protein 6.6

494. Maple Chicken Thighs

Preparation Time: 10 minutes
Cooking Time: 30 minutes
Servings: 4
Ingredients
- large chicken thighs, bone-in
- tablespoons French mustard
- tablespoons Dijon mustard
- 1 clove minced garlic
- tablespoons maple syrup

Directions:
- Mix chicken with everything in a bowl and coat it well.
- Place the chicken along with its marinade in the baking pan.
- Press "Power Button" of the Air Fryer Grill and turn the dial to select the "Bake" mode.
- Press the Time button and again turn the dial to set the Cooking Time to 30 minutes.
- Now push the Temp button and rotate the dial to set the temperature at 370 degrees F.
- Once preheated, place the baking pan inside and close its lid.
- Serve warm.

Nutrition:
Calories 301 Total Fat 15.8 g
Saturated Fat 2.7 g Cholesterol 75 mg
Sodium 189 mg
Total Carbs 31.7 g
Fiber 0.3 g
Sugar 0.1 g
Protein 28.2 g

495. Italian Chicken Bake

Preparation Time: 10 minutes
Cooking Time: 25 minutes
Servings: 6
Ingredients:
- ¾ lbs. chicken breasts
- tablespoons pesto sauce
- ½ (14 oz) can tomatoes, diced
- 1 cup Mozzarella cheese, shredded
- tablespoon fresh basil, chopped

Directions:
- Place the flattened chicken breasts in a baking pan and top them with pesto.
- Add tomatoes, cheese, and basil on top of each chicken piece.
- Press "Power Button" of the Air Fryer Grill and turn the dial to select the "Bake" mode.
- Press the Time button and again turn the dial to set the Cooking Time to 25 minutes.
- Now push the Temp button and rotate the dial to set the temperature at 355 degrees F.
- Once preheated, place the baking dish inside and close its lid.
- Serve warm.

Nutrition:
Calories 537 Total Fat 19.8 g
Saturated Fat 1.4 g Cholesterol 10 mg
Sodium 719 mg Total Carbs 25.1 g
Fiber 0.9 g Sugar 1.4 g
Protein 37.8 g

496. Pesto Chicken Bake

Preparation Time: 10 minutes
Cooking Time: 35 minutes
Servings: 3
Ingredients
- chicken breasts
- 1 (6 oz.) jar basil pesto
- medium fresh tomatoes, sliced
- mozzarella cheese slices

Directions:
- Spread the tomato slices in a casserole dish and top them with chicken.
- Add pesto and cheese on top of the chicken and spread evenly.
- Press "Power Button" of the Air Fryer Grill and turn the dial to select the "Air Fry" mode.
- Press the Time button and again turn the dial to set the Cooking Time to 30 minutes.
- Now push the Temp button and rotate the dial to set the temperature at 350 degrees F.
- Once preheated, place the casserole dish inside and close its lid.
- After it is baked, switch the oven to broil mode and broil for 5 minutes.
- Serve warm.

Nutrition:
Calories 452 Total Fat 4 g
Saturated Fat 2 g Cholesterol 65 mg
Sodium 220 mg Total Carbs 23.1 g
Fiber 0.3 g Sugar 1 g
Protein 26g

497. Lemon Garlic Chicken

Preparation Time: 15 minutes
Cooking Time: 40 minutes
Servings: 4
Ingredients:
- chicken breast fillets
- 1 tablespoon lemon juice
- 1 tablespoon melted butter
- 1 teaspoon garlic powder
- Salt and pepper to taste

Directions:
- Mix lemon juice and melted butter in a bowl.
- Brush both sides of chicken with this mixture.
- Season with garlic powder, salt and pepper.
- Insert grill grate to your Ninja Foodi Grill.
- Place chicken on top of the grill.
- Close the hood.
- Grill at 350 degrees F for 15 to 20 minutes per side.

Nutrition:
Calories: 553 kcal
Protein: 62.46 g
Fat: 31.26 g
Carbohydrates: 1.89 g

498. Grilled Ranch Chicken

Preparation Time: 30 minutes
Cooking Time: 30 minutes
Servings: 6
Ingredients:
- chicken thigh fillets
- tablespoons ranch dressing
- Garlic salt and pepper

Directions:
- Spread both sides of chicken with ranch dressing.
- Sprinkle with garlic salt and pepper.
- Set your Ninja Foodi Grill to grill.
- Preheat it to medium.
- Add chicken to the grill grate.
- Cook for 15 minutes per side.

Nutrition:
Calories: 475 kcal
Protein: 33.16 g
Fat: 36.43 g
Carbohydrates: 1.66 g

499. Chicken Breast Pita Sandwiches

Preparation Time: 20 minutes
Cooking Time: 10 minutes
Servings: 4
Ingredients:
- boneless, skinless chicken breasts, cut into 1-inch cubes
- pita pockets, split in half
- 1 red bell pepper, sliced
- 1 small red onion, sliced
- ⅓ cup Italian salad dressing
- ½ teaspoon dried thyme
- 1 cup cherry tomatoes, chopped
- cups butter lettuce, tear into slices
- Cooking spray

Directions:
- Place the chicken, bell pepper and onion in the air fryer basket. Sprinkle with 1 tablespoon Italian salad dressing and thyme. Spritz with cooking spray.
- Put the air fryer lid on and bake in the preheated air fryer at 375ºF for 9 to 11 minutes. Shake the basket once when it shows 'TURN FOOD' on the air fryer lid screen halfway through cooking time, or until the chicken is cooked through.
- Transfer the chicken to a bowl and pour in the remaining salad dressing. Combine well.
- To assemble the sandwiches, start with the pita halves, then add the butter lettuce slices, and cherry tomatoes. Serve immediately.

Nutrition:
Calories: 1493
Total Fat: 146.77g
Saturated Fat: 75.456g
Total Carbs: 36.38g
Fiber: 3.7g
Protein: 46.36g
Sugar: 9.78g
Sodium: 1611mg

500. Asian Style Turkey Meatballs

Preparation Time: 24 minutes
Cooking Time: 13 minutes
Servings: 4
Ingredients:
- 1-pound ground turkey
- 1 small onion, minced
- tablespoons peanut oil
- ¼ cup water chestnuts, finely chopped
- tablespoons low-sodium soy sauce
- ½ teaspoon ground ginger
- ¼ cup panko bread crumbs
- 1 egg, beaten

Directions:
- In a 6×6×2 inch baking pan, add the onion and peanut oil. Stir well.
- Place the pan in the air fryer and put the air fryer lid on. Cook in the preheated air fryer at 375ºF for 1 to 2 minutes, or until the onion is soft and translucent. Transfer the cooked onion into a large bowl. Add the water chestnuts, soy sauce, ground ginger, and bread crumbs into the onion. Stir in the beaten egg and whisk well, then add in the turkey. Toss until well combined.
- On your cutting board, scoop out the mixture and shape into 1-inch meatballs.
- Arrange the meatballs in the pan and drizzle with the oil.
- Place the pan in the air fryer and put the air fryer lid on. Bake in batches at 400ºF for 10 to 12 minutes, or until the meatballs are cooked through. Remove the meatballs from the pan to a plate. Let cool for 3 minutes before serving.

Nutrition:
Calories: 683 Total Fat: 33.29gSaturated Fat: 15.591g Total Carbs: 3.23gFiber: 0.6g Protein: 24.77gSugar: 1.17g Sodium: 342mgCholesterol: 271mg

501. Sweet And Spicy Chicken Stir-Fry

Preparation Time: 15 minutes
Cooking Time: 15 minutes
Servings: 4
Ingredients:
- ¾ pound boneless, skinless chicken thighs, cut into 1-inch pieces
- 1 small red onion, sliced
- 1 yellow bell pepper, cut into 1½-inch pieces
- ¼ cup chicken stock
- 1 tablespoon olive oil
- to 3 teaspoons curry powder
- tablespoons honey
- ¼ cup orange juice
- 1 tablespoon cornstarch

Directions:
- Place the red onion, chicken thighs, and pepper in the air fryer basket and drizzle with olive oil.
- Put the air fryer lid on and cook in the preheated air fryer at 375ºF for 12 to 14 minutes. Flip the chicken thighs when it shows 'TURN FOOD' on the lid screen halfway through cooking time, or until the chicken reaches 1650F.
- Transfer the chicken and vegetables to a 6-inch metal bowl. Add the chicken stock, curry powder, honey, orange juice, and cornstarch into the bowl. Combine well.
- Place the metal bowl inside the basket and put the air fryer lid on. Cook for 3 minutes more.
- Remove the bowl from the basket. Let cool for 3 minutes before serving.

Nutrition:
Calories: 746 Total Fat: 22.98g
Saturated Fat: 16.852g
Total Carbs: 25.2g Fiber: 2.1g
Protein: 12.61g
Sugar: 14.48g
Sodium: 471mg

502. Crispy Chicken Parmigiana

Preparation Time: 15 minutes
Cooking Time: 15 minutes
Servings: 4
Ingredients:
- (4-ounce) boneless, skinless chicken breasts
- ½ cup grated Parmesan cheese
- 1 cup Italian bread crumbs
- teaspoons Italian seasoning
- Salt and pepper to taste
- egg whites - ¾ cup marinara sauce
- ½ cup shredded mozzarella cheese
- Cooking spray

Directions:
- On a flat work surface, pound the chicken into ¼-inch pieces.
- In a large bowl, mix together the bread crumbs, Parmesan cheese, Italian seasoning, salt and pepper. Stir until well combined. In another bowl, pour in the egg whites. Set aside.
- Spritz the air fryer basket with cooking spray.
- Dredge the chicken cutlets in the egg whites, and then in the bread crumbs mixture to coat.
- Arrange the breaded cutlets in the air fryer basket and mist with cooking spray.
- Put the air fryer lid on and cook in the preheated air fryer at 375ºF for 7 minutes. Transfer the fried chicken cutlets to a serving plate.
- Drizzle with the marinara sauce and sprinkle mozzarella cheese on top. Cook for an additional 3 minutes until the cheese is bubbly. Let cool for 3 minutes and serve.

Nutrition:
Calories: 944 Total fat: 70g
Saturated fat: 3g Cholesterol: 46mg
Sodium: 593mg Carbohydrates: 220g
Fiber: 1g, Protein: 105g

503. Chicken Fajitas With Avocados

Preparation Time: 15 minutes
Cooking Time: 10 minutes
Servings: 4
Ingredients:
- boneless, skinless chicken breasts, sliced
- avocados, peeled and chopped
- 1 small red onion, sliced
- red bell peppers, sliced
- ½ cup spicy ranch salad dressing
- ½ teaspoon dried oregano
- corn tortillas
- cups torn butter lettuce

Directions:
- Put the onion, chicken and pepper in the air fryer basket. Drizzle with 1 tablespoon of salad dressing and sprinkle with the oregano.
- Put the air fryer lid on and grill in the preheated air fryer at 375ºF for 10 to 14 minutes. Flip the chicken when it shows 'TURN FOOD' on the lid screen halfway through cooking time, or until the chicken is browned and slightly charred.
- Remove the vegetables and chicken from the basket to a serving dish. Drizzle over the remaining salad dressing.
- Serve warm.

Nutrition:
Calories: 887, Total Fat: 34.25g
Saturated Fat: 22.931g Total Carbs: 14.29g
Fiber: 7.3g Protein: 22.2g
Sugar: 4.2g Sodium: 2841mg

504. Fried Chicken With Buttermilk

Preparation Time: 15 minutes
Cooking Time: 15 minutes
Servings: 4
Ingredients:
- chicken pieces: drumsticks, breasts, and thighs
- ⅓ cup buttermilk
- 1 cup flour
- teaspoons paprika
- eggs, beaten
- 1½ cups bread crumbs
- tablespoons olive oil
- Freshly ground black pepper and salt to taste

Directions:
- On your cutting board, thoroughly dry the chicken with paper towels. In a shallow bowl, mix the flour, paprika, salt and pepper.
- In another bowl, whisk the eggs and buttermilk until well combined.
- In a third bowl, combine the bread crumbs with olive oil.
- Dredge the chicken in the flour mixture, then dip into the eggs, and finally dunk into the bread crumbs. Gently but firmly press the crumbs onto the skin of chicken pieces to fully coat.
- Place the breaded chicken into the air fryer basket. Put the air fryer lid on and cook in the preheated air fryer at 375ºF for 15 minutes. Flip the chicken when it shows 'TURN FOOD' on the lid screen halfway through cooking time.
- Transfer the chicken to a serving dish. Let cool for 5 minutes before serving.

Nutrition:
Calories: 651 Total Fat: 22.34g
Saturated Fat: 13.684g Total Carbs: 27.54g
Fiber: 2.2g Protein: 14.38g
Sugar: 6.14g Sodium: 1257mg

505. Panko-Crusted Chicken Nuggets

Preparation Time: 15 minutes
Cooking Time: 15 minutes
Servings: 4
Ingredients:
- 1-pound boneless, skinless chicken breasts

Chicken seasoning or rub
Salt and pepper to taste
eggs
tablespoons bread crumbs
tablespoons panko bread crumbs
Cooking spray

Directions:

On your cutting board, slice the chicken breast into 1-inch cutlets.

In a large bowl, mix together the chicken cutlets, chicken seasoning, salt and pepper. Toss to fully coat. Set aside.

In another bowl, whisk the eggs. In a third bowl, combine the bread crumbs with panko.

Dredge the chicken cutlets in the whisked eggs, and then into the bread crumbs to coat well.

Arrange the breaded chicken cutlets in the air fryer basket and spray them with cooking spray.

Put the air fryer lid on and cook in batches in the preheated air fryer at 400ºF for 4 minutes. Shake the air fryer basket when the lid screen indicates 'TURN FOOD' during cooking time, and cook for an additional 4 minutes.

Transfer the cooked chicken cutlets to a serving bowl. Let cool for 3 minutes and serve.

Nutrition:
Calories: 508 Total Fat: 24g
Saturated Fat: 1g Cholesterol: 147mg
Sodium: 267mg Carbohydrates: 67g
Fiber: 1g
Protein: 24g

506. Crusted Chicken Tenders

Preparation Time: 27 minutes
Cooking Time: 12 minutes
Servings: 4
Ingredients:
chicken tenders
½ cup all-purpose flour
1 egg
½ cup dry bread crumbs
tablespoons vegetable oil

Directions:

Put the flour in a bowl. Set aside.

In a second bowl, whisk the egg. Set aside.

In a third bowl, mix the bread crumbs and oil together. Set aside.

Dredge the chicken tenders in the flour, then in the whisked egg, and finally in the crumb mixture to coat well.

Lay the tenders in the air fryer basket. Put the air fry lid on and cook in the preheated air fryer at 350ºF for about 12 minutes or until lightly browned.

Remove the chicken tenders from the basket and serve on a platter.

Nutrition:
Calories: 253
Total Fat: 11.4g
Carbohydrates: 9.8g
Protein: 26.2g
Cholesterol: 109mg
Sodium: 171mg

507. Chicken With Greek Yogurt Buffalo Sauce

Preparation Time: 36 minutes
Cooking Time: 15 minutes
Servings: 4
Ingredients:
1-pound skinless, boneless chicken breasts, cut into 1-inch strips
½ cup plain fat-free Greek yogurt
1 cup panko bread crumbs
1 tablespoon sweet paprika
1 tablespoon cayenne pepper
1 tablespoon garlic pepper
¼ cup egg substitute
1 tablespoon hot sauce
1 teaspoon hot sauce

Directions:

- In a bowl, mix the bread crumbs, sweet paprika, cayenne pepper, and garlic pepper. Set aside.
- In a second bowl, whisk together the Greek yogurt, egg substitute, and 1 tablespoon plus 1 teaspoon hot sauce.
- Dunk the chicken strips into the buffalo sauce, then coat with bread crumb mixture.
- Arrange the well-coated chicken strips in the air fryer basket. Put the air fry lid on and cook in the preheated air fryer at 400ºF for 15 minutes or until well browned. Flip the strips when the lid screen indicates 'TURN FOOD' halfway through.
- Remove the chicken from the basket and serve on a plate.

Nutrition:
Calories: 234, Fat: 4.6g,
Carbohydrates: 22.1g
Protein: 31.2g
Cholesterol: 65mg
Sodium: 696mg

508. Baked Chicken Fajita Roll-Ups

Preparation Time: 35 minutes
Cooking Time: 12 minutes
Servings: 4
Ingredients:
- (4-ounce) boneless, skinless chicken breasts
- Juice of ½ lime
- tablespoons fajita seasoning
- ½ red bell pepper, cut into strips
- ½ green bell pepper, cut into strips
- ¼ onion, sliced
- Cooking spray
- toothpicks, soaked for at least 30 minutes

Directions:
- On a flat work surface, carefully butterfly or pound the chicken into ¼-inch cutlets.
- Sprinkle the lemon juice over cutlets and season with fajita seasoning to taste. Toss well.
- To make the chicken roll-ups, evenly spread the bell pepper strips and onion slices on each chicken cutlet. Roll each cutlet into a tight cylinder and secure with a toothpick through the center.
- Arrange 4 chicken roll-ups in the air fryer basket. Spray them with cooking spray.
- Put the air fryer lid on and cook in the preheated air fryer at 400ºF for 12 minutes.
- Transfer to a serving dish and cool for 5 minutes before serving.

Nutrition:
Calories: 770Total Fat: 65g
Saturated Fat: 0g
Cholesterol: 32mg
Sodium: 302mg
Carbohydrates: 212g
Fiber: 0g
Protein: 94g

509. Garlicky Chicken And Potatoes

Preparation Time: 15 minutes
Cooking Time: 15 minutes
Servings: 4
Ingredients:
- 1 broiler-fryer whole chicken (2½ to 3 pounds)
- to 16 creamer potatoes, scrubbed
- cloves garlic, peeled
- tablespoons olive oil
- ½ teaspoon garlic salt
- 1 slice of lemon
- ½ teaspoon dried thyme
- ½ teaspoon dried marjoram

Directions:
- Rinse the chicken and pat it dry using paper towels.

- In a small bowl, combine 1 tablespoon of the olive oil and salt. Rub half of the olive mixture evenly on all sides of the chicken. Stuff the lemon slice and garlic cloves inside the chicken. Sprinkle the thyme and marjoram on top.
- Arrange the chicken in the air fryer basket and spread out the scrubbed potatoes. Drizzle the remaining olive oil mixture on top.
- Put the air fryer lid on and roast in the preheated air fryer at 375ºF for 25 minutes, or until the chicken registers 165ºF on a meat thermometer (inserted into the center of the chicken's thickest part). If not fully cooked through, return the chicken to the basket and roast for another 5 minutes.
- Transfer the chicken and potatoes to a plate. Let rest for 5 minutes before serving.

Nutrition:
Calories: 1523
Total Fat: 22.77g
Saturated Fat: 14.11g
Total Carbs: 24.16g
Fiber: 1.5g
Protein: 13.35g
Sugar: 0.24g
Sodium: 1013mg

510. Chicken Thighs With Lemon Garlic

Preparation Time: 15 minutes
Cooking Time: 20 minutes
Servings: 4
Ingredients:
- skin-on, bone-in chicken thighs
- lemon wedges
- ¼ cup lemon juice
- cloves garlic, minced
- tablespoons olive oil
- 1 teaspoon Dijon mustard
- ¼ teaspoon salt
- ⅛ teaspoon ground black pepper

Directions:
- Mix the lemon juice, Dijon mustard, olive oil, garlic, salt, and pepper together in a bowl. Refrigerate to marinate for an hour.
- Put the chicken thighs into a zip lock bag and pour the marinade all over the chicken and zip the bag. Refrigerate for at least 2 hours.
- Take the chicken out from the bag. Pat dry with paper towels. Arrange them in the air fryer basket.
- Put the air fry lid on and cook in batches in the preheated air fryer at 350ºF for 15 to 18 minutes or until cooked through.
- Transfer the chicken thighs to a platter. Squeeze the lemon wedges over before serving.

Nutrition:
Calories: 258,
Total Fat: 18.6g,
Cholesterol: 71mg,
Carbohydrates: 3.6g,
Sodium: 242mg,
Protein: 19.4g

511. Lemony Chicken With Barbecue Sauce

Preparation Time: 10 minutes
Cooking Time: 12 minutes
Servings: 4
Ingredients:
- boneless, skinless chicken thighs
- tablespoons lemon juice
- ¼ cup barbecue sauce, gluten-free
- cloves garlic, minced

Directions:
- In a medium bowl, mix together the chicken, cloves, barbecue sauce and lemon juice. Set aside for 10 minutes to marinate.

Transfer the marinated chicken thighs into the air fryer basket, shaking off excess sauce. You may need to work in batches to avoid overcrowding.

Put the air fryer lid on and grill in the preheated air fryer at 375ºF for 12 minutes. Flip the chicken thighs when it shows 'TURN FOOD' on the lid screen halfway through cooking time, or until the chicken registers at least 165ºF using a meat thermometer inserted into the center of the chicken.

Transfer to a platter and repeat with remaining chicken thighs. Serve warm.

Nutrition:
Calories: 113
Total Fat: 12.31g
Saturated Fat: 8.531g
Total Carbs: 27g
Fiber: 0.2g
Protein: 6.61g
Sugar: 2.874g
Sodium: 803mg

512. Chicken Popcorn

Preparation time: 10 minutes
Cooking time: 10 minutes
Servings: 6
Ingredients:
- eggs
- 1 1/2 lb. Chicken breasts, cut into small chunks
- 1 tsp paprika
- 1/2 tsp garlic powder
- 1 tsp onion powder
- 1/2 cups pork rind, crushed
- 1/4 cup coconut flour
- Pepper
- Salt

Directions:
In a small bowl, mix together coconut flour, pepper, and salt.
In another bowl, whisk eggs until combined.
Take one more bowl and mix together pork panko, paprika, garlic powder, and onion powder.
Add chicken pieces in a large mixing bowl. Sprinkle coconut flour mixture over chicken and toss well.
Dip chicken pieces in the egg mixture and coat with pork panko mixture and place on a plate.
Spray air fryer basket with cooking spray.
Preheat the air fryer to 400 f.
Add half prepared chicken in air fryer basket and cook for 10-12 minutes. Shake basket halfway through.
Cook remaining half using the same method.
Serve and enjoy.

Nutrition:
Calories 265 Fat 11 g
Carbohydrates 3 g Sugar 0.5 g
Protein 35 g
Cholesterol 195 mg

513. Quick & Easy Meatballs

Preparation time: 10 minutes
Cooking time: 10 minutes
Servings: 4
Ingredients:
- 1 lb. Ground chicken
- 1 egg, lightly beaten
- 1/2 cup mozzarella cheese, shredded
- 1 1/2 tbsp taco seasoning
- garlic cloves, minced
- tbsp fresh parsley, chopped
- 1 small onion, minced
- Pepper
- Salt

Directions:
Add all ingredients into the large mixing bowl and mix until well combined.
Make small balls from mixture and place in the air fryer basket.

Cook meatballs for 10 minutes at 400 f.
Serve and enjoy.
Nutrition:
Calories 253
Fat 10 g
Carbohydrates 2 g
Sugar 0.9 g
Protein 35 g
Cholesterol 144 mg

514. Lemon Pepper Chicken Wings

Preparation time: 10 minutes
Cooking time: 16 minutes
Servings: 4
Ingredients:
- 1 lb. Chicken wings
- 1 tsp lemon pepper
- 1 tbsp. olive oil
- 1 tsp salt

Directions:
- Add chicken wings into the large mixing bowl.
- Add remaining ingredients over chicken and toss well to coat.
- Place chicken wings in the air fryer basket.
- Cook chicken wings for 8 minutes at 400 f.
- Turn chicken wings to another side and cook for 8 minutes more.
- Serve and enjoy.

Nutrition:
Calories 247 Fat 11 g
Carbohydrates 0.3 g Sugar 0 g
Protein 32 g
Cholesterol 101 mg

515. Bbq Chicken Wings

Preparation time: 10 minutes
Cooking time: 20 minutes
Servings: 4
Ingredients:
- 1 1/2 lbs. Chicken wings
- tbsp unsweetened bbq sauce
- 1 tsp paprika
- 1 tbsp. olive oil
- 1 tsp garlic powder
- Pepper
- Salt

Directions:
- In a large bowl, toss chicken wings with garlic powder, oil, paprika, pepper, and salt.
- Preheat the air fryer to 360 f.
- Add chicken wings in air fryer basket and cook for 12 minutes.
- Turn chicken wings to another side and cook for 5 minutes more.
- Remove chicken wings from air fryer and toss with bbq sauce.
- Return chicken wings in air fryer basket and cook for 2 minutes more.
- Serve and enjoy.

Nutrition: Calories 372
Fat 16.2 g
Carbohydrates 4.3g
Sugar 3.7 g
Protein 49.4 g
Cholesterol 151 mg

516. Yummy Chicken Nuggets

Preparation time: 10 minutes
Cooking time: 12 minutes
Servings: 4

Ingredients:
- 1 lb. Chicken breast, skinless, boneless and cut into chunks
- tbsp sesame seeds, toasted
- egg whites
- 1/2 tsp ground ginger
- 1/4 cup coconut flour
- 1 tsp sesame oil
- Pinch of salt

Directions:
- Preheat the air fryer to 400 f.
- Toss chicken with oil and salt in a bowl until well coated.

Add coconut flour and ginger in a zip-lock bag and shake to mix. Add chicken to the bag and shake well to coat.

In a large bowl, add egg whites. Add chicken in egg whites and toss until well coated.

Add sesame seeds in a large zip-lock bag.

Shake excess egg off from chicken and add chicken in sesame seed bag. Shake bag until chicken well coated with sesame seeds.

Spray air fryer basket with cooking spray.

Place chicken in air fryer basket and cook for 6 minutes.

Turn chicken to another side and cook for 6 minutes more.

Serve and enjoy.

Nutrition:
Calories 265
Fat 11.5 g
Carbohydrates 8.6 g
Sugar 0.3 g
Protein 31.1 g
Cholesterol 73 mg

517. Italian Seasoned Chicken Tenders

Preparation time: 10 minutes
Cooking time: 10 minutes
Servings: 2
Ingredients:
- eggs, lightly beaten
- 1 1/2 lbs. Chicken tenders
- 1/2 tsp onion powder
- 1/2 tsp garlic powder
- 1 tsp paprika
- 1 tsp italian seasoning
- tbsp ground flax seed
- 1 cup almond flour
- 1/2 tsp pepper
- 1 tsp sea salt

Directions:
Preheat the air fryer to 400 f.
Season chicken with pepper and salt.
In a medium bowl, whisk eggs to combine.
In a shallow dish, mix together almond flour, all seasonings, and flaxseed.
Dip chicken into the egg then coats with almond flour mixture and place on a plate.
Spray air fryer basket with cooking spray.
Place half chicken tenders in air fryer basket and cook for 10 minutes. Turn halfway through.
Cook remaining chicken tenders using same steps.
Serve and enjoy.

Nutrition:
Calories 315
Fat 21 g
Carbohydrates 12 g
Sugar 0.6 g
Protein 17 g
Cholesterol 184 mg

518. Classic Chicken Wings

Preparation time: 10 minutes
Cooking time: 40 minutes
Servings: 4
Ingredients:
- lbs. Chicken wings
- For sauce:
- 1/4 tsp tabasco
- 1/4 tsp worcestershire sauce
- tbsp. butter, melted
- oz. hot sauce

Directions:
Spray air fryer basket with cooking spray.
Add chicken wings in air fryer basket and cook for 25 minutes at 380 f. Shake basket after every 5 minutes.
After 25 minutes turn temperature to 400 f and cook for 10-15 minutes more.
Meanwhile, in a large bowl, mix together all sauce ingredients.
Add cooked chicken wings in a sauce bowl and toss well to coat.

Serve and enjoy.
Nutrition:
Calories 593
Fat 34.4 g
Carbohydrates 1.6 g
Sugar 1.1 g
Protein 66.2 g
Cholesterol 248 mg

519. Simple Spice Chicken Wings

Preparation time: 10 minutes
Cooking time: 30 minutes
Servings: 3
Ingredients:
- 1 1/2 lbs. Chicken wings
- 1 tbsp. baking powder, gluten-free
- 1/2 tsp onion powder
- 1/2 tsp garlic powder
- 1/2 tsp smoked paprika
- 1 tbsp. olive oil
- 1/2 tsp pepper
- 1/4 tsp sea salt

Directions:
- Add chicken wings and oil in a large mixing bowl and toss well.
- Mix together remaining ingredients and sprinkle over chicken wings and toss to coat.
- Spray air fryer basket with cooking spray.
- Add chicken wings in air fryer basket and cook at 400 f for 15 minutes. Toss well.
- Turn chicken wings to another side and cook for 15 minutes more.
- Serve and enjoy.

Nutrition:
Calories 280
Fat 19 g
Carbohydrates 2 g
Sugar 0 g
Protein 22 g
Cholesterol 94 mg

520. Herb Seasoned Turkey Breast

Preparation time: 10 minutes
Cooking time: 35 minutes
Servings: 4
Ingredients:
- lbs. Turkey breast
- 1 tsp fresh sage, chopped
- 1 tsp fresh rosemary, chopped
- 1 tsp fresh thyme, chopped
- Pepper
- Salt

Directions:
- Spray air fryer basket with cooking spray.
- In a small bowl, mix together sage, rosemary, and thyme.
- Season turkey breast with pepper and salt and rub with herb mixture.
- Place turkey breast in air fryer basket and cook at 390 f for 30-35 minutes.
- Slice and serve.

Nutrition:
Calories 238
Fat 3.9 g
Carbohydrates 10 g
Sugar 8 g
Protein 38.8 g
Cholesterol 98 mg

521. Tasty Rotisserie Chicken

Preparation time: 10 minutes
Cooking time: 20 minutes
Servings: 6
Ingredients:
- lbs. Chicken, cut into eight pieces
- 1/4 tsp cayenne
- 1 tsp paprika
- tsp onion powder
- 1 1/2 tsp garlic powder
- 1 1/2 tsp dried oregano
- 1/2 tbsp dried thyme
- Pepper
- Salt

Directions:
- Season chicken with pepper and salt.
- In a bowl, mix together spices and herbs and rub spice mixture over chicken pieces.
- Spray air fryer basket with cooking spray.
- Place chicken in air fryer basket and cook at 350 f for 10 minutes.
- Turn chicken to another side and cook for 10 minutes more or until the internal temperature of chicken reaches at 165 f.
- Serve and enjoy.

Nutrition:
Calories 350 Fat 7 g
Carbohydrates 1.8 g Sugar 0.5 g
Protein 66 g Cholesterol 175 mg

522. Spicy Asian Chicken Thighs

Preparation time: 10 minutes
Cooking time: 20 minutes
Servings: 4
Ingredients:
- chicken thighs, skin-on, and bone-in
- tsp ginger, grated
- 1 lime juice
- tbsp. chili garlic sauce
- 1/4 cup olive oil
- 1/3 cup soy sauce

Directions:
- In a large bowl, whisk together ginger, lime juice, chili garlic sauce, oil, and soy sauce.
- Add chicken in bowl and coat well with marinade and place in the refrigerator for 30 minutes.
- Place marinated chicken in air fryer basket and cook at 400 f for 15-20 minutes or until the internal temperature of chicken reaches at 165 f. Turn chicken halfway through.
- Serve and enjoy.

Nutrition:
Calories 403 Fat 23.5 g
Carbohydrates 3.2 g Sugar 0.6 g
Protein 43.7 g Cholesterol 130 mg

523. Tomato, Eggplant 'N Chicken Skewers

Preparation time: 10 minutes
Cooking time: 30 minutes
Servings: 4
Ingredients:
- ¼ teaspoon cayenne pepper
- ¼ teaspoon ground cardamom
- 1 ½ teaspoon ground turmeric
- 1 can coconut milk
- 1 cup cherry tomatoes
- 1 medium eggplant, cut into cubes
- 1 onion, cut into wedges
- 1-inch ginger, grated
- pounds boneless chicken breasts, cut into cubes - tablespoons fresh lime juice
- tablespoons tomato paste
- teaspoons lime zest
- cloves of garlic, minced
- Salt and pepper to taste

Directions:
- Place in a bowl the garlic, ginger, coconut milk, lime zest, lime juice, tomato paste, salt, pepper, turmeric, cayenne pepper, cardamom, and chicken breasts. Allow to marinate in the fridge for at least for 2 hours.
- Preheat the air fryer to 3900F.
- Place the grill pan accessory in the air fryer.
- Skewer the chicken cubes with eggplant, onion, and cherry tomatoes on bamboo skewers.
- Place on the grill pan and cook for 25 minutes making sure to flip the chicken every 5 minutes for even cooking.

Nutrition:
Calories:485 Carbs:19.7 g
Protein: 55.2g Fat: 20.6g

524. Teriyaki Glazed Chicken Bake

Preparation time: 10 minutes
Cooking time: 30 minutes
Servings: 2
Ingredients:
- tablespoons cider vinegar
- skinless chicken thighs
- 1-1/2 teaspoons cornstarch
- 1-1/2 teaspoons cold water
- 1/2 clove garlic, minced
- 1/4 cup white sugar
- 1/4 cup soy sauce
- 1/4 teaspoon ground ginger
- 1/8 teaspoon ground black pepper

Directions:
- Lightly grease baking pan of air fryer with cooking spray. Add all Ingredients and toss well to coat. Spread chicken in a single layer on bottom of pan.
- For 15 minutes, cook on 390oF.
- Turnover chicken while brushing and covering well with the sauce.
- Cook for 15 minutes at 330oF.
- Serve and enjoy.

Nutrition:
Calories: 267
Carbs: 19.9g
Protein: 24.7g
Fat: 9.8g

525. Sriracha-Ginger Chicken

Preparation time: 10 minutes
Cooking time: 35 minutes
Servings: 3
Ingredients:
- ¼ cup fish sauce
- ¼ cup sriracha
- ½ cup light brown sugar
- ½ cup rice vinegar
- 1 ½ pounds chicken breasts, pounded
- 1/3 cup hot chili paste
- teaspoons grated and peeled ginger

Directions:
- Place all Ingredients in a Ziploc bag and allow to marinate for at least 2 hours in the fridge.
- Preheat the air fryer to 3900F.
- Place the grill pan accessory in the air fryer.
- Grill the chicken for 25 minutes.
- Flip the chicken every 10 minutes for even grilling.
- Meanwhile, pour the marinade in a saucepan and heat over medium flame until the sauce thickens.
- Before serving the chicken, brush with the sriracha glaze.

Nutrition:
Calories: 415
Carbs: 5.4g
Protein: 49.3g
Fat: 21.8g

526. Naked Cheese, Chicken Stuffing 'N Green Beans

Preparation time: 10 minutes
Cooking time: 20 minutes
Servings: 3
Ingredients:
- 1 cup cooked, cubed chicken breast meat
- 1/2 (10.75 ounce) can condensed cream of chicken soup
- 1/2 (14.5 ounce) can green beans, drained
- 1/2 cup shredded Cheddar cheese
- 6-ounce unseasoned dry bread stuffing mix
- salt and pepper to taste

Directions:
- Mix well pepper, salt, soup, and chicken in a medium bowl.
- Make the stuffing according to package Directions: for Cooking.
- Lightly grease baking pan of air fryer with cooking spray. Evenly spread chicken mixture on bottom of pan. Top evenly with stuffing. Sprinkle cheese on top.
- Cover pan with foil.

For 15 minutes, cook on 390oF.

Remove foil and cook for 5 minutes at 390oF until tops are lightly browned.

Serve and enjoy.

Nutrition:
Calories: 418
Carbs: 48.8g
Protein: 27.1g
Fat: 12.7g

527. Grilled Chicken Pesto

Preparation time: 10 minutes
Cooking time: 30 minutes
Servings: 8
Ingredients:
- 1 ¾ cup commercial pesto
- chicken thighs
- Salt and pepper to taste

Directions:
- Place all Ingredients in the Ziploc bag and allow to marinate in the fridge for at least 2 hours.
- Preheat the air fryer to 3900F.
- Place the grill pan accessory in the air fryer.
- Grill the chicken for at least 30 minutes.
- Make sure to flip the chicken every 10 minutes for even grilling.

Nutrition:
Calories: 477
Carbs: 3.8g
Protein: 32.6g
Fat: 36.8g

528. Healthy Turkey Shepherd's Pie

Preparation time: 10 minutes
Cooking time: 50 minutes
Servings: 2
Ingredients:
- 1 tablespoon butter, room temperature
- 1/2 clove garlic, minced
- 1/2 large carrot, shredded
- 1/2 onion, chopped
- 1/2 teaspoon chicken bouillon powder
- 1/2-pound ground turkey
- 1/8 teaspoon dried thyme
- 1-1/2 large potatoes, peeled
- 1-1/2 teaspoons all-purpose flour
- 1-1/2 teaspoons chopped fresh parsley
- 1-1/2 teaspoons olive oil
- tablespoons warm milk
- 4.5-ounce can sliced mushrooms
- ground black pepper to taste
- salt to taste

Directions:
- Until tender, boil potatoes. Drain and transfer to a bowl. Mash with milk and butter until creamy. Set aside.
- Lightly grease baking pan of air fryer with olive oil. Add onion and for 5 minutes, cook on 360oF. Add chicken bouillon, garlic, thyme, parsley, mushrooms, carrot, and ground turkey. Cook for 10 minutes while stirring and crumbling halfway through cooking time.
- Season with pepper and salt. Stir in flour and mix well. Cook for 2 minutes.
- Evenly spread turkey mixture. Top with mashed potatoes, evenly.
- Cook for 20 minutes or until potatoes are lightly browned.
- Serve and enjoy.

Nutrition:
Calories: 342
Carbs: 38.0g
Protein: 18.3g
Fat: 12.9g

529. Chicken Fillet Strips

Preparation time: 10 minutes
Cooking time: 11 minutes
Servings: 4
Ingredients:
- 1 lb. Chicken fillets
- 1 tsp. Paprika
- 1 tbsp. Heavy cream

.5 tsp. Black pepper
Butter (as needed)

Directions:
- Heat the Air Fryer at 365º Fahrenheit.
- Slice the fillets into strips and dust with salt and pepper.
- Add a light coating of butter to the basket.
- Arrange the strips in the basket and air-fry for six minutes.
- Flip the strips and continue frying for another five minutes.
- When done, garnish with the cream and paprika. Serve warm.

Nutrition:
Calories: 162 kcal
Protein: 24.85 g
Fat: 6.05 g
Carbohydrates: 0.65 g

530. Chicken Chili Verde

Preparation time: 10 minutes
Cooking time: 25 minutes
Servings: 6
Ingredients:
- pounds of chicken breasts or thighs
- ½ of a teaspoon of cumin, ground
- ¼ of a teaspoon of garlic powder
- ounces of salsa verde
- Salt and pepper, to taste

Directions:
- Place the chicken meat inside the cooker. Sprinkle with seasonings and pour the salsa on top.
- Set the pressure to high and cook for 25 minutes.
- After that time, release the pressure quickly. Using two forks, shred the meat inside the pot and mix with the juices and salsa. Taste for seasoning and adjust as necessary.

Nutrition:
Cal.: 206   Total fat: 4.8 g
Total Carbs: 3.9 g   Proteins: 33 g

531. Lemon Curry Chicken

Preparation time: 5 minutes
Cooking time: 35 minutes
Servings: 6
Ingredients:
- 1 can of coconut milk
- ¼ of a cup of cup freshly squeezed lemon juice - 1 tablespoon of curry powder
- 1 teaspoon of turmeric
- pounds chicken thighs and/or breasts

Directions:
- In a measuring cup (or a bowl – but the cup makes it easier later) combine the coconut milk, spices and lemon juice.
- First, pour a little of the coconut milk mix into the pot. Place the meat over it, and cover it with the rest of the milk. Don't worry about little lumps in the cream. Close the lid and seal the valve.
- Choose the poultry setting and set the pressure to high and the timer for 15 minutes. Add 10 extra minutes if you're using frozen chicken meat.
- Once it finishes cooking, quickly release the pressure. Check the chicken by cutting through the thickest part – you should not see any pink. If it looks pinkish, close the lid back, again select high pressure and cook for 10-15 more minutes.
- When the chicken is cooked through, shred it with two forks without removing it from the pot. Mix it well with the sauce. If you find it hard to manoeuvre inside the pot, take the meat to the plate and add it shredded to the sauce. Taste for seasoning and adjust as necessary with salt and pepper.
- This chicken goes great served with your favourite vegetables – roasted or steamed!

Nutrition:
Cal.: 615   Fat: 25.2 g
Carbs: 3.3 g   Protein: 89.6 g

532. Turkey Joint

Preparation time: 10 minutes
Cooking time: 11 minutes
Servings: 6
Ingredients:
- lb. Turkey breast
- tbsp. Melted butter
- cloves Garlic
- 1 tsp. Thyme
- 1 tsp. Rosemary

Directions:
- Warm the Air Fryer to reach 375° Fahrenheit.
- Pat the turkey breast dry. Mince the garlic and chop the rosemary and thyme.
- Melt the butter and mix with the garlic, thyme, and rosemary in a small mixing bowl. Brush the butter over turkey breast.
- Place in the Air Fryer basket, skin side up, and cook for 40 minutes or until internal temperature reaches 160° Fahrenheit, flipping halfway through.
- Wait for five minutes before slicing.

Nutrition:
Calories: 321 kcal
Protein: 34.35 g
Fat: 19.32 g
Carbohydrates: 0.56 g

533. Cilantro Drumsticks

Preparation time: 12 minutes
Cooking time: 18 minutes
Servings: 4
Ingredients:
- chicken drumsticks
- ½ cup chimichurri sauce
- ¼ cup lemon juice

Directions:
- Coat the chicken drumsticks with chimichurri sauce and refrigerate in an airtight container for no less than an hour, ideally overnight.
- When it's time to cook, pre-heat your fryer to 400°F.
- Remove the chicken from refrigerator and allow return to room temperature for roughly twenty minutes.
- Cook for eighteen minutes in the fryer. Drizzle with lemon juice to taste and enjoy.

Nutrition:
Calories: 452 kcal Protein: 49.16 g
Fat: 25.53 g Carbohydrates: 3.52 g

534. Mozzarella Turkey Rolls

Preparation time: 10 minutes
Cooking time: 10 minutes
Servings: 4
Ingredients:
- slices turkey breast
- 1 cup sliced fresh mozzarella
- 1 tomato, sliced
- ½ cup fresh basil
- chive shoots

Directions:
- Pre-heat your Air Fryer to 390°F.
- Lay the slices of mozzarella, tomato and basil on top of each turkey slice.
- Roll the turkey up, enclosing the filling well, and secure by tying a chive shoot around each one.
- Put in the Air Fryer and cook for 10 minutes. Serve with a salad if desired.

Nutrition:
Calories: 3616 kcal Protein: 506.27 g
Fat: 160.48 g Carbohydrates: 1.21 g

535. Sage & Onion Turkey Balls

Preparation time: 25 minutes
Cooking time: 15 minutes
Servings: 2
Ingredients:
- oz. turkey mince

½ small onion, diced
1 medium egg
1 tsp. sage
½ tsp. garlic, pureed
tbsp. friendly bread crumbs
Salt to taste
Pepper to taste

Directions:
- Put all of the ingredients in a bowl and mix together well.
- Take equal portions of the mixture and mold each one into a small ball. Transfer to the Air Fryer and cook for 15 minutes at 350°F.
- Serve with tartar sauce and mashed potatoes.

Nutrition:
Calories: 516 kcal
Protein: 22.1 g
Fat: 30.22 g
Carbohydrates: 37.75 g

536. Turkey Loaf

Preparation time: 10 minutes
Cooking time: 40 minutes
Servings: 4

Ingredients:
- 2/3 cup of finely chopped walnuts
- 1 egg
- 1 tbsp. organic tomato paste
- 1 ½ lb. turkey breast, diced
- 1 tbsp. Dijon mustard
- ½ tsp. dried savory or dill
- 1 tbsp. onion flakes
- ½ tsp. ground allspice
- 1 small garlic clove, minced
- ½ tsp. sea salt
- ¼ tsp. black pepper
- 1 tbsp. liquid aminos
- tbsp. grated parmesan cheese

Directions:
- Pre-heat Air Fryer to 375°F.
- Coat the inside of a baking dish with a little oil.
- Mix together the egg, dill, tomato paste, liquid aminos, mustard, salt, dill, garlic, pepper and allspice using a whisk. Stir in the diced turkey, followed by the walnuts, cheese and onion flakes.
- Transfer the mixture to the greased baking dish and bake in the Air Fryer for 40 minutes.
- Serve hot.

Nutrition:
Calories: 432 kcal Protein: 44.43 g
Fat: 25.61 g Carbohydrates: 5.18 g

537. Moroccan Chicken

Preparation time: 15 minutes
Cooking time: 15 minutes
Servings: 2

Ingredients:
- ½ lb. shredded chicken
- 1 cup broth
- 1 carrot
- 1 broccoli, chopped
- Pinch of cinnamon
- Pinch of cumin
- Pinch of red pepper
- Pinch of sea salt

Directions:
- In a bowl, cover the shredded chicken with cumin, red pepper, sea salt and cinnamon.
- Chop up the carrots into small pieces. Put the carrot and broccoli into the bowl with the chicken.
- Add the broth and stir everything well. Set aside for about 30 minutes.
- Transfer to the Air Fryer. Cook for about 15 minutes at 390°F. Serve hot.

Nutrition:
Calories: 212 kcal
Protein: 30.03 g Fat: 7.1 g
Carbohydrates: 5.96 g

538. Herbed Cornish Game Hen

Preparation Time: 15 minutes
Cooking Time: 35 minutes
Servings: 4
Ingredients:
- 2 tbsp. avocado oil
- ½ tsp. dried oregano
- ½ tsp. dried rosemary
- ½ tsp. dried thyme
- ½ tsp. dried basil
- Salt and ground black pepper, as required
- 2 Cornish game hens

Directions:
- In a bowl, mix together the oil, dried herbs, salt and black pepper.
- Rub each hen with the herb mixture evenly.
- Press the "Power" button of the Air Fryer Oven and turn the dial to select "Air Fry" mode.
- Press the "Time" button and again turn the dial to set the cooking time to 35 minutes.
- Now push the "Temp" button and rotate the dial to set the temperature at 360°F.
- Press the "Start/Pause" button to start.
- When the unit beeps to show that it is preheated, open the lid and grease the air fry basket.
- Arrange the hens into the prepared basket breast-side down, and insert in the Air Fryer Oven.
- When the cooking time is completed, open the lid and transfer the hens onto a platter.
- Cut each hen into pieces and serve.

Serving Suggestion: Serve alongside roasted veggies.
Variation Tip: You can use fresh herbs instead of dried herbs.
Nutrition:
- Calories: 895
- Fats: 62.9 g
- Saturated Fats: 17.4 g
- Carbs: 0.7 g
- Fiber: 0.5 g
- Protein: 75.9 g

539. Cajun Spiced Whole Chicken

Preparation Time: 15 minutes
Cooking Time: 1 hour 10 minutes
Servings: 6
Ingredients:
- ¼ cup butter, softened
- 2 tsp. dried rosemary
- 2 tsp. dried thyme
- 1 tbsp. Cajun seasoning
- 1 tbsp. onion powder
- 1 tbsp. garlic powder
- 1 tbsp. paprika
- 1 tsp. cayenne pepper
- Salt, as required
- 1 (3-lb.) whole chicken, neck and giblets removed

Directions:

1. In a bowl, add the butter, herbs, spices and salt and mix well. Rub the chicken with spicy mixture generously. With the help of kitchen twines, tie off the wings and legs. Press the "Power" button of the Air Fryer Oven and turn the dial to select "Air Bake" mode. Press the "Time" button and again turn the dial to set the cooking time to 70 minutes. Now push the "Temp" button and rotate the dial to set the temperature at 380°F.
2. Press the "Start/Pause" button to start.
3. Open the unit when it has reached the temperature, when it beeps.
4. Arrange the chicken over the wire rack and insert them in the Air Fryer Oven.
5. When the cooking time is completed, open the lid and place the chicken onto a platter for about 10 minutes before cutting. Cut into desired sized pieces and serve.

Serving Suggestions: Serve alongside a fresh green salad.
Variation Tip: You can adjust the ratio of spices according to your choice.
Nutrition:
Calories: 421 Fats: 14.8 g
Saturated Fats: 6.9 g Carbs: 2.3 g
Fiber: 0.9 g Sugar: 0.5 g Protein: 66.3 g

540. Lemony Whole Chicken

Preparation Time: 15 minutes
Cooking Time: 1 hour 20 minutes
Servings: 8

Ingredients:
- 1 (5-lb.) whole chicken, neck and giblets removed
- Salt and ground black pepper, as required
- 2 fresh rosemary sprigs
- 1 small onion, peeled and quartered
- 1 garlic clove, peeled and cut in half
- 4 lemon zest slices
- 1 tbsp. extra-virgin olive oil
- 1 tbsp. fresh lemon juice

Directions:

1. Rub the inside and outside of chicken with salt and black pepper evenly.
2. Place the rosemary sprigs, onion quarters, garlic halves and lemon zest in the cavity of the chicken. With the help of kitchen twines, tie off the wings and legs.
3. Arrange the chicken onto a greased baking pan and drizzle with the oil and lemon juice. Press the "Power" button of the Air Fryer Oven and turn the dial to select "Air Bake" mode. Press the "Time" button and again turn the dial to set the cooking time to 20 minutes. Now push the "Temp" button and rotate the dial to set the temperature at 400°F. Press the "Start/Pause" button to start.
4. Open the unit when it has reached the temperature, when it beeps.
5. Arrange the pan over the wire rack and insert them in the oven.
6. After 20 minutes of cooking, set the temperature to 375°F for 60 minutes.
7. When cooking time is completed, open the lid and place the chicken onto a platter for about 10 minutes before cutting.
8. Cut into desired piece sizes and serve.

Serving Suggestions: Serve alongside the steamed veggies.
Variation Tip: Lemon can be replaced with lime.
Nutrition:
Calories: 448 Fats: 10.4 g
Saturated Fats: 2.7 g Carbs: 1 g
Fiber: 0.4 g Sugar: 0.2 g Protein: 82 g

541. Crispy Chicken Legs

Preparation Time: 15 minutes
Cooking Time: 20 minutes
Servings: 3
Ingredients:
- 3 (8-oz.) chicken legs
- 1 cup buttermilk
- 2 cups white flour
- 1 tsp. garlic powder
- 1 tsp. onion powder
- 1 tsp. ground cumin
- 1 tsp. paprika
- Salt and ground black pepper, as required
- 1 tbsp. olive oil

Directions:
- In a bowl, place the chicken legs and buttermilk and refrigerate for about 2 hours.
- In a shallow dish, mix together the flour and the spices.
- Remove the chicken from buttermilk.
- Coat the chicken legs with flour mixture, then dip them into buttermilk and finally, coat with the flour mixture again.
- Press the "Power" of the Air Fryer Oven and turn the dial to select "Air Fry" mode.
- Press the "Time" button and again turn the dial to set the cooking time to 20 minutes.
- Now push the "Temp" button and rotate the dial to set the temperature to 355°F.
- Press the "Start/Pause" button to start.
- When the unit beeps to show that it is preheated, open the lid and grease the air fry basket.
- Arrange the chicken legs into the prepared air fry basket and drizzle with the oil.
- Insert the basket in the Air Fryer Oven.
- When cooking time is completed, open the lid and serve hot.

Serving Suggestions: Serve with your favorite dip.
Variation Tip: White flour can be replaced with almond flour too.
Nutrition:
Calories: 817 Fats: 23.3 g
Saturated Fats: 5.9 g Carbs: 69.5 g
Fiber: 2.7 g Sugar: 4.7 g
Protein: 77.4 g

542. Marinated Spicy Chicken Legs

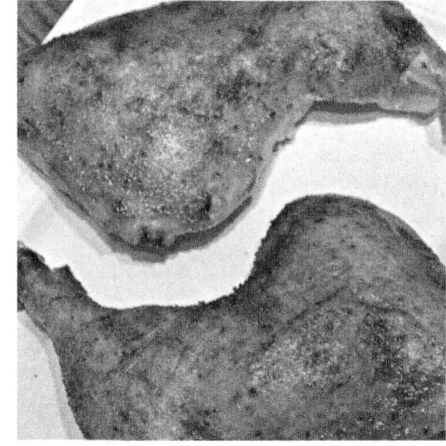

Preparation Time: 10 minutes
Cooking Time: 20 minutes
Servings: 4
Ingredients:
- 4 chicken legs
- 3 tbsp. fresh lemon juice
- 3 tsp. ginger paste
- 3 tsp. garlic paste

Salt, as required
4 tbsp. plain yogurt
2 tsp. red chili powder
1 tsp. ground cumin
1 tsp. ground coriander
1 tsp. ground turmeric
Ground black pepper, as required

Directions:

In a bowl, mix together the chicken legs, lemon juice, ginger, garlic and salt. Set aside for about 15 minutes.

Meanwhile, in another bowl, mix together the yogurt and the spices.

Add the chicken legs and coat with the spice mixture generously.

Cover the bowl and refrigerate for at least 10–12 hours.

Press the "Power" button of the Air Fryer Oven and turn the dial to select "Air Fry" mode.

Press the "Time" button and again turn the dial to set the cooking time to 20 minutes.

Now push the "Temp" button and rotate the dial to set the temperature to 440°F.

Press the "Start/Pause" button to start.

When the unit beeps to show that it is preheated, open the lid and grease the air fry basket.

Place the chicken legs into the prepared air fry basket and insert them in the Air Fryer Oven .

When cooking time is completed, open the lid and serve hot.

Serving Suggestions: Serve with fresh greens.
Variation Tip: Lemon juice can be replaced with vinegar.
Nutrition:

Calories: 461 Fats: 17.6 g
Saturated Fats: 5 g Carbs: 4.3 g
Fiber: 0.9 g
Sugar: 1.5 g
Protein: 67.1 g

543. Gingered Chicken Drumsticks

Preparation Time: 10 minutes
Cooking Time: 25 minutes
Servings: 3
Ingredients:

¼ cup full-fat coconut milk
2 tsp. fresh ginger, minced
2 tsp. galangal, minced
2 tsp. ground turmeric
Salt, as required
3 (6-oz.) chicken drumsticks

Directions:

Place the coconut milk, galangal, ginger, and spices in a large bowl and mix well.

Add the chicken drumsticks and coat with the marinade generously.

Refrigerate to marinate for at least 6–8 hours.

Press the "Power" button of the Air Fryer Oven and turn the dial to select "Air Fry" mode.

Press the "Time" button and again turn the dial to set the cooking time to 25 minutes.

Now push the "Temp" button and rotate the dial to set the temperature at 375°F.

Press the "Start/Pause" button to start.

When the unit beeps to show that it is preheated, open the lid and grease the air fry basket.

Place the chicken drumsticks into the prepared air fry basket and insert them in the Air Fryer Oven .

When the cooking time is completed, open the lid and serve hot.

Serving Suggestions: Serve alongside the lemony couscous.

Variation Tip: Coconut milk can be replaced with cream.

Nutrition:
Calories: 347 Fats: 14.8 g
Saturated Fats: 6.9 g Carbs: 3.8 g
Fiber: 1.1 g Sugar: 0.8 g Protein: 47.6 g

---

544. Crispy Chicken Drumsticks

Preparation Time: 15 minutes
Cooking Time: 25 minutes
Servings: 4

Ingredients:
- 4 chicken drumsticks
- 1 tbsp. adobo seasoning
- Salt, as required
- 1 tbsp. onion powder
- 1 tbsp. garlic powder
- ½ tbsp. paprika
- Ground black pepper, as required
- 2 eggs
- 2 tbsp. milk
- 1 cup all-purpose flour
- ¼ cup cornstarch

Directions:
- Season the chicken drumsticks with the adobo seasoning and a pinch of salt.
- Set aside for about 5 minutes.
- In a small bowl, add the spices, salt and black pepper and mix well.
- In a shallow bowl, add the eggs, milk and 1 tsp. of the spice mixture and beat until well combined.
- In another shallow bowl, add the flour, cornstarch and the remaining spice mixture.
- Coat the chicken drumsticks with the flour mixture and tap off excess.
- Now, dip the chicken drumsticks in the egg mixture.
- Again coat the chicken drumsticks with the flour mixture.
- Arrange the chicken drumsticks onto a wire rack-lined baking sheet and set aside for about 15 minutes.
- Now, arrange the chicken drumsticks onto a sheet pan and spray the chicken with cooking spray lightly.
- Press the "Power" button of the Air Fryer Oven and turn the dial to select "Air Fry" mode.
- Press the "Time" button and again turn the dial to set the cooking time to 25 minutes.
- Now push the "Temp" button and rotate the dial to set the temperature at 350°F.
- Press the "Start/Pause" button to start.
- When the unit beeps to show that it is preheated, open the lid and grease the air fry basket.
- Place the chicken drumsticks into the prepared air fry basket and insert them in the Air Fryer Oven.
- When the cooking time is completed, open the lid and serve hot.

Serving Suggestions: Serve with French fries.
Variation Tip: Make sure to coat chicken pieces completely.

Nutrition:
Calories: 483 Fats: 12.5 g
Saturated Fats: 3.4 g Carbs: 35.1 g
Fiber: 1.6 g
Sugar: 1.8 g
Protein: 53.7 g

545. Lemony Chicken Thighs

Preparation Time: 15 minutes
Cooking Time: 20 minutes
Servings: 6
Ingredients:
- 6 (6-oz.) chicken thighs
- 2 tbsp. olive oil
- 2 tbsp. fresh lemon juice
- 1 tbsp. Italian seasoning
- Salt and ground black pepper, as required
- 1 lemon, sliced thinly

Directions:
- In a large bowl, add all the ingredients except for the lemon slices and toss to coat well.
- Refrigerate to marinate for 30 minutes or overnight.
- Remove the chicken thighs and let any excess marinade drip off.
- Press the "Power" button of the Air Fryer Oven and turn the dial to select "Air Fry" mode.
- Press the "Time" button and again turn the dial to set the cooking time to 20 minutes.
- Now push the "Temp" button and rotate the dial to set the temperature at 350°F.
- Press the "Start/Pause" button to start.
- When the unit beeps to show that it is preheated, open the lid and grease the air fry basket.
- Place the chicken thighs into the prepared air fry basket and insert them in the Air Fryer Oven .
- After 10 minutes of cooking, flip the chicken thighs.
- When cooking time is completed, open the lid and serve hot alongside the lemon slices.

Serving Suggestions: Serve alongside your favorite dipping sauce.
Variation Tip: Select chicken with a pinkish hue.
Nutrition:
Calories: 472 Fats: 18 g
Saturated Fats: 4.3 g Carbs: 0.6 g
Fiber: 0.1 g Sugar: 0.4 g Protein: 49.3 g

546. Chinese Chicken Drumsticks

Preparation Time: 10 minutes
Cooking Time: 20 minutes
Servings: 4
Ingredients:
- 1 tbsp. oyster sauce
- 1 tsp. light soy sauce
- ½ tsp. sesame oil
- 1 tsp. Chinese five-spice powder
- Salt and ground black pepper, as required
- 4 (6-oz.) chicken drumsticks
- 1 cup corn flour

Directions:
- In a bowl, mix together the sauces, oil, five-spice powder, salt, and black pepper.
- Add the chicken drumsticks and coat them generously with the marinade.
- Refrigerate for at least 30–40 minutes.
- In a shallow dish, place the corn flour.

- Remove the chicken from marinade and lightly coat with corn flour.
- Press the "Power" button of the Air Fryer Oven and turn the dial to select "Air Fry" mode.
- Press the "Time" button and again turn the dial to set the cooking time to 20 minutes.
- Now push the "Temp" button and rotate the dial to set the temperature at 390°F.
- Press the "Start/Pause" button to start.
- When the unit beeps to show that it is preheated, open the lid and grease the air fry basket.
- Place the chicken drumsticks into the prepared air fry basket and insert them in the Air Fryer Oven.
- When the cooking time is completed, open the lid and serve hot.

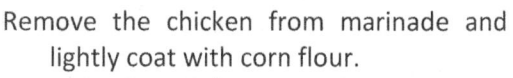

Serving Suggestions: Serve with fresh greens.
Variation Tip: Use best quality sauces.
Nutrition:
Calories: 287 Fats: 13.8 g
Saturated Fats: 7.1 g Carbs: 1.6 g
Fiber: 0.2 g Sugar: 0.1 g Protein: 38.3 g

547. Crispy Chicken Thighs

Preparation Time: 15 minutes
Cooking Time: 25 minutes
Servings: 4
Ingredients:
- ½ cup all-purpose flour
- 1½ tbsp. Cajun seasoning
- 1 tsp. seasoning salt
- 1 egg
- 4 (4-oz.) chicken thighs, skin-on

Directions:
- In a shallow bowl, mix together the flour, Cajun seasoning, and seasoning salt.
- In another bowl, crack the egg and beat well.
- Coat each chicken thigh with the flour mixture, then dip them into the beaten egg and finally, coat them with the flour mixture again.
- Shake off the excess flour thoroughly.
- Press the "Power" button of the Air Fryer Oven and turn the dial to select "Air Fry" mode.
- Press the "Time" and again turn the dial to set the cooking time to 25 minutes.
- Now push the "Temp" and rotate the dial to set the temperature at 390°F.
- Press the "Start/Pause" button to start.
- When the unit beeps to show that it is preheated, open the lid and grease the air fry basket.
- Place the chicken thighs into the prepared air fry basket and insert them in the Air Fryer Oven.
- When cooking time is completed, open the lid and serve hot.

Serving Suggestions: Serve with ketchup.
Variation Tip: Feel free to use seasoning of your choice.
Nutrition:
Calories: 288
Fats: 9.6 g
Saturated Fats: 2.7 g
Carbs: 12 g
Fiber: 0.4 g
Sugar: 0.1 g
Protein: 35.9 g

548. Oat Crusted Chicken Breasts

Preparation Time: 15 minutes
Cooking Time: 12 minutes
Servings: 2
Ingredients:
- 2 (6-oz.) chicken breasts
- Salt and ground black pepper, as required
- ¾ cup oats
- 2 tbsp. mustard powder
- 1 tbsp. fresh parsley
- 2 medium eggs

Directions:
- Place the chicken breasts onto a cutting board, and with a meat mallet, flatten each into an even thickness.
- Then, cut each chicken breast in half.
- Sprinkle the chicken pieces with salt and black pepper and set aside.
- In a blender, add the oats, mustard powder, parsley, salt and black pepper and pulse until a coarse breadcrumb-like mixture is formed.
- Transfer the oat mixture into a shallow bowl.
- In another bowl, crack the eggs and beat well.
- Coat the chicken with oat mixture, dip into beaten eggs, and coat with the oat mixture again.
- Press the "Power" button of the Air Fryer Oven and turn the dial to select "Air Fry" mode.
- Press the "Time" button and again turn the dial to set the cooking time to 12 minutes.
- Now push the "Temp" and rotate the dial to set the temperature at 350°F.
- Press the "Start/Pause" button to start.
- When the unit beeps to show that it is preheated, open the lid and grease the air fry basket.
- Place the chicken breasts into the prepared air fry basket and insert them in the Air Fryer Oven.
- Flip the chicken breasts once halfway through.
- When cooking time is completed, open the lid and serve hot.

Serving Suggestions: Serve with mashed potatoes.
Variation Tip: Check the meat "best by" date.
Nutrition:
Calories: 556 Fats: 22.2 g
Saturated Fats: 5.3 g Carbs: 25.1 g
Fiber: 4.8 g
Sugar: 1.4 g
Protein: 61.6 g

549. Crispy Chicken Cutlets

Preparation Time: 15 minutes
Cooking Time: 30 minutes
Servings: 4
Ingredients:
- ¾ cup flour
- 2 large eggs

1½ cups breadcrumbs
¼ cup Parmesan cheese, grated
1 tbsp. mustard powder
Salt and ground black pepper, as required
4 (6-oz.) (¼-inch thick) skinless, boneless chicken cutlets

Directions:
In a shallow bowl, add the flour.
In a second bowl, crack the eggs and beat them well.
In a third bowl, mix together the breadcrumbs, cheese, mustard powder, salt, and black pepper.
Season the chicken with salt, and black pepper.
Coat the chicken with flour, then dip them into beaten eggs and finally coat them with the breadcrumbs mixture.
Press the "Power" button of the Air Fryer Oven and turn the dial to select "Air Fry" mode.
Press the "Time" button and again turn the dial to set the cooking time to 30 minutes.
Now push the "Temp" button and rotate the dial to set the temperature at 355°F.
Press the "Start/Pause" button to start.
When the unit beeps to show that it is preheated, open the lid and grease the air fry basket.
Place the chicken cutlets into the prepared air fry basket and insert them in the Air Fryer Oven.
When the cooking time is completed, open the lid and serve hot.

Serving Suggestions: Serve with favorite greens.
Variation Tip: Parmesan cheese can be replaced with your favorite cheese.
Nutrition:
Calories: 526 ats: 13 g
Saturated Fats: 4.2 g
Carbs: 48.6 g Fiber: 3 g
Sugar: 3 g
Protein: 51.7 g

550. Brie Stuffed Chicken Breasts

Preparation Time: 15 minutes
Cooking Time: 15 minutes
Servings: 4
Ingredients:
2 (8-oz.) skinless, boneless chicken fillets
Salt and ground black pepper, as required
4 brie cheese slices - 1 tbsp. fresh chive, minced
4 bacon slices

Directions:
Cut each chicken fillet in 2 equal-sized pieces. Carefully, make a slit in each chicken piece horizontally, about ¼-inch from the edge. Open each chicken piece and season them with salt and black pepper. Place 1 cheese slice in the open area of each chicken piece and sprinkle with the chives. Close the chicken pieces and wrap each one with a bacon slice. Secure with toothpicks.
Press the "Power" button of th Air Fryer Oven and turn the dial to select "Air Fry" mode. Press the "Time" button and again turn the dial to set the cooking time to 15 minutes. Now push the "Temp" button and rotate the dial to set the temperature at 355°F.
Press the "Start/Pause" button to start.
When the unit beeps to show that it is preheated, open the lid and grease the

air fry basket. Place the chicken pieces into the prepared air fry basket and insert them in the oven. When the cooking time is completed, open the lid and place the rolled chicken breasts onto a cutting board.

Cut into desired slice sizes and serve.

Serving Suggestions: Serve with creamy mashed potatoes.

Variation Tip: Season the chicken breasts slightly.

Nutrition:

Calories: 394 Fats: 24 g
Saturated Fats: 10.4 g Carbs: 0.6 g
Sugar: 0.1 g Protein: 42 g

551. Chicken Kabobs

Preparation Time: 15 minutes
Cooking Time: 9 minutes
Servings: 2
Ingredients:

- 1 (8-oz.) chicken breast, cut into medium-sized pieces - 1 tbsp. fresh lemon juice
- 3 garlic cloves, grated
- 1 tbsp. fresh oregano, minced
- ½ tsp. lemon zest, grated
- Salt and ground black pepper, as required
- 1 tsp. plain Greek yogurt - 1 tsp. olive oil

Directions:

In a large bowl, add the chicken, lemon juice, garlic, oregano, lemon zest, salt and black pepper and toss to coat well.

Cover the bowl and refrigerate overnight.

Remove the bowl from the refrigerator and stir in the yogurt and oil. Thread the chicken pieces onto the metal skewers.

Press the "Power" button of the Air Fryer Oven and turn the dial to select "Air Fry" mode. Press the "Time" button and again turn the dial to set the cooking time to 9 minutes. Now push the "Temp" button and rotate the dial to set the temperature at 350°F.

Press "Start/Pause" button to start.

When the unit beeps to show that it is preheated, open the lid and grease the air fry basket. Place the skewers into the prepared air fry basket and insert them in the oven. Flip the skewers once halfway through. When cooking time is completed, open the lid and serve hot.

Serving Suggestions: Serve alongside fresh salad.

Variation Tip: Make sure to tri the chicken pieces.

Nutrition:

Calories: 167 Fats: 5.5 g
Saturated Fats: 0.5 g Carbs: 3.4 g
Fiber: 0.5 g Sugar: 1.1 g Protein: 24.8 g

552. Simple Turkey Breast

Preparation Time: 10 minutes
Cooking Time: 1 hour 20 minutes
Servings: 6
Ingredients:

- 1 (2 ¾-lb.) turkey breast half, bone-in, skin-on
- Salt and ground black pepper, as required

Directions:
- Rub the turkey breast with the salt and black pepper evenly.
- Arrange the turkey breast into a greased baking pan.
- Press the "Power" button of the Air Fryer Oven and turn the dial to select "Air Bake" mode. Press the "Time" and again turn the dial to set the cooking time to 1 hour 20 minutes. Now push the "Temp" button and rotate the dial to set the temperature at 450ºF.
- Press the "Start/Pause" button to start.
- Open the unit when it has reached the temperature, when it beeps.
- Arrange the pan over the wire rack and insert it in the oven. When cooking time is completed, open the lid and place the turkey breast onto a cutting board. With a piece of foil, cover the turkey breast for about 20 minutes before slicing.
- With a sharp knife, cut the turkey breast into desired size slices and serve.

Serving Suggestions: Serve alongside the steamed veggies.

Variation Tip: Beware of flat spots on meat, which can indicate thawing and refreezing.

Nutrition:
Calories: 221 Fats: 0.8 g Protein: 51.6 g

---

553. Herbed Duck Breast

Preparation Time: 15 minutes
Cooking Time: 20 minutes
Servings: 2
Ingredients:
- 1 (10-oz.) duck breast
- Olive oil cooking spray
- ½ tbsp. fresh thyme, chopped
- ½ tbsp. fresh rosemary, chopped
- 1 cup chicken broth
- 1 tbsp. fresh lemon juice
- Salt and ground black pepper, as required

Directions:
- Spray the duck breast with cooking spray evenly.
- In a bowl, mix well the remaining ingredients.
- Add the duck breast and coat it with the marinade generously.
- Refrigerate it covered for about 4 hours.
- With a piece of foil, cover the duck breast.
- Press the "Power" of the Air Fryer Oven and turn the dial to select "Air Fry" mode.
- Press the "Time" button and again turn the dial to set the cooking time to 15 minutes.
- Now push the "Temp" and rotate the dial to set the temperature at 390ºF.
- Press the "Start/Pause" button to start.
- When the unit beeps to show that it is preheated, open the lid and grease the air fry basket.
- Place the duck breast into the prepared air fry basket and insert them in the Air Fryer Oven.
- After 15 minutes of cooking, set the temperature to 355ºF for 5 minutes.
- When the cooking time is completed, open the lid and serve hot.

Serving Suggestions: Serve with spiced potatoes.

Variation Tip: Don't undercook the duck meat.

Nutrition:
Calories: 209
Fats: 6.6 g
Saturated Fats: 0.3 g
Carbs: 1.6 g
Fiber: 0.6 g
Sugar: 0.5 g
Protein: 33.8 g

CHAPTER 9:

Seafood

554. Citrusy Branzini On The Grill

Preparation Time: 5 minutes
Cooking Time: 15 minutes
Servings: 4
Ingredients:
- branzini fillets
- Salt and pepper to taste
- lemons, juice freshly squeezed
- oranges, juice freshly squeezed

Directions:
- Place all ingredients in a Ziploc bag. Keep it in the fridge for 2 hours.
- Preheat the air fryer at 3900F.
- Place the grill pan attachment in the air fryer.
- Place the fish on the grill pan and cook for 15 minutes until the fish is flaky.

Nutrition:
Calories: 318; Carbs: 20.8g; Protein: 23.5g; Fat: 15.6g

555. Cajun-Seasoned Lemon Salmon

Preparation Time: 5 minutes
Cooking Time: 10 minutes
Servings: 4
Ingredients:
- 1 salmon fillet - 1 teaspoon Cajun seasoning
- lemon wedges, for serving
- 1 teaspoon liquid stevia
- ½ lemon, juiced

Directions:
- Preheat your air fryer to 350Fahrenheit. Combine lemon juice and liquid stevia and coat salmon with this mixture. Sprinkle Cajun seasoning all over salmon. Place salmon on parchment paper in air fryer and cook for 7-minutes. Serve with lemon wedges.

Nutrition:
Calories: 287, Total Fat: 9.3g, Carbs: 8.4g, Protein: 15.3g

556. Grilled Salmon Fillets

Preparation Time: 5 minutes
Cooking Time: 10 minutes
Servings: 4
Ingredients:
- salmon fillets
- tablespoons olive oil
- 1/3 cup of light soy sauce
- 1/3 cup of water
- Salt and black pepper to taste

Directions:
- Season salmon fillets with salt and pepper. Mix what's left of the ingredients in a bowl. Allow the salmon fillets to marinate in mixture for 2-hours. Preheat your air fryer to 355Fahrenheit for 5-minutes. Drain salmon fillets and air fry for 8-minutes.

Nutrition:
Calories: 302, Total Fat: 8.6g, Carbs: 7.3g, Protein: 15.3g

557. Cheesy Breaded Salmon

Preparation Time: 5 minutes
Cooking Time: 20 minutes
Servings: 4
Ingredients:
- cups breadcrumbs
- salmon fillets
- eggs, beaten
- 1 cup Swiss cheese, shredded

Directions:
- Preheat your air fryer to 390Fahrenheit. Dip each salmon filet into eggs. Top with Swiss cheese. Dip into breadcrumbs, coating entire fish. Put into an oven-safe dish and cook for 20-minutes.

Nutrition:
Calories: 296, Total Fat: 9.2g, Carbs: 8.7g, Protein: 15.2g

558. Coconut Crusted Shrimp

Preparation Time: 15 minutes
Cooking Time: 40 minutes
Servings: 4
Ingredients:
- ounces coconut milk
- ½ cup sweetened coconut, shredded
- ½ cup panko breadcrumbs
- 1-pound large shrimp, peeled and deveined
- Salt and black pepper, to taste

Directions:
- Preheat the Air fryer to 350 o F and grease an Air fryer basket.
- Place the coconut milk in a shallow bowl.
- Mix coconut, breadcrumbs, salt, and black pepper in another bowl.
- Dip each shrimp into coconut milk and finally, dredge in the coconut mixture.
- Arrange half of the shrimps into the Air fryer basket and cook for about 20 minutes.
- Dish out the shrimps onto serving plates and repeat with the remaining mixture to serve.

Nutrition:
Calories: 408,
Fats: 23.7g,
Carbohydrates: 11.7g,
Sugar: 3.4g,
Proteins: 31g,

559. Rice Flour Coated Shrimp

Preparation Time: 20 minutes
Cooking Time: 20 minutes
Servings: 3
Ingredients:
- tablespoons rice flour
- 1-pound shrimp, peeled and deveined
- tablespoons olive oil
- 1 teaspoon powdered sugar
- Salt and black pepper, as required

Directions:
- Preheat the Air fryer to 325 o F and grease an Air fryer basket.
- Mix rice flour, olive oil, sugar, salt, and black pepper in a bowl.
- Stir in the shrimp and transfer half of the shrimp to the Air fryer basket.
- Cook for about 10 minutes, flipping once in between.
- Dish out the mixture onto serving plates and repeat with the remaining mixture.

Nutrition:
Calories: 299,
Fat: 12g,
Carbohydrates: 11.1g,
Sugar: 0.8g,
Protein: 35g,
Sodium: 419mg

560. Buttered Scallops

Preparation Time: 15 minutes
Cooking Time: 4 minutes
Servings: 2
Ingredients:
- ¾ pound sea scallops, cleaned and patted very dry
- 1 tablespoon butter, melted
- ½ tablespoon fresh thyme, minced
- Salt and black pepper, as required

Directions:
- Preheat the Air fryer to 390 o F and grease an Air fryer basket.
- Mix scallops, butter, thyme, salt, and black pepper in a bowl.
- Arrange scallops in the Air fryer basket and cook for about 4 minutes.
- Dish out the scallops in a platter and serve hot.

Nutrition:
Calories: 202,
Fat: 7.1g,
Carbohydrates: 4.4g,
Sugar: 0g,
Protein: 28.7g,

561. Fish Sticks

Preparation Time: 5 minutes
Cooking Time: 20 minutes
Servings: 4
Ingredients:
- 1 lb. cod fillet; cut into 3/4-inch strips
- 1 oz. pork rinds, finely ground
- 1 large egg.
- ¼ cup blanched finely ground almond flour.
- 1 tbsp. coconut oil

Directions:
- Place ground pork rinds, almond flour, and coconut oil into a large bowl and mix together. Take a medium bowl, beat egg
- Dip each fish stick into the egg and then coat with the flour mixture, covering as fully and evenly as possible. Place fish sticks into the basket of air fryer
- Fix the temperature to 400 F and set the timer for 10 minutes or until golden. Serve immediately.

Nutrition:
Calories: 205;
Protein: 24.4g;
Fiber: 0.8g;
Fat: 10.7g;
Carbs: 1.6g

562. Butter Trout

Preparation Time: 5 minutes
Cooking Time: 20 minutes
Servings: 4
Ingredients:
- trout fillets; boneless
- Juice of 1 lime
- 1 tbsp. parsley; chopped.
- tbsp. butter; melted
- Salt and black pepper to taste.

Directions:
- Mix the fish fillets with the melted butter, salt and pepper, rub gently, put the fish in your air fryer's basket and cook at 390°F for 6 minutes on each side.
- Divide between plates and serve with lime juice drizzled on top and with parsley sprinkled at the end.

Nutrition:
Calories: 221;
Fat: 11g;
Fiber: 4g;
Carbs: 6g;
Protein: 9g

563. Pesto Almond Salmon

Preparation Time: 5 minutes
Cooking Time: 15 minutes
Servings: 4
Ingredients:
- 2: 1 ½-inch-thicksalmon fillets: about 4 oz. each
- ¼ cup sliced almonds, roughly chopped
- ¼ cup pesto
- tbsp. unsalted butter; melted.

Directions:
- In a small bowl, mix pesto and almonds. Set aside. Place fillets into a 6-inch round baking dish
- Brush each fillet with butter and place half of the pesto mixture on the top of each fillet. Place dish into the air fryer basket. Change the temperature to 390 ° F and set the timer for 12 minutes
- Salmon will easily flake when fully cooked and reach an internal temperature of at least 145 Degrees F. Serve warm.

Nutrition:
Calories: 433; Protein: 23.3g;
Fiber: 2.4g; Fat: 34.0g;
Carbs: 6.1g

564. Garlic Lemon Shrimp

Preparation Time: 5 minutes
Cooking Time: 10 minutes
Servings: 4
Ingredients:
- 8 oz. medium shelled and deveined shrimp

1 medium lemon.
2 tbsp. unsalted butter; melted.
½ tsp. minced garlic
½ tsp. Old Bay seasoning

Directions:

Zest lemon and then cut in half. Place shrimp in a large bowl and squeeze juice from ½ lemon on top of them.

Add lemon zest to bowl along with remaining ingredients. Toss shrimp until fully coated

Pour bowl contents into 6-inch round baking dish. Place into the air fryer basket.

Adjust the temperature to 400 Degrees F and set the timer for 6 minutes. Shrimp will be bright pink when fully cooked. Serve warm with pan sauce.

Nutrition:
Calories: 190;
Protein: 16.4g;
Fiber: 0.4g;
Fat: 11.8g;
Carbs: 2.9g

565. Air-Fried Crab Sticks

Preparation Time: 5 minutes
Cooking Time: 10 minutes
Servings: 4
Ingredients:

Crab sticks: 1 package
Cooking oil spray: as needed

Directions:

Take each of the sticks out of the package and unroll until flat. Tear the sheets into thirds.

Arrange them on a plate and lightly spritz using cooking spray. Set the timer for 10 minutes.

Note: If you shred the crab meat; you can cut the time in half, but they will also easily fall through the holes in the basket.

Nutrition:
Calories: 220 Carbs: 11 g
Fat: 13 g Protein: 23 g

566. Cajun Salmon

Preparation Time: 5 minutes
Cooking Time: 10 minutes
Servings: 4
Ingredients:

Salmon fillet – ¾-inch thick: 1)
Juice of ¼ lemon
For Breading: Cajun seasoning for coating
Optional: Sprinkle of sugar

Directions:

Warm the Air Fryer to 356º Fahrenheit: approx. 5 min.).

Rinse and pat the salmon dry. Thoroughly coat the fish with the coating mix.

Arrange the fillet in the fryer basket and set the timer for seven minutes with the skin side facing upward.

Serve with a drizzle of lemon.

Nutrition:
Calories: 370
Carbs: 12 g
Fat: 10 g
Protein: 28 g

567. E-Z Catfish

Preparation Time: 5 minutes
Cooking Time: 25 minutes
Servings: 3
Ingredients:

Olive oil: 1 tbsp.
Seasoned fish fry: .25 cup
Catfish fillets: 4

Directions:

Prepare the fryer to 400º Fahrenheit.

First, wash the fish, and dry with a paper towel.

Dump the seasoning into a large zip-type baggie. Add the fish and shake to cover each fillet. Spray with a spritz of cooking oil spray. Add to the basket.

Set the timer for ten minutes. Flip, and reset the timer for ten more minutes. Flip once more and cook for two to three minutes.

Once it reaches the desired crispiness, transfer to a plate to serve.

Nutrition:
Calories: 290
Carbs: 14 g
Fat: 16 g
Protein: 30 g

568. Fish Nuggets

Preparation Time: 5 minutes
Cooking Time: 20 minutes
Servings: 4
Ingredients:
Cod fillet: 1 lb.
Eggs: 3
Olive oil: 4 tbsp.
Almond flour: 1 cup
Gluten-free breadcrumbs: 1 cup

Directions:
Fix the temperature of the Air Fryer at 390º Fahrenheit.

Cut the cod into nuggets.

Prepare three dishes. Beat the eggs in one. Combine the oil and breadcrumbs in another. The last one will be almond flour.

Cover each of the nuggets using the flour, a dip in the eggs, and the breadcrumbs.

Arrange the prepared nuggets in the basket and set the timer for 20 minutes. Serve.

Nutrition:
Calories: 220
Carbs: 10 g
Fat: 12 g
Protein: 23 g

569. Grilled Shrimp

Preparation Time: 5 minutes
Cooking Time: 10 minutes
Servings: 4
Ingredients:
Medium shrimp/prawns: 8
Melted butter: 1 tbsp.
Rosemary: 1 sprig
Pepper and salt: as desired
Minced garlic cloves: 3

Directions:
Combine all of the fixings in a mixing bowl. Toss well and arrange in the fryer basket.

Set the timer for 7 minutes: 356º Fahrenheit and serve.

Nutrition:
Calories: 180
Carbs: 2 g
Fat: 10 g
Protein: 15 g

570. Honey & Sriracha Tossed Calamari

Preparation Time: 10 minutes
Cooking Time: 20 minutes
Servings: 2
Ingredients:
Calamari tubes - tentacles if you prefer: .5 lb.
Club soda: 1 cup
Flour: 1 cup
Salt - red pepper & black pepper: 2 dashes each
Honey: .5 cup+ 1-2 tbsp. Sriracha

Directions:
Fully rinse the calamari and blot it dry using a bunch of paper towels. Slice into rings: .25-inch wide). Toss the rings into a bowl. Pour in the club soda and stir until all are submerged. Wait for about 10 minutes.

- Sift the salt, flour, red & black pepper. Set aside for now.
- Dredge the calamari into the flour mixture and set on a platter until ready to fry.
- Spritz the basket of the Air Fryer with a small amount of cooking oil spray. Arrange the calamari in the basket, careful not to crowd it too much.
- Set the temperature at 375º Fahrenheit and the timer for 11 minutes.
- Shake the basket twice during the cooking process, loosening any rings that may stick.
- Remove from the basket, toss with the sauce, and return to the fryer for two more minutes.
- Serve with additional sauce as desired.
- Make the sauce by combining honey, and sriracha, in a small bowl, mix until fully combined.

Nutrition:
Calories: 210
Carbs: 5 g
Fat: 12 g
Protein: 19 g

571. Salmon Croquettes

Preparation Time: 5 minutes
Cooking Time: 10 minutes
Servings: 4
Ingredients:
- Red salmon: 1 lb. can
- Breadcrumbs: 1 cup
- Vegetable oil: .33 cup
- Chopped parsley: half of 1 bunch
- Eggs: 2

Directions:
- Set the Air Fryer at 392º Fahrenheit.
- Drain and mash the salmon. Whisk and add the eggs and parsley.
- In another dish, mix the breadcrumbs and oil.
- Prepare 16 croquettes using the breadcrumb mixture.
- Arrange in the preheated fryer basket for seven minutes.
- Serve.

Nutrition:
Calories: 240 Carbs: 7 g
Fat: 16 g Protein: 30 g

572. Spicy Cod

Preparation Time: 5 minutes
Cooking Time: 10 minutes
Servings: 4
Ingredients:
- 4 cod fillets; boneless
- 2 tbsp. assorted chili peppers
- 1 lemon; sliced
- Juice of 1 lemon
- Salt and black pepper to taste

Directions:
In your air fryer, mix the cod with the chili pepper, lemon juice, salt and pepper
Arrange the lemon slices on top and cook at 360°F for 10 minutes. Divide the fillets between plates and serve.

Nutrition:
Calories: 250
Carbs: 13 g
Fat: 13 g
Protein: 29 g

573. Air Fried Lobster Tails

Preparation Time: 5 minutes
Cooking Time: 10 minutes
Servings: 2
Ingredients:
- 2 tablespoons unsalted butter, melted
- 1 tablespoon minced garlic
- 1 teaspoon salt
- 1 tablespoon minced fresh chives
- 2 (4- to 6-ounce) frozen lobster tails

Directions:
Preparing the Ingredients

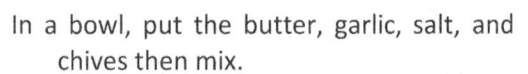

In a bowl, put the butter, garlic, salt, and chives then mix.

Butterfly the lobster tail: Starting at the meaty end of the tail, use kitchen shears to cut down the center of the top shell. Stop when you reach the fanned, wide part of the tail. Carefully spread apart the meat and the shell along the cut line, but keep the meat attached where it connects to the wide part of the tail. Use your hand to gently disconnect the meat from the bottom of the shell. Lift the meat up and out of the shell (keeping it attached at the wide end). Close the shell under the meat, so the meat rests on top of the shell.

Place the lobster in the air fryer basket and generously brush the butter mixture over the meat.

Air Frying. Set the temperature of your AF to 380°F. Set the timer and steam for 4 minutes.

Open the air fryer and rotate the lobster tails. Brush them with more of the butter mixture. Reset the timer and steam for 4 minutes more. The lobster is done when the meat is opaque.

Nutrition:
Calories: 255;
Fat: 13g;
Carbohydrate: 2g;
Protein: 32g;
Sodium: 1453mg

574. Air Fryer Salmon

Preparation Time: 5 minutes
Cooking Time: 10 minutes
Servings: 2
Ingredients:
½ tsp. salt
½ tsp. garlic powder
½ tsp. smoked paprika
Salmon

Directions:
Preparing the Ingredients. Mix spices together and sprinkle onto salmon. Place seasoned salmon into the Air fryer.

Air Frying. Close crisping lid. Set temperature to 400°F, and set time to 10 minutes.

Nutrition:
Calories: 185; Fat: 11g; Protein:21g; Sugar:0g

575. Simple Scallops

Preparation Time: 5 minutes
Cooking Time: 5 minutes
Servings: 4
Ingredients:
12 medium sea scallops
1 teaspoon fine sea salt
ground black pepper as desired
Fresh thyme leaves, for garnish (optional)

Directions:
Preparing the Ingredients. Grease the air fryer basket with avocado oil. Preheat the air fryer to 390°F. Rinse the scallops and pat completely dry. Spray avocado oil on the scallops and season them with the salt and pepper.

Air Frying. Place them in the air fryer basket, spacing them apart (if you're using a smaller air fryer, work in batches if necessary). Flip the scallops after cooking for 2 minutes, and cook for another 2 minutes, or until cooked through and no longer translucent. Garnish with ground black pepper and thyme leaves, if desired. Best served fresh.

Nutrition:
Calories: 170
Carbs: 8 g
Fat: 11 g
Protein: 17 g

576. 3-Ingredient Air Fryer Catfish

Preparation Time: 5 minutes
Cooking Time: 15 minutes
Servings: 4
Ingredients:
- 1 tbsp. chopped parsley
- 1 tbsp. olive oil
- ¼ C. seasoned fish fry
- 4 catfish fillets

Directions:
- Preparing the Ingredients. Ensure your air fryer is preheated to 400 degrees.
- Rinse off catfish fillets and pat dry. Add fish fry seasoning to Ziploc baggie, then catfish. Shake bag and ensure fish gets well coated. Spray each fillet with olive oil. Add fillets to air fryer basket.
- Air Frying. Set temperature to 400°F, and set time to 10 minutes. Cook 10 minutes. Then flip and cook another 2-3 minutes.

Nutrition:
Calories: 208;
Fat: 5g;
Protein:17g;
Sugar:0.5g

577. Pecan-Crusted Catfish

Preparation Time: 5 minutes
Cooking Time: 12 minutes
Servings: 4
Ingredients:
- ½ cup pecan meal
- 1 teaspoon fine sea salt
- ¼ teaspoon ground black pepper
- 4 (4-ounce) catfish fillets
- FOR GARNISH (OPTIONAL):
- Fresh oregano

Directions:
- Preparing the Ingredients. Grease the air fryer basket with avocado oil. Preheat the air fryer to 375°F. In a large bowl, mix the pecan meal, salt, and pepper. One at a time, dredge the catfish fillets in the mixture, coating them well. Use your hands to press the pecan meal into the fillets. Spray the fish with avocado oil and place them in the air fryer basket.
- Air Frying. Cook the coated catfish for 12 minutes, or until it flakes easily and is no longer translucent in the center, flipping halfway through. Garnish with oregano sprigs and pecan halves, if desired.

Nutrition:
Calories 162; Fat 11g;
Protein 17g; Total carbs 1g; Fiber 1g

578. Flying Fish

Preparation Time: 5 minutes
Cooking Time: 12 minutes
Servings: 4
Ingredients:
- Tbsp Oil
- 3–4 oz Breadcrumbs
- 1 Whisked Whole Egg in a Saucer/Soup Plate
- 4 Fresh Fish Fillets
- Fresh Lemon (For serving)

Directions:
- Preparing the Ingredients. Warm up the air fryer to 350° F. Mix the crumbs and oil until it looks nice and loose. Dip the fish in the egg and coat lightly, then move on to the crumbs. Make sure the fillet is covered evenly.
- Air Frying. Cook in the air fryer basket for roughly 12 minutes – depending on the size of the fillets you are using. Serve with fresh lemon & chips to complete the duo.

Nutrition:
Calories: 180
Carbs: 9 g
Fat: 12 g
Protein: 19 g

579. Air Fryer Fish Tacos

Preparation Time: 5 minutes
Cooking Time: 15 minutes
Servings: 4
Ingredients:
- 1 pound cod
- 1 tbsp. cumin
- ½ tbsp. chili powder
- 1 ½ C. coconut flour
- 10 ounces Mexican beer
- 2 eggs

Directions:
- Preparing the Ingredients. Whisk beer and eggs together. Whisk flour, pepper, salt, cumin, and chili powder together. Slice cod into large pieces and coat in egg mixture then flour mixture.
- Air Frying. Spray bottom of your air fryer basket with olive oil and add coated codpieces. Cook 15 minutes at 375 degrees.
- Serve on lettuce leaves topped with homemade salsa.

Nutrition:
Calories: 178;
Carbs: 61g;
Fat: 10g;
Protein: 19g;
Sugar: 1g

580. Bacon Wrapped Scallops

Preparation Time: 5 minutes
Cooking Time: 5 minutes
Servings: 4
Ingredients:
- 1 tsp. paprika
- 1 tsp. lemon pepper
- 5 slices of center-cut bacon
- 20 raw sea scallops

Directions:
- Preparing the Ingredients. Rinse and drain scallops, placing on paper towels to soak up excess moisture. Cut slices of bacon into 4 pieces. With a piece of bacon, wrap each scallop, then using toothpicks to secure. Sprinkle wrapped scallops with paprika and lemon pepper.
- Air Frying. Spray air fryer basket with olive oil and add scallops.
- Cook 5-6 minutes at 400 degrees, making sure to flip halfway through.

Nutrition:
Calories: 389; Carbs: 63g;
Fat: 17g; Protein: 21g; Sugar: 1g

581. Quick Fried Catfish

Preparation Time: 5 minutes
Cooking Time: 15 minutes
Servings: 4
Ingredients:
- 3/4 cups Original Bisquick™ mix
- 1/2 cup yellow cornmeal
- 1 tablespoon seafood seasoning
- 4 catfish fillets (4-6 oz. each)
- 1/2 cup ranch dressing

Directions:
- Preparing the Ingredients.
- In a bowl mix the Bisquick mix, cornmeal, and seafood seasoning together. Pat the filets dry, then brush them with ranch dressing. Press the filets into the Bisquick mix on both sides until the filet is evenly coated.
- Air Frying.
- Cook in your air fryer at 360 degrees for 15 minutes, flip the filets halfway through. Serve.

Nutrition:
Calories: 372;
Fat: 16g;
Protein: 28g;
Fiber: 1.7g

582. Air-Fried Herbed Shrimp

Preparation Time: 2 minutes
Cooking Time: 5 minutes
Servings: 4
Ingredients:
- One ¼ lb. shrimp, peeled and deveined
- ½ teaspoon paprika
- One tablespoon olive oil
- ¼ cayenne pepper
- ½ teaspoon Old Bay seasoning

Directions:
Preheat air fryer to 400Fahrenheit. Mix all the ingredients in a bowl. Place the seasoned shrimp into the air fryer basket and cook for 5-minutes.

Nutrition:
Calories: 300
Total Fat: 9.3g
Carbs: 8.2g
Protein: 14.6g

583. Creamy Air Fryer Salmon

Preparation Time: 5 minutes
Cooking Time: 10 minutes
Servings: 2
Ingredients:
- ¾ lb. salmon, cut into six pieces
- ¼ cup plain yogurt
- One tablespoon dill, chopped
- Three tablespoons light sour cream
- One tablespoon olive oil

Directions:
Flavor the salmon with salt and put it in an air fryer. Drizzle the salmon with olive oil. Air-fry salmon at 285Fahrenheit and cook for 10-minutes. Mix the dill, yogurt, sour cream, and some salt(optional). Place salmon on serving dish and drizzle with creamy sauce.

Nutrition:
Calories: 289 Total Fat: 9.8g
Carbs: 8.6 Protein: 14.7g

584. Barbecued Lime Shrimp

Preparation Time: 5 minutes
Cooking Time: 15 minutes
Servings: 4
Ingredients:
- 4 cups of shrimp
- 1 ½ cups barbeque sauce
- One fresh lime, cut into quarters

Directions:
Preheat your air fryer to 360Fahrenheit. Place the shrimp in a bowl with barbeque sauce. Stir gently. Allow shrimps to marinade for at least 5-minutes. Place the shrimp in the air fryer and cook for 15-minutes. Remove from air fryer and squeeze lime over shrimps.

Nutrition:
Calories: 289,
Total Fat: 9.8g,
Carbs: 8.7g,
Protein: 14.9g

585. Spicy Air-Fried Cheese Tilapia

Preparation Time: 5minutes
Cooking Time: 10 minutes
Servings: 4
Ingredients:
- 1 lb. tilapia fillets
- One tablespoon olive oil
- Salt and pepper to taste
- Two teaspoons paprika
- ¾ cup parmesan cheese, grated

Directions:
Preheat your air fryer to 400Fahrenheit. Mix the parmesan cheese, paprika, salt, and pepper. Drizzle olive oil over the tilapia fillets and coat with paprika and cheese mixture. Place the coated tilapia fillets on aluminum foil.

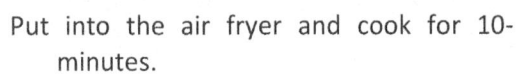

Put into the air fryer and cook for 10-minutes.

Nutrition:
Calories: 289,
Total Fat: 8.9g,
Carbs: 7.8g,
Protein: 14.9g

586. Cheese Salmon

Preparation Time: 4 minutes
Cooking Time: 11 minutes
Servings: 6
Ingredients:
- 2 lbs. salmon fillet
- Salt and pepper to taste
- ½ cup parmesan cheese, grated
- ¼ cup parsley, fresh, chopped
- Two garlic cloves, minced

Directions:
Preheat your air fryer to 350Fahrenheit. Put the salmon skin side facing down on aluminum foil and cover with another piece of foil. Cook salmon for 10-minutes. Remove the salmon from foil and top it with minced garlic, parsley, parmesan cheese, and pepper.
Return salmon to air fryer for 1-minute cook time.

Nutrition:
Calories: 297,
Total Fat: 9.5g,
Carbs: 8.3g,
Protein: 14.9g

587. Air-Fryer Baked Salmon & Asparagus

Preparation Time: 5 minutes
Cooking Time: 15 minutes
Servings: 4
Ingredients:
- Four salmon fillets
- Four asparagus
- Two tablespoons butter
- Three lemons, sliced
- Salt and pepper to taste

Directions:
Preheat the air fryer to 300Fahrenheit. Take four pieces of aluminum foil. Add asparagus, half lemon juice, pepper, and salt in a bowl and toss. Divide seasoned asparagus evenly on four aluminum foil pieces. Put one salmon fillet asparagus. Put some lemon slices on top of salmon fillets. Fold foil tightly to seal the parcel. Place in an air fryer basket and cook for 15-minutes. Serve warm.

Nutrition:
Calories: 291,
Total Fat: 16g,
Carbs: 1g,
Protein: 35g

588. Parmesan Baked Salmon

Preparation Time: 5 minutes
Cooking Time: 11 minutes
Servings: 5
Ingredients:
- 2 lbs. fresh salmon fillet
- Salt and pepper to taste
- ½ cup parmesan cheese, grated
- ¼ cup fresh parsley, chopped
- Two garlic cloves, minced

Directions:
Preheat the air fryer to 300Fahrenheit. Put some salmon with the skin side down on foil and cover with more foil. Bake the salmon in the air fryer basket for 10-minutes. Open the foil and top salmon with cheese, garlic, pepper, salt, and parsley. Return for an additional minute in the air fryer.

Nutrition:
Calories: 267, Total Fat: 12g,
Carbs: 6g,
Protein: 37g

589. Grilled Prawns

Preparation Time: 5 minutes
Cooking Time: 15 minutes
Servings: 4
Ingredients:
- Eight medium prawns
- Salt and pepper to taste
- Three garlic cloves, minced
- One tablespoons butter, melted
- One rosemary sprig

Directions:
- Add ingredients to a bowl and toss well. Add the marinated prawns to the air fryer basket and cook at 300Fahrenheit for 7-minutes. Serve hot!

Nutrition:
Calories: 137,
Total Fat: 4g,
Carbs: 3g,
Protein: 20g

590. Pesto Scallops

Preparation Time: 10 minutes
Cooking Time: 7 minutes
Servings: 4
Ingredients:
- 1 lb. Scallops
- 3 tbsp heavy cream
- 1/4 cup basil pesto
- 1 tbsp olive oil
- Salt and Pepper

Directions:
- Spray air fryer multi-level air fryer basket with cooking spray.
- Season scallops with pepper and salt and adds into the air fryer basket and place basket into the air fryer.
- Seal pot with air fryer lid and select air fry mode then set the temperature to 320 f and timer for 5 minutes. Turn scallops after 3 minutes.
- Meanwhile, in a small pan, heat olive oil over medium heat. Add pesto and heavy cream and cook for 2 minutes. Remove from heat.
- Add scallops into the mixing bowl. Pour pesto sauce over scallops and toss well. Serve and enjoy.

Nutrition:
Calories 171
Fat 8.5 g
Carbohydrates 3.5 g
Sugar 0 g
Protein 19.4 g
Cholesterol 53 mg

591. Creamy Parmesan Shrimp

Preparation Time: 10 minutes
Cooking Time: 5 minutes
Servings: 4
Ingredients:
- 1 lb. Shrimp, deveined and cleaned
- 1 oz parmesan cheese, grated
- 1 tbsp garlic, minced
- 1 tbsp lemon juice
- 1/4 cup salad dressing

Directions:
- Spray air fryer multi-level air fryer basket with cooking spray.
- Add shrimp into the air fryer basket and place basket into the air fryer.
- Seal pot with air fryer lid and select air fry mode then set the temperature to 400 f and timer for 5 minutes.
- Transfer shrimp into the mixing bowl. Add remaining ingredients over shrimp and stir for 1 minute.
- Serve and enjoy.

Nutrition:
Calories 219
Fat 8.4 g
Carbohydrates 6.3 g
Sugar 1 g
Protein 28.4 g
Cholesterol 248 mg

592. Delicious Garlic Butter Salmon

Preparation Time: 10 minutes
Cooking Time: 7 minutes
Servings: 4
Ingredients:
- 1 lb. Salmon fillets
- 2 tbsp garlic, minced
- 1/4 cup parmesan cheese, grated
- 1/4 cup butter, melted
- Salt and Pepper

Directions:
- Season salmon with pepper and salt.
- In a bowl, mix butter, cheese, and garlic together, and brush over salmon fillets.
- Place the dehydrating tray in a multi-level air fryer basket and place basket in the air fryer.
- Place salmon fillets on dehydrating tray.
- Seal pot with air fryer lid and select air fry mode then set the temperature to 400 f and timer for 7 minutes.
- Serve and enjoy.

Nutrition:
Calories 277 Fat 19.8 g
Carbohydrates 1.7 g
Sugar 0.1 g Protein 24.3 g
Cholesterol 85 mg

593. Horseradish Salmon

Preparation Time: 10 minutes
Cooking Time: 7 minutes
Servings: 2
Ingredients:
- salmon fillets
- 1/4 cup breadcrumbs
- 2 tbsp olive oil
- 1 tbsp horseradish
- Salt and Pepper

Directions:
- Place the dehydrating tray in a multi-level air fryer basket and place basket in the air fryer.
- Place salmon fillets on dehydrating tray.
- In a small bowl, mix together breadcrumbs, oil, horseradish, pepper, and salt and spread over salmon fillets.
- Seal pot with air fryer lid and select air fry mode then set the temperature to 400 f and timer for 7 minutes.
- Serve and enjoy.

Nutrition:
Calories 413
Fat 25.8 g
Carbohydrates 10.6 g
Sugar 1.4 g
Protein 36.4 g
Cholesterol 78 mg

594. Pesto Shrimp

Preparation Time: 10 minutes
Cooking Time: 5 minutes
Servings: 6
Ingredients:
- 1 lb. Shrimp, defrosted
- 14 oz basil pesto

Directions:
- Add shrimp and pesto into the mixing bowl and toss well.
- Spray air fryer multi-level air fryer basket with cooking spray.
- Add shrimp into the air fryer basket and place basket into the air fryer.
- Seal pot with air fryer lid and select air fry mode then set the temperature to 400 f and timer for 5 minutes.
- Serve and enjoy.

Nutrition:
Calories 105
Fat 1.7 g
Carbohydrates 2.9 g
Sugar 0.2 g
Protein 19.3 g
Cholesterol 159 mg

595. Garlic Butter Shrimp

Preparation Time: 10 minutes
Cooking Time: 10 minutes
Servings: 4
Ingredients:
- 1 lb. Shrimp, peeled and deveined
- 2 tbsp olive oil
- 1/4 cup butter, melted
- 4 tbsp garlic, minced
- Salt and Pepper

Directions:
- Add shrimp into the mixing bowl. Add remaining ingredients and toss well.
- Line air fryer multi-level air fryer basket with aluminum foil.
- Add shrimp into the air fryer basket and place basket into the air fryer.
- Seal pot with air fryer lid and select air fry mode then set the temperature to 400 f and timer for 10 minutes. Mix halfway through.
- Serve and enjoy.

Nutrition:
Calories 309 Fat 20.5 g
Carbohydrates 4.5 g Sugar 0.1 g
Protein 26.5 g
Cholesterol 269 mg

596. Honey Mustard Salmon

Preparation Time: 10 minutes
Cooking Time: 9 minutes
Servings: 2
Ingredients:
- 2 salmon fillets
- 2 tbsp Dijon mustard
- 2 tbsp honey
- 1/4 cup mayonnaise
- Salt and Pepper

Directions:
- In a small dish, mix mustard, honey, mayonnaise, pepper, and salt together and brush over salmon.
- Place the dehydrating tray in a multi-level air fryer basket and place basket in the air fryer.
- Place salmon fillets on dehydrating tray.
- Seal pot with air fryer lid and select air fry mode then set the temperature to 350 f and timer for 9 minutes.
- Serve and enjoy.

Nutrition:
Calories 424
Fat 21.4 g
Carbohydrates 25.2 g
Sugar 19.3 g
Protein 35.5 g
Cholesterol 86 mg

597. Classic Tilapia

Preparation Time: 10 minutes
Cooking Time: 8 minutes
Servings: 2
Ingredients:
- 2 tilapia fillets
- 1 cup breadcrumbs
- 2 tbsp olive oil

Directions:
- Brush fish fillets with oil then coat with breadcrumbs.
- Place the dehydrating tray in a multi-level air fryer basket and place basket in the air fryer.
- Place coated fish fillets on dehydrating tray.
- Seal pot with air fryer lid and select air fry mode then set the temperature to 370 f and timer for 8 minutes.
- Serve and enjoy.

Nutrition:
Calories 426
Fat 17.9 g
Carbohydrates 38.9 g
Sugar 3.4 g
Protein 28.2 g
Cholesterol 55 mg

598. Coconut Crusted Fish Fillets

Preparation Time: 10 minutes
Cooking Time: 8 minutes
Servings: 2
Ingredients:
- 2 tilapia fillets - 1 egg, lightly beaten
- 1/4 cup coconut flour
- 1/2 cup flaked coconut
- Salt

Directions:
- In a small dish, mix coconut flour, flaked coconut, and salt together.
- Dip fish fillets in egg then coat with coconut flour mixture.
- Place the dehydrating tray in a multi-level air fryer basket and place basket in the air fryer.
- Place coated fish fillets on dehydrating tray.
- Seal pot with air fryer lid and select air fry mode then set the temperature to 400 f and timer for 8 minutes. Turn fish fillets halfway through.
- Serve and enjoy.

Nutrition:
Calories 255 Fat 11.4 g
Carbohydrates 13.2 g
Sugar 1.4 g Protein 26.5 g
Cholesterol 137 mg

599. Tuna Patties

Preparation Time: 10 minutes
Cooking Time: 6 minutes
Servings: 4
Ingredients:
- 1 egg, lightly beaten
- 1/4 cup breadcrumbs
- 1 tbsp mustard
- Oz can tuna, drained
- Salt and Pepper

Directions:
- Put all of the ingredients into the mixing bowl and mix until well combined.
- Make four patties from mixture and place on a plate.
- Place the dehydrating tray in a multi-level air fryer basket and place basket in the air fryer.
- Place tuna patties on dehydrating tray.
- Seal pot with air fryer lid and select air fry mode then set the temperature to 400 f and timer for 6 minutes. Turn patties halfway through.
- Serve and enjoy.

Nutrition:
Calories 113
Fat 2.7 g
Carbohydrates 5.9 g
Sugar 0.7 g
Protein 15.6 g
Cholesterol 56 mg

600. Fish With Vegetables

Preparation Time: 10 minutes
Cooking Time: 25 minutes
Servings: 4
Ingredients:
- 1/2 lb. Cod fillet, cut into four pieces
- 1 cup cherry tomatoes
- 2 tbsp olive oil
- 1 cup baby potatoes, diced
- Salt and Pepper

Directions:
- Line air fryer multi-level air fryer basket with aluminum foil.
- Toss potatoes with half olive oil and add into the air fryer basket and place basket into the air fryer.
- Seal pot with air fryer lid and select bake mode then set the temperature to 380 f and timer for 15 minutes.
- Add cod and cherry tomatoes in the basket.
- Drizzle with the excess oil and season with pepper and salt.

Seal pot with air fryer lid and select bake mode then set the temperature to 380 f and timer for 10 minutes.

Serve and enjoy.

Nutrition:
Calories 146
Fat 7.7 g
Carbohydrates 8.8 g
Sugar 1.2 g
Protein 12 g
Cholesterol 28 mg

601. Balsamic Salmon

Preparation Time: 10 minutes
Cooking Time: 3 minutes
Servings: 2
Ingredients:
- 2 salmon fillets
- 1 cup of water
- 2 tbsp balsamic vinegar
- 1 1/2 tbsp honey
- Salt and Pepper

Directions:
Season salmon with pepper and salt.
Mix together vinegar and honey.
Brush fish fillets with vinegar honey mixture.
Transfer water into the fryer then place trivet into the basket.
Place fish fillets on top of the trivet.
Seal fryer and cook on manual high pressure for 3 minutes.
As soon as the cooking is done, release pressure using the quick-release method then open the lid.
Garnish with parsley and serve.

Nutrition:
Calories 278
Fat 7.8 g
Carbohydrates 3.3 g
Sugar 0.5 g
Protein 46.8 g
Cholesterol 341 mg

602. Dijon Fish Fillets

Preparation Time: 10 minutes
Cooking Time: 3 minutes
Servings: 2
Ingredients:
- 2 halibut fillets
- 1 tbsp Dijon mustard
- 1 1/2 cups water
- Pepper
- Salt

Directions:
Transfer water into the air fryer then place steamer basket
Season fish fillets with pepper and salt and brush with Dijon mustard.
Place fish fillets in the steamer basket.
Seal fryer and cook on manual high pressure for 3 minutes.
After the cooking is done, release pressure using the quick-release method than open the lid.
Serve and enjoy.

Nutrition:
Calories 323
Fat 7 g
Carbohydrates 0.5 g
Sugar 0.1 g
Protein 60.9 g
Cholesterol 93 mg

603. Perfect Salmon Dinner

Preparation Time: 10 minutes
Cooking Time: 2 minutes
Servings: 3
Ingredients:
- 1 lb. Salmon fillet, cut into three pieces
- 2 garlic cloves, minced
- 1/2 tsp ground cumin
- 1 tsp red chili powder
- Salt and Pepper

Directions:
Discharge 1 1/2 cups water into the air fryer then place trivet into the pot.

In a small bowl, mix together garlic, cumin, chili powder, pepper, and salt.

Rub salmon with spice mixture and place on top of the trivet.

Seal pot with lid and cook on steam mode for 2 minutes.

After the cooking is done, release pressure using the quick-release method than open the lid.

Serve and enjoy.

Nutrition:
Calories 211
Fat 7 g
Carbohydrates 0.5 g
Sugar 0.1 g
Protein 60.9 g
Cholesterol 93 mg

604. Steam Clams

Preparation Time: 10 minutes
Cooking Time: 3 minutes
Servings: 3
Ingredients:
- 1 lb. Mushy shell clams
- 2 tbsp butter, melted
- 1/4 cup white wine
- 1/2 tsp garlic powder
- 1/4 cup fresh lemon juice

Directions:

Add white wine, lemon juice, garlic powder, and butter into the air fryer.

Place trivet into the pot.

Arrange clams on top of the trivet.

Seal pot and cook on manual high pressure for 3 minutes.

Once done then allow to release pressure naturally then open the lid.

Serve and enjoy.

Nutrition:
Calories 336 Fat 7 g
Carbohydrates 0.5 g Sugar 0.1 g
Protein 60.9 g
Cholesterol 93 mg

605. Breaded Coconut Shrimp

Preparation Time: 5 minutes
Cooking Time: 15 minutes
Servings: 4
Ingredients:
- 1 lb. shrimp
- 1 cup panko breadcrumbs
- 1 cup coconut, shredded
- 2 eggs
- ⅓ cup all-purpose flour

Directions:

Fix the temperature of the Air Fryer at 360º Fahrenheit.

Peel and devein the shrimp.

Whisk the seasonings with the flour as desired. In another bowl, whisk the eggs, and in the third bowl, combine the breadcrumbs and coconut.

Dip the cleaned shrimp into the flour, egg wash, and finish it off with the coconut mixture.

Lightly, spray the basket of the Air Fryer Oven and set the timer for 10–15 minutes.

Air-fry until it's a golden brown before serving.

Nutrition:
Calories: 285
Fats: 12.8 g
Carbs: 3.7 g
Protein: 38.1 g

606. Breaded Cod Sticks

Preparation Time: 5 minutes
Cooking Time: 20 minutes
Servings: 4
Ingredients:
- 2 large eggs
- 3 tbsp. milk
- 2 cups breadcrumbs
- 1 cups almond flour
- 1 lb. cod

Directions:
- Heat the Air Fryer Oven to 350ºF.
- Prepare 3 bowls; one with the milk and eggs, one with the breadcrumbs (salt and pepper if desired), and another with almond flour.
- Dip the sticks in the flour, egg mixture, and breadcrumbs.
- Place in the basket and set the timer for 12 minutes. Toss the basket halfway through the cooking process.
- Serve with your favorite sauce.

Nutrition:
- Calories: 254 Fats: 14.2 g
- Carbs: 5.7 g Protein: 39.1 g

607. Cajun Shrimp

Preparation Time: 5 minutes
Cooking Time: 5 minutes
Servings: 6
Ingredients:
- 16–20 (1 ¼-lb.) tiger shrimp
- 1 tbsp. olive oil
- .5 tsp. OLD BAY® seasoning
- .25 tsp. smoked paprika
- .25 tsp. cayenne pepper

Directions:
- Set the Air Fryer Oven to 390º Fahrenheit.
- Cover the shrimp using the oil and spices.
- Toss them into the Air Fry basket and set the timer for 5 minutes.
- Serve with your favorite side dish.

Nutrition:
- Calories: 356 Fats: 18 g
- Carbs: 5 g Protein: 34 g

608. Cod Fish Nuggets

Preparation Time: 5 minutes
Cooking Time: 20 minutes
Servings: 4
Ingredients:
- 1 lb. cod fillet
- 3 eggs
- 4 tbsp. olive oil
- 1 cup almond flour
- 1 cup breadcrumbs, gluten-free

Directions:
- Heat the Air Fryer Oven to 390ºF.
- Slice the cod into nuggets.
- Prepare 3 bowls and whisk the eggs in one of them. Combine the salt, oil, and breadcrumbs in another bowl. Sift the almond flour into the third bowl.
- Cover each of the nuggets with the flour, dip in the eggs, and the breadcrumbs.
- Arrange the nuggets in the basket and set the timer for 20 minutes.
- Serve the fish with your favorite dips or sides.

Nutrition:
- Calories: 334 Fats: 10 g
- Carbs: 8 g Protein: 32 g

609. Creamy Salmon

Preparation Time: 5 minutes
Cooking Time: 20 minutes
Servings: 4
Ingredients:
- 1 tbsp. dill, chopped
- 1 tbsp. olive oil
- 1 ¾ oz. plain yogurt
- 6 pieces (¾-lb.) salmon

Directions:
- Heat the Air Fryer Oven and wait for it to reach 285ºF.
- Shake the salt over the salmon and add them to the fryer basket with the olive oil to air-fry for 10 minutes.
- Whisk the yogurt, salt, and dill.
- Serve the salmon with the sauce or side dish of your preference.

Nutrition:
- Calories: 340 Carbs: 5 g
- Fats: 16 g
- Protein: 32 g

610. Crumbled Fish
Preparation Time: 5 minutes
Cooking Time: 15 minutes
Servings: 4
Ingredients:
- .5 cup breadcrumbs
- 4 tbsp. vegetable oil
- 1 egg
- 4 fish fillets
- 1 lemon

Directions:
Heat the Air Fryer Oven to 356ºF.
Whisk the oil and breadcrumbs until crumbly.
Dip the fish into the egg, then in the crumb mixture. Arrange the fish fillets in the Air Fryer Oven and air-fry for 12 minutes.
Garnish with the lemon.

Nutrition:
Calories: 320 Carbs: 8 g
Fats: 10 g Protein: 28 g

611. Easy Crab Sticks
Preparation Time: 5 minutes
Cooking Time: 10 minutes
Servings: 4
Ingredients:
- 1 package crab sticks
- Cooking oil spray as needed

Directions:
Take each of the sticks out of the package and unroll it until the sticks are flat. Tear the sheets into thirds.
Arrange them on the air fryer basket and spray lightly with the cooking oil. Set the timer for 10 minutes.

Tip: If you shred the crab meat, you can cut the time in half, but they will also easily fall through the holes in the basket.

Nutrition:
Calories: 285 Fats: 12.8 g
Carbs: 3.7 g Protein: 38.1 g

612. Fried Catfish
Preparation Time: 5 minutes
Cooking Time: 15 minutes
Servings: 4
Ingredients:
- 1 tbsp. olive oil
- .25 cup seasoned fish fry
- 4 catfish fillets

Directions:
Heat the Air Fryer Oven to 400ºF before 'fry' time.
Rinse the catfish and pat dry using a paper towel.
Dump the seasoning into a sizeable Ziploc® bag. Add the fish and shake to cover each fillet. Spray with the cooking oil spray and add to the basket.
Set the timer for 10 minutes. Flip, and reset the timer for ten additional minutes. Turn the fish once more and cook for 2–3 minutes.
Once it reaches the desired crispiness, transfer to a plate and serve.

Nutrition:
Calories: 376 Fats: 9 g
Carbs: 10 g Protein: 28 g

613. Grilled Sardines
Preparation Time: 5 minutes
Cooking Time: 20 minutes
Servings: 4
Ingredients:
- 5 sardines

Directions:
Preheat the Air Fryer Oven to 320ºF.
Place the sardines in the air fry basket.
Set the timer to 14 minutes. After 7 minutes, remember to turn the sardines so that they are roasted on both sides.

Nutrition:
Calories: 189 g Fats: 10 g
Protein: 22 g
Cholesterol: 128 mg

614. Zucchini with Tuna

Preparation Time: 10 minutes
Cooking Time: 30 minutes
Servings: 4
Ingredients:
- 4 medium zucchinis
- 4 1/5 oz. tuna in oil (canned) drained
- 1 oz. grated cheese
- 1 tsp. pine nuts
- Salt, pepper to taste

Directions:
- Cut the zucchini in half, laterally, and empty it with a small spoon (set aside the pulp that will be used for filling); place them in the basket.
- In a food processor, put the zucchini pulp, drained tuna, pine nuts and grated cheese. Mix everything until you get a homogeneous and dense mixture.
- Fill the zucchini. Set the Air Fryer Oven to 356ºF.
- Simmer for 20 min, depending on the size of the zucchini. Let cool before serving.

Nutrition:
- Calories: 389 Carbs: 10 g
- Fats: 29 g
- Sugar: 5 g
- Protein: 23 g
- Cholesterol: 40 mg

615. Caramelized Salmon Fillet

Preparation Time: 5 minutes
Cooking Time: 25 minutes
Servings: 4
Ingredients:
- 2 salmon fillets
- 2 oz. cane sugar
- 4 tbsp. soy sauce
- 1 ¾50g sesame seeds
- Fresh ginger

Directions:
- Preheat the Air Fryer Oven at 356ºF for 5 minutes.
- Put the cane sugar and soy sauce in the basket.
- Cook everything for 5 minutes.
- In the meantime, wash the salmon fillets well, pass it through the sesame seeds to cover it completely and place it inside the tank and add the fresh ginger.
- Cook for 12 minutes.
- Turn the fish over and finish cooking for another 8 minutes.

Nutrition:
- Calories: 569
- Fats: 14.9 g
- Carbs: 40 g
- Sugar: 27.6 g
- Protein: 66.9 g
- Cholesterol: 165.3 mg

616. Deep Fried Prawns

Preparation Time: 15 minutes
Cooking Time: 20 minutes
Servings: 6
Ingredients:
- 12 prawns
- 2 eggs
- ½ tsp. Flour to taste
- 1 tbsp Breadcrumbs
- 4 tbsp Yogurt
- 2 tbsp Mayonnaise sauce

Directions:
- Remove the head of the prawns and shell carefully.
- Dip the prawns first in the flour, then in the beaten eggs and then in the breadcrumbs.
- Preheat the Air Fryer Oven for 1 minute at 302ºF.
- Add the prawns and cook for 4 minutes. If the prawns are large, it will be necessary to cook 6 at a time.
- Turn the prawns and cook for another 4 minutes.

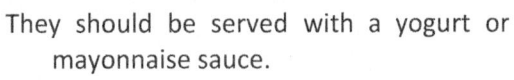

They should be served with a yogurt or mayonnaise sauce.

Nutrition:
Calories: 2385.1
Fats: 23
Carbs: 52.3 g
Sugar: 0.1 g
Protein: 21.4 g

617. Mussels with Pepper

Preparation Time: 15 minutes
Cooking Time: 20 minutes
Servings: 5
Ingredients:
1 ½ lb. mussels
1 clove garlic
1 tsp. oil
½ tsp. Pepper to taste
½ tsp. Parsley Taste

Directions:
Clean and scrape the mussels cover and remove the byssus (the "beard" that comes out of the mussels.)
Pour the oil, clean the mussels and the crushed garlic in the air fryer basket. Set the temperature to 392ºF and simmer for 12 minutes. Towards the end of cooking, add the black pepper and the chopped parsley.
Finally, distribute the mussel juice well at the bottom of the basket, shaking the basket.

Nutrition:
Calories: 150 Carbs: 2 g
Fats: 8 g Protein: 15 g

618. Monkfish with Olives and Capers

Preparation Time: 25 minutes
Cooking Time: 40 minutes
Servings: 4
Ingredients:
1 monkfish
10 cherry tomatoes
1 ¾ cailletier olives
5 capers

Directions:
Spread aluminum foil inside the air fry basket and place the monkfish clean and skinless.
Chop the tomatoes and add them with the olives, capers, oil, and salt.
Set the temperature to 320ºF.
Cook the monkfish for about 40 minutes.

Nutrition:
Calories: 404
Fats: 29 g
Carbs: 36 g
Sugar: 7 g
Protein: 24 g
Cholesterol: 36 mg

619. Shrimp, Zucchini and Cherry Tomato Sauce

Preparation Time: 5 minutes
Cooking Time: 30 minutes
Servings: 4
Ingredients:
2 zucchinis
300 shrimps
7 cherry tomatoes
Salt and pepper to taste
1 garlic clove

Directions:
Pour the oil in the Air Fryer Oven, and add the garlic clove and diced zucchini.
Cook for 15 minutes at 302ºF.
Add the shrimps and the tomato pieces, salt, and spices.
Cook for another 5–10 minutes or until the shrimp water evaporates.

Nutrition:
Calories: 214.3 Fats: 8.6 g
Carbs: 7.8 g Sugar: 4.8 g
Protein: 27.0 g
Cholesterol: 232.7 mg

620. Salmon with Pistachio Bark

Preparation Time: 10 minutes
Cooking Time: 30 minutes
Servings: 4
Ingredients:
- 1 ⅓ lb. salmon fillet
- 1 ⅓ oz. pistachios
- Salt to taste

Directions:
- Put the parchment paper on the bottom of the air fryer basket and place the salmon fillet in it (it can be cooked whole or already divided into four portions).
- Cut the pistachios in thick pieces, grease the top of the fish, and salt (little because the pistachios are already salted), and cover everything with the pistachios.
- Set the air fryer to 356ºF and simmer for 25 minutes.

Nutrition:
Calories: 371.7 Fats: 21.8 g
Carbs: 9.4 g Sugar: 2.2 g
Protein: 34.7 g
Cholesterol: 80.5 mg

621. Salted Marinated Salmon

Preparation Time: 10 minutes
Cooking Time: 30 minutes
Servings: 4
Ingredients:
- 1 lb. salmon fillet
- 16 lb. coarse salt
- 1 tbsp Oil

Directions:
- Place some baking paper on the air fry basket and the salmon on top (skin-side up) covered with coarse salt.
- Set the air fryer to 302ºF.
- Cook everything for 25–30 minutes. At the end of cooking, remove the fish and serve with a drizzle of oil.

Nutrition:
Calories: 290 Fats: 13 g
Carbs: 3 g
Protein: 40 g
Cholesterol: 196 mg

622. Sautéed Trout with Almonds

Preparation Time: 35 minutes
Cooking Time: 20 minutes
Servings: 4
Ingredients:
- 1 1/5 lb. salmon trout
- 15 black peppercorns
- 2 Dill leaves to taste
- 1 oz. almonds
- ½ tsp. Salt to taste
- 1 tbsp Oil

Directions:
- Cut the trout into cubes and marinate it for half an hour with the rest of the ingredients (except salt).
- Cook in air fryer for 17 minutes at 320ºF. Drizzle with oil and salt and serve.

Nutrition:
Calories: 238.5
Fats: 20.1 g
Carbs: 11.5 g
Sugar: 1.0 g
Protein:4.0 g
Cholesterol: 45.9 mg

623. Calamari Slices

Preparation Time: 5 minutes
Cooking Time: 12 minutes
Servings: 4
Ingredients:
- 16 calamari slices
- 1 egg
- 1 tbsp Breadcrumbs
- ½ tsp. Salt, pepper, sweet paprika

Directions:
- Put the calamari slices in the air fryer to boil for 2 minutes.
- Remove and dry them well.
- Beat the egg and season to taste. Add the egg mixture to the calamari slices and serve with the breadcrumbs.

Nutrition:
- Calories: 356 Fats: 18 g
- Carbs: 5 g Protein: 34 g

624. Honey Glazed Salmon

Preparation Time: 10 minutes
Cooking Time: 8 minutes
Servings: 2
Ingredients:
- 2 (6-oz.) salmon fillets
- ½ tsp. Salt, as required
- 2 tbsp. honey

Directions:
- Sprinkle the salmon fillets with salt and then, coat with honey.
- Press the "Power" button of the Air Fryer Oven and turn the dial to select the "Air Fry" mode.
- Press the "Time" button and again turn the dial to set the cooking time to 8 minutes.
- Now push the "Temp" button and rotate the dial to set the temperature at 355ºF.
- Press the "Start/Pause" button to start.
- Open the unit when it is already hot, when it beeps.
- Arrange the salmon fillets in a greased air fry basket and insert them in the Air Fryer Oven .
- Serve hot.

Nutrition:
- Calories: 289
- Fats: 10.5 g
- Carbs: 17.3 g
- Protein: 33.1 g

625. Sweet & Sour Glazed Salmon

Preparation Time: 12 minutes
Cooking Time: 20 minutes
Servings: 2
Ingredients:
- ⅓ cup soy sauce
- ⅓ cup honey
- 3 tsp. rice wine vinegar
- 1 tsp. water
- 4 (3 ½-oz.) salmon fillets

Directions:
- Mix the soy sauce, honey, vinegar, and water together in a bowl.
- In another small bowl, reserve about half of the mixture.
- Add the salmon fillets in the remaining mixture and coat them well.
- Cover the bowl and refrigerate to marinate for about 2 hours.
- Press the "Power" button of the Air Fryer Oven and turn the dial to select the "Air Fry" mode.
- Press the "Time" button and again turn the dial to set the cooking time to 12 minutes.
- Now push the "Temp" button and rotate the dial to set the temperature at 355ºF.
- Press the "Start/Pause" button to start.
- Open the unit when it is already hot, when it beeps.
- Arrange the salmon fillets in greased air fry basket" and insert them in the Air Fryer Oven .
- Flip the salmon fillets once halfway through and coat them with the reserved marinade after every 3 minutes.
- Serve hot.

Nutrition:
- Calories: 462 Fats: 12.3 g
- Carbs: 49.8 g
- Protein: 41.3 g

626. Ranch Tilapia

Preparation Time: 15 minutes
Cooking Time: 13 minutes
Servings: 4
Ingredients:
- ¾ cup cornflakes, crushed
- 1 (1-oz.) packet dry ranch-style dressing mix
- 2 ½ tbsp. vegetable oil
- 2 eggs
- 4 (6-oz.) tilapia fillets

Directions:
- In a shallow bowl, beat the eggs.
- In another bowl, add the cornflakes, ranch dressing, and oil and mix until a crumbly mixture form.
- Dip the tilapia fillets into the egg mixture and then, and coat them with the bread crumbs mixture.
- Press the "Power" button of the Air Fryer Oven and turn the dial to select the "Air Fry" mode.
- Press the "Time" button and again turn the dial to set the cooking time to 13 minutes.
- Now push the "Temp" button and rotate the dial to set the temperature at 356ºF.
- Press the "Start/Pause" button to start.
- Open the unit when it is already hot, when it beeps.
- Arrange the tilapia fillets in greased air fry basket and insert them in the Air Fryer Oven .
- Serve hot.

Nutrition:
Calories: 267 Fats: 12.2 g
Carbs: 5.1 g Protein: 34.9 g

627. Breaded Flounder

Preparation Time: 15 minutes
Cooking Time: 12 minutes
Servings: 3
Ingredients:
- 1 egg
- 1 cup dry breadcrumbs
- ¼ cup vegetable oil
- 3 (6-oz.) flounder fillets
- 1 lemon, sliced

Directions:
- In a shallow bowl, beat the egg.
- In another bowl, add the breadcrumbs and oil and mix until the crumbly mixture is formed.
- Dip the flounder fillets into the beaten egg and then coat with the breadcrumb mixture.
- Press the "Power" button of the Air Fryer Oven and turn the dial to select the "Air Fry" mode.
- Press the "Time" button and again turn the dial to set the cooking time to 12 minutes.
- Now push the "Temp" button and rotate the dial to set the temperature at 356ºF.
- Press the "Start/Pause" button to start.
- Open the unit when it is already hot, when it beeps.
- Arrange the flounder fillets in a greased air fry basket and insert them in the Air Fryer Oven .
- Plate with lemon slices and serve hot.

Nutrition:
Calories: 524 Fats: 24.2 g
Saturated Fats: 5.1 g
Cholesterol: 170 mg
Sodium: 463 mg
Carbs: 26.5 g Fiber: 1.5 g
Sugar: 2.5 g Protein: 47.8 g

628. Simple Haddock

Preparation Time: 15 minutes
Cooking Time: 8 minutes
Servings: 2
Ingredients:
- 2 (6-oz.) haddock fillets
- 1 tbsp. olive oil
- Salt and ground black pepper, as required

Directions:

- Coat the haddock fillets with oil and then sprinkle with salt and black pepper.
- Press the "Power" button of the Air Fryer Oven and turn the dial to select the "Air Fry" mode.
- Press the "Time" button and again turn the dial to set the cooking time to 8 minutes.
- Now push the "Temp" button and rotate the dial to set the temperature at 355ºF.
- Press the "Start/Pause" button to start.
- Open the unit when it is already hot, when it beeps.
- Arrange the haddock fillets in a greased air fry basket and insert them in the Air Fryer Oven.
- Serve hot.

Nutrition:

Calories: 251
Fats: 8.6 g
Saturated Fats: 1.3 g
Cholesterol: 126 mg
Sodium 226: mg
Protein: 41.2 g

629. Breaded Hake

Preparation Time: 15 minutes
Cooking Time: 12 minutes
Servings: 4
Ingredients:

- 1 egg
- 4 oz. breadcrumbs
- 2 tbsp. vegetable oil
- 4 (6-oz.) hake fillets
- 1 lemon, cut into wedges

Directions:

- Beat the egg in a large bowl.
- In another bowl, add the breadcrumbs, and oil and mix until a crumbly mixture forms.
- Dip hake fillets into the egg and then coat with the bread crumbs mixture.
- Press the "Power" button of the Air Fryer Oven and turn the dial to select the "Air Fry" mode.
- Press the "Time" button and again turn the dial to set the cooking time to 12 minutes.
- Now push the "Temp" button and rotate the dial to set the temperature at 350ºF.
- Press the "Start/Pause" button to start.
- Open the unit when it is already hot, when it beeps.
- Arrange the hake fillets in a greased air fry basket and insert them in the Air Fryer Oven.
- Serve hot.

Nutrition:

Calories: 297
Fats: 10.6 g
Saturated Fats: 2 g
Cholesterol: 89 mg
Sodium: 439 mg
Carbs: 22 g
Fiber: 1.4 g
Sugar: 1.9 g
Protein: 29.2 g

630. Sesame Seeds Coated Tuna

Preparation Time: 15 minutes
Cooking Time: 6 minutes
Servings: 2
Ingredients:

- 1 egg white
- ¼ cup white sesame seeds
- 1 tbsp. black sesame seeds
- Salt and ground black pepper, as required
- 2 (6-oz.) tuna steaks

Directions:

- Beat the egg white in a large bowl.
- In another bowl, mix together the sesame seeds, salt, and black pepper.
- Dip the tuna steaks into the beaten egg white and then coat with the sesame seeds mixture.

- Press the "Power" button of the Air Fryer Oven and turn the dial to select the "Air Fry" mode.
- Press the "Time" button and again turn the dial to set the cooking time to 6 minutes.
- Now push the "Temp" button and rotate the dial to set the temperature at 400 degrees F.
- Press the "Start/Pause" button to start.
- Open the unit when it is already hot, when it beeps.
- Arrange the tuna steaks in greased "Air Fry Basket" and insert them in the Air Fryer Oven.
- Flip the tuna steaks once halfway through.
- Serve hot.

Nutrition:
Calories: 450
Total Fats: 21.9 g
Saturated Fats: 4.3 g
Cholesterol: 83 mg
Sodium: 182 mg
Carbs: 5.4 g
Fiber: 2.7 g
Sugar: 0.2 g
Protein: 56.7 g

631. Cheese and Ham Patties

Preparation Time: 10 minutes
Cooking Time: 10 minutes
Servings: 4
Ingredients:
- 1 puff pastry sheet
- 4 handfuls mozzarella cheese, grated
- 4 tsp. mustard
- 8 ham slices, chopped

Directions:
- Spread out the puff pastry on a clean surface and cut it into 12 squares.
- Divide the cheese, ham, and mustard on half of them, top with the other halves, and seal the edges.
- Place all the patties in your air fry basket and cook at 370ºF for 10 minutes.
- Divide the patties between plates and serve.

Nutrition:
Calories: 212 Fats: 12 g Fiber: 7 g
Carbs: 14 g Protein: 8 g

632. Air-Fried Seafood

Preparation Time: 10 minutes
Cooking Time: 10 minutes
Servings: 4
Ingredients:
- 1 lb. fresh scallops, mussels, fish fillets, prawns, shrimp
- 2 eggs, lightly beaten
- Salt and black pepper
- 1 cup breadcrumbs mixed with the zest of 1 lemon
- Cooking spray

Directions:
- Clean the seafood as needed.
- Dip each piece into the egg mixture and season with salt and pepper.
- Coat the seafood in the crumbs and spray with oil.
- Arrange the seafood in the Air Fryer Oven and cook for 6 minutes at 400ºF. turning once halfway through.
- Serve and Enjoy!

Nutrition:
Calories: 133 Protein: 17.4 g
Fats: 3.1 g Carbs: 8.2 g

633. Fish with Chips

Preparation Time: 5 minutes
Cooking Time: 20 minutes
Servings: 2
Ingredients:
- 1 (6-oz.) cod fillet
- 3 cups salt
- 3 cups vinegar-flavored kettle cooked chips
- ¼ cup buttermilk
- Salt and pepper to taste

Directions:

Mix to combine the buttermilk, pepper, and salt in a bowl. Put the cod and leave to soak for 5 minutes Put the chips in a food processor and process until crushed. Transfer the chips to a shallow bowl. Coat the fillet with the crushed chips. Put the coated fillet in the air fry basket. Cook for 12 minutes at 400ºF. Serve and Enjoy!

Nutrition:

Calories: 646 Protein: 41 g
Fats: 33 g Carbs: 48 g

634. Crumbly Fishcakes

Preparation Time: 5 minutes
Cooking Time: 10 minutes
Servings: 4
Ingredients:

8 oz. salmon, cooked
1 ½ oz. potatoes, mashed
A handful of parsley, chopped
1 lemon zest
1 ¾ oz. plain flour

Directions:

Carefully, flake the salmon. In a bowl, mix the flaked salmon, zest, capers, dill, and mashed potatoes.

Form small cakes using the mixture and dust the cakes with flour; refrigerate for 60 minutes. Preheat your Air Fryer Oven to 350ºF. and cook the cakes for 7 minutes. Serve chilled.

Nutrition:

Calories: 210 Protein: 10 g
Fats: 7 g Carbs: 25 g

635. Bacon Wrapped Shrimp

Preparation Time: 10 minutes
Cooking Time: 20 minutes
Servings: 4
Ingredients:

16 bacon slices, thin
16 pieces tiger shrimp, peeled and deveined

Directions:

Wrap each shrimp with a slice of bacon. Put all the finished pieces in tray and chill for 20 minutes.

Arrange the bacon-wrapped shrimp in the air frying basket. Cook for 7 minutes at 390ºF. Transfer to a plate lined with paper towels to drain before serving.

Nutrition:

Calories: 436 Protein: 32 g
Fats: 41.01 g Carbs: 0.8 g

636. Crab Legs

Preparation Time: 10 minutes
Cooking Time: 10 minutes
Servings: 4
Ingredients:

3 lb. crab legs
¼ cup salted butter, melted and divided
½ lemon, juiced
¼ tsp. garlic powder

Directions:

In a bowl, toss the crab legs and 2 tbsp. of the melted butter together. Place the crab legs in the air fry basket

Cook at 400°F for 15 minutes, giving the basket a good shake halfway through.

Combine the remaining butter with the lemon juice and garlic powder.

Crack open the cooked crab legs and remove the meat. Serve with the butter dip on the side, and enjoy!

Nutrition:

Calories: 272 Fats: 19 g
Fiber: 9 g Carbs: 18 g Protein: 12 g

637. Fish Sticks

Preparation Time: 5 minutes
Cooking Time: 10 minutes
Servings: 4
Ingredients:

1 lb. whitefish

2 tbsp. Dijon mustard
¼ cup mayonnaise
1 ½ cup pork rinds, finely ground
¾ tsp. Cajun seasoning

Directions:

Place the whitefish on a tissue to dry it off, then cut it up into slices about 2 inches thick.

In one bowl, combine the mustard and mayonnaise, and in another, the Cajun seasoning and pork rinds.

Coat the fish firstly in the mayo-mustard mixture, then in the Cajun-pork rind mixture. Give each slice a shake to remove any surplus. Then place the fish sticks in the basket of the air flyer.

Cook at 400°F for 5 minutes. Turn the fish sticks over and cook for another 5 minutes on the other side.

Serve warm with a dipping sauce of your choice and enjoy.

Nutrition:
Calories: 212
Fats: 12 g
Fiber: 7 g
Carbs: 14 g
Protein: 8 g

638. Crusty Pesto Salmon

Preparation Time: 5 minutes
Cooking Time: 10 minutes
Servings: 2
Ingredients:

¼ cup almonds, roughly chopped
¼ cup pesto
2 (4-oz.) salmon fillets
2 tbsp. unsalted butter, melted

Directions:

Mix the almonds and pesto together.

Place the salmon fillets in a round baking dish, roughly 6 inches in diameter.

Brush the fillets with butter, followed up by the pesto mixture, ensuring to coat both the top and bottom of the filets. Put the baking dish inside the Air Fryer Oven.

Cook for 12 minutes at 390°F.

The salmon is ready when it flakes easily when prodded with a fork. Serve warm.

Nutrition:
Calories: 354 Fats: 21 g
Carbs: 23 g Protein: 19 g

639. Salmon Patties

Preparation Time: 5 minutes
Cooking Time: 10 minutes
Servings: 4
Ingredients:

1 tsp. chili powder
2 tbsp. full-fat mayonnaise
¼ cup ground pork rinds
2 (5-oz.) pouches cooked pink salmon
1 egg

Directions:

Stir everything together to prepare the patty mixture. If the mixture is dry or falling apart, add in more pork rinds as necessary.

Take equal-sized amounts of the mixture to form 4 patties, before placing the patties in the air fry basket.

Cook at 400°F for 8 minutes.

Halfway through cooking, flip the patties over. Once they are crispy, serve with the toppings of your choice and enjoy.

Nutrition:
Calories: 325
Fats: 21 g
Carbs: 18 g
Protein: 29 g

640. Cajun Salmon

Preparation Time: 5 minutes
Cooking Time: 10 minutes
Servings: 4
Ingredients:

2 (4-oz) skinless salmon fillets

2 tbsp. unsalted butter, melted
1 pinch ground cayenne pepper
1 tsp. paprika
½ tsp. garlic pepper

Directions:
- Using a brush, apply the butter to the salmon fillets.
- Combine the other ingredients and massage this mixture into the fillets. Place the fish inside you're the Air Fryer Oven.
- Cook for seven minutes at 390°F.
- When the salmon is ready, it should flake apart easily.
- Enjoy with the sides of your choosing.

Nutrition:
Calories: 383
Fats: 12 g
Carbs: 29 g
Protein: 31 g

641. Buttery Cod

Preparation Time: 5 minutes
Cooking Time: 10 minutes
Servings: 4
Ingredients:
- 2 (4-oz.) cod fillets
- 2 tbsp. salted butter, melted
- 1 tsp. OLD BAY® seasoning
- ½ medium lemon, sliced

Directions:
- Place the cod fillets in a dish.
- Brush with melted butter, season with OLD BAY® and top with some lemon slices.
- Wrap the fish in aluminum foil and put into your Air Fryer Oven
- Cook for 8 minutes at 350°F.
- The cod is ready when it flakes easily. Serve hot.

Nutrition:
Calories: 354
Fats: 21 g
Carbs: 23 g
Protein: 19 g

642. Sesame Tuna Steak

Preparation Time: 5 minutes
Cooking Time: 10 minutes
Servings: 4
Ingredients:
- 1 tbsp. coconut oil, melted
- 2 (6-oz.) tuna steaks
- ½ tsp. garlic powder
- 2 tsp. black sesame seeds
- 2 tsp. white sesame seeds

Directions:
- Apply the coconut oil to the tuna steaks with a brush, then season with the garlic powder.
- Combine the black and the white sesame seeds. Embed them in the tuna steaks, covering the fish all over. Place the tuna into your Air Fry.
- Cook for 8 minutes at 400°F, turning the fish halfway through.
- The tuna steaks are ready when they have reached a temperature of 145°F. Serve straightaway.

Nutrition:
Calories: 343 Fats: 11 g
Carbs: 27 g Protein: 25 g

643. Lemon Garlic Shrimp

Preparation Time: 5 minutes
Cooking Time: 10 minutes
Servings: 4
Ingredients:
- 1 medium lemon
- ½ lb. medium shrimp, shelled and deveined
- ½ tsp. OLD BAY® seasoning
- 2 tbsp. unsalted butter, melted

Directions:
- Grate the lemon rind into a bowl. Cut the lemon in half then juice it in the same bowl. Toss in the shrimp, OLD BAY®, and butter, mixing everything to make sure the shrimp is completely covered.

Transfer to a round baking dish roughly 6 inches wide, then place this dish in your Air Fryer Oven.

Cook at 400°F for 6 minutes. The shrimp is ready when it becomes a bright pink color.

Serve hot, drizzling any leftover sauce over the shrimp.

Nutrition:

Calories: 374 Fats: 14 g
Carbs: 18 g Protein: 21 g

644. Foil Packet Salmon

Preparation Time: 5 minutes
Cooking Time: 10 minutes
Servings: 4
Ingredients:

- 2 (4-oz.) salmon fillets, skinless
- 2 tbsp. unsalted butter, melted
- ½ tsp. garlic powder
- 1 medium lemon
- ½ tsp. dried dill

Directions:

Take a sheet of foil and cut into two squares measuring roughly 5"x5". Lay each of the salmon fillets at the center of each piece. Brush both fillets with 1 tbsp. of butter and season with ¼ tsp. of garlic powder.

Halve the lemon and grate the skin of one half over the fish. Cut four half-slices of lemon, using two to top each fillet. Season each fillet with ¼ tsp. of dill.

Fold the tops and sides of the aluminum foil over the fish to create a kind of packet. Place each one in the fryer.

Cook for 12 minutes at 400°F.

The salmon is ready when it flakes easily. Serve hot.

Nutrition:

Calories: 365 Fats: 16 g
Carbs: 18 g Protein: 23 g

645. Foil Packet Lobster Tail

Preparation Time: 5 minutes
Cooking Time: 10 minutes
Servings: 4
Ingredients:

- 2 (6-oz.) lobster tail halves
- 2 tbsp. salted butter, melted
- ½ medium lemon, juiced
- ½ tsp. OLD BAY® seasoning
- 1 tsp. dried parsley

Directions:

Lay each lobster on a sheet of aluminum foil. Add ½ of the butter and lemon juice over each one, and season with OLD BAY®.

Fold down the sides and ends of the foil to seal the lobster. Place each one in the fryer.

Cook at 375°F for 12 minutes.

Just before serving, top the lobster with dried parsley.

Nutrition:

Calories: 369 Fats: 19 g Carbs: 25 g Protein: 28 g

646. Avocado Shrimp

Preparation Time: 5 minutes
Cooking Time: 10 minutes
Servings: 4
Ingredients:

- ½ cup onion, chopped
- 2 lb. shrimp
- 1 tbsp. seasoned salt
- 1 avocado
- ½ cup pecans, chopped

Directions:

Preheat the fryer to 400°F.

Put the chopped onion in the basket of the fryer and spritz with some cooking spray. Let cook for 5 minutes.

Add the shrimp and set the timer for a further 5 minutes. Sprinkle with some seasoned salt, then allow to cook for an additional 5 minutes.

During these last 5 minutes, halve your avocado and remove the pit. Cube each half, then scoop out the flesh.

Take care when removing the shrimp from the Air Fryer Oven . Place it on a dish and top with the avocado and the chopped pecans.

Nutrition:
Calories: 384
Fats: 24 g
Carbs: 13 g
Protein: 39 g

647. Lemon Butter Scallops

Preparation Time: 1 hour 5 minutes
Cooking Time: 10 minutes
Servings: 4
Ingredients:
- 1 lemon
- 1 lb. scallops
- ½ cup butter
- ¼ cup parsley, chopped

Directions:

Juice the lemon into a Ziploc® bag.

Wash your scallops, dry them, and season to taste. Put them in the bag with the lemon juice. Refrigerate for 1 hour.

Remove the bag from the refrigerator and leave for about 12 minutes, or until it returns to room temperature. Transfer the scallops into a foil pan that is small enough to be placed inside the fryer.

Preheat the fryer to 400°F and put the rack inside.

Place the foil pan on the rack, and cook for five minutes.

In the meantime, melt the butter in a saucepan over medium heat. Zest the lemon over the saucepan, then add in the chopped parsley. Mix well.

Be careful when removing the pan from the Air Fryer Oven . Transfer the contents to a plate and drizzle with the lemon-butter mixture. Serve hot.

Nutrition:
Calories: 412
Fats: 17 g
Carbs: 18 g
Protein: 26 g

648. Cheesy Lemon Halibut

Preparation Time: 5 minutes
Cooking Time: 10 minutes
Servings: 4
Ingredients:
- 1 lb. halibut fillet
- ½ cup butter
- 2 ½ tbsp. mayonnaise
- 2 ½ tbsp. lemon juice
- ¾ cup parmesan cheese, grated
- ½ tsp. Cooking spray

Directions:

Preheat your fryer to 375°F.

Spritz the halibut fillets with cooking spray and season as desired.

Put the halibut in the fryer and cook for 12 minutes.

In the meantime, combine the butter, mayonnaise, and lemon juice in a bowl with a hand mixer. Ensure a creamy texture is achieved.

Stir in the grated parmesan.

When the halibut is ready, open the Air Fryer Oven and spread the butter over the fish with a butter knife. Let it cook for a couple more minutes, then serve hot.

Nutrition:
Calories: 354
Fats: 21 g
Carbs: 23 g
Protein: 19 g

649. Spicy Mackerel

Preparation Time: 5 minutes
Cooking Time: 10 minutes
Servings: 4
Ingredients:
- 2 mackerel fillets
- 2 tbsp. red pepper flakes
- 2 tsp. garlic, minced
- 1 tsp. lemon juice

Directions:
- Season the mackerel fillets with the red pepper flakes, minced garlic, and a drizzle of lemon juice. Allow to sit for 5 minutes.
- Preheat your fryer at 350°F.
- Cook the mackerel for 5 minutes, before opening the Air Fryer Oven to flip the fillets, allow to cook on the other side for another 5 minutes.
- Plate the fillets, making sure to spoon any remaining juice over them before serving.

Nutrition:
- Calories: 393
- Fats: 12 g
- Carbs: 13 g
- Protein: 35 g

CHAPTER 10:

Vegetabes

650. Zucchini Curry
Preparation Time: 5 Minutes
Cooking Time: 8-10 Minutes
Servings: 3
Ingredients:
- 2 Zucchinis, Washed & Sliced
- 1 Tablespoon Olive Oil
- Pinch Sea Salt
- Curry Mix, Pre-Made

Directions:
- Turn on your air fryer to 390.
- Combine your zucchini slices, salt, oil, and spices.
- Put the zucchini into the air fryer, cooking for eight to ten minutes.
- You can serve alone or with sour cream.

Nutrition:
Calories: 100 Fat: 1
Carbs: Four Protein: Two

651. Healthy Carrot Fries
Preparation Time: 5 Minutes
Cooking Time: 12-15 Minutes
Servings: 3
Ingredients:
- 5 Large Carrots
- 1 Tablespoon Olive Oil
- ½ Teaspoon Sea Salt

Directions:
- Heat your air fryer to 390, and then wash and peel your carrots. Cut them in a way to form fries.
- Combine your carrot sticks with your olive oil and salt, coating evenly.
- Place them into the air fryer, cooking for twelve minutes. If they are not as crispy as you desire, then cook for two to three more minutes.
- Serve with sour cream, ketchup or just with your favorite main dish.

Nutrition:
Calories: 140 Fat: three
Carbs: Six Protein: Seven

652. Simple Stuffed Potatoes
Preparation Time: 15 Minutes
Cooking Time: 35 Minutes
Servings: 3
Ingredients:
- 4 Large Potatoes, Peeled
- 2 Bacon, Rashers
- ½ Brown Onion, Diced
- ¼ Cup Cheese, Grated

Directions:
- Start by heating your air fryer to 350.
- Cut your potatoes in half, and then brush the potatoes with oil.
- Put it in your air fryer, and cook for ten minutes. Brush the potatoes with oil again and bake for another ten minutes.
- Make a whole in the baked potato to get them ready to stuff.
- Sauté the bacon and onion in a frying pan. You should do this over medium heat, adding cheese and stir. Remove from heat.
- Stuff your potatoes, and cook for four to five minutes.

Nutrition:
Calories: 180
Fat: eight
Carbs: 10
Protein: 11

653. Simple Roasted Carrots
Preparation Time: 5 Minutes
Cooking Time: 35 Minutes
Servings: 3
Ingredients:
- 4 Cups Carrots, Chopped
- 1 Teaspoon Herbs de Provence
- 2 Teaspoons Olive Oil
- 4 Tablespoons Orange Juice

Directions:
- Start by preheating your air fryer to 320 degrees.

Combine your carrot pieces with your herbs and oil.

Cook for twenty-five to twenty-eight minutes.

Take it out and dip the pieces in orange juice before frying for an additional seven minutes.

Nutrition:
Calories: 125 Fat: two
Carbs: Five
Protein: Six

654. Broccoli & Cheese
Preparation Time: 5 Minutes
Cooking Time: 9 Minutes
Servings: 3
Ingredients:
- 1 Head Broccoli, Washed & Chopped
- Salt & Pepper to Taste
- 1 Tablespoon Olive oil
- Sharp Cheddar Cheese, Shredded

Directions:
Start by putting your air fryer to 360.

Combine your broccoli with your olive oil and sea salt.

Place it in the air fryer, and cook for six minutes.

Take it out, and then top with cheese, cooking for another three minutes.

Serve with your choice of protein.

Nutrition:
Calories: 170 Fat: five
Carbs: Nine Protein: Seven

655. Fried Plantains
Preparation Time: 5 minutes
Cooking Time: 10 minutes
Servings: two
Ingredients:
- 2 ripe plantains, peeled and cut at a diagonal into ½-inch-thick pieces
- 3 tablespoons ghee, melted
- ¼ teaspoon kosher salt

Directions:
Preparing the Ingredients. In a bowl, mix the plantains with the ghee and salt.

Air Frying. Arrange the plantain pieces in the air fryer basket. Set the air fryer to 400°F for 8 minutes. The plantains are done when they are soft and tender on the inside, and have plenty of crisp, sweet, brown spots on the outside.

Nutrition:
Calories: 180
Fat: 5
Carbs: 10
Protein: 7

656. Bacon-Wrapped Asparagus
Preparation Time: 5 minutes
Cooking Time: 10 minutes
Servings: 4
Ingredients:
- 1 pound asparagus, trimmed (about 24 spears)
- 4 slices bacon or beef bacon
- ½ cup Ranch Dressin for serving
- 3 tablespoons chopped fresh chives, for garnish

Directions:
Preparing the Ingredients. Grease the air fryer basket with avocado oil. Preheat the air fryer to 400°F.

Slice the bacon down the middle, making long, thin strips. Wrap 1 slice of bacon around 3 asparagus spears and secure each end with a toothpick. Repeat with the remaining bacon and asparagus.

Air Frying. Place the asparagus bundles in the air fryer in a single layer. (If you're using a smaller air fryer, cook in batches if necessary.) Cook for 8 minutes for thin stalks, 10 minutes for medium to thick stalks, or until the asparagus is slightly charred on the ends and the bacon is crispy.

Serve with ranch dressing and garnish with chives. Best served fresh.

Nutrition:
Calories 241; Fat 22g;
Protein 7g; Total carbs 6g;
Fiber 3g

657. Air Fried Roasted Corn On The Cob

Preparation Time: 5 minutes
Cooking Time: 10 minutes
Servings: 4
Ingredients:
- 1 tablespoon vegetable oil
- 4 ears of corn
- Unsalted butter, for topping
- Salt, for topping
- Freshly ground black pepper, for topping

Directions:
Preparing the Ingredients. Rub the vegetable oil onto the corn, coating it thoroughly.

Air Frying. Set the temperature of your AF to 400°F. Set the timer and grill for 5 minutes.

Using tongs, flip or rotate the corn.

Reset the timer and grill for 5 minutes more.

Serve with a pat of butter and a generous sprinkle of salt and pepper.

Nutrition:
Calories: 265; Fat: 17g;
Carbohydrate: 29g; Fiber: 4g;
Sugar: 5g; Protein: 5g;

658. Green Beans & Bacon

Preparation Time: 15 minutes
Cooking Time: 20 minutes
Servings: 4
Ingredients:
- 3 cups frozen cut green beans
- 1 medium onion, chopped
- 3 slices bacon, chopped
- ¼ cup water
- Kosher salt and black pepper

Directions:
Preparing the Ingredients

In a 6 × 3-inch round heatproof pan, combine the frozen green beans, onion, bacon, and water. Toss to combine. Place the saucepan in the basket.

Air Frying

Set the air fryer to 375°F for 15 minutes.

Raise the air fryer temperature to 400°F for 5 minutes. Season the beans with salt and pepper to taste and toss well.

Remove the pan from the air fryer basket and cover with foil. Let it rest for 5 minutes then serve.

Nutrition:
Calories: 230
Fat: 10
Carbs: 14
Protein: 17

659. Air Fried Honey Roasted Carrots

Preparation Time: 5 minutes
Cooking Time: 15 minutes
Servings: 4
Ingredients:
- 3 cups baby carrots
- 1 tablespoon extra-virgin olive oil
- 1 tablespoon honey
- Salt
- Freshly ground black pepper
- Fresh dill (optional)

Directions:
Preparing the Ingredients. In a bowl, combine honey, olive oil, carrots, salt, and pepper. Make sure that the carrots are thoroughly coated with oil. Place the carrots in the air fryer basket.

Air Frying. Set the temperature of your AF to 390°F. Set the timer and roast for 12 minutes, or until fork-tender.

Remove the air fryer drawer and release the air fryer basket. Pour the carrots into a bowl, sprinkle with dill, if desired, and serve.

Nutrition:
Calories: 140 Fat: 3
Carbs: 7 Protein: 9

660. Air Fried Roasted Cabbage

Preparation Time: 5 minutes
Cooking Time: 10 minutes
Servings: 4
Ingredients:
- 1 head cabbage, sliced in 1-inch-thick ribbons - 1 tablespoon olive oil
- salt and freshly ground black pepper
- 1 teaspoon garlic powder
- 1 teaspoon red pepper flakes

Directions:

Preparing the Ingredients. In a bowl, combine the olive oil, cabbage, salt, pepper, garlic powder, and red pepper flakes. Make sure that the cabbage is thoroughly coated with oil. Place the cabbage in the air fryer basket.

Air Frying. Set the temperature of your Air Fryer to 350°F. Set the timer and roast for 4 minutes.

Using tongs, flip the cabbage. Reset the timer and roast for 3 minutes more.

Nutrition:
Calories: 100 Fat: 1
Carbs: 3 Protein: 3

661. Burrata-Stuffed Tomatoes

Preparation Time: 5 minutes
Cooking Time: 5 minutes
Servings: 4
Ingredients:
- 4 medium tomatoes
- ½ teaspoon fine sea salt
- 4 (2-ounce) Burrata balls
- Fresh basil leaves, for garnish
- Extra-virgin olive oil, for drizzling

Directions:

Preparing the Ingredients. Preheat the air fryer to 300°F.

Scoop out the tomato seeds and membranes using a melon baller or spoon. Sprinkle the insides of the tomatoes with the salt. Stuff each tomato with a ball of Burrata.

Air Frying. Put it in the fryer and cook for 5 minutes, or until the cheese has softened.

Garnish with olive oil and basil leaves. Serve warm.

Nutrition:
Calories 108; Fat 7g;
Protein 6g; Total Carbs 5g; Fiber 2g

662. Broccoli With Parmesan Cheese

Preparation Time: 5 minutes
Cooking Time: 5 minutes
Servings: 4
Ingredients:
- 1 pound broccoli florets
- 2 teaspoons minced garlic
- 2 tablespoons olive oil
- ¼ cup grated or shaved Parmesan cheese

Directions:

Preparing the Ingredients. Preheat the air fryer to 360°F. In a bowl, mix together the broccoli florets, garlic, olive oil, and Parmesan cheese.

Air Frying. Place the broccoli in the air fryer basket in a single layer and set the timer and steam for 4 minutes.

Nutrition:
Calories: 130 Fat: 3
Carbs: 5 Protein: 4

663. Caramelized Broccoli
Preparation Time: 5 minutes
Cooking Time: 10 minutes
Servings: 4
Ingredients:
- 4cups broccoli florets
- 3tablespoons melted ghee or butter-flavored coconut oil
- 1½ teaspoons fine sea salt or smoked salt
- Mayonnaise, for serving (optional; omit for egg-free)

Directions:
- Preparing the Ingredients. Grease the basket with avocado oil. Preheat the air fryer to 400°F. Place the broccoli in a large bowl. Drizzle it with the ghee, toss to coat, and sprinkle it with the salt.
- Air Frying. Transfer the broccoli to the air fryer basket and cook for 8 minutes, or until tender and crisp on the edges.

Nutrition:
Calories: 120
Fat: 2
Carbs: 4
Protein: 3

664. Brussels Sprouts With Balsamic Oil
Preparation Time: 5 minutes
Cooking Time: 15 minutes
Servings: 4
Ingredients:
- ¼ teaspoon salt
- 1 tablespoon balsamic vinegar
- 2cups Brussels sprouts, halved
- 3tablespoons olive oil

Directions:
- Preparing the Ingredients. Preheat the air fryer for 5 minutes. Mix all ingredients in a bowl until the zucchini fries are well coated.
- Air Frying. Place in the air fryer basket. Close and cook for 15 minutes for 350°F.

Nutrition:
Calories: 82;
Fat: 6.8g;
Protein: 1.5g

665. Spiced Butternut Squash
Preparation Time: 10 minutes
Cooking Time: 15 minutes
Servings: 4
Ingredients:
- 4cups 1-inch-cubed butternut squash
- 2tablespoons vegetable oil
- 1 to 2 tablespoons brown sugar
- 1 teaspoon Chinese five-spice powder

Directions:
- Preparing the Ingredients. In a bowl, combine the oil, sugar, squash, and five-spice powder. Toss to coat.
- Place the squash in the air fryer basket.
- Air Frying. Set the air fryer to 400°F for 15 minutes or until tender.

Nutrition:
Calories: 160
Fat: 5
Carbs: 9
Protein: 6

666. Garlic Thyme Mushrooms
Preparation Time: 5 minutes
Cooking Time: 10 minutes
Servings: 4
Ingredients:
- 3tablespoons unsalted butter, melted
- 1 (8-ounce) package button mushrooms, sliced
- 2cloves garlic, minced
- 3sprigs fresh thyme leaves
- ½ teaspoon fine sea salt

Directions:
- Preparing the Ingredients. Grease the basket with avocado oil. Preheat the air fryer to 400°F.

Place all the ingredients in a medium-sized bowl. Use a spoon or your hands to coat the mushroom slices.

Air Frying. Put the mushrooms in the basket in one layer; work in batches if necessary. Cook for 10 minutes, or until slightly crispy and brown. Garnish with thyme sprigs before serving.

Reheat in a warmed up 350°F air fryer for 5 minutes, or until heated through.

Nutrition:
Calories 82;
Fat 9g;
Protein 1g;
Total carbs 1g;
Fiber 0.2g

667. Zucchini Parmesan Chips

Preparation Time: 10 minutes
Cooking Time: 10 minutes
Servings: 10
Ingredients:
- ½ tsp. paprika
- ½ C. grated parmesan cheese
- ½ C. Italian breadcrumbs
- 1 lightly beaten egg
- 2 thinly sliced zucchinis

Directions:

Preparing the Ingredients. Use a very sharp knife or mandolin slicer to slice zucchini as thinly as you can. Pat off extra moisture. Beat egg with a pinch of pepper and salt and a bit of water.

Combine paprika, cheese, and breadcrumbs in a bowl. Dip slices of zucchini into the egg mixture and then into breadcrumb mixture. Press gently to coat.

Air Frying. With olive oil cooking spray, mist coated zucchini slices. Place into your Air fryer in a single layer. Set temperature to 350°F, and set time to 8 minutes. Sprinkle with salt and serve with salsa.

Nutrition:
Calories: 130
Fat: 2
Carbs: 5
Protein: 3

668. Jicama Fries

Preparation Time: 10 minutes
Cooking Time: 5 minutes
Servings: 4
Ingredients:
- 1 tbsp. dried thyme
- ¾ C. arrowroot flour
- ½ large Jicama
- Eggs

Directions:

Preparing the Ingredients. Sliced jicama into fries.

Whisk eggs together and pour over fries. Toss to coat.

Mix a pinch of salt, thyme, and arrowroot flour together. Toss egg-coated jicama into dry mixture, tossing to coat well.

Air Frying. Spray the air fryer basket with olive oil and add fries. Set temperature to 350°F, and set time to 5 minutes. Toss halfway into the cooking process.

Nutrition:
Calories: 211;
Fat: 19g;
Carbs: 16g;
Protein: 9g

669. Cauliflower Pizza Crust

Preparation Time: 5 minutes
Cooking Time: 20 minutes
Servings: 6
Ingredients:
- 1 (12-oz.) Steamer bag cauliflower
- 1 large egg
- ½ cup shredded sharp cheddar cheese
- 2 tbsp. Blanched finely ground almond flour
- 1 tsp. Italian blend seasoning

Directions:

- Cook cauliflower according to package. Take out from bag and place into a paper towel to remove excess water. Place cauliflower into a large bowl.
- Add almond flour, cheese, egg, and italian seasoning to the bowl and mix well
- Cut a piece of parchment to fit your air fryer basket. Press cauliflower into 6-inch round circle. Place into the air fryer basket. Adjust the temperature to 360 degrees f and set the timer for 11 minutes. After 7 minutes, flip the pizza crust
- Add preferred toppings to pizza. Place back into air fryer basket and cook an additional 4 minutes or until fully cooked and golden. Serve immediately.

Nutrition:
Calories: 230;
Protein: 14.9g;
Fiber: 4.7g;
Fat: 14.2g;
Carbs: 10.0g

670. Savoy Cabbage And Tomatoes

Preparation Time: 5 minutes
Cooking Time: 20 minutes
Servings: 4
Ingredients:

- 2 spring onions; chopped.
- 1 savoy cabbage, shredded
- 1 tbsp. Parsley; chopped.
- 2 tbsp. Tomato sauce
- Salt and black pepper to taste.

Directions:

- In a pan that fits your air fryer, mix the cabbage the rest of the ingredients except the parsley, toss, put the pan in the fryer and cook at 360°f for 15 minutes
- Divide between plates and serve with parsley sprinkled on top.

Nutrition:
Calories: 163;
Fat: 4g;
Fiber: 3g;
Carbs: 6g;
Protein: 7g

671. Cauliflower Steak

Preparation Time: 5 minutes
Cooking Time: 10 minutes
Servings: 4
Ingredients:

- 1 medium head cauliflower
- ¼ cup blue cheese crumbles
- ¼ cup hot sauce
- ¼ cup full-fat ranch dressing
- 2 tbsp. Salted butter; melted.

Directions:

- Remove cauliflower leaves. Slice the head in ½-inch-thick slices.
- In a small bowl, mix hot sauce and butter. Brush the mixture over the cauliflower.
- Place each cauliflower steak into the air fryer, working in batches if necessary. Adjust the temperature to 400 degrees f and set the timer for 7 minutes
- When cooked, edges will begin turning dark and caramelized. To serve, sprinkle steaks with crumbled blue cheese. Drizzle with ranch dressing.

Nutrition:
Calories: 122; Protein: 4.9g;
Fiber: 3.0g; Fat: 8.4g; Carbs: 7.7g

672. Tomato, Avocado And Green Beans

Preparation Time: 5 minutes
Cooking Time: 20 minutes
Servings: 4
Ingredients:

- ¼ lb. Green beans, trimmed and halved

1 avocado, peeled, pitted and cubed
1 pint mixed cherry tomatoes; halved
2tbsp. Olive oil

Directions:

In a pan that fits your air fryer, mix the tomatoes with the rest of the ingredients, toss.

Put the pan in the fryer and cook at 360°f for 15 minutes. Transfer to bowls and serve

Nutrition:
Calories: 151;
Fat: 3g;
Fiber: 2g;
Carbs: 4g;
Protein: 4g

673. Dill And Garlic Green Beans

Preparation Time: 5 minutes
Cooking Time: 20 minutes
Servings: 4
Ingredients:

1 lb. Green beans, trimmed
½ cup bacon, cooked and chopped.
2garlic cloves; minced
2tbsp. Dill; chopped.
Salt and black pepper to taste.

Directions:

In a pan that fits the air fryer, combine the green beans with the rest of the ingredients, toss.

Put the pan in the fryer and cook at 390°f for 15 minutes

Divide everything between plates and serve.

Nutrition:
Calories: 180;
Fat: 3g;
Fiber: 2g;
Carbs: 4g;
Protein: 6g

674. Eggplant Stacks

Preparation Time: 5 minutes
Cooking Time: 15 minutes
Servings: 4
Ingredients:

2large tomatoes; cut into ¼-inch slices
¼ cup fresh basil, sliced
4oz. Fresh mozzarella; cut into ½-oz. Slices
1 medium eggplant; cut into ¼-inch slices
2tbsp. Olive oil

Directions:

In a 6-inch round baking dish, place four slices of eggplant on the bottom. Put a slice of tomato on each eggplant round, then mozzarella, then eggplant. Repeat as necessary.

Drizzle with olive oil. Cover dish with foil and place dish into the air fryer basket. Adjust the temperature to 350 degrees f and set the timer for 12 minutes.

When done, eggplant will be tender. Garnish with fresh basil to serve.

Nutrition:
Calories: 195;
Protein: 8.5g;
Fiber: 5.2g;
Fat: 12.7g;
Carbs: 12.7g

675. Air Fried Spaghetti Squash

Preparation Time: 5 minutes
Cooking Time: 50 minutes
Servings: 4
Ingredients:

½ large spaghetti squash
2tbsp. Salted butter; melted.
1 tbsp. Coconut oil
1tsp. Dried parsley.
½tsp. Garlic powder.

Directions:

Brush shell of spaghetti squash with coconut oil. Place the skin side down and brush

the inside with butter. Sprinkle with garlic powder and parsley.
- Place squash with the skin side down into the air fryer basket. Adjust the temperature to 350 degrees f and set the timer for 30 minutes
- When the timer beeps, flip the squash so skin side is up and cook an additional 15 minutes or until fork tender. Serve warm.

Nutrition:
Calories: 182;
Protein: 1.9g;
Fiber: 3.9g;
Fat: 11.7g;
Carbs: 18.2g

676. Beets And Blue Cheese Salad

Preparation Time: 10 minutes
Cooking Time: 15 minutes
Servings: 6
Ingredients:
- 6 beets, peeled and quartered
- Salt and black pepper to the taste
- ¼ cup blue cheese, crumbled
- 1 tablespoon olive oil

Directions:
- Put beets in your air fryer, cook them at 350 degrees F for 14 minutes and transfer them to a bowl. Add blue cheese, salt, pepper and oil, toss and serve. Enjoy!

Nutrition:
Calories 100, Fat 4,
Fiber 4, Carbs 10, Protein 5

677. Broccoli Salad

Preparation Time: 10 minutes
Cooking Time: 10 minutes
Servings: 4
Ingredients:
- 1 broccoli head, with separated florets
- 1 tbsp. peanut oil
- 6 cloves of garlic, minced
- 1 tbsp. Chinese rice wine vinegar
- Salt and black pepper to taste

Directions:
- In a bowl, mix broccoli half of the oil with salt, pepper and, toss, transfer to your air fryer and cook at 350 degrees F for 8 minutes. Halfway through, shake the fryer. Take the broccoli out and put it into a salad bowl, add the rest of the peanut oil, garlic and rice vinegar, mix really well and serve. Enjoy!

Nutrition:
Calories 121,
Fat 3,
Fiber 4,
Carbs 4,
Protein 4

678. Roasted Brussels Sprouts With Tomatoes

Preparation Time: 5 minutes
Cooking Time: 10 minutes
Servings: 4
Ingredients:
- 1-pound Brussels sprouts, trimmed
- Salt and black pepper to the taste
- 6 cherry tomatoes, halved
- ¼ cup green onions, chopped
- 1 tablespoon olive oil

Directions:
- Season Brussels sprouts with salt and pepper, put them in your air fryer and cook at 350 degrees F for 10 minutes. Transfer them to a bowl, add salt, pepper, cherry tomatoes, green onions and olive oil, toss well and serve. Enjoy!

Nutrition:
Calories 121, Fat 4,
Fiber 4, Carbs 11,
Protein 4

679. Cheesy Brussels Sprouts

Preparation Time: 10 minutes
Cooking Time: 10 minutes
Servings: 4
Ingredients:
- 1-pound Brussels sprouts, washed
- Juice of 1 lemon
- Salt and black pepper to the taste
- 2 tablespoons butter
- 3 tablespoons parmesan, grated

Directions:
Put Brussels sprouts in your air fryer, cook them at 350 degrees F for 8 minutes and transfer them to a bowl. Warm up a pan over moderate heat with the butter, then add lemon juice, salt and pepper, whisk well and add to Brussels sprouts. Add parmesan, toss until parmesan melts and serve. Enjoy!

Nutrition:
Calories 152, Fat 6,
Fiber 6, Carbs 8,
Protein 12

680. Sweet Baby Carrots Dish

Preparation Time: 10 minutes
Cooking Time: 10 minutes
Servings: 4
Ingredients:
- 2 cups baby carrots
- A pinch of salt and black pepper
- 1 tablespoon brown sugar
- ½ tablespoon butter, melted

Directions:
In a dish that fits your air fryer, mix baby carrots with butter, salt, pepper and sugar, toss, introduce in your air fryer and cook at 350 degrees F for 10 minutes. Divide among plates and serve. Enjoy!

Nutrition:
Calories 100, Fat 2,
Fiber 3, Carbs 7, Protein 4

681. Seasoned Leeks

Preparation Time: 10 minutes
Cooking Time: 10 minutes
Servings: 4
Ingredients:
- 4 leeks, washed, halved
- Salt and black pepper to taste
- 1 tbsp. butter, melted
- 1 tbsp. lemon juice

Directions:
Rub leeks with melted butter, season with salt and pepper, put in your air fryer and cook at 350 degrees F for 7 minutes. Arrange on a platter, drizzle lemon juice all over and serve. Enjoy!

Nutrition:
Calories 100,
Fat 4,
Fiber 2,
Carbs 6,
Protein 2

682. Crispy Potatoes And Parsley

Preparation Time: 10 minutes
Cooking Time: 10 minutes
Servings: 4
Ingredients:
- 1-pound gold potatoes, cut into wedges
- Salt and black pepper to the taste
- 2 tablespoons olive
- Juice from ½ lemon
- ¼ cup parsley leaves, chopped

Directions:
Rub potatoes with salt, pepper, lemon juice and olive oil, put them in your air fryer and cook at 350 degrees F for 10 minutes. Divide among plates, sprinkle parsley on top and serve. Enjoy!

Nutrition:
Calories 152, Fat 3,
Fiber 7, Carbs 17,
Protein 4

683. Garlic Tomatoes

Preparation Time: 10 minutes
Cooking Time: 15 minutes
Servings: 4
Ingredients:
- 4 garlic cloves, crushed
- 1-pound mixed cherry tomatoes
- 3 thyme springs, chopped
- Salt and black pepper to the taste
- ¼ cup olive oil

Directions:
In a bowl, mix tomatoes with salt, black pepper, garlic, olive oil and thyme, toss to coat, introduce in your air fryer and cook at 360 degrees F for 15 minutes. Divide tomatoes mix on plates and serve. Enjoy!

Nutrition:
Calories 100, Fat 0,
Fiber 1, Carbs 1, Protein 6

684. Easy Green Beans And Potatoes

Preparation Time: 10 minutes
Cooking Time: 15 minutes
Servings: 5
Ingredients:
- 2 pounds green beans
- 6 new potatoes, halved
- Salt and black pepper to the taste
- A drizzle of olive oil
- 6 bacon slices, cooked and chopped

Directions:
In a bowl, mix green beans with potatoes, salt, pepper and oil, toss, transfer to your air fryer and cook at 390 degrees F for 15 minutes. Divide among plates and serve with bacon sprinkled on top. Enjoy!

Nutrition:
Calories 374, Fat 15,
Fiber 12, Carbs 28,
Protein 12

685. Green Beans And Tomatoes

Preparation Time: 10 minutes
Cooking Time: 15 minutes
Servings: 4
Ingredients:
- 1 pint cherry tomatoes
- 1 pound green beans
- 2 tablespoons olive oil
- Salt and black pepper to the taste

Directions:
In a bowl, mix cherry tomatoes with green beans, olive oil, salt and pepper, toss, transfer to your air fryer and cook at 400 degrees F for 15 minutes. Divide among plates and serve right away. Enjoy!

Nutrition:
Calories 162,
Fat 6,
Fiber 5,
Carbs 8,
Protein 9

686. Flavored Asparagus

Preparation Time: 5 minutes
Cooking Time: 30 minutes
Servings: 2
Ingredients:
- Nutritional yeast
- Olive oil non-stick spray
- One bunch of asparagus

Directions:
Wash asparagus and then cut off the bushy, woody ends. Drizzle asparagus with olive oil spray and sprinkle with yeast. In your air fryer, lay asparagus in a singular layer. Cook 8 minutes at 360 degrees.

Nutrition:
Calories: 17 Cal
Fat: 4 g
Carbs: 32 g
Protein: 24 g

687. Avocado Fries

Preparation Time: 5 minutes
Cooking Time: 5 minutes
Servings: 6
Ingredients:
- 1 avocado
- ½ tsp. salt
- ½ C. panko breadcrumbs
- Bean liquid (aquafaba) from a 15-ounce can of white or garbanzo beans

Directions:
Peel, pit, and slice up avocado. Toss salt and breadcrumbs together in a bowl. Place aquafaba into another bowl. Dredge slices of avocado first in aquafaba and then in panko, making sure you get an even coating. Place coated avocado slices into a single layer in the air fryer. Cook 5 minutes at 390 degrees, shaking at 5 minutes. Serve with your favorite keto dipping sauce!

Nutrition:
Calories: 102
Fat: 22g
Protein: 9g
Sugar: 1g

688. Spaghetti Squash Tots

Preparation Time: 5 minutes
Cooking Time: 15 minutes
Servings: 10
Ingredients:
- ¼ tsp. pepper
- ½ tsp. salt
- 1 thinly sliced scallion
- 1 spaghetti squash

Directions:
Wash and cut the squash in lengthwise. Scrape out the seeds. With a fork, remove spaghetti meat by strands and throw out skins. In a clean towel, toss in squash and wring out as much moisture as possible. Place in a bowl and with a knife slice through meat a few times to cut up smaller. Add pepper, salt, and scallions to squash and mix well. Create "tot" shapes with your hands and place in air fryer. Spray with olive oil. Cook 15 minutes at 350 degrees until golden and crispy!

Nutrition:
Calories: 231
Fat: 18g
Protein: 5g
Sugar: 0g

689. Cinnamon Butternut Squash Fries

Preparation Time: 10 minutes
Cooking Time: 10 minutes
Servings: 2
Ingredients:
- 1 pinch of salt
- 1 tbsp. powdered unprocessed sugar
- 2tsp. cinnamon
- 1 tbsp. coconut oil
- 10ounces pre-cut butternut squash fries

Directions:
In a plastic bag, pour in all ingredients. Coat fries with other components till coated and sugar is dissolved. Spread coated fries into a single layer in the air fryer. Cook 10 minutes at 390 degrees until crispy.

Nutrition:
Calories: 175 Fat: 8g
Protein: 1g Sugar: 5g

690. Lemon Bell Peppers

Preparation Time: 20 minutes
Cooking Time: 15 minutes
Servings: 4
Ingredients:
- 1 ½ lb. Mixed bell peppers; halved and deseeded
- 2tbsp. Lemon juice

2tbsp. Balsamic vinegar
2tsp. Lemon zest, grated
A handful parsley; chopped.

Directions:
Put the peppers in your air fryer's basket and cook at 350°f for 15 minutes. Peel the bell peppers, mix them with the rest of the ingredients, toss and serve

Nutrition:
Calories: 151;Fat: 2g;
Fiber: 3g; Carbs: 5g; Protein: 5g

691. Pesto Tomatoes

Preparation Time: 5 minutes
Cooking Time: 10 minutes
Servings: 4
Ingredients:
Large heirloom tomatoes – 3, cut into ½ inch thick slices.
Pesto – 1 cup
Feta cheese – 8 oz. cut into ½ inch thick slices
Red onion – ½ cup, sliced thinly
Olive oil – 1 tbsp.

Directions:
Spread some pesto on each slice of tomato. Top each tomato slice with a feta slice and onion and drizzle with oil. Arrange the tomatoes onto the greased rack and spray with cooking spray. Arrange the drip pan in the bottom of the Air Fryer Grill cooking chamber. Select "Air Fry" and then set the temperature to 390 °F. Set the time for 14 minutes and press "Start". When the display shows "Add Food" insert the rack in the center position. When the display shows "Turn Food" do not turn food. When Cooking Time is complete, remove the rack from the Air Fryer Grill. Serve warm.

Nutrition:
Calories 480, Carbs 13g,
Fat 41.9g, Protein 15.4g

692. Seasoned Potatoes

Preparation Time: 5 minutes
Cooking Time: 40 minutes
Servings: 2
Ingredients:
Russet potatoes – 2, scrubbed
Butter – ½ tbsp. melted
Garlic & herb blend seasoning – ½ tsp.
Garlic powder – ½ tsp.
Salt, as required

Directions:
In a bowl, mix all of the spices and salt. With a fork, prick the potatoes. Coat the potatoes with butter and sprinkle with spice mixture. Arrange the potatoes onto the cooking rack. Arrange the drip pan in the bottom of the Air Fryer Grill cooking chamber. Choose "Air Fry" and then set the temperature to 400 °F. Set the time for 40 minutes and press "Start". When the display shows "Add Food" insert the cooking rack in the center position. When the display shows "Turn Food" do nothing. Once cooking is done, remove the tray from the Air Fryer Grill. Serve hot.

Nutrition:
Calories 176,
Carbs 34.2g,
Fat 2.1g,
Protein 3.8g

693. Spicy Zucchini

Preparation Time: 10 minutes
Cooking Time: 15 minutes
Servings: 4
Ingredients:
Zucchini – 1 lb. cut into ½-inch thick slices lengthwise
Olive oil – 1 tbsp.
Garlic powder – ½ tsp.
Cayenne pepper – ½ tsp.
Salt and ground black pepper, as required

Directions:

Put all of the ingredients into a bowl and toss to coat well. Arrange the zucchini slices onto a cooking tray. Arrange the drip pan in the bottom of the Air Fryer Grill cooking chamber. Choose "Air Fry" and then set the temperature to 400 °F. Set the time for 12 minutes and press "Start". When the display shows "Add Food" insert the cooking tray in the center position. When the display shows "Turn Food" do nothing. Once cooking is done, remove the tray from the Air Fryer Grill. Serve hot.

Nutrition:
Calories 67,
Carbs 5.6g,
Fat 5g,
Protein 2g

694. Seasoned Yellow Squash

Preparation Time: 5 minutes
Cooking Time: 10 minutes
Servings: 4
Ingredients:

- Large yellow squash – 4, cut into slices
- Olive oil – ¼ cup
- Onion – ½, sliced
- Italian seasoning – ¾ tsp.
- Garlic salt – ½ tsp.
- Seasoned salt – ¼ tsp.

Directions:

In a bowl, mix all the ingredients together. Place the veggie mixture in the greased cooking tray. Arrange the drip pan in the bottom of the Air Fryer Grill cooking chamber. Choose "Air Fry" and then set the temperature to 400 °F. Set the time for 10 minutes and press "Start". When the display shows "Add Food" insert the cooking tray in the center position. When the display shows "Turn Food" turn the vegetables. Once cooking is done, remove the tray from the Air Fryer Grill. Serve hot.

Nutrition:
Calories 113,
Carbs 8.1g,
Fat 9g,
Protein 4.2g

695. Buttered Asparagus

Preparation Time: 5 minutes
Cooking Time: 10 minutes
Servings: 4
Ingredients:

- Fresh thick asparagus spears – 1 lb. trimmed
- Butter – 1 tbsp. melted
- Salt and ground black pepper, as required

Directions:

Put all of the ingredients into a bowl and toss to coat well. Arrange the asparagus onto a cooking tray. Arrange the drip pan in the bottom of the Air Fryer Grill cooking chamber. Choose "Air Fry" and then set the temperature to 350 °F. Set the time for 10 minutes and press "Start". When the display shows "Add Food" insert the cooking tray in the center position. When the display shows "Turn Food" turn the asparagus. Once cooking is done, remove the tray from the Air Fryer Grill. Serve hot.

Nutrition:
Calories 64,
Carbs 5.9g,
Fat 4g,
Protein 3.4g

696. Buttered Broccoli

Preparation Time: 5 minutes
Cooking Time: 15 minutes
Servings: 4
Ingredients:

- Broccoli florets – 1 lb.
- Butter – 1 tbsp. melted

Red pepper flakes – ½ tsp. crushed
Salt and ground black pepper, as required

Directions:

Gather all of the ingredients in a bowl and toss to coat well. Place the broccoli florets in the rotisserie basket and attach the lid. Arrange the drip pan in the bottom of the Air Fryer Grill cooking chamber. Choose "Air Fry" and then set the temperature to 400 °F. Fix the time for 15 minutes and press "Start". Then, close the door and touch "Rotate". When the display shows "Add Food" arrange the rotisserie basket, on the rotisserie spit. Then, close the door and touch "Rotate". When Cooking Time is complete, press the red lever to release the rod. Remove from the Air Fryer Grill. Serve immediately.

Nutrition:
Calories 55, Carbs 6.1g,
Fat 3g, Protein 2.3g

697. Seasoned Carrots With Green Beans

Preparation Time: 5 minutes
Cooking Time: 10 minutes
Servings: 4
Ingredients:

Green beans – ½ lb. trimmed
Carrots – ½ lb. peeled and cut into sticks
Olive oil – 1 tbsp.
Salt and ground black pepper, as required

Directions:

Gather all the ingredients into a bowl and toss to coat well. Place the vegetables in the rotisserie basket and attach the lid. Arrange the drip pan in the bottom of the Air Fryer Grill cooking chamber. Choose "Air Fry" and then set the temperature to 400 °F. Set the time for 10 minutes and press "Start". Then, close the door and touch "Rotate". When the display shows "Add Food" arrange the rotisserie basket, on the rotisserie spit. Then, close the door and touch "Rotate". When Cooking Time is complete, press the red lever to release the rod. Remove from the Air Fryer Grill. Serve hot.

Nutrition:
Calories 94, Carbs 12.7g,
Fat 4.8g, Protein 2g

698. Sweet Potato With Broccoli

Preparation Time: 5 minutes
Cooking Time: 20 minutes
Servings: 4
Ingredients:

Medium sweet potatoes – 2, peeled and cut in 1-inch cubes
Broccoli head – 1, cut in 1-inch florets
Vegetable oil – 2 tbsps.
Salt and ground black pepper, as required

Directions:

Grease a baking dish that will fit in the Air Fryer Grill. Gather all of the ingredients into a bowl and toss to coat well. Place the veggie mixture into the prepared baking dish in a single layer. Arrange the drip pan in the bottom of Air Fryer Grill cooking chamber. Select "Roast" and then adjust the temperature to 415 °F. Set the time for 20 minutes and press "Start". When the display shows "Add Food" insert the baking dish in the center position. When the display shows "Turn Food" turn the vegetables. When Cooking Time is complete, remove the baking dish from the Air Fryer Grill. Serve hot.

Nutrition:
Calories 170, Carbs 25.2g,
Fat 7.1g,
Protein 2.9g

699. Seasoned Veggies

Preparation Time: 5 minutes
Cooking Time: 12 minutes
Servings: 4
Ingredients:
- Baby carrots – 1 cup
- Broccoli florets – 1 cup
- Cauliflower florets – 1 cup
- Olive oil – 1 tbsp.
- Italian seasoning – 1 tbsp.
- Salt and ground black pepper, as required

Directions:
Gather all of the ingredients into a bowl and toss to coat well. Place the vegetables in the rotisserie basket and attach the lid. Arrange the drip pan in the bottom of the Air Fryer Grill cooking chamber. Choose "Air Fry" and then set the temperature to 380 °F. Set the time for 18 minutes and press "Start". Then, close the door and touch "Rotate". When the display shows "Add Food" arrange the rotisserie basket, on the rotisserie spit. Then, close the door and touch "Rotate". When Cooking Time is complete, press the red lever to release the rod. Remove from the Air Fryer Grill. Serve.

Nutrition:
Calories 66, Carbs 5.7g,
Fat 4.7g,
Protein 1.4g

700. Potato Gratin

Preparation Time: 5 minutes
Cooking Time: 20 minutes
Servings: 4
Ingredients:
- Large potatoes – 2, sliced thinly
- Cream – 5½ tbsps.
- Eggs – 2
- Plain flour – 1 tbsp.
- Cheddar cheese – ½ cup, grated

Directions:
Arrange the potato cubes onto the greased rack. Arrange the drip pan in the bottom of the Air Fryer Grill cooking chamber. Choose "Air Fry" and then set the temperature to 355 °F. Set the time for 10 minutes and press "Start". When the display shows "Add Food" insert the cooking rack in the center position. When the display shows "Turn Food" do not turn food. Meanwhile, in a bowl, add cream, eggs and flour and mix until a thick sauce form. Once cooking is done, remove the tray from the Air Fryer Grill. Divide the potato slices into 4 lightly greased ramekins evenly and top with the egg mixture, followed by the cheese. Arrange the ramekins on top of a cooking rack. Again, select "Air Fry" and then adjust the temperature to 390 °F. Set the time for 10 minutes and press "Start". When the display shows "Add Food" insert the cooking rack in the center position. When the display shows "Turn Food" do not turn food. When Cooking Time is complete, remove the ramekins from the Air Fryer Grill. Serve warm.

Nutrition:
Calories 233, Carbs 31.g,
Fat 8g,
Protein 9.7g

701. Garlic Edamame

Preparation Time: 5 minutes
Cooking Time: 10 minutes
Servings: 4
Ingredients:
- Olive oil
- 1 (16-ounce) bag frozen edamame in pods
- salt and freshly ground black pepper
- ½ teaspoon garlic salt
- ½ teaspoon red pepper flakes (optional)

Directions:
- Spray a fryer basket lightly with olive oil.
- In a medium bowl, add the frozen edamame and lightly spray with olive oil. Toss to coat.
- In a bowl, combine together the garlic salt, salt, black pepper, and red pepper flakes (if using). Add the mixture to the edamame and toss until evenly coated.
- Place half the edamame in the fryer basket. Do not overfill the basket.
- Air fry for 5 minutes. Shake the basket and cook until the edamame is starting to brown and get crispy, 3 to 5 more minutes.
- Repeat with the remaining edamame and serve immediately.
- Pair It With: These make a nice side dish to almost any meal.
- Air Fry Like a Pro: If you use fresh edamame, reduce the air fry time by 2 to 3 minutes to avoid overcooking. Air-fried edamame do not retain their crisp texture, so it's best to eat them right after cooking.

Nutrition:
Calories: 100;
Total Fat: 3g;
Saturated Fat: 0g;
Carbohydrates: 9g;
Protein: 8g;
Fiber: 4g;
Sodium: 496mg

702. Spicy Chickpeas

Preparation Time: 5 minutes
Cooking Time: 20 minutes
Servings: 4
Ingredients:
- Olive oil
- ½ teaspoon ground cumin
- ½ teaspoon chili powder
- ¼ teaspoon cayenne pepper
- ¼ teaspoon salt
- 1 (19-ounce) can chickpeas, drained and rinsed

Directions:
- Spray a fryer basket lightly with olive oil.
- In a bowl, combine the chili powder, cumin, cayenne pepper, and salt.
- In a medium bowl, add the chickpeas and lightly spray them with olive oil. Add the spice mixture and toss until coated evenly.
- Transfer the chickpeas to the fryer basket. Air fry until the chickpeas reach your desired level of crunchiness, 15 to 20 minutes, making sure to shake the basket every 5 minutes.
- Air Fry Like a Pro: I find 20 minutes to be the sweet spot for very crunchy chickpeas. If you prefer them less crispy, cook for about 15 minutes. These make a great vehicle for experimenting with different seasoning mixes such as Chinese 5-spice, a mixture of curry and turmeric, or herbs de Provence.

Nutrition:
Calories: 122; Total Fat: 1g;
Saturated Fat: 0g; Carbohydrates: 22g;
Protein: 6g; Fiber: 6g; Sodium: 152mg

703. Egg Roll Pizza Sticks

Preparation Time: 10 minutes
Cooking Time: 5 minutes
Servings: 4
Ingredients:
- Olive oil
- 8 pieces reduced-fat string cheese
- 8 egg roll wrappers
- 24 slices turkey pepperoni
- Marinara sauce, for dipping (optional)

Directions:
- Spray a fryer basket lightly with olive oil. Fill a small bowl with water.

- Place each egg roll wrapper diagonally on a work surface. It should look like a diamond.
- Place 3 slices of turkey pepperoni in a vertical line down the center of the wrapper.
- Place 1 mozzarella cheese stick on top of the turkey pepperoni.
- Fold the top and bottom corners of the egg roll wrapper over the cheese stick.
- Fold the left corner over the cheese stick and roll the cheese stick up to resemble a spring roll. Dip a finger in the water and seal the edge of the roll
- Repeat with the rest of the pizza sticks.
- Place them in the fryer basket in a single layer, making sure to leave a little space between each one. Lightly spray the pizza sticks with oil.
- Air fry until the pizza sticks are lightly browned and crispy, about 5 minutes.
- These are best served hot while the cheese is melted. Accompany with a small bowl of marinara sauce, if desired.

Nutrition:
Calories: 362; Total Fat: 8g;
Saturated Fat: 4g;
Cholesterol: 43mg;
Carbohydrates: 40g;
Protein: 23g;
Fiber: 1g;
Sodium: 1,026mg

704. Cajun Zucchini Chips

Preparation Time: 10 minutes
Cooking Time: 15 minutes
Servings: 4
Ingredients:
   Olive oil
   2 large zucchinis, cut into ⅛-inch-thick slices
   2 teaspoons Cajun seasoning

Directions:
- Spray a fryer basket lightly with olive oil.
- Put the zucchini slices in a medium bowl and spray them generously with olive oil.
- Sprinkle the Cajun seasoning over the zucchini and stir to make sure they are evenly coated with oil and seasoning.
- Place slices in a single layer in the fryer basket, making sure not to overcrowd.
- Air fry for 8 minutes. Flip the slices over and air fry until they are as crisp and brown as you prefer, an additional 7 to 8 minutes.
- Air Fry Like a Pro: In order to achieve the best result, it is important not to overcrowd the fryer basket. The zucchini chips turn out best if there is room for the air to circulate around each slice. You can add Cooking Time if you like very brown and crunchy zucchini chips.

Nutrition:
Calories: 26;
Total Fat: <1g;
Carbohydrates: 5g;
Protein: 2g;
Fiber: 2g;
Sodium: 286mg

705. Crispy Old Bay Chicken Wings

Preparation Time: 10 minutes
Cooking Time: 15 minutes
Servings: 4
Ingredients:
   Olive oil
   2 tablespoons Old Bay seasoning
   2 teaspoons baking powder
   2 teaspoons salt
   2 pounds chicken wings

Directions:
- Spray a fryer basket lightly with olive oil.
- In a big resealable bag, combine together the Old Bay seasoning, baking powder, and salt.

Pat the wings dry with paper towels.

Place the wings in the zip-top bag, seal, and toss with the seasoning mixture until evenly coated.

Place the seasoned wings in the fryer basket in a single layer. Lightly spray with olive oil.

Air fry for 7 minutes. Turn the wings over, lightly spray them with olive oil, and air fry until the wings are crispy and lightly browned, 5 to 8 more minutes. Using a meat thermometer, check to make sure the internal temperature is 165°F or higher.

Nutrition:
Calories: 501;
Total Fat: 36g;
Saturated Fat: 10g;
Cholesterol: 170mg;
Carbohydrates: 1g;
Protein: 42g;
Sodium: 2,527mg

706. Cinnamon And Sugar Peaches

Preparation Time: 10 minutes
Cooking Time: 13 minutes
Servings: 4
Ingredients:
- Olive oil
- 2 tablespoons sugar
- ¼ teaspoon ground cinnamon
- 4 peaches, cut into wedges

Directions:

Spray a fryer basket lightly with olive oil.

In a bowl, combine the cinnamon and sugar. Add the peaches and toss to coat evenly.

Place the peaches in a single layer in the fryer basket on their sides.

Air fry for 5 minutes. Turn the peaches skin side down, lightly spray them with oil, and air fry until the peaches are lightly brown and caramelized, 5 to 8 more minutes.

Make it Even Lower Calorie: Use a zero-calorie sugar substitute such as Nutrisweet or monk fruit sweetener instead of granulated sugar.

Air Fry Like a Pro: These do not get truly crispy, but rather they remain soft, sweet, and caramelized. They are truly delightful and make a wonderful dessert option.

Nutrition:
Calories: 67;
Total Fat: <1g;
Carbohydrates: 17g;
Protein: 1g;
Fiber: 2g;
Sodium: 0mg

707. Chicken Wings With Provencal Herbs In Air Fryer

Preparation Time: 15 minutes
Cooking Time: 20 minutes
Servings: 4
Ingredients:
- 1kg chicken wings
- Provencal herbs
- Extra virgin olive oil
- Salt
- Ground pepper

Directions:

We put the chicken wings in a bowl, clean and chopped.

Add a few threads of oil, salt, ground pepper and sprinkle with Provencal herbs.

We linked well and let macerate a few minutes, I had them 15 minutes.

We put the wings in the basket of the Air fryer.

We select 180 degrees, 20 minutes.

From time to time we remove so that they are done on all their faces.

If we see that they have been little golden, we put a few more minutes.

We serve

Nutrition:
Calories: 160 Fat: 6
Carbs: 8 Protein: 13

---

708. Spiced Chicken Wings In Airfryer

Preparation Time: 15 minutes
Cooking Time: 30 minutes
Servings: 4
Ingredients:
- 1 kg chicken wings
- Salt
- Ground pepper
- Extra virgin olive oil
- Spices, I put roasted chicken or roast chicken spices.

Directions:
- We clean the wings and chop, throw the tip and place in a bowl the other two parts of the wings that have more meat.
- We season and add some extra virgin olive oil threads.
- Sprinkle with spices, we can put whatever we want, put spices for roast chicken that they sell as is in supermarkets, in regular spice cans.
- We flirt well and leave for 30 minutes to rest in the refrigerator.
- We put the wings in the basket of the Air fryer and select 180 degrees, about 30 minutes. From 20 minutes, we are checking if we have to remove them before. From time to time, we shake the basket so that the wings move and are made all over their faces.
- We serve

Nutrition:
Calories: 170 Fat: 6
Carbs: 8
Protein: 15

709. Rosti (Swiss Potatoes)

Preparation Time: 10 minutes
Cooking Time: 15 minutes
Servings: 4
Ingredients:
- 250 g peeled white potatoes
- 1 tablespoon finely chopped chives
- Freshly ground black pepper
- 1 tablespoon of olive oil
- 2 tablespoons of sour cream

Directions:
- Preheat the air fryer to 180 ° C. Grate the thick potatoes in a bowl and add three quarters of the chives and salt and pepper to taste. Mix it well.
- Grease the pizza pan with olive oil and spread the potato mixture evenly through the pan. Press the grated potatoes against the pan and spread the top of the potato cake with some olive oil.
- Place the pizza pan inside the fryer basket and insert it into the air fryer. Set the timer to 15 mins and fry the rosti until it has a nice brownish color on the outside and is soft and well done inside.
- Cut the rosti into 4 quarters and place each quarter on a plate. Garnish with a spoonful of sour cream. Spread the remaining of the scallions over the sour cream and add a touch of ground pepper.

Nutrition:
Carbs: 25.2g Fat: 11.7g
Fatty sat: 5.9g Protein: 2.5g
Fibers: 1.9g Sugar: 2.2g

710. Crispy Brussels Sprouts

Preparation Time: 5 minutes
Cooking Time: 10 minutes
Servings: 2
Ingredients:
- ½ lb. Brussels sprouts, cut in half

½ tbsp. oil
½ tbsp. unsalted butter, melted

Directions:
Rub the sprouts with oil.
Place them into the air fry basket.
Cook at 400ºF for 10 minutes. Stir once at the halfway mark.
Remove the air fry basket and drizzle with the melted butter.
Serve.

Nutrition:
Calories: 90
Fats: 6.1 g
Carb: 4 g
Protein: 2.9 g

711. Flatbread

Preparation Time: 5 minutes
Cooking Time: 7 minutes
Servings: 2

Ingredients:
1 cup shredded mozzarella cheese
¼ cup almond flour
1 oz. full-fat cream cheese, softened

Directions:
Melt the mozzarella in the microwave for 30 seconds. Stir in the almond flour until smooth.
Add the cream cheese. Continue mixing until a dough forms. Knead with your wet hands if necessary.
Divide the dough into two pieces and roll out to ¼-inch thickness between two pieces of parchment.
Cover the air fry basket with parchment and place the flatbreads into the air fry basket. Work in batches if necessary.
Cook at 320ºF for 7 minutes. Flip once at the halfway mark.
Serve.

Nutrition:
Calories: 296 Fats: 22.6 g
Carb: 3.3 g Protein: 16.3 g

712. Creamy Cabbage

Preparation Time: 10 minutes
Cooking Time: 20 minutes
Servings: 2

Ingredients:
½ green cabbage head, chopped
½ yellow onion, chopped
Salt and black pepper, to taste
½ cup whipped cream
1 tbsp. cornstarch

Directions:
Put the cabbage and the onion in the Air Fryer Oven.
In a bowl, mix cornstarch with the whipped cream, salt, and pepper. Stir and pour over cabbage.
Toss and cook at 400ºF for 20 minutes.
Serve.

Nutrition:
Calories: 208
Fats: 10 g
Carb: 16 g
Protein: 5 g

713. Creamy Potatoes

Preparation Time: 10 minutes
Cooking Time: 20 minutes
Servings: 2

Ingredients:
¾ lb. potatoes, peeled and cubed
1 tbsp. olive oil
Salt and black pepper, to taste
½ tbsp. hot paprika
½ cup Greek yogurt
1 cup Water

Directions:
Place the potatoes in a bowl, pour the water to cover, and leave aside for 10 minutes. Drain, pat dry and transfer to another bowl.
Add the salt, pepper, paprika, and half of the oil to the potatoes and mix.

Put the potatoes in the air fry basket and cook at 360ºF for 20 minutes.

In a bowl, mix the yogurt with salt, pepper, and the rest of the oil and whisk.

Divide the potatoes onto plates, drizzle with yogurt dressing, mix, and serve.

Nutrition:
Calories: 170
Fats: 3 g
Carb: 20 g
Protein: 5 g

714. Green Beans and Cherry Tomatoes

Preparation Time: 10 minutes
Cooking Time: 15 minutes
Servings: 2
Ingredients:
- 8 oz. cherry tomatoes
- 8 oz. green beans
- 1 tbsp. olive oil
- Salt and black pepper, to taste

Directions:
In a bowl, mix the cherry tomatoes with green beans, olive oil, salt, and pepper. Mix.

Cook in the air fryer at 400ºF for 15 minutes. Shake once.

Serve.

Nutrition:
Calories: 162
Fats: 6 g
Carb: 8 g
Protein: 9 g

715. Crispy Brussels Sprouts and Potatoes

Preparation Time: 10 minutes
Cooking Time: 8 minutes
Servings: 2
Ingredients:
- ¾ lb. Brussels sprouts, washed and trimmed
- ½ cup new potatoes, chopped
- 2 tsp. breadcrumbs
- Salt and black pepper, to taste
- 2 tsp. butter

Directions:
In a bowl, add the Brussels sprouts, potatoes, bread crumbs, salt, pepper, and butter. Mix well.

Place the mixture in the Air Fryer Oven and cook at 400ºF for 8 minutes.

Serve.

Nutrition:
Calories: 152
Fats: 3 g
Carb: 17 g
Protein: 4 g

716. Herbed Tomatoes

Preparation Time: 10 minutes
Cooking Time: 15 minutes
Servings: 2
Ingredients:
- 2 big tomatoes, halved and insides scooped out
- Salt and black pepper, to taste
- ½ tbsp. olive oil
- 1 garlic clove, minced
- ¼ tsp. thyme, chopped

Directions:
In the air fry basket, mix the tomatoes with thyme, garlic, oil, salt, and pepper.

Mix and cook at 390ºF for 15 minutes.

Serve.

Nutrition:
Calories: 112 Fats: 1 g
Carb: 4 g Protein: 4 g

717. Air Fried Leeks

Preparation Time: 10 minutes
Cooking Time: 7 minutes
Servings: 2
Ingredients:
- 2 leeks, washed, ends cut, and halved
- Salt and black pepper, to taste

½ tbsp. butter, melted
½ tbsp. lemon juice

Directions:
Rub the leeks with the melted butter and season with salt and pepper.
Lay them inside the air fryer and cook at 350ºF for 7 minutes.
Arrange them on a platter. Drizzle them with the lemon juice and serve.

Nutrition:
Calories: 100
Fats: 4 g
Carb: 6 g
Protein: 2 g

---

718. Crispy Broccoli

Preparation Time: 10 minutes
Cooking Time: 10 minutes
Servings: 4
Ingredients:
1 large head fresh broccoli
2 tsp. olive oil
2 tpsp Lemon juice

Directions:
Rinse the broccoli and pat it dry. Cut off the florets and separate them (you can also use the broccoli stems too). Cut them into 1-inch chunks and peel them.
Toss the broccoli, olive oil, and lemon juice in a large bowl until coated.
Roast the broccoli in the Air Fry Basket in batches for 10–14 minutes or until the broccoli is crisp-tender and slightly brown around the edges. Repeat with the remaining broccoli. Serve immediately.

Nutrition:
Calories: 63
Fats: 2 g
Protein: 4 g
Carbs: 10 g
Sodium: 50 mg
Fiber: 4 g

719. Garlic-Roasted Bell Peppers

Preparation Time: 5 minutes
Cooking Time: 20 minutes
Servings: 4
Ingredients:
4 bell peppers, any colors, stemmed, seeded, membranes removed, and cut into fourths
1 tsp. olive oil
4 garlic cloves, minced
½ tsp. dried thyme

Directions:
Put the peppers in the air fry basket and drizzle with olive oil. Toss gently. Roast for 15 minutes.
Sprinkle with the garlic and thyme. Roast for 3–5 minutes more, or until tender. Serve immediately.

Nutrition:
Calories: 36
Fats: 1 g
Protein: 1 g
Carbs: 5 g
Sodium: 21 mg
Fiber: 2 g

---

720. Asparagus with Garlic

Preparation Time: 5 minutes
Cooking Time: 10 minutes
Servings: 4
Ingredients:
1-lb. asparagus, rinsed, ends snapped off where they naturally break (see Tip)
2 tsp. olive oil
3 garlic cloves, minced
2 tbsp. balsamic vinegar
½ tsp. dried thyme

Directions:
In a huge bowl, mix the asparagus with olive oil. Transfer to the air fry basket.
Sprinkle with garlic. Roast for 4–5 minutes for crisp-tender or for 8–11 minutes for

the asparagus to get crisp on the outside and tender on the inside.

Drizzle with the balsamic vinegar and the thyme leaves. Serve immediately.

Nutrition:
- Calories: 41
- Fats: 1 g
- Protein: 3 g
- Carbs: 6 g
- Sodium: 3 mg

---

721. Cheesy Roasted Sweet Potatoes

Preparation Time: 5 minutes
Cooking Time: 20 minutes
Servings: 4
Ingredients:
- 2 large sweet potatoes, peeled and sliced
- 1 tsp. olive oil
- 1 tbsp. white balsamic vinegar
- 1 tsp. dried thyme
- ¼ cup grated Parmesan cheese

Directions:
In a big bowl, shower the sweet potato slices with the olive oil and toss.

Sprinkle with the balsamic vinegar and thyme and toss again.

Sprinkle the potatoes with the Parmesan cheese and toss to coat.

Roast the slices in the air fryer basket in batches for 18–23 minutes, tossing the sweet potato slices in the basket during cooking, until tender.

Repeat with the remaining sweet potato slices. Serve immediately.

Nutrition:
- Calories: 100
- Fats: 3 g
- Protein: 4 g
- Carbs: 15 g
- Sodium: 132 mg

---

722. Salty Lemon Artichokes

Preparation Time: 15 minutes
Cooking Time: 45 minutes
Servings: 2
Ingredients:
- 1 lemon
- 2 artichokes
- 1 tsp. kosher salt
- 1 garlic head
- 2 tsp. olive oil

Directions:
Cut off the edges of the artichokes.

Cut the lemon into the halves.

Peel the garlic head and chop the garlic cloves roughly.

Then place the chopped garlic in the artichokes.

Sprinkle the artichokes with the olive oil and kosher salt.

Then squeeze the lemon juice into the artichokes.

Wrap the artichokes in the foil.

Preheat the Air Fryer Oven to 330ºF.

Place the wrapped artichokes in the air fryer and cook for 45 minutes.

When the artichokes are cooked, discard the foil and serve.

Enjoy!

Nutrition:
- Calories: 133
- Fats: 5 g
- Fiber: 9.7 g
- Carbs: 21.7 g
- Protein: 6 g

---

723. Asparagus & Parmesan

Preparation Time: 10 minutes
Cooking Time: 6 minutes
Servings: 2
Ingredients:
- 1 tsp. sesame oil
- 11 oz. asparagus
- 1 tsp. chicken stock

½ tsp. ground white pepper
3 oz. Parmesan

Directions:

Wash the asparagus and chop them roughly.

Sprinkle the chopped asparagus with the chicken stock and ground white pepper.

Then sprinkle the asparagus with the sesame oil and shake them.

Place the asparagus in the air fry basket.

Cook the vegetables for 4 minutes at 400ºF.

Meanwhile, shred the Parmesan cheese.

When the time is over, shake the asparagus gently and sprinkle with the shredded cheese.

Cook the asparagus for 2 minutes more at 400ºF.

After this, transfer the cooked asparagus in the serving plates.

Serve and taste it!

Nutrition:

Calories: 189
Fats: 11.6 g
Fiber: 3.4 g
Carbs: 7.9 g
Protein: 17.2 g

724. Corn on Cobs

Preparation Time: 10 minutes
Cooking Time: 10 minutes
Servings: 2
Ingredients:

2 fresh corn on cobs
2 tsp. butter
1 tsp. salt
1 tsp. paprika
¼ tsp. olive oil

Directions:

Preheat the Air Fryer Oven to 400ºF.

Rub the corn on cobs with the salt and paprika.

Then sprinkle the corn on cobs with the olive oil.

Place the corn on cobs in the air fry basket.

Cook the corn on cobs for 10 minutes.

When the time is over, transfer the corn on cobs in the serving plates and rub with the butter gently.

Serve the meal immediately.

Enjoy!

Nutrition:

Calories: 122
Fats: 5.5 g
Fiber: 2.4 g
Carbs: 17.6 g
Protein: 3.2 g

725. Onion Green Beans

Preparation Time: 10 minutes
Cooking Time: 12 minutes
Servings: 2
Ingredients:

11 oz green beans
1 tbsp. onion powder
1 tbsp. olive oil
½ tsp. salt
¼ tsp. chili flakes

Directions:

Wash the green beans carefully and place them in a bowl.

Sprinkle the green beans with the onion powder, salt, chili flakes, and olive oil.

Shake the green beans carefully.

Preheat the Air Fryer Oven to 400ºF.

Put the green beans in the Air Fryer Oven and cook for 8 minutes.

After this, shake the green beans and cook them for 4 minutes more at 400ºF.

When the time is over, shake the green beans.

Serve the side dish and enjoy!

Nutrition:

Calories: 1205
Fats: 7.2 g
Fiber: 5.5 g
Carbs: 13.9 g
Protein: 3.2 g

726. Dill Mashed Potato

Preparation Time: 10 minutes
Cooking Time: 15 minutes
Servings: 2

Ingredients:
- 2 potatoes
- 2 tbsp. fresh dill, chopped
- 1 tsp. butter
- ½ tsp. salt
- ¼ cup half and half

Directions:
- Preheat the air fryer to 390ºF.
- Rinse the potatoes thoroughly and place them in the Air Fryer Oven.
- Cook the potatoes for 15 minutes.
- After this, remove the potatoes from the Air Fryer Oven.
- Peel the potatoes.
- Mash the potatoes well with the help of the fork.
- Then add the chopped fresh dill and salt.
- Stir it gently and add the butter and half and half.
- Take the hand blender and blend the mixture well.
- When the mashed potato is cooked, serve it immediately. Enjoy!

Nutrition:
- Calories: 211 Fats: 5.7 g
- Fiber: 5.5 g
- Carbs: 36.5 g
- Protein: 5.1 g

727. Cream Potato

Preparation Time: 15 minutes
Cooking Time: 20 minutes
Servings: 2

Ingredients:
- 3 medium potatoes, scrubbed
- ½ tsp. kosher salt
- 1 tbsp. Italian seasoning
- ⅓ cup cream
- ½ tsp. ground black pepper

Directions:
- Slice the potatoes.
- Preheat the air fryer to 365 F.
- Make the first layer from the sliced potato in the air fry basket.
- Sprinkle the potato layer with the kosher salt and ground black pepper.
- After this, make the second layer of the potato and sprinkle it with the Italian seasoning.
- Make the last layer of the sliced potato and pour the cream.
- Cook the scallop potato for 20 minutes.
- When the scalloped potato is cooked, let it chill till the room temperature. Enjoy!

Nutrition:
- Calories: 269
- Fats: 4.7 g
- Fiber: 7.8 g
- Carbs: 52.6 g
- Protein: 5.8 g

728. Chili Squash Wedges

Preparation Time: 10 minutes
Cooking Time: 18 minutes
Servings: 2

Ingredients:
- 11 oz Acorn squash
- ½ tsp. salt
- 1 tbsp. olive oil
- ½ tsp. chili pepper
- ½ tsp. paprika

Directions:
- Cut the Acorn squash into the wedges.
- Sprinkle the wedges with the salt, olive oil, chili pepper, and paprika.
- Massage the wedges gently.
- Preheat the Air Fryer Oven to 400ºF.
- Put the Acorn squash wedges in the air fry basket and cook for 18 minutes.
- Flip the wedges onto another side after 9 minutes of cooking.

Serve the cooked meal hot. Enjoy!

Nutrition:
Calories: 125 Fats: 7.2 g
Fiber: 2.6 g Carbs: 16.7 g
Protein: 1.4 g

729. Honey Carrots with Greens

Preparation Time: 7 minutes
Cooking Time: 12 minutes
Servings: 2
Ingredients:
1 cup baby carrot
½ tsp. salt
½ tsp. white pepper
1 tbsp. honey
1 tsp. sesame oil

Directions:
Preheat the Air Fryer Oven to 385ºF.
Combine the baby carrot with the salt, white pepper, and sesame oil.
Shake the baby carrot and transfer in the air fry basket.
Cook the vegetables for 10 minutes.
After this, add the honey and shake the carrots.
Cook the meal for 2 minutes.
After this, shake the carrots and serve immediately.
Enjoy!

Nutrition:
Calories: 83 Fats: 2.4 g
Fiber: 2.6 g Carbs: 16 g
Protein: 0.6 g

730. South Asian Cauliflower Fritters

Preparation Time: 5 minutes
Cooking Time: 20 minutes
Servings: 4
Ingredients:
1 large chopped into florets cauliflower
3 tbsp. Greek yogurt
3 tbsp. flour
½ tsp. ground turmeric
½ tsp. ground cumin
½ tsp. ground paprika
12 tsp. ground coriander
½ tsp. salt
½ tsp. black pepper

Directions:
Using a large bowl, add and mix the Greek yogurt, flour, and seasonings properly.
Add the cauliflower florets and toss it until it is well covered
Heat up your air fryer to 390ºF.
Grease your air fry basket with a non-stick cooking spray and add half of the cauliflower florets to it.
Cook it for 10 minutes or until it turns golden brown and crispy, then shake it after 5 minutes. (Repeat this with the other half).
Serve and enjoy!

Nutrition:
Calories: 120 Fats: 4 g
Protein: 7.5 g
Carbs: 14 g
Fiber: 3.4 g

731. Supreme Air-Fried Tofu

Preparation Time: 5 minutes
Cooking Time: 50 minutes
Servings: 4
Ingredients:
1 block extra-firm tofu, pressed and sliced into 1-inch cubes
2 tbsp. soy sauce
1 tsp. seasoned rice vinegar
2 tsp. toasted sesame oil
1 tbsp. cornstarch

Directions:
Using a bowl, add and toss the tofu, soy sauce, seasoned rice vinegar, sesame oil until they are properly covered.

Place it inside your refrigerator and allow to marinate for 30 minutes.

Preheat your air fryer to 370ºF.

Add the cornstarch to the tofu mixture and toss it until it is properly covered.

Grease your air fryer basket with a non-stick cooking spray and add the tofu inside the basket.

Cook it for 20 minutes at a 370ºF, and shake it after 10 minutes.

Serve and enjoy!

Nutrition:
Calories: 80
Fats: 5.8 g
Protein: 5 g
Carbs: 3 g
Fiber: 1.2 g

732. Not Your Average Zucchini Parmesan Chips

Preparation Time: 5 minutes
Cooking Time: 10 minutes
Servings: 4
Ingredients:
- 2 thinly sliced zucchinis
- 1 beaten egg
- ½ cup panko breadcrumbs
- ½ cup grated Parmesan cheese
- Salt and black pepper

Directions:

Prepare the zucchini by using a mandolin or a knife to slice them thinly.

Use a cloth to pat dry the zucchini chips.

Then using a bowl, add the egg and beat it properly. After that, pick another bowl, and add the breadcrumbs, Parmesan cheese, salt, and black pepper.

Dredge the zucchini chips into the egg mixture and then cover it with the Parmesan-breadcrumb mixture.

Grease the battered zucchini chips with a non-stick cooking spray and place it inside your Air Fryer Oven.

Cook it for 8 minutes at 350ºF.

Once done, carefully remove it from your Air Fryer Oven and sprinkle another tsp. of salt to give it some taste.

Serve and enjoy!

Nutrition:
Calories: 100
Fats: 6 g
Protein: 4 g
Carbs: 9 g
Fiber: 1.8 g

733. Sky-High Roasted Corn

Preparation Time: 5 minutes
Cooking Time: 10 minutes
Servings: 4
Ingredients:
- 4 ears of husk-less corn
- 1 tbsp. olive oil
- 1 tsp. salt
- 1 tsp. black pepper

Directions:

Heat up your Air Fryer Oven to 400ºF.

Sprinkle the ears of corn with the olive oil, salt and black pepper.

Place it inside your air fryer and cook it for 10 minutes at 400ºF.

Serve and enjoy!

Nutrition:
Calories: 100
Fats: 1 g
Protein: 3 g
Fiber: 3 g
Carbs: 22 g

734. Ravishing Air-Fried Carrots with Honey Glaze

Preparation Time: 5 minutes
Cooking Time: 10 minutes
Servings: 1
Ingredients:
- 3 cups carrots chopped into ½-inch pieces
- 1 tbsp. olive oil

2 tbsp. honey
1 tbsp. brown sugar
Salt and black pepper

Directions:

Heat up your Air Fryer Oven to 390ºF.

Using a bowl, add and toss the carrot pieces, olive oil, honey, brown sugar, salt, and the black pepper until the carrots are properly covered.

Place it inside your Air Fryer Oven and add the carrots.

Cook it for 12 minutes at 390ºF, and then shake after 6 minutes. Serve and enjoy!

Nutrition:

Calories: 90
Fats: 3.5 g
Fiber: 2 g
Carbs: 13 g
Protein: 1 g

735. Flaming Buffalo Cauliflower Bites

Preparation Time: 5 minutes
Cooking Time: 20 minutes
Servings: 4

Ingredients:

1 cauliflower head, large and chopped into florets
3 beaten eggs
2/3 cup cornstarch
2 tbsp. melted butter
¼ cup hot sauce

Directions:

Heat up your Air Fryer Oven to 360ºF.

Using a large mixing bowl, add and mix the eggs and the cornstarch a properly.

Add the cauliflower, gently toss it until it is properly covered with the batter, shake it off in case of any excess batter and set it aside.

Grease your air fry basket with a non-stick cooking spray and add the cauliflower bites, which will require you to work in batches.

Cook the cauliflower bites for 15–20 minutes or until it has a golden-brown color and a crispy texture, while still shaking occasionally.

Then, in a small mixing bowl, add and mix the melted butter and hot sauce properly.

Once the cauliflower bites are done, remove it from your Air Fryer Oven and place it into a large bowl. Pour the buffalo sauce over the cauliflower bites and toss it until it is properly covered.

Serve and enjoy!

Nutrition:

Calories: 240
Fats: 5.5 g
Fiber: 6.3 g
Protein: 8.8 g
Carbs: 37 g

736. Pleasant Air-Fried Eggplant

Preparation Time: 5 minutes
Cooking Time: 20 minutes
Servings: 4

Ingredients:

2 eggplants, thinly sliced or chopped into chunks
1 tsp. salt
1 tsp. black pepper
1 cup rice flour
1 cup white wine

Directions:

In a bowl, add the rice flour, white wine and mix properly until it gets smooth.

Add the salt, black pepper and stir again.

Dredge the eggplant slices or chunks into the batter and remove any excess batter.

Heat up your Air Fryer Oven to 390ºF.

Grease the air fry basket with a non-stick cooking spray.

Add the eggplant slices or chunks into your Air Fryer Oven and cook it for 15–20 minutes or until it has a golden brown and crispy texture, while still shaking it occasionally.

Carefully, remove it from your air fryer and allow it to cool off. Serve and enjoy!

Nutrition:
Calories: 380
Fats: 15 g
Protein: 13 g
Fiber: 6.1 g
Carbs: 51 g

737. Cauliflower Hash

Preparation Time: 10 minutes
Cooking Time: 15 minutes
Servings: 6
Ingredients:
- 1 lb. cauliflower
- 2 eggs
- 1 tsp. salt
- ½ tsp. ground paprika
- 4 oz. turkey fillet, chopped

Directions:

Wash the cauliflower, chop, and set aside.

In a different bowl, crack the eggs and whisk well.

Add the salt and ground paprika and stir.

Place the chopped turkey in the air fryer basket and cook it for 4 minutes at 365°F, stirring halfway through.

After this, add the chopped cauliflower and stir the mixture.

Cook the turkey-cauliflower mixture for 6 minutes more at 370°F, stirring it halfway through.

Then pour in the whisked egg mixture and stir it carefully.

Cook the cauliflower hash for 5 minutes more at 365°F.

When the cauliflower hash is done, let it cool and transfer to serving bowls. Serve and enjoy!

Nutrition:
Calories: 143 g Fats: 9.5 g
Fiber: 2 g Carbs: 4.5 g
Protein: 10.4 g

738. Asparagus with Almonds

Preparation Time: 10 minutes
Cooking Time: 5 minutes
Servings: 2
Ingredients:
- 9 oz. asparagus
- 1 tsp. almond flour
- 1 tbsp. almond flakes
- ¼ tsp. salt
- 1 tsp. olive oil

Directions:

Combine the almond flour and almond flakes and stir the mixture well.

Sprinkle the asparagus with the olive oil and salt.

Shake it gently and coat in the almond flour mixture.

Place the asparagus in the air fry basket and cook at 400°F for 5 minutes, stirring halfway through.

Then cool a little and serve.

Nutrition:
Calories: 143 g
Fats: 11 g
Fiber: 4.6 g
Carbs: 8.6 g
Protein: 6.4 g

739. Zucchini Cubes

Preparation Time: 7 minutes
Cooking Time: 8 minutes
Servings: 2
Ingredients:
- 1 zucchini
- ½ tsp. ground black pepper

1 tsp. oregano
2 tbsp. chicken stock
½ tsp. coconut oil

Directions:

Chop the zucchini into cubes.

Combine the ground black pepper, and oregano; stir the mixture.

Sprinkle the zucchini cubes with the spice mixture and stir well.

After this, sprinkle the zuchini with the chicken stock.

Place the coconut oil in the air fry basket and preheat it to 360°F for 20 seconds.

Then add the zucchini cubes and cook them for 8 minutes at 390°F, stirring halfway through.

Transfer to serving plates and enjoy!

Nutrition:

Calories: 30
Fats: 1.5 g
Fiber: 1.6 g
Carbs: 4.3 g
Protein: 1.4 g

740. Sweet Potato & Onion Mix

Preparation Time: 10 minutes
Cooking Time: 15 minutes
Servings: 4
Ingredients:

2 sweet potatoes, peeled
1 red onion, peeled
1 white onion, peeled
1 tsp. olive oil
¼ cup almond milk

Directions:

Chop the sweet potatoes and the onions into cubes.

Sprinkle the sweet potatoes with olive oil.

Place the sweet potatoes in the air fry basket and cook for 5 minutes at 400°F.

Then stir the sweet potatoes and add the chopped onions.

Pour in the almond milk and stir gently.

Cook the mix for 10 minutes more at 400°F.

When the mix is cooked, let it cool a little and serve.

Nutrition:

Calories: 56
Fats: 4.8 g
Fiber: 0.9 g
Carbs: 3.5 g
Protein: 0.6 g

741. Spicy Eggplant Cubes

Preparation Time: 10 minutes
Cooking Time: 20 minutes
Servings: 2
Ingredients:

12 oz. eggplants
½ tsp. cayenne pepper
½ tsp. ground black pepper
½ tsp. cilantro
½ tsp. ground paprika

Directions:

Rinse the eggplants and slice them into cubes.

Sprinkle the eggplant cubes with the cayenne pepper and ground black pepper.

Add the cilantro and ground paprika.

Stir the mixture well and let it rest for 10 minutes.

After this, sprinkle the eggplants with olive oil and place in the air fry basket.

Cook the eggplants for 20 minutes at 380°F, stirring halfway through.

When the eggplant cubes are done, serve them right away!

Nutrition:

Calories: 67
Fats: 2.8 g
Fiber: 6.5 g
Carbs: 10.9 g
Protein: 1.9 g

742. Roasted Garlic Head

Preparation Time: 5 minutes
Cooking Time: 10 minutes
Servings: 4
Ingredients:
- 1 lb. garlic head
- 1 tbsp. olive oil
- 1 tsp. thyme

Directions:
- Cut the ends of the garlic head and place it in the air fry basket.
- Then sprinkle the garlic head with the olive oil and thyme.
- Cook the garlic head for 10 minutes at 400°F.
- When the garlic head is cooked, it should be soft and aromatic.
- Serve immediately.

Nutrition:
- Calories: 200
- Fats: 4.1 g
- Fiber: 2.5 g
- Carbs: 37.7 g
- Protein: 7.2 g

743. Wrapped Asparagus

Preparation Time: 10 minutes
Cooking Time: 5 minutes
Servings: 4
Ingredients:
- 12 oz. asparagus
- ½ tsp. ground black pepper
- 3 oz. turkey fillet, sliced
- ¼ tsp. chili flakes

Directions:
- Sprinkle the asparagus with the ground black pepper and chili flakes.
- Stir carefully.
- Wrap the asparagus in the sliced turkey fillet and place in the air fry basket.
- Cook the asparagus at 400°F for 5 minutes, turning halfway through cooking.
- Let the wrapped asparagus cool for 2 minutes before serving.

Nutrition:
- Calories: 133
- Fats: 9 g
- Fiber: 1.9 g
- Carbs: 3.8 g
- Protein: 9.8 g

744. Baked Yams with Dill

Preparation Time: 10 minutes
Cooking Time: 8 minutes
Servings: 2
Ingredients:
- 2 yams
- 1 tbsp. fresh dill
- 1 tsp. coconut oil
- ½ tsp. minced garlic

Directions:
- Wash the yams carefully and cut them into halves.
- Sprinkle the yam halves with the coconut oil and then rub with the minced garlic.
- Place the yams in the air fry basket and cook for 8 minutes at 400°F.
- After this, mash the yams gently with a fork and then sprinkle with the fresh dill.
- Serve the yams immediately.

Nutrition:
- Calories: 25
- Fats: 2.3 g Fiber: 0.2 g
- Carbs: 1.2 g Protein: 0.4 g

745. Honey Onions

Preparation Time: 10 minutes
Cooking Time: 20 minutes
Servings: 2
Ingredients:
- 2 white onions, large
- 1 tbsp. raw honey
- 1 tsp. water
- 1 tbsp. paprika

Directions:
- Peel the onions, and using a knife, make cuts in the shape of a cross.
- Then combine the raw honey and water; stir.
- Add the paprika and stir the mixture until smooth.
- Place the onions in the air fryer basket and sprinkle them with the honey mixture.
- Cook the onions for 16 minutes at 380°F.
- When the onions are cooked, they should be soft.
- Transfer the cooked onions to serving plates and serve.

Nutrition:
- Calories: 10
- Fats: 0.6 g Fiber: 4.5 g
- Carbs: 24.6 g
- Protein: 2.2 g

746. Delightful Roasted Garlic Slices

Preparation Time: 10 minutes
Cooking Time: 8 minutes
Servings: 4
Ingredients:
- 1 tsp. coconut oil
- ½ tsp. cilantro, dried
- ¼ tsp. cayenne pepper
- 12 oz. garlic cloves, peeled

Directions:
- Sprinkle the garlic cloves with the cayenne pepper and the dried cilantro.
- Mix the garlic up with the spices, and then transfer to the air fry basket.
- Add the coconut oil and cook the garlic for 8 minutes at 400°F, stirring halfway through.
- When the garlic cloves are done, transfer them to serving plates and serve.

Nutrition:
- Calories: 137 Fats: 1.6 g
- Fiber: 1.8 g Carbs: 28.2 g Protein: 5.4 g

747. Coconut Oil Artichokes

Preparation Time: 10 minutes
Cooking Time: 13 minutes
Servings: 4
Ingredients:
- 1 lb. artichokes
- 1 tbsp. coconut oil
- 1 tbsp. water
- ½ tsp. minced garlic
- ¼ tsp. cayenne pepper

Directions:
- Trim the ends of the artichokes, sprinkle them with the water, and rub them with the minced garlic.
- Sprinkle with the cayenne pepper and the coconut oil.
- After this, wrap the artichokes in foil and place in the air fryer basket.
- Cook for 10 minutes at 370°F.
- Then remove the artichokes from the foil and cook them for 3 minutes more at 400°F.
- Transfer the cooked artichokes to serving plates and let them cool a little.
- Serve!

Nutrition:
- Calories: 83
- Fats: 3.6 g
- Fiber: 6.2 g
- Carbs: 12.1 g
- Protein: 3.7 g

748. Roasted Mushrooms

Preparation Time: 10 minutes
Cooking Time: 5 minutes
Servings: 2
Ingredients:
- 12 oz. mushroom hats
- ¼ cup fresh dill, chopped
- ¼ tsp. onion, chopped
- 1 tsp. olive oil
- ¼ tsp. turmeric

Directions:
- Combine the chopped dill and onion.
- Add the turmeric and stir the mixture.
- After this, add the olive oil and mix until homogenous.
- Then fill the mushroom hats with the dill mixture and place them in the air fry basket.
- Cook the mushrooms for 5 minutes at 400°F.
- When the vegetables are cooked, let them cool to room temperature before serving.

Nutrition:
Calories: 73 Fats: 3.1 g
Fiber: 2.6 g Carbs: 9.2 g Protein: 6.6 g

749. Mashed Yams

Preparation Time: 10 minutes
Cooking Time: 10 minutes
Servings: 5
Ingredients:
- 1 lb. yams
- 1 tsp. olive oil
- 1 tbsp. almond milk
- ¾ tsp. salt
- 1 tsp. dried parsley

Directions:
- Peel the yams and chop them.
- Place the chopped yams in the air fry basket and sprinkle with the salt and dried parsley.
- Add the olive oil and stir the mixture.
- Cook the yams at 400°F for 10 minutes, stirring twice during cooking.
- When the yams are done, blend them well with a hand blender until smooth.
- Add the almond milk and stir carefully.
- Serve, and enjoy!

Nutrition:
Calories: 120 Fats: 1.8 g
Fiber: 3.6 g Carbs: 25.1 g
Protein: 1.4 g

750. Cauliflower Rice

Preparation Time: 10 minutes
Cooking Time: 12 minutes
Servings: 4
Ingredients:
- 14 oz. cauliflower heads
- 1 tbsp. coconut oil
- 2 tbsp. fresh parsley, chopped

Directions:
- Wash the cauliflower heads carefully and chop them into small pieces of rice.
- Place the cauliflower in the air fry and add coconut oil.
- Stir carefully and cook for 10 minutes at 370°F.
- Then add the fresh parsley and stir well.
- Cook the cauliflower rice for 2 minutes more at 400°F.
- After this, gently toss the cauliflower rice and serve immediately.

Nutrition:
Calories: 55
Fats: 3.5 g
Fiber: 2.5 g
Carbs: 5.4 g
Protein: 2 g

751. Shredded Cabbage

Preparation Time: 15 minutes
Cooking Time: 15 minutes
Servings: 4
Ingredients:
- 15 oz. cabbage
- ¼ tsp. salt
- ¼ cup chicken stock
- ½ tsp. paprika

Directions:
- Shred the cabbage and sprinkle it with the salt and paprika.
- Stir the cabbage and let it sit for 10 minutes.
- Then transfer the cabbage to the air fry basket and add the chicken stock.

Cook the cabbage for 15 minutes at 250°F, stirring halfway through.
When the cabbage is soft, it is done.
Serve immediately, while still hot.

Nutrition:
Calories: 132
Fats: 2.1 g
Carbs: 32.1 g
Protein: 1.78 g

752. Fried Leeks Recipe

Preparation Time: 5 minutes
Cooking Time: 10 minutes
Servings: 4
Ingredients:
4 leeks; ends cut off and halved

1 tbsp. butter; melted
1 tbsp. lemon juice
Salt and black pepper to taste

Directions:
Coat the leeks with the melted butter, flavor with salt and black pepper, put in your Air Fryer Oven and cook at 350°F, for 7 minutes.
Arrange on a platter, drizzle the lemon juice all over and serve.

Nutrition:
Calories: 100
Fats: 4 g
Fiber: 2 g
Carbs: 6 g
Protein: 2 g

753. Brussels Sprouts and Tomatoes Mix Recipe

Preparation Time: 5 minutes
Cooking Time: 10 minutes
Servings: 4
Ingredients:
1 lb. Brussels sprouts; trimmed
6 cherry tomatoes; halved
¼ cup green onions; chopped.
1 tbsp. olive oil
Salt and black pepper to the taste

Directions:
Season Brussels sprouts with salt and pepper, put them in your Air Fryer Oven and cook at 350°F for 10 minutes.
Transfer them to a bowl, add the salt, pepper, cherry tomatoes, green onions and olive oil, toss well and serve.

Nutrition:
Calories: 121
Fats: 4 g
Fiber: 4 g
Carbs: 11 g
Protein: 4 g

754. Radish Hash Recipe

Preparation Time: 5 minutes
Cooking Time: 15 minutes
Servings: 4
Ingredients:
½ tsp. onion powder
⅓ cup parmesan, grated
4 eggs
1 lb. radishes, sliced
Salt and black pepper to taste

Directions:
In a bowl; mix the radishes with salt, pepper, onion, eggs and parmesan and stir well.
Transfer the radishes to a pan that fits your air fryer and cook at 350°F for 7 minutes.
Divide the hash on plates and serve.

Nutrition:
Calories: 80 Fats: 5 g
Fiber: 2 g Carbs: 5 g Protein: 7 g

755. Broccoli Salad Recipe

Preparation Time: 5 minutes
Cooking Time: 20 minutes
Servings: 4
Ingredients:
1 broccoli head, florets separated

1 tbsp. Chinese rice wine vinegar
1 tbsp. peanut oil
6 garlic cloves, minced
Salt and black pepper to taste

Directions:
In a bowl, mix broccoli with salt, pepper and half of the oil, toss, transfer to your Air Fryer Oven and cook at 350°F for 8 minutes, shaking the fryer halfway

Transfer the broccoli to a salad bowl, add the rest of the peanut oil, garlic and rice vinegar, toss really well and serve.

Nutrition:
Calories: 121 Fats: 3 g
Fiber: 4 g Carbs: 4 g
Protein: 4 g

756. Chili Broccoli

Preparation Time: 5 minutes
Cooking Time: 15 minutes
Servings: 4
Ingredients:
1-lb. broccoli florets
2 tbsp. olive oil
2 tbsp. chili sauce
Juice of 1 lime
A pinch of salt and black pepper

Directions:
Combine all of the ingredients in a bowl, and toss well.

Put the broccoli in your air fryer's basket and cook at 400 degrees F for 15 minutes.

Divide between plates and serve.

Nutrition:
Calories: 173 Fats: 6 g
Fiber: 2 g Carbs: 6 g Protein: 8 g

757. Parmesan Broccoli and Asparagus

Preparation Time: 5 minutes
Cooking Time: 15 minutes
Servings: 4
Ingredients:

1 broccoli head, florets separated
½ lb. asparagus, trimmed
Juice of 1 lime
Salt and black pepper to the taste
2 tbsp. olive oil
3 tbsp. parmesan, grated

Directions:
In a small bowl, combine the asparagus with the broccoli and all the other ingredients except the parmesan, toss, transfer to your air fry basket and cook at 400ºF for 15 minutes.

Divide between plates, sprinkle the parmesan on top and serve.

Nutrition:
Calories: 172
Fats: 5 g
Fiber: 2 g
Carbs: 4 g
Protein: 9 g

758. Butter Broccoli Mix

Preparation Time: 5 minutes
Cooking Time: 15 minutes
Servings: 4
Ingredients:
1 lb. broccoli florets
A pinch of salt and black pepper
1 tsp. sweet paprika
½ tbsp. butter, melted

Directions:
In a small bowl, combine the broccoli with the rest of the ingredients, and toss.

Put the broccoli in your air fry basket, cook at 350ºF for 15 minutes, divide between plates and serve.

Nutrition:
Calories: 130
Fats: 3 g
Fiber: 3 g
Carbs: 4 g
Protein: 8 g

759. Balsamic Kale
Preparation Time: 2 minutes
Cooking Time: 12 minutes
Servings: 6
Ingredients:
- 2 tbsp. olive oil
- 3 garlic cloves, minced
- 2 ½ lb. kale leaves
- Salt and black pepper to taste
- 2 tbsp. balsamic vinegar

Directions:
- In a pan that fits the Air Fryer Oven, combine all the ingredients and toss.
- Put the pan in your Air Fryer Oven and cook at 300ºF for 12 minutes.
- Divide between plates and serve.

Nutrition:
- Calories: 122 Fats: 4 g
- Fiber: 3 g Carbs: 4 g
- Protein: 5 g

760. Kale and Olives
Preparation Time: 5 minutes
Cooking Time: 15 minutes
Servings: 4
Ingredients:
- 1 ½ lb. kale, torn
- 2 tbsp. olive oil
- Salt and black pepper to taste
- 1 tbsp. hot paprika
- 2 tbsp. black olives, pitted and sliced

Directions:
- In a pan that fits the Air Fry, combine all the ingredients and toss.
- Put the pan in your Air Fry, cook at 370ºF for 15 minutes, divide between plates and serve.

Nutrition:
- Calories: 154
- Fats: 3 g
- Fiber: 2 g
- Carbs: 4 g
- Protein: 6 g

761. Kale and Mushrooms Mix
Preparation Time: 5 minutes
Cooking Time: 15 minutes
Servings: 4
Ingredients:
- 1 lb. brown mushrooms, sliced
- 1 lb. kale, torn
- Salt and black pepper to the taste
- 2 tbsp. olive oil
- 14 oz. coconut milk

Directions:
- In a pot that fits your Air Fryer Oven, mix the kale with the rest of the ingredients and toss.
- Put the pan in the fryer, cook at 380ºF for 15 minutes, divide between plates and serve.

Nutrition:
- Calories: 162
- Fats: 4 g
- Fiber: 1 g
- Carbs: 3 g
- Protein: 5 g

762. Oregano Kale
Preparation Time: 5 minutes
Cooking Time: 10 minutes
Servings: 4
Ingredients:
- 1 lb. kale, torn
- 1 tbsp. olive oil
- A pinch of salt and black pepper
- 2 tbsp. oregano, chopped

Directions:
- In a pan that fits the Air Fryer Oven, combine all the ingredients and toss.
- Put the pan in the air fryer and cook at 380ºF for 10 minutes.
- Divide between plates and serve.

Nutrition:
- Calories: 140 Fat : 3 g
- Fiber: 2 g Carbs: 3 g
- Protein: 5 g

763. Kale and Brussels Sprouts

Preparation Time: 5 minutes
Cooking Time: 15 minutes
Servings: 8
Ingredients:
- 1 lb. Brussels sprouts, trimmed
- 2 cups kale, torn
- 1 tbsp. olive oil
- Salt and black pepper to taste
- 3 oz. mozzarella, shredded

Directions:
- In a pan that fits the Air Fryer Oven, combine all the ingredients except the mozzarella and toss.
- Put the pan in the Air Fryer Oven and cook at 380ºF for 15 minutes.
- Divide between plates, sprinkle the cheese on top and serve.

Nutrition:
- Calories: 170
- Fats: 5 g
- Fiber: 3 g
- Carbs: 4 g
- Protein: 7 g

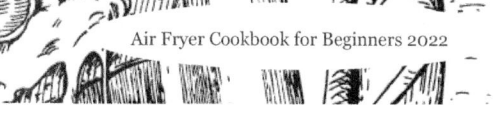

CHAPTER 11:

Soups and Stews

764. Potato And Cheese Soup

Preparation Time: 10 minutes
Cooking Time: 10 minutes
Servings: 6
Ingredients:
- 6 cups potatoes, cubed
- 2 tablespoons butter
- ½ cup yellow onion, chopped
- 28 ounces chicken stock
- Salt and ground black pepper, to taste
- 2 tablespoons dried parsley
- 1/8 teaspoon red pepper flakes
- 2 tablespoons cornstarch
- 2 tablespoons water
- 3 ounces cream cheese, cubed
- 2 cups half and half
- 1 cup cheddar cheese, shredded
- 1 cup corn
- 6 bacon slices, cooked and crumbled

Directions:
Put the air fryer on Sauté mode, add the butter and melt it. Put in the onion, stir, and cook 5 minutes. Add half of the stock, salt, pepper, pepper flakes, and parsley and stir. Put the potatoes in the steamer basket, cover the Air fryer and cook on the Steam setting for 4 minutes. Naturally release the pressure, uncover the Air fryer, and transfer the potatoes to a bowl. In another bowl, mix the cornstarch with water and stir well. Put the air fryer to Manual mode, add the cornstarch slurry, cream cheese, and shredded cheese and stir well. Add the rest of the stock, corn, bacon, potatoes, half and half. Stir, bring to a simmer, ladle into bowls, and serve.

Nutrition:
Calories – 188
Protein – 9 g.
Fat – 7.14 g.
Carbs – 22 g.

765. Split Pea Soup

Preparation Time: 10 minutes
Cooking Time: 20 minutes
Servings: 6
Ingredients:
- 2 tablespoons butter
- 1 pound chicken sausage, ground
- 1 yellow onion, peeled and chopped
- ½ cup carrots, peeled and chopped
- ½ cup celery, chopped
- 2 garlic cloves, peeled and minced
- 29 ounces chicken stock
- Salt and ground black pepper, to taste
- 2 cups water
- 16 ounces split peas, rinsed
- ½ cup half and half
- ¼ teaspoon red pepper flakes

Directions:
Put the air fryer on Sauté mode, add the sausage, brown it on all sides and transfer to a plate. Put the butter in the Air fryer and melt it. Add the celery, onions, and carrots, stir, and cook 4 minutes. Mix in the garlic, stir and cook for 1 minute. Add the water, stock, peas and pepper flakes, stir, cover and cook on the Soup setting for 10 minutes. Release the pressure, puree the mix using an immersion blender and Put the air fryer on Manual mode. Add the sausage, salt, pepper, and half and half, stir, bring to a simmer, and ladle into soup bowls.

Nutrition:
Calories – 30 Protein – 20 g.
Fat – 11 g. Carbs – 14 g.

766. Corn Soup

Preparation Time: 10 minutes
Cooking Time: 15 minutes
Servings: 4
Ingredients:
- 2 leeks, chopped

2 tablespoons butter
2 garlic cloves, peeled and minced
6 ears of corn, cobs reserved, kernels cut off,
2 bay leaves
4 tarragon sprigs, chopped
1-quart chicken stock
Salt and ground black pepper, to taste
Extra virgin olive oil
1 tablespoon fresh chives, chopped

Directions:
Put the air fryer on Sauté mode, add the butter and melt it. Add the leeks and garlic, stir, and cook for 4 minutes. Add the corn, corn cobs, bay leaves, tarragon, and stock to cover everything, cover the Air fryer and cook on the Soup setting for 15 minutes. Release the pressure, uncover the Air fryer, discard the bay leaves and corn cobs, and transfer everything to a blender. Pulse well to obtain a smooth soup, add the rest of the stock and blend again. Add the salt and pepper, stir well, divide into soup bowls, and serve cold with chives and olive oil on top.

Nutrition:
Calories – 300
Protein – 13 g.
Fat – 8.3 g.
Carbs – 50 g.

767. Beef And Rice Soup

Preparation Time: 10 minutes
Cooking Time: 15 minutes
Servings: 6
Ingredients:
1 pound ground beef
3 garlic cloves, peeled and minced
1 yellow onion, peeled and chopped
1 tablespoon vegetable oil
1 celery stalk, chopped
28 ounces beef stock
14 ounces canned crushed tomatoes
½ cup white rice
12 ounces spicy tomato juice
15 ounces canned garbanzo beans, rinsed
1 potato, cubed
Salt and ground black pepper, to taste
½ cup frozen peas
2 carrots, peeled and sliced thin

Directions:
Put the air fryer on Sauté mode, add the beef, stir, cook until it browns, and transfer to a plate. Add the oil to the Air fryer and heat it up. Add the celery and onion, stir, and cook for 5 minutes. Put in the garlic, stir and cook for 1 minute. Add the tomato juice, stock, tomatoes, rice, beans, carrots, potatoes, beef, salt, and pepper, stir, cover and cook on the Manual setting for 5 minutes. Release the pressure, uncover the Air fryer, and set it on Manual mode. Dash more salt and pepper, if desired, and the peas, stir, bring to a simmer, transfer to bowls, and serve hot.

Nutrition:
Calories – 230
Protein – 3 g.
Fat – 7 g.
Carbs – 10 g.

768. Chicken Noodle Soup

Preparation Time: 10 minutes
Cooking Time: 12 minutes
Servings: 6
Ingredients:
1 yellow onion, peeled and chopped
1 tablespoon butter
1 celery stalk, chopped
4 carrots, peeled and sliced
Salt and ground black pepper, to taste
6 cups chicken stock
cups chicken, already cooked and shredded
Egg noodles, already cooked

Directions:

Put the air fryer on Sauté mode, add the butter and heat it up. Put in the onion, stir, and cook 2 minutes. Add the celery and carrots, stir, and cook 5 minutes. Add the chicken and stock, stir, cover the Air fryer and cook on the Soup setting for 5 minutes. Release the pressure, uncover the Air fryer, add salt and pepper to taste, and stir. Divide the noodles into soup bowls, add the soup over them, and serve.

Nutrition:
Calories – 100
Protein – 7 g.
Fat – 1 g.
Carbs – 4 g.

769. Zuppa Toscana

Preparation Time: 10 minutes
Cooking Time: 17 minutes
Servings: 8
Ingredients:
- 1 pound chicken sausage, ground
- 6 bacon slices, chopped
- 3 garlic cloves, peeled and minced
- 1 cup yellow onion, peeled and chopped
- 1 tablespoon butter
- 40 ounces chicken stock
- Salt and ground black pepper, to taste
- Red pepper flakes
- 3 potatoes, cubed
- 3 tablespoons cornstarch
- 12 ounces evaporated milk
- 1 cup Parmesan, shredded
- 2 cup spinach, chopped

Directions:

Put the air fryer on Sauté mode, add the bacon, stir, cook until it's crispy, and transfer to a plate. Add the sausage to the Air fryer, stir, cook until it browns on all sides, and also transfer to a plate. Add the butter to the Air fryer and melt it. Put in the onion, stir, and cook for 5 minutes. Put in the garlic, stir, and cook for a minute. Pour in ⅓ of the stock, salt, pepper, and pepper flakes and stir. Place the potatoes in the steamer basket of the Air fryer, cover and cook on the Steam setting for 4 minutes. Release the pressure, uncover the Air fryer, and transfer the potatoes to a bowl. Add the rest of the stock to the Air fryer with the cornstarch mixed with the evaporated milk, stir, and Put the air fryer on Manual mode. Add the cheese, sausage, bacon, potatoes, spinach, more salt and pepper, if needed, stir, divide into bowls, and serve.

Nutrition:
Calories – 170 Protein – 10 g.
Fat – 4 g.
Carbs – 24 g.

770. Minestrone Soup

Preparation Time: 10 minutes
Cooking Time: 15 minutes
Servings: 8
Ingredients:
- 1 tablespoon extra virgin olive oil
- 1 celery stalk, chopped
- 2 carrots, peeled and chopped
- 1 onion, peeled and chopped
- 1 cup corn kernels
- 1 zucchini, chopped
- 3 pounds tomatoes, cored, peeled, and chopped
- 4 garlic cloves, peeled and minced
- 29 ounces chicken stock
- 1 cup uncooked pasta
- Salt and ground black pepper, to taste
- 1 teaspoon Italian seasoning
- 2 cups baby spinach
- 15 ounces canned kidney beans
- 1 cup Asiago cheese, grated
- 2 tablespoons fresh basil, chopped

Directions:

Put the air fryer on Sauté mode, add the oil and heat it up. Put in the onion, stir, and cook for 5 minutes. Add the carrots, garlic, celery, corn, and zucchini, stir, and cook 5 minutes. Add the tomatoes, stock, Italian seasoning, pasta, salt, and pepper, stir, cover, and cook on the Soup setting for 4 minutes. Naturally release the pressure, uncover, add the beans, basil, and spinach. Dash more salt and pepper, if desired, divide into bowls, add the cheese on top, and serve.

Nutrition:
Calories –110 Protein – 5 g.
Fat – 2 g. Carbs – 18 g.

771. Chicken And Wild Rice Soup

Preparation Time: 10 minutes
Cooking Time: 15 minutes
Servings: 6
Ingredients:

- 1 cup yellow onion, peeled and chopped
- tablespoons butter
- 1 cup celery, chopped
- 1 cup carrots, chopped
- 28ounces chicken stock
- 2chicken breasts, skinless, boneless and chopped
- 6ounces wild rice
- Red pepper flakes
- Salt and ground black pepper, to taste
- 1 tablespoon dried parsley
- 2tablespoons cornstarch
- 2tablespoons water
- 1 cup milk
- 1 cup half and half
- 4ounces cream cheese, cubed

Directions:

Put the air fryer on Sauté mode, add the butter and melt it. Add the carrot, onion, and celery, stir and cook for 5 minutes. Add the rice, chicken, stock, parsley, salt, and pepper, stir, cover, and cook on the Soup setting for 5 minutes. Release the pressure, uncover, add the cornstarch mixed with water, stir, and Put the air fryer on Manual mode. Add the cheese, milk, and half and half, stir, heat up, transfer to bowls, and serve.

Nutrition:
Calories – 200
Protein – 5 g.
Fat – 7 g.
Carbs – 19 g.

772. Creamy Tomato Soup

Preparation Time: 10 minutes
Cooking Time: 6 minutes
Servings: 8
Ingredients:

- 1 yellow onion, peeled and chopped
- 3tablespoons butter
- 1 carrot, peeled and chopped
- 2celery stalks, chopped
- 2garlic cloves, peeled and minced
- 29ounces chicken stock
- Salt and ground black pepper, to taste
- ¼ cup fresh basil, chopped
- 3pounds tomatoes, peeled, cored, and cut into quarters
- 1 tablespoon tomato paste
- 1 cup half and half
- ½ cup Parmesan cheese, shredded

Directions:

Put the air fryer on Sauté mode, add the butter and melt it. Mix in the onion, carrots, and celery, stir, and cook for 3 minutes. Put in the garlic, stir, and cook for 1 minute. Put in the tomatoes, tomato paste, stock, basil, salt, and pepper, stir, cover, and cook on the Soup setting for 5 minutes. Release the pressure, uncover the Air fryer and puree the soup using and immersion blender. Add the cheese and half and half, stir, Put the air fryer on Manual mode and heat everything up.

Divide the soup into soup bowls, and serve.

Nutrition:
Calories – 280
Protein – 24 g.
Fat – 8 g.
Carbs – 32 g.

773. Tomato Soup

Preparation Time: 10 minutes
Cooking Time: 45 minutes
Servings: 6
Ingredients:
- For the roasted tomatoes:
- 14 garlic cloves, peeled and crushed
- 3 pounds cherry tomatoes, cut into halves
- Salt and ground black pepper, to taste
- 2 tablespoons extra virgin olive oil
- ½ teaspoon red pepper flakes

For the soup:
- 1 yellow onion, peeled and chopped
- 2 tablespoons olive oil
- 1 red bell pepper, seeded and chopped
- 3 tablespoons tomato paste
- 2 celery ribs, chopped
- 2 cups chicken stock
- 1 teaspoon garlic powder
- 1 teaspoon onion powder
- ½ tablespoon dried basil
- ½ teaspoon red pepper flakes
- Salt and ground black pepper, to taste
- 1 cup heavy cream

For Servings:
- Fresh basil leaves, chopped
- ½ cup Parmesan cheese, grated

Directions:
Take the tomatoes and garlic in a baking tray, drizzle 2 tablespoons oil, season with salt, pepper and a ½ teaspoon of red pepper flakes, toss to coat, introduce in the oven at 425ºF, and roast for 25 minutes. Take the tomatoes out of the oven and set aside. Put the air fryer on Sauté mode, add the oil, and heat it up. Add the onion, bell pepper, celery, salt, pepper, garlic powder, onion powder, basil, the remaining red pepper flakes, stir, and cook for 3 minutes. Add the tomato paste, roasted tomatoes, and garlic and stir. Add the stock, cover the Air fryer, and cook on the Manual setting for 10 minutes. Release the pressure, uncover the Air fryer and set it on Sauté mode. Add the heavy cream and blend everything using an immersion blender. Divide in bowls, add basil and cheese on top, and serve.

Nutrition:
Calories – 150
Protein – 4 g.
Fat – 1 g.
Carbs – 3 g.

774. Carrot Soup

Preparation Time: 10 minutes
Cooking Time: 16 minutes
Servings: 4
Ingredients:
- 1 tablespoon vegetable oil
- 1 onion, peeled and chopped
- 1 tablespoon butter
- 1 garlic clove, peeled and minced
- 1 pound carrots, peeled and chopped
- 1 small ginger piece, peeled and grated
- Salt and ground black pepper, to taste
- ¼ teaspoon brown sugar
- 2 cups chicken stock
- 1 tablespoon Sriracha
- 14 ounces canned coconut milk
- Cilantro leaves, chopped, for serving

Directions:
Put the air fryer on Sauté mode, add the butter and oil, and heat them up. Put in

the onion, stir and cook for 3 minutes. Add the ginger and garlic, stir, and cook for 1 minute. Add the sugar, carrots, salt, and pepper, stir, and cook 2 minutes. Add the sriracha, coconut milk, stock, stir, cover, and cook on the Soup setting for 6 minutes. Naturally release the pressure for 10 minutes, uncover the Air fryer, blend the soup with an immersion blender, add more salt and pepper, if needed, and divide into soup bowls. Add the cilantro on top, and serve.

Nutrition:
Calories – 60
Protein – 2 g.
Fat – 1 g.
Carbs – 12 g.

775. Cabbage Soup
Preparation Time: 10 minutes
Cooking Time: 10 minutes
Servings: 4
Ingredients:
- 1 cabbage head, chopped
- 12 ounces baby carrots
- 3 celery stalks, chopped
- ½ onion, peeled and chopped
- 1 packet vegetable soup mix
- 2 tablespoons olive oil
- 12 ounces soy burger
- 3 teaspoons garlic, peeled and minced
- ¼ cup cilantro, chopped
- 4 cups chicken stock
- Salt and ground black pepper, to taste

Directions:
In the Air fryer, mix the cabbage with the celery, carrots, onion, soup mix, soy burger, stock, olive oil, and garlic, stir, cover, and cook on Soup mode for 5 minutes. Release the pressure, uncover the Air fryer, add the salt, pepper, and cilantro, stir again well, divide into soup bowls, and serve.

Nutrition:
Calories – 100
Protein – 10 g.
Fat – 1 g.
Carbs – 10 g.

776. Cream Of Asparagus
Preparation Time: 10 minutes
Cooking Time: 25 minutes
Servings: 4
Ingredients:
- 2 pounds green asparagus, trimmed, tips cut off and cut into medium pieces
- 3 tablespoons butter
- 1 yellow onion, peeled and chopped
- 6 cups chicken stock
- ¼ teaspoon lemon juice
- ½ cup crème fraiche
- Salt and ground white pepper, to taste

Directions:
Put the air fryer on Sauté mode, add the butter and melt it. Add the asparagus, salt, and pepper, stir, and cook for 5 minutes. Add 5 cups of the stock, cover the Air fryer, and cook on Soup mode for 15 minutes. Release the pressure, uncover the Air fryer and transfer soup to a blender. Pulse several times and return to the Air fryer. Put the air fryer on Manual mode, add the crème fraiche, the rest of the stock, salt, pepper, and lemon juice, bring to a boil, divide into soup bowls, and serve.

Nutrition:
Calories – 80
Protein – 6.3 g.
Fat – 8 g.
Carbs – 16 g.

777. Veggie Noodle Soup

Preparation Time: 5 minutes
Cooking Time: 10 minutes
Servings: 4
Ingredients:
- Celery – 4 stalks, chopped into bite-sized pieces
- Carrots – 4, chopped into bite-sized pieces
- Sweet potatoes – 2, peeled and chopped
- Sweet onion – 1, chopped
- Broccoli florets – 1 cup
- Tomato – 1, diced
- Garlic – 2 cloves, minced
- Bay leaf – 1
- Dried oregano – 1 tsp.
- Dried thyme – 1 tsp.
- Dried basil – 1 tsp.
- Salt – 1 to 2 tsp.
- Ground black pepper
- Dried pasta – 1 cup
- Vegetable stock – 4 cups, plus more as needed
- Water – 1 to ½ cups, plus more as needed
- Chopped fresh parsley, for garnish
- Lemon zest for garnish
- Crackers, for serving

Directions:
- In the Air fryer, combine the water, stock, pasta, salt, pepper, basil, thyme, oregano, bay leaf, garlic, tomato, broccoli, onion, sweet potatoes, carrots, and celery.
- Cover the Air fryer.
- Cook on High for 3 minutes.
- Do a natural release and then a quick release.
- Remove the lid and stir the soup.
- Discard the bay leaf, garnish and serve.

Nutrition:
Calories – 120
Protein – 8 g.
Fat – 10 g.
Carbs – 22 g.

778. Carrot Ginger Soup

Preparation Time: 5 minutes
Cooking Time: 10 minutes
Servings: 2
Ingredients:
- Carrots – 7 chopped
- Fresh ginger – 1-inch, peeled and chopped
- Sweet onion – ½, chopped
- Vegetable stock – 1 ¼ cups
- Salt – ½ tsp.
- Sweet paprika – ½ tsp.
- Ground black pepper
- Cashew sour cream for garnish
- Fresh herbs for garnish

Directions:
- In the Air fryer, combine the paprika, salt, stock, onion, ginger, and carrots. Season with pepper.
- Cover the Air fryer.
- Cook on High for 3 minutes.
- Do a natural release and then a quick release.
- Open and blend with a hand mixer until smooth.
- Garnish and serve.

Nutrition:
Calories – 85
Protein – 6.7 g.
Fat – 8.5 g.
Carbs – 18 g.

779. Creamy Tomato Basil Soup

Preparation Time: 5 minutes
Cooking Time: 4 minutes
Servings: 4
Ingredients:
- Vegan butter – 2 Tbsp.
- Small sweet onion – 1, chopped
- Garlic – 2 cloves, minced
- Carrot – 1, chopped
- Celery – 1 stalk, chopped
- Vegetable stock – 3 cups

- Tomatoes – 3 pounds, quartered
- Fresh basil – ¼ cup, plus more for garnishing
- Nutritional yeast – ¼ cup
- Salt and ground black pepper
- Nondairy milk – ½ to 1 cup

Directions:
- Press Sauté on the Air fryer, add butter and melt.
- Put in the garlic and onion and stir-fry for 3 to 4 minutes.
- Add celery and carrot and cook 2 minutes more. Stir continuously.
- Add the stock and deglaze the pot.
- Add salt, yeast, basil, and tomatoes. Stir to mix. Cover the Air fryer.
- Cook on High for 4 minutes.
- Do a natural release than a quick release.
- Open and blend with a hand mixer until smooth.
- Stir in milk. Taste and adjust seasoning.
- Garnish and serve.

Nutrition:
Calories – 70 Protein – 5.6 g. Fat – 7.4g. Carbs – 13 g.

780. Cream Of Mushroom Soup

Preparation Time: 5 minutes
Cooking Time: 4 minutes
Servings: 4
Ingredients:
- Vegan butter – 2 Tbsp.
- Small sweet onion – 1, chopped
- White button mushrooms – 1 ½ pound, sliced
- Garlic – 2 cloves, minced
- Dried thyme – 2 tsp.
- Sea salt -1 tsp.
- Vegetable stock – 1 ¾ cup
- Silken tofu – ½ cup
- Chopped fresh thyme for garnishing

Directions:
- Press Sauté on the Air fryer. Melt the butter and add the onion. Stir-fry for 2 minutes. Add the salt, dried thyme, garlic, and mushrooms. Stir-fry for 2 minutes more and press Cancel.
- Stir in the stock. Cover the Air fryer.
- Cook on High for 5 minutes.
- Meanwhile, process the tofu in a food processor until smooth. Set aside.
- Do a natural release, then quick release.
- Open and blend with a hand mixer until smooth.
- Garnish and serve.

Nutrition:
Calories – 80
Protein – 6.2 g.
Fat – 9 g.
Carbs – 17 g.

781. Chipotle Sweet Potato Chowder

Preparation Time: 3 minutes
Cooking Time: 2 minutes
Servings: 4
Ingredients:
- Vegetable stock – 1 ¼ cups
- Lite coconut milk – 1 (14-ounce) can
- Sweet potatoes – 2, peeled and diced
- Canned chipotle peppers – 2 to 4 (in adobo sauce), diced
- Red bell pepper – 1, diced
- Small onion – 1, diced
- Ground cumin – 1 tsp.
- Salt – ½ to 1 tsp.
- Frozen sweet corn – 1 ½ cups
- Adobo sauce from the canned peppers, to taste

Directions:
- Whisk the coconut milk and stock in a bowl. Mix well.
- Pour into the Air fryer. Add the salt, cumin, onion, bell pepper, chipotles, and sweet potatoes.
- Cover the Air fryer.
- Cook on High for 2 minutes.
- Do a natural release, then quick release.

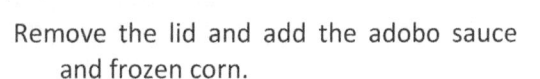

Remove the lid and add the adobo sauce and frozen corn.

Warn the corn and serve.

Nutrition:
Calories – 95
Protein – 8.5 g.
Fat – 9.2 g.
Carbs – 23 g.

782. Coconut Sweet Potato Stew

Preparation Time: 5 minutes
Cooking Time: 4 minutes
Servings: 4
Ingredients:

- Avocado oil – 2 Tbsp.
- Sweet onion – ½, diced
- Sweet potatoes – 2, peeled and cubed
- Garlic – 2 cloves, minced
- Salt – 1 to 1 ½ tsp.
- Ground turmeric – 1 tsp.
- Paprika – 1 tsp.
- Ground cumin – ½ tsp.
- Dried oregano – ½ tsp.
- Chili powder – 1 to 2 dashes
- Roma tomatoes – 2, chopped
- Lite coconut milk – 1 (14-ounce) can, shaken well
- Water – 1 ¼ cups, plus more as needed
- Chopped kale – 1 to 2 cups

Directions:

- Choose Sauté on the Air fryer and add oil.
- Add onion and stir-fry for 3 minutes.
- Stir in chili powder, oregano, cumin, paprika, turmeric, salt, garlic, and sweet potatoes. Stir-fry for 1 minute.
- Add the water, tomatoes, and coconut milk and mix.
- Cover the Air fryer.
- Cook on High for 4 minutes.
- Do a natural release than a quick release.
- Open and stir in the kale. Mix.
- Serve.

Nutrition:
Calories – 105
Protein – 9.3 g.
Fat – 10 g.
Carbs – 25 g.

783. Italian Vegetable Stew

Preparation Time: 5 minutes
Cooking Time: 7 minutes
Servings: 4
Ingredients:

- Olive oil – 2 Tbsp.
- Leeks – 2, white and very light green parts only, chopped
- Sweet onion – 1, chopped
- Carrot – 1, chopped
- Celery – 1, sliced
- White mushrooms – 1 cup, sliced
- Small eggplant – 1, chopped
- Garlic – 3, cloves, minced
- Yukon gold potatoes – 3, chopped
- Roma tomatoes – 3, chopped
- Vegetable stock – 4 cups
- Dried oregano – 1 tsp.
- Salt – ½ tsp. plus more as needed
- Torn kale leaves – 2 cups
- Ground black pepper
- Fresh basil for garnishing

Directions:

- Choose Sauté on the Air fryer and add oil.
- Add eggplant, mushrooms, celery, carrot, onion, and leeks. Stir-fry for 2 minutes.
- Add the garlic.
- Cook 30 seconds more.
- Add the salt, oregano, stock, tomatoes, and potatoes.
- Cover the Air fryer.
- Cook on High for 7 minutes.
- Do a natural release and then a quick release.
- Open and stir in the kale.
- Taste and adjust seasoning.

Serve.
Nutrition:
Calories – 115
Protein – 10 g.
Fat – 12 g.
Carbs – 28 g.

784. Spinach Mint Stew
Preparation Time: 5 minutes
Cooking Time: 15 minutes
Servings: 4
Ingredients:
- 2 cups heavy cream
- 1 tablespoon lemon juice
- 1 small onion, chopped
- 2 cups fresh spinach, chopped
- 2 garlic cloves, minced
- 1/2 teaspoon black pepper, (finely ground)
- 1 tablespoon mint leaves, torn
- 1 teaspoon salt
- 1 cup celery leaves, chopped
- 2 tablespoon butter
- 1 cup celery stalks, chopped

Directions:
- Arrange Air fryer over a dry platform in your kitchen. Open its top lid and switch it on.
- Find and press "SAUTE" cooking function; add the butter in it and allow it to heat.
- In the pot, add the onions, garlic, and celery stalks; cook (while stirring) until turns translucent and softened for around 2 minutes.
- Add celery leaves and spinach; season to taste and stir-cook for 2-3 minutes.
- Add in the heavy cream; gently stir to mix well.
- Close top lid to create a locked chamber; make sure that safety valve is in locking position.
- Find and press "MANUAL" cooking function; timer to 5 minutes with default "HIGH" pressure mode.
- Allow the pressure to build to cook the ingredients.
- After cooking time is over, press "CANCEL" setting. Find and press "QPR" cooking function. This setting is for quick release of inside pressure.
- Slowly open the lid, stir in the mint and lemon juice. Take out the cooked recipe in serving plates or serving bowls and enjoy the keto recipe.

Nutrition:
Calories – 85
Protein – 7.1 g.
Fat – 8 g.
Carbs – 18.6 g.

785. Creamy Cauliflower And Sage Soup
Preparation Time: 10 minutes
Cooking Time: 10 minutes
Servings: 4
Ingredients:
- 1 teaspoon butter
- 1 large onion, chopped
- 4 cloves garlic, minced
- 1 teaspoon ground sage
- 8 cups cauliflower florets
- 3 cups low-sodium chicken broth
- ½ teaspoon salt
- Pepper to taste
- ½ cup unsweetened coconut milk

Directions:
- Select the Sauté setting and heat the butter. Mix in the onion and cook until clear, about 3-5 minutes. Add the garlic and sage and cook for 1 minute. Add the cauliflower, chicken broth, salt, and pepper, and stir well.
- Press Cancel to reset the cooking Directions:. Secure the lid and fix the Pressure Release to Sealing. Select the Pressure Cook or Manual setting and set

the cooking time to 10 minutes at high pressure.
- Once the timer is done, let sit for at least 10 minutes; the pressure will release naturally. Then switch the Pressure Release to Venting to allow any last steam out.
- Open the lid and puree the soup using an immersion blender or by transferring it to a stand blender. Stir in the unsweetened coconut milk and add salt and pepper to taste.

Nutrition:
Calories – 171
Protein – 8.8 g.
Fat – 9.2 g.
Carbs – 18.1 g.

786. Curried Pumpkin Soup
Preparation Time: 10 minutes
Cooking Time: 5 minutes
Servings: 4
Ingredients:
- 2 tablespoons butter
- 1 onion, chopped
- 2 tablespoons curry powder
- 1/8 teaspoon cayenne pepper (optional)
- 4 cups vegetable broth
- 4 cups low-sodium pumpkin puree
- 1 tablespoon tamari
- Salt to taste
- Pepper to taste
- 1½ cups unsweetened coconut milk
- 1 teaspoon lemon juice
- Optional: ¼ cup roasted pumpkin seeds for serving

Directions:
- Select the Sauté setting on the Air fryer and heat the butter. Add the onion and cook until translucent, 3-4 minutes.
- Add the curry powder and cayenne (if using), and stir until fragrant 1-2 minutes. Pour in the vegetable broth and the cup of water. Stir in the pumpkin puree and tamari. Season to taste with salt and pepper.
- Press Cancel to reset the cooking Directions:. Secure the lid and fix the Pressure Release to Sealing. Select the Pressure Cook or Manual setting and set the cooking time to 5 minutes at high pressure.
- Once done, set aside for at least 10 minutes; the pressure will release naturally. Then switch the Pressure Release to Venting to allow any last steam out.
- Open the lid and puree the soup using an immersion blender or by transferring it to a stand blender. Stir in the unsweetened coconut milk and add salt and pepper to taste.
- Ladle into bowls and top with roasted pumpkin seeds, if desired.

Nutrition:
Calories – 340
Protein – 5.8 g.
Fat – 24.9 g.
Carbs – 30.9 g.

787. My Signature Lemon Chicken Soup
Preparation Time: 10 minutes
Cooking Time: 6 minutes
Servings: 4
Ingredients:
- 1 tablespoon olive oil
- 1 medium onion, chopped
- 3 cloves garlic, roughly chopped
- 2 medium carrots, peeled and sliced
- 6 stalks celery, sliced
- 8 cups fat-free chicken broth
- 1 teaspoon dried thyme
- Salt to taste
- Pepper to taste
- 1½ lbs. boneless skinless chicken breasts

- 4oz. whole wheat spaghetti, broken in 1-inch pieces
- 1 bunch kale, stemmed and roughly chopped, to yield 1.5 cups
- 2 lemons, juiced
- Optional: lemon wedges for serving

Directions:
- Select the Sauté setting and heat the olive oil. Add the onion, garlic, carrots, and celery and sauté for 4-6 minutes. Add the chicken broth and thyme. Add salt and pepper to taste. Add the chicken breasts and stir well.
- Press Cancel to reset the cooking Directions:. Secure the lid and fix the Pressure Release to Sealing. Select the Soup setting and set the cooking time to 6 minutes at high pressure.
- Once done, set aside for at least 10 minutes; the pressure will release naturally. Then switch the Pressure Release to Venting to allow any last steam out.
- Open the lid andtake out the chicken and shred. Add the broken spaghetti and stir; cook for time indicated on package. Add the chicken back to the pot and stir in the kale and lemon juice.
- Ladle into bowls and serve with an extra squeeze of lemon, drizzle of olive oil, or fresh cracked pepper.

Nutrition:
Calories – 388 Protein – 45 g.
Fat – 7 g. Carbs – 35.1 g.

788. Fuss-Free French Onion Soup

Preparation Time: 5 minutes
Cooking Time: 20 minutes
Servings: 4
Ingredients:
- 3 tablespoons unsalted butter
- 3 large yellow onions, halved and then thinly sliced
- 2 tablespoons balsamic vinegar
- 6 cups beef broth
- 2 large sprigs fresh thyme
- 1 teaspoon salt

Directions:
- Select the Sauté setting and heat the butter. Add the onions and stir constantly until completely cooked down and caramelized. This can take 20-30 minutes or more, depending on your onions and the heat of your Air fryer. You're looking for a deep caramel color. If the onions begin to blacken at the edges, use the Adjust button to reduce the heat to Less.
- Once the onions have caramelized, add the balsamic vinegar, red wine vinegar, broth, thyme, and salt, and scrape up any browned bits from the bottom of the pot.
- Press Cancel to reset the cooking Directions:. Secure the lid and fix the Pressure Release to Sealing. Select the Soup setting and set the cooking time to 10 minutes at high pressure.
- Once done, set aside for at least 10 minutes; the pressure will release naturally. Then switch the Pressure Release to Venting to allow any last steam out.
- Open the Air fryer and discard the thyme stems. Flavor with salt and pepper to taste and serve warm.

Nutrition:
Calories – 151 Protein – 5.5 g.
Fat – 9.4 g. Carbs – 11.5 g.

789. Creamy Broccoli And Apple Soup

Preparation Time: 5 minutes
Cooking Time: 5 minutes
Servings: 4
Ingredients:
- 2 tablespoons butter

- 3 medium leeks, white parts only (frozen is fine!)
- 2 shallots, chopped, about 3 tablespoons
- 1 large head broccoli, cut into florets
- 1 large apple, peeled, cored, and diced
- 4 cups vegetable broth
- 1 cup unsweetened coconut milk
- Pepper to taste
- Salt to taste
- Optional: ¼ cup walnuts, toasted
- Optional: ¼ cup coconut cream

Directions:
- Select the Sauté setting and heat the butter. Add the leeks and shallots and cook, stirring constantly, until softened, 4-6 minutes. Add the broccoli and apple and sauté another 5-6 minutes. Add the vegetable broth and stir well.
- Press Cancel to reset the cooking Directions:. Secure the lid and fix the Pressure Release to Sealing. Select the Pressure Cook or Manual setting and set the cooking time to 5 minutes at high pressure.
- Once done, set aside for at least 10 minutes; the pressure will release naturally. Then switch the Pressure Release to Venting to allow any last steam out.
- Open the lid and puree the soup using an immersion blender or by transferring it to a stand blender. Stir in the unsweetened coconut milk and add salt and pepper to taste.
- Ladle into bowls and top with toasted walnuts or a drizzle of coconut cream.

Nutrition:
Calories – 259
Protein – 6.8 g.
Fat – 14.3 g.
Carbs – 32.3 g.

790. Immune-Boost Chard And Sweet Potato Stew

Preparation Time: 10 minutes
Cooking Time: 8 minutes
Servings: 2
Ingredients:
- 2 tablespoons olive oil
- 1 tsp cumin seeds, or 1 tsp ground cumin
- 1 medium onion, diced
- 2 medium sweet potatoes, peeled and in ½ inch cubes
- ½ teaspoon turmeric
- 1 tablespoon fresh ginger, peeled and minced
- 1 teaspoon salt
- 1 teaspoon ground coriander
- 2 cups vegetable broth
- 1 bunch Swiss chard (about 12 oz)
- Optional: lemon wedges for serving

Directions:
- Select the Sauté setting and heat the olive oil. Mix in the onion and cook until clear, 3-5 minutes. If using cumin seeds, add them now and toast them for 1-3 minutes, until fragrant. Otherwise, add the ground cumin in the next step.
- Add the sweet potato, ground cumin (if using), ginger, turmeric, coriander, and salt and cook for 3-4 minutes. Add the vegetable broth and chard. Add more salt and pepper if needed.
- Press Cancel to reset the cooking Directions:. Secure the lid and fix the Pressure Release to Sealing. Select the Pressure Cook or Manual setting and set the cooking time to 8 minutes at high pressure.
- Once done, set aside for at least 10 minutes; the pressure will release naturally. Then switch the Pressure Release to Venting to allow any last steam out.

Scoop into bowls and serve warm with a squeeze of lemon juice, if desired.

Nutrition:
Calories – 308
Protein – 6.2 g.
Fat – 14.4 g.
Carbs – 42.6 g.

791. Moroccan Lentil Soup

Preparation Time: 10 minutes
Cooking Time: 10 minutes
Servings: 4
Ingredients:
- 1 tablespoon olive oil
- 1 small onion, chopped
- cloves garlic, minced
- 3/4 lb. ground turkey
- 1 tablespoon cumin
- 1 teaspoon garlic powder
- 1 teaspoon chili powder
- 1 teaspoon salt, plus more to taste
- ¼ teaspoon cinnamon
- Pepper to taste
- cups beef broth
- 1 cup green or brown lentils

Directions:
- Select the Sauté setting and heat the olive oil. Put in the onion and garlic and sauté until fragrant, 2-3 minutes. Add the ground beef and cumin, garlic powder, chili powder, salt, cinnamon, and pepper. Cook until very well-browned and beginning to sear. Add the beef broth and scrape up any browned bits from the bottom of the pot. Add the lentils and stir well.
- Press Cancel to reset the cooking Directions:. Secure the lid and fix the Pressure Release to Sealing. Select the Soup setting and set the cooking time to 10 minutes at high pressure.
- Once done, set aside for at least 10 minutes; the pressure will release naturally. Then switch the Pressure Release to Venting to allow any last steam out.
- Open the Air fryer and taste; add more salt and pepper to taste. Ladle into bowls and serve with a drizzle of olive oil or fresh cracked pepper.

Nutrition:
Calories – 364
Protein – 31.3 g.
Fat – 12 g.
Carbs – 32.2 g.

792. Salmon Meatballs Soup

Preparation Time: 6 minutes
Cooking Time: 10 minutes
Servings: 5
Ingredients:
- 2 cups hot water
- 2 beaten large eggs
- 1 lb. ground salmon
- 2 minced garlic cloves
- 2 tbsps. butter

Directions:
- In a bowl, mix butter, garlic, eggs and salmon. Apply a seasoning of pepper and salt.
- Combine the mixture and use your hands to form small balls.
- Place the fish balls in the freezer to set for 2 hours or until frozen.
- Pour the hot water in the Air fryer and drop in the frozen fish balls.
- Apply pepper and salt for seasoning.
- Set lid in place and ensure vent is on "Sealing."
- On "Manual" mode, set timer to 10 minutes.

Nutrition:
Calories – 199
Protein – 13.3 g.
Fat – 19.4 g.
Carbs – 0.6 g.

793. Turmeric Chicken Soup

Preparation Time: 6 minutes
Cooking Time: 15 minutes
Servings: 3
Ingredients:
- 1 bay leaf
- ½ cup coconut milk
- 2½ tsps. turmeric powder
- 4 cups water
- 3 boneless chicken breasts

Directions:
- Place all ingredients in the Air fryer.
- Give a good stir to mix everything.
- Set lid in place and ensure vent points to "Sealing."
- Set to "Poultry" mode and set timer to 15 minutes.
- Do natural pressure release.

Nutrition:
Calories – 599
Protein – 46.8 g.
Fat – 61.4 g.
Carbs – 3.8 g.

794. Egg Drop Soup With Shredded Chicken

Preparation Time: 6 minutes
Cooking Time: 15 minutes
Servings: 6
Ingredients:
- 4 beaten eggs
- cups shredded chicken
- 2 tbsps. coconut oil
- 1 chopped celery
- 1 minced onion

Directions:
- Choose the "Sauté" button on the Air fryer and heat the oil.
- Sauté the onion and celery for 2 minutes or until fragrant.
- Add the chicken and 4 cups water.
- Apply pepper and salt for seasoning.
- Set lid in place and ensure vent points to "Sealing."
- Press the "Poultry" button and adjust the time to 10 minutes.
- Do natural pressure release.
- Once the lid is open, press the "Sauté" button and allow the soup to simmer.
- Very gently, gradually pour in the beaten eggs and allow to simmer for 3 more minutes.

Nutrition:
Calories – 154 Protein – 9.6 g.
Fat – 12.8 g.
Carbs – 2.9 g.

795. Asian Egg Drop Soup

Preparation Time: 6 minutes
Cooking Time: 9 minutes
Servings: 3
Ingredients:
- 2 beaten eggs
- 1 tsp. grated ginger
- 3 cups water
- 2 cups chopped kale
- 3 tbsps. coconut oil

Directions:
- Place all ingredients except for the beaten eggs in the Air fryer.
- Apply pepper and salt for seasoning.
- Set lid in place and ensure vent points to "Sealing."
- On "Manual" mode, set timer to 6 minutes.
- Do natural pressure release.
- Once the lid is open, press the "Sauté" button and allow the soup to simmer.
- Very gently, gradually pour in the beaten eggs and allow to simmer for 3 more minutes.

Nutrition:
Calories – 209
Protein – 6.5 g.
Fat – 20.3 g.
Carbs – 1.7 g.

796. Leek And Salmon Soup

Preparation Time: 6 minutes
Cooking Time: 10 minutes
Servings: 4
Ingredients:
- 1 lb. sliced salmon
- 1¾ cup coconut milk
- 2 tbsps. avocado oil
- 3 minced garlic cloves
- 4 trimmed and chopped leeks

Directions:
- Place all ingredients in the Air fryer.
- Apply pepper and salt for seasoning.
- Stir to combine all ingredients.
- Set lid in place and ensure vent points to "Sealing."
- On "Manual" mode, cook for 10 minutes.

Nutrition:
Calories – 535
Protein – 27.3 g.
Fat – 40.9 g.
Carbs – 19.5 g.

797. Thai Coconut Soup

Preparation Time: 6 minutes
Cooking Time: 6 minutes
Servings: 2
Ingredients:
- 6 oz. shrimps
- 1 cup fresh cilantro
- 2 cups water
- 3 kaffir limes
- 1 ½ cups organic coconut milk

Directions:
- In the air fryer, add in all ingredients excluding cilantro.
- Set lid in place and ensure vent points to "Sealing."
- While on "Manual" mode, set timer to 6 minutes.
- Do natural pressure release.
- Once the lid is open, garnish with the fresh cilantro.

Nutrition:
Calories – 517
Protein – 21.9 g.
Fat – 44.6 g.
Carbs – 15.4 g.

798. Ginger Halibut Soup

Preparation Time: 6 minutes
Cooking Time: 12 minutes
Servings: 4
Ingredients:
- 2 cups water
- 2 tbsps. minced fresh ginger
- 2 tbsps. coconut oil
- 1 lb. sliced halibut
- 1 chopped large onion

Directions:
- Choose the "Sauté" button on the Air fryer and heat the oil.
- Sauté the onion until fragrant.
- Pour in the water and the rest of the ingredients. Apply pepper and salt for seasoning.
- Set lid in place and ensure vent points to "Sealing."
- While on "Manual" mode, set timer to 10 minutes.

Nutrition:
Calories – 259
Protein – 10.9 g.
Fat – 22.8 g.
Carbs – 7.9 g.

799. Salmon Head Soup

Preparation Time: 6 minutes
Cooking Time: 12 minutes
Servings: 1
Ingredients:
- 1 sliced onion
- 3-inch slivered ginger piece
- 4 tbsps. coconut oil
- 1 salmon head
- 3 cups water

Directions:
- Choose the "Sauté" button on the Air fryer and heat the oil.
- Sauté the onion until fragrant.
- Pour in the water and add the salmon head and ginger.
- Apply pepper and salt for seasoning.
- Set lid in place and ensure vent points to "Sealing."
- While on "Manual" mode, set timer to 10 minutes.
- Do quick pressure release.

Nutrition:
Calories – 474
Protein – 15.3 g.
Fat – 54.4 g.
Carbs – 1.8 g.

800. Chicken Curry Soup
Preparation Time: 7 minutes
Cooking Time: 25 minutes
Servings: 3-4
Ingredients:
- 1½ bone-in chicken halved breast
- 3 Diagonally sliced medium carrots
- 2 bay leaves
- 1 Pinch of Kosher salt
- 6 cups of low-sodium chicken broth
- 2 tablespoons of unsalted butter
- 1 thinly sliced large onion
- 1 teaspoon of sugar
- 1 and ½ teaspoons of Madras curry powder
- 1/3 Cup of jasmine rice
- 3 tablespoons of finely chopped fresh mint
- 3 tablespoons of chopped fresh dill
- 1 lemon sliced into thin wedges

Directions:
- Combine your chicken, the carrots, the bay leaf and 1 pinch of salt into your Air fryer.
- Add around 3 cups of broth and press boil at a medium heat.
- Close the lid and set at high pressure to around 10 to 15 minutes.
- In the meantime; heat the quantity of butter over a medium low heat in a deep sauce pan.
- Add the sugar and the onion with 1 pinch of salt and cook for around 5 minutes
- Add the powder of curry and cook for around 2 minutes
- When the timer beeps, add the broth and the rice; then set the heat to high and let simmer for 10 minutes
- Remove the chicken out of the broth and shred the chicken meat into small pieces; then place it back in the broth.
- Puree the mixture of the rice with a blender until it becomes smooth and then pour it into the mixture of the shredded chicken and the broth and let simmer for around 5 minutes
- Once the soup is ready, garnish with herbs and then serve it with lemon
- Enjoy!

Nutrition:
Calories – 147.2
Protein – 16 g.
Fat – 5.1 g.
Carbs – 7.6 g.

801. Salmon Stew
Preparation Time: 6 minutes
Cooking Time: 13 minutes
Servings: 3
Ingredients:
- 48oz. salmon fillets
- 3 cups spinach leaves
- 3 tbsps. olive oil
- 3 cups water
- 3 minced garlic cloves

Directions:
- Choose the "Sauté" button on the Air fryer and heat the olive oil.
- Sauté the garlic until fragrant.

Add the water and salmon fillets. Apply pepper and salt for seasoning.
Set lid in place and ensure vent points to "Sealing."
While on "Manual" mode, set timer to 10 minutes.
Do quick pressure release.
Once the lid is open, press the "Sauté" button and add the spinach.
Allow to simmer for 3 minutes.

Nutrition:
Calories – 825 Protein 46.1 g.
Fat – 94.5 g.
Carbs – 2.1 g.

802. Coconut Seafood Soup

Preparation Time: 6 minutes
Cooking Time: 8 minutes
Servings: 5
Ingredients:
- 1 cup coconut milk
- 10 peeled and deveined shrimps
- 1 crushed thumb-size ginger
- 4 tilapia fillets
- 2 cups water

Directions:
Place all ingredients in the Air fryer.
Stir in pepper and salt.
Set lid in place and ensure vent points to "Sealing."
While on "Manual" mode, set timer to 8 minutes.

Nutrition:
Calories – 238 Protein – 13.6 g.
Fat – 28.8 g. Carbs – 2.7 g.

803. Chicken Soup

Preparation Time: 6 minutes
Cooking Time: 20 minutes
Servings: 4
Ingredients:
- 3 lb of pastured chicken
- 2 roughly chopped carrots
- 1 roughly chopped celery stalk
- ½ radish or turnip chopped into small cubes
- 1 Tbsp of dried parsley
- 1 Tbsp of thyme
- 1 Tbsp of thyme and rosemary
- 1 Tbsp of rosemary
- 2 bay leaves
- 3 crushed garlic cloves
- 1 Medium sliced red or white onion
- 1 Tbsp of sea salt
- 1 teaspoon of freshly ground black pepper
- 1 Finely chopped scallion or chopped green onion

Directions:
In the liner of your Air fryer, arrange the vegetables; then add the chicken and then add the herbs on the top.
Add around 4 to Cups of water.
Tightly Make sure to lock the lid and then close the vent.
Press the setting of SOUP
When the timer beeps, naturally release the pressure for around 20 minutes.
Open the lid, take out the chicken and debone it; then reserve it to prepare the broth Place the meat back into the Air fryer Smash the carrots and the celery against the side of the pot
Add 1 pinch of salt and 1 pinch pepper according to the taste.
Garnish the soup with the scallion and the sliced onion Ladle the soup into bowls
Serve and enjoy your soup!

Nutrition:
Calories – 90 Protein – 11 g.
Fat – 2 g. Carbs – 6 g.

804. Poached Egg Soup

Preparation Time: 6 minutes
Cooking Time: 36 minutes
Servings: 2
Ingredients:
- Pepper

Salt
1 lb. chicken bones
1 chopped romaine lettuce head
2 whole eggs

Directions:

Place 2 cups water and chicken bones in the Air fryer.
Set lid in place and ensure vent points to "Sealing."
Set to "Poultry" mode and the timer to 30 minutes.
Do quick pressure release.
Take the bones out and discard.
Press the "Sauté" button and allow the soup to simmer.
Once simmered, carefully crack the eggs open and stir for 3 minutes.
Add the lettuce and season with salt and pepper.
Allow to simmer for 3 more minutes.

Nutrition:
Calories – 443
Protein – 58.3 g.
Fat – 39.2 g.
Carbs – 4.3 g.

805. Simple Chicken And Kale Soup

Preparation Time: 6 minutes
Cooking Time: 20 minutes
Servings: 4
Ingredients:

1 lb. boneless chicken breasts
4 cups chopped kale
3 tbsps. coconut oil
2 chopped celery stalks
1 diced onion

Directions:

Choose the "Sauté" button on the Air fryer and heat the oil.
Sauté the onions and celery until fragrant.
Add the chicken breasts and sear for 2 minutes on each side.
Pour in 3 cups water and Apply pepper and salt for seasoning.
Set lid in place and ensure vent points to "Sealing."
Set to "Poultry" mode and the timer to 15 minutes.
Use a natural pressure release and open the lid.
Once the lid is open, press the "Sauté" button and add the kale.
Allow to simmer for 3 minutes.

Nutrition:
Calories – 303
Protein – 20.8 g.
Fat – 29.3 g.
Carbs – 2.2 g.

806. Asparagus Soup

Preparation Time: 6 minutes
Cooking Time: 10 minutes
Servings: 4
Ingredients:

½ lb of fresh asparagus cut into pieces. Make sure to remove the woody ends of the asparagus.
1 Sliced or chopped medium sized yellow onion.
3 Chopped or minced cloves of garlic cloves.
3 tbsp of coconuts oil.
½ teaspoon of dried thyme
5 Cups of bone broth
Zest + 1 Tbsp of juice of organic lemon
1 Teaspoon of sea salt
2 Cups of organic sour cream*

Directions:

Prepare your asparagus, the onion and the garlic. Remove all the woody ends from the asparagus stalks and discard it.
Chop the asparagus into pieces of 1 inch each.
Slice the onion into halves and chop it.
Smash the garlic cloves or chop it.
Set the ingredients aside.

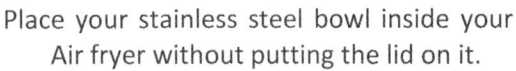

Place your stainless steel bowl inside your Air fryer without putting the lid on it.

Put the air fryerto the button "Sauté" and then add the coconut oil; the add onions and the garlic. Cook the mixture for 5 minutes and keep stirring occasionally; add the thyme and the cook for 1 more minutes.

Add the broth, the asparagus and the lemon zest with the salt.

Lock the lid of the Air fryer and press the button "Manual" high pressure.

Set the pressure timer to 5 minutes and when the timer goes off, add the sour cream and stir; of course after the air fryer releases the steam.

Serve and enjoy

Nutrition:
Calories – 161.2
Protein – 6.3 g.
Fat – 8.2 g.
Carbs – 16.4 g.

807. Leftover Shredded Chicken Soup

Preparation Time: 6 minutes
Cooking Time: 12 minutes
Servings: 3
Ingredients:
- 7cups water
- 2cups shredded leftover chicken meat
- 2tbsps. coconut oil
- 8minced garlic cloves
- 1 chopped onion

Directions:
Choose the "Sauté" button on the Air fryer and heat the oil.

Sauté the onions and garlic until fragrant.

Add the chicken meat and Apply pepper and salt for seasoning.

Pour in the water. Season with more salt and pepper.

Set lid in place and ensure vent points to "Sealing."

While on "Manual" mode, set timer to 10 minutes.

Nutrition:
Calories – 356 Protein – 23.4 g.
Fat – 32.1 g.
Carbs – 2.5 g.

808. Cream Of Broccoli Soup

Preparation Time: 6 minutes
Cooking Time: 34 minutes
Servings: 5
Ingredients:
- 1 sliced small avocado
- 1 tsp. paprika powder
- ½ lb. chicken bones
- 2heads broccoli florets
- 4cups water

Directions:
Place the chicken bones and water in the Air fryer.

Apply pepper and salt for seasoning

Set lid in place and ensure vent points to "Sealing."

While on "Manual" mode, set timer to 30 minutes.

Do quick pressure release.

Once the lid is open, discard the bones.

Stir in the broccoli.

Close the lid once more and choose the "Manual" button and cook for 4 minutes.

Do quick pressure release.

Transfer all contents into a blender then add avocado slices.

Pulse until smooth and set in a bowl.

Apply a sprinkle of paprika powder.

Nutrition:
Calories – 118
Protein – 7.3 g.
Fat – 10.3 g.
Carbs – 1.9 g.

809. Turkey With Ginger And Turmeric Soup

Preparation Time: 6 minutes
Cooking Time: 17 minutes
Servings: 4
Ingredients:
- 1 lb. chopped turkey meat
- 3 tbsps. coconut oil
- 1 tsp. turmeric powder
- 1 sliced thumb-size ginger
- 2 chopped stalks of celery

Directions:
- Choose the "Sauté" button on the Air fryer and heat the oil.
- Stir in the celery, ginger, and turmeric powder until fragrant.
- Add the turkey meat and stir for another minute.
- Pour in 3 cups of water and Apply pepper and salt for seasoning.
- Set lid in place and ensure vent points to "Sealing."
- While on "Manual" mode, set timer to 15 minutes.
- Do natural pressure release.

Nutrition:
Calories – 287
Protein – 22.8 g.
Fat – 24.3 g.
Carbs – 0.8 g.

810. Butternut Squash Soup

Preparation Time: 5 minutes
Cooking Time: 10 minutes
Servings: 4
Ingredients:
- 1 Peeled and diced Butternut squash.
- 1 Peeled and diced apple
- 1 Tbsp of Ginger powder or you can use pureed ginger
- 4 Cups of chicken broth
- 2 Tbsp of Coconut oil to taste

Directions:
- Start by hitting the sauté button on the Instant you are using so that you pre-heat it.
- When you become able to see the word "HOT", add the coconuts oil and add some of the butternut squash cubes to it then brown it ever lightly for approximately 5 minutes. Now, add the remaining quantity of squash and also add the rest of your ingredients.
- Close; then lock your Air fryer.
- Now, press your manual and use the + for you to add 10 more minutes at high pressure to the cooking time.
- When the time is over, open the air fryer by using the Quick Release.
- Puree your mixture by using a blender right in your air fryer or you can also take the mixture out of the air fryer and place it into a blender.
- Serve and enjoy your delicious and healthy soup.

Nutrition:
Calories – 110
Protein – 2 g.
Fat – 2.5 g.
Carbs – 22 g.

CHAPTER 12:

Desserts

811. Apple Chips
Preparation Time: 10 minutes
Cooking Time: 20 minutes
Servings: 2
Ingredients:
- 1 apple, sliced thinly
- Salt to taste
- ¼ teaspoon ground cinnamon

Directions:
- Preheat the air fryer to 350 degrees F.
- Toss the apple slices in salt and cinnamon.
- Add to the air fryer.
- Let cool before serving.

Nutrition:
Calories – 59 Protein – 0.3 g.
Fat – 0.2 g.
Carbs – 15.6 g.

812. Sweetened Plantains
Preparation Time: 5 minutes
Cooking Time: 8 minutes
Servings: 4
Ingredients:
- 2 ripe plantains, sliced
- 2 teaspoons avocado oil
- Salt to taste
- Maple syrup

Directions:
- Toss the plantains in oil.
- Season with salt.
- Cook in the air fryer basket at 400 degrees F for 10 minutes, shaking after 5 minutes.
- Drizzle with maple syrup before serving.

Nutrition:
Calories – 125 Protein – 1.2 g.
Fat – 0.6 g. Carbs – 32 g.

813. Roasted Bananas
Preparation Time: 5 minutes
Cooking Time: 5 minutes
Servings: 2
Ingredients:
- 2 cups bananas, cubed
- 1 teaspoon avocado oil
- 1 tablespoon maple syrup
- 1 teaspoon brown sugar
- 1 cup almond milk

Directions:
- Coat the banana cubes with oil and maple syrup.
- Sprinkle with brown sugar.
- Cook at 375 F in the air fryer for 5 minutes.
- Drizzle milk on top of the bananas before serving.

Nutrition:
Calories – 107 Protein – 1.3 g.
Fat – 0.7 g. Carbs – 27 g.

814. Pear Crisp
Preparation Time: 10 minutes
Cooking Time: 25 minutes
Servings: 2
Ingredients:
- 1 cup flour
- 1 stick vegan butter
- 1 tablespoon cinnamon
- ½ cup sugar - 2 pears, cubed

Directions:
- Mix flour and butter to form crumbly texture.
- Add cinnamon and sugar.
- Put the pears in the air fryer.
- Pour and spread the mixture on top of the pears.
- Cook at 350 degrees F for 25 minutes.

Nutrition:
Calories – 544 Protein – 7.4 g.
Fat – 0.9 g. Carbs – 132.3 g.

815. Easy Pears Dessert
Preparation Time: 10 minutes
Cooking Time: 25 minutes
Servings: 12
Ingredients:
- 6 big pears, cored and chopped
- ½ cup raisins

1 teaspoon ginger powder
¼ cup coconut sugar
1 teaspoon lemon zest, grated

Directions:

In a container that fits your air fryer, mix pears with raisins, ginger, sugar and lemon zest, stir, introduce in the fryer and cook at 350 degrees F for 25 minutes.

Divide into bowls and serve cold.

Enjoy!

Nutrition:

Calories – 200 Protein – 6 g.
Fat – 3 g. Carbs – 6 g.

816. Vanilla Strawberry Mix

Preparation Time: 10 minutes
Cooking Time: 20 minutes
Servings: 10
Ingredients:

2 tablespoons lemon juice
2 pounds strawberries
4 cups coconut sugar
1 teaspoon cinnamon powder
1 teaspoon vanilla extract

Directions:

In a pot that fits your air fryer, mix strawberries with coconut sugar, lemon juice, cinnamon and vanilla, stir gently, introduce in the fryer and cook at 350 degrees F for 20 minutes

Divide into bowls and serve cold.

Enjoy!

Nutrition:

Calories – 140 Protein – 2 g.
Fat – 0 g. Carbs – 5 g.

817. Sweet Bananas And Sauce

Preparation Time: 10 minutes
Cooking Time: 20 minutes
Servings: 4
Ingredients:

Juice of ½ lemon
3 tablespoons agave nectar
1 tablespoon coconut oil
4 bananas, peeled and sliced diagonally
½ teaspoon cardamom seeds

Directions:

Arrange bananas in a pan that fits your air fryer, add agave nectar, lemon juice, oil and cardamom, introduce in the fryer and cook at 360 degrees F for 20 minutes

Divide bananas and sauce between plates and serve.

Enjoy!

Nutrition:

Calories – 210
Protein – 3 g.
Fat – 1 g.
Carbs – 8 g.

818. Cinnamon Apples And Mandarin Sauce

Preparation Time: 10 minutes
Cooking Time: 20 minutes
Servings: 4
Ingredients:

4 apples, cored, peeled and cored
2 cups mandarin juice
¼ cup maple syrup
2 teaspoons cinnamon powder
1 tablespoon ginger, grated

Directions:

In a pot that fits your air fryer, mix apples with mandarin juice, maple syrup, cinnamon and ginger, introduce in the fryer and cook at 365 degrees F for 20 minutes

Divide apples mix between plates and serve warm.

Enjoy!

Nutrition:

Calories – 170 Protein – 4 g.
Fat – 1 g. Carbs – 6 g.

819. Chocolate Vanilla Bars
Preparation Time: 10 minutes
Cooking Time: 7 minutes
Servings: 12
Ingredients:
- 1 cup sugar free and vegan chocolate chips
- 2 tablespoons coconut butter
- 2/3 cup coconut cream
- tablespoons stevia
- ¼ teaspoon vanilla extract

Directions:
- Put the cream in a bowl, add stevia, butter and chocolate chips and stir
- Leave aside for 5 minutes, stir well and mix the vanilla.
- Transfer the mix into a lined baking sheet, introduce in your air fryer and cook at 356 degrees F for 7 minutes.
- Leave the mix aside to cool down, slice and serve.
- Enjoy!

Nutrition:
Calories – 120
Protein – 1 g.
Fat – 5 g.
Carbs – 6 g.

820. Raspberry Bars
Preparation Time: 10 minutes
Cooking Time: 6 minutes
Servings: 12
Ingredients:
- ½ cup coconut butter, melted
- ½ cup coconut oil
- ½ cup raspberries, dried
- ¼ cup swerve
- ½ cup coconut, shredded

Directions:
- In your food processor, blend dried berries very well.
- In a bowl that fits your air fryer, mix oil with butter, swerve, coconut and raspberries, toss well, introduce in the fryer and cook at 320 degrees F for 6 minutes.
- Spread this on a lined baking sheet, keep in the fridge for an hour, slice and serve.
- Enjoy!

Nutrition:
Calories – 164 Protein – 2 g.
Fat – 22 g. Carbs – 4 g.

821. Cocoa Berries Cream
Preparation Time: 10 minutes
Cooking Time: 10 minutes
Servings: 4
Ingredients:
- 3 tablespoons cocoa powder
- 14 ounces coconut cream
- 1 cup blackberries
- 1 cup raspberries
- 2 tablespoons stevia

Directions:
- In a bowl, whisk cocoa powder with stevia and cream and stir.
- Add raspberries and blackberries, toss gently, transfer to a pan that fits your air fryer, introduce in the fryer and cook at 350 degrees F for 10 minutes.
- Divide into bowls and serve cold.
- Enjoy!

Nutrition:
Calories – 205 Protein – 2 g.
Fat – 34 g. Carbs – 6 g.

822. Cocoa Pudding
Preparation Time: 10 minutes
Cooking Time: 20 minutes
Servings: 2
Ingredients:
- 2 tablespoons water
- ½ tablespoon agar
- 4 tablespoons stevia
- 4 tablespoons cocoa powder
- 2 cups coconut milk, hot

Directions:
- In a bowl, mix milk with stevia and cocoa powder and stir well.
- In a bowl, mix agar with water, stir well, add to the cocoa mix, stir and transfer to a pudding pan that fits your air fryer.
- Introduce in the fryer and cook at 356 degrees F for 20 minutes.
- Serve the pudding cold.
- Enjoy!

Nutrition:
Calories – 170 Protein – 3 g.
Fat – 2 g. Carbs – 4 g.

823. Blueberry Coconut Crackers

Preparation Time: 10 minutes
Cooking Time: 30 minutes
Servings: 12
Ingredients:
- ½ cup coconut butter
- ½ cup coconut oil, melted
- 1 cup blueberries
- 3 tablespoons coconut sugar

Directions:
- In a pot that fits your air fryer, mix coconut butter with coconut oil, raspberries and sugar, toss, introduce in the fryer and cook at 367 degrees F for 30 minutes
- Spread on a lined baking sheet, keep in the fridge for a few hours, slice crackers and serve.
- Enjoy!

Nutrition:
Calories – 174 Protein – 7 g.
Fat – 5 g. Carbs – 4 g.

824. Cauliflower Pudding

Preparation Time: 10 minutes
Cooking Time: 30 minutes
Servings: 4
Ingredients:
- 2½ cups water
- 1 cup coconut sugar
- 2 cups cauliflower rice
- 2 cinnamon sticks
- ½ cup coconut, shredded

Directions:
- In a pot that fits your air fryer, mix water with coconut sugar, cauliflower rice, cinnamon and coconut, stir, introduce in the fryer and cook at 365 degrees F for 30 minutes
- Divide pudding into cups and serve cold.
- Enjoy!

Nutrition:
Calories – 203 Protein – 4 g.
Fat – 4 g. Carbs – 9 g.

825. Sweet Vanilla Rhubarb

Preparation Time: 10 minutes
Cooking Time: 10 minutes
Servings: 4
Ingredients:
- 5 cups rhubarb, chopped
- 2 tablespoons coconut butter, melted
- 1/3 cup water
- 1 tablespoon stevia
- 1 teaspoon vanilla extract

Directions:
- Put rhubarb, ghee, water, stevia and vanilla extract in a pan that fits your air fryer, introduce in the fryer and cook at 365 degrees F for 10 minutes
- Divide into small bowls and serve cold.
- Enjoy!

Nutrition:
Calories – 103 Protein – 2 g.
Fat – 2 g. Carbs – 6 g.

826. Pineapple Pudding

Preparation Time: 10 minutes
Cooking Time: 5 minutes
Servings: 8
Ingredients:
- 1 tablespoon avocado oil

- 1 cup rice - 14 ounces milk
- Sugar to the taste
- 8 ounces canned pineapple, chopped

Directions:

- In your air fryer, mix oil, milk and rice, stir, cover and cook on High for 3 minutes.
- Add sugar and pineapple, stir, cover and cook on High for 2 minutes more.
- Divide into dessert bowls and serve.

Nutrition:

Calories – 154 Protein – 8 g.
Fat – 4 g. Carbs – 14 g.

827. Blueberry Jam

Preparation Time: 10 minutes
Cooking Time: 11 minutes
Servings: 2
Ingredients:

- ½ pound blueberries
- 1/3 pound sugar
- Zest from ½ lemon, grated
- ½ tablespoon butter
- A pinch of cinnamon powder

Directions:

- Put the blueberries in your blender, pulse them well, strain, transfer to your pressure cooker, add sugar, lemon zest and cinnamon, stir, cover and simmer on sauté mode for 3 minutes.
- Add butter, stir, cover the fryer and cook on High for 8 minutes.
- Transfer to a jar and serve.

Nutrition:

Calories – 211 Protein – 5 g.
Fat – 3 g. Carbs – 6 g.

828. Plum Jam

Preparation Time: 20 minutes
Cooking Time: 8 minutes
Servings: 12
Ingredients:

- 3 pounds plums, stones removed and roughly chopped
- 2 tablespoons lemon juice
- 2 pounds sugar
- 1 teaspoon vanilla extract
- 3 ounces water

Directions:

- In your air fryer, mix plums with sugar and vanilla extract, stir and leave aside for 20 minutes
- Add lemon juice and water, stir, cover and cook on High for 8 minutes.
- Divide into bowls and serve cold.

Nutrition:

Calories – 191 Protein – 13 g.
Fat – 3 g. Carbs – 12 g.

829. Coconut Pancake

Preparation Time: 10 minutes
Cooking Time: 20 minutes
Servings: 4
Ingredients:

- 2 cups self-raising flour
- 2 tablespoons sugar - 2 eggs
- 1 and ½ cups coconut milk
- A drizzle of olive oil

Directions:

- In a bowl, mix eggs with sugar, milk and flour and whisk until you obtain a batter.
- Grease your air fryer with the oil, add the batter, spread into the pot, cover and cook on Low for 20 minutes.
- Slice pancake, divide between plates and serve cold.

Nutrition:

Calories – 162 Protein – 8 g.
Fat – 3 g. Carbs – 7 g.

830. Apples And Red Grape Juice

Preparation Time: 10 minutes
Cooking Time: 10 minutes
Servings: 2
Ingredients:

- 2 apples

½ cup natural red grape juice
2 tablespoons raisins
1 teaspoon cinnamon powder
½ tablespoons sugar

Directions:

Put the apples in your air fryer, add grape juice, raisins, cinnamon and stevia, toss a bit, cover and cook on High for 10 minutes.

Divide into 2 bowls and serve.

Nutrition:

Calories – 110 Protein – 3 g.
Fat – 1 g. Carbs – 3 g.

831. Coconut And Avocado Pudding

Preparation Time: 2 hours
Cooking Time: 2 minutes
Servings: 3
Ingredients:

½ cup avocado oil
4 tablespoons sugar
1 tablespoon cocoa powder
14 ounces canned coconut milk
1 avocado, pitted, peeled and chopped

Directions:

In a bowl, mix oil with cocoa powder and half of the sugar, stir well, transfer to a lined container, keep in the fridge for 1 hour and chop into small pieces.

In your air fryer, mix coconut milk with avocado and the rest of the sugar, blend using an immersion blender, cover cooker and cook on High for 2 minutes.

Add chocolate chips, stir, divide pudding into bowls and keep in the fridge until you serve it.

Nutrition:

Calories – 140
Protein – 4 g.
Fat – 3 g.
Carbs – 3 g.

832. Cinnamon Rolls

Preparation Time: 2 hours
Cooking Time: 15 minutes
Servings: 8
Ingredients:

1 pound vegan bread dough
¾ cup coconut sugar
1 and ½ tablespoons cinnamon powder
2 tablespoons vegetable oil

Directions:

Roll dough on a floured working surface, shape a rectangle and brush with the oil.

In a bowl, mix cinnamon with sugar, stir, sprinkle this over dough, roll into a log, seal well and cut into 8 pieces.

Leave rolls to rise for 2 hours, place them in your air fryer's basket, cook at 350 degrees F for 5 minutes, flip them, cook for 4 minutes more and transfer to a platter.

Enjoy!

Nutrition:

Calories – 170
Protein – 6 g.
Fat – 1 g.
Carbs – 7 g.

833. Cherries And Rhubarb Bowls

Preparation Time: 10 minutes
Cooking Time: 35 minutes
Servings: 4
Ingredients:

2 cups cherries, pitted and halved
1 cup rhubarb, sliced
1 cup apple juice
2 tablespoons sugar
½ cup raisins.

Directions:

In a pot that fits your air fryer, combine the cherries with the rhubarb and the other ingredients, toss, cook at 330 degrees F for 35 minutes, divide into bowls, cool down and serve.

Nutrition:
Calories – 212
Protein – 7 g.
Fat – 8 g.
Carbs – 13 g.

834. Pumpkin Bowls
Preparation Time: 10 minutes
Cooking Time: 15 minutes
Servings: 4
Ingredients:
- 2 cups pumpkin flesh, cubed
- 1 cup heavy cream
- 1 teaspoon cinnamon powder
- 3 tablespoons sugar
- 1 teaspoon nutmeg, ground

Directions:
In a pot that fits your air fryer, combine the pumpkin with the cream and the other ingredients, introduce in the fryer and cook at 360 degrees F for 15 minutes. Divide into bowls and serve.

Nutrition:
Calories – 212
Protein – 7 g.
Fat – 5 g.
Carbs – 15 g.

835. Apple Jam
Preparation Time: 10 minutes
Cooking Time: 25 minutes
Servings: 4
Ingredients:
- 1 cup water
- ½ cup sugar
- 1-pound apples, cored, peeled and chopped
- ½ teaspoon nutmeg, ground

Directions:
In a pot that suits your air fryer, mix the apples with the water and the other ingredients, toss, introduce the pan in the fryer and cook at 370 degrees F for 25 minutes.
Blend a bit using an immersion blender, divide into jars and serve.

Nutrition:
Calories – 204
Protein – 4 g.
Fat – 3 g.
Carbs – 12 g.

836. Yogurt And Pumpkin Cream
Preparation Time: 10 minutes
Cooking Time: 30 minutes
Servings: 4
Ingredients:
- 1 cup yogurt
- 1 cup pumpkin puree
- 2 eggs, whisked
- 2 tablespoons sugar
- ½ teaspoon vanilla extract

Directions:
In a large bowl, mix the puree and the yogurt with the other ingredients, whisk well, pour into 4 ramekins, put them in the air fryer and cook at 370 degrees F for 30 minutes.
Cool down and serve.

Nutrition:
Calories – 192 Protein – 4 g.
Fat – 7 g.
Carbs – 12 g.

837. Raisins Rice Mix
Preparation Time: 10 minutes
Cooking Time: 25 minutes
Servings: 6
Ingredients:
- 1 cup white rice
- 2 cups coconut milk
- 3 tablespoons sugar
- 1 teaspoon vanilla extract
- ½ cup raisins

Directions:
In the air fryer's pan, combine the rice with the milk and the other ingredients, introduce the pan in the fryer and cook at 320 degrees F for 25 minutes.
Divide into bowls and serve warm.

Nutrition:
Calories – 132
Protein – 7 g.
Fat – 6 g.
Carbs – 11 g.

838. Orange Bowls
Preparation Time: 10 minutes
Cooking Time: 10 minutes
Servings: 4
Ingredients:
- 1 cup oranges, peeled and cut into segments
- 1 cup cherries, pitted and halved
- 1 cup mango, peeled and cubed
- 1 cup orange juice
- 2 tablespoon sugar

Directions:
In the air fryer's pan, mix the oranges with the cherries and the other ingredients, toss and cook at 320 degrees F for 10 minutes.
Divide into bowls and serve cold.

Nutrition:
Calories – 191
Protein – 4 g.
Fat – 7 g.
Carbs – 14 g.

839. Strawberry Jam
Preparation Time: 10 minutes
Cooking Time: 25 minutes
Servings: 8
Ingredients:
- 1 pound strawberries, chopped
- 1 tablespoon lemon zest, grated
- 1 and ½ cups water
- ½ cup sugar
- ½ tablespoon lemon juice

Directions:
In the air fryer's pan, mix the berries with the water and the other ingredients, stir, introduce the pan in your air fryer and cook at 330 degrees F for 25 minutes.
Divide into bowls and serve cold.

Nutrition:
Calories – 202
Protein – 7 g.
Fat – 8 g.
Carbs – 6 g.

840. Caramel Cream
Preparation Time: 10 minutes
Cooking Time: 15 minutes
Servings: 4
Ingredients:
- 1 cup heavy cream
- 3 tablespoons caramel syrup
- ½ cup coconut cream
- 1 tablespoon sugar
- ½ teaspoon cinnamon powder

Directions:
In a bowl, mix the cream with the caramel syrup and the other ingredients, whisk, divide into small ramekins, introduce in the fryer and cook at 320 degrees F and bake for 15 minutes.
Divide into bowls and serve cold.

Nutrition:
Calories – 234 Protein – 5 g.
Fat – 13 g. Carbs – 11 g.

841. Wrapped Pears
Preparation Time: 10 minutes
Cooking Time: 15 minutes
Servings: 4
Ingredients:
- 4 puff pastry sheets
- 14 ounces vanilla custard
- 2 pears, halved

1 egg, whisked

2tbsp. sugar

Directions:
- Put the puff pastry slices on a clean surface, add spoonful of vanilla custard in the center of each, top with pear halves and wrap.
- Brush pears with egg, sprinkle sugar and place them in your air fryer's basket and cook at 320 °F for 15 minutes.
- Divide parcels on plates and serve.

Nutrition:

Calories – 200 Protein – 6 g.

Fat – 7 g. Carbs – 6 g.

842. Lemon Bars

Preparation Time: 10 minutes
Cooking Time: 35 minutes
Servings: 8
Ingredients:
- ½ cup butter, melted
- 1 cup erythritol
- 1 and ¾ cups almond flour
- 3eggs, whisked
- Juice of 3 lemons

Directions:
- In a bowl, mix 1 cup flour with half of the erythritol and the butter, stir well and press into a baking dish that fits the air fryer lined with parchment paper.
- Put the dish in your air fryer and cook at 350 degrees F for 10 minutes.
- For the meantime, in a bowl, blend the rest of the flour with the remaining erythritol and the other ingredients and whisk well.
- Spread this over the crust, put the dish in the air fryer once more and cook at 350 degrees F for 25 minutes.
- Cool down, cut into bars and serve.

Nutrition:

Calories – 210 Protein – 8 g.

Fat – 12 g. Carbs – 4 g.

843. Coconut Donuts

Preparation Time: 5 minutes
Cooking Time: 15 minutes
Servings: 4
Ingredients:
- 8ounces coconut flour
- 1 egg, whisked
- and ½ tablespoons butter, melted
- 4ounces coconut milk
- 1 teaspoon baking powder

Directions:
- In a bowl, put all of the ingredients and mix well.
- Shape donuts from this mix, place them in your air fryer's basket and cook at 370 degrees F for 15 minutes.
- Serve warm.

Nutrition:

Calories – 190 Protein – 6 g.

Fat – 12 g. Carbs – 4 g.

844. Blueberry Cream

Preparation Time: 4 minutes
Cooking Time: 20 minutes
Servings: 6
Ingredients:
- 2cups blueberries
- Juice of ½ lemon
- 2tablespoons water
- 1 teaspoon vanilla extract
- 2tablespoons swerve

Directions:
- In a large bowl, put all ingredients and mix well.
- Divide this into 6 ramekins, put them in the air fryer and cook at 340 degrees F for 20 minutes
- Cool down and serve.

Nutrition:

Calories – 123

Protein – 3 g.

Fat – 2 g.

Carbs – 4 g.

845. Blackberry Chia Jam
Preparation Time: 10 minutes
Cooking Time: 30 minutes
Servings: 12
Ingredients:
- 3 cups blackberries
- ¼ cup swerve
- 4 tablespoons lemon juice
- 4 tablespoons chia seeds

Directions:
- In a pan that suits the air fryer, combine all the Ingredients: and toss.
- Put the pan in the fryer and cook at 300 degrees F for 30 minutes.
- Divide into cups and serve cold.

Nutrition:
Calories – 100
Protein – 1 g.
Fat – 2 g.
Carbs – 3 g.

846. Mixed Berries Cream
Preparation Time: 5 minutes
Cooking Time: 30 minutes
Servings: 6
Ingredients:
- 12 ounces blackberries
- 6 ounces raspberries
- 12 ounces blueberries
- ¾ cup swerve
- 2 ounces coconut cream

Directions:
- In a bowl, put all the Ingredients: and mix well.
- Divide this into 6 ramekins, put them in your air fryer and cook at 320 degrees F for 30 minutes.
- Cool down and serve it.

Nutrition:
Calories – 100
Protein – 2 g.
Fat – 1 g.
Carbs – 2 g.

847. Air Fried Crumbed Fish
Preparation Time: 10 minutes
Cooking Time: 12 minutes
Servings: 4
Ingredients:
- Bread crumbs: 1 cup
- Vegetable oil: ¼ cup
- 4 Flounder fillets
- 1 Beaten egg
- 1 Sliced Lemon

Directions:
- Preheat an air fryer to 350 °F (180 °C).
- In a cup, add the bread crumbs and the oil. Stir until the mixture becomes crumbly and loose.
- Dip the fish fillets in the egg mixture; shake off any excesses. Dip the fillets into a mixture of bread crumbs; until evenly and thoroughly coated.
- Gently lay coated fillets in the preheated air fryer. Cook, about 12 minutes, with a fork, until fish flakes easily. Garnish with sliced lemon.

Nutrition:
Calories: 354 Cal
Fat: 17.7 g
Carbohydrates: 22.5 g
Protein: 26.9 g

848. Air Fryer Meatloaf
Preparation Time: 10 minutes
Cooking Time: 25 minutes
Servings: 4
Ingredients:
- 1-pound lean beef
- 1 lightly beaten egg
- 3 tablespoons. bread crumbs
- 1 small, finely chopped onion
- 1 tablespoon. chopped fresh thyme
- 1 teaspoon salt
- 1 pinch ground black pepper to taste
- 2 thickly sliced mushrooms
- 1 tablespoon. olive oil

Directions:

- Preheat an air fryer up to 200 degrees C (392 degrees F).
- In a bowl, combine ground beef, egg, bread crumbs, ointment, thyme, salt, and pepper. Knead and mix well.
- Move the mixture of beef into a baking pan and smooth the rim—press chestnuts into the top and coat with olive oil. Place the saucepan in the basket of the air fryer and slide into the air fryer.
- Set 25-minute air fryer timer and roast meatloaf until well browned.
- Set aside the meatloaf for at least 10 minutes before slicing and serving into wedges.

Nutrition:
Calories: 296.8
Protein: 24.8 g
Carbohydrates: 5.9 g
Cholesterol: 125.5 mg

849. Air Fryer Shrimp A La Bang

Preparation Time: 10 minutes
Cooking Time: 12 minutes
Servings: 2
Ingredients:

- 1/2 cup mayonnaise
- 1/4 cup sweet chili sauce
- 1 tablespoon. sriracha sauce
- 1/4 cup all-purpose flour
- 1 cup panko bread crumbs
- Raw shrimp: 1 pound, peeled and deveined
- 1 leaf lettuce
- 2 green, chopped onions or to taste (optional)

Directions:

- Set temperature of air fryer to 400 degrees F (200 degrees C).
- In a bowl, stir in mayonnaise, chili sauce, and sriracha sauce until smooth. Put some bang sauce, if desired, in a separate bowl for dipping.
- Take a plate and place flour on it. Use a separate plate and place panko bread crumbs on it.
- First coat the shrimp with flour, then mayonnaise mixture, then panko. Place shrimp covered on a baking sheet.
- Place shrimp, without overcrowding, in the air fryer basket.
- Cook for approximately 12 minutes. Repeat with shrimp leftover.
- Use lettuce wraps for serving, garnished with green onion.

Nutrition:
Calories: 415
Fat: 23.9 g
Carbohydrates: 32.7 g
Protein: 23.9 g

850. Balsamic-Glazed Carrots

Preparation Time: 5 minutes
Cooking Time: 18 minutes
Servings: 3
Ingredients:

- 3 medium-size carrots, cut into 2-inch × ½-inch sticks
- 1 tablespoon orange juice
- 2 teaspoons balsamic vinegar
- 1 teaspoon maple syrup
- 1 teaspoon avocado oil
- ½ teaspoon dried rosemary
- ¼ teaspoon sea salt
- ¼ teaspoon lemon zest

Directions:

- Put the carrots in the baking pan and sprinkle with the orange juice, balsamic vinegar, maple syrup, avocado oil, rosemary, sea salt, finished by the lemon zest. Toss well.
- Slide the baking pan into Rack Position 1, select Convection Bake, set

temperature to 375ºF (190ºC), and set time to 18 minutes.
- Stir the carrots several times during the cooking process.
- When cooking is complete, the carrots should be nicely glazed and tender. Remove from the oven and serve hot.

Nutrition:
Calories: 191 Cal
Fat: 6g
Carbohydrates: 31.4g
Protein: 3.7g
Cholesterol: 3mg
Sodium: 447mg

851. Baked Potatoes With Yogurt And Chives

Preparation Time: 5 minutes
Cooking Time: 35 minutes
Servings: 4
Ingredients:
- 4(7-ounce / 198-g) russet potatoes, rinsed
- Olive oil spray
- ½ teaspoon kosher salt, divided
- ½ cup 2% plain Greek yogurt
- ¼ cup minced fresh chives
- Freshly ground black pepper

Directions:
- Pat the potatoes dry and pierce them all over with a fork. Spritz the potatoes with olive oil spray. Sprinkle with ¼ teaspoon of the salt.
- Transfer the potatoes to the baking pan.
- Slide the baking pan into Rack Position 1, select Convection Bake, set temperature to 400ºF (205ºC), and set time to 35 minutes.
- When cooking is complete, the potatoes should be fork-tender. Remove from the oven and split open the potatoes. Top with the yogurt, chives, the remaining ¼ teaspoon of salt, and finish with the black pepper. Serve immediately.

Nutrition:
Calories: 172 Cal Fat: 9.8g
Carbohydrates: 17.5g Protein: 3.9g
Cholesterol: 84mg
Sodium: 112mg

852. Buttered Broccoli With Parmesan

Preparation Time: 5 minutes
Cooking Time: 4 minutes
Servings: 4
Ingredients:
- 1 pound (454 g) broccoli florets
- 1 medium shallot, minced
- 2 tablespoons olive oil
- 2 tablespoons unsalted butter, melted
- 2 teaspoons minced garlic
- ¼ cup grated Parmesan cheese

Directions:
- Combine the broccoli florets with the shallot, olive oil, butter, garlic, and Parmesan cheese in a medium bowl and toss until the broccoli florets are thoroughly coated.
- Place the broccoli florets in the baking pan in a single layer.
- Slide the baking pan into Rack Position 1, select Convection Bake, set temperature to 350ºF (180ºC), and set time to 4 minutes.
- When cooking is complete, the broccoli florets should be crisp-tender. Remove from the oven and serve warm.

Nutrition:
Calories: 191 Cal
Fat: 6g
Carbohydrates: 31.4g
Protein: 3.7g
Cholesterol: 3mg
Sodium: 447mg

853. Creamy Corn Casserole

Preparation Time: 5 minutes
Cooking Time: 15 minutes
Servings: 4
Ingredients:
- 2 cups frozen yellow corn
- 1 egg, beaten
- 3 tablespoons flour
- ½ cup grated Swiss or Havarti cheese
- ½ cup light cream
- ¼ cup milk
- Pinch salt
- Freshly ground black pepper, to taste
- 2 tablespoons butter, cut into cubes
- Nonstick cooking spray

Directions:
- Spritz the baking pan with nonstick cooking spray.
- Stir together the remaining ingredients except the butter in a medium bowl until well incorporated. Transfer the mixture to the prepared baking pan and scatter with the butter cubes.
- Slide the baking pan into Rack Position 1, select Convection Bake, set temperature to 320ºF (160ºC), and set time to 15 minutes.
- When cooking is complete, the top should be golden brown and a toothpick inserted in the center should come out clean. Remove from the oven. Let the casserole cool for 5 minutes before slicing into wedges and serving.

Nutrition:
Calories: 172 Cal
Fat: 9.8g
Carbohydrates: 17.5g
Protein: 3.9g
Cholesterol: 84mg
Sodium: 112mg

854. Charred Green Beans With Sesame Seeds

Preparation Time: 5 minutes
Cooking Time: 8 minutes
Servings: 4
Ingredients:
- 1 tablespoon reduced-sodium soy sauce or tamari
- ½ tablespoon Sriracha sauce
- 4 teaspoons toasted sesame oil, divided
- 12 ounces (340 g) trimmed green beans
- ½ tablespoon toasted sesame seeds

Directions:
- Whisk together the soy sauce, Sriracha sauce, and 1 teaspoon of sesame oil in a small bowl until smooth. Set aside.
- Toss the green beans with the remaining sesame oil in a large bowl until evenly coated.
- Place the green beans in the air fryer basket in a single layer.
- Put the air fryer basket on the baking pan and slide into Rack Position 2, select Air Fry, set temperature to 375ºF (190ºC), and set time to 8 minutes.
- Stir the green beans halfway through the cooking time.
- When cooking is complete, the green beans should be lightly charred and tender. Remove from the oven to a platter. Pour the prepared sauce over the top of green beans and toss well. Serve sprinkled with the toasted sesame seeds.

Nutrition:
Calories: 191 Cal
Fat: 6g
Carbohydrates: 31.4g
Protein: 3.7g
Cholesterol: 3mg
Sodium: 447mg

855. Cinnamon-Spiced Acorn Squash

Preparation Time: 5 minutes
Cooking Time: 15 minutes
Servings: 2
Ingredients:
- 1 medium acorn squash, halved crosswise and deseeded
- 1 teaspoon coconut oil
- 1 teaspoon light brown sugar
- Few dashes of ground cinnamon
- Few dashes of ground nutmeg

Directions:
- On a clean work surface, rub the cut sides of the acorn squash with coconut oil. Scatter with the brown sugar, cinnamon, and nutmeg.
- Put the squash halves in the air fryer basket, cut-side up.
- Put the air fryer basket on the baking pan and slide into Rack Position 2, select Air Fry, set temperature to 325ºF (163ºC), and set time to 15 minutes.
- When cooking is complete, the squash halves should be just tender when pierced in the center with a paring knife. Remove from the oven.
- Rest for 5 to 10 minutes and serve warm.

Nutrition:
Calories: 172 Cal
Fat: 9.8g
Carbohydrates: 17.5g
Protein: 3.9g
Cholesterol: 84mg
Sodium: 112mg

856. Parmesan Asparagus Fries

Preparation Time: 15 minutes
Cooking Time: 6 minutes
Servings: 4
Ingredients:
- 2 egg whites
- ¼ cup water
- ¼ cup plus 2 tablespoons grated Parmesan cheese, divided
- ¾ cup panko bread crumbs
- ¼ teaspoon salt
- 12 ounces (340 g) fresh asparagus spears, woody ends trimmed
- Cooking spray

Directions:
- In a shallow dish, whisk together the egg whites and water until slightly foamy. In a separate shallow dish, thoroughly combine ¼ cup of Parmesan cheese, bread crumbs, and salt.
- Dip the asparagus in the egg white, then roll in the cheese mixture to coat well.
- Place the asparagus in the air fryer basket in a single layer, leaving space between each spear. Spritz the asparagus with cooking spray.

Put the air fryer basket on the baking pan and slide into Rack Position 2, select Air Fry, set temperature to 390ºF (199ºC), and set time to 6 minutes.

When cooking is complete, the asparagus should be golden brown and crisp. Remove from the oven. Sprinkle with the remaining 2 tablespoons of cheese and serve hot.

Nutrition:
Calories: 191 Cal
Fat: 6g
Carbohydrates: 31.4g
Protein: 3.7g
Cholesterol: 3mg
Sodium: 447mg

857. Chili Corn On The Cob

Preparation Time: 10 minutes
Cooking Time: 15 minutes
Servings: 4
Ingredients:

- 2 tablespoon olive oil, divided
- 2 tablespoons grated Parmesan cheese
- 1 teaspoon garlic powder
- 1 teaspoon chili powder
- 1 teaspoon ground cumin
- 1 teaspoon paprika
- 1 teaspoon salt
- ¼ teaspoon cayenne pepper (optional)
- 4 ears fresh corn, shucked

Directions:

Grease the air fryer basket with 1 tablespoon of olive oil. Set aside.

Combine the Parmesan cheese, garlic powder, chili powder, cumin, paprika, salt, and cayenne pepper (if desired) in a small bowl and stir to mix well.

Lightly coat the ears of corn with the remaining 1 tablespoon of olive oil. Rub the cheese mixture all over the ears of corn until completely coated.

Arrange the ears of corn in the greased basket in a single layer.

Put the air fryer basket on the baking pan and slide into Rack Position 2, select Air Fry, set temperature to 400ºF (205ºC), and set time to 15 minutes.

Flip the ears of corn halfway through the cooking time.

When cooking is complete, they should be lightly browned. Remove from the oven and let them cool for 5 minutes before serving.

Nutrition:
Calories: 172 Cal Fat: 9.8g
Carbohydrates: 17.5g
Protein: 3.9g
Cholesterol: 84mg
Sodium: 112mg

858. Spicy Cabbage

Preparation Time: 5 minutes
Cooking Time: 7 minutes
Servings: 4
Ingredients:

- 1 head cabbage, sliced into 1-inch-thick ribbons
- 1 tablespoon olive oil
- 1 teaspoon garlic powder
- 1 teaspoon red pepper flakes
- 1 teaspoon salt
- 1 teaspoon freshly ground black pepper

Directions:

Toss the cabbage with the olive oil, garlic powder, red pepper flakes, salt, and pepper in a large mixing bowl until well coated.

Transfer the cabbage to the baking pan.

Slide the baking pan into Rack Position 1, select Convection Bake, set temperature to 350ºF (180ºC), and set time to 7 minutes.

Flip the cabbage with tongs halfway through the cooking time.

When cooking is complete, the cabbage should be crisp. Remove from the oven to a plate and serve warm.

Nutrition:
Calories: 172 Cal
Fat: 9.8g
Carbohydrates: 17.5g
Protein: 3.9g
Cholesterol: 84mg
Sodium: 112mg

859. Spicy Broccoli With Hot Sauce

Preparation Time: 5 minutes
Cooking Time: 14 minutes
Servings: 6
Ingredients:
Broccoli:
- 1 medium-sized head broccoli, cut into florets
- 1½ tablespoons olive oil
- 1 teaspoon shallot powder
- 1 teaspoon porcini powder
- ½ teaspoon freshly grated lemon zest
- ½ teaspoon hot paprika
- ½ teaspoon granulated garlic
- ⅓ teaspoon fine sea salt
- ⅓ teaspoon celery seeds

Hot Sauce:
- ½ cup tomato sauce
- 1 tablespoon balsamic vinegar
- ½ teaspoon ground allspice

Directions:
In a mixing bowl, combine all the ingredients for the broccoli and toss to coat. Transfer the broccoli to the air fryer basket.

Put the air fryer basket on the baking pan and slide into Rack Position 2, select Air Fry, set temperature to 360ºF (182ºC), and set time to 14 minutes.

Meanwhile, make the hot sauce by whisking together the tomato sauce, balsamic vinegar, and allspice in a small bowl.

When cooking is complete, remove the broccoli from the oven and serve with the hot sauce.

Nutrition:
Calories: 191 Cal
Fat: 6g
Carbohydrates: 31.4g
Protein: 3.7g
Cholesterol: 3mg
Sodium: 447mg

860. Cheesy Broccoli Gratin

Preparation Time: 5 minutes
Cooking Time: 14 minutes
Servings: 2
Ingredients:
- ⅓ cup fat-free milk
- 1 tablespoon all-purpose or gluten-free flour
- ½ tablespoon olive oil
- ½ teaspoon ground sage
- ¼ teaspoon kosher salt
- ⅛ teaspoon freshly ground black pepper
- 2 cups roughly chopped broccoli florets
- 6 tablespoons shredded Cheddar cheese
- 2 tablespoons panko bread crumbs
- 1 tablespoon grated Parmesan cheese
- Olive oil spray

Directions:
Spritz the baking pan with olive oil spray.

Mix the milk, flour, olive oil, sage, salt, and pepper in a medium bowl and whisk to combine. Stir in the broccoli florets, Cheddar cheese, bread crumbs, and Parmesan cheese and toss to coat.

Pour the broccoli mixture into the prepared baking pan.

Slide the baking pan into Rack Position 1, select Convection Bake, set temperature to 330ºF (166ºC), and set time to 14 minutes.

When cooking is complete, the top should be golden brown and the broccoli should be tender. Remove from the oven and serve immediately.

Nutrition:
Calories: 172 Cal
Fat: 9.8g
Carbohydrates: 17.5g
Protein: 3.9g
Cholesterol: 84mg
Sodium: 112mg

861. Perfect Cinnamon Toast
Preparation Time: 10 minutes
Cooking Time: 5 minutes
Servings: 6
Ingredients:
   2 tsp. pepper
   1 ½ tsp. cinnamon
   ½ cup sweetener of choice
   1 cup coconut oil
   12 slices whole wheat bread

Directions:
   Melt the coconut oil and mix it with the sweetener until dissolved. Mix in the remaining ingredients except bread until incorporated.
   Spread mixture onto the bread slices, covering all the areas.
   Pour the coated bread pieces into the oven rack/basket. Place the rack on the middle shelf of the Air Fryer Oven. Set temperature to 400°F, and set the time to 5 minutes.
   Remove and cut diagonally. Enjoy!

Nutrition:
Calories: 124
Fats: 2 g
Carbs: 5 g

862. Angel Food Cake
Preparation Time: 5 minutes
Cooking Time: 30 minutes
Servings: 12
Ingredients:
   ¼ cup butter, melted
   1 cup powdered erythritol
   1 tsp. strawberry extract
   12 egg whites
   2 tsp. cream of tartar

Directions:
   Preheat the Air Fryer Oven for 5 minutes.
   Blend the cream of tartar and the egg whites.
   Use a hand mixer and whisk until white and fluffy.
   Add the rest of the ingredients except for the butter and whisk for another minute.
   Pour into a baking dish.
   Place in the air fry basket and cook for 30 minutes at 400°F or if a toothpick inserted in the middle comes out clean.
   Drizzle with the melted butter once cooled.

Nutrition:
Calories: 65
Protein: 3.1 g
Fats: 5 g
Carbs: 6.2 g

863. Apple Dumplings
Preparation Time: 10 minutes
Cooking Time: 25 minutes
Servings: 4
Ingredients:
   2 tbsp. melted coconut oil
   2 puff pastry sheets
   1 tbsp. brown sugar
   2 tbsp. raisins
   2 small apples of choice

Directions:
   Preheat the Air Fryer Oven to 356ºF.

- Core and peel the apples and mix with the raisins and sugar.
- Place a bit of the apple mixture into the puff pastry sheets and brush the sides with the melted coconut oil.
- Place into the Air Fryer Oven. Cook for 25 minutes, turning halfway through. They will be golden when done.

Nutrition:
Calories: 367
Protein: 2 g
Fats: 7 g
Carbs: 10 g

864. Chocolate Donuts

Preparation Time: 5 minutes
Cooking Time: 20 minutes
Servings: 8–10
Ingredients:
- (8-oz.) can Jumbo® biscuits
- 1 tbsp Cooking oil
- 2 tbsp Chocolate sauce, such as Betty Crocker™

Directions:
- Form 8 donuts out of the dough and place them on a flat worksurface. Use a small circle cookie cutter or a biscuit cutter to cut a hole in the center of each donut. You can also cut the holes using a knife.
- Grease the basket with cooking oil.
- Place 4 donuts in the Air Fryer Oven. Do not stack. Spray with cooking oil. Cook for 4 minutes.
- Open the Air Fryer Oven and flip the donuts. Cook for an additional 4 minutes.
- Remove the cooked donuts from the Air Fryer Oven, then repeat for the remaining 4 donuts.
- Drizzle chocolate sauce over the donuts and enjoy while warm.

Nutrition:
Calories: 181 Protein: 3 g
Fats: 98 g Carbs: 42 g

865. Apple Hand Pies

Preparation Time: 5 minutes
Cooking Time: 8 minutes
Servings: 6
Ingredients:
- 15 oz. apple pie filling, no-sugar-added
- 1 store-bought pie crust

Directions:
- Lay out the pie crust and slice them into equal-sized squares.
- Place 2 tbsp. of apple pie filling into each square and seal the crust with a fork.
- Place the Rack on the middle shelf of the Air Fryer Oven. Set temperature to 390°F, and set the time to 8 minutes, or until golden in color.

Nutrition:
Calories: 278 Protein: 5 g
Fats: 10 g Carbs: 17 g

866. Sweet Cream Cheese Wontons

Preparation Time: 5 minutes
Cooking Time: 5 minutes
Servings: 16
Ingredients:
- 1 egg with a little water
- 2 Wonton wrappers
- ½ cup powdered erythritol
- 8 oz. softened cream cheese
- 1 tbsp Olive oil

Directions:
- Mix the sweetener and the cream cheese together.
- Lay out 4 wontons at a time and cover with a dish towel to prevent them from drying out.
- Place ½ of a tsp. of cream cheese mixture into each wrapper.
- Dip your finger into the egg-water mixture and fold it diagonally to form a triangle. Seal the edges well.
- Repeat with the remaining ingredients.

Place filled wontons into the Air Fryer Oven and cook 5 minutes at 400ºF, shaking halfway through cooking.

Nutrition:
Calories: 303 Protein: 0.5 g
Fats: 3 g Carbs: 3 g

867. French Toast Bites
Preparation Time: 5 minutes
Cooking Time: 15 minutes
Servings: 8
Ingredients:
- 3 tbsp Almond milk
- 1 tbsp Cinnamon sugar to taste
- ⅓ cup sweetener
- 3 eggs
- 4 pieces wheat bread

Directions:
Preheat the Air Fryer Oven to 360ºF.
Whisk the eggs and thin out with almond milk.
Mix ⅓ cup of sweetener with lots of cinnamon.
Tear the bread in half, ball up pieces and press together to form a ball.
Soak the bread balls in the egg mixture, and then into cinnamon sugar, making sure to thoroughly coat.
Place the coated bread balls into the Air Fryer Oven and bake for 15 minutes.

Nutrition:
Calories: 289 Fats: 11 g Carbs: 17 g

868. Cinnamon Sugar Roasted Chickpeas
Preparation Time: 5 minutes
Cooking Time: 10 minutes
Servings: 2
Ingredients:
- 1 tbsp. sweetener
- 1 tbsp. cinnamon
- 1 cup chickpeas

Directions:
Preheat th Air Fryer Oven to 390ºF.
Rinse and drain the chickpeas.
Mix all the ingredients together and add to the Air Fryer Oven.
Pour into the oven rack/basket. Place the rack on the middle shelf of the Air Fryer Oven. Set temperature to 390°F, and set time to 10 minutes.

Nutrition:
Calories: 111
Protein: 16 g
Fats: 19 g
Carbs: 18 g

869. Brownie Muffins
Preparation Time: 10 minutes
Cooking Time: 10 minutes
Servings: 12
Ingredients:
- 1 package Betty Crocker™ Fudge Brownie Mix
- ¼ cup walnuts, chopped
- 1 egg
- ⅓ cup vegetable oil
- 2 tsp. water

Directions:
Grease a 12-cavity muffin pan and set it aside.
In a bowl, put all the ingredients together.
Place the mixture into the prepared muffin pan.
Press the "Power" of the Air Fryer Oven and turn the dial to select the "Air Fry" mode.
Press the "Time" button and again turn the dial to set the cooking time to 10 minutes.
Now push the "Temp" button and rotate the dial to set the temperature at 300ºF.
Press the "Start/Pause" button to start.
Open the unit when it has reached the temperature, when it beeps.

Arrange the muffin pan in the air fry basket and insert it in the oven.

Place the muffin pan onto a wire rack to cool for about 10 minutes.

Carefully, invert the muffins onto the wire rack to completely cool before serving.

Nutrition:
Calories: 168 Protein: 2 g
Fats: 8.9 gCarbs: 20.8 g

870. Chocolate Mug Cake

Preparation Time: 15 minutes
Cooking Time: 13 minutes
Servings: 1
Ingredients:
¼ cup self-rising flour
5 tbsp. caster sugar
1 tbsp. cocoa powder
3 tbsp. coconut oil
3 tbsp. whole milk

Directions:
In a shallow mug, add all the ingredients and mix until well combined.

Press the "Power" of the Air Fryer Oven and turn the dial to select the "Air Fry" mode.

Press the "Time" button and again turn the dial to set the cooking time to 13 minutes.

Now push the "Temp" button and rotate the dial to set the temperature at 392ºF.

Press the "Start/Pause" button to start.

Open the unit when it has reached the temperature, when it beeps.

Arrange the mug in the air fry basket and insert it in the Air Fryer Oven.

Place the mug onto a wire rack to cool slightly before serving.

Nutrition:
Calories: 729
Protein: 5.7 g
Fats: 43.3 g
Carbs: 88.8 g

871. Grilled Peaches

Preparation Time: 10 minutes
Cooking Time: 10 minutes
Servings: 2
Ingredients:
2 peaches, cut into wedges and remove pits
¼ cup butter, diced into pieces
¼ cup brown sugar
¼ cup Graham Cracker® crumbs

Directions:
Arrange the peach wedges on Air Fryer Oven rack and air-fry at 350ºF for 5 minutes.

In a bowl, add the butter, Graham Cracker® crumbs, and brown sugar and mix well.

Place the pecans skin-side down.

Spoon the butter mixture over top of the peaches and air-fry for 5 minutes more.

Top with the whipped cream and serve.

Nutrition:
Calories: 378
Protein: 2.3 g
Fats: 24.4 g
Carbs: 40.5 g

872. Simple & Delicious Spiced Apples

Preparation Time: 10 minutes
Cooking Time: 10 minutes
Servings: 4
Ingredients:
4 apples, sliced
1 tsp. apple pie spice
2 tbsp. sugar
2 tbsp. ghee, melted
2 lb. Ice cream

Directions:
Add the apple slices into the mixing bowl.

Add the remaining ingredients on top of the apple slices and toss until well coated.

Transfer apple slices on the Air Fryer Ovenpan and air-fry at 350ºF for 10 minutes.

Top with the ice cream and serve.
Nutrition:
Calories: 196
Protein: 0.6 g
Fats: 6.8 g
Carbs: 37.1 g

873. Tangy Mango Slices
Preparation Time: 10 minutes
Cooking Time: 12 hours
Servings: 6
Ingredients:
4 mangoes, peeled and cut into ¼-inch slices
¼ cup fresh lemon juice
1 tbsp. honey
Directions:
In a big bowl, combine together the honey and lemon juice and set aside.
Add the mango slices in the lemon-honey mixture and coat them well.
Arrange the mango slices on the Air Fryer Oven rack and dehydrate them at 135ºF for 12 hours.
Nutrition:
Calories: 147
Protein: 1.9 g
Fats: 0.9 g
Carbs: 36.7 g

874. Dried Raspberries
Preparation Time: 10 minutes
Cooking Time: 15 hours
Servings: 4
Ingredients:
4 cups raspberries, washed and dried
¼ cup fresh lemon juice
Directions:
Add the raspberries and lemon juice in a bowl and toss well.
Arrange the raspberries on the Air Fryer Oven tray and dehydrate them at 135ºF for 12–15 hours.
Store in an air-tight container.

Nutrition:
Calories: 68
Protein: 1.6 g
Fats: 0.9 g
Carbs: 15 g

875. Sweet Peach Wedges
Preparation Time: 10 minutes
Cooking Time: 8 hours
Servings: 4
Ingredients:
3 peaches, cut and remove pits and sliced
½ cup fresh lemon juice
Directions:
Add the lemon juice and the peach slices into the bowl and toss well.
Arrange the peach slices on the Air Fryer Ovenrack and dehydrate them at 135ºF for 6–8 hours.
Serve and enjoy.
Nutrition:
Calories: 52
Protein: 1.3 g
Fats: 0.5 g
Carbs: 11.1 g

876. Air Fryer Oreo Cookies
Preparation Time: 5 minutes
Cooking Time: 5 minutes
Servings: 9
Ingredients:
½ cup pancake mix:
½ cup water:
Cooking spray
9 chocolate sandwich cookies: (e.g. Oreo®)
1 tbsp. (or to taste) confectioners' sugar
Directions:
Blend the pancake mix with the water until well mixed.
Line the parchment paper on the air fry basket. Spray non-stick cooking spray on the parchment paper. Dip each cookie in the pancake mix and place them in the

basket. Make sure they do not touch; if possible, cook in batches.

Preheat the Air Fryer Oven to 400°F. Cook for 4–5 minutes; flip until golden brown, 2–3 more minutes. Sprinkle the confectioners' sugar over the cookies and serve.

Nutrition:
Calories: 77
Protein: 1.2 g
Fats: 2.1 g
Carbs: 13.7 g

877. Air Fried Butter Cake

Preparation Time: 10 minutes
Cooking Time: 15 minutes
Servings: 4
Ingredients:

7 tbsp. butter, at ambient temperature
¼ cup white sugar, plus 2 tbsp.
1 ⅔ cups all-purpose flour
1 pinch salt, or to taste
6 tbsp. milk

Directions:

Preheat the Air Fryer Oven to 350ºF. Spray the cooking spray on a tiny fluted tube pan.

Take a large bowl and add ¼ cup butter and 2 tbsp. of sugar in it.

Take an electric mixer to beat the sugar and butter until smooth and fluffy. Stir in the salt and flour. Stir in the milk and thoroughly combine the batter. Transfer the batter to the prepared saucepan; use a spoon back to level the surface.

Place the pan inside the air fry basket. Set the timer within 15 minutes. Bake the batter until a toothpick comes out clean when inserted into the cake.

Turn the cake out of the saucepan and allow it to cool for about 5 minutes.

Nutrition:
Calories: 470
Protein: 7.9 g
Fats: 22.4 g
Carbs: 59.7 g

878. Air Fryer S'mores

Preparation Time: 5 minutes
Cooking Time: 3 minutes
Servings: 4
Ingredients:

4 Graham Crackers®, each half split to make 2 squares, for a total of 8 squares
8 squares chocolate bar Hershey's®, broken into squares
4 marshmallows

Directions:

Take deliberate steps. Air-fryers use hot air for cooking food. Marshmallows are light and fluffy, and this should keep the marshmallows from flying around the basket if you follow these steps.

Put 4 squares of Graham Crackers® on a basket of the air fryer.

Place 2 squares of chocolate bars on each cracker.

Place the basket back into the Air Fryer Oven and fry at 390°F for 1 minute. It is barely long enough for the chocolate to melt. Remove basket from air fryer.

Top with a marshmallow over each cracker. Throw the marshmallow down a little bit into the melted chocolate. This will help in making the marshmallow stay over the chocolate.

Put the basket back into the Air Fryer Oven and fry at 390°F for 2 minutes. (The marshmallows should be puffed up and browned at the tops).

Using tongs to carefully remove each cracker from the air fry basket and place it on a platter. Top each marshmallow with another square of Graham Crackers®.

Enjoy it right away!

Nutrition:
Calories: 200
Protein: 2.6 g
Fats: 3.1 g
Carbs: 15.7 g

879. Peanut Butter Cookies

Preparation Time: 2 minutes
Cooking Time: 5 minutes
Servings: 10
Ingredients:
- 1 cup peanut butter
- 1 cup sugar
- 1 egg

Directions:
- Blend all of the ingredients with a hand mixer.
- Spray the air fry basket with canola oil. (Alternatively, parchment paper can also be used, but it will take longer to cook your cookies)
- Set the Air Fryer Oven temperature to 350ºF.
- Place rounded dough balls onto air fryer trays. Press down softly with the back of a fork.
- Place air fry basket in your Air Fryer Oven in the middle shelf. Cook for 5 minutes.
- Serve the cookies with milk.

Nutrition:
Calories: 236 Protein: 6 g
Fats: 13 g
Carbs: 26 g

880. Sweet Pear Stew

Preparation Time: 10 minutes
Cooking Time: 15 minutes
Servings: 4
Ingredients:
- 4 pears, cored and cut into wedges
- 1 tsp. vanilla
- ¼ cup apple juice
- 2 cups grapes, halved

Directions:
- Put all of the ingredients in the Air Fryer Ovenand stir well.
- Close the Air Fryer Ovenand cook on high for 15 minutes.
- As soon as the cooking is done, let it release pressure naturally for 10 minutes, then release the remaining pressure using "Quick Release." Remove the lid.
- Stir and serve.

Nutrition:
Calories: 162 Protein: 1.1 g
Fats: 0.5 g
Carbs: 41.6 g

881. Vanilla Apple Compote

Preparation Time: 10 minutes
Cooking Time: 15 minutes
Servings: 6
Ingredients:
- 3 cups apples, cored and cubed
- 1 tsp. vanilla
- ¾ cup coconut sugar
- 1 cup water
- 2 tbsp. fresh lime juice

Directions:
- Put all of the ingredients in the instnt pot and stir well.
- Close the Air Fryer Ovenand cook on high for 15 minutes.
- As soon as the cooking is done, let it release pressure naturally for 10 minutes, then release the remaining pressure using "Quick Release." Remove the lid.
- Stir and serve.

Nutrition:
Calories: 76 Protein: 0.5 g
Fats: 0.2 g
Carbs: 19.1 g

882. Apple Dates Mix

Preparation Time: 10 minutes
Cooking Time: 15 minutes
Servings: 4
Ingredients:
- 4 apples, cored and cut into chunks
- 1 tsp. vanilla
- 1 tsp. cinnamon
- ½ cup dates, pitted
- 1 ½ cups apple juice

Directions:
- Put all of the ingredients in the Air Fryer Oven and stir well.
- Close the Air Fryer Oven and cook on high for 15 minutes.
- As soon as the cooking is done, let release pressure naturally for 10 minutes, then release the remaining pressure using "Quick Release." Remove the lid.
- Stir and serve.

Nutrition:
- Calories: 226
- Protein: 1.3 g
- Fats: 0.6 g
- Carbs: 58.6 g

883. Chocolate Rice

Preparation Time: 10 minutes
Cooking Time: 20 minutes
Servings: 4
Ingredients:
- 1 cup rice
- 1 tbsp. cocoa powder
- 2 tbsp. maple syrup
- 2 cups almond milk

Directions:
- Put all of the ingredients in the Air Fryer Oven and stir well.
- Close the Air Fryer Oven and cook on high for 20 minutes.
- As soon as the cooking is done, let it cool naturally for 10 minutes, then release the remaining pressure using "Quick Release." Remove the lid.
- Stir and serve.

Nutrition:
- Calories: 474
- Protein: 6.3 g
- Fats: 29.1 g
- Carbs: 51.1 g

884. Raisins Cinnamon Peaches

Preparation Time: 10 minutes
Cooking Time: 15 minutes
Servings: 4
Ingredients:
- 4 peaches, cored and cut into chunks
- 1 tsp. vanilla
- 1 tsp. cinnamon
- ½ cup raisins
- 1 cup water

Directions:
- Put all of the ingredients in the Air Fryer Oven and stir well.
- Close the Air Fryer Oven and cook on high for 15 minutes.
- As soon as the cooking is done, let it release pressure naturally for 10 minutes, then release the remaining pressure using "Quick Release." Remove the lid.
- Stir and serve.

Nutrition:
- Calories: 118
- Protein: 2 g
- Fats: 0.5 g
- Carbs: 29 g

885. Lemon Pear Compote

Preparation Time: 10 minutes
Cooking Time: 15 minutes
Servings: 6
Ingredients:
- 3 cups pears, cored and cut into chunks
- 1 tsp. vanilla

1 tsp. liquid stevia
1 tbsp. lemon zest, grated
2 tbsp. lemon juice

Directions:
- Put all of the ingredients in the Air Fryer Oven and stir well.
- Close the Air Fryer Oven and cook on high for 15 minutes.
- As soon as the cooking is done, let it release pressure naturally for 10 minutes, then release the remaining pressure using "Quick Release." Remove the lid.
- Stir and serve.

Nutrition:
Calories: 50 Protein: 0.4 g
Fats: 0.2 g
Carbs: 12.7 g

886. Strawberry Stew

Preparation Time: 10 minutes
Cooking Time: 15 minutes
Servings: 4

Ingredients:
- 12 oz. fresh strawberries, sliced
- 1 tsp. vanilla
- 1 ½ cups water
- 1 tsp. liquid stevia
- 2 tbsp. lime juice

Directions:
- Put all of the ingredients in the Air Fryer Oven and stir well.
- Close the Air Fryer Oven and cook on high for 15 minutes.
- As soon as the cooking is done, let it release pressure naturally for 10 minutes, then release the remaining pressure using "Quick Release." Remove the lid.
- Stir and serve.

Nutrition:
Calories: 36
Protein: 0.7 g
Fats: 0.3 g
Carbs: 8.5 g

887. Walnut Apple Pear Mix

Preparation Time: 10 minutes
Cooking Time: 10 minutes
Servings: 4

Ingredients:
- 2 apples, cored and cut into wedges
- ½ tsp. vanilla
- 1 cup apple juice
- 2 tbsp. walnuts, chopped
- 2 apples, cored and cut into wedges

Directions:
- Put all of the ingredients in the Air Fryer Oven and stir well.
- Close the Air Fryer Oven and cook on high for 10 minutes.
- As soon as the cooking is done, let it release pressure naturally for 10 minutes, then release the remaining pressure using "Quick Release." Remove the lid.
- Serve and enjoy.

Nutrition:
Calories: 132
Protein: 1.3 g
Fats: 2.6 g
Carbs: 28.3 g

888. Cinnamon Pear Jam

Preparation Time: 10 minutes
Cooking Time: 4 minutes
Servings: 12

Ingredients:
- 8 pears, cored and cut into quarters
- 1 tsp. cinnamon
- ¼ cup apple juice
- 2 apples, peeled, cored and diced

Directions:
- Put all of the ingredients in the Air Fryer Oven and stir well.
- Close the Air Fryer Oven and cook on high for 4 minutes.
- As soon as the cooking is done, let it release pressure naturally. Remove the lid.

Blend the pear apple mixture using an immersion blender until smooth.

Serve and enjoy.

Nutrition:
Calories: 103 Protein: 0.6 g
Fats: 0.3 g
Carbs: 27.1 g

889. Pear Sauce
Preparation Time: 10 minutes
Cooking Time: 15 minutes
Servings: 6
Ingredients:
10 pears, sliced
1 cup apple juice
1 ½ tsp. cinnamon
¼ tsp. nutmeg

Directions:
Put all of the ingredients in the Air Fryer Oven and stir well.

Close the Air Fryer Oven and cook on high for 15 minutes.

Once done, allow to release pressure naturally for 10 minutes, then release the remaining using "Quick Release." Remove the lid.

Blend the pear mixture using an immersion blender until smooth.

Serve and enjoy.

Nutrition:
Calories: 222
Protein: 1.3 g
Fats: 0.6 g
Carbs: 58.2 g

890. Sweet Peach Jam
Preparation Time: 10 minutes
Cooking Time: 16 minutes
Servings: 20
Ingredients:
1 ½ lb. fresh peaches, pitted and chopped
½ tbsp. vanilla
¼ cup maple syrup

Directions:
Put all of the ingredients in the Air Fryer Oven and stir well.

Close the Air Fryer Oven and cook on high for 1 minute.

Once done, allow to release pressure naturally. Remove the lid.

Set pot on "Sauté" mode and cook for 15 minutes, or until the jam is thickened.

Pour into the container and store it in the fridge.

Nutrition:
Calories: 16
Protein: 0.1 g
Carbs: 3.7 g

891. Warm Peach Compote
Preparation Time: 10 minutes
Cooking Time: 1 minute
Servings: 4
Ingredients:
4 peaches, peeled and chopped
1 tbsp. water
½ tbsp. cornstarch
1 tsp. vanilla

Directions:
Add the water, vanilla, and peaches into the Air Fryer Oven oven.

Close the Air Fryer Oven and cook on high for 1 minute.

Once done, allow to release pressure naturally. Remove the lid.

In a small bowl, whisk together 1 tbsp. of water and the cornstarch and pour into the pot and stir well.

Serve and enjoy.

Nutrition:
Calories: 66
Protein: 1.4 g
Fats: 0.4 g
Carbs: 15 g

892. Spiced Pear Sauce

Preparation Time: 10 minutes
Cooking Time: 6 hours
Servings: 12
Ingredients:
- 8 pears, cored and diced
- ½ tsp. ground cinnamon
- ¼ tsp. ground nutmeg
- ¼ tsp. ground cardamom
- 1 cup water

Directions:
- Put all of the ingredients in the Air Fryer Oven and stir well.
- Close the Air Fryer Oven with its lid and select "Slow Cook" mode and cook on low for 6 hours.
- Mash the sauce using a potato masher.
- Pour into the container and store.

Nutrition:
Calories: 81
Protein: 0.5 g
Fats: 0.2 g
Carbs: 21.4 g

893. Honey Fruit Compote

Preparation Time: 10 minutes
Cooking Time: 3 minutes
Servings: 4
Ingredients:
- ⅓ cup honey
- 1 ½ cups blueberries
- 1 ½ cups raspberries

Directions:
- Put all of the ingredients in the Air Fryer Oven and stir well.
- Close the Air Fryer Oven with lid and cook on high for 3 minutes.
- Once done, allow to release pressure naturally. Remove the lid.
- Serve and enjoy.

Nutrition:
Calories: 141 Protein: 1 g
Fats: 0.5 g Carbs: 36.7 g

Printed in Great Britain
by Amazon